Java

A Framework for Program Design and Data Structures

SECOND EDITION

Kenneth A. Lambert
Washington and Lee University

Martin Osborne
Western Washington State University

THOMSON

BROOKS/COLE

Australia • Canada • Mexico • Singapore • Spain
United Kingdom • United States

THOMSON

BROOKS/COLE

Editor: Kallie Swanson
Editorial Assistant: Aarti Jayaraman
Technology Project Manager: Burke Taft
Executive Marketing Manager: Tom Ziolkowski
Marketing Assistant: Jennifer Gee
Advertising Project Manager: Vicky Wan
Project Manager, Editorial Production: Kelsey McGee
Print/Media Buyer: Jessica Reed

Permissions Editor: Kiely Sexton
Production Service: Dustine Friedman/The Book Company
Text Designer: Lisa Devenish/Devenish Design
Copy Editor: Frank Hubert
Cover Designer: Laurie Albrecht
Cover Image: J. A. Kraulis/Masterfile
Compositor: ATLIS Graphics
Cover Printing, Printing and Binding: Webcom

For more information about our products, contact us at:
Thomson Learning Academic Resource Center
1-800-423-0563

For permission to use material from this text, contact us by:

Phone: 1-800-730-2214

Fax: 1-800-730-2215

Web: http://www.thomsonrights.com

Library of Congress Control Number: 2003102164

ISBN 0-534-39285-7

Brooks/Cole—Thomson Learning
10 Davis Drive
Belmont, CA 94002
USA

Asia
Thomson Learning
5 Shenton Way #01-01
UIC Building
Singapore 068808

Australia/New Zealand
Thomson Learning
102 Dodds Street
Southbank, Victoria 3006
Australia

Canada
Nelson
1120 Birchmount Road
Toronto, Ontario M1K 5G4
Canada

Europe/Middle East/Africa
Thomson Learning
High Holborn House
50/51 Bedford Row
London WC1R 4LR
United Kingdom

Latin America
Thomson Learning
Seneca, 53
Colonia Polanco
11560 Mexico D.F.
Mexico

Spain/Portugal
Paraninfo
Calle Magallanes, 25
28015 Madrid, Spain

CONTENTS

Overview

This text is intended for a second course in programming and problem solving, commonly known as Data Structures or CS2. We want students to focus on traditional computer science topics while writing object-oriented programs with graphical user interfaces. The text covers six major aspects of computing:

1. **Data structures:** Fundamental abstract data types (ADTs) are discussed. These include strings, vectors, linked lists, sets, tables, files, stacks, queues, and trees.

2. **Complexity analysis:** Tools for analyzing and predicting run time and memory usage are introduced.

3. **Object-oriented programming:** OOP is today's dominant programming paradigm. All the essentials of this subject are covered.

4. **Software development lifecycle:** Rather than isolate software development techniques in separate chapters, our book deals with them throughout in the context of numerous case studies.

5. **Graphical user interfaces and event-driven programming:** Many books at this level cling to what has now become an antiquated mode of programming—character-based terminal I/O. The reason is simple. Graphical user interfaces and event-driven programming are too complex for beginning students. In this book, we overcome the barrier of complexity in the manner explained below.

6. **Networking:** Multithreading and simple client/server applications are introduced.

Java™ 2 Collections and Extensions

This text covers all of the Java 2 collection classes, such as lists, sets, and maps. As of this writing, Java 2 collections do not include traditional ADTs such as queues, trees, and graphs. We develop these as extensions or analogs of the Java 2 classes in a special package called `lamborne`.

Prototype and Professional Versions of Collections

Each collection class is introduced in the form of a prototype that contains the essential features of the collection. The use of prototypes allows students to focus on implementation strategies without worrying about such issues as completeness and error handling. These issues are then discussed when the more professional versions are developed later in each chapter.

Alternative I/O Styles: The Terminal and GUIs

In Java, one can choose between two very different I/O styles. Terminal I/O is appropriate for sequential, text-based input and output, usually in the context of testing algorithms. More realistic programs require graphical user interfaces. Although Java has a wide range of classes that support both I/O styles, their use can be complicated for first-year students. This edition of the text shows how to write code from scratch that uses both styles. We also show how to simplify this code by developing a package called `ioutil`. This package provides a `KeyboardReader` class that simplifies terminal I/O and several classes that simplify GUIs. Thus, students can use either I/O style without being overwhelmed and distracted from the basic business of software development: algorithm design and factoring code into classes. In addition, students can gain sustained exposure to the model, view, controller pattern, one of the basic components of software design.

Use of Java to Present Traditional Topics in a Contemporary Context

The text covers the traditional topics of CS2: data structures, algorithm analysis, and software design. However, the use of Java allows these topics to have a contemporary presentation. Here are three examples:

1. The use of GUIs supports the principled introduction of the model, view, controller pattern for structuring large software systems.
2. Wherever possible, an ADT is situated in a class hierarchy, and its connections to other ADTs are explored via modern interfaces such as iterators and collection-views.
3. The use of sockets and network applications supports the principled introduction of the client/server pattern as another mechanism for structuring large software systems.

Case Studies

The book contains numerous case studies (complete Java programs), ranging from the simple to the substantial. To emphasize the importance and reality of the software development life cycle, case studies are always presented in the framework of a user request, analysis, design, and implementation, with well-defined tasks performed at each stage. Some case studies are carried through several chapters or extended in end-of-chapter programming projects.

How to Use the Book

We have organized the book to satisfy different time frames and topic preferences. We recommend that every student read Chapter 1, which provides an overview of the main topics of CS2. Students who have had a thorough introduction to object-oriented programming with Java in CS1 can skip Chapter 2. Students who wish to use terminal I/O only can skip Chapter 3, which introduces GUI programming. Chapters 4 and 5 give an overview of complexity analysis and the use of arrays and linked structures in Java. All students should read Chapter 4, but those who have already worked with arrays and linked structures might skip Chapter 5. Chapter 6, which provides an overview of Java's collections framework, is required reading. There we introduce the interfaces, hierarchies, and other important concepts such as iterators that play a large role in subsequent chapters. Chapters 7, 8, and 9 cover stacks, queues, and lists. They could be read in any order. Recursion (Chapter 10) could be read earlier, but should be read before Chapters 11 and 12, which discuss tree structures. Chapters 13 through 15 provide a transition to advanced topics in the computer science curriculum, such as hashing, graph algorithms, concurrent programming, and client/server applications.

We have made every effort to produce an error-free text and take full responsibility for any errors or omissions. Readers are encouraged to report errors to klambert@wlu.edu. A listing of errata, should they exist, and other information about the book will be posted on the author's Web site, http://www.wlu.edu/ ~lambertk/ CS2Java/.

Acknowledgments

Our thanks to the reviewers of this second edition and, again, to those of the first edition. We are especially grateful to Pete Peterson, of Texas A & M University, who gave us extra insight and guidance.

Our editorial and production staff working with Brooks/Cole also deserves thanks for making this book possible: Kallie Swanson, Brooks/Cole editor; Dusty Friedman, production service; Frank Hubert, copyeditor; Debra Gates, proofreader; and Julie Nemer, indexer.

Kenneth A. Lambert
Martin Osborne

To Carolyn
Ken

To Ann
Martin

CHAPTER 1

Overview

Upon completion of this chapter, you should be able to

- Describe the principal features of four categories of collections

- Explain the purpose and importance of algorithm design and analysis

- Summarize the steps in the software development process

- Give an overview of the main ideas of object-oriented programming

- Discuss the different ways in which software is tested

In this chapter, we introduce the major topics covered in this book. These topics include collections, abstract data types, and the analysis of algorithms. In addition, we give a brief overview of object-oriented programming and the software development process.

1.1   Collections

The principal topic of this book is collections. A collection, as the name implies, is a group of items that we wish to treat as a conceptual unit. Nearly every nontrivial piece of software involves the use of collections, and while much of what you learn in computer science comes and goes with changes in technology, the basic principles of organizing collections endure. In your first computer science course, you undoubtedly worked extensively with arrays, which are the most common and fundamental type of collection. Other important types of collections include stacks, lists, queues, binary search trees, heaps, graphs, maps, sets, and bags. Collections can be homogeneous, meaning that all items in the collection must be of the same type, or heterogeneous, meaning the items can be of different types. In most languages, arrays are homogeneous. In some collections, the items are restricted to objects, whereas in others, the items can be objects or primitive types such as integers and doubles.

1.1.1 Categories of Collections

An important distinguishing characteristic of collections is the manner in which they are organized. In this book, we explore four main categories of collections.

Linear Collections

The items in a linear collection are, like people in a line, ordered by position. Each item except the first has a unique predecessor, and each item except the last has a unique successor. As shown in Figure 1.1, D2's predecessor is D1, and its successor is D3. Everyday examples of linear collections are grocery lists, stacks of dinner plates, and a line of customers waiting at a bank.

Figure 1.1   **A linear collection**

Hierarchical Collections

Data items in hierarchical collections are ordered in a structure reminiscent of an upside-down tree. Each data item, except the one at the top, has just one predecessor, its **parent,** but potentially many successors, called its **children.** As shown in Figure 1.2, D3's predecessor (parent) is D1, and its successors (children) are D4, D5, and D6. A company's organization tree and a book's table of contents are examples of hierarchical collections.

Figure 1.2   **A hierarchical collection**

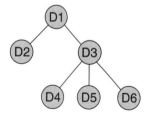

Graphs

A collection in which each data item can have many predecessors and many successors is called a graph. As shown in Figure 1.3, all elements connected to D3 are considered to be both its predecessors and successors. Examples of graphs are maps of airline routes between cities and electrical wiring diagrams for buildings.

Figure 1.3 **A graph collection**

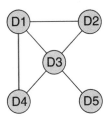

Unordered Collections

As the name implies, items in an unordered collection are not in any particular order, and one cannot meaningfully speak of an item's predecessor or successor. Figure 1.4 shows such a structure. A bag of marbles is an example of an unordered collection. Although one can put marbles into and take marbles out of a bag, once in the bag, the marbles are in no particular order.

Figure 1.4 **An unordered collection**

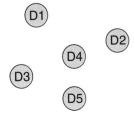

1.1.2 Operations on Collections

Collections are typically dynamic rather than static, and their contents change throughout the course of a program. The actual manipulations that can be performed on a collection vary with the type of collection being used, but generally, the operations fall into several broad categories:

Search and retrieval: These operations search a collection for a given target item or for an item at a given position. If the item is found, either it or its position is returned. If the item is not found, a distinguishing value such as null or −1 is returned.

Removal: This operation deletes a given item or the item at a given position.

Insertion: This operation adds an item to a collection and usually at a particular position within the collection.

Replacement:

This operation combines removal and insertion into a single operation.

Traversal:

This operation visits each item in a collection. Depending on the type of collection, the order in which the items are visited can vary. During a traversal, items can be accessed or modified. Some traversals also permit the insertion or removal of items from the underlying collection.

Test for equality:

If items can be tested for equality, then the collections containing them can also be tested for equality. To be equal, two collections must contain equal items at corresponding positions. For unordered collections, of course, the requirement of corresponding positions can be ignored. Some collections, such as strings, can also be tested for their position in a natural ordering by using the comparisons less than and greater than.

Determination of size:

Every collection contains a finite number of items. This number is the collection's size. Some collections also have a maximum capacity, or number of places available for storing items. An egg carton is a familiar example of a container with a maximum capacity.

Cloning:

This operation creates a copy of an existing collection. The copy usually shares the same items as the original, a feat that is impossible in the real world. In the real world, a copy of a bag of marbles could not contain the same marbles as the original bag, given a marble's inability to be in two places at once. However, the rules of cyberspace are more flexible, and there are many situations in which we make these strange copies of collections. What we are copying is the structure of the collection, not the elements it contains. However, it is possible, and sometimes useful, to produce a ***deep copy*** of a collection in which both the structure and the items are copied.

Exercises 1.1

1. Give three real-world examples of each of the following types of collections:
   a. linear
   b. hierarchical
   c. graph

2. How does replacement of an item in a collection differ from its removal?

3. State two criteria for the equality of two collections.

4. Describe two ways in which a collection can be cloned.

1.2   Abstract Data Types

From the foregoing discussion, we see that a collection consists of data organized in a particular manner together with methods for manipulating the data. However, those who use collections in their programs have a rather different perspective on collections than those who are responsible for implementing them in the first place.

Users of collections need to know how to declare and use each type of collection. From their perspective, a collection is a means for storing and accessing data in some predetermined manner, without concern for the details of the collection's implementation. From the users' perspective, a collection is an *abstraction,* and for this reason, in computer science, collections are called *abstract data types.*

Developers of collections, on the other hand, are concerned with implementing a collection's behavior in the most efficient manner possible, with the goal of providing the best performance to users of the collections. Throughout this book, we consider collections from both angles. For each category of collections (linear, hierarchical, etc.), we define one or more abstract data types and one or more implementations of that type.

The idea of abstraction is not unique to a discussion of collections. It is an important principle in many endeavors both in and out of computer science. For example, when studying the effect of gravity on a falling object, we try to create an experimental situation in which we can ignore incidental details such as the color and taste of the object (what sort of apple was it anyway that hit Newton on the head?). When studying mathematics, we do not concern ourselves with what the numbers might be used to count, fishhooks or arrowheads, but try to discover abstract and enduring principles of numbers. A house plan is an abstraction of the physical house, and it allows us to focus on structural elements without being overwhelmed by incidental details such as the color of the kitchen cabinets, which is important to the eventual house but not to the house's structural relationships. In computer science, we also use abstraction as a technique for ignoring or hiding details that are for the moment inessential, and we often build up a software system layer by layer, each layer being treated as an abstraction by the layers above that utilize it. Without abstraction, we would need to consider all aspects of a software system simultaneously, an impossible task. Of course, the details must be considered eventually, but in a small and manageable context.

In Java, methods are the smallest unit of abstraction, classes are the next, and packages the largest. We will implement abstract data types as classes and gather them together in a package called `lamborne`. The `lamborne` package in turn supplements and extends the package `java.util`, which is a key component of the Java development library.

Exercise 1.2

Give an example of the use of abstraction from your everyday life.

1.3 Algorithm Analysis

As we are going to implement abstract data types in several different ways, we need some basis for comparing their implementations. We must ask: What are the qualities that make one implementation preferable to another, assuming that each implementation is correct to begin with? More generally, how can we choose between competing algorithms for any computer process? There are several criteria for measuring algorithms, the most important of which are simplicity, clarity, and efficiency.

1.3.1 Simplicity and Clarity

All things being equal, and they never are, we prefer algorithms that are as simple and clear as possible; however, attempts to improve space and time efficiency usually come at the cost of increased programming complexity. As people are fond of saying, there is no such thing as a free lunch.

1.3.2 Space Efficiency

When we discuss space efficiency, we are not talking about the memory occupied by the code. Rather, we are concerned with memory allocated to data and to supporting method calls. The space requirements for the latter become significant whenever recursive methods are used. The memory requirements for an ideal implementation of a collection would be exactly equal to the space occupied by the data being stored in the collection. However, in practice, there is nearly always additional overhead. As we present various implementations of collections, we compare the actual space used to the ideal.

1.3.3 Time Efficiency

The amount of time it takes to perform a task can vary greatly depending on the algorithm used. For example, consider how long it takes to search a list of names. The most obvious approach is to start at the top of the list and work down until either the name or the end of the list is encountered. On average, when a name is in the list, this linear search process entails looking at half the list. However, if the list is sorted alphabetically, a much more efficient binary search algorithm can be used. First, look at the name in the middle of the list. If it equals the name desired, the search is over. If it is later in alphabetical order, repeat the search in the first half of the list, and if it is earlier in alphabetical order, search in the second half. At each stage, this process halves the portion of the list remaining to be examined, and it terminates quickly. Table 1.1 shows the maximum number of comparisons needed by both methods as a function of the list's size.

Because the two search algorithms are fundamentally different in their speed, they are said to be of a different **order**. Later, we define this term precisely, but basically, two algorithms are of a different order if there is a point beyond which one is always better than the other. For instance, consider Figure 1.5, which graphs the run times of two algorithms based on the size of the collection they are processing. For values of n less than N_1, algorithm A is faster than algorithm B, but after that, B is always superior.

Table 1.1   **The Number of Comparisons as a Function of a List's Size**

Size of List	Maximum Number of Comparisons Made during a Binary Search	Maximum Number of Comparisons Made during a Linear Search
10	4	10
100	7	100
1,000	10	1,000
10,000	13	10,000
n	smallest m such that $n \leq 2^m$	n

Figure 1.5   **The run times of two algorithms**

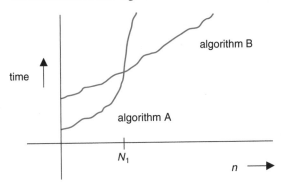

Exercise 1.3

There are three algorithms that operate on a collection of size n. They have running speeds that are expressed as $\log_2 n$, n, and n^2. Which algorithm is the fastest, which is the slowest, and why?

1.4   Algorithm Types

Computer scientists sometimes classify algorithms according to the design strategies they employ. Three of the most common types of algorithms are *greedy* algorithms, *divide-and-conquer* algorithms, and *backtracking* algorithms.

1.4.1   Greedy Algorithms

At each step, a greedy algorithm does whatever is most profitable or most urgent or most gratifying at that instant without regard to future consequences. A greedy algorithm repeats this process until the task has been completed. An everyday example occurs when we work through a list of things to do. At each step, we select the most urgent item.

As a more complex example, consider the task of connecting several cities with a network of fiberoptic cables in the cheapest manner possible (Figure 1.6). The connection between two cities does not have to be direct. For instance, the path from Seattle to Philadelphia could pass through Denver. Obviously, there will not be any looping paths in the final network because, if there were, we could remove one of the cables in the loop without isolating any cities, thereby obtaining a cheaper network. So how do we construct the network? The answer is surprisingly simple. Start by installing the cheapest stretch of cable. At each subsequent step, install the cheapest stretch that does not introduce a loop. Continue until all cities are part of the network.

Figure 1.6   **Cable routes between several cities**

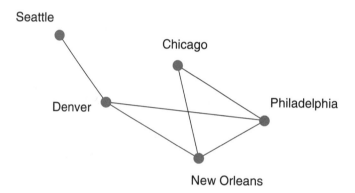

Later in the book, we prove that this simple algorithm actually produces the desired result. Although it is fairly easy to write greedy algorithms, there are many situations in which they do not work as intended. In general, we can hardly expect a sequence of locally optimal decisions to lead to a globally optimal result. For instance, when one hikes up a mountain, taking the easiest path at each juncture is as likely to lead to the base of an unscalable cliff as it is to the peak.

1.4.2   Divide-and-Conquer Algorithms

In a divide-and-conquer algorithm, we divide a large problem into smaller subproblems. We then solve each subproblem separately and combine the results into a solution to the whole problem. The procedure is particularly attractive when each subproblem is of the same type as the original so that it can be solved by reapplying the technique until sub-subproblems are finally reached which are trivially simple to solve. This particular approach to divide-and-conquer algorithms is called ***recursion.***

As an everyday example, suppose we are asked to look for a needle in a haystack. We divide the haystack in two and look for the needle in each half separately. We reapply the technique to each half in turn and repeat until the pieces are so small that we can tell at a glance if the needle is in one of them. Despite being tediously slow, the technique should work, although the authors cannot claim to have actually tried it. However, we have all used a similar technique to find words in a dictionary, where the fact that the words are in order allows us to eliminate blocks of pages at each stage.

1.4.3 Backtracking Algorithms

Backtracking algorithms involve nothing more than an organized approach to trial and error. At any point, when confronted by several alternatives, we select one at random. If it does not work out, we backup to the last place that still has an untried alternative and try again.

We mentioned earlier that a greedy algorithm approach to mountain climbing was inadvisable; however, a backtracking algorithm is guaranteed to get us to the top provided there is at least one climbable path from the parking lot to the summit. We begin by taking any path from the parking lot. At each junction in the trail, we take any direction that has not already been tried. Whenever we reach a location beyond which we cannot advance, we backup to the last place at which there is an untried choice and take it. The drawback of this approach is that it is probably going to be inefficient. Unless we get lucky, we will not go directly to the mountaintop on the shortest path possible, but at least we will get there eventually.

We will encounter many examples of these different types of algorithms throughout the book.

Exercise 1.4

Give an example of a greedy algorithm, a divide-and-conquer algorithm, and a backtracking algorithm from your daily life.

1.5 The Software Development Process

For the remainder of this chapter, we consider various aspects of the software development process. As this is not a book on software engineering, the coverage is somewhat superficial, but the ideas presented give you greater insight into software development and introduce you to techniques that you can begin to apply to your own programs. To get started, we note that computer software has some interesting features that distinguish it from other human artifacts.

1.5.1 Complexity

Software is unique in its complexity. No other human construct approaches the number of parts and interdependencies common to large software systems. Even computer hardware is a distant second.

1.5.2 Fragility

Software systems are fragile. No logic error is so small that it does not have the potential for crashing some immense and critical program. Imagine if houses could collapse because of one misplaced nail. Even worse, imagine a house that stands for years and then tumbles over one day because an untested sequence of events has occurred, such as flushing the toilet, taking a shower, and turning on the dishwasher in quick succession. It sounds preposterous, but unfortunately, analogous situations occasionally crash software systems. An unforeseen and perhaps innocent sequence of events causes some portion of a program to be executed for the first time or with values never encountered before, and the program dies.

An obvious way to reduce the risk of errors associated with software complexity and fragility is to test programs thoroughly before putting them into production. But as we see later, this remedy is not as easy as it sounds.

Even when a program is tested completely and thoroughly or is known to be perfectly correct by virtue of some other technique, such as a mathematical proof of correctness, there is still no guarantee that it will operate as planned when exposed to real-world situations. For instance, back in the early days of America's early-warning defense system, the rising of the moon was mistaken for a swarm of Soviet missiles. How could such a thing happen? It was not a logic error. The software designers had forgotten to take the moon's existence into consideration, and radar beams bouncing off the moon where mistaken for incoming rockets. The first American to blast into space landed several hundred miles from the intended splashdown because again the software designers had made a slight oversight. They never stopped to consider that the earth's motion around the sun would have an effect on the space capsule's reentry path.

Our favorite story of this type concerns a fail-safe torpedo guidance system. The torpedo's guidance program was designed to trigger a self-destruct mechanism in the unlikely event that the torpedo accidentally got turned around. After all, you would not want the torpedo to sink the ship that launched it. A destroyer with forward torpedo tubes was assigned the task of testing the new guidance system. Everything went fine until one day the firing mechanism failed, the torpedo got stuck in the tube, and the destroyer turned around and headed back to port. Boom! It certainly is hard to think of everything, and we probably never do, but thankfully, the consequences are usually not so dramatic.

1.5.3 Malleability

Another problem faced by software engineers is that software is highly malleable. At first glance, this seems to be an advantage compared with the situation in the early days of computing, when programmers had to rewire the hardware each time they ran a new application. However, the malleability of software has a downside. Customers think nothing of asking for changes that are unthinkable for any other type of product. An airline manufacturer is not asked to toss in a couple of extra engines at the last minute, and a building contractor is not expected to retrofit a basement. But requests of similar magnitude are common in the computer world, and developers are magically supposed to accommodate them.

1.5.4 Interconnectivity

Finally, software is more than just lines of code. The interactions between the parts are significant, but these interactions are invisible. Imagine being asked to modify a large system. Your boss begins by tossing a 200-page listing on your desk. Where do you go from there? How can you possibly conceptualize the dynamic behavior of such a system? But until you have, you dare not change a single line of code.

In the next several sections, we discuss techniques that will help you build reliable and maintainable software.

Exercise 1.5

Discuss several respects in which software is different from hardware.

1.6 Introduction to Object-Oriented Programming

There are several general approaches to programming. Among the most common are the procedural, the functional, and the object-oriented approaches.

1.6.1 Procedural Programming

The procedural approach decomposes a software system into a hierarchy of subprograms called *procedures.* Subprograms at an intermediate level provide a service to those above it and obtain the support of those below it. Each procedure solves a piece of the overall problem. Frequently, many of the procedures manipulate a common pool of data. The structure of a procedural program is like an upside-down bushy tree that spreads out from a single procedure at the top. Each procedure on one level typically depends on several procedures at the next lower level in the tree. Some procedures may also have dependency links to other procedures at the same level in the tree. When a procedural program is large, these dependencies can make it hard to maintain. Furthermore, the fact that many procedures tend to operate on a common pool of data can produce unexpected and erroneous side effects.

1.6.2 Functional Programming

The functional approach decomposes a software system into a set of subprograms called *functions.* Unlike procedures, the functions in a functional program do not tend to access global data, so unexpected side effects are fewer. Moreover, well-structured functional programs are not treelike, but layered. There tend to be fewer connections and dependencies between layers of functions than there are between individual procedures in a tree. Thus, large functional programs are easier to design and maintain than large procedural programs.

1.6.3 Object-Oriented Programming (OOP)

The object-oriented approach decomposes a software system into a set of communicating *objects.* Unlike functions or procedures, objects contain both data and methods for manipulating these data. To prevent unexpected side effects, objects can *encapsulate* or hide their data, allowing access to them only through a restricted set of operations. To maximize the reuse of existing code, new classes of objects can *inherit* behavior from existing classes. Finally, because objects tend to be more loosely connected than either functions or procedures, software engineers have found that object-oriented programs are the most easily designed and maintained.

1.6.4   An Intuitive Overview of Object-Oriented Programming

Just in case your memory of OOP is a little rusty, we now review some of OOP's major concepts by means of an extended analogy. Imagine you are in charge of putting on a wedding reception. Because you cannot do the whole thing yourself, you hire the help of various specialists. For example, you will need

- A band to play the music
- A caterer to supply the food
- A bartender to serve the drinks
- A maintenance person to clean up afterward

After the initial planning, the great day arrives, and thanks to the flawless participation of the specialists, the reception comes off without a hitch. As Table 1.2 shows, there is much in this situation that has meaningful parallels in the development and running of an object-oriented system.

A more detailed review of object-oriented programming appears in Chapter 2.

Table 1.2   **An Object-Oriented View of a Wedding Reception**

The World of the Wedding Reception	*The World of OOP*
Planning the reception.	Designing and programming the system.
Carrying out the reception.	Running the program.
Determining the different types of specialists needed, for instance, musicians and caterers. This process is based on the fact that each type of specialist has particular skills and accessories.	Determining the different types of software components needed in the system, or *classes* as they are usually called. For each class, we must specify its rules of behavior and data requirements in terms of *methods* and *instance variables,* respectively.
The actual reception involves individual specialists, for instance, a bartender named Bob and a trumpeter named Jill, rather than types of specialists.	The running program involves *objects,* each of which is an *instance* of a particular class. A class acts as a template that describes the capabilities of the objects derived from that class.
During the reception, specialists communicate and ask each other to do things. A specialist's response to a request sometimes depends on the	When the program is running, objects send each other *messages.* An object responds to a message by executing the code in a corresponding method.

Table 1.2   **An Object-Oriented View of a Wedding Reception** *(Continued)*

The World of the Wedding Reception	*The World of OOP*
current situation. For instance, when asked to play, a musician looks at the score; however, everyone is careful not to ask any individual to do something for which he or she is not trained.	The outcome often depends on the object's **current state,** as reflected in the values of its instance variables, also called **attributes.** However, when writing the program, we are careful not to send a message to an object unless its class has a corresponding method.
At the start of the reception, the bandleader tells each band member to play the newlyweds' favorite tune. All members understand this request, but their responses depend on their types. The trumpeter toots, and the drummer bangs.	Different types of objects also can understand the same message. This is referred to as **polymorphism.** However, an object's response to a message depends on which class it belongs to.
A bartender not only knows how to mix drinks but also controls the various bottles from which the drinks are made.	An object contains the instance variables on which its methods act. This combination of behavior and data within a single software unit is called **encapsulation.**
A bartender could be called a server, and someone who asks for a drink might be called a client.	In an object-oriented system, an object that receives a message is called a **server** and the one that sends the message is called a **client.** During the course of a program, an object might fill both roles.
Someone who orders a drink needs to know just its name, but not the ingredients or how they are mixed.	When requesting a service, a client object needs to know what message to send to the server, but not the server's internal state or the coding details of its methods. In fact, from the client's perspective, it does not matter if the server's internal details were to change radically, just so long as the end result remains the same. A server's ability to hide internal details from its clients is called **information hiding.**
The band contains several different types of members. All band members share some common skills, for instance, the ability to read music and follow the beat; however, some specialize in the saxophone and others in the trumpet. Thus, there is a hierarchy of band members.	Classes can also be organized in a hierarchy. A class at any point in the hierarchy defines methods and attributes that are shared by all classes below it. The classes below are **subclasses,** while the one above is a **superclass.** Each subclass defines additional methods and attributes that distinguish it from its superclass. This process of sharing is called **inheritance.**

continued

Table 1.2   **An Object-Oriented View of a Wedding Reception** *(Continued)*

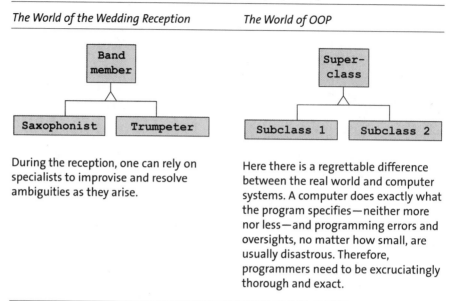

The World of the Wedding Reception	*The World of OOP*
During the reception, one can rely on specialists to improvise and resolve ambiguities as they arise.	Here there is a regrettable difference between the real world and computer systems. A computer does exactly what the program specifies—neither more nor less—and programming errors and oversights, no matter how small, are usually disastrous. Therefore, programmers need to be excruciatingly thorough and exact.

Exercise 1.6

Describe three types of problems for which procedural programming, functional programming, and object-oriented programming would be appropriate.

1.7   The Software Development Life Cycle

Over the years, computer scientists have developed a view of the software development process known as the *software life cycle.* We now present a particular version of this life cycle called the *waterfall model,* which consists of several phases:

1. **User request:** In this phase, the programmers receive a broad statement of a problem that is potentially amenable to a computerized solution. This step is also called the *user requirements* phase.

2. **Analysis:** The programmers determine what the program will do. This is sometimes viewed as a process of clarifying the specifications for the problem.

3. **Design:** The programmers determine how the program will do its task.

4. **Implementation:** They write the program. This step is also called the *coding* phase.

5. **Integration:** Large programs have many parts. These parts must be brought together into a smoothly functioning product, and this is usually not an easy task.

6. **Maintenance:** Programs usually have a long life; 5 to 15 years are common. During this time, requirements change and minor or major modifications must be made.

The interaction between these phases is shown in Figure 1.7. Note that the figure resembles a waterfall in which the results of each step trickle down to the next phase. A mistake detected in one phase often requires the developer to back up and redo some work in the previous phase. Modifications made during maintenance also require backing up to an earlier phase.

Figure 1.7   **The waterfall model of software development**

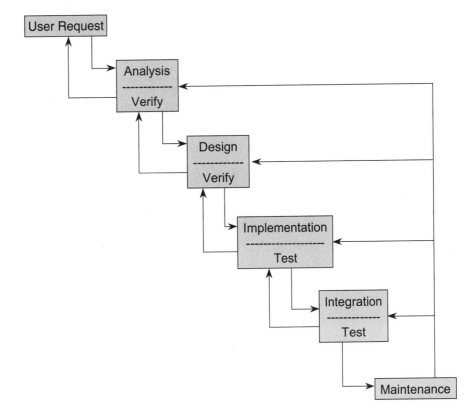

Exercise 1.7

Why should substantial time be invested in analysis and design before a piece of software is coded?

1.8   **Our Approach to Software Development**

This book includes numerous case studies, all of which are presented from a lifecycle perspective.

1.8.1　　　Request

We begin case studies with a supposed customer request. These requests are usually fairly brief, and we must then apply analysis to spell out more precisely what the program will do.

1.8.2　　　Analysis

During analysis, we describe exactly what the system will do and delineate any assumptions and conditions that might apply. During this phase, we always design a user interface. At the beginning of the software development process, it is important to discover exactly the customer's expectations of the system. This could be accomplished by means of pages and pages of written specifications. However, it would be very hard for a customer to make coherent sense of such a document, and there is the very real danger that the system, when it is finally completed months or years later, will be quite different from what the customer envisioned. Mock-ups of the user interface, on the other hand, are readily understood by the customer and can be the basis for a fruitful discussion of the system's capabilities. In fact, it is common to go one step further and make a prototype of the system. Normally, a prototype is an executable program that imitates the system's user interface. It needs to be developed rapidly and is thrown away once it has served its purpose of clarifying the system's requirements.

During analysis, we also determine the major software components from which the system will be built. Because we are using an object-oriented approach, these components are, of course, classes. We describe each class's responsibilities and draw an object model to show the relationship between the classes.

Generally, in our case studies, the user interface consists of a single window that is supported by a *view class.* If there are several windows, then there are an equal number of view classes. Even if the application is trivial, there is also a *model class,* which represents the data being manipulated and in turn works with a number of other application-specific classes.

1.8.3　　　Design

During design, we determine the variables and methods for each class. In Chapter 2, we discuss the overall strategy for doing this. In a view class, there are variables representing the view's visual components (command buttons, menu items, text boxes, etc.), and there are methods that respond to user-initiated events such as menu and command button activations. In addition, the view contains a reference to the model. The methods included in the model are determined by the overall data manipulation requirements of the application. Most of these manipulations occur in response to messages from the view, which in turn is responding to user-initiated events.

1.8.4　　　Implementation

Finally, we present an implementation that conforms to our analysis and design decisions.

1.9 Testing during Analysis and Design

Testing is integral to all phases of the software development process and is not an activity restricted only to the coding phase. During analysis, we must review our work and make sure we are satisfying the customer's specifications and taking all real-world constraints into consideration. This process often requires a deep understanding of the problem domain. To develop a computerized financial system, we must understand and incorporate fundamental accounting principles. When creating an early-warning defense system, we must consider the impact of the rising of the moon. During design, we must continually verify that we are adhering to the requirements and guidelines established during analysis.

But how should we conduct this process of verification? There is no way to "run" the specifications created during analysis and design through a computer in order to "see" if the results are correct and complete, an approach we depend on when we test code. We might instead just check our work very carefully by hand; however, it is nearly impossible to do so effectively. The false assumptions and oversights that led to the inclusion of an error in the first place tend to be repeated during the review. For programmers working in a team, there is a way out of this dilemma. It is called a *walk-through.*

1.9.1 Walk-Throughs

During a walk-through, one team member presents his or her work to the others. Everyone focuses on discovering flaws. Most frequently, it is the person doing the presentation who, suddenly in the midst of explaining some point, discovers an oversight, inconsistency, or contradiction, despite the fact that the presenter may have glided over this error any number of times previously without noticing anything wrong.

There are several important guidelines for conducting a walk-through. First, management should never use the walk-through as an opportunity to evaluate the presenter's competence or productivity. To do so inhibits the free flow of ideas and shifts the focus away from the product being examined to the person doing the presentation, who now has a vested interest in covering up shortcomings. Second, the people listening must be careful not to make their comments personal, and in a like spirit, the presenter must not take comments personally. Third, it is very important not to try to correct errors during the walk-through. Correcting errors is always a separate process.

1.10 Testing Code

Remarkably, walk-throughs are also an excellent way to test code. At first blush, walk-throughs for code seem like an inordinate waste of everyone's time. Surely, one might think, it is faster and more effective to run the code against test data. Although test data are required, the construction of completely effective test data is nearly impossible, so many defects go undetected, even after all tests have been passed flawlessly. Walk-throughs of code take time, but it is time well spent. Overall, higher quality software is obtained in less rather than more time.

1.10.1 Unit, Integration, and Acceptance Testing

There are three points in the coding process at which test data should be used. These are called ***unit testing, integration testing,*** and ***acceptance testing.***

Unit testing: In an object-oriented setting, it is possible to test classes in isolation. To perform a unit test, we write code that instantiates an object of the desired type and then send the object a series of messages that subject it to a thorough workout.

Integration testing: After all classes have been tested in isolation, we need to confirm that they work together properly. To the extent possible, it is best to bring classes into the test environment one at a time. If classes are tossed together too soon, it is difficult to track down the source of errors. By bringing new classes into the test environment one at a time, we have a better chance of isolating errors quickly. But this strategy does raise a tricky question: How can we run the system before all the classes are included? There are two answers. First, we can implement the system in a stepwise fashion, at each stage adding features, until we work our way up to the complete system. Second, for some of the classes, we can substitute simplified prototypes that have the same interfaces as the classes they replace but without all of their internal processing capabilities.

Acceptance testing: Once the system has been completed, it must go through one final phase of testing under conditions identical to those in which it will eventually be used on a daily basis. Whereas during integration testing, the system runs against data artificially designed to exercise specific features, now it must be determined if the system functions adequately in a real-life setting.

1.10.2 What to Test

Before we begin testing, we must determine which aspects of our program we wish to verify. At first blush, this seems obvious. We should test to see if the program is correct. A reasonable definition of "correct" is that the program produces the expected outputs when operating on inputs that fall within specified limits. However, there are several other aspects of a program's performance that we might also wish to consider:

1. Is the program ***user friendly?*** No matter how correct a program, if it is difficult to use, it is unacceptable.

2. Is the program ***robust,*** by which we mean does it behave well when presented with invalid or unexpected inputs? A program is inadequate if it crashes when the user misunderstands the input requirements or makes a keyboard error. In contrast, a robust program rejects invalid inputs and signals the user to try again.

3. Is the program *reliable?* How often does it fail and how severe are the consequences of a failure? A program that frequently destroys half a day's work is not reliable.

4. Does the program have *acceptable performance?* A program that takes 10 hours to sort a list of numbers might be correct, but it is not very useful.

1.10.3   How to Design Test Data

There are three basic approaches to testing: *haphazard, black box,* and *white box.*

Haphazard testing: The haphazard approach is the one you might be tempted to use late the night before a program is due. Just bang on the program until it breaks, fix the bugs that show up, and call it good. Considering that the possible combinations of inputs frequently run into the billions and beyond, randomly trying only a few obviously is not very effective.

Black box testing: In black box testing, we try to be more organized in our choice of inputs. Consider the very simple example of a payroll program that computes pay differently for regular hours and overtime hours. Although there are many possible values for hours worked, we do not need to try all of them to feel confident that the program works correctly. When constructing the test data, we observe that all hours between 0 and 40 are in some sense equivalent, as are all hours over 40. So we might decide to test the program with just the inputs 30 and 50. Generally, inputs can be partitioned into clusters of equivalent data, such that if a program works correctly on one set of values from a cluster, it works equally well for all other values in the same cluster. To be on the safe side, we should also test the program for values on the boundaries between clusters. For the payroll problem, this means adding the values 0 and 40 to our test data. Finally, we should consider data that we know are unreasonable. For the payroll problem, we could include −15, 3045, and "3ax6" in the test data.

There are difficulties with black box testing. It is easy to overlook some clusters, and worse, the number of clusters can be so large that we cannot possibly consider them all. It is important to note that the construction of the test data is made without consideration or knowledge of the program's internal workings. It is for this reason that the process is called black box testing.

White box testing: In white box testing, we attempt to concoct test data that exercise all parts of our program. To do so, we examine the code closely and then formulate the test data, but the task can be difficult. Image a program consisting of a dozen `if-else` statements following each other in sequence. When testing this program, prudence recommends using test data that cause each branch of each `if-else` statement to be executed at least once. This is called *code coverage* and perhaps could be achieved with as few as two sets of inputs. The first set might exercise all the `if` clauses, while the second set exercises all the `else` clauses. However, such an approach is woefully inadequate. What we really need are test data that exercise every possible combination of `if` clauses and `else` clauses, of which there are 2^{12}, or 4,096. That is, we need test data that exercise every possible path through the program. This is just a simple example. A typical program might contain an enormous number of paths. Unfortunately, the fact that every path through a program has been tested tells us nothing about whether or not the program's logic takes into account all the different combinations of inputs. Thus, we should combine black box with white box testing.

By the way, once we devise a good set of test data for a program, we should keep it. Then, anytime we change the program, we should rerun it on the test data to make sure that our modifications have not unintentionally broken some feature that previously worked correctly. This process is called *regression testing.*

1.11   Proofs of Correctness

The difficulty of testing programs leads us to look for other approaches to establish program correctness. One of these consists of trying to prove that a program is correct in a strictly mathematical sense. The form of the statement we attempt to prove might be something like this: Given inputs of type X, then program Y produces outputs of type Z. Regrettably, proving even the simplest program correct is quite tedious, and most programmers are much worse at mathematics than they are at programming. Their proofs of correctness might be even more suspect than their code. Nonetheless, programs of significant size have been proven correct, and an understanding of the basic processes involved can help anyone reason more effectively about the programs he or she writes.

At this point, people sometimes wonder why we do not automate the process of determining program correctness. There are, after all, theorem-proving programs. However, before investing a lot of effort in trying to write a general-purpose correctness-proving program, you need to keep a rather amazing fact in mind. It is a proven, incontestable, mathematical truth that it is impossible to write a program that performs the following seemingly much simpler task. To wit, write a program that takes as input the listing for an arbitrary program, X, and a list of arbitrary inputs for that program, Y, and then determines if X will stop or run forever when presented with Y. This is called the ***halting problem.*** And it is impossible, not just difficult, to write a program that can solve it, not only at this time and place but at any time and in any place by any species in the universe.

But wait a minute, you say. How can one ever rule out the possibility of doing something? How can one know that some future genius will not break through the seeming barrier of impossibility? Such are the wonders of mathematics that it is possible to prove something impossible. Another task that mathematical analysis has proven impossible comes from the realm of plain old high school geometry, discovered over 2,000 years ago by the early Greeks. As you may remember, it is easy to bisect an angle using nothing more than a compass and straight edge. However, centuries of effort have never revealed a way to trisect an angle using the same tools. Now, thanks to a branch of mathematics called Galois theory, we know that it can never be done. The French mathematician and genius Évariste Galois, who developed the theory, died in a duel at the age of 21 in the year 1832.

The moral of this discussion of testing and proofs of correctness is not, "Hey, you can't ever be certain your software is correct, so just put it out there and see what happens." No, the responsible programmer must take a disciplined approach to software development. It is possible to write high-quality software, although there are limits to the confidence we should place in complex systems.

1.12 Some Other Aspects of the Software Development Process

We now consider two more things we can do to improve the quality of our software. First, we can follow some well-accepted coding conventions, and second, we can use preconditions and postconditions.

1.12.1 Coding Conventions

The use of good coding conventions leads to more readable, maintainable programs. Good programmers adhere to the following conventions.

Meaningful class, variable, and method names: Class and variable names should be nouns or noun phrases that suggest the purpose of the class or variable, for instance, `salesTaxRate` rather than `tax` or `str`. Method names should be verbs or verb phrases that describe the method's action, such as `computePay` rather than just `pay` or `compute`.

Symbolic constants: A symbolic constant names a value that does not change throughout the course of a program. Using a name, such as `MAX_ACCOUNTS`, instead of a "magic number," such as 25, greatly enhances program readability and maintainability.

Indentation: Modern programming languages are free-format, and most modern programming environments come with syntax-directed editors that format code according to standard conventions. Examples of this format for Java abound throughout this book.

Capitalization conventions: The conventions Java programmers use for capitalizing identifiers are shown in Table 1.3.

Table 1.3

Java Conventions for Capitalizing Identifiers

Kind of Identifier	Spelling Convention	Examples
Constants	All uppercase. Words are separated by an underscore.	`MAX_VALUE, PI`
Variables and methods	Begin with a lowercase letter. Words after the first one begin with a capital letter and are not separated by spaces.	`length, getBalance`
Classes	Begin each word with a capital letter.	`JMenuItem, SalariedEmployee`

Program comments: It is usually difficult to figure out what a program does just by reading the code, unless you happen to be the author and the program is fresh in your mind. Well-placed comments, on the other hand, help both the original programmer and those who must maintain the program in years to come. However, excessive comments, especially those that repeat the obvious, can be worse than none. Over time, programmers often ignore the comments and change the code without updating the comments.

What sort of comments are useful? A class's definition usually begins with an overview of the class's responsibilities. Each variable declaration can be followed by a brief comment that explains the variable's role. A tricky section of code should be preceded by comments that explains what it is doing. Methods can include a short description of what they do. This description often has a fixed format consisting of:

■ a brief description of what the method does
■ a list of the method's preconditions
■ a list of the method's postconditions
■ a description of the value returned by the method

1.12.2 Preconditions and Postconditions

A *precondition* is a statement of what must be true before a method is invoked if the method is to run correctly. A *postcondition* is a statement of what will be true after the method has finished execution. One can think of preconditions and postconditions as the subject of an imaginary conversation between a method's author and user:

Author: Here are the things that you must guarantee to be true before my method is invoked. They are its preconditions.

User: Fine. And what do you guarantee will be the case if I do that?

Author: Here are the things that I guarantee to be true when my method finishes execution. They are its postconditions.

Preconditions usually describe the state of any parameters and instance variables that a method is about to access. Postconditions describe the state of any parameters and instance variables that the method has changed.

Preconditions and postconditions can also be set up as executable statements in Java. Such statements have the following form:

```
if (<condition is not satisfied>)
    throw new <exception type> (<message string>);
```

Let's examine the use of preconditions, postconditions, and exceptions in a hypothetical square root method. If you are not yet familiar with Java, refer to Appendix A for a discussion of syntax.

```
double squareRoot (double x, double tolerance)
// Computes the square root of x to within the specified tolerance
//
// Precondition:    x >= 0 and tolerance > 0
// Postcondition:   If the computed value is called v, then
//                  |x - v * v| < tolerance.
// Returns:         The computed value v.
{
    if (x < 0)
        throw new ArithmeticException ("Error: x is negative");
    if (tolerance <= 0)
        throw new ArithmeticException ("Error: tolerance not positive");

    . . . code computing the square root goes here . . .

    if (Math.abs(x - v * v) >= tolerance)
        throw new ArithmeticException(
            "Error: root not computed to required tolerance");
    return v;
}
```

In this code, each condition is enforced in the following way:

1. The *logical complement* of the precondition or postcondition is evaluated.
2. If that condition returns `true`, then the precondition or postcondition is not satisfied.
3. An exception of the appropriate type (in this case, an `ArithmeticException`) is thrown if the condition is true.

A client program in Java can catch these exceptions and handle them gracefully, or they can be allowed to propagate to the Java Virtual Machine, which terminates the program.

Preconditions and postconditions are especially helpful when used in conjunction with the many methods needed to implement an abstract data type. Preconditions and postconditions form a contract between

- the designer trying to develop a set of manipulative methods that are consistent and complete
- the programmer trying to write the code
- users of the ADT trying to determine how it works

1.13 Development of Hierarchical Systems

For the sake of completeness, we address one last topic concerning software development. Back in the days before object-oriented languages pushed procedural languages aside, software systems were organized as a hierarchy of methods calling each other. In this hierarchy, methods near the top were responsible for the overall control of the system, and those near the bottom tended to do the nitty-gritty work. In some sense, all of this was analogous to the manner in which many human organizations function, be they armies or large manufacturing concerns. The design task of software decomposition then consisted primarily of determining the structure of a reasonable hierarchy. If designed well, some of the methods in such a hierarchy could be used in more than one system. Some of the ideas from this approach to software development are still useful in an object-oriented context. In particular, we can decompose a complex method into a hierarchy of simpler ones.

A question now arises: In which order should one design such a hierarchy of methods? The most popular approach consists of starting at the top and working down. The process is called ***top-down development.*** The opposite approach, ***bottom-up development,*** can also be used. It seems rather artificial to adhere rigidly to either approach. When we think about a problem of any complexity, we get ideas in no fixed order and probably end up using a ***mixed approach.***

Having designed a hierarchy of methods, we must implement and test the methods in some order. Writing them all at once and bringing them together untested often generates numerous errors that are difficult to locate. Instead we could begin by writing and testing the top-level method in isolation. After it has been debugged, we write one of its subordinates, introduce the subordinate into the hierarchy, and test again. In this way, we work down the hierarchy one method at a time. Errors, when they occur, are located quickly. A top-down implementation does raise the question, however, of how to test a method before its subordinates have been written. The solution is to write a ***stub*** as a stand-in for a subordinate. The stub returns some fixed values representative of the method it is replacing. After the stub has served its purpose, it is replaced by the actual method.

Alternatively, we could work up the hierarchy using ***drivers.*** A driver tests another method vigorously by calling it with various combinations of parameters. Actually, it is easier to test low-level methods using drivers than by using a top-down approach. In a top-down approach, it is often difficult to create all the circumstances to which the lowest level methods must respond. Again, a mixed approach may be preferable with top-down for the upper region of the hierarchy and bottom-up for the lower.

KEY TERMS

abstract data type	graph collection	recursion
acceptance testing	greedy algorithms	regression testing
algorithm	hierarchical collection	stub
black box testing	integration testing	top-down development
bottom-up development	linear collection	unit testing
code coverage	object-oriented	unordered collection
divide-and-conquer	programming	waterfall model
algorithms	postcondition	white box testing
driver	precondition	

CHAPTER SUMMARY

There are several major topics that are covered in a second course in computer science. The primary focus is on organizing data with collections. Collections can be viewed from a purely theoretical perspective and classified as linear, hierarchical, graph, and unordered. These broad categories have various subtypes as well, such as lists, stacks, and queues. The formal properties of collections suit them for various applications and have implications for alternative implementation strategies. These strategies in turn form the basis for an exploration of algorithm design and analysis, the software development process, and object-oriented programming.

REVIEW QUESTIONS

1. Which types of collections did you use in your first programming course? If you used more than one type, how did they differ?

2. Describe three types of operations on collections.

3. What is an abstract data type? Give an example.

4. Give one example of a backtracking algorithm that you have used to solve a problem in everyday life.

5. Explain why computer scientists go to the trouble of analyzing algorithms for their efficiency instead of gathering data on actual run times.

6. Think of a complex event in your life and write a description of it from an object-oriented perspective similar to the wedding reception example in Table 1.2.

7. Describe three characteristics of software that make its development different from the development of hardware.

8. What are the major phases of the software life cycle and what happens during each one?

9. What are preconditions and postconditions? Give an example of each.

10. Describe the differences between black box testing and white box testing.

CHAPTER 2

Overview of Object-Oriented Programming and Basic I/O in Java

OBJECTIVES Upon completion of this chapter, you should be able to

- Create classes in Java with the appropriate attributes and behavior
- Describe the roles of constructors, accessor methods, and mutator methods
- Use visibility modifiers to control clients' access to a class's variables and methods
- Throw exceptions to handle error conditions
- Understand the role of interfaces in designing and implementing classes
- Write methods for comparing two objects and for cloning objects
- Employ techniques for serializing objects to transfer them to and from files
- Organize classes in a hierarchy to exploit the features of inheritance and polymorphism
- Explain the restrictions on the use of objects in Java assignment statements and method parameters and when to use the cast operator and `instanceof` operator to overcome these restrictions
- Construct a set of classes for performing basic terminal and text file input and output

2.1 Introduction

Object-oriented programming is a popular way to organize large software systems. A major advantage of this approach is that classes, the basic building blocks of object-oriented systems, *encapsulate* or enclose both data and code. Prior to the development of object-oriented programming, data and code were represented by separate software abstractions, and consequently, it was much harder to subdivide software systems into manageable units.

This chapter provides an overview of object-oriented programming in Java with an emphasis on those features needed to implement data structures. The chapter also reviews basic input/output (I/O) facilities in Java. Although I/O is not part of data structures per se, most programs entail either an interaction with the user or the transfer of data to and from files. Here we present two major approaches to I/O: character-based I/O (involving the keyboard, the console, and files) and serialization. In Chapter 3, we add graphical user interfaces to the I/O mix. While this does not exhaust the possibilities, it is sufficient for our purposes. Much of this material will be a review for students who used Java in CS1, but the examples are simple enough to be grasped even by those who used C++ or a non-object-oriented language in CS1. In addition, supplementary material on Java's most basic features is presented in Appendix A.

The primary features of object-oriented programming are encapsulation, inheritance, and polymorphism. We begin with a discussion of classes and objects and then demonstrate the role of serialization in transferring objects to and from files. We next show how to organize classes in a hierarchy so that the resulting system can exploit inheritance and polymorphism. This concludes the material on the mechanics of object-oriented programming and is followed by a section on object-oriented analysis and design. We finish with a discussion of character-based stream I/O via the console and files.

2.2   Classes and Objects

When building an object-oriented system, a programmer asks the following questions: What are the classes of objects needed for this system? What behavior do these objects exhibit? A *class* is a software package that describes the characteristics of similar objects. An *object* is a run-time entity that contains data and responds to *messages* sent to it by the object's users. A class has two parts:

1. Variable declarations that define an object's data requirements. When a variable refers to memory for data that belong to a single object, it is an *instance variable.* When a variable refers to memory for data that are shared by all objects of a class, it is a *class variable* or *static variable.*

2. *Methods* that define an object's behavior in response to messages. A method is a chunk of code that is activated when an object or a class receives a message. When a method responds to a message sent to an object, it is an *instance method.* When a method responds to a message sent to a class, it is a *class method* or *static method.*

Classes can represent real-world objects such as students and employees or computational objects such as arrays and strings. To give an overview of some of these concepts, we briefly examine the use of two standard Java classes: `String` and `System`.

2.2.1   Example: String Objects

Strings represent collections of characters such as "The cat sat on the mat." Each string in a Java program is an object and instance of the class `String`. The next code segment declares a `String` variable, initializes it to "The cat sat on the mat.", and displays the string and its length in the terminal window:

```
1 String str = "The cat sat on the mat.";
2 int length = str.length();
3 System.out.println(str + " " + length);
4 char ch = str.charAt(2);
```

The first line of code instantiates a `String` and establishes a variable reference, `str`, to this object. The second line sends the message `length` to the string object. In response, the string executes a method that returns its length, or the number of characters it contains. This value, an `int`, is then used to build a new string in the third line of code. The expression in this line contains two string concatenation operators (`+`), which use the characters in the string, a string containing a blank space, and the length to generate a new, longer string. The concatenation operator requires that at least one of its operands be a string. The fourth line retrieves the character at index position 2 within the string, namely, 'e'. Indexing begins at 0.

In this example, all the messages sent to the string object are accessor messages. An *accessor* method returns information about an object's state or content without modifying the object. In contrast, a *mutator* method modifies an object's state. Because strings in Java are *immutable,* meaning they cannot be changed, they recognize no mutator messages.

The next code segment shows how we can use another Java class, `StringBuffer`, to modify the character data within a string:

```
1 String str = "The cat sat on the mat.";
2 StringBuffer buf = new StringBuffer(str);
3 buf.setCharAt(4, 'b');
4 str = buf.toString();
5 System.out.println(str);  // Prints "The bat sat on the mat."
```

Here, the programmer

1. Constructs a string buffer object with the string as its initial contents *(line 2)*.

2. Sends the mutator message `setCharAt` to the string buffer to change 'c' to 'b' at position 4 (actually, the fifth character) *(line 3)*.

3. Resets the string variable to the buffer's modified string *(line 4)*.

4. Displays the string *(line 5)*.

An important point about these examples is that a string's implementation details are hidden from the programmer using the class. This is formally called *information hiding.* Thus, a programmer does not need to know how the collection of characters is represented within a string object, nor does she need to know how the methods are coded. In fact, a programmer needs to know only two things to use a given class:

1. How to create an instance or object of the class. To do this, she invokes one of the class's *constructor methods.*

2. A list of the class's methods including return types and parameters. This is called the class's *interface.* The interfaces for all of Java's standard classes can be found in Sun's Java documentation (see Appendix A for details).

2.2.2   Example: Terminal Output

Our code examples thus far have displayed output to the terminal with a statement of the form

```
System.out.println(<some data>);
```

This code exhibits several features of the use of objects:

- `System` is the name of a class that contains information about the terminal window.
- `out` is the name of a `static` variable in the `System` class. A `static` variable is referenced by using the class name followed by the **selector operator** (.) followed by the variable name, as in `System.out`.
- `System.out` is an instance of the class `PrintStream` and represents the terminal window.
- The method `println` has one parameter, which can be either an object of any type or a value of a primitive data type (such as `int`, `double`, or `String`). When the parameter is a primitive value, `println` converts it to a string if necessary; when the parameter is an object, `println` sends the `toString` message to the object to obtain the object's string representation.
- `println` then writes this string to the terminal window.
- The method `println` is **overloaded,** meaning that the parameter list can vary in either type or number from one call to the next.

2.2.3   Objects, Classes, and Computer Memory

When a Java program is executing, the computer's memory must hold

- executable code for all the classes used (in their compiled form)
- variables that refer to the objects
- objects

Memory for methods is allocated within a class's code block. Memory for data is allocated within objects. Although a class's code must be in memory at all times, individual objects can come and go. An object first appears and occupies memory when instantiated, and it disappears automatically when no longer needed. Java keeps track of whether or not objects are referenced. Because unreferenced objects cannot be used, Java assumes that it is okay to delete them from memory. Java does this during a process called **garbage collection.**

2.2.4   Three Characteristics of an Object

An object has three characteristics worth emphasizing. First, an object has **behavior** as defined by the methods of its class. Second, an object has **state,** which is another way of saying that at any particular moment its instance variables have particular values. Typically, the state changes over time in response to mutator messages sent to the object. Third, an object has its own unique **identity,** which distinguishes it from all other objects in the computer's memory, even those that might momentarily have the same state. An object's identity is handled behind the scenes by the Java Virtual Machine (JVM) and should not be confused with the variables that might refer to the object. Of these, there can be none, one, or several. When there are none, the garbage collector soon purges the object from memory. Later, we will see an example in which two variables refer to the same object.

2.2.5 Clients and Servers

When messages are sent, two objects are involved: the sender and the receiver, also called the ***client*** and ***server.*** A client's interactions with a server are limited to sending messages; consequently, a client needs to know nothing about the internal workings of a server. The server's data requirements and the implementation of its methods are hidden from the client, an approach which we previously saw is called ***information hiding.*** From the client's perspective, the server is a ***black box.*** Information hiding allows a class's users to focus on the services it provides, while only the class's implementer needs to understand its internal workings. Another term used to refer to a server is ***abstract data type*** (ADT). An ADT is abstract in that a client knows only the interface of the data type: the set of messages that objects of that type understand.

Exercise 2.2

Browse the documentation for the Java Development Kit (JDK) and locate the `String` and `StringBuffer` classes. Write a short essay that describes the differences between the two classes.

2.3   An `Employee` Class

Having gained a general understanding of basic object-oriented terminology, we are now ready to develop a class from scratch. We begin by considering the class from the perspective of a client; that is, we describe the class's interface. Then we show how to implement the class.

2.3.1 User Requirements

As an example, we consider the requirements of a personnel department that needs to manipulate employee information. In our simple system, each employee has a name, an hourly pay rate, and the number of hours worked for each of 5 working days. Table 2.1 summarizes these attributes.

The user of an employee object should be able to access and modify each of its attributes. In addition, the user should be able to ask an employee for the total hours worked and the total weekly pay. Any hours worked over 40 are paid at 1.5 times the employee's hourly rate. Finally, the client should be able to

- create new employee objects
- make copies of them

- compare them based on ordering by name
- ask for a summary of an employee's data as a string
- save and retrieve employee objects from files

Table 2.1

The Attributes of an Employee

Employee Attribute	What It Represents
Name	The employee's name
Pay rate	The employee's hourly wage
Hours worked	The number of hours worked for each of 5 days

Table 2.2 lists methods in the interface of the `Employee` class and thus summarizes its behavior from the client's perspective. Note that the `Employee` methods `setPayRate`, `setHours`, and `getHours` have preconditions, which are implemented in the class as executable statements.

Table 2.2

The Methods of the Interface for the `Employee` Class

Employee Method	How It Is Used and What It Does
`Employee()`	Example: `Employee emp = new Employee();` Returns a new `Employee` object.

`Employee(String name,`
`        double payRate,`
`        int[] days)`
	Example:
	`int[] hours = {8, 6, 10, 8, 8};`
	`Employee emp = new Employee("Mary", 8.50,`
	`                                    hours);`
	Preconditions: `payRate > 0` and length of `days` equals 5.
	Returns a new `Employee` object.
	Reminder: Arrays and other Java basics are presented in Appendix A.

`void setName(String` `newName)`	Example: `emp.setName ("Sue");` Sets the name of `employee` to `newName`.
`String getName()`	Example: `String str = emp.getName();` Returns the name of `emp`.
`setPayRate` `(double newRate)`	Example: `emp.setPayRate(10.50);` Precondition: `newRate > 0`. Sets pay rate of `emp` to `newRate`.
`double getPayRate()`	Example: `rate = emp.getPayRate();` Returns the pay rate of `emp`.
`void setHours(int` `whichDay, int hours)`	Example: `emp.setHours (3, 8);` Preconditions: `1 <= whichDay <= 5` and `hours >= 0`. Sets the hours on `whichDay` to `hours`.

Table 2.2   **The Methods of the Interface for the Employee Class (Continued)**

Employee Method	How It Is Used and What It Does
int getHours(int whichDay)	**Example:** `int hours = emp.getHours (3);`
	Precondition: `1 <= whichDay <= 5.` Returns the hours on `whichDay.`
int getTotalHours()	**Example:** `int totalHrs = emp.getTotalHours();` Returns the total hours worked.
double computePay()	**Example:** `double pay = emp.computePay();` Returns the weekly pay.
boolean equals(Object obj)	**Example:** `boolean yes = emp1.equals(emp2);`
	Compares two employees for equality using their names. Returns `true` if the names are equal or `false` otherwise.
int compareTo(Object obj)	**Example:** `int relation = emp1.compareTo(emp2);` Compares two employees for ordering using their names. The result is 0 if the names are equal, >0 if the first name is greater than the second name, or <0 if the first name is less than the second name.
Object clone()	**Example:** `Employee emp2 = (Employee)emp1.clone();` Creates and returns a shallow copy of the employee.
String toString()	**Example:** `str = emp.toString();` Returns a string that describes the employee.

Here is a short Java application that tests some of the features of the Employee class.

```java
public class EmployeeTester{

    public static void main(String[] args){

        // Create a default employee object
        Employee emp1 = new Employee();

        // Create an employee object with given attributes
        int [] hours = {8, 10, 6, 8, 9};
        Employee emp2 = new Employee("Sue", 6.50, hours);

        // Display some information about emp2
        System.out.println(emp2.toString());
        System.out.println("Total hours: " + emp2.getTotalHours());
        System.out.println("Weekly pay : " + emp2.computePay());

        // Compare the employees for equality before and after cloning
        System.out.println("Equals: " + emp1.equals(emp2));
        emp1 = (Employee)emp2.clone();
```

Continued

Continued

```
        System.out.println("Equals: " + emp1.equals(emp2));
    }
}
```

The program's output looks like this:

```
Name:      Sue
Pay rate: 6.5
Hours worked:
Day 1: 8
Day 2: 10
Day 3: 6
Day 4: 8
Day 5: 9

Total hours: 41
Weekly pay : 269.75
Equals: false
Equals: true
```

2.3.2   Structure of a Class Template

Before implementing the Employee class, we describe the general form or *template* of all class definitions.

A class template consists of four parts:

1. the class's name and some modifying phrases

2. a description of the class and its instance variables

3. one or more constructor methods

4. one or more methods that specify how an object responds to messages

Here is a typical format for a class template:

```
import <package name>.*;

public class <name of class> extends <some other class>
                            implements <an interface>{

    // Declaration of class and instance variables
    private <type> <name>;
    ...

    // Code for the constructor methods
    public <name of class>() {
       // Initialize the instance variables
       . . .
    }
    . . .

    // Code for the other methods
    public <return type> <name of method> (<parameter list>){
       . . .
    }
    ...
}
```

Some of the phrases used in the template need to be explained:

- import <package name>.*;: This statement gives a class access to all of the classes in a ***package.*** A package is a group of classes that are related in some way. Examples are lamborne, a package of collection classes written by the authors, and java.io, a standard Java package of file management classes. There may be several import statements at the beginning of a class implementation. An alternative form for importing just a single class from a package is

```
import <package name>.<class name>;
```

- public class: Class definitions usually begin with the reserved word public, indicating that the class is accessible to all clients desiring access. There are some alternatives to public that we overlook for now.
- <name of class>: Class names are user-defined symbols, and thus, they must adhere to the rules for naming variables and methods. It is common to start class names with a capital letter and variable and method names with a lowercase letter. The names of variables that are declared to be final, and therefore act as constants that cannot be changed, are often completely capitalized.
- extends <some other class>: Java organizes its classes in a ***hierarchy.*** At the ***root,*** or ***base,*** of this hierarchy is a class called Object. In the hierarchy, if a class A is immediately above another class B, we say that A is the ***superclass,*** or ***parent,*** of B and B is a ***subclass,*** or ***child,*** of A (Figure 2.1).

Figure 2.1 **A simple class hierarchy**

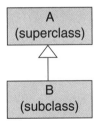

Whenever a new class is created, it must be incorporated into the hierarchy by extending an existing class. The new class's exact placement in the hierarchy is important because a new class inherits the characteristics of its superclass through a process called ***inheritance.*** The new class then adds to and modifies these inherited characteristics, or in other words, the new class ***extends*** the superclass. If the clause extends <some other class> is omitted from the new class's definition, then by default, the new class is assumed to be a subclass of Object, the highest class in Java's class hierarchy.

- implements <an interface>: In addition, a new class may optionally ***implement*** an interface. An ***interface*** is a list of methods that the implementing class must define. Examples are the interfaces: Cloneable, which requires its implementers to define the method `clone`; `Comparable`, which requires its implementers to define the method `compareTo`; and `Serializable`, which allows an object to be transferred to and from a file but does not require a new method to be defined. When appropriate, the programmer can also write code that defines new interfaces, as we shall see in Chapter 6.

■ `private <type> <name>`: Instance variables are nearly always declared to be `private`. This prevents the class's clients from referring to the instance variables directly. Making instance variables private is an important aspect of information hiding.

■ `public <return type> <name of method>`: Methods are usually declared to be `public`, which allows the class's clients to refer to them.

`private` and `public` are called *visibility modifiers.* If both `private` and `public` are omitted, the visibility varies with the circumstances. Without explaining why, suffice it to say that omitting the visibility modifier is often equivalent to using `public`.

To illustrate the difference between `private` and `public`, suppose the class `Employee` has a private instance variable `name` and a public method `setName`. Then

```
Employee e;
e = new Employee();
e.name = "Alice";      // Compiler error -- name is private
e.setName ("Alice")    // No error -- setName is public
```

2.3.3   Design and Implementation of the `Employee` Class

From the user requirements, we know the attributes and the methods of an employee object. During design, we determine the data representation for the attributes and how the methods will be implemented. Table 2.3 shows the types of data.

Table 2.3   **The Attributes of an Employee and Their Data Representation**

Employee Attribute	Data Representation
Name	`String`
Pay rate	`double`
Hours worked	Array of 5 `int`

These data are realized as instance variables. In addition, it is convenient to define final class variables to represent the size of the array, the regular weekly hours, and the overtime pay rate. Class variables, as mentioned previously, are shared by all objects of the class, and the qualifier `final` indicates that once initialized these variables cannot be changed by later code. To support copying, comparisons, and saving employees to files, the `Employee` class implements the interfaces `Cloneable`,

`Comparable`, and `Serializable`. Here is the start of the code for the Employee class:

```
import java.io.Serializable;     // Obtains Serializable interface

public class Employee implements Cloneable,
                                 Comparable,
                                 Serializable{

    // Class variables (actually, constants)
    static public final int MAX_DAYS = 5;
    static public final int MAX_REGULAR_HOURS = MAX_DAYS * 8;
    static public final double OVERTIME_RATE = 1.5;

    // Instance variables
    private String name;
    private double payRate;
    private int[] days;

. . . constructors and methods follow . . .
```

2.3.4 Constructor Methods and Exceptions

The purpose of a constructor is to initialize the instance variables of a newly instantiated object. It is activated when the keyword `new` is used and in no other way. It can never be used with an existing object to reset the object's instance variables.

A class template can include more than one constructor provided that each has a unique parameter list; however, all the constructors must have the same name—that is, the name of the class. The constructors we have seen so far have had empty parameter lists and are called ***default constructors.***

If a class template contains no constructors, the Java Virtual Machine provides a primitive default constructor behind the scenes. This constructor initializes numeric variables to zero and object variables to `null`, a special value that indicates the object variable currently references no object. However, if a class template contains even one constructor, the Java Virtual Machine no longer provides a default constructor automatically.

Here are the two constructors for the `Employee` class:

```
// Constructor methods

    // Initialize a new employee's name to the empty string and her
    // pay rate and hours worked to 0
    public Employee(){
        name = "";
        payRate = 0;
        days = new int[MAX_DAYS];
        for (int i = 0; i < MAX_DAYS; i++)
            days[i] = 0;
    }

    // Initialize a new employee's attributes to the given parameters
```

Continued

Continued

```
     // Preconditions: payRate > 0
     //                 size of array == MAX_DAYS
     public Employee (String name, double payRate, int[] hoursWorked){
        if (hoursWorked.length != MAX_DAYS)
           throw new IllegalArgumentException(
                "Array must have " + MAX_DAYS + " days");
        if (payRate <= 0)
           throw new IllegalArgumentException("Pay rate must be > 0");
        this.name = name;
        this.payRate = payRate;
        days = new int[MAX_DAYS];
        for (int i = 0; i < MAX_DAYS; i++)
           days[i] = hoursWorked[i];
     }
```

Note that the second constructor enforces its preconditions in the following way:

1. The *logical complement* of the precondition is evaluated.

2. If that condition returns `true`, then the precondition is not satisfied.

3. An *exception* of the appropriate type (in this case, an `IllegalArgumentException`) is thrown if the condition is true.

A client program in Java can catch these exceptions and handle them gracefully, or they can be allowed to propagate to the Java Virtual Machine, which terminates the program. The next two short programs and screen shots illustrate these options. Both programs feed an oversized array to the `Employee` constructor. The first program allows Java to handle the exception. Here is the listing followed by the output:

```
public class Oversize1{

   public static void main(String[] args){

      // Create an employee object with an oversized array
      // and let Java handle the exception
      int [] hours = {1, 2, 3, 4, 5, 6};
      Employee emp = new Employee("Sue", 6.50, hours);
   }
}
```

```
java.lang.IllegalArgumentException: Array must have 5 days
     at Employee.<init>(Employee.java:34)
     at Oversize1.main(Oversize1.java:8)
Exception in thread "main"
 ----jGRASP wedge2: exit code for process is 1.
 ----jGRASP: operation complete.
```

The second program uses a `try-catch` statement to recover from the exception under program control. Again, here is the listing followed by the output:

```
public class Oversize2{
   public static void main(String[] args){
```

Continued

Continued

```
        // Create an employee object with an oversized array
        // and handle the exception ourselves
        try{
            int [] hours = {1, 2, 3, 4, 5, 6};
            Employee emp = new Employee("Sue", 6.50, hours);
        }catch (IllegalArgumentException e){
            System.out.println ("Caught the error:\n" + e.toString());
        }
    }
}
```

```
Caught the error:
java.lang.IllegalArgumentException: Array must have 5 days
```

As you can see, the program does not terminate when the exception is thrown but allows other actions to occur.

2.3.5   What Is **This**?

The implementation of the second `Employee` constructor method uses the following statements to initialize the employee's instance variables:

```
public Employee (String name, double payRate, int[] hoursWorked){
    .
    .
    .
    this.name = name;
    this.payRate = payRate;
```

Note the use of the reserved word `this`. The word `this` refers to the object itself. Thus, the expression `this.name` refers to the current employee object's instance variable, whereas the expression `name` refers to the constructor method's parameter. In addition to helping resolve name conflicts, the reserved word `this` is often used to implement additional constructor methods. For example, suppose the implementer wanted to provide a constructor that accepts just the employee's name from the client. The code for this method is:

```
public Employee (String name){
    this();
    this.name = name;
}
```

Instead of initializing the instance variables to their default values in this method, we invoke the default constructor to do so. The expression `this()` refers to the default constructor for the `Employee` class.

In general, there are three forms for using the reserved word `this`:

1. `this.<variable name>`: References an instance variable.
2. `this(<parameters>)`: References a constructor method.
3. `this.<method name>(<parameters>)`: References an instance method.

2.3.6 Accessors, Mutators, and `toString`

The next code segment shows the implementation of the `Employee` accessor methods, mutator methods, and the method `toString`. Note the use of exceptions to enforce preconditions:

```java
//Public methods

  // Set an employee's name
  public void setName (String name){
     this.name = name;
  }

  // Get an employee's name
  public String getName (){
     return name;
  }

  // Set an employee's pay rate
  // Precondition: newRate > 0
  public void setPayRate (double newRate){
     if (newRate < 0)
        throw new IllegalArgumentException("new rate must be > 0");
     payRate = newRate;
  }

  // Get an employee's pay rate
  public double getPayRate (){
     return payRate;
  }

  // Set the hours worked on the indicated day
  // Preconditions: 1 <= whichDay <= MAX_DAYS
  //                hours >= 0
  public void setHours (int whichDay, int hours){
     if (whichDay < 1 || whichDay > MAX_DAYS)
        throw new IllegalArgumentException(
              "Day must be >= 1 and <= " + MAX_DAYS);
     if (hours < 0)
        throw new IllegalArgumentException("hours must be >= 0");

     days[whichDay - 1] = hours;
  }

  // Get the hours worked on the indicated day
  // Precondition: 1 <= whichDay <= MAX_DAYS
  public int getHours (int whichDay){
     if (whichDay < 1 || whichDay > MAX_DAYS)
        throw new IllegalArgumentException(
              "Day must be >= 1 and <= " + MAX_DAYS);
     return days[whichDay - 1];
  }

  // Compute and return an employee's total hours
  public int getTotalHours(){
     int total = 0;
```

Continued

Continued

```
      for (int i = 0; i < MAX_DAYS; i++)
         total += days[i];
      return total;
   }


   // Compute and return an employee's weekly pay
   public double computePay(){
      int total = getTotalHours();
      int overtimeHours = total - MAX_REGULAR_HOURS;
      if (overtimeHours > 0)
         return payRate * OVERTIME_RATE * overtimeHours +
                payRate * MAX_REGULAR_HOURS;
         else
            return payRate * total;
   }

   // Return a string representation of a employee's name, pay rate
   // and hours worked.
   public String toString(){
      String str = "Name:        " + name + "\n" +
                   "Pay rate: " + payRate + "\n" +
                   "Hours worked:\n";
      for (int i = 0; i < MAX_DAYS; i++)
         str += "Day " + (i + 1) + ": " + days[i] + "\n";
      return str;
   }
```

The method `toString` is also defined in the `Object` class, so if we had not re-defined it here, an `Employee` object would still recognize the `toString` message; however, the default implementation in `Object` only returns the class name.

2.3.7 Testing for Equality

A Java programmer should be careful when comparing two objects for equality. There are two ways to do this:

1. Use the equality operator = =.
2. Use the instance method `equals`. This method is defined in the `Object` class and uses the = = operator by default, but the method is often overridden as we shall illustrate shortly.

Consider the following rather surprising code segment which instantiates a `String` object and then checks its value in two different ways:

```
String str = new String("Java");          // Instantiate a String
                                           // object and let str
                                           // reference it.


System.out.println (str == "Java");        // Displays false.

System.out.println (str.equals ("Java"));  // Displays true.

System.out.println (str != "Java");        // Displays true.
```

Here is an explanation:

1. The objects referenced by the variable `str` and the literal `"Java"` are two different objects in memory, even though the characters they contain are the same.

2. The operator `==` compares the references to the objects, not the contents of the objects. Thus, if the two references do not point to the same object in memory, `==` returns `false`. Because the two strings in our example are not the same object in memory, `==` returns `false`.

3. The method `equals` is redefined in the `String` class and returns `true` if two `String` objects have exactly the same content.

4. A corollary of these facts is that the operator `!=` can return `true` for two strings even though the method `equals` also returns `true`.

The operator `==` can be used with objects of any type. In these cases, too, the `==` operator tests for object identity: a reference to the same object in memory. Thus, we usually avoid using `==` when comparing objects. For instance, to test two employee objects for equality, we implement the method `equals` in the `Employee` class as follows:

```java
// Compare two employees for equality
public boolean equals (Object other){
    if (this == other)
        return true;
    if (! (other instanceof Employee))
        return false;
    Employee employee = (Employee)other;
    return name.equals (employee.name);
}
```

Note that the method expects an `Object` as a parameter. This means the user can pass an object of any class when the method is called. However, the method should compare the two objects only if the parameter object is in fact of class `Employee`. Therefore, the method must do one of three things:

1. Return `true` if the two objects are identical (using `==` for the test).

2. Return `false` if the parameter object is not an instance of class `Employee`.

3. If the parameter object is an instance of class `Employee`, cast its class down from `Object` to `Employee` before accessing the data within it. We explore the technique of casting in more detail shortly.

2.3.8   Comparisons and the `Comparable` Interface

Some objects have a natural ordering. For example, one can sort a list of strings in ascending or descending order. To do this, one must compare objects for less than or greater than, as well as equal to. Some Java classes, such as `String`, implement the `Comparable` interface to provide this capability. This interface requires the server to implement a single method, `compareTo`. Its form is:

```
// Returns 0 if objects are equal, < 0 if less than, > 0 if
// greater than

int compareTo(Object other)
```

The following code segment illustrates the use of this method:

```
String s1 = "Ali";
String s2 = "Ann";

int aliToAnn = s1.compareTo(s2);    // < 0 because "Ali" < "Ann"
int annToAli = s2.compareTo(s1);    // > 0 because "Ann" > "Ali"
int aliToAli = s1.compareTo("Ali"); // == 0 because "Ali" equals "Ali"
```

Here is the code for the Employee method compareTo:

```
// Compare two employees for order
public int compareTo (Object other){
    if (! (other instanceof Employee))
        throw new IllegalArgumentException("Parameter must be an Employee");

    Employee employee = (Employee)other;
    return name.compareTo(employee.name);
}
```

Because Employee objects are comparable, we can implement a method that sorts an array of employees by name. The following code uses a *selection sort algorithm,* which is discussed in detail in Chapter 4.

```
void sortByName(Employee[] employees, int employeeCount){
    for (int i = 0; i < employeeCount - 1; i++){
        int minIndex = i;

        // Find smallest name
        for (int j = i + 1; j < employeeCount; j++){
            Employee e1 = employees[j];
            Employee e2 = employees[minIndex];

            // Compare two employees
            if (e1.compareTo(e2) < 0)
                minIndex = j;
        }

        // Swap employees if necessary
        if (minIndex != i){
            Employee temp = employees[i];
            employees [i] = employees[minIndex];
            employees [minIndex] = temp;
        }
    }
}
```

2.3.9 Copying Objects and the `Cloneable` Interface

The attempt to copy an object with a simple assignment statement can cause a problem. The following code creates two references to one `Employee` object when the intent is to copy the contents of one `Employee` object to another:

```
Employee e1, e2;
int[] days = {8, 8, 8, 8, 8};
e1 = new Employee ("Mary", 8.50, days);
e2 = e1;                      // e1 and e2 refer to the same object
```

If clients of the `Employee` class need to copy `Employee` objects, the class should implement the interface `Cloneable`. Including this interface allows objects to respond to the message `clone`. A default version of `clone` already exists in the class `Object` and constructs a *shallow* or bit-wise *copy* of an object. A shallow copy causes problems if a class's instance variables are themselves references to objects because then a bitwise copy of an object results in two objects whose instance variables reference, and thus share, common instance objects. In such situations, we must override the default `clone` method and write a new version that begins by copying the instance objects. The result, when coded properly, is a *deep copy.* A shallow copy of an `Employee` object would create two employees sharing the same array of `days`, whereas with a deep copy each employee has his own array even though the two arrays initially contain the same values. Assuming we have already written a suitable `clone` method for `Employee`, here is how we would use it:

```
Employee e1, e2;
int[] days = {8, 8, 8, 8, 8};
e1 = new Employee ("Mary", 8.50, days);
e2 = e1.clone();              // e1 and e2 refer to different objects
```

Note that `==` returns `false` and `equals` returns `true` for an object and its clone.

The implementation of `clone` creates and returns an instance of an `Employee` with copies of the current employee's attributes. Here is the code for the method `clone`:

```
// Clone a new employee
public Object clone(){
    return new Employee (name, payRate, days);
}
```

If you now look again at the `Employee` constructor, you will see that a deep copy has indeed been created.

2.3.10 Object Serialization

Objects are called *persistent* if they survive between runs of an application. Obviously, objects must be saved to a file and loaded from a file if they are to be considered persistent. When objects are complex, the code for transferring them to and from files is in turn complex. Java provides excellent file management capabilities that would allow writing such code; however, Java also provides a feature called *serialization* that supports persistence with a minimum of coding on our part. To use serialization, we do two things:

1. Make each user-defined data class in the program serializable.

2. Use the classes `ObjectInputStream` and `ObjectOutputStream` to load and save the data model.

For example, to serialize the `Employee` class, we import the package `java.io` and add `Serializable` to the list of interfaces implemented by the class. That is it. Most standard Java data classes also implement the `Serializable` interface.

When we are ready to save a particular `Employee` object to a file, we write code like this:

```
import java.io.*;

public class TestSaveEmployee{
    public static void main (String[] args){

        // Create an Employee object
        int[] days = {8, 10, 6, 8, 8};
        Employee emp = new Employee("Bill", 8.50, days);

        // Open the appropriate streams and write the object to the file
        try{
            FileOutputStream foStream = new FileOutputStream ("employee.dat");
            ObjectOutputStream ooStream = new ObjectOutputStream (foStream);
            ooStream.writeObject (emp);
            foStream.flush();
            foStream.close();
        }catch (Exception e){
            System.out.println ("Error during output: " + e.toString());
        }
    }
}
```

The details of opening file streams are explained in Appendix A. The method `writeObject` outputs the `Employee` object to the object output stream. Likewise, the method `readObject` can input an entire object from an object input stream, as shown in the next program:

```
import java.io.*;

public class TestLoadEmployee{
    public static void main (String[] args){

        Employee emp;
        try{
            FileInputStream fiStream = new FileInputStream ("employee.dat");
            ObjectInputStream oiStream = new ObjectInputStream (fiStream);
```

Continued

Continued

```
        emp = (Employee) oiStream.readObject();
        fiStream.close();
        System.out.println (emp);
    }catch (Exception e){
        System.out.println ("Error during input: " + e.toString());
    }
  }
}
```

The method `readObject` returns a generic `Object`, which must be cast to an `Employee` object before being stored in an `Employee` variable. We can save multiple objects to the same file and load them back later, provided we remember their positions in the input stream and their types as we assign them to variables.

Occasionally, an object contains data that are unwise to save to disk. For example, an array's cells might not all be occupied, so it wastes disk space to make the entire array persistent. To indicate that a variable should not be persistent or serialized, we add the reserved word `transient` to its declaration, as in the following example:

```
private transient double[] data;   // This array will not be saved
```

We will see several examples of the use of transient variables in Chapters 6 to 14 on collections.

2.3.11   The Methods `finalize` and `dispose`

Just as a class's constructors are called automatically when an object is instantiated, the method `finalize`, if defined, is called automatically when an object is swept away by the garbage collector. The method usually contains code to free certain types of computer resources that are not recovered by the garbage collector. File handles, about which you may know nothing yet, are an example.

However, using `finalize` in this or any other way has a serious flaw. Programmers have no control over how long the garbage collector waits before doing its job, and during the delay, an important resource may be unavailable. Consequently, programmers sometimes include a method called `dispose` instead. The `dispose` method is not called automatically, so it is the programmer's responsibility to call it when an object is no longer needed, which introduces the risk of calling it too soon. When included, both methods are declared `public void` and take no parameters. Because there is no need to implement these methods in the `Employee` class, we do not include them.

2.3.12   Some Helpful Hints for Working with Objects

1. When developing a user-defined class, write a short tester program that does the following:

a. Creates objects of that class, using each of the different constructor methods.

b. Runs the accessor methods and displays the values of the objects' instance variables.

c. Runs the mutator methods and then displays the values of the variables again.

d. Tests any class variables and class methods in a similar manner.

2. In general, it simplifies testing and debugging if we write a `toString` method for each new user-defined class. The `toString` method returns a formatted string that contains the values of an object's instance variables.

3. Be sure that constructors initialize all of an object's instance variables.

4. When clients need to copy objects, provide a `clone` method. Remember that the simple assignment of variables causes multiple references to the same object.

Exercises 2.3

1. Explain the role of constructors, accessors, and mutators in a class definition.

2. Add the constructor to initialize a name to the `Employee` class and test it with a tester program.

3. Why is it a good idea to declare instance variables as `private`?

4. Explain the use of `this` in a class definition.

5. What are the issues involved in comparing two objects for equality?

6. What are the issues involved in copying objects?

2.4   Inheritance and Polymorphism

Java organizes classes in an ***inheritance hierarchy.*** Classes inherit the instance variables and methods of the classes above them in the hierarchy. A class can extend its inherited characteristics by adding instance variables and methods and by overriding inherited methods. Some classes in a hierarchy must never be instantiated. They are called ***abstract classes.*** Their sole purpose is to define features and behavior common to their subclasses. On the other hand, classes that are instantiated are ***concrete classes.***

Methods with a similar function, but in different classes, are usually given the same name. This is called ***polymorphism.*** Polymorphism makes classes easier to use because programmers need to memorize fewer method names. In a well-designed class hierarchy, polymorphism is employed as much as possible. A good example of a polymorphic message is `toString`. Every object, no matter which class it belongs to, understands the `toString` message and responds by returning a string that describes the object.

Inheritance and polymorphism provide a mechanism for reusing code and can greatly reduce the effort required to implement a new class. We examine these ideas in the context of a simple inheritance structure.

2.5   Implementing a Simple Shape Hierarchy

To illustrate the use of inheritance and polymorphism, we now develop a hierarchy of classes. Suppose we need to perform some basic manipulations on circles and rectangles. These manipulations include positioning, moving, and stretching these basic geometric shapes. In addition, we want to determine a shape's area, and we want to flip the dimensions of rectangles—that is, interchange a rectangle's width and height. For good measure, we require each shape to respond to the `toString` message by returning a description of the shape's attributes.

We proceed by defining classes for circles and rectangles. These classes are called `Circle` and `Rectangle`, respectively. To minimize the coding involved, we first implement a class `Shape` and from it derive the subclasses `Circle` and `Rectangle` (Figure 2.2). Because we never instantiate a generic shape object, we designate the Shape class as `abstract`. The classes `Circle` and `Rectangle`, on the other hand, are concrete.

Figure 2.2   **The Shape class hierarchy**

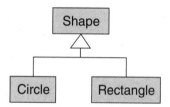

2.5.1   Implementing the Shape Class

Before implementing the hierarchy, we determine which characteristics are shared by `Circle` and `Rectangle`. We gather these together in the `Shape` class. Here is our list of common features:

- **Position:** All shapes have an *x, y* position in an underlying coordinate system. This position can be stored in the instance variables `xPos` and `yPos`. The Shape class's constructors initialize the variables, and its accessor methods make their values available to clients.

- **Movement:** All shapes are movable. Moving a shape is accomplished by changing its *x, y* coordinates. A method `moveTo` performs this task.

- **Area computation:** All shapes are able to calculate their areas; however, this is done differently for circles and rectangles. Consequently, we cannot write code in the Shape class to perform the needed calculations, but we can designate in the Shape class that all subclasses must implement an `area` method. To do this, we declare `area` as an ***abstract method*** in the Shape class. Now, the Java compiler will complain if a subclass of Shape forgets to implement an `area` method.

- **Stretching:** All shapes are stretchable. This is achieved by changing a circle's radius or by changing a rectangle's width and height. The code cannot be written in the Shape class, so we declare an abstract method called `stretchBy`.

- **toString**: All shapes must respond to the `toString` message. The response should include a shape's position. Other details differ for circles and rectangles. Therefore, the `Shape` class implements a `toString` method that indicates only the position. The subclasses need to extend this method to include the other information.

That exhausts the list of attributes shared by circles and rectangles, so we are ready to present a complete listing for the `Shape` class:

```
1 abstract public class Shape extends Object{
2
3     private double xPos;
4     private double yPos;
5
6     public Shape (){
7         xPos = 0;
8         yPos = 0;
9     }
10
11     public Shape (double x, double y){
12         xPos = x;
13         yPos = y;
14     }
15
16     abstract public double area();
17
18     abstract public void stretchBy (double factor);
19
20     public final double getXPos(){
21         return xPos;
22     }
23
24     public final double getYPos(){
25         return yPos;
26     }
27
28     public void moveTo (double xLoc, double yLoc){
29         xPos = xLoc;
30         yPos = yLoc;
31     }
32
33     public String toString(){
34         String str = "(X,Y) Position: (" + xPos + "," + yPos + ")\n";
35         return str;
36     }
37
38 }
```

There are two features worth noting in this listing:

1. **Abstract methods:** On *lines 16* and *18,* the methods `area` and `stretchBy` begin with the word `abstract`, end with a semicolon, and include no code. The purpose of an abstract method is to notify subclasses that they must implement the method or they will not compile successfully. If a class contains an abstract method, that class itself must be abstract as indicated in *line 1.*

2. We have already seen that a constant is specified as a `final` variable. This means that once it is defined, its value cannot be changed. A similar syntax is used to define methods that cannot be redefined in subclasses. For example, the accessor methods for the instance variables of the `Shape` class are defined as `final` *(lines 20–26)*. Classes can also be declared as final. This implies that such classes cannot have subclasses.

2.5.2 Implementing the `Circle` Class

To implement the `Circle` class, we extend the `Shape` class. Only those features of a circle not shared with a rectangle are considered. Thus, the `Circle` class must do the following:

■ Declare a variable to keep track of a circle's radius.

■ Implement the abstract methods `area` and `stretchBy`.

■ Extend `Shape`'s constructors and `toString` method.

Here is the listing:

```java
public class Circle extends Shape{

    private double radius;

    public Circle(){
        super();
        radius = 0;
    }

    public Circle (double xLoc, double yLoc, double rds){
        super (xLoc, yLoc);
        radius = rds;
    }

    public double getRadius(){
        return radius;
    }

    public double area(){
        return Math.PI * radius * radius;
    }

    public void stretchBy (double factor){
        radius = radius * factor;
    }

    public String toString(){
        String str = "CIRCLE\n"
                    + super.toString()
                    + "Radius: " + radius + "\n"
                    + "Area: " + area();
        return str;
    }
}
```

The word `super` in this listing activates code in the superclass. The details of how this is done are different in constructors than in other methods, as we explain next.

2.5.3 Constructors and `super`

When an object is instantiated, a constructor is activated to initialize the object's variables. The constructor is, of course, located in the object's class. If variables are declared in the superclass, these also need to be initialized. This initialization is achieved most easily by activating the constructor in the superclass. To activate the default constructor in the superclass, use the method `super`:

```
super();
```

To activate a different constructor in the superclass, use the reserved word `super` together with the parameter list of the desired constructor; for instance,

```
super (xLoc, yLoc);
```

2.5.4 Other Methods and `super`

The `Circle` class also uses `super` in a completely different manner. Any method can include code that looks like this:

```
super.<method name> (<parameter list>);
```

This code activates the named method in the superclass. In contrast, the code

```
<method name> (<parameter list>);
```

activates the named method in the actual class of the receiver object. We saw an example in *line 29* of the `Circle` class's `toString` method:

```
+ super.toString.
```

2.5.5 Implementing the `Rectangle` Class

The `Rectangle` class's implementation is similar to that of the `Circle` class. There is one minor difference. The `Rectangle` class includes a method, `flipDimensions`, that is not part of either the `Shape` or `Circle` class. Here is the code:

```
public class Rectangle extends Shape{

    private double width;
    private double height;

    public Rectangle(){
        super();
        width = 0;
        height = 0;
    }

    public Rectangle (double xLoc, double yLoc, double wdth, double hght){
```

Continued

Continued

```
      super (xLoc, yLoc);
      width = wdth;
      height = hght;
   }

   public double area(){
      return width * height;
   }

   public void flipDimensions(){
      double temp = width;
      width = height;
      height = temp;
   }

   public void stretchBy (double factor){
      width = width * factor;
      height = height * factor;
   }

   public String toString(){
      String str = "RECTANGLE\n"
               + super.toString()
               + "Width & Height: " + width + " & " + height +"\n"
               + "Area: " + area();
      return str;
   }
}
```

2.5.6   Protected Variables and Methods

Earlier, we discussed the difference between `public` and `private` visibility. A name can be declared `public` in a class and thus be visible to the rest of an application. Or a name can be declared `private` in a class and be visible only within that class's implementation. Subclasses cannot see `private` names declared in their parent classes.

To make a method or variable visible to subclasses or other classes within the same package, but not to the rest of an application, we declare it to be `protected`. There are two mechanisms for placing classes in the same package. The first, which we are not going to explore, requires:

■ A package statement is placed at the beginning of each listing.

■ At the time of compilation, the class is in a folder with the same name as the package.

■ After compilation, the bytecode is in a folder with the same name as the package or is gathered together into a `jar` file.

■ The compiler and run-time environment are told where to find the package.

■ Finally, classes using the package import it.

The fact that these rules vary slightly for different integrated development environments (IDEs) adds to the complexity. We will make no further mention of this approach and leave it to the interested reader to explore the details.

The second mechanism is automatic and implicit. All classes compiled together in the same folder are considered to be in a default package even though there is no explicit mention of packages or import statements. To demonstrate protected variables, we could modify the Shape class as follows:

```
abstract public class Shape extends Object{

    protected double xPos;
    protected double yPos;
    . . .
}
```

The variables xPos and yPos are now visible to all descendants of Shape, including Circle, so we could rewrite Circle's constructors as follows:

```
public Circle (){
    xPos = 0;
    yPos = 0;
    radius = 0;
}

public Circle (double xLoc, double yLoc, double rds){
    xPos = xLoc;
    yPos = yLoc;
    radius = rds;
}
```

Obviously, this is not an improvement over our previous manner of coding Circle's constructors. Generally, it is best to limit the visibility of instance variables as much as possible, so private instance variables are preferred to protected and public ones in most situations.

2.5.7 Implementation, Extension, Overriding, and Finality

From the foregoing discussion, we can see that there are four ways in which methods in a subclass can be related to methods in a superclass:

1. *Implementation* of an abstract method: As we have seen, each subclass is forced to implement the abstract methods specified in its superclass. Abstract methods are thus a means of requiring certain behavior in all subclasses.

2. *Extension:* There are two kinds of extension:
   a. The subclass method does not exist in the superclass.
   b. The subclass method invokes the same method in the superclass and then extends the superclass's behavior with its own operations.

3. *Overriding:* In this case, the subclass method does not invoke the superclass method. Instead, the subclass method is intended as a complete replacement of the superclass method.

4. *Finality:* The method in the superclass is complete and cannot be modified by the subclasses. We declare such a method to be final.

Exercises 2.5

1. Explain the purpose of abstract classes and abstract methods.

2. Where should the reserved words `public`, `private`, and `protected` be used?

3. Explain the cases in which a method would be inherited, in contrast to the cases in which a method is overridden.

4. Describe how the reserved word `super` is used in a class definition.

5. Add a new class, `Cylinder`, to the `Shape` hierarchy. Like other shapes, a cylinder has an area. Unlike other shapes, a cylinder has a volume, so include a method called `volume` that returns a cylinder's volume. Try to exploit inheritance, perhaps by making `Cylinder` a subclass of `Circle`.

2.6   Using the Shape Classes

Here is a little program that tests the shape classes.

```
public class ShapeTester {

    public static void main (String[] args){
        Circle circ;
        circ = new Circle (0, 0, 1);
        System.out.println ("Creating\n" + circ.toString());
        circ.moveTo (1, 2);
        System.out.println ("Moving\n" + circ.toString());
        circ.stretchBy (2);
        System.out.println ("Stretching\n" + circ.toString());

        Rectangle rect;
        rect = new Rectangle (0, 0, 1, 2);
        System.out.println ("Creating\n" + rect.toString());
        rect.moveTo (1, 2);
        System.out.println ("Moving\n" + rect.toString());
        rect.stretchBy (2);
        System.out.println ("Stretching\n" + rect.toString());
        rect.flipDimensions();
        System.out.println ("Flipping dimensions\n" + rect.toString());
    }
}
```

The program produces the following output:

```
Creating
CIRCLE
(X,Y) Position: (0.0,0.0)
Radius: 1.0
Area: 3.141592653589793
Moving
CIRCLE
(X,Y) Position: (1.0,2.0)
Radius: 1.0
```

Continued

Continued

```
Area: 3.141592653589793
Stretching
CIRCLE
(X,Y) Position: (1.0,2.0)
Radius: 2.0
Area: 12.566370614359172
Creating
RECTANGLE
(X,Y) Position: (0.0,0.0)
Width & Height: 1.0 & 2.0
Area: 2.0
Moving
RECTANGLE
(X,Y) Position: (1.0,2.0)
Width & Height: 1.0 & 2.0
Area: 2.0
Stretching
RECTANGLE
(X,Y) Position: (1.0,2.0)
Width & Height: 2.0 & 4.0
Area: 8.0
Flipping dimensions
RECTANGLE
(X,Y) Position: (1.0,2.0)
Width & Height: 4.0 & 2.0
Area: 8.0
```

2.6.1 Finding the Right Method

When a message is sent to an object, Java looks for a matching method. The search starts in the object's class and, if necessary, continues up the class hierarchy. Consequently, in the preceding program, when the moveTo message is sent to a circle or a rectangle, the moveTo method in the Shape class is activated. There is no moveTo method in either the Circle or Rectangle class. On the other hand, when the stretchBy message is sent to a circle, Java finds a corresponding method in the Circle class.

2.6.2 Arrays of Shapes

There are many situations in which we might want to work with arrays of shapes. In this section, we learn some simple rules that must be observed when doing so.

Declaring an Array of Shapes

Suppose we want to work with an array of circles. We might begin as follows:

```
Circle[] circles;                    // Declare an array variable
circles = new Circle[10];            // Reserve space for 10 circles
circles[0] = new Circle (1,1,2);     // Assign a circle to the 1st element
circles[1] = new Circle (6,3,15);    // Assign a circle to the 2nd element
. . .
```

For greater flexibility, we might prefer an array that can hold all the different types of shapes simultaneously—that is, circles, rectangles, and cylinders (see the exercises in the previous section), as demonstrated next:

```
Shape[] shapes;                      // Declare an array variable
shapes = new Shape[10];              // Reserve space for 10 shapes
shapes[0] = new Circle (1,1,1);      // Assign a circle to the 1st element
shapes[1] = new Rectangle (2,2,2,2); // Assign a rectangle to the 2nd
shapes[2] = new Circle (5,5,5);      // Assign a circle to the 3rd
shapes[3] = new Rectangle (4,4,4,4); // Assign a rectangle to the 4th
. . .
```

An important rule must be followed when objects of different classes are mixed in an array:

Rule for Mixing Objects of Different Classes in an Array: If we declare an array variable of type ClassX

```
ClassX[] theArray = new ClassX[10];
```

then we can store in the array objects of ClassX or objects of any class below ClassX in the class hierarchy.

```
theArray[0] = new ClassX();
theArray[1] = new ClassY(); // where ClassY is a subclass of ClassX
theArray[2] = new ClassZ(); // where ClassZ is a subclass of ClassY
. . . etc . . .
```

A similar rule applies to nonarray variables:

Rule for Assigning Objects of Different Classes to a Variable: If we declare a variable of type ClassX

```
ClassX theVariable;
```

then we can assign to the variable objects of ClassX or objects of any class below ClassX in the class hierarchy.

```
theVariable = new ClassX();
theVariable = new ClassY(); // where ClassY is a subclass of ClassX
theVariable = new ClassZ(); // where ClassZ is a subclass of ClassY
. . . etc . . .
```

Sending Messages to Objects in an Array of Shapes

Suppose we have an array of various shapes: circles, rectangles, and cylinders. We can easily find the combined area of all the shapes by sending each an area message.

```
Shape[] shapes = new Shape[10];
shapes[0] = new Circle (...);
shapes[1] = new Rectangle (...);
```

Continued

Continued

```
. . .
totalArea = 0;
for (int i = 0; i < 10; i++)
    totalArea += shapes[i].area();
```

This works because the `area` method is declared in the `Shape` class and implemented in each of the concrete classes actually stored in the array. Because the `area` method is polymorphic throughout the `Shape` hierarchy, each object in the array knows what to do when it is sent the `area` message.

The `instanceof` *Operator*

In the last exercise set, you developed a `Cylinder` class that recognizes a `volume` message. Now, suppose we add volume objects to our array of shapes. We might try to find the combined volume of all the shapes; however, we are now confronted with a problem. Some shapes do not have a volume and do not recognize the `volume` message. We can overcome this difficulty by sending the `volume` message only to those shapes that have a volume—that is, to the cylinder objects. Java provides an operator that allows us to determine an object's class. It is called `instanceof`. Here, then, is a first attempt at finding the total volume of all the shapes:

```
Shape[] shapes = new Shape[10];
shapes[0] = new Circle (...);
shapes[1] = new Cylinder (...);
. . .
totalVolume = 0;
for (int i = 0; i < 10; i++){
    if (shape[i] instanceof Cylinder)
        totalVolume += shapes[i].volume(); // <<<<<< Problem here
}
```

That looks good, but there is a problem in the indicated line. There is no `volume` method in the `Shape` class, so the Java compiler will complain. We did not have a similar problem when we were computing the `totalArea` because the `Shape` class does have an `area` method, even if it is an abstract method. Hence, the Java compiler accepts the line of code:

```
totalArea += shapes[i].area();
```

When the preceding line of code is executed, the `area` method used depends on the actual shape being processed at that moment: circle, rectangle, or cylinder.

Casting to the Rescue

We overcome our problem by using the cast operator. We replace the line of code

```
totalVolume += shapes[i].volume();       // <<<<<< Problem here
```

with the line

```
totalVolume += ((Cylinder)shapes[i]).volume(); // <<<<<< No problem
```

However, the cast operator must be used with caution, and two rules must be observed:

1. Before casting an object, be sure that the object is of the target type. Thus, before casting a generic shape to a cylinder, we must be certain that the shape is in fact a cylinder; otherwise, there is a run-time error.

2. Never cast up; only cast down. Thus, it is okay to cast a Shape to a Cylinder, but not vice versa. Class Cylinder is below class Shape in the hierarchy.

Exercises 2.6

1. State the rule for assigning objects of different classes to the same variable.
2. How can polymorphism be used effectively in processing arrays of objects?
3. When is the use of the instanceof operator necessary?
4. Describe the cases in which the casting of objects is necessary and the pitfalls to avoid when casting.

2.7   Shapes as Parameters and Return Values

Objects can be passed to and returned from methods. Objects are passed to methods as parameters and passed back in return statements. Actually, objects themselves are not passed—rather, references to objects are—although we do not usually bother to make the distinction.

It is obvious that an object must exist before it is passed to a method. Less obvious is the fact that the changes the method makes to the object are permanent. The changes are still in effect after the method stops executing. An object returned by a method is usually created in the method, and the object continues to exist after the method stops executing.

If a parameter specifies that an incoming object belongs to ClassX, then an object of any subclass can be substituted. Similarly, if a method's return type is ClassX, then objects of ClassX or any subclass can be returned.

We now illustrate these ideas with some examples.

2.7.1   Example: Rectangle In, Circle Out

For our first example, we write a method that takes a rectangle as an input parameter and returns a circle. The circle has the same area and position as the rectangle. Here is a short program that shows the method in action, followed by a copy of the program's output.

```
public class TestShapes {

   public static void main (String[] args){
      Circle circ;
```

Continued

Continued

```
      Rectangle rectangle;

      rectangle = new Rectangle (1,1,4,6);
      circ = makeCircleFromRectangle (rectangle);

      System.out.println ("\nRectangle Area: " + rectangle.area() +
                          "\nCircle Area:    " + circ.area());
   }

   static private Circle makeCircleFromRectangle (Rectangle rectangle){
      double area = rectangle.area();
      double radius = Math.sqrt (area / Math.PI);
      Circle circle = new Circle (rectangle.getXPos(),
                                  rectangle.getYPos(),
                                  radius);

      return circle;
   }
}
```

```
Rectangle Area: 24.0
Circle Area:    24.000000000000004
```

2.7.2   Example: Any Shape In, Circle Out

We now modify the previous method so that it accepts any shape as an input parameter—circles, rectangles, or cylinders. The fact that all shapes understand the `area` method makes the task easy:

```
static private Circle makeCircleFromAnyShape (Shape shape){
   double area = shape.area();
   double radius = Math.sqrt (area / Math.PI);
   Circle circle = new Circle (shape.getXPos(),
                               shape.getYPos(),
                               radius);

   return circle;
}
```

2.7.3   Example: Any Shape In, Any Shape Out

It is also possible for a method to return any shape rather than a specified one. The next method has two input parameters. The first parameter is a shape, and the second indicates the type of shape to return:

```
static private Shape makeOneShapeFromAnother (Shape inShape,
                                              String returnType){

   Shape outShape = null;
   double area, radius, width, height;
   double x = inShape.getXPos();
   double y = inShape.getYPos();

   area = inShape.area();
   if (returnType.equals ("circle")){
```

Continued

Continued

```
        radius = Math.sqrt (area / Math.PI);
        // Assign a circle
        outShape = new Circle (x, y, radius);
    }else if (returnType.equals ("rectangle")){
        width = height = Math.sqrt (area);
        // Assign a rectangle
        outShape = new Rectangle (x, y, width, height);
    }
    return outShape;
}
```

In this code, notice that outShape is declared to be of type Shape, an abstract class; however, when it comes time to assign a value to outShape, one of the concrete shapes is used—Circle or Rectangle. This is consistent with the rule stated earlier in the chapter:

> If we declare a variable of type ClassX, then we can assign to the variable objects of ClassX or objects of any class below ClassX in the class hierarchy.

Here is a test of the foregoing method followed by a copy of the program's output:

```
public class TestShapes {

    public static void main (String[] args){
        Rectangle rectangle;
        Shape shape1, shape2;

        rectangle = new Rectangle (1,1,4,6);
        shape1 = makeOneShapeFromAnother (rectangle, "circle");
        shape2 = makeOneShapeFromAnother (rectangle, "rectangle");

        System.out.println ("\nRectangle Area: " + rectangle.area() +
                            "\nCircle Area:    " + shape1.area() +
                            "\nRectangle Area: " + shape2.area());
    }

    static private Shape makeOneShapeFromAnother
                    (Shape inShape, String returnType)

        . . . Code as shown above . . .

    }
}
```

```
Rectangle Area: 24.0
Circle Area:    24.000000000000004
Rectangle Area: 23.999999999999996
```

Exercises 2.7

1. Describe the rule for passing different classes of objects to the same parameter of a method.

2. Describe the rule for returning different classes of objects from a method.

2.8   **Decomposition of Object-Oriented Systems**

The major task in software development, as in any large, complex endeavor, consists of breaking the job down into manageable components that can later be recombined to yield a working whole. In an object-oriented setting, this entails determining the classes, their responsibilities, and their interactions. There are several formal methodologies that can assist in this process, but the Unified Modeling Language (UML) seems to be the most widely used. Regardless of the methodology, it is important to take a disciplined and organized approach to software development and to benefit from the experiences of others as distilled in these methodologies. Because the systems we develop in this book are relatively small and because this is not a book on software engineering, we take a somewhat informal, yet effective, approach based on UML.

2.8.1   Finding Classes

The first and most obvious task in developing a system consists of determining the classes from which the system will be composed. But how can we identify the classes? There are several useful sources of information. We can:

■   read the requirements and look for nouns

■   develop potential screen layouts with an eye to identifying data items needed in the system, for instance, customer name and address on a data entry screen

■   consider nouns that are common to the problem domain in general

From this, we will find:

■   the names of classes

■   the names of attributes of classes

■   synonyms for classes and attributes already identified

■   things irrelevant to the problem

At first, it might seem strange that such a mechanical process could lead to a genuinely useful result; however, the experience of many people shows that it does. For the most part, it is not difficult to distinguish between a class and an attribute. For instance, if the problem talks about customers and their balances, it is fairly obvious that there needs to be a `Customer` class with a `balance` attribute. It is common for people, when describing a situation, to use several different words to refer to the same things; in other words, people use synonyms. At one point, a problem's requirements might talk of *customers* and at the next refer to *clients*. As programmers, we must settle on one of the terms and use it as the name of our class. Problem requirements commonly mention things that are not part of the eventual software system but which are nonetheless part of the overall problem context. For instance, a requirement might speak of the showroom in which a sales transaction is negotiated. In this context, we are probably interested in the sales transaction, so we have a `SalesTransaction` class that has attributes specifying the *date, amount,* and *customer* involved; however, the location at which the transaction occurs is probably immaterial, so we do not need a `Showroom` class with attributes describing the *furniture, carpet,* and *wallpaper.*

The classes discovered in this process can represent:

- people, things, places, events/transactions, organizations, abstractions
- collection classes
- user interface classes
    - windows and dialogs
    - window components: buttons, list boxes, edit boxes, and so on
- resource encapsulation classes

Being aware of general categories helps us identify all the classes involved in a system and gives us confidence that we have chosen wisely. The category called **abstractions** is very broad and, in a drawing system, might refer to lines, rectangles, and ovals, whereas in an airline reservation system, it might refer to flight schedules.

Collection classes are, of course, the major topic of this book. Generally, when creating a new object-oriented system, we use existing collection classes rather than create new ones; however, upon completing this book, you will be ready to develop your own when needed.

We rarely develop new user interface classes, as these highly specialized classes are nearly always part of our development environment. In this book, we use Java's standard classes for graphical user interfaces, called the Abstract Window Toolkit (AWT) and Swing. Because there are a large number of classes in the AWT and Swing and because the intricacies of their use can become a major distraction, consuming most of your programming energies, in Chapter 3 we present a streamlined and straightforward approach to graphical user interface (GUI) development that will meets our needs throughout the book.

Resource encapsulation classes are the final category mentioned earlier. Most major programs need to use the computer's files system, access a database, communicate across the Internet, or interact with some other major resource. Fortunately, there are usually packages of classes for dealing with situations of this type, and we do not have to write them ourselves, unless we happen to be specialists in one of those areas and are developing a package for the sake of others.

2.8.2   Assigning Responsibilities

Having identified the classes needed by a new system, we next attempt to make a general statement about each class's role or responsibilities within the system. For instance, the overall responsibility of a `BankAccount` class might be to keep accurate track of a customer's balance. This in turn suggests subsidiary responsibilities of knowing how to handle deposits, withdrawals, and calculations of interest. The manner in which we assign responsibilities can have a significant impact on the overall quality of the final product. Because there are usually many ways in which responsibilities can be allocated, we need to develop guidelines that help us distinguish between good and bad choices. Here are three we have found useful:

Equitable sharing: The work of the system should be shared equitably among the classes. At one extreme, we try to avoid classes that are little more than repositories for data. These are classes that have no methods other than those needed to access the data items. At the other extreme, we avoid classes that try to do too much. Think, by way of analogy, of two companies. In the first company, the boss insists on having direct control over every detail of the company's operations. Responsibility is never delegated. For a task to get done, each employee involved is told exactly what to do. The employees do not communicate with each other. In the second company, each employee has a well-understood area of responsibility and interacts freely with others in the completion of a task, the interactions being guided by the overall responsibilities of each. The boss initiates a task and then steps back and allows employees to get the job done. A well-designed object-oriented system is more like the second company than the first.

Coherence: Each employee in a well-run company and each class in a well-designed system should have a coherent or related set of responsibilities, not a grab bag of miscellaneous ones. Stated differently, each class should have high **cohesion.**

Coupling: Communications between employees and between classes should be parsimonious—that is, minimal, while still achieving the desired end. Communications, although essential, introduce complexity. All things being equal, it is preferable to achieve a result by sending four messages rather than eight. Aside from the number of messages, it is more complicated to invoke a method that has eight parameters than one that has four or fewer. This type of complexity is referred to as **coupling,** and we strive to design systems in which the coupling is low.

The next time you are planning a party, you can experiment with the impact that coherence and coupling have on a successful outcome. Suppose it is a large party, and you have three helpers. Divide the work among the four of you as follows: (1) decorating; (2) buying snacks and drinks; (3) borrowing extra tables, chairs, and eating utensils; (4) organizing the menu. This sounds like a good plan. Each person needs to take care of a group of related activities (high coherence), and there should be little need for communication and coordination among you (low coupling).

On the other hand, just for the sake of the experiment, you could instead make a detailed list of all the individual tasks that need to be completed: Buy mustard, arrange for someone to bring a chicken casserole, ask someone to bring extra chairs (number not known yet), hang colored crepe paper around the room, get some more extra chairs, get some soft drinks, and so forth. Now write each of these individual tasks on a little piece of paper, mix the papers up in a hat, and then each of you in turn picks from the hat until the papers are gone. This is not going to work well. You are each responsible for unrelated tasks (low cohesion), and you all need to be in constant communication with each other to make sure that nothing is forgotten or done incorrectly (high coupling).

In the context of our example, the issues seem so obvious; however, good organization, whether in everyday life or in software development, is critical and difficult to achieve.

2.8.3   Finding Data Attributes

Once the responsibilities of the classes have been determined, we focus on finding the attributes of each class. The attributes are represented by the instance variables within a class, and they are of three types:

1. Attributes that refer to atomic data types. For example,

- weight, height, age, and bank balance can be represented by numbers
- sex and marital status can be represented by characters

2. Attributes that refer to types already in our class libraries. For example,

- name, address, and phone number can be represented by instances of a `String` class
- birthday and employment date can be represented by instances of a `Date` class
- list box, radio button, and edit control are instances of common interface classes
- file, socket, and database table are instances of classes that encapsulate resources

3. Attributes that refer to classes that we are developing as part of the project. For example,

- a `SalesTransaction` class might have as an attribute the customer object who is making the purchase, where `Customer` is another class that we have developed as part of the application

Attributes in the third category involve relationships between the classes we are creating; for instance, every sales transaction involves a customer. We will speak more of this soon when we discuss the object model.

2.8.4   Finding Methods

Everything that happens in an object-oriented system gets done by means of objects sending messages to each other. To determine these messages and the methods that support them, we begin by defining the term *system operation.* A system operation consists of everything the system does in response to a user-triggered event, such as the selection of a menu option.

To find the methods, we need to analyze each system operation in turn and determine a sequence of messages, sent from object to object, that can achieve the needed result. This is a little like writing a play. The objects are the actors, and the messages they send comprise the dialog. In this process, we are guided by the overall role of each class as delineated in an earlier step where we assigned responsibilities to each class. In other words, the messages sent to an object should be consistent with the object's responsibilities or role. In the context of a play, this principle is taken for granted, and we would think it very peculiar if the dialog did not match the characters. That said, there are usually several possible scripts for each system operation, and we attempt to choose the one that is in some sense the most elegant, the one that gets the job done with the least overall effort.

In small systems, and all programs in this book fall into that category, we never actually write any of these scripts. Instead, we rely on our ability to imagine the various situations in which a class must act and then provide it with methods that support its role in those situations.

2.8.5   Relationships Between Classes and the Object Model

A diagram called an *object model* can represent relationships between the classes in a system. The relationships are of two general types in Table 2.4.

Table 2.4	**Two General Types of Relationships among Objects**		
	Type of Relationship	*Shorthand Description*	*Example*
	inheritance	is-a	a robin **is a** bird
	aggregation	has-a	a car **has an** engine

Relationships between classes can also have a *cardinality,* such as one-to-one, one-to-many, or many-to-many. To keep track of this, we can draw *class diagrams.* In the diagrams shown in Figure 2.3, we indicate that:

- eagles, wrens, and robins are types of birds
- a car has from 2 to 4 doors, 4 wheels, and an engine

Figure 2.3   **Features of an object model**

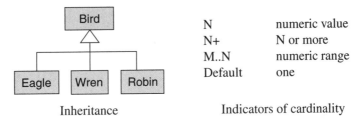

Inheritance   Indicators of cardinality

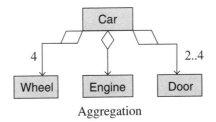

Aggregation

The case studies in the remaining chapters occasionally make use of diagrams of this sort in analysis and design.

2.9   Character-Based Stream I/O

Java's many I/O classes allow programmers to deal flexibly with even the most complex I/O problems; however, somewhat mysteriously, there are no simple ways to handle the most commonplace I/O situations. To illustrate, consider a program that asks the user for degrees Fahrenheit and displays the equivalent degrees Celsius. Here is a sample run:

```
Enter degrees Fahrenheit: 212
The equivalent in Celsius is 100.0
```

And here is the listing of corresponding program:

```
1 import java.io.*;
2 public class FToCFromKeyboard{
3    public static void main (String[] args){
4        double fahrenheit;
5        double celsius;
6        try{
7            InputStreamReader reader = new InputStreamReader(System.in);
8            BufferedReader buffer = new BufferedReader(reader);
9            System.out.print("Enter degrees Fahrenheit: ");
10           fahrenheit = Double.parseDouble(buffer.readLine());
11           celsius = (fahrenheit - 32.0) * 5.0 / 9.0;
12           System.out.println("The equivalent in Celsius is " + celsius);
13       }catch(Exception e){
14           System.err.println("Input error -- " + e.toString());
15       }
16   }
17 }
```

The most obvious feature of this program, and of all programs involving I/O, is that the code is embedded in a `try-catch` statement *(lines 6, 13, 15)*. The actual input is obtained by sending a `readLine` message to a `buffer` object *(line 10)*. This message returns a string, which is then converted into a `double` before being assigned to the variable `fahrenheit` *(line 10)*. The `buffer` object is obtained by a sequence of instantiations *(lines 7, 8)*.

This code is ungainly, and it supports the entry of only a single number per input line. Greater flexibility, at the cost of greater complexity, is obtained by reading a single character at a time from the buffer and then aggregating these characters into numeric strings. However, there is a natural and elegant escape from this tiresome situation that is completely in keeping with the spirit of object-oriented programming. We can build a new class better suited to our needs using the `InputStreamReader` and `BufferedReader` classes.

2.9.1   Introduction to a Keyboard Reader

To illustrate our plan, we present a class called `KeyboardReader` that initially consists of a constructor and one public method:

Method	What It Does and How It Is Used
`KeyboardReader ()`	Creates an instance of the class.
	`KeyboardReader reader =` `    new KeyboardReader ();`

double readDouble()   Reads the next double from the keyboard input stream. If the user enters several doubles on a line, they can be retrieved sequentially by a series of readDouble messages. Throws a NumberFormatException if the double is not well-formed.

```
double d = reader.readDouble();
```

Rewriting the temperature conversion program to use our new class yields less cumbersome code. *Line 1* imports the package containing the KeyboardReader class:

```
 1 import ioutil.*;
 2 public class FToCUsingKeyboardReader{
 3     public static void main (String[] args){
 4         double fahrenheit;
 5         double celsius;
 6         KeyboardReader reader = new KeyboardReader();
 7         System.out.print("Enter degrees Fahrenheit: ");
 8         fahrenheit = reader.readDouble();
 9         celsius = (fahrenheit - 32.0) * 5.0 / 9.0;
10         System.out.println("The equivalent in Celsius is " + celsius);
11     }
12 }
```

The implementation of the class KeyboardReader is somewhat strenuous because of the complexities associated with reading the input stream one character at a time and aggregating the numeric characters into numbers; however, this class is written just once and thereafter is available whenever we need it. Here is a preliminary listing. We call the listing preliminary because we will make it part of a package and incorporate it into a small class hierarchy:

```
import java.io.*;

abstract public class KeyboardReader{

    // Instance variable .........................................

    protected BufferedReader  buffer;

    // Constructor ...............................................

    public KeyboardReader(){
        InputStreamReader reader = new InputStreamReader(System.in);
        buffer = new BufferedReader(reader);
    }

    // Public method .............................................

    public double readDouble(){
        return Double.parseDouble(getWord());
    }

    // Private methods ...........................................

    private char getCharacter(){
```

Continued

Continued

```
    int ch = -1;    // The compiler insists that we
                    // initialize the variable.
    try {
        ch = buffer.read();
    }catch (IOException e){
        System.out.println(e);
        System.exit(0);
    }
    return (char) ch;
}

private char getNonSpaceCharacter(){
    char ch;
    do
        ch = getCharacter();
    while (isWhiteSpace(ch));
    return ch;
}

private String getWord(){
    String word = "";
    char ch = getNonSpaceCharacter();

    do{
        word = word + ch;
        ch = getCharacter();
    }while (!isWhiteSpace(ch));

    return word;
}

private boolean isWhiteSpace(char ch){
    return ch == ' ' || ch == '\t' || ch == '\n' || ch == '\r';
}
}
```

2.9.2　Extending the Keyboard Reader

Now that we see the potential of a `KeyboardReader` class, it is natural to extend it to cover other input situations. The modifications are straightforward, so we do not bother to show the listing; however, it is available on the book's CD. Here is a list of all the public methods in our extended `KeyboardReader` class.

Method	What It Does and How It Is Used

`KeyboardReader ()`	Creates an instance of the class.
	
	`KeyboardReader reader =`
	　　`new KeyboardReader ();`

`char getChar()`	Gets the next character from the keyboard input stream. `char ch = reader.getChar();`

`char readChar()`	Reads the next non-white-space character from the keyboard input stream. White space consists of the characters space (' '), tab ('\t'), newline ('\n'), and return ('\r') `char ch = reader.readChar();`
`double readDouble()`	Reads the next double from the keyboard input stream. Throws a `NumberFormat Exception` if the double is not well-formed. Numbers are separated by white space. `double d = reader.readDouble();`
`int readInt()`	Reads the next integer from the keyboard input stream. Throws a `NumberFormat Exception` if the integer is not well-formed. Numbers are separated by white space. `int i = reader.readDouble();`
`String readLine()`	Reads a complete line from the keyboard input stream. The current line, if any, is first discarded. `String s = reader.readLine();`
`String readWord()`	Reads the next word from the keyboard input stream. Words are separated by white space. `String word = reader.readWord();`
`... read ... (Stringprompt)`	Same as the preceding read methods but first displays the indicated prompt on the console.

From the perspective of these methods, numbers and words are delimited by white space. Character inputs do not need to be separated by white space, but they can be. We now present a short program that illustrates use of the `KeyboardReader` class. Here are two samples of the interface interaction:

```
Enter your name: Bill Smith
Enter three integers: 11 22 33
Bill Smith the sum of the numbers is 66
```

```
Enter your name: Bill Smith
Enter three integers:
          11     22
   33
Bill Smith the sum of the numbers is 66
```

Notice that the user can enter the numbers across multiple lines. Here is the program listing:

```
import ioutil.*;
public class AddThreeIntegers {

    public static void main(String[] args){
        String name;
        int sum, num1, num2, num3;
        KeyboardReader reader = new KeyboardReader();

        name = reader.readLine("Enter your name: ");
        num1 = reader.readInt("Enter three integers: ");
        num2 = reader.readInt();
        num3 = reader.readInt();
        sum = num1 + num2 + num3;
        System.out.println(name + " the sum of the number is " + sum);
    }
}
```

2.9.3 A File Reader

Our success in constructing a `KeyboardReader` class encourages us to explore the possibility of doing something similar for text files. Fortunately, due to the thoughtful manner in which Java supports I/O, this task is very easy. To start, we rewrite our original temperature conversion program to use a file called `in.dat` for input and `out.dat` for output. The input file, created with any text editor, consists of a single line containing a single number. The output file consists of a single line with the format "xx degrees Fahrenheit equals yy degrees Celsius." Here is the code:

```
1  import java.io.*;
2  public class FToCFromFile{
3      public static void main (String[] args){
4          double fahrenheit;
5          double celsius;
6          try{
7              FileInputStream stream = new FileInputStream("in.dat");
8              InputStreamReader reader = new InputStreamReader(stream);
9              BufferedReader buffer = new BufferedReader(reader);
10
11             FileOutputStream fileOutputStream = new FileOutputStream("out.dat");
12             PrintWriter printWriter = new PrintWriter(fileOutputStream, true);
13
14             fahrenheit = Double.parseDouble(buffer.readLine());
15             celsius = (fahrenheit - 32.0) * 5.0 / 9.0;
16
17             printWriter.println(fahrenheit + " degrees Fahrenheit equals " +
18                                 celsius + " degrees Celsius.");
19
20             buffer.close();
21             printWriter.close();
22
23         }catch(Exception e){
```

Continued

Continued

```
24            System.err.println("Input error -- " + e.toString());
25        }
26    }
27 }
```

The differences between the keyboard and file versions of the program are slight. The program still uses a `BufferedReader` for input, but the code leading to its instantiation requires an extra step *(lines 7–9)*. Output is sent to a `PrintWriter`, instantiated in *lines 11–12,* rather than `System.out`, which just happens to be a `PrintWriter` attached to the console rather than to a file   Therefore, we can use `print` and `println` messages just as before. When a program terminates, open files are closed automatically, but we can also close files explicitly as shown in *lines 20–21.*

Because of these similarities between file and console I/O, the code to implement a `FileReader` class is nearly identical to the code for our `KeyboardReader` class. There are some differences between the classes, however.

1. The constructor for a `FileReader` requires a file name parameter:

> `FileReader(String inputFileName)`

2. Read methods never have a prompt parameter.

3. There are two new methods:

> `boolean iseof()`   Returns `true` if the last read failed due to the end-of-file being encountered.
>
> `void close()`   Closes the file reader.

To maximize code reuse, the classes `KeyboardReader` and `FileReader` are subclasses of an abstract class called `TextReader`. We do not list these classes here, but they are on the book's CD.

A short program illustrates the use of the `FileReader` class. The program begins by asking the user for the names of input and output files. It then adds the integers in the input file and prints the sum to the output file. Pay particular attention to the manner in which the end-of-file is detected. The end-of-file condition occurs as soon as the program attempts to read an input that is not present in the file. Notice that the program does not know ahead of time how many integers are in the input file nor does it know how many integers appear on each line. Here is the code:

```
1 import ioutil.*;
2 import java.io.*;
3
4 public class AddIntegersInAFile {
5
6    public static void main(String[] args){
7
8        // Ask the user for the file names
9        KeyboardReader keyboard = new KeyboardReader();
10       String inFileName = keyboard.readWord("Enter name of input file: ");
11       String outFileName = keyboard.readWord("Enter name of output file: ");
12
13       // Sum the integers in the input file
```

Continued

Continued

```
14      ioutil.FileReader inFile = new ioutil.FileReader(inFileName);
15      int sum = 0;
16      int num = inFile.readInt();
17      while (!inFile.iseof()){
18          sum += num;
19          num = inFile.readInt();
20      }
21      inFile.close();
22
23      // Print the sum to the output file
24      try{
25          FileOutputStream
26              fileOutputStream = new FileOutputStream(outFileName);
27          PrintWriter printWriter = new PrintWriter(fileOutputStream, true);
28          printWriter.println("The sum of the integers is " + sum + ".");
29          printWriter.close();
30      }catch(Exception e){
31        System.err.println("Input error -- " + e.toString());
32      }
33   }
34 }
```

In this listing, *line 14* requires some explanation. Both ioutil.* and java.io.* include a class called FileReader. To distinguish between them, we prefix the name of the class with the name of the package from which it is to be obtained. We could avoid the problem by renaming our class, but this sort of thing is fairly common, so there is more to be learned by leaving the name as is.

2.9.4   Formatting the Output

Sometimes it is desirable to format output in columns. This otherwise tedious process is greatly simplified by the introduction of a Format class. The interested reader can view the code on the book's CD. Here we content ourselves with describing the class's methods and presenting two short illustrative programs. The class, which is part of the ioutil package, is limited to static class methods as follows:

String **Format.**justify(char leftRight, long x, int width)

> Converts a long to a string and returns it formatted according to the justification type and specified width.
>
> > leftRight the type of justification ('l', 'c', 'r' — left, center, right)
> >
> > x the number to be formatted.
> >
> > width the length of the returned string.
>
> If the result exceeds the width, a string of *s is returned.

String **Format.**justify(char   leftRight,   char ch,   int width)

> Same as above but for char instead of long.

String **Format.**justify(char   leftRight, String str,   int width)

> Same as above but for String instead of long.

```
String Format.justify(char  leftRight,  double  x,  int
     width, int precision)
```

Same as above but for `double` instead of `long`. Precision indicates the number of digits after the decimal point.

The first demonstration program repeatedly prints the number 1.23456 right justified in a field of width 10 with a varying number of digits after the decimal point:

```
import ioutil.*;

public class VaryingPrecision {

    public static void main(String[] args){

        FileReader reader = new FileReader("in.dat");
        double number = 1.23456;
        for (int i = 0; i < 10; i++){
            String str = "The number with precision " + i + ":"
                       + Format.justify('r', number, 10, i);
            System.out.println(str);
        }
    }
}
```

Here is the program's output:

```
The number with precision 0:         1
The number with precision 1:       1.2
The number with precision 2:      1.23
The number with precision 3:     1.235
The number with precision 4:    1.2346
The number with precision 5:   1.23456
The number with precision 6:  1.234560
The number with precision 7: 1.2345600
The number with precision 8:1.23456000
The number with precision 9:**********
```

The second program reads a file containing sales data and displays the data and totals on the console. The input file looks like this:

```
Catherine 23415
Ken 321
Martin 4384.75
Tess 3595.74
```

And the console output looks like this:

```
NAME               SALES   COMMISSIONS
Catherine       23415.00       2341.50
Ken               321.00         32.10
Martin           4384.75        438.48
Tess             3595.74        359.57
                ----------    ----------
Totals          31716.49       3171.65
```

While not a model of the object-oriented approach, the program is short and simple.

```java
import ioutil.*;

public class PrintSales {

    // Declare variables shared by several methods
    private static String name;
    private static double sales, totalSales = 0,
                            commission, totalCommissions = 0;
    private static FileReader reader = new FileReader("in.dat");

    public static void main(String[] args){

        // Display the headings
        displayText("NAME", "SALES", "COMMISSIONS");

        // Read sales figures, compute commisions,
        // increment totals, and display
        readNameAndSales();
        while (!reader.iseof()){
            commission = sales * 0.10;
            totalSales += sales;
            totalCommissions += commission;
            displayNumbers(name, sales, commission);
            readNameAndSales();
        }

        // Display totals
        displayText("", "----------", "----------");
        displayNumbers("Totals", totalSales, totalCommissions);
    }

    private static void readNameAndSales(){
        name = reader.readWord();
        sales = reader.readDouble();
    }

    private static void displayText(String s1, String s2, String s3){
        String str = Format.justify('l', s1, 12) +
                     Format.justify('r', s2, 15) +
                     Format.justify('r', s3, 15);
        System.out.println(str);
    }

    private static void displayNumbers(String s, double num1, double num2){
        String str = Format.justify('l', s, 12) +
                     Format.justify('r', num1, 15, 2) +
                     Format.justify('r', num2, 15, 2);
        System.out.println(str);
    }
}
```

2.9.5 Using the Support Classes

The programs presented in this section have used several support classes: KeyboardReader, FileReader, and Format. There are several different ways to make support classes accessible to the Java compiler and run-time environment.

1. Include the `class` files in the same directory as the program using them.
2. Place the `class` files in a directory of support classes and modify the `CLASSPATH` environment variable to point at this directory.
3. Include the `class` files in a package of utilities and place this package in the appropriate directory or directories. This is the approach we have taken by placing the classes in the package `ioutil.jar`. When this option is chosen, programs must import the `jar` file in the usual manner (`import ioutil.*;`).

The first option is the simplest to implement. The second and third options are the most convenient to use but require a deeper knowledge of how to install Java. The installation instructions that come with Java and/or your integrated development environment (IDE) usually contain all the information needed to implement options 2 and 3.

Exercises 2.9

1. Study the code for the method `readInt` in the class `KeyboardReader`. Explain where the exceptions might occur and what happens when they occur. *Tip:* Browse the Java documentation on the `Integer` class and the `BufferedReader class`.
2. Explain why the `TestIO` program is shorter and easier to read than an equivalent program that does not use the `KeyboardReader` class.
3. Add a method `pause(<a message>)` to the class `KeyboardReader`. This method should display the message and wait for the user to press the Enter or Return key.
4. Add methods to the class `KeyboardReader` that input characters, integers, doubles, and strings without prompts. *Tip:* These new methods should call the existing methods with empty strings as prompts.

KEY TERMS

abstract class	deep copy	message
abstract method	encapsulation	method
accessor	exception	mutator
casting	extension	overriding
class	final method	package
class method	final variable	parameter
class variable	garbage collection	persistence
client	identity	polymorphism
cohesion	information hiding	serialization
concrete class	inheritance	server
constructor	instance variable	shallow copy
coupling	interface	visibility modifier

CHAPTER SUMMARY

An object-oriented software system consists of a set of objects. Objects communicate by sending messages to each other. Senders of messages are called clients, whereas receivers of messages are called servers. In response to a message, an object executes a method, which performs a task. Objects can contain their own storage for data. These data are encapsulated, and thus secure, when they can be accessed only by sending the appropriate messages. Each object is an instance of a class, which is a template that defines the methods and types of data for that object. An object is created by a process called instantiation, which allows a client to initialize data with particular values.

A final variable behaves like a constant. Once it is declared and initialized, its value cannot be changed.

Static methods and data are associated with a class rather than an instance of a class. A static variable provides a common area of data storage for all instances of a class. A static method allows the client of a class to send a message to that class without instantiating an object.

A class can extend another class and thereby inherit its methods and data. Programmers develop object-oriented software by extending existing class hierarchies, thereby reusing code. Programmers use visibility modifiers to control access to data and methods. Public data and methods can be accessed by any client of a class. Protected data and methods can be accessed only by subclasses of a class. Private data and methods can be accessed only within the defining class.

Some classes are said to be abstract. They are never instantiated. Instead, they provide a place to define a set of data and methods common to several subclasses. Some methods are also abstract. These methods are included in abstract classes and have no implementation. Each subclass is required to provide an implementation.

The set of public methods of a class is called its interface. Several classes can implement the same interface. When two or more classes implement the same interface, that interface's methods are said to be polymorphic. This means that the same messages can be understood by objects of several different classes. Programmers can also define methods in a subclass that override the same methods in a superclass. These methods are also polymorphic. Polymorphic methods allow the programmer to reuse existing interfaces, thereby greatly simplifying the structure of a software system.

Several commonly used interfaces support the comparison, copying, and serialization of objects.

An object-oriented software system handles terminal input and output and text file input and output by sending messages to the appropriate objects.

REVIEW QUESTIONS

1. State three characteristics of an object.

2. What are accessors and mutators? Give an example of each.

3. What is a final variable?

4. Explain the difference between instance variables and static variables.

5. What is data encapsulation? Give an example.

6. Describe the appropriate use of the visibility modifiers public, private, and protected.

7. Give two examples of class hierarchies.

8. A message is sent to an object. Describe how the computer finds the appropriate method to execute.

9. What is an interface? Give two examples.

10. What are polymorphic methods? Give two examples.

11. How does the programmer configure a set of objects so they can be transferred to and from a file?

12. When must the programmer use a cast operator with objects?

13. What are the main issues to be concerned about when comparing two objects for equality?

14. What is the difference between a shallow copy and a deep copy of an object?

15. The computer detects an error condition at run time and throws an exception. Describe what happens next.

CHAPTER 3

Introduction to GUI-Based Applications with Java

OBJECTIVES Upon completion of this chapter, you should be able to

- Create and lay out the components of a simple but realistic graphical user interface (GUI)

- Write the methods for handling user events in a GUI

- Explain the roles and responsibilities of the different parts of the model, view, controller pattern

- Choose the appropriate components, such as buttons, menus, and scrolling lists, for GUI applications

- Write classes that hide the details of layouts and numeric input and output in GUI applications

- Create multiwindow applications

This chapter shows how to create a graphical user interface (GUI). The chapter takes a first look at GUI-based Java applications but does not to provide a complete survey of Java language features for dealing with GUIs. There are many ways in which a GUI-based program can be structured, each with its strengths, weaknesses, and level of complexity. Here we strive to present the simplest structure possible while providing a reasonable degree of generality. The classes that support GUIs are found in the Java packages `java.awt`, `javax.swing`, and `java.awt.event`. This chapter presents the fundamentals of using these packages. Additional details can be found in many advanced books on Java.

Having completed the chapter, you will have the freedom to develop either terminal-based or GUI-based applications. It takes more effort to develop a GUI-based than a terminal-based application, but a GUI's greater ease of use frequently justifies the extra work required to create it.

The best way to use this chapter is to read Sections 3.1–3.6 and 3.10 carefully. Then take just a quick look at the other sections and return to them for a more careful reading when you need the features they discuss. For your convenience, Section 3.11 provides a compendium of the GUI-based methods presented throughout the chapter.

To simplify the coding of several often-repeated tasks, we have written several support classes. These are included on the book's CD in three forms: source code, class files, and in the package `ioutil.jar`. Appendix C explains how to make I/O support classes accessible to the compiler and run-time environment.

3.1 Model, View, Controller Pattern

GUI-based applications are usually organized around the model, view, controller (MVC) pattern. A ***pattern*** is a particular arrangement of classes designed to deal efficiently with a frequently encountered programming situation. A pattern embodies a standard solution to a common problem. The idea of patterns did not originate in programming. For instance, many patterns are employed in architecture. Kitchens in American houses are organized in just a handful of standard ways, and the same can be said for bathrooms and bedrooms. A visit to a foreign country immediately reveals that there are other possibilities. The principal advantage of using patterns is that we spend less time "reinventing the wheel" and more time dealing with each problem's new and unique aspects. Additionally, many widely used patterns have been honed over time by the best programmers until they are efficient, straightforward, and maintainable.

In the model, view, controller pattern, the model represents the data structure or resource being manipulated by the programmer. The view is a visual presentation of the model's current state. The controller responds to commands from the user, usually given in the form of button clicks and menu selections.

The temperature conversion program in Figure 3.1 provides an example. The user enters a temperature, say 212 degrees Fahrenheit, and clicks the F to C button. The program then displays 100 in the Celsius field. Similarly, the program can convert degrees Celsius to degrees Fahrenheit.

Model—The model for this application is a `Thermometer` object that knows a temperature and can return its value in either Celsius or Fahrenheit degrees.

View—The view displays the GUI we see in Figure 3.1.

Controller—The controller consists of classes, called listeners, that are activated when the user clicks the command buttons F to C and C to F and on the icon for closing the

Figure 3.1 **Temperature conversion program**

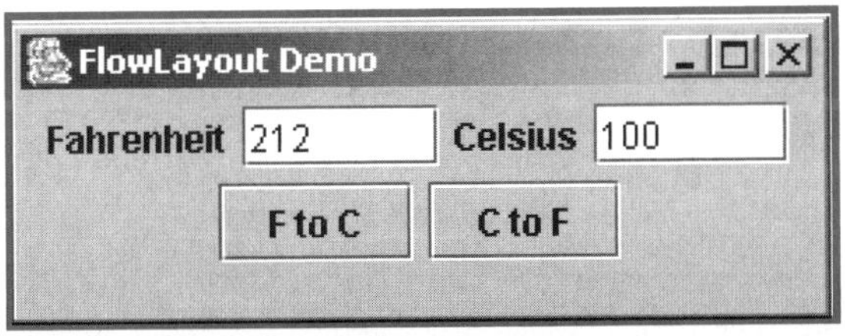

window. Typically, a listener asks the view for the value of one or more data fields, sends messages to the model, and finishes by sending updated values to the view.

3.2   Code for a Temperature Conversion Program

We now examine the code for a temperature conversion program. Even this very simple GUI application has many parts, but fortunately, the parts occur in exactly the same relationship in all programs of this general type. Thus, the complexities need to be mastered only once.

3.2.1   The Model

The model in this example is as short and simple as possible. Here is the code:

```
 1 // Model class
 2
 3 public class Thermometer {
 4
 5    private double degreesCelsius;
 6
 7    public void setCelsius(double degrees){
 8       degreesCelsius = degrees;
 9    }
10
11    public void setFahrenheit(double degrees){
12       degreesCelsius = (degrees - 32.0) * 5.0 / 9.0;
13    }
14
15    public double getCelsius(){
16       return degreesCelsius;
17    }
18
19    public double getFahrenheit(){
20       return getCelsius() * 9.0 / 5.0 + 32.0;
21    }
22 }
```

Line 5 defines the class's single instance variable `degreesCelsius`, which stores the temperature in Celsius. *Lines 7* and *11* provide mutator methods for setting the temperature from either Celsius or Fahrenheit input. *Lines 15* and *19* define accessor methods for retrieving the temperature in either Celsius or Fahrenheit.

3.2.2   The View

The view is a subclass of a standard Java class called `JFrame`. A frame provides a container for the various components that comprise the user interface (labels, data entry fields, lists, command buttons, radio buttons, check boxes, menu bars, etc.). In the present example, the view class is declared as follows:

```
public class DemoFlowLayout extends JFrame{
```

The rational for the rather strange name will become clear shortly.

Sharing the Model with the View. In our approach to writing GUI-based programs, the view instantiates the model and stores it as an instance variable:

```
private Thermometer thermo = new Thermometer();
```

Components. The components that comprise the view are declared as instance variables within the view class:

```
          Type          Name                Instantiate and initialize
private Jlabel       lbFahrenheit = new JLabel ("Fahrenheit");
private JTextField tfFahrenheit = new JTextField ("212", 6);
private JLabel       lbCelsius    = new JLabel ("Celsius");
private JTextField tfCelsius    = new JTextField ("100", 6);
private JButton      btFtoC       = new JButton ("F to C");
private JButton      btCtoF       = new JButton ("C to F");
```

Here we have declared

- two labels initialized to "Fahrenheit" and "Celsius"
- two data entry text fields initialized to "212" and "100", each six characters wide
- two command buttons labeled "F to C" and "C to F"

When the program is running, the user enters numbers in the text fields and clicks the command buttons.

Container and Layout Manager. The view, as a subclass of JFrame, includes a container object to which the components must be added. This is done under the control of a layout manager, which determines the manner in which the components are organized within the container. There are a several different layout options. The easiest to use is a FlowLayout. Components controlled by a FlowLayout are displayed left to right, top to bottom, in the order added to the container. As many components as will fit are displayed on the container's first line. Additional components are then displayed on the second line and so on. If the window is resized, the components move around as shown in Figure 3.2. The resulting appearance is often quite confusing.

Here is the code for adding the components to the container. It appears in the view's constructor:

```
// Create container and layout
Container contentPane = getContentPane();
contentPane.setLayout (new FlowLayout());

// Add controls to container
contentPane.add (lbFahrenheit);
contentPane.add (tfFahrenheit);
contentPane.add (lbCelsius);
contentPane.add (tfCelsius);
contentPane.add (btFtoC);
contentPane.add (btCtoF);
```

Figure 3.2   **Various appearances of a window under control of a `FlowLayout`**

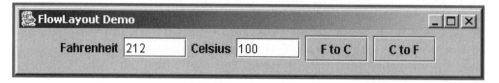

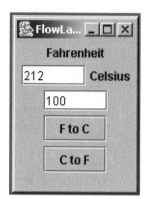

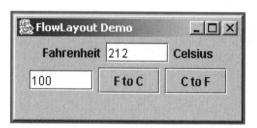

Events and Listeners. The application responds to three user-initiated events corresponding to clicking the command buttons (F to C and C to F) and the window's close icon. To handle these events, we associate listener objects with the command buttons and close icon:

```
// Specify listeners
btFtoC.addActionListener(new FtoCListener());
btCtoF.addActionListener(new CtoFListener());
addWindowListener(new MyWindowAdapter());
```

This code is also part of the view's constructor. The third listener (`MyWindowAdapter`) is associated with the frame class (`DemoFlowLayout`).

3.2.3   The Controller

The controller is implemented by the listener classes. A listener is instantiated in the view and acts when its corresponding event occurs. Listeners for command buttons implement the interface `ActionListener`, which consists of a single method. Here is the code for the F to C button listener:

```
// Fahrenheit button listener
private class FtoCListener implements ActionListener{
    public void actionPerformed (ActionEvent event){
        String inStr = tfFahrenheit.getText().trim();
        double f = Double.parseDouble(inStr);
        thermo.setFahrenheit(f);
```

Continued

Continued

```
        String outStr =
            Format.justify ('1', thermo.getCelsius(), 0, 2);
        tfCelsius.setText (outStr);
    }
}
```

The `actionPerformed` method begins by querying the Fahrenheit field (`tfFahrenheit.getText`). The resulting string is trimmed of spaces and converted to a double. The thermometer object is then updated using `setFahrenheit`, and an equivalent Celsius value is retrieved using `getCelsius`. The static method `Format.justify`, as explained in Chapter 2, converts a number to a formatted string with two digits after the decimal point. Finally, the formatted string is displayed in the Celsius field (`tfCelsius.setText`). The code for the C to F button listener is similar. In Section 3.11, Compendium of Methods, we say more about the methods `getText`, `setText`, and other related methods.

The listener that closes the window extends the class `WindowAdapter`. We merely need to specify the code for the `windowClosing` method:

```
// Window listener
private class MyWindowAdapter extends WindowAdapter{
    public void windowClosing (WindowEvent e){
        System.exit(0);
    }
}
```

Private Classes. The listener classes are defined as private inner classes of the view class. This means that they occupy the same source file as the view class and, very conveniently, have access to all the private instance variables in the view class. It is possible to restructure the program so that the listener classes are public classes, each in its own source file; however, communication between the classes then becomes more awkward. Using private classes keeps things as simple as possible while still maintaining reasonable standards.

Although the inner classes share the same source file as the view class, the compiler places the bytecodes for each class in a separate file. The name of the class file for an inner class is formed by concatenating the name of the view class, the character $, and the name of the inner class as in `DemoFlowLayout$FtoCListener.class`.

3.2.4 Complete Listing for the View and Controller

We are now ready to present a complete listing for the view and controller. After the listing, we make a few additional observations about the code.

```
1 import java.awt.*;
2 import javax.swing.*;
3 import java.awt.event.*;
4
5 public class DemoFlowLayout extends JFrame{
```

Continued

Continued

```
 6
 7      /////////////////////////////////////////////////////// main
 8
 9      public static void main (String[] args){
10         JFrame theFrame = new DemoFlowLayout();
11         theFrame.setSize (200, 125);
12         theFrame.setVisible (true);
13      }
14
15      /////////////////////////////////////////////////////// Model
16
17      private Thermometer thermo = new Thermometer();
18
19      /////////////////////////////////////////////////////// View
20
21      // Create controls
22      private JLabel      lbFahrenheit = new JLabel ("Fahrenheit");
23      private JTextField tfFahrenheit = new JTextField ("212", 6);
24      private JLabel      lbCelsius    = new JLabel ("Celsius");
25      private JTextField tfCelsius    = new JTextField ("100", 6);
26      private JButton    btFtoC       = new JButton ("F to C");
27      private JButton    btCtoF       = new JButton ("C to F");
28
29      public DemoFlowLayout(){
30
31         // Set title
32         setTitle("FlowLayout Demo");
33
34         // Create container and layout
35         Container contentPane = getContentPane();
36         FlowLayout layout = new FlowLayout();
37         contentPane.setLayout (layout);
38
39         // Add controls to container
40         contentPane.add (lbFahrenheit);
41         contentPane.add (tfFahrenheit);
42         contentPane.add (lbCelsius);
43         contentPane.add (tfCelsius);
44         contentPane.add (btFtoC);
45         contentPane.add (btCtoF);
46
47         // Specify listeners
48         btFtoC.addActionListener(new FtoCListener());
49         btCtoF.addActionListener(new CtoFListener());
50         addWindowListener(new MyWindowAdapter());
51      }
52
53      /////////////////////////////////////////////////////// Controller
54
55      // Fahrenheit button listener
56      private class FtoCListener implements ActionListener{
57         public void actionPerformed (ActionEvent event){
58            String inStr = tfFahrenheit.getText().trim();
59            double f = Double.parseDouble(inStr);
60            thermo.setFahrenheit(f);
61            String outStr
```

Continued

Continued

```
62              = Format.justify ('l', thermo.getCelsius(), 0, 2);
63          tfCelsius.setText (outStr);
64      }
65  }
66
67  // Celsius button listener
68  private class CtoFListener implements ActionListener{
69      public void actionPerformed (ActionEvent event){
70          String inStr = tfCelsius.getText().trim();
71          double c = Double.parseDouble(inStr);
72          thermo.setCelsius(c);
73          String outStr
74              = Format.justify('l', thermo.getFahrenheit(), 0, 2);
75          tfFahrenheit.setText (outStr);
76      }
77  }
78
79  // Window listener
80  private class MyWindowAdapter extends WindowAdapter{
81      public void windowClosing (WindowEvent e){
82          System.exit(0);
83      }
84  }
85 }
```

Lines 1–3 of the code import classes needed to support GUIs. *Lines 9–13* contain the static method `main`. Because it is where execution begins, `main` is a necessary part of every application. Here the method instantiates a `DemoFlowLayout` view object, sets the size of the view's window, makes the view visible, and terminates. The code we have written is then inactive until the user triggers an event. The window's size is specified in terms of its width and height as measured in pixels.

3.3   GridBagLayout **Class**

The `FlowLayout` in the preceding program, while simple to use, often yields a rather confusing interface. Better results are achieved by using the more sophisticated `GridBagLayout`. The `GridBagLayout` divides the view into cells, and the programmer then specifies the cell or cells occupied by each component. For instance, consider Figure 3.3, which shows a `GridBagLayout`-based interface for

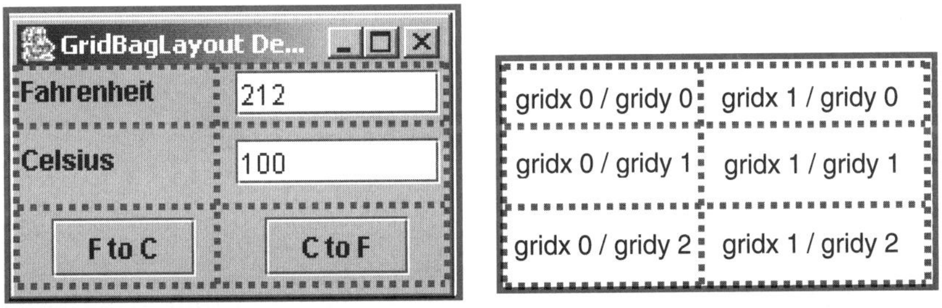

Figure 3.3   A **GridBayLayout** for the temperature conversion program

the temperature conversion program. We have superimposed a grid over the interface to facilitate the discussion that follows. A cell's location in the grid is indicated by its *x* and *y* position, with numbering starting at 0. As each component is added to the layout, its grid position and several other characteristics are specified.

To use the `GridBagLayout`, we replace *lines 34–37* of the preceding code with the much longer code that follows. All the remaining code in the view class is unchanged. The replacement code is a little overwhelming, but do not panic. In the next section, we show how to encapsulate most of the mess in a separate class that we then use in all our GUI applications. Here is the code followed by an explanation:

```
34      // Create container and layout
35      Container contentPane = getContentPane();
36      GridBagLayout layout = new GridBagLayout();
37      contentPane.setLayout (layout);
38
39      // Set basic constraints
40      GridBagConstraints gbc = new GridBagConstraints();
41
42      gbc.insets.bottom = 1;
43      gbc.insets.left = 2;
44      gbc.insets.right = 2;
45      gbc.insets.top = 1;
46
47      gbc.weightx = 100;
48      gbc.weighty = 100;
49      gbc.gridwidth = 1;
50      gbc.gridheight = 1;
51
52      // Set label constraints
53      gbc.fill = GridBagConstraints.NONE;
54      gbc.anchor = GridBagConstraints.NORTHWEST;
55      gbc.gridx = 0;
56      gbc.gridy = 0;
57      layout.setConstraints(lbFahrenheit, gbc);
58      gbc.gridx = 0;
59      gbc.gridy = 1;
60      layout.setConstraints(lbCelsius, gbc);
61
62      // Set text field constraints
63      gbc.fill = GridBagConstraints.HORIZONTAL;
64      gbc.anchor = GridBagConstraints.NORTHWEST;
65      gbc.gridx = 1;
66      gbc.gridy = 0;
67      layout.setConstraints(tfFahrenheit, gbc);
68      gbc.gridx = 1;
69      gbc.gridy = 1;
70      layout.setConstraints(tfCelsius, gbc);
71
72      // Set button constraints
73      gbc.fill = GridBagConstraints.NONE;
74      gbc.anchor = GridBagConstraints.CENTER;
75      gbc.gridx = 0;
76      gbc.gridy = 2;
77      layout.setConstraints(btFtoC, gbc);
78      gbc.gridx = 1;
```

Continued

Continued

```
79          gbc.gridy = 2;
80          layout.setConstraints(btCtoF, gbc);
```

Lines 34–37 are essentially the same as before except that we specify a `GridBagLayout` rather than a `FlowLayout`. *Line 40* instantiates a `GridBagConstraints` object. The position of a component within the grid and several other display characteristics are specified by setting the parameters of the constraint object. The meaning of these parameters is as follows:

gridx, gridy	The position of the component within the grid. If the component spans several cells, then this is the location of the top left cell. Values start at 0.
gridwidth, gridheight	The width and height of the component's enclosing area as measured in grid cells.
insets	The space between the component and the invisible edges of its containing cells.
weightx, weighty	This determines how the space occupied by a component grows and shrinks when the view's size is changed. Our standard weight is 100, but all components do not need the same weight. A weight of 0 specifies that the space occupied by a component remains constant.
fill	This parameter specifies the manner in which a component stretches to fill its containing area. The possibilities are NONE, HORIZONTAL, VERTICAL, and BOTH.
anchor	This controls a component's position within its containing area. The possibilities are CENTER, NORTH, NORTHWEST, and so forth.

Lines 42–50 set constraints that will be shared by all the components. *Lines 53–56* indicate additional constraints for the "Fahrenheit" label. *Line 57* tells the layout to associate the current set of constraints with the "Fahrenheit" label. *Lines 58–80* repeat this process for the remaining components.

3.4   EasyGridLayout Class

The complex code needed to specify a `GridBagLayout` is easily encapsulated in a separate class called `EasyGridLayout`. We first show how to use this class and then present its listing. To use an `EasyGridLayout`, we replace *lines 34–37* of our original listing (see the code for the `FlowLayout`) with the following:

```
34          // Create container and layout
35          Container contentPane = getContentPane();
```

Continued

Continued

```
36        EasyGridLayout layout = new EasyGridLayout();
37        contentPane.setLayout (layout);
38
39        // Set constraints
40        layout.setConstraints(lbFahrenheit ,1,1,1,1);
41        layout.setConstraints(tfFahrenheit ,1,2,1,1);
42        layout.setConstraints(lbCelsius    ,2,1,1,1);
43        layout.setConstraints(tfCelsius    ,2,2,1,1);
44        layout.setConstraints(btFtoC       ,3,1,1,1);
45        layout.setConstraints(btCtoF       ,3,2,1,1);
```

As we set the constraints for each component, we indicate its row position, column position, width in cells, and height in cells. Here rows and columns are numbered starting from 1 rather than 0. The other constraints are set to appropriate default values within the `EasyGridLayout` class.

The listing for `EasyGridLayout` follows. As *line 1* indicates, it is part of the `ioutil` package, which must be imported into any program using `EasyGridLayout`. For the most part, the code is self-explanatory. `JLabel`, `JButton`, and `JTextField` are subclasses of `JComponent`. Other component types that we encounter later in the chapter are also included. If you want to use components not included here, you can modify the class.

```
1 package ioutil;
2
3 import javax.swing.*;
4 import java.awt.*;
5
6 public class EasyGridLayout extends GridBagLayout {
7
8     public void setConstraints (JLabel c, int row, int col,
9                                 int width, int height){
10        finishSet (c, row, col, width, height,
11                0, 0,
12                GridBagConstraints.NONE,
13                GridBagConstraints.NORTHWEST);
14     }
15
16     public void setConstraints (JButton c, int row, int col,
17                                 int width, int height){
18        finishSet (c, row, col, width, height,
19                0,0,
20                GridBagConstraints.NONE,
21                GridBagConstraints.CENTER);
22     }
23
24     public void setConstraints (JTextField c, int row, int col,
25                                 int width, int height){
26        finishSet (c, row, col, width, height,
27                100, 0,
28                GridBagConstraints.HORIZONTAL,
29                GridBagConstraints.NORTHWEST);
30     }
```

Continued

Continued

```
31
32     public void setConstraints (JScrollPane c, int row, int col,
33                            int width, int height){
34        finishSet (c, row, col, width, height,
35                    100, 100,
36                    GridBagConstraints.BOTH,
37                    GridBagConstraints.NORTHWEST);
38     }
39
40     public void setConstraints (JTextArea c, int row, int col,
41                            int width, int height){
42        finishSet (c, row, col, width, height,
43                    100, 100,
44                    GridBagConstraints.BOTH,
45                    GridBagConstraints.NORTHWEST);
46     }
47
48     public void setConstraints (JList c, int row, int col,
49                            int width, int height){
50        finishSet (c, row, col, width, height,
51                    100, 100,
52                    GridBagConstraints.BOTH,
53                    GridBagConstraints.NORTHWEST);
54     }
55
56     public void setConstraints (JCheckBox c, int row, int col,
57                            int width, int height){
58        finishSet (c, row, col, width, height,
59                  0, 0,
60                    GridBagConstraints.HORIZONTAL,
61                    GridBagConstraints.NORTHWEST);
62     }
63
64     public void setConstraints (JRadioButton c, int row, int col,
65                            int width, int height){
66        finishSet (c, row, col, width, height,
67                  0, 0,
68                    GridBagConstraints.HORIZONTAL,
69                    GridBagConstraints.NORTHWEST);
70     }
71
72     public void setConstraints (JPanel c, int row, int col,
73                            int width, int height){
74        finishSet (c, row, col, width, height,
75                    100, 100,
76                    GridBagConstraints.BOTH,
77                    GridBagConstraints.NORTHWEST);
78     }
79
80
81     private void finishSet (Component c, int y, int x, int w, int h,
82                            int weightx, int weighty,
83                            int fill, int anchor){
84
85        GridBagConstraints gbc = new GridBagConstraints();
86
```

Continued

Continued

```
 87        gbc.insets.bottom = 5;
 88        gbc.insets.left = 5;
 89        gbc.insets.right = 5;
 90        gbc.insets.top = 5;
 91
 92        gbc.weightx = weightx;
 93        gbc.weighty = weighty;
 94
 95        gbc.fill = fill;
 96        gbc.anchor = anchor;
 97
 98        gbc.gridx = x-1;
 99        gbc.gridy = y-1;
100
101        gbc.gridwidth = w;
102        gbc.gridheight = h;
103
104        setConstraints(c, gbc);
105    }
106 }
```

The book's accompanying CD includes the source for this file, the corresponding `class` file, and the `jar` file (`ioutil.jar`) containing this and other I/O support classes (see Section 3.11).

3.5   `IntegerField` and `DoubleField` Classes

Many of the book's GUI programs manipulate numeric data. To make the entry and display of numbers as easy as possible, we have developed two subclasses of `JTextField`. These are `IntegerField` and `DoubleField`, and they provide two advantages over `JTextField` when dealing with numeric data. First, their contents can be retrieved and set without the bother of explicitly converting between strings and numbers. Second, invalid nonnumeric characters entered by the user are disregarded rather than causing an exception when the input string is converted to a number.

As an example, we modify the temperature conversion program to use `DoubleField`. Double fields are declared and instantiated as follows:

```
private DoubleField dfFahrenheit = new DoubleField (212);
private DoubleField dfCelsius     = new DoubleField (100);
```

Constraints are specified in the same manner as for a `JTextField`:

```
layout.setConstraints(dfFahrenheit ,1,2,1,1);
layout.setConstraints(dfCelsius     ,2,2,1,1);
```

The Fahrenheit button listener illustrates the simplification in coding:

```
// Fahrenheit button listener
private class FtoCListener implements ActionListener{
```

Continued

Continued

```
public void actionPerformed (ActionEvent event){
    double f = dfFahrenheit.getNumber();
    thermo.setFahrenheit(f);
    dfCelsius.setPrecision(2);
    dfCelsius.setNumber(thermo.getCelsius());
    }
}
```

In place of the getText and setText methods of JTextField, we have substituted the methods getNumber and setNumber. The method setPrecision controls the number of digits displayed after the decimal point. The class IntegerField is used in a similar manner. We omit the listings of both classes, but interested readers can find the source code on the book's CD. They are part of the ioutil package.

3.6 Pop-up Messages

GUI programs sometimes communicate with the user by popping up a small window containing a message. After reading the message, the user dismisses the window by clicking an OK button. To simplify this process, we have added the class MessageBox to ioutil. We now illustrate its use in a short program. Figure 3.4 shows the interface for the program and the pop-up message triggered when the user clicks the command button Save Me. The listing and an explanation follow.

Figure 3.4   **Demonstration of pop-up messages**

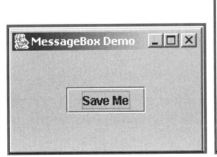
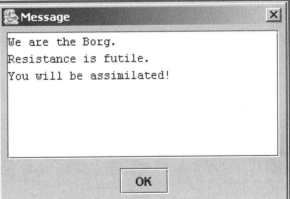

```
1 import java.awt.*;
2 import javax.swing.*;
3 import java.awt.event.*;
4 import ioutil.*;
5
6 public class DemoMessageBox extends JFrame {
```

Continued

Continued

```
 7
 8    //////////////////////////////////////////////////// main
 9
10    public static void main (String[] args){
11        JFrame theFrame = new DemoMessageBox();
12        theFrame.setSize (200, 125);
13        theFrame.setVisible (true);
14    }
15
16    //////////////////////////////////////////////////// Model
17
18    // none
19
20    //////////////////////////////////////////////////// View
21
22    // Create controls
23    private JButton btPressMe = new JButton ("Save Me");
24
25    public DemoMessageBox(){
26
27        // Set title
28        setTitle("MessageBox Demo");
29
30        // Create container and layout
31        Container contentPane = getContentPane();
32        EasyGridLayout layout = new EasyGridLayout();
33        contentPane.setLayout (layout);
34
35        // Add controls to container
36        layout.setConstraints(btPressMe ,1,1,1,1);
37        contentPane.add (btPressMe);
38
39        // Specify listeners
40        btPressMe.addActionListener(new SaveMeButtonListener());
41        addWindowListener(new MyWindowAdapter());
42    }
43
44    //////////////////////////////////////////////////// Controller
45
46    // Fahrenheit button listener
47    private class SaveMeButtonListener implements ActionListener{
48        public void actionPerformed (ActionEvent event){
49            new MessageBox(DemoMessageBox.this,
50                            "We are the Borg.\n" +
51                            "Resistance is futile.\n" +
52                            "You will be assimilated!\n"
53                            , 300, 200);
54        }
55    }
56
57    // Window listener
58    private class MyWindowAdapter extends WindowAdapter{
59        public void windowClosing (WindowEvent e){
60            System.exit(0);
61        }
62    }
63 }
```

Lines 49–54 show how to activate a pop-up message. A message box constructor requires three parameters. The first is a reference to the frame from which the message is being displayed. The second is the actual message. And the third specifies the width and height of the message window as measured in pixels. The message window is a modal dialog, meaning that access to the main window (the one containing the Press Me button) is blocked until the user dismisses the message window. You can see a listing of the `MessageBox` source code on the book's CD. It is part of the `ioutil` package. The `MessageBox` class was created by subclassing class `JDialog` (for more information about modal dialogs see Section 3.8). Message boxes can be used only from inside a class that extends `JFrame` or `JDialog`. In particular, they cannot be used in terminal-based applications.

3.7   Additional Window Components

In this section, we introduce several additional window components. You have encountered all of them before in commercial software, so you are already familiar with their behavior from a user's perspective. Here we give a brief description of each and illustrate its use in a short program. The components presented here and in the previous section will enable you to develop fairly sophisticated and professional looking GUIs. We recommend that you skim this section the first time you read it. Later, when you need to use one of the components, read the explanation more carefully. Here is a list of the new components and related classes:

`JMenuBar, JMenu,` `JMenuItem`	Windows can include a menu bar that displays one or more menus. When a menu is selected, a list of menu items drops down. A listener is associated with each item.
`JTextArea,` `JScrollPane`	A text area is a multiline text field and responds to the same messages as a text field, plus a few additional ones. Optional horizontal and vertical scroll bars are added by embedding the text area in a scroll pane. The scroll bars do not appear until they are needed.
`JCheckBox`	Check boxes are either checked or unchecked. A program can check and/or get the status of a check box.
`JRadioButton,` `ButtonGroup`	Radio buttons are organized in groups. Selecting one button in a group deselects the others. A program can check and/or get the status of a radio button.
`JList, DefaultListModel,` `JScrollPane`	A list displays a list of strings. The listener associated with a list is activated when a user clicks or double-clicks an item. This is called selecting. Under program control, items can be added to or removed from a list. The items are actually stored

in a list model associated with the list. Selecting items is not restricted to the user. A program can select an item or determine which item, if any, has been selected by sending messages directly to a list. A selected item is highlighted, whether it is selected by the user or by the program. Horizontal and vertical scroll bars are added by embedding the list in a scroll pane. A list model can store objects of any type. The associated list then displays a description of each object as obtained by sending the object a `toString` message.

3.7.1   Menus and Text Areas

Figure 3.5 shows the interface for a program that uses a text area and menu bar. The menu options are:

File/New   Clears the text area.

Edit/Append   Appends "Appending one more line." to the text area.

Edit/Replace Replaces the content of the text area with "Setting a new line of text."

Figure 3.5   **A text area and menu bar demo program**

Initially, the text area displays "Greetings!" Here is a listing followed by some brief remarks:

```
1 import java.awt.*;
2 import javax.swing.*;
3 import java.awt.event.*;
4 import ioutil.*;
5
6 public class DemoMenusAndTextAreas extends JFrame{
7 )
8     //////////////////////////////////////////////////////// main
```

Continued

Continued

```
9
10     public static void main(String[] args){
11        JFrame theFrame = new DemoMenusAndTextAreas();
12        theFrame.setSize(350, 250);
13        theFrame.setVisible(true);
14     }
15
16     ///////////////////////////////////////////////////// Model
17
18     // none
19
20     ///////////////////////////////////////////////////// View
21
22     // Create controls
23     private JTextArea taDisplay      = new JTextArea("Greetings!\n");
24
25     private JMenu     muFile      = new JMenu("File");
26     private JMenuItem miFileNew   = new JMenuItem("New");
27
28     private JMenu     muEdit      = new JMenu("Edit");
29     private JMenuItem miEditAppend  = new JMenuItem("Append");
30     private JMenuItem miEditReplace = new JMenuItem("Replace");
31
32     public DemoMenusAndTextAreas(){
33
34        // Set title
35        setTitle("Menus and TextArea Demo");
36
37        // Create container and layout
38        Container contentPane = getContentPane();
39        EasyGridLayout layout = new EasyGridLayout();
40        contentPane.setLayout (layout);
41
42        // Set constraints and add controls to container
43        JScrollPane spDisplay = new JScrollPane(taDisplay);
44        layout.setConstraints(spDisplay  , 1,1,1,1);
45        contentPane.add(spDisplay);
46
47        // Create the menu bar and add menus and menu items
48        JMenuBar menuBar = new JMenuBar();
49        setJMenuBar(menuBar);
50        menuBar.add(muFile);
51        menuBar.add(muEdit);
52        muFile.add(miFileNew);
53        muEdit.add(miEditAppend);
54        muEdit.add(miEditReplace);
55
56        // Specify listeners
57        miFileNew.addActionListener(new FileNewListener());
58        miEditAppend.addActionListener(new EditAppendListener());
59        miEditReplace.addActionListener(new EditReplaceListener());
60        addWindowListener(new MyWindowAdapter());
61     }
62
63     ///////////////////////////////////////////////////// Controller
64
65     // File-new listener
```

Continued

Continued

```
66   private class FileNewListener implements ActionListener{
67       public void actionPerformed(ActionEvent e){
68           taDisplay.setText("");
69       }
70   }
71
72   // Edit-append listener
73   private class EditAppendListener implements ActionListener{
74       public void actionPerformed(ActionEvent e){
75           taDisplay.append("Appending one more line.\n");
76       }
77   }
78
79   // Edit-modify listener
80   private class EditReplaceListener implements ActionListener{
81       public void actionPerformed(ActionEvent e){
82           taDisplay.setText("Setting a new line of text.\n");
83       }
84   }
85
86   // Window listener
87   private class MyWindowAdapter extends WindowAdapter{
88       public void windowClosing (WindowEvent e){
89           System.exit(0);
90       }
91   }
92 }
```

First, we consider the lines associated with the text area. *Line 23* instantiates the text area, and *line 43* instantiates a scroll pane with the text area embedded in it. *Line 44* sets the scroll pane's constraints. *Lines 68, 75,* and *82* change the contents of the text area.

Second, we look at the lines related to the menus. *Lines 25–30* instantiate the menus and menu items. *Lines 48–49* create the menu bar and add it to the view. *Lines 50–51* add the two menus (`File` and `Edit`) to the menu bar. *Lines 52–54* add the menu items to their respective menus. *Lines 57–59* associate a listener with each menu item. When the user selects a menu item, the corresponding listener is activated. The listeners are defined in *lines 65–84*. Each listener implements the single method `actionPerformed`.

It is sometimes convenient to select the font used in a text area and/or prevent the user from modifying its content. Both of these features are illustrated next:

```
String message = "Some message goes here.";
textArea.setText(message);
textArea.setFont(new Font("Courier", Font.PLAIN, 12));
textArea.setEditable(false);
```

For more information, see Section 3.11 or explore Java's online documentation.

3.7.2 Check Boxes and Radio Buttons

The next program illustrates the use of check boxes and radio buttons. Any number of check boxes can be selected at once; however, radio buttons are organized in groups, and only one member of a group can be selected at a time. Selecting one button in a group deselects the others. Figure 3.6 shows the program's interface. The

Figure 3.6   **A check box and radio button demo program**

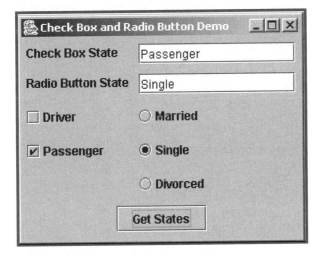

user selects zero, one, or two check boxes and one radio button. When the user presses the Get States command button, the program displays the labels of all selected check boxes and the single selected radio button. The listing is followed by an explanation of the features new to this program.

```
1 import java.awt.*;
2 import javax.swing.*;
3 import java.awt.event.*;
4 import ioutil.*;
5
6 public class DemoCheckBox extends JFrame{
7
8     ///////////////////////////////////////////////// main
9
10    public static void main (String[] args){
11       JFrame theFrame = new DemoCheckBox();
12       theFrame.setSize(300, 250);
13       theFrame.setVisible(true);
14    }
15
16    ///////////////////////////////////////////////// Model
17
18    // none
19
20    ///////////////////////////////////////////////// View
21
22    // Create controls
23
24    // Fields to display states of boxes and buttons
25    private JLabel        lbCheck  = new JLabel("Check Box State");
26    private JLabel        lbRadio  = new
27                                     JLabel("Radio Button State");
28    private JTextField    tfCheck  = new JTextField("");
```

Continued

Continued

```java
29      private JTextField    tfRadio  = new JTextField("");
30
31      // Check boxes
32      private JCheckBox      cbDriver    = new JCheckBox("Driver");
33      private JCheckBox      cbPassenger = new JCheckBox("Passenger");
34
35      // Radio buttons
36      private JRadioButton rbMarried  = new JRadioButton("Married");
37      private JRadioButton rbSingle   = new JRadioButton("Single");
38      private JRadioButton rbDivorced = new JRadioButton("Divorced");
39
40      // Command button
41      private JButton       btGetStates = new JButton("Get States");
42
43      public DemoCheckBox(){
44
45          // Set title
46          setTitle("Check Box and Radio Button Demo");
47
48          // Mark the default check box and radio button
49          cbDriver.setSelected(true);
50          rbSingle.setSelected(true);
51
52          // Add the radio buttons to a button group
53          ButtonGroup bgMaritalStatus = new ButtonGroup();
54          bgMaritalStatus.add(rbMarried);
55          bgMaritalStatus.add(rbSingle);
56          bgMaritalStatus.add(rbDivorced);
57
58          // Create container and layout
59          Container contentPane = getContentPane();
60          EasyGridLayout layout = new EasyGridLayout();
61          contentPane.setLayout(layout);
62
63          // Set constraints
64          layout.setConstraints(lbCheck     ,1,1,1,1);
65          layout.setConstraints(lbRadio     ,2,1,1,1);
66          layout.setConstraints(tfCheck     ,1,2,1,1);
67          layout.setConstraints(tfRadio     ,2,2,1,1);
68          layout.setConstraints(cbDriver    ,3,1,1,1);
69          layout.setConstraints(cbPassenger ,4,1,1,1);
70          layout.setConstraints(rbMarried   ,3,2,1,1);
71          layout.setConstraints(rbSingle    ,4,2,1,1);
72          layout.setConstraints(rbDivorced  ,5,2,1,1);
73          layout.setConstraints(btGetStates ,6,1,2,1);
74
75          // Add controls to container
76          contentPane.add(lbCheck);
77          contentPane.add(lbRadio);
78          contentPane.add(tfCheck);
79          contentPane.add(tfRadio);
80          contentPane.add(cbDriver);
81          contentPane.add(cbPassenger);
82          contentPane.add(rbMarried);
83          contentPane.add(rbSingle);
84          contentPane.add(rbDivorced);
```

Continued

Continued

```
85          contentPane.add(btGetStates);
86
87      // Specify listeners
88      btGetStates.addActionListener(new GetStatesListener());
89      addWindowListener(new MyWindowAdapter());
90  }
91
92  ///////////////////////////////////////////////////// Controller
93
94  //Get States button listener
95  private class GetStatesListener implements ActionListener{
96      public void actionPerformed (ActionEvent event){
97          String cbStr = "", rbStr = "";
98          if (cbDriver.isSelected())
99              cbStr = "Driver ";
100         if (cbPassenger.isSelected())
101             cbStr = cbStr + "Passenger";
102         tfCheck.setText(cbStr);
103         if (rbMarried.isSelected())
104             rbStr = "Married";
105         else if (rbDivorced.isSelected())
106             rbStr = "Divorced";
107         else if (rbSingle.isSelected())
108             rbStr = "Single";
109         tfRadio.setText(rbStr);
110     }
111 }
112
113 // Window listener
114 private class MyWindowAdapter extends WindowAdapter{
115     public void windowClosing (WindowEvent e){
116         System.exit(0);
117     }
118 }
119 }
```

Lines 24–41 declare and instantiate the components in the usual manner. *Lines 48–50* show how to set check boxes and radio buttons under program control. *Lines 52–56* create a radio button group and add our three radio buttons to the group. We could, if we wished, have divided the buttons among several groups. Listeners can be associated with check boxes and radio buttons, but we never use that feature in the book. The `isSelected` method (*lines 98, 100,* etc.) allows the program to determine which buttons have been selected.

3.7.3   Lists

List components are more complex to use than the other components discussed here. There are two reasons for this. First, list components have a richer set of features than the other components. Second, adding and removing items from a list are done via an associated list model, while retrieving and selecting items are done by sending messages directly to the list object itself. Remembering which messages get sent to which object increases the programmer's burden. The list model is typically an instance of `DefaultListModel`. Although other possibilities exist, we do not address them here.

The next program, whose interface is shown in Figure 3.7, illustrates a list's major features. As usual, the code is followed by an explanation.

Figure 3.7   **A list demo program**

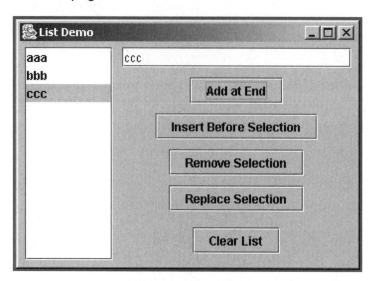

```
 1 import java.awt.*;
 2 import javax.swing.*;
 3 import java.awt.event.*;
 4 import ioutil.*;
 5
 6 public class DemoList extends JFrame{
 7
 8    ///////////////////////////////////////////////////// main
 9
10    public static void main(String[] args){
11       JFrame theFrame = new DemoList();
12       theFrame.setSize(350, 250);
13       theFrame.setVisible(true);
14    }
15
16    ///////////////////////////////////////////////////// Model
17
18    // none
19
20    ///////////////////////////////////////////////////// View
21
22    // Create controls
23    private DefaultListModel lmNames = new DefaultListModel();
24    private JList            ltNames = new JList(lmNames);
25
26    private JTextField tfName    = new JTextField("");
27    private JButton    btAdd     = new JButton("Add at End");
28    private JButton    btInsert  =
```

Continued

Continued

```
29                         new JButton("Insert Before Selection");
30     private JButton     btRemove  = new JButton("Remove Selection");
31     private JButton     btReplace = new JButton("Replace Selection");
32     private JButton     btClear   = new JButton("Clear List");
33
34     public DemoList(){
35
36        // Set window title
37        setTitle("List Demo");
38
39        // Set the list selection mode
40        ltNames.setSelectionMode
41          (ListSelectionMode.SINGLE_SELECTION);
42
43        // Disable all but the add button
44        enableDisableButtons();
45
46        // Create container and layout
47        Container contentPane = getContentPane();
48        EasyGridLayout layout = new EasyGridLayout();
49        contentPane.setLayout (layout);
50
51        // Set constraints
52        JScrollPane spName = new JScrollPane(ltNames);
53        layout.setConstraints(spName    ,1,1,1,6);
54        layout.setConstraints(tfName    ,1,2,1,1);
55        layout.setConstraints(btAdd     ,2,2,1,1);
56        layout.setConstraints(btInsert  ,3,2,1,1);
57        layout.setConstraints(btRemove  ,4,2,1,1);
58        layout.setConstraints(btReplace ,5,2,1,1);
59        layout.setConstraints(btClear   ,6,2,1,1);
60
61        // Add controls to container
62        contentPane.add(spName);
63        contentPane.add(tfName);
64        contentPane.add(btAdd);
65        contentPane.add(btInsert);
66        contentPane.add(btRemove);
67        contentPane.add(btReplace);
68        contentPane.add(btClear);
69
70        // Specify listeners
71        ltNames.addMouseListener(new ListMouseListener());
72        btAdd.addActionListener(new AddListener());
73        btInsert.addActionListener(new InsertListener());
74        btRemove.addActionListener(new RemoveListener());
75        btReplace.addActionListener(new ReplaceListener());
76        btClear.addActionListener(new ClearListener());
77        addWindowListener(new MyWindowAdapter());
78     }
79
80     // Enable and disable buttons as appropriate
81     private void enableDisableButtons(){
82        if (lmNames.size() == 0){
83           btInsert.setEnabled(false);
84           btRemove.setEnabled(false);
```

Continued

Continued

```
 85         btReplace.setEnabled(false);
 86         btClear.setEnabled(false);
 87      }else{
 88         btClear.setEnabled(true);
 89      }
 90      if (ltNames.getSelectedIndex() == -1){
 91         btInsert.setEnabled(false);
 92         btRemove.setEnabled(false);
 93         btReplace.setEnabled(false);
 94      }else{
 95         btInsert.setEnabled(true);
 96         btRemove.setEnabled(true);
 97         btReplace.setEnabled(true);
 98      }
 99   }
100
101   ///////////////////////////////////////////////////// Controller
102
103   private void messageBox(String msg){
104      new MessageBox(this, msg, 300, 100);
105   }
106
107   // Determine if the new name is OK
108   private boolean isNameOK(String name){
109      if (name.equals("")){
110         messageBox("Please enter a name.");
111         return false;
112      }else if (lmNames.contains(name)){
113         messageBox("The name " + name +
114                    " is already in the list.");
115         return false;
116      }else
117         return true;
118   }
119
120   // List mouse listener
121   private class ListMouseListener extends MouseAdapter{
122      public void mouseClicked(MouseEvent e) {
123         if (lmNames.isEmpty())
124            return;
125         int index = ltNames.getSelectedIndex();
126         String name = (String)lmNames.get(index);
127         if (e.getClickCount() == 2)
128            messageBox("You double clicked " + name + ".");
129         else if (e.getClickCount() == 1){
130            tfName.setText(name);
131            enableDisableButtons();
132         }
133      }
134   }
135
136   // Add listener
137   private class AddListener implements ActionListener{
138      public void actionPerformed(ActionEvent e){
139         String name = tfName.getText().trim();
140         if (!isNameOK(name))
141            return;
```

Continued

Continued

```
142              lmNames.addElement(name);
143              ltNames.setSelectedIndex(lmNames.size() - 1);
144              enableDisableButtons();
145         }
146      }
147
148      // Insert listener
149      private class InsertListener implements ActionListener{
150         public void actionPerformed(ActionEvent e){
151              int index = ltNames.getSelectedIndex();
152              String name = tfName.getText().trim();
153              if (!isNameOK(name))
154                 return;
155              lmNames.add(index, name);
156              ltNames.setSelectedIndex(index);
157         }
158      }
159
160      // Remove listener
161      private class RemoveListener implements ActionListener{
162         public void actionPerformed(ActionEvent e){
163              int index = ltNames.getSelectedIndex();
164              lmNames.remove(index);
165              tfName.setText("");
166              enableDisableButtons();
167         }
168      }
169
170      // Replace listener
171      private class ReplaceListener implements ActionListener{
172         public void actionPerformed(ActionEvent e){
173              int index = ltNames.getSelectedIndex();
174              String name = tfName.getText().trim();
175              if (!isNameOK(name))
176                 return;
177              lmNames.set(index, name);
178         }
179      }
180
181      // Clear listener
182      private class ClearListener implements ActionListener{
183         public void actionPerformed(ActionEvent e){
184              lmNames.clear();
185              tfName.setText("");
186              enableDisableButtons();
187         }
188      }
189
190      // Window listener
191      private class MyWindowAdapter extends WindowAdapter{
192         public void windowClosing (WindowEvent e){
193              System.exit(0);
194         }
195      }
196 }
```

Line 23 declares and instantiates a list model, and *line 24* ties the list model to the list. *Lines 40–41* specify that only a single item in the list can be selected at a time.

Selection of multiple items is also possible but is beyond the scope of this book. *Line 52* places the list in a scroll pane. *Line 71* associates a mouse listener with the list. This listener is activated whenever the user clicks or double-clicks on the list. *Lines 121–134* define the list's mouse listener. The listener needs to define just one method, `mouseClicked`. This method begins by checking to see if the list is empty and returns immediately if it is. When the user double-clicks, two events are usually triggered—a single click event followed by a double click event—so the `mouseClicked` method is executed twice. You will need to keep this in mind when using list components. *Lines 120–188* illustrate methods for manipulating a list and its model.

3.8   Working with Modal Dialogs

Some applications require several windows. Modal dialogs provide one mechanism for providing this facility. A modal dialog is a window that pops up under program control. Once it appears, other windows in the application refuse to respond until the modal dialog is dismissed. As already mentioned, the `MessageBox` class is implemented as a modal dialog. In this section, we show how to write modal dialogs and how to exchange information between a main window and its modal dialogs.

In Figure 3.8, the main window on the left displays the name and age of a dog. When the user selects the Modify button, the dialog on the right pops up, and the user can then modify the dog's name and/or age. If the user clicks the OK button, the dialog

Figure 3.8   **A modal dialog demo program**

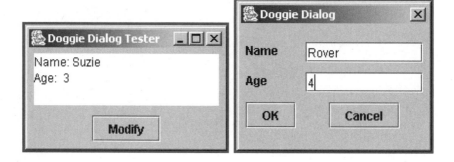

closes and the modified data are transferred back to the main window. But if the user closes the dialog or clicks the Cancel button, the dialog terminates without transferring any data back to the main window. In our program, the main window and the dialog transfer data to and fro by means of a shared dog object. Thus, there are three principal classes in this application: a dog class and two GUI classes (the main window and the dialog). In addition, the two GUI classes include the private listener classes.

We begin by listing the `Dog` class. The code is straightforward and requires no explanation:

```
 1 public class Dog {
 2
 3    private String name;
 4    private int age;
 5
 6    public void setName(String name){
 7       this.name = name;
 8    }
 9
10    public String getName(){
11       return name;
12    }
13
14    public void setAge(int age){
15       this.age = age;
16    }
17
18    public int getAge(){
19       return age;
20    }
21
22    public String toString(){
23       return "Name: " + name  + "\n" + "Age:   " + age;
24    }
25 }
```

Next we list the class that implements the main window. For the most part, this code uses familiar features, so we restrict our discussion to the code that activates and communicates with the dialog.

```
 1 import java.awt.*;
 2 import javax.swing.*;
 3 import java.awt.event.*;
 4 import ioutil.*;
 5
 6 public class DemoDialogTester extends JFrame{
 7
 8    /////////////////////////////////////////////////// main
 9
10    public static void main (String[] args){
11       JFrame theFrame = new DemoDialogTester();
12       theFrame.setSize (125, 125);
13       theFrame.setVisible (true);
14    }
15
16    /////////////////////////////////////////////////// Model
17
18    private Dog dog;
19
20    /////////////////////////////////////////////////// View
21
22    // Create controls
23    private JTextArea taDisplayDog = new JTextArea ("");
24    private JButton btModify       = new JButton ("Modify");
25
```

Continued

Continued

```
26      public DemoDialogTester(){
27
28          // Set title
29          setTitle("Doggie Dialog Tester");
30
31          // Initialize the dog object
32          dog = new Dog();
33          dog.setName("Suzie"); dog.setAge(3);
34
35          // Initialize the taDisplayDog
36          taDisplayDog.setText(dog.toString());
37          taDisplayDog.setEditable(false);
38
39          // Create container and layout
40          Container contentPane = getContentPane();
41          EasyGridLayout layout = new EasyGridLayout();
42          contentPane.setLayout (layout);
43
44          // Set constraints
45          layout.setConstraints(taDisplayDog ,1,1,1,1);
46          layout.setConstraints(btModify     ,2,1,1,1);
47
48          // Add controls to container
49          contentPane.add (taDisplayDog);
50          contentPane.add (btModify);
51
52          // Specify listeners
53          btModify.addActionListener(new btModifyListener());
54          addWindowListener(new MyWindowAdapter());
55      }
56
57      /////////////////////////////////////////////////// Controller
58
59      // Modify button listener
60      private class btModifyListener implements ActionListener{
61          public void actionPerformed (ActionEvent event){
62              DemoDialog dlg =
63                  new DemoDialog(DemoDialogTester.this, dog);
64              dlg.show();
65              if (dlg.getDlgCloseIndicator().equals("OK")){
66                  taDisplayDog.setText(dog.toString());
67              }
68          }
69      }
70
71      // Window listener
72      private class MyWindowAdapter extends WindowAdapter{
73          public void windowClosing (WindowEvent e){
74              System.exit(0);
75          }
76      }
77  }
```

The code involving the dialog is in the Modify button's listener class *(lines 60–69)*. When the user selects the Modify button, the listener instantiates a dialog and passes it a reference to the main window and a previously initialized dog *(lines 62–63)*, after which *line*

64 displays the dialog. The listener then suspends execution until the user dismisses the dialog. When the listener resumes execution in *line 65,* it asks the now invisible dialog how it was closed. If the user clicked the dialog's OK button, the main window assumes that the dialog modified the dog object and redisplays the dog's name and age.

We complete this discussion by examining the dialog class. In most respects, the dialog's code is similar to the main window's. Both include visual components and listeners; however, there are a few new details that we explain at the end of the listing.

```
 1 import java.awt.*;
 2 import javax.swing.*;
 3 import java.awt.event.*;
 4 import ioutil.*;
 5
 6 public class DemoDialog extends JDialog{
 7
 8     /////////////////////////////////////////////////// Model
 9
10     private Dog dog;
11
12     /////////////////////////////////////////////////// View
13
14     // Create controls
15     private JLabel        lbName    = new JLabel("Name");
16     private JTextField    tfName    = new JTextField("");
17     private JLabel        lbAge     = new JLabel("Age");
18     private IntegerField  ifAge     = new IntegerField(0);
19     private JButton       btOK      = new JButton("OK");
20     private JButton       btCancel  = new JButton("Cancel");
21
22     public DemoDialog(Frame parent, Dog dog){
23
24         // Do some initialization in the superclass JDialog
25         super(parent, true);
26
27         // Place the dog's state information in the
28         // dialog's data controls
29         this.dog = dog;
30         tfName.setText(dog.getName());
31         ifAge.setNumber(dog.getAge());
32
33         // Create container and layout
34         Container contentPane = getContentPane();
35         EasyGridLayout layout = new EasyGridLayout();
36         contentPane.setLayout (layout);
37
38         // Set constraints
39         layout.setConstraints(lbName   ,1,1,1,1);
40         layout.setConstraints(tfName   ,1,2,1,1);
41         layout.setConstraints(lbAge    ,2,1,1,1);
42         layout.setConstraints(ifAge    ,2,2,1,1);
43         layout.setConstraints(btOK     ,3,1,1,1);
44         layout.setConstraints(btCancel ,3,2,1,1);
45
```

Continued

Continued

```
46         // Add controls to the container
47         contentPane.add(lbName);
48         contentPane.add(tfName);
49         contentPane.add(lbAge);
50         contentPane.add(ifAge);
51         contentPane.add(btOK);
52         contentPane.add(btCancel);
53
54         // Specify listeners
55         btOK.addActionListener(new OKButtonListener());
56         btCancel.addActionListener(new CancelButtonListener());
57         addWindowListener(new MyWindowAdapter());
58
59         // Set the title and make the dialog visible
60         setTitle("Doggie Dialog");
61         dlgCloseIndicator = "Cancel";      // The default is "Cancel"
62         setSize(200, 150);
63     }
64
65     /////////////////////////////////////////////////////// Controller
66
67     private String dlgCloseIndicator;
68
69     public String getDlgCloseIndicator(){
70         return dlgCloseIndicator;
71     }
72
73     // OK button listener
74     private class OKButtonListener implements ActionListener{
75         public void actionPerformed (ActionEvent event){
76             dog.setName(tfName.getText());
77             dog.setAge(ifAge.getNumber());
78             dlgCloseIndicator = "OK";
79             dispose();
80         }
81     }
82
83     // Cancel button listener
84     private class CancelButtonListener implements ActionListener{
85         public void actionPerformed (ActionEvent event){
86             dispose();
87         }
88     }
89
90     // Window listener
91     private class MyWindowAdapter extends WindowAdapter{
92         public void windowClosing (WindowEvent e){
93             dispose();
94         }
95     }
96 }
```

A dialog extents `JDialog` *(line 6)* and receives a reference to its main window (or parent) and to the object it is displaying via the constructor's parameters *(line 22)*. A dialog can include any number of command buttons, but we typically use two. The constructor must begin by calling the superclass's constructor *(line 25)*. Pressing the OK button indicates that changes should be recorded, and pressing Cancel indicates that changes should be ignored. The listener for the OK button *(lines 74–81)* updates the dog object with data retrieved from the dialog's data entry fields, sets the close indicator to "OK," disposes of (i.e., closes) the dialog's window, and relinquishes control to the main window. The listener for the Cancel button disposes of the dialog's window, the close indicator previously having been set to "Cancel" in the dialog's constructor.

3.9 Multiwindow Applications

An application can include multiple windows, all of which have equal status, no window being a modal dialog. In this type of application, each window provides a separate view of the model. Figure 3.9 illustrates the approach. Here the model is a dog that is shared by the two views. The first view allows the user to change the dog's age and the second view the dog's name. Of course, the views in a realistic multiwindow application differ more than the windows shown here, but the techniques illustrated in this trivial example apply elsewhere. The principal challenge in this type of application is keeping the two views in synchronization. Both views need to show the current state of the model. Thus, if the user changes the age using the window on the left, the new age needs to be displayed immediately in the window on the right.

Figure 3.9   **A multiwindow demo program**

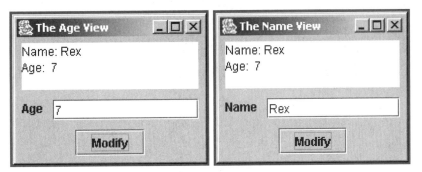

The application consists of four public classes plus the usual private listeners. The public classes are a `Dog` class, a class for the age view, a class for the name view, and a class that coordinates the other three. We have already listed the `Dog` class in a previous section, so here we begin our examination of the code by looking at the coordinating class:

```
1 import java.awt.*;
2 import javax.swing.*;
3 import java.awt.event.*;
4
5 public class DemoMultiViewApp{
```

Continued

Continued

```
 6
 7        /////////////////////////////////////////////// main
 8
 9     public static void main (String[] args){
10        DemoMultiViewApp theApp = new DemoMultiViewApp();
11     }
12
13
14        /////////////////////////////////////////////// Model
15
16     private Dog dog;
17
18        /////////////////////////////////////////////// Views
19
20     private DemoNameView nameView;
21     private DemoAgeView ageView;
22
23        /////////////////////////////////////////////// Startup
24
25     public DemoMultiViewApp(){
26        dog = new Dog();
27        dog.setName("Suzie");
28        dog.setAge(3);
29        nameView = new DemoNameView(this, dog);
30        ageView = new DemoAgeView(this, dog);
31     }
32
33        /////////////////////////////////////////////// Synchronize
34
35     public void updateAllViews(){
36        nameView.updateView();
37        ageView.updateView();
38     };
39 }
```

The coordinating class contains instance variables representing the model (a dog) and the two views. The public method main is in this coordinating class *(lines 9–11)* and does nothing more than instantiate a coordinating object. The coordinator object's constructor initializes the model and instantiates the two views. Each view is passed a reference to the model and the coordinator. As we will see shortly, the views are responsible for displaying themselves. Anytime a view changes the model, it sends the updateAllViews message to the coordinator. The corresponding method in the coordinator *(lines 35–38)* then tells each view to update itself. In this way, changes are broadcast to all views.

We now look at one of the two view classes. They are so similar that there is no point in listing both; however, the code for both is on the book's CD.

```
1 import java.awt.*;
2 import javax.swing.*;
3 import java.awt.event.*;
4 import ioutil.*;
5
6 public class DemoAgeView extends JFrame{
```

Continued

Continued

```
 7
 8      ///////////////////////////////////////////////// Model
 9
10      private Dog dog;
11
12      ///////////////////////////////////////////////// The App
13
14      private DemoMultiViewApp app;
15
16      ///////////////////////////////////////////////// View
17
18      // Create controls
19      private JTextArea     taDisplayDog = new JTextArea("");
20      private JLabel        lbAge        = new JLabel("Age");
21      private IntegerField ifAge        = new IntegerField(0);
22      private JButton       btModify     = new JButton("Modify");
23
24      public DemoAgeView(DemoMultiViewApp app, Dog dog){
25
26          this.dog = dog;
27          this.app = app;
28
29          // Set title
30          setTitle("The Age View");
31
32          // Initialize taDisplayDog
33          taDisplayDog.setText(dog.toString());
34          taDisplayDog.setEditable(false);
35
36          // Create container and layout
37          Container contentPane = getContentPane();
38          EasyGridLayout layout = new EasyGridLayout();
39          contentPane.setLayout (layout);
40
41          // Set constraints
42          layout.setConstraints(taDisplayDog ,1,1,2,1);
43          layout.setConstraints(lbAge        ,2,1,1,1);
44          layout.setConstraints(ifAge        ,2,2,1,1);
45          layout.setConstraints(btModify     ,3,1,2,1);
46
47          // Add controls to container
48          contentPane.add(taDisplayDog);
49          contentPane.add(lbAge);
50          contentPane.add(ifAge);
51          contentPane.add(btModify);
52
53          // Specify listeners
54          btModify.addActionListener(new btModifyListener());
55          addWindowListener(new MyWindowAdapter());
56
57          // Display the view
58          setSize(200, 150);
59          setLocation (200, 300);
60          setVisible(true);
61      }
62
63      public void updateView(){
```

Continued

Continued

```
64        taDisplayDog.setText(dog.toString());
65      }
66
67      ///////////////////////////////////////////////////// Controller
68
69      // Modify button listener
70      private class btModifyListener implements ActionListener{
71          public void actionPerformed (ActionEvent event){
72              int age = ifAge.getNumber();
73              dog.setAge(age);
74              app.updateAllViews();
75          }
76      }
77
78      // Window listener
79      private class MyWindowAdapter extends WindowAdapter{
80          public void windowClosing (WindowEvent e){
81              System.exit(0);
82          }
83      }
84 }
```

The view maintains a reference to the model and to the coordinator *(lines 10 and 14)*. These references are set in the view's constructor *(lines 26–27)*. The view's modify button listener modifies the dog object *(lines 72–73)* and sends the `updateAllViews` message to the coordinator, called `app` here *(line 74)*. The view updates itself when it receives the `updateView` message from the coordinator *(lines 63–65)*.

That concludes the explanation. There are other ways to organize multiwindow applications and to synchronize views, but the one shown here has the virtue of simplicity.

3.10   Sharing Listeners

Until now, each command button and menu item has had its own listeners; however, it is possible for several of these to share a single listener. Doing so reduces slightly the amount of code we must write, but there is a cost. When the listener is activated, it must begin by determining which event triggered its activation using a series of nested `if-then-else` statements. Some programmers object strongly to sharing listeners in this way, claiming reasonably that it violates one of the basic tenets of object-oriented programming—namely, a method should not need to determine on whose behalf it is acting. Other programmers say that while general rules are important, they can sometimes be broken if it is done thoughtfully and infrequently.

Without taking sides in this debate, we now show how to rewrite the temperature conversion program so that one listener services both command buttons. Here is the code:

```
1 import java.awt.*;
2 import javax.swing.*;
3 import java.awt.event.*;
```

Continued

Continued

```
 4 import ioutil.*;
 5
 6 public class DemoCombineListeners extends JFrame{
 7
 8     /////////////////////////////////////////////////// main
 9
10     public static void main (String[] args){
11         JFrame theFrame = new DemoCombineListeners();
12         theFrame.setSize (200, 125);
13         theFrame.setVisible (true);
14     }
15
16     /////////////////////////////////////////////////// Model
17
18     private Thermometer thermo = new Thermometer();
19
20     /////////////////////////////////////////////////// View
21
22     // Create controls
23     private JLabel        lbFahrenheit = new JLabel ("Fahrenheit");
24     private DoubleField dfFahrenheit = new DoubleField (212);
25     private JLabel        lbCelsius    = new JLabel ("Celsius");
26     private DoubleField dfCelsius     = new DoubleField (100);
27     private JButton       btFtoC       = new JButton ("F to C");
28     private JButton       btCtoF       = new JButton ("C to F");
29
30     public DemoCombineListeners(){
31
32         // Set title
33         setTitle("DoubleField Demo");
34
35         // Create container and layout
36         Container contentPane = getContentPane();
37         EasyGridLayout layout = new EasyGridLayout();
38         contentPane.setLayout (layout);
39
40         // Set constraints
41         layout.setConstraints(lbFahrenheit ,1,1,1,1);
42         layout.setConstraints(dfFahrenheit ,1,2,1,1);
43         layout.setConstraints(lbCelsius     ,2,1,1,1);
44         layout.setConstraints(dfCelsius     ,2,2,1,1);
45         layout.setConstraints(btFtoC        ,3,1,1,1);
46         layout.setConstraints(btCtoF        ,3,2,1,1);
47
48         // Add controls to container
49         contentPane.add (lbFahrenheit);
50         contentPane.add (dfFahrenheit);
51         contentPane.add (lbCelsius);
52         contentPane.add (dfCelsius);
53         contentPane.add (btFtoC);
54         contentPane.add (btCtoF);
55
56         // Specify listeners
57         btFtoC.addActionListener(new CombinedListener());
58         btCtoF.addActionListener(new CombinedListener());
59         addWindowListener(new MyWindowAdapter());
```

Continued

Continued

```
60        }
61
62        ///////////////////////////////////////////////////// Controller
63
64        // Combined button listener
65        private class CombinedListener implements ActionListener{
66            public void actionPerformed (ActionEvent event){
67                if (event.getSource() == btFtoC){
68                    double f = dfFahrenheit.getNumber();
69                    thermo.setFahrenheit(f);
70                    dfCelsius.setPrecision(2);
71                    dfCelsius.setNumber(thermo.getCelsius());
72                }else{
73                    double c = dfCelsius.getNumber();
74                    thermo.setCelsius(c);
75                    dfFahrenheit.setPrecision(2);
76                    dfFahrenheit.setNumber(thermo.getFahrenheit());
77                }
78            }
79        }
80
81        // Window listener
82        private class MyWindowAdapter extends WindowAdapter{
83            public void windowClosing (WindowEvent e){
84                System.exit(0);
85            }
86        }
87 }
```

In this program, the first lines of interest are *lines 57–58,* where we associate each button with the same listener. The combination listener is defined in *lines 64–79.* Notice that the `actionPerformed` method has a parameter: the event that triggered the listener *(line 66).* One of this event's attributes is the object that fired the event. In *line 67,* we ask the event for this object and compare it to a command button, thereby determining which button fired the event. The rest is obvious.

3.11   Compendium of Methods

This section is intended as a reference. It lists all the major methods used in the chapter, plus a few additional ones. We organize the information in two ways. First, we list the classes according to their hierarchical relationships, and beside each class, we list its methods. A method applies to its class and the class's subclasses. Second, we give a brief description of each method, taken when possible directly from Java's online documentation (see www.sun.com). The online documentation on which this section is based can also be downloaded from Sun's Web site and installed on your personal computer. If you read the documentation, you will see that the methods presented here are just a small percentage of those available. Java provides many advanced and sophisticated methods for manipulating GUIs, and in this chapter, we have merely presented the basics.

Here then is a hierarchical list of the classes and associated methods.

Class	Methods
ActionEvent	getSource
ActionListener	actionPerformed
ButtonGroup	constructor, add
Container	add, setLayout
DefaultListModel	constructor, add, addElement, clear, contains, get, isEmpty, remove, removeElement, set, size, toArray
EasyGridLayout	constructor, setConstraints
Font	constructor
Jcomponent	setEnabled, setFont, setVisible
. . . AbstractButton	addActionListener
. . . . . . JButton	constructor
. . . . JMenuItem	constructor
. . . . JMenu	constructor, add
. . . . JToggleButton	isSelected, setSelected
. . . . JCheckBox	constructor
. . . . JRadioButton	constructor
. . . JLabel	constructor
. . . JList	constructor, addMouseListener, getModel, getSelectedIndex, getSelectedValue, setSelected Index, setSelectedValue, setSelectionMode,
. . . JMenuBar	constructor, add
. . . JTextComponent	getText, setEditable, setText
. . . . . . JTextArea	constructor, append, setLineWrap
. . . . . . JTextField	constructor

Class	Methods
. . . . IntegerField	constructor, getNumber, isValid, setNumber,
. . . . DoubleField	constructor, getNumber, getPrecision, isValid, setNumber, setPrecision
JscrollPane	constructor
MessageBox	constructor
MouseAdapter	mouseClicked
MouseEvent	getClickCount
Various superclasses	addWindowListener, getContentPane, setJMenuBar, setLocation, setSize, setTitle, setVisible
. . . JDialog	dispose, show
. . . JFrame	

We now describe the methods. They are grouped by class. Constructors are shown only if we call them explicitly in our code.

ActionEvent

Object **getSource**()

The object on which the event initially occurred.

ActionListener

void **actionPerformed**(ActionEvent e)

Invoked when an action occurs.

ButtonGroup

ButtonGroup()

Creates a new ButtonGroup.

void **add**(AbstractButton b)

Adds the button to the group.

Container

Component **add**(Component comp)

Appends the specified component to the end of this container.

void **setLayout**(LayoutManager mgr)

Sets the layout manager for this container.

DefaultListModel

DefaultListModel()

Creates a new `DefaultListModel`.

void **add**(int index, Object element)

Inserts the specified element at the specified position in this list. Counting starts at 0.

void **addElement**(Object obj)

Adds the specified component to the end of this list.

void **clear**()

Removes all of the elements from this list.

boolean **contains**(Object elem)

Tests whether the specified object is a component in this list.

Object **get**(int index)

Returns the element at the specified position in this list.

boolean **isEmpty**()

Tests whether this list has any components.

Object **remove**(int index)

Removes the element at the specified position in this list.

boolean **removeElement**(Object obj)

Removes the first (lowest indexed) occurrence of the argument from this list.

Object **set**(int index, Object element)

Replaces the element at the specified position in this list with the specified element.

int **size()**

Returns the number of components in this list.

Object[] **toArray**()

Returns an array containing all of the elements in this list in the correct order.

EasyGridLayout

EasyGridLayout()

Creates a new `EasyGridLayout`.

void **setConstraints**(Component comp, int row, int col, int height, int width)

Places the component in the grid at position `row`, `col` and occupies `height`, `width` cells of the grid. Row and column numbers start at 1. The component is restricted to one of the following or to a subclass of these: `JLabel`, `JButton`, `JTextField`, `JScrollPane`, `JTextArea`, `JList`, `JCheckBox`, `JRadioButton`, `JPanel`. To deal with other components, the user must modify the class.

Font

Font(String name, int style, int size)

Creates a new `Font` from the specified name, style, and point size. To get a list of font names available on your computer, open Word and drop down the font list. Styles include `Font.BOLD`, `Font.ITALIC`, `Font.PLAIN`. Combine styles with the bitwise union operator (|).

JComponent

void **setEnabled**(boolean enabled)

Sets whether or not this component is enabled.

void **setFont**(Font font)

Sets the font for this component.

void **setVisible**(boolean aFlag)

Makes the component visible or invisible.

JComponent...AbstractButton

void **addActionListener**(ActionListener l)

Adds an `ActionListener` to the button.

JComponent...JButton

JButton(String label)

Creates a new `JButton` with the designated label.

JComponent...JMenuItem

JMenuItem(String label)

Creates a new `JMenuItem` with the designated label.

JComponent...JMenu

JMenu(String label)

Creates a new `JMenu` with the designated label.

JMenuItem **add**(JMenuItem menuItem)

Appends a menu item to the end of this menu.

JComponent ...JToggleButton

boolean **isSelected**()

Returns the state of the button: `true` if selected, else `false`.

void **setSelected**(boolean b)

Sets the state of the button.

JComponent ...JCheckBox

JCheckBox(String label)

Creates a new `JCheckBox` with the designated label.

JComponent ...JRadioButton

JRadioButton(String label)

Creates a new `JRadioButton` with the designated label.

JComponent ...JLabel

JLabel(String label)

Creates a new `JLabel` with the designated label.

JComponent ... JList

JList(ListModel dataModel)

Constructs a JList that displays the elements in the specified, non-null model.

void **addMouseListener**(MouseListener l)

Adds the specified mouse listener to receive mouse events from this component.

ListModel **getModel**()

Returns the data model that holds the list of items displayed by the JList component.

int **getSelectedIndex**()

Returns the first selected index; returns −1 if there is no selected item.

Object **getSelectedValue**()

Returns the first selected value or null if the selection is empty.

void **setSelectedIndex**(int index)

Selects a single cell.

void **setSelectedValue**(Object anObject, boolean shouldScroll)

Selects the specified object from the list.

void **setSelectionMode**(int selectionMode)

Determines whether single-item or multiple-item selections are allowed. (We use only the mode ListSelectionModel. SINGLE_SELECTION)

JComponent ... JMenuBar

JMenuBar()

Creates a new JMenuBar.

JMenu **add**(JMenu c)

Appends the specified menu to the end of the menu bar.

JComponent ... JTextComponent

String **getText**()

Returns the text contained in this JtextComponent.

void **setEditable**(boolean b)

Sets the specified boolean to indicate whether or not this JTextComponent should be editable.

void **setText**(String t)

Sets the text of this JTextComponent to the specified text.

JComponent ... JTextArea

JTextArea(String content)

Creates a new JTextArea with the designated content.

void **append**(String str)

> Appends the given text to the end of the text area.

void **setLineWrap**(boolean wrap)

> Sets the line-wrapping policy of the text area. If set to `true`, the lines will be wrapped if they are too long to fit within the allocated width. If set to `false`, the lines will always be unwrapped.

JComponent ... JTextField

JTextField(String content)

> Creates a new `JTextField` with the designated content.

JTextField(String content, int width)

> Creates a new `JTextField` with the designated content and character width.

JComponent ... IntegerField

IntegerField(int number)

> Creates a new `IntegerField` displaying the designated number converted to a string.

int **getNumber**()

> Converts the characters in the field to an integer and returns it. If the characters do not constitute a valid integer, they are replaced by the string "0" and zero is returned.

boolean **isValid**()

> Returns `true` if the characters in the field constitute a valid integer, else returns `false`.

void **setNumber**(int number)

> Sets the field to the designated `number` after converting it to a string.

JComponent ... DoubleField

DoubleField(double number)

> Creates a new `DoubleField` displaying the designated `number` converted to a string.

double **getNumber**()

> Converts the characters in the field to a double and returns it. If the characters do not constitute a valid double, they are replaced by the string "0.0" and zero is returned.

int **getPrecision**()

> Returns the number of digits after the decimal point when numbers are displayed in this field.

boolean **isValid**()

> Returns `true` if the characters in the field constitute a valid double, else returns `false`.

void **setNumber**(double number)

> Sets the field to the designated `number` after converting it to a string.

void **setPrecision**(int precision)

>Sets the number of digits to be displayed after the decimal point.

JComponent . . . JScrollPane

JScrollPane(Component view)

>Creates a JScrollPane that displays the contents of the specified component, where both horizontal and vertical scroll bars appear whenever the component's contents are larger than the view. Component is a superclass of JComponent.

JComponent . . . MessageBox

MessageBox(JFrame sender, String message, int width, int height)

>Pops up a modal dialog displaying the indicated message. The dialog's pixel dimensions are given by width and height. Message boxes can be used only from inside classes that extend JFrame or JDialog.

JComponent . . . Various superclasses

void **addWindowListener**(WindowListener l)

>Adds the specified window listener to receive window events from this window.

Container **getContentPane**()

>Returns the Container which is the contentPane for this window.

void **setJMenuBar**(JMenuBar menubar)

>Sets the menu bar.

void **setLocation**(int x, int y)

>Sets the *x, y* pixel location of a window's top left corner.

void **setSize**(int width, int height)

>Sets a window's width and height as measured in pixels.

void **setTitle**(String title)

>Sets a window's title.

void **setVisible**(boolean visible)

>Sets a window's visibility.

JComponent . . . JDialog

void **dispose**()

>Closes a dialog's window and returns control to the code immediately following the show method that displayed the dialog's window in the first place.

void **show**()

>Makes a dialog's window visible and blocks until the user disposes of the dialog's window.

KEY TERMS

container	layout manager	model, view, controller (MVC) pattern
controller	listener	
event	modal dialog	pattern
graphical user interface (GUI)	model	view

CHAPTER SUMMARY

Software systems can be structured using the model, view, controller pattern. In a system that uses a graphical user interface, the view consists of windows, window objects, and their layouts. Window objects such as text fields and list boxes display the model's data to the user. The view's components can also allow the user to input information or browse through it. Buttons and menu items allow users to select commands. A layout provides rules for organizing window objects in a window.

The controller consists of listener objects. A listener object receives a message when an event occurs in an associated window object. The method that executes in response to this message can perform a task, such as updating the data in the model.

A dialog is a special type of window that can force the user to perform a task before closing the window.

Multiwindow applications use several windows or dialogs to present several views of a data model simultaneously.

REVIEW QUESTIONS

1. Explain the difference between a text field and a text area.
2. How do you make a text field be output-only?
3. Describe the work that must be done when using a text field to support the input and output of numeric data.
4. Describe a situation in which the use of menus would be more appropriate than the use of buttons.
5. What is a listener object? Give an example of such an object and its use in a program.
6. Explain the roles and responsibilities of the different parts of the model, view, controller pattern.
7. In what respect does a dialog differ from an application window?
8. How are window objects organized in a flow layout?
9. Describe an application that makes appropriate use of a scrolling list box.
10. What is the difference between a check box and a radio button?

CHAPTER 4

Complexity

OBJECTIVES Upon completion of this chapter, you should be able to

- Explain the difference between the timing of algorithms and their complexity analysis and know when each method of measuring their efficiency is appropriate

- Determine the growth rate or order of complexity of an algorithm

- State the common growth rates of algorithms

- Describe the conditions under which the use of different search and sort algorithms is appropriate

Algorithms are implemented as programs that run on real computers with finite resources. Computer programs consume two resources: processing time and memory. Obviously, when run with the same inputs or data sets, programs that consume less of these two resources are in some sense "better" than programs that consume more. In this chapter, we introduce tools for analyzing the computational complexity or efficiency of algorithms. These tools are used throughout the book to assess the trade-offs in using different implementations of ADTs.

4.1   Measuring the Efficiency of Algorithms

Some algorithms use so little time and memory that their performance is not an issue. For example, most users are happy with any algorithm that loads a file in less than 1 second. Then, any algorithm that meets this requirement is as good as any other. Other algorithms are so slow or use so much memory that they are totally impractical on inputs of a realistic size, taking perhaps thousands of years to finish on the fastest computer imaginable. In such cases, we must either find better algorithms or live without a solution.

In algorithm design, there is often a trade-off between time and memory, allowing speed to be exchanged for memory, or vice versa. Some clients might be willing to pay for more memory to get a faster algorithm, whereas others would rather settle for a slower algorithm that economizes on memory. In any case, because efficiency is a desirable feature of algorithms, it is important to pay attention to their performance.

When attempting to select between two algorithms on the basis of their execution time, we are immediately confronted with a dilemma. We cannot run the algorithms on all possible inputs, so how do we decide which is best? The standard approach is to find a function, called the ***growth rate,*** that expresses execution time as a function of input size. We then choose the algorithm whose growth rate is smaller for inputs of the size we are dealing with. For instance, consider the problem of sorting arrays of integers. The input size equals the number of elements in the array, and there are many standard sorting algorithms whose growth rates are already known. However, there is a further complication. The execution times of many sort algorithms vary even for inputs of the same size, so when comparing these algorithms, do we consider their best, average, or worst performance? In the sections that follow, we look at this and related questions in more detail.

4.1.1   Measuring Execution Time of an Algorithm

One way to measure an algorithm's growth rate is to use the computer's clock to obtain actual run times for several inputs of the same size and then repeat the process for inputs of increasing size. From these data, we attempt to generalize and predict how the algorithm behaves in general. Consider the simple, if unrealistic, example of a program that repeats a calculation numerous times. Here the input size is the number of repetitions. We start with 1 million repetitions, time the algorithm, and output the run time to the terminal window. We then double the number of repetitions and repeat the process. After five doublings, we have a set of results from which we can generalize. Here is the code for our tester program followed by the output:

```
1 import java.util.*;
2
3 public class TimeTester{
4
5    public static void main(String[] args){
6        long inputSize = 1000000;
7        int work = 0;
8
9        for (int i = 1; i <= 5; i++){
10           Date d1 = new Date();
11
12           // The start of "the algorithm"
13           for (int j = 1; j <= inputSize; j++){
14               work++;                              // Do a constant amount
15               work--;                              // of work on each pass
16           }
17           // The end of "the algorithm"
18
19           Date d2 = new Date();
20           long msec = d2.getTime() - d1.getTime();
21           System.out.println("Input size = " + inputSize + "\n" +
22                             "   Time in msec = " + msec);
```

Continued

Continued

```
23              inputSize = inputSize * 2;
24        }
25    }
26 }
```

```
Input size = 1000000
    Time in msec = 10
Input size = 2000000
    Time in msec = 30
Input size = 4000000
    Time in msec = 50
Input size = 8000000
    Time in msec = 100
Input size = 16000000
    Time in msec = 200
```

The tester program uses the Date class defined in the package java.util to track the run times. The constructor for Date returns a Date object containing the time at which it was created to the nearest millisecond (*lines 10* and *19*). The Date method getTime returns the number of milliseconds between that time and January 1, 1970 *(line 20)*. Thus, the difference between the times of the two dates represents the elapsed time in milliseconds *(line 20)*. Note also that the program does a constant amount of "work" on each pass through the loop (*lines 14* and *15*). This work consumes enough time on each pass to make the total run time significant.

A quick glance at the results reveals that the run time more or less doubles when the input size doubles. Thus, we predict that the run time for an input of size 32 million will be approximately 400 milliseconds.

As another example, consider the following change in the tester program's algorithm:

```
for (int j = 1; j <= inputSize; j++){
    for (int k = 1; k <= inputSize; k++){
        work++;
        work--;
    }
}
```

We have moved the "work" instructions into a nested loop. Each loop iterates inputSize times. When left to run overnight, this program was still hard at work the next morning, having output results for only the first input size of 1 million. Obviously, the presence of nested loops has a very dramatic effect on the program's run time. Starting with a more reasonable initial input size of 1,000 yields the following results:

```
Input size = 1000
    Time in msec = 20
Input size = 2000
    Time in msec = 60
Input size = 4000
    Time in msec = 210
```

Continued

Continued

```
Input size = 8000
    Time in msec = 631
Input size = 16000
    Time in msec = 2464
```

Note that when the input size doubles, the number of milliseconds of run time more or less quadruples. At this rate, the program should run for months with an initial input size of 1 million!

Recording run times allows us to make accurate predictions about an algorithm's speed; however, there are two major problems with this technique:

1. Different hardware platforms have different processing speeds, so the run times of an algorithm differ from machine to machine. Also, the run time of a program varies with the type of operating system that lies between it and the hardware. Finally, different programming languages and compilers produce code whose performance varies. For example, an algorithm coded in C and compiled into machine code usually runs faster than the same algorithm written in Java and compiled into bytecode.

2. It is impractical to time some algorithms on data sets of increasing size because the algorithms are just too slow regardless of the programming language or computer used.

Despite its deficiencies, a timing algorithm is often a useful tool, but in addition, we would like an estimate of algorithmic efficiency that is independent of a particular hardware or software platform. This estimate would tell us how well or how poorly an algorithm performs on any platform.

4.1.2   Counting Instructions

Counting instruction executions provides an alternative to timing. A count provides a good indicator of the amount of abstract "work" done by an algorithm no matter what platform the algorithm runs on. Of course, when we count instruction executions, we are referring to instructions in the high-level code in which the algorithm is written, not instructions in the executable machine language program.

When analyzing an algorithm in this way, we distinguish between two classes of instructions:

1. instructions that execute the same number of times regardless of the input size

2. instructions whose execution count varies with the input size

Following an established convention, we ignore instructions in the first class because they usually do not increase the total significantly. Instructions in the second class normally are found in loops or recursive methods (see Chapter 10). In the case of loops, instructions performed in the most deeply nested loops contribute much more to the total count than those in outer loops, which suggests a further simplification. Focus on a single instruction, which we call the ***representative instruction,*** whose execution count is proportional to the overall execution count of the algorithm. For example, we now modify the previous program to track and display the number of times the instruction `count++;` executes as the input size varies:

```
for (int i = 1; i <= 5; i++){
   int count = 0;
   for (int j = 1; j <= inputSize; j++)
      for (int k = 1; k <= inputSize; k++){
         count++;
         work++;
         work--;
      }
      System.out.println("Input size = " + inputSize + "\n" +
                         "   Instr. count = " + count);
      inputSize = inputSize * 2;
}
```

As we can see from the results, the number of times the representative instruction executes is the square of the input size:

```
Input size = 1000
   Instr. count = 1000000
Input size = 2000
   Instr. count = 4000000
Input size = 4000
   Instr. count = 16000000
Input size = 8000
   Instr. count = 64000000
Input size = 16000
   Instr. count = 256000000
```

Here is a similar program that tracks the number of calls to a recursive `fibonacci` method for several input sizes. The output follows the listing.

```
 1 public class CountTester2{
 2
 3     private static int count = 0;
 4
 5     public static void main(String[] args){
 6         int inputSize = 2;
 7
 8         for (int i = 1; i <= 5; i++){
 9             count = 0;
10             fibonacci(inputSize);
11             System.out.println("Input size = " + inputSize + "\n" +
12                                "   Instr. count = " + count);
13             inputSize = inputSize * 2;
14         }
15     }
16
17     private static int fibonacci(int n){
18         count++;
19         if (n < 3)
20             return 1;
21         else
22             return fibonacci(n - 1) + fibonacci(n - 2);
23     }
24 }
```

```
Input size = 2
   Instr. count = 1
Input size = 4
   Instr. count = 5
Input size = 8
   Instr. count = 41
Input size = 16
   Instr. count = 1973
Input size = 32
   Instr. count = 4356617
```

As the input size doubles, the instruction count (number of recursive calls) grows slowly at first and then grows very rapidly. At first, the instruction count is less than the square of the input size, but the instruction count of 1973 is significantly larger than the square of the input size 16. (For a thorough discussion of the design and analysis of recursive algorithms, see Chapter 10.) Indeed, we are left to wonder about the relationship between input size and instruction count. The answer is revealed in Chapter 10.

4.1.3   Deriving the Growth Rate Algebraically

The two previous approaches to determining growth rate share three drawbacks. To analyze an algorithm, we must actually write a running program, for some algorithms the run times become intolerably large very quickly, and from the output we may not be able to discover a function that relates input size to execution time or instruction count.

The solution to these problems is to take a more algebraic approach to determining execution time as we illustrate next. We begin by returning to our original algorithm and deriving a formula that relates input size directly to execution time. Here is a listing of the algorithm with execution times written to the right of each instruction. As we cannot know these times exactly, we represent them by the variables $t1$ through $t4$.

```
long inputSize = 1000000;                    //      t1
int work = 0;                                //      t2

for (int j = 1; j <= inputSize; j++){        //      t3
   work++;                                    //      t4
   work--;                                    //      t4
}
```

In the above, $t3$ represents the time expended by the loop control mechanisms on each iteration. For the algorithm as a whole, the execution time is

$$t1 + t2 + n(t3 + 2t4)$$

where n equals `inputSize`. Now regardless of the actual values of $t1$ through $t4$, we can see that as n gets large, the contribution of $t1$ and $t2$ to the overall execution becomes less significant. Thus, for large n, the formula is approximated by

$$nt$$

where t equals $t3 + 2t4$. This last formula brings us back to the idea of judging the performance of an algorithm by the executions of a single representative instruction.

4.1.4 Measuring the Memory Used by an Algorithm

A complete analysis of the resources used by an algorithm includes the amount of memory required. Once again, we focus on rates of potential growth. Some algorithms require the same amount of memory to solve any problem. Other algorithms require more memory as the input size gets larger. We consider several of these algorithms in later chapters, particularly in Chapter 10. For now, we assume that the ideal data structure contains a reference to each object in it and nothing more. We thus ignore the space requirements for the actual objects. For example, an array of n objects requires n references (these might be 4 bytes each).

Exercises 4.1

1. Write a tester program that counts and displays the number of instructions in the body of the following loop:

```
while (inputSize > 0)
   inputSize = inputSize / 2;
```

Run the program with input sizes of 1,000, 2,000, 4,000, 10,000, and 100,000. As the input size doubles or increases by a factor of 10, what happens to the number of instructions?

2. The `Date` method `getTime` returns the elapsed time. Because the operating system might use the CPU for part of this time, the elapsed time might not reflect the actual time that a Java code segment uses the CPU. Browse the Java documentation for an alternative way of recording the processing time and describe how this would be done.

3. An optimizing compiler might eliminate the "work" instructions (`work++` and `work--`) used in the example algorithms of this section. Suggest an alternative for these instructions that does not depend on the number of iterations of the loop and is not optimized away.

4.2 Comparing Growth Rates

Having established several techniques for determining algorithmic growth rates, we turn to the task of comparing them. The manner in which computer scientists do this is not completely intuitive, but it has proven practical.

4.2.1 Comparing Growth Rates Algebraically

We say that two growth functions f and g have the ***same growth rate*** or ***same order of complexity*** if the ratio of $f(n)/g(n)$ is bounded by positive constants as n gets large, or stated more formally

$$c \leq \lim_{n \to \infty} \frac{f(n)}{g(n)} \leq d$$

where c and d are positive constants and n represents the input size.

For those unfamiliar with the notation of limits, we can reexpress the preceding in a somewhat longer form as follows. There exist constants $0 < c < d$ and a natural number n_0 such that for all $n > n_0$,

$$c \leq \frac{f(n)}{g(n)} \leq d$$

As a consequence of this definition, we can see that

$$f(n) = 10n + 2000 \qquad \text{and} \qquad g(n) = 0.01n + 2$$

have the same growth rate even though for all values of n, $f(n)$ is 1,000 times larger than $g(n)$.

Similarly, we say that f and g have **different growth rates** or **different orders of complexity** if either the ratio of $f(n)/g(n)$ or $g(n)/f(n)$ tends to 0 as n gets large, or again stated more formally, either

$$\lim_{n \to \infty} \frac{f(n)}{g(n)} = 0 \qquad \text{or} \qquad \lim_{n \to \infty} \frac{g(n)}{f(n)} = 0$$

In the former case, we say that f's **growth rate is less than** g's or that f's **order of complexity is less than** g's.

As a consequence of this definition, if

$$f(n) = 1,000,000n + 2,000,000 \qquad \text{and} \qquad g(n) = n^2 + n + 1$$

then f's growth rate is less than g's even though for all values of n less than 1,000 or so, $f(n)$ is in fact greater than $g(n)$. Of course, eventually, for sufficiently large values of n, $f(n)$ is less than $g(n)$ and so much so that the limit of $f(n)/g(n)$ goes to 0.

With these definitions in mind, let us consider two polynomial growth functions

$$f(n) = a_m x^m + a_{m-1} x^{m-1} + \ldots + a_1 x + a_0 \qquad \text{where } a_m > 0$$

and

$$f(n) = b_n x^n + b_{n-1} x^{n-1} + \ldots + b_1 x + b_0 \qquad \text{where } b_n > 0$$

Then

- if $m < n$, f's growth rate is less than g's
- if $m = n$, f and g have the same growth rate
- f's growth is the same as x^m and g's is the same as x^n

From all of this, we conclude that when comparing growth rates, we only consider what happens for large values of n. In practice, however, when the input size is relatively small, we might prefer the "worse" algorithm with the greater growth rate.

Table 4.1 lists some common growth rates in increasing order of complexity and situations in which they occur. Table 4.2 shows some representative values for these. For growth rates involving log, it does not matter which base we choose because logs

Table 4.1   **Some Typical Growth Rates**

Growth Rates	A Corresponding Problem
1	Determine the larger of two numbers.
$\log n$	Find a number in an array using a binary search.
n	Find a number in an array using a linear search.
$n \log n$	Sort the numbers in an array using a merge sort.
n^2	Sort the numbers in an array using a selection sort.
n^3	Find the shortest path between every pair of vertices in a graph.
2^n	Process all subsets of a set with n elements.
$n!$	Process all permutations of n objects.

Table 4.2   **Representative Values for Growth Functions**

n	1	$\log_{10} n$	n	$n \log_{10} n$	n^2	n^3	2^n	$n!$
10	1	1	10	10	10^2	10^3	1024	3,628,800
100	1	2	100	200	10^4	10^6	1.2E30	9.3E157
1000	1	3	1000	3000	10^6	10^9	1.1E301	4.0E2567
10000	1	4	10000	40000	10^8	10^{12}	2.0E3010	2.8E35659

taken in two different bases are always proportional. We encounter some of these growth rates later in the chapter, others later in the book, and others not at all. Growth rates that are exponential or greater grow so fast that the corresponding algorithms are impractical. In these situations, we must either develop more efficient algorithms, forgo a computer solution, or settle for an algorithm that produces an approximate result in a more reasonable time.

4.2.2   Big-O Notation

When talking about growth rates, computer scientists customarily use **_big-O notation._** A growth function f is said to be big-O of g, written $f = O(g)$, if the growth rate of f is less than or equal to the growth rate of g. More formally, $f = O(g)$ means that

$$0 \le \lim_{n \to \infty} \frac{f(n)}{g(n)} \le c$$

for some constant $c > 0$. The "O" in big-O stands for "on the order of."

Usually, when we analyze the time complexity of an algorithm, we do not require an exact statement of the growth function f, but settle instead for the simplest and least function g such that $f = O(g)$. For instance, from the definition of big-O, we see that all polynomial growth functions of degree k are equivalent to n^k, or in other words

$$f(n) = a_k n^k + a_{k-1} n^{k-1} + \ldots + a_1 n + a_0, \qquad \text{where } a_k > 0$$
$$= O(n^k)$$

In selecting n^k, we are using the simplest and least polynomial that will work. It is equally true that

$$f(n) = a_k n^k + a_{k-1} n^{k-1} + \ldots + a_1 n + a_0, \qquad \text{where } a_k > 0$$
$$= O(n^{k+1})$$

But n^{k+1} is not the least polynomial that works.

To verify the accuracy of our claim that $f(n) = O(n^k)$, we apply the definition of big-O:

$$0 \leq \lim_{n \to \infty} \frac{a_k n^k + a_{k-1} n^{k-1} + \ldots + a_1 n + a_0}{n^k} = a_k \leq c$$

Table 4.3 provides some additional examples of big-O equivalents.

Table 4.3

Some Functions and Their Big-O Equivalents

Function f	Simplest Big-O Equivalent g
547	1
$0.1n^2$	n^2
$30{,}000n^2 + 12{,}000n + 179$	n^2
$34n \log n + 42n + 8$	$n \log n$
$172^n + 3n^2 + 16n + 24$	2^n

Taking advantage of big-O notation, we can now express the growth rate of the chapter's first algorithm as:

$$f(n) = t1 + t2 + n(t3 + 2t4)$$
$$= a_1 n + a_0, \text{ where } a_1 = t3 + 2t4 \text{ and } a_0 = t1 + t2$$
$$= O(n)$$

The fact that the growth rate is $O(n)$ further justifies our practice of computing growth rates based on a single representative instruction.

4.2.3 Best, Worst, and Average Behavior

Now that we know how to talk about growth rates, we must remind ourselves that for many algorithms execution times can vary even for inputs of the same size. Therefore, instead of talking about a single growth rate function for an algorithm, we should determine growth rate functions for the best, worst, and average behavior of the algorithm. For example, a linear search algorithm does less work to find a target at the beginning of an array than at the end of the array. In general, we are more interested in the average and worst-case behaviors than in the best-case behavior. In the examples that follow, we show how to analyze algorithms for all three cases.

Exercises 4.2

1. Assume that each of the following expressions indicates the number of operations performed by an algorithm for a input size of n. Point out the dominant term of each algorithm and use big-O notation to classify it.

   a. $2^n - 4n^2 + 5n$

   b. $3n^2 + 6$

   c. $n^3 + n^2 - n$

2. For input size n, algorithms A and B perform exactly n^2 and $\frac{1}{2}n^2 + \frac{1}{2}n$ instructions, respectively. Which algorithm does more work? Are there particular input sizes for which one algorithm performs significantly better than the other? Are there particular input sizes for which both algorithms perform approximately the same amount of work?

3. Suppose there are three algorithms that have n^4, n^3, and n^2 behaviors, respectively. Explain why the three algorithms do not basically do the same amount of work.

4.3 Search Algorithms

We now present and discuss several typical algorithms for searching and sorting arrays. We first discuss the design of an algorithm, then show its implementation as a Java method, and finally provide an analysis of the algorithm's computational complexity. To keep things simple, each method processes a filled array of integers. Arrays of different sizes can be passed as parameters to the methods. The methods are declared as `public` and `static`, so they can be included in a class that can be used like Java's `Math` class. We use these methods in the case study later in the chapter.

4.3.1 Linear Search of an Array

Assume that items in an array are in random order. Then the only way to search for a target item is to begin with the item at the first position and compare it to the target. If the items are the same, we return the position of the current item. Otherwise, we move on to the next position. If we arrive at the last position and still cannot find the target, we return -1. This kind of search is called linear search or sequential search. Here is the Java code for the linear search method:

```java
public static int linearSearch(int target, int[] array){
    for (int i = 0; i < array.length; i++){
        if (array[i] == target)
            return i;
    }
    return -1;
}
```

The comparison in the body of the loop is the representative instruction for our analysis, which considers three cases:

1. In the worst case, the target item is at the end of the list or not in the list at all. Then the algorithm must make n comparisons for an array of size n. Thus, the worst-case complexity of linear search is $O(n)$.

2. In the best case, the algorithm finds the target at the first position, after making one comparison, for an $O(1)$ complexity.

3. In the average case, the algorithm performs $(n + n - 1 + n - 2 + \ldots + 1) / n = (n + 1) / 2$ comparisons for $O(n)$ complexity. Even though for large n the difference between n and $(n + 1) / 2$ is great, they are both $O(n)$.

Clearly, the best-case behavior of linear search is rare when compared with the average and worst-case behaviors, which have the same order of complexity.

When the data in the array are objects rather than values of a primitive type, we must alter the comparison instruction. In Java, the operator $==$ returns `true` only if the two objects are identical, and this is hardly ever the case in a search situation. We must use the `equals` method instead, as shown in the following code:

```
public static int linearSearch(Object target, Object[] array){
    for (int i = 0; i < array.length; i++){
        if (array[i].equals(target))
            return i;
    }
    return -1;
}
```

The effect of `equals` from an efficiency standpoint is to increase the run time of each comparison. For example, when applied to `strings`, `equals` compares each pair of characters within two strings rather than the references to the string objects. However, this change simply increases the constant of proportionality and has no effect on the order of complexity of the search.

4.3.2 Binary Search of an Array

When you look up a person's number in a phone book, you don't do a linear search. Instead, you estimate the portion of pages to pull over based on the name's alphabetical position in the book and open the book there. If the names on that page come before the target name, you look on later pages; if the names come after the target name, you look on earlier pages. You repeat this process until you find the name or find that it's not in the book. You search this way rather than using linear search because the items in the phone book are in sorted order.

Let us assume that the items in the array are sorted in ascending order. Our new search algorithm now goes directly to the middle position in the array and compares the target to the item. If there is a match, the algorithm returns the position. Otherwise, if the current item is less than the target, the algorithm searches the portion of the array after the middle position. If the current item is greater than the target, the algorithm searches the portion of the array before the middle position. The search process stops when the algorithm finds the target or cannot continue to subdivide the array. Here is the code for the binary search method:

```java
public static int binarySearch(int target, int[] array){
    int low = 0;
    int high = array.length - 1;
    while (low <= high){
        int middle = (low + high) / 2;
        if (array[middle] == target)              // Representative instruction
            return middle;
        else if (array[middle] < target)
            low = middle + 1;                      // Search to right of middle
        else
            high = middle - 1;                     // Search to left of middle
    }
    return -1;
}
```

Figure 4.1 shows all the different ways an array containing the numbers 1, 2, ..., 9 might be subdivided during a search, and from this figure, we can quickly determine how many equality comparisons are needed to find a target value or determine that it is not there. For instance, we can see that a search for the target value 5 is resolved on the first equality comparison, a search for 7 on the second equality comparison, 8 on the third, and 9 on the fourth. A search for 10 fails on the fourth equality comparison.

Figure 4.1   **The items of an array visited during a binary search for 10**

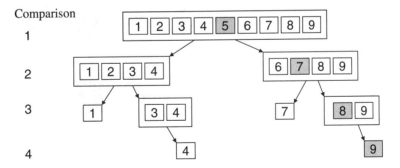

Can you convince yourself that a search for 1 is completed on the third equality comparison, and a search for 2.5 (assuming we modify the method to work with doubles instead of integers) is resolved on the third equality comparison?

The worst case occurs when the target value is not in the array, and we now derive the algorithm's growth rate in the worst case using the equality comparison as our representative instruction. We proceed by observing that there is one equality comparison for each subdivision of the array. We count the original array as the first subdivision. So the problem of maximizing the number of equality comparisons is equivalent to maximizing the number of times the array is subdivided. Each subdivision more or less halves its predecessor, and once it reaches a size of one, it can be subdivided no further. Thus, starting with an array of 9 elements we can form subarrays of size 9, 4, 2, 1, and the worst-case number of comparisons is four.

In general, we can form subarrays whose sizes are

$$n, n/2, n/2^2, n/2^3, \ldots, n/2^{k-1} = 1$$

keeping mind that integer division discards fractional amounts. The length of this sequence is k, and k is the first integer for which $n < 2^k$, or stated differently, k is the first integer greater than $\log_2 n$.

We have now established that in the worst case the complexity of binary search is $O(\log n)$. Because logs in different bases are proportional, we have omitted the reference to base 2. It can be shown, although we will not do so, that the average complexity is also $O(\log n)$. Obviously, in the best case, the complexity is $O(1)$.

As was the case with linear search, when the data in the array are objects rather than values of a primitive type, we must alter the way in which the comparisons are performed. In Java, the programmer must satisfy two requirements:

1. The objects in the array must implement the `Comparable` interface.
2. The search method must use the method `compareTo` to perform the comparisons. This method returns 0 if the objects are equal (using method `equals`), a positive integer if the first object is greater than the second object, or a negative integer if the first object is less than the second object.

Here is the modified code for the binary search of an array of objects:

```
// Assumes that the objects implement Comparable
public static int binarySearch(Object target, Object[] array){
    int low = 0;
    int high = array.length - 1;
    while (low <= high){
        int middle = (low + high) / 2;
        int result = ((Comparable)array[middle]).compareTo(target);
        if (result == 0)
            return middle;
        else if (result < 0)
            low = middle + 1;
        else
            high = middle - 1;
    }
    return -1;
}
```

Binary search is obviously much more efficient than linear search. However, the kind of search algorithm we choose depends on the organization of data in the array. There is some additional cost in the overall system if we use binary search. That cost lies in maintaining a sorted array. In the next section, we examine several strategies for sorting an array, and we analyze their complexity.

Exercises 4.3

1. Suppose that an array contains the values

20 44 48 55 62 66 74 88 93 99

at index positions 0 through 9. Trace the values of the variables `low`, `high`, and `middle` in a nonrecursive binary search of this array for the target value 90. Repeat for the target value 44.

2. The method we usually use to look up an entry in a phone book is not exactly the same as a binary search because we don't always go to the midpoint of the sublist being searched in a phone book. Instead, we estimate the position of the target based on the alphabetical position of the first letter of the person's last name. For example, when looking up a number for Smith, we first look toward the middle of the second half of the phone book instead of the middle of the entire book. Suggest a modification of the binary search algorithm that emulates this strategy for an array of names. Is its computational complexity any better than that of the standard binary search?

4.4   Sort Algorithms

Computer scientists have devised many ingenious strategies for sorting an array of items. We won't consider all of them here. In this chapter, we examine some algorithms that are easy to write but inefficient. In Chapter 10, we look at some algorithms that are harder to write but more efficient. Each of the Java sort methods that we develop here operates on an array of integers and uses a `swap` method to exchange the positions of two items in the array. Here is the code for the `swap` method:

```
public static void swap(int[] array, int i, int j){
    int temp = array[i];
    array[i] = array[j];
    array[j] = temp;
}
```

4.4.1   Selection Sort

Perhaps the simplest strategy is to search the entire array for the smallest item. If it is not in the first position, we swap it with the item at the first position. We then start at the second position and repeat the process, swapping the smallest remaining item with the item at the second position if necessary. When we reach the last position in this overall process, the array is sorted. The algorithm is called **selection sort** because each pass through the main loop selects a single item to be moved. Table 4.4 shows the states of an array of five items after each search and swap pass of selection sort. The two items just swapped on each pass have an asterisk next to them, and the sorted portion of the array is shaded.

Table 4.4 **A Trace of the Data during a Selection Sort**

Unsorted Array	After 1st Pass	After 2nd Pass	After 3rd Pass	After 4th Pass
5	1*	1	1	1
3	3	2*	2	2
1	5*	5	3*	3
2	2	3*	5*	4*
4	4	4	4	5*

Here is the Java method for selection sort:

```java
public static void selectionSort(int[] array){
    for (int i = 0; i < array.length - 1; i++){
        int minIndex = i;
        for (int j = i + 1; j < array.length; j++)
            if (array[j] < array[minIndex])
                minIndex = j;
        if (minIndex != i)
            swap(array, minIndex, i);
    }
}
```

Selection sort has a nested loop within which we find our representative instruction, the comparison, for analysis. For an array of size n, the outer loop executes $n - 1$ times. On the first pass through the outer loop, the inner loop executes $n - 1$ times. On the second pass through the outer loop, the inner loop executes $n - 2$ times. On the last pass through the outer loop, the inner loop executes once. Thus, the total number of comparisons for an array of size n is

$$(n - 1) + (n - 2) + \ldots + 1 = n\,(n - 1)\,/\,2 = \tfrac{1}{2}\,n^2 - \tfrac{1}{2}\,n$$

So selection sort is $O(n^2)$ in all cases. For large data sets, the cost of swapping items might also be significant. Because data items are swapped only in the outer loop, this additional cost for selection sort is linear in the worst and average cases.

As was the case for binary search, when the array contains objects, the objects must implement the `Comparable` interface, and the sort method must use the `compareTo` method.

4.4.2   Bubble Sort

Another sort algorithm that is easy to conceive and code is **bubble sort.** The strategy is to start at the beginning of the array and compare pairs of data items as we move down to the end. Each time the items in the pair are out of order, we swap them. This process has the effect of "bubbling" the largest items down to the end of the array. We then repeat the process from the beginning of the array and go to the next to last item, and so on, until we begin with the last item. At that point, the array is sorted.

Table 4.5 shows a trace of the bubbling process through an array of five items. This process makes four comparisons to bubble the largest item down to the end of the array. Once again, items just swapped are marked with an asterisk, and the sorted portion is shaded.

Table 4.5 **A Trace of the Data during a Bubble Sort**

Unsorted Array	After 1st Comparison	After 2nd Comparison	After 3rd Comparison	After 4th Comparison
5	4*	4	4	4
4	5*	2*	2	2
2	2	5*	1*	1
1	1	1	5*	3*
3	3	3	3	5*

Here is the Java method for bubble sort:

```
public static void bubbleSort(int[] array){
    for (int i = 0; i < array.length - 1; i++)
        for (int j = 0; j < array.length - i - 1; j++)
            if (array[j] > array[j + 1])
                swap(array, j, j + 1);
}
```

As with selection sort, bubble sort has a nested loop within which we find our representative instruction, a comparison. The sorted portion of the array now grows from the end of the array up to the beginning, but the behavior of bubble sort is quite similar to that of selection sort: The inner loop executes $\frac{1}{2} n^2 - \frac{1}{2} n$ times for an array of size n. Thus, bubble sort is $O(n^2)$ in all cases. Like selection sort, bubble sort won't perform any swaps if the array is already sorted. However, bubble sort's worst-case behavior for exchanges is greater than linear. The proof of this is left as an exercise.

We can make a minor adjustment to bubble sort to improve its best-case behavior to linear. If no swaps occur during a pass through the main loop, then the array is sorted. This can happen on any pass and, in the best case, will happen on the first pass. We can track the presence of swapping with a Boolean flag and return from the method when the inner loop does not set this flag. Here is the modified bubble sort method:

```
public static void bubbleSort(int[] array){
    for (int i = 0; i < array.length - 1; i++){
        boolean swapped = false;
        for (int j = 0; j < array.length - i - 1; j++)
            if (array[j] > array[j + 1]){
                swap(array, j, j + 1);
                swapped = true;
```

Continued

Continued

```
        }
    if (! swapped)
        return;
    }
}
```

Note that this modification only improves best-case behavior. On the average, the be-havior of bubble sort is still O(n^2).

4.4.3   Insertion Sort

Our modified bubble sort performs better than selection sort for arrays that are al-ready sorted or only have a few items out of order. In these cases, the modified bub-ble sort is O(n). Another algorithm called ***insertion sort*** attempts to exploit the par-tial ordering of arrays in a different way. The strategy is as follows:

■ On the ith pass through the array, the ith item should be inserted into its proper place among the first i items in the array.

■ After the ith pass, the first i items should be in sorted order.

■ This process is analogous to the way in which many people organize playing cards in their hands. That is, if one holds the first $i - 1$ cards in order, one picks the ith card and compares it to these cards until its proper spot is found.

■ As with our other sort algorithms, insertion sort consists of two loops. The outer loop traverses the positions from 1 to $n - 1$. For each position i in this loop, we save the item and start the inner loop at position $i - 1$. For each position j in this loop, we move the item to position $j + 1$ until we find the insertion point for the saved (ith) item.

Here is the code for the `insertionSort` method:

```
public static void insertionSort(int[] array){
    for (int i = 1; i < array.length; i++){
        int itemToInsert = array[i];
        int j = i - 1;
        while (j >= 0){
            if (itemToInsert < array[j]){
                array[j + 1] = array[j];
                j--;
            }
            else
                break;
        }
        array[j + 1] = itemToInsert;
    }
}
```

Table 4.6 shows the states of an array of five items after each major pass in an in-sertion sort. The item to be inserted on the next pass is marked with an arrow; after it is inserted, this item is marked with an asterisk.

Once again, analysis focuses on the comparison in the nested loop as the represen-tative instruction. The outer loop executes $n - 1$ times. In the worst case, when all of the data are out of order, the inner loop executes once on the first pass, twice on

Table 4.6 | **A Trace of the Data during an Insertion Sort**

Unsorted Array	After 1st Pass	After 2nd Pass	After 3rd Pass	After 4th Pass
2	2	1*	1	1
5←	5 (no insertion)	2	2	2
1	1←	5	4*	3*
4	4	4←	5	4
3	3	3	3←	5

the second pass, and so on, for a total of $\frac{1}{2}n^2 - \frac{1}{2}n$ times. Thus, the worst-case behavior of insertion sort is $O(n^2)$.

The more items in the array are in order, the better insertion sort gets until, in the best case of a sorted array, the algorithm is linear. In the average case, however, insertion sort is still quadratic.

Exercises 4.4

1. Rewrite the sorting methods so that they sort an array of objects.

2. Which configuration of data in an array causes the smallest number of exchanges in a selection sort? Which configuration of data causes the largest number of exchanges?

3. Explain the role that the number of data exchanges plays in the analysis of selection sort and bubble sort. What role, if any, does the size of the data objects play?

4. Explain why the modified bubble sort still exhibits $O(n^2)$ behavior on the average.

5. Explain why insertion sort works well on partially sorted arrays.

4.5 Case Study: Recording Run Times and Counting Instructions

The purpose of this case study is to provide a test bed in which we can compare the behavior of the various search and sort algorithms presented in the chapter.

4.5.1 Request

Write a program that allows the user to profile different search and sort algorithms.

4.5.2 Analysis

The program allows the user to create arrays of integers of any size. The items in an array are randomly generated, and the user can specify that the array should contain duplicates or unique items. The user can display the contents of the array at any time.

The program allows the user to select an algorithm to run from a pull-down menu. The options are the selection, bubble, and insertion sorts and linear and binary search. If the menu selection is a search algorithm, the program runs the search for a user-specified target in the array. The results displayed are the run time, a count of the comparisons made during the search, and the position of the target or −1 if the target is not in the array. If the menu selection is a sort algorithm, the program runs the algorithm on the array. The results displayed are the run time and the counts of the number of comparisons and exchanges of items during the sort. Figure 4.2 shows the proposed interface after a bubble sort on an array of 900 integers.

The program uses two classes:

1. `AlgorithmProfiler` This class sets up the interface and handles user interaction.
2. `Algorithms` This class implements the search and sort algorithms as well as various utilities for setting up arrays and maintaining statistics.

Figure 4.2   **The interface for the algorithm profiler**

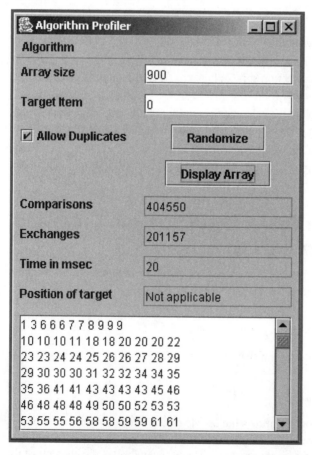

4.5.3   Design of the `Algorithms` Class

The `Algorithms` class is set up much like Java's `Math` class, with several static methods. The search and sort methods have the same design as those discussed earlier in this chapter, with the exception that they access and update variables to maintain a record of the run time and the counts of comparisons and exchanges. These variables are declared `public` and `static` so as to be easily accessible to the `AlgorithmProfiler` class.

The method `getRandomArray` returns a new array of integers of the specified size. The caller can also specify whether or not this array should contain duplicate values. The integers are positioned in random order and range from 1 to the size of the array.

The method `toString` returns a string containing the integers in the array. This string is formatted so that at most 10 integers print on a line when the string is output.

4.5.4   Implementation of the `Algorithms` Class

Here is an implementation of the `Algorithms` class. We omit most of the search and sort algorithms developed earlier in this chapter but include one, `selectionSort`, to show how the statistics are updated.

```
1 import java.util.*;
2
3 public class Algorithms {
4
5     public static long comparisons = 0,
6                        exchanges   = 0,
7                        runningTime = 0;
8
9     public static void selectionSort(int[] array){
10        comparisons = exchanges = 0;
11        Date d1 = new Date();
12        for (int i = 0; i < array.length - 1; i++){
13            int minIndex = i;
14            for (int j = i + 1; j < array.length; j++){
15                comparisons++;
16                if (array[j] < array[minIndex])
17                    minIndex = j;
18            }
19            if (minIndex != i)
20                swap(array, minIndex, i);
21        }
22        Date d2 = new Date();
23        runningTime = d2.getTime() - d1.getTime();
24    }

    . . . Other sort and search methods presented in the chapter
    . . . go here.

101    public static int[] getRandomArray(int size, boolean duplicates){
102        int[] array = new int[size];
```

Continued

Continued

```
103        int i = 0;
104        while (i < size){
105            int value = 1 + (int)(Math.random() * size);
106            if (duplicates || (linearSearch(value, array, i) == -1)){
107                array[i] = value;
108                i++;
109            }
110        }
111        return array;
112    }
113
114    public static String toString(int[] array){
115        String str = "";
116        for (int i = 0; i < array.length; i++){
117            str += array[i] + " ";
118            if (i != 0 && i % 10 == 0)
119                str += "\n";
120        }
121        return str;
122    }
123
124 }
```

4.5.5 Design and Implementation of the `AlgorithmProfiler` Class

The development of the `AlgorithmProfiler` class is the same as most other view classes. Here is a complete listing of the code:

```
 1 import java.awt.*;
 2 import javax.swing.*;
 3 import java.awt.event.*;
 4
 5 public class AlgorithmProfiler extends JFrame{
 6
 7     ///////////////////////////////////////////////////// main
 8
 9     public static void main (String[] args){
10         JFrame theFrame = new AlgorithmProfiler();
11         theFrame.setSize(300, 500);
12         theFrame.setVisible(true);
13     }
14
15     ///////////////////////////////////////////////////// Model
16
17     private int[] array;
18     private int targetItem, targetPosition;
19
20     ///////////////////////////////////////////////////// View
21
22     // Create controls
23     private JLabel        lbArraySize    = new JLabel("Array size");
24     private IntegerField ifArraySize    = new IntegerField(100);
25     private JLabel        lbTargetItem   = new JLabel("Target Item");
```

Continued

Continued

```java
26    private IntegerField ifTargetItem   = new IntegerField(0);
27    private JCheckBox     cbDuplicates   = new JCheckBox("Allow Duplicates");
28    private JButton       btRandomize    = new JButton("Randomize");
29    private JButton       btDisplayArray = new JButton("Display Array");
30    private JLabel        lbComparisons  = new JLabel("Comparisons");
31    private JTextField    tfComparisons  = new IntegerField(0);
32    private JLabel        lbExchanges    = new JLabel("Exchanges");
33    private JTextField    tfExchanges    = new IntegerField(0);
34    private JLabel        lbTime         = new JLabel("Time in msec");
35    private JTextField    tfTime         = new IntegerField(0);
36    private JLabel        lbPosition     = new JLabel("Position of target");
37    private JTextField    tfPosition     = new IntegerField(0);
38    private JTextArea     taDisplayArray = new JTextArea("");
39
40    private JMenu     muAlgorithm      = new JMenu("Algorithm");
41    private JMenuItem miSelectionSort  = new JMenuItem("Selection Sort");
42    private JMenuItem miBubbleSort     = new JMenuItem("Bubble Sort");
43    private JMenuItem miInsertionSort  = new JMenuItem("Insertion Sort");
44    private JMenuItem miLinearSearch   = new JMenuItem("Linear Search");
45    private JMenuItem miBinarySearch   = new JMenuItem("Binary Search");
46
47    public AlgorithmProfiler(){
48
49        // Initialize
50        tfComparisons.setEditable(false);
51        tfExchanges.setEditable(false);
52        tfPosition.setEditable(false);
53        tfTime.setEditable(false);
54        cbDuplicates.setSelected(true);        // Allow duplicates by default
55        setTitle("Algorithm Profiler");
56        targetItem = 0;
57        targetPosition = -1;
58        array = Algorithms.getRandomArray(100, true);  // Default size of 100
59
60        // Create container and layout
61        Container contentPane = getContentPane();
62        EasyGridLayout layout = new EasyGridLayout();
63        contentPane.setLayout (layout);
64
65        // Set constraints
66        JScrollPane spDisplayArea = new JScrollPane(taDisplayArray);
67        layout.setConstraints(lbArraySize     ,1,1,1,1);
68        layout.setConstraints(ifArraySize     ,1,2,1,1);
69        layout.setConstraints(lbTargetItem    ,2,1,1,1);
70        layout.setConstraints(ifTargetItem    ,2,2,1,1);
71        layout.setConstraints(cbDuplicates    ,3,1,1,1);
72        layout.setConstraints(btRandomize     ,3,2,1,1);
73        layout.setConstraints(btDisplayArray  ,4,2,1,1);
74        layout.setConstraints(lbComparisons   ,5,1,1,1);
75        layout.setConstraints(tfComparisons   ,5,2,1,1);
76        layout.setConstraints(lbExchanges     ,6,1,1,1);
77        layout.setConstraints(tfExchanges     ,6,2,1,1);
78        layout.setConstraints(lbTime          ,7,1,1,1);
79        layout.setConstraints(tfTime          ,7,2,1,1);
80        layout.setConstraints(lbPosition      ,8,1,1,1);
81        layout.setConstraints(tfPosition      ,8,2,1,1);
```

Continued

Continued

```
82       layout.setConstraints(spDisplayArea   ,9,1,2,1);
83
84       // Add controls to container
85       contentPane.add(lbArraySize);
86       contentPane.add(ifArraySize);
87       contentPane.add(lbTargetItem);
88       contentPane.add(ifTargetItem);
89       contentPane.add(cbDuplicates);
90       contentPane.add(btRandomize);
91       contentPane.add(btDisplayArray);
92       contentPane.add(lbComparisons);
93       contentPane.add(tfComparisons);
94       contentPane.add(lbExchanges);
95       contentPane.add(tfExchanges);
96       contentPane.add(lbTime);
97       contentPane.add(tfTime);
98       contentPane.add(lbPosition);
99       contentPane.add(tfPosition);
100      contentPane.add(spDisplayArea);
101
102      // Create the menu bar and add menus and menu items
103      JMenuBar menuBar = new JMenuBar();
104      setJMenuBar(menuBar);
105      menuBar.add(muAlgorithm);
106      muAlgorithm.add(miSelectionSort);
107      muAlgorithm.add(miBubbleSort);
108      muAlgorithm.add(miInsertionSort);
109      muAlgorithm.add(miLinearSearch);
110      muAlgorithm.add(miBinarySearch);
111
112      // Specify listeners
113      miSelectionSort.addActionListener(new MenuActionListener());
114      miBubbleSort.addActionListener(new MenuActionListener());
115      miInsertionSort.addActionListener(new MenuActionListener());
116      miLinearSearch.addActionListener(new MenuActionListener());
117      miBinarySearch.addActionListener(new MenuActionListener());
118      btRandomize.addActionListener(new ButtonActionListener());
119      btDisplayArray.addActionListener(new ButtonActionListener());
120      addWindowListener(new MyWindowAdapter());
121    }
122
123    ///////////////////////////////////////////////////////// Controller
124
125    private void updateDisplay(String type){
126       if (type == "sort"){
127          tfComparisons.setText("" + Algorithms.comparisons);
128          tfExchanges.setText("" + Algorithms.exchanges);
129          tfTime.setText("" + Algorithms.runningTime);
130          tfPosition.setText("Not applicable");
131       }else{ // "search"
132          tfComparisons.setText("" + Algorithms.comparisons);
133          tfExchanges.setText("Not applicable");
134          tfTime.setText("Not applicable");
135          tfPosition.setText("" + targetPosition);
136       }
```

Continued

Continued

```
137    }
138
139    // Menu action listener
140    private class MenuActionListener implements ActionListener{
141       public void actionPerformed(ActionEvent e){
142          String type = "sort";
143          Object menuItem= e.getSource();
144          targetItem = ifTargetItem.getNumber();
145          if (menuItem== miSelectionSort)
146             Algorithms.selectionSort(array);
147          else if (menuItem== miBubbleSort)
148             Algorithms.bubbleSort(array);
149          else if (menuItem== miInsertionSort)
150             Algorithms.insertionSort(array);
151          else if (menuItem== miLinearSearch){
152             type = "search";
153             targetPosition = Algorithms.linearSearch(targetItem,
154                                            array, array.length);
155          }else if (menuItem== miBinarySearch){
156             type = "search";
157             targetPosition = Algorithms.binarySearch(targetItem,
158                                     array, array.length);
159          }
160          updateDisplay(type);
161       }
162    }
163
164    // Button action listener
165    private class ButtonActionListener implements ActionListener{
166       public void actionPerformed(ActionEvent e){
167          Object button= e.getSource();
168          if (button== btRandomize){
169             array = Algorithms.getRandomArray(ifArraySize.getNumber(),
170                                         cbDuplicates.isSelected());
171             taDisplayArray.setText("");
172          }else
173             taDisplayArray.setText(Algorithms.toString(array));
174       }
175    }
176
177    // Window listener
178    private class MyWindowAdapter extends WindowAdapter{
179       public void windowClosing (WindowEvent e){
180          System.exit(0);
181       }
182    }
183 }
```

Exercise 4.5

Modify the profiler program so that it allows the user to run different sort algorithms on the same data set. Tip: Maintain a backup copy of the array and provide an additional check box for this option.

KEY TERMS

average case	bubble sort	selection sort
best case	growth rate	worst case
big-O notation	insertion sort	
binary search	order of complexity	

CHAPTER SUMMARY

There are two ways to determine the efficiency of an algorithm. The first method is empirical and involves obtaining the run time of the algorithm on a real computer. Because run times vary with the type of programming language and the type of hardware, a more independent measure of efficiency is desirable. The second method is analytical. One performs an analysis of the algorithm to derive its order of complexity. This is a measure of the abstract work an algorithm does as a function of the size of its data or problem size. Because an algorithm's order of complexity is machine and language independent, it can be used to predict the behavior of an algorithm with different data sets on any machine.

There are several common orders of complexity, such as logarithmic, linear, and quadratic. Search algorithms are generally either linear or logarithmic, whereas sort algorithms generally are either quadratic or $n\log n$.

The memory requirements of an algorithm can also be analyzed for their complexity, although this is not as great an issue as the run time.

REVIEW QUESTIONS

1. Explain why obtaining the actual run times of an algorithm is usually a poor method of determining its efficiency.
2. Draw diagrams that illustrate the rates of growth of logarithmic, linear, and quadratic algorithms.
3. Jayne claims that her algorithm, which has a complexity of $\frac{1}{2} n^2 + \frac{1}{2} n$, is generally faster than Bill's algorithm, which is exactly n^2. Is she right, and why?
4. Why is bubble sort a really bad algorithm?
5. Assume that bubble sort takes 5 seconds to sort an array of 10,000 elements on a given computer. How long will it take to sort an array of 1 million elements?

CHAPTER 5

Arrays and Linked Data Structures

OBJECTIVES Upon completion of this chapter, you should be able to

- Describe the basic features of arrays that account for the cost/benefit trade-offs in their use

- Describe the basic features of linked structures that account for the cost/benefit trade-offs in their use

- Design and implement methods for performing insertions and removals of items from an array

- Design and implement methods for increasing or decreasing the length of an array in an efficient manner

- Design and implement various methods for manipulating linked structures

- Explain the difference between singly linked, doubly linked, and circular linked structures

As mentioned in Chapter 1, an *abstract data type* (ADT) provides a programmer with an interface or set of operations. An ADT hides from the programmer details of how the operations are implemented and how the data within objects of that type are represented. The terms *data structure* and *concrete data type* refer to the internal representation of an ADT's data. This chapter covers operations on two data structures that are used to implement abstract data types: arrays and linked structures. We begin by reviewing operations on arrays that CS1 students may have covered briefly. We then introduce the ideas of pointers and linked structures and some common operations on them. Throughout, we assess the time/space trade-offs in using these two kinds of data structures.

5.1 Characteristics of Arrays

The array is probably the most common data structure in programs. In this section, we discuss several characteristics that programmers must keep in mind when using an array to implement an ADT.

5.1.1 Random Access and Contiguous Memory

As you know, an array represents a sequence of items that can be accessed by index position. The index operation makes storing or retrieving an item at a given position easy for the programmer. The index operation is also very fast. Indexing is a *random access* operation. During random access, the computer obtains the location of the *i*th item by performing a constant number of steps. Thus, no matter how large the array, it takes the same amount of time to access the first item as it does to access the last item.

The computer supports random access for arrays by allocating a block of *contiguous memory* cells for the array's items. One such block is shown in Figure 5.1. For simplicity, the figure assumes that each data item occupies a single memory cell, although this is not often the case.

Figure 5.1   **A block of contiguous memory**

Block of contiguous memory for array

Machine address		Array index
10011101		0
10011110		1
10011111		2
10100000		3
10100001		4

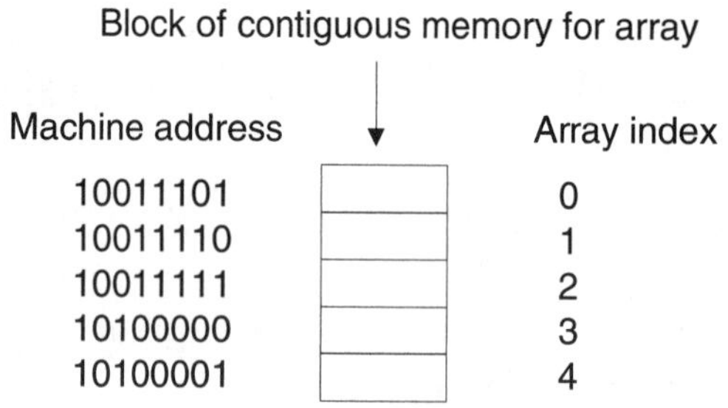

Because the addresses of the items are in numeric sequence, the address of an array item can be computed by adding two values: the array's *base address* and the item's *offset*. The array's base address is the machine address of the first item. An item's offset is equal to its index multiplied by a constant representing the number of memory cells required by an array item. To summarize, the index operation has two steps:

```
Fetch the base address of the array's memory block
Return the result of adding the index * k to this address
```

For example, suppose the base address of an array's memory block is 10011101, and each item requires a single cell of memory. Then the addresses of the first three data items are 10011101, 10011110, and 10011111, respectively.

The important point to note about random access is that the computer does not have to search for a given cell in an array, where one starts with the first cell and counts cells until the *i*th cell is reached. Random access in constant time is perhaps the most desirable feature of an array. However, this feature requires that the array be represented in a block of contiguous memory. As we will see shortly, this requirement leads to some costs when we implement other operations on arrays.

5.1.2   Static Memory and Dynamic Memory

Arrays in older languages such as FORTRAN and Pascal were *static* data structures. The size of the array was determined at compile time, so the programmer needed to specify this size with a constant. Because the size of an array could not be changed at run time, the programmer needed to predict how much array memory would be needed by all applications of the program. If the program always expected a known, fixed number of items in the array, there was no problem. But in the other cases, where the number of data items varied, programmers had to ask for enough memory to cover the cases when the largest number of data items would be stored in an array. Obviously, this requirement resulted in programs that wasted memory for many applications. Worse still, when the number of data items exceeded the size of the array, the best a program could do was to return an error message.

Modern languages such as Java and C++ provide a remedy for these problems by allowing the programmer to create *dynamic arrays*. Like a static array, a dynamic array occupies a contiguous block of memory and supports random access. However, the size of a dynamic array need not be known until run time. Thus, the programmer can specify the size of a dynamic array with a variable. For example, the following Java code segment allows the user of a program to input the size of an array from the console:

```
KeyboardReader reader = new KeyboardReader();
int[] array;
int size = reader.readInt("Enter the size of the array:");
array = new int[size];
```

In addition, the programmer can readjust the size of an array to an application's data requirements at run time. These adjustments can take three forms:

1. Create an array with a reasonable default size at program startup.

2. When the array cannot hold more data, increase its size.

3. When the array seems to be wasting memory (some data have been removed by the application), decrease its size.

We show how to resize an array shortly.

5.1.3   Physical Size and Logical Size

When working with an array, programmers must often distinguish between its *physical size* and its *logical size*. The physical size of an array is its total number of array cells, or the number used to specify its capacity when the array is created. The logical size of an array is the number of items in it that should be currently available to the application. In cases when the array is always full, the programmer need not worry about this distinction. However, such cases are rare. Figure 5.2 shows three arrays with the same physical size but different logical sizes. The cells currently occupied by data are shaded. As you can see, it is possible to access cells in the first two arrays that contain *garbage,* or data not currently meaningful to the application. Thus, the programmer must take care to track both the physical size and the logical size of an array in most applications.

Figure 5.2   **Arrays with different logical sizes**

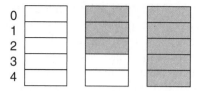

The public instance variable `length` contains the physical size of a Java array. In cases when the logical size may differ from the physical size, the application must use its own variable to track the number of items currently stored in an array. We did just that in the case study program of Chapter 3, where we used an array to maintain a list of employees. In that program, we declared two instance variables: one for the array and the other for the number of employees currently in the array. Here is the relevant code:

```
public static final int MAX_EMPLOYEES = 20;     // Physical size

private Employee[] employees;                    // Array variable
private int employeeCount;                       // Logical size

public EmployeeModel(){                          // Initialize
    employees = new Employee[MAX_EMPLOYEES];
    employeeCount = 0;
}
```

In this application, the physical size of the array is a constant, `MAX_EMPLOYEES`, which is 20. The logical size is a variable, `employeeCount`, which is initialized to 0. Whenever an employee is added to the array, we increment `employeeCount` by 1. Whenever an employee is removed from the array (although the case study did not do this), we decrement `employeeCount` by 1. In general, the logical size and the physical size tell us several important things about the state of the array:

1. If the logical size is 0, the array is empty. That is, the array contains no data items.

2. Otherwise, at any given time, the index of the last item in the array is the logical size minus 1.

3. If the logical size equals the physical size, there is no more room for data in the array.

To keep the case study simple, we returned an error message when the array ran out of room rather than attempting to resize it. Moreover, we did not allow insertions of items before the end of the array and did not support removals of items. In the next section, we show how a programmer can add these capabilities to an array-based implementation.

Exercises 5.1

1. Explain how random access works and why it is an efficient means of accessing data.

2. Describe the consequences of the difference between the logical size and the physical size of an array.

5.2 Operations on Arrays

In this section, we discuss the implementation of several array operations. For generality, we assume that the programmer is working with an array of objects, although one can modify the code to cover arrays of integers, employees, or whatever element type is desired. We assume the following data declarations:

```
final int DEFAULT_CAPACITY = 5;
int logicalSize = 0;
Object[] array = new Object[DEFAULT_CAPACITY];
```

As you can see, the array has an initial logical size of 0 and a default physical capacity of 5. For each operation that uses this array, we provide a description of the implementation strategy and an annotated Java code segment. At the end of this section, we develop some `static` methods to perform these operations on arrays.

5.2.1 Increasing the Size of an Array

When a new item is about to be inserted and the array's logical size equals its physical size, it is time to increase the size of the array. The resizing process consists of three steps:

1. Create a new, larger array.

2. Copy the data from the old array to the new array.

3. Reset the old array variable to the new array object.

Here is the code for this operation:

```
if (logicalSize == array.length){
   Object[] tempArray = new Object[array.length + 1];     // Create a new array
   for (int i = 0; i < logicalSize; i++)                  // Copy data from the old
      tempArray[i] = array[i];                            // array to the new array
   array = tempArray;            // Reset the old array variable to the new array
}
```

Note that the old array's memory is left out for the garbage collector. We also take the natural course of increasing the array's size by one cell to accommodate each new item. However, consider the performance implications of this decision. When the array is resized, the number of copy operations is linear. Thus, the overall time performance for adding n items to an array is $1 + 2 + 3 + \ldots + n$ or $n(n+1)/2$ or n^2.

We can achieve more reasonable time performance by doubling the size of the array each time we increase its size as follows:

```
Object[] tempArray = new Object[array.length * 2];   // Create new array
```

The analysis of the time performance of this version is left as an exercise. The gain in time performance is of course achieved at the cost of wasting some memory. However, the overall space performance of this operation is linear because a temporary array is required no matter what our strategy is.

5.2.2 Decreasing the Size of an Array

When the logical size of an array shrinks, cells go to waste. When an item is about to be removed and the number of these unused cells reaches or exceeds a certain threshold, say, three-fourths of the physical size of the array, it is time to decrease the physical size. The process of decreasing the size of an array is just the inverse of increasing it. Here are the steps:

1. Create a new, smaller array.

2. Copy the data from the old array to the new array.

3. Reset the old array variable to the new array object.

The code for this process kicks in when the logical size of the array is less than or equal to one-fourth of its physical size and its physical size is greater than the default capacity that we have established for the array. The algorithm reduces the physical size of the array either to one-half of its physical size or to its default capacity, whichever is greater. Here is the code:

```
if (logicalSize <= array.length / 4 && array.length > DEFAULT_CAPACITY){
    int newSize = Math.max(DEFAULT_CAPACITY, array.length / 2);
    Object[] tempArray = new Object[newSize];        // Create new array
    for (int i = 0; i < logicalSize; i++)            // Copy data from old array
        tempArray[i] = array[i];                     // to new array
    array = tempArray;                       // Reset old array variable to new array
}
```

Note that this strategy allows some memory to be wasted when shrinking the array. Whenever we decrease the size of an array, we leave its physical size at twice its logical size. This strategy tends to decrease the likelihood of further resizings in either direction. The time/space analysis of the contraction operation is left as an exercise.

5.2.3 Inserting an Item into an Array That Grows

Inserting an item into an array differs from replacing an item in an array. In the case of a replacement, an item already exists at the given index position and a simple assignment suffices. Moreover, the logical size of the array does not change. In the case of an insertion, we must do four things:

1. Check for available space before attempting an insertion and increase the size of the array if necessary.

2. Shift the items from the logical end of the array to the target index position down by one.

3. Assign the new item to the target index position.

4. Increment the logical size by one.

Figure 5.3 shows these steps for the insertion of an item at position 1 in an array of four items. As you can see, the order in which the items are shifted is critical. If we had started at the target index and copied down from there, we would have lost two items. Thus, we must start at the logical end of the array and work back up to the target index, copying each item to the cell of its successor. Here is the Java code for the insertion operation:

```java
// Increase size of array if necessary

// Shift items down by one position
for (int i = logicalSize; i > targetIndex; i--)
    array[i] = array[i - 1];
// Add new item and increment logical size
array[targetIndex] = newItem;
logicalSize++;
```

The time performance for shifting items during an insertion is linear on the average, so the insertion operation is linear.

Figure 5.3   **Inserting an item into an array**

Shift down item at	Shift down item at	Shift down item at	Now safe to	Array after
$n - 1$	$n - 2$	i	replace item at	insertion is
			position 1	finished

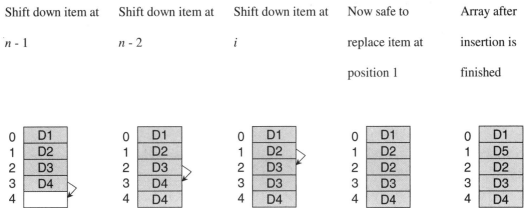

5.2.4   Removing an Item from an Array

Removing an item from an array involves the inverse process of inserting an item into the array. Here are the steps in this process:

1. Shift the items from the target index position to the logical end of the array up by one.

2. Decrement the logical size by one.

3. Check for wasted space and decrease the size of the array if necessary.

Figure 5.4 shows these steps for the removal of an item at position 1 in an array of five items. As with insertions, the order in which we shift items is critical. For a removal, we begin at the item following the target position and move toward the logical end of the array, copying each item to the cell of its predecessor. Here is the Java code for the removal operation:

```
// Shift items up by one position
for (int i = targetIndex; i < logicalSize - 1; i++)
    array[i] = array[i + 1];
// Decrement logical size
logicalSize--;

// Decrease size of array if necessary
```

Once again, because the time performance for shifting items is linear on average, the time performance for the removal operation is linear.

Figure 5.4   **Removing an item from an array**

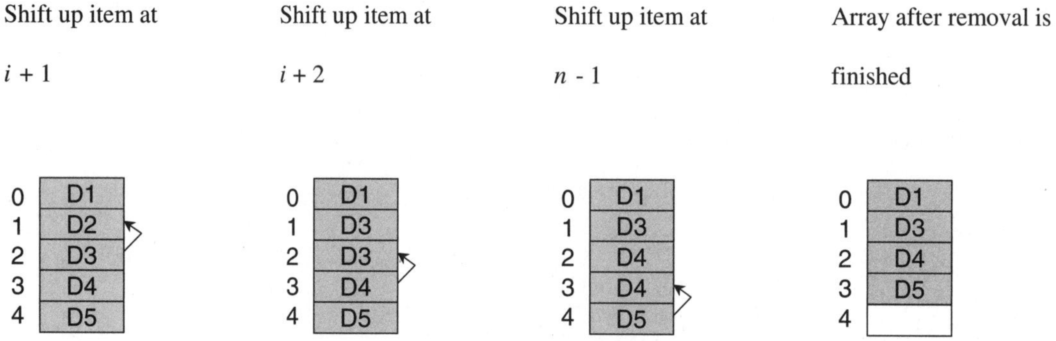

Shift up item at	Shift up item at	Shift up item at	Array after removal is
$i + 1$	$i + 2$	$n - 1$	finished

5.2.5   A Tester Program for Array Methods

The operations just discussed are so frequently used that it is a good idea to provide methods for them. Ideally, one implements them as `static` methods in a class that serves a utility function similar to Java's `Math` class. We now specify two of these methods in the context of a tester program and leave their complete development as an exercise.

The tasks of increasing or decreasing an array can be packaged in a single method called `resizeIfNeeded`. This method expects three parameters:

1. An array of objects, which is the array to be resized.

2. An integer representing the array's current logical size.

3. An integer representing the array's default capacity.

If the method finds that the array does not need resizing, it returns the original array. Otherwise, the method expands or contracts the array in the manner described earlier and returns this new array.

A method to insert a new item at a given index position is now easily written. The method `insertItem` expects the array, its logical size, its default capacity, the target index, and the new item as parameters. `insertItem` returns the array with the new item inserted at the given position. However, the method does not increment the array's logical size; that is the responsibility of the user of the method.

Here is a short tester program that uses these methods (*lines 12* and *14*):

```
 1 public class Tester{
 2
 3    public static int DEFAULT_CAPACITY = 3;
 4
 5    public static void main(String[] args){
 6
 7       // Create an initial array with 3 strings.
 8       Object[] array = {"hi", "there", "Mary"};
 9       int logicalSize = 3;
10
11       // Insert strings at positions 0 and 1.
12       array = insertItem(array, logicalSize, DEFAULT_CAPACITY, 0, "Jack");
13       logicalSize++;
14       array = insertItem(array, logicalSize, DEFAULT_CAPACITY, 1, "says");
15       logicalSize++;
16
17       // Display new physical size and contents.
18       System.out.println(array.length);
19       for (int i = 0; i < logicalSize; i++)
20          System.out.print(array[i] + " ");
21    }
22
23    // Definitions of array methods go here
24 }
```

5.2.6   Complexity Trade-off: Searching and Modifying an Array

As mentioned earlier, most of the benefits of using arrays flow from random access. Access to an item by position is in constant time. As shown in Chapter 4, when the items in an array are sorted, the binary search for a given item runs in logarithmic time in the worst case. The reason is that the location of the array's midpoint item requires constant time due to random access. Thus, arrays work very well as implementation structures for applications that must access items by position or by value.

However, the requirement that array items be stored in contiguous memory limits the performance of insertions and removals. The basic problem, if we can call it that, is that the user of an array must maintain a one-to-one correspondence between the logical positions of the items in the array and their physical positions in the underlying memory. That is why the user must shift items during insertions or removals. In the next section, we explore a way of solving this problem.

Exercises 5.2

1. Draw a picture of the memory used by the array insertion method that doubles the size of the array when the array must be expanded. Assume that the array's logical and physical sizes equal 5 before the insertion is performed.

2. Analyze the time complexity of the array insertion method that doubles the size of the array when the array must be expanded.

3. Analyze the time and space complexity of the array removal method discussed in this section.

4. Implement and test the static methods for insertion, removal, and resizing discussed in this section.

5. Compare the static methods of Exercise 4 to the methods in the `Utilities` class of the `lamborne` package. Discuss any differences in performance that might be evident.

6. The case study program of Chapter 3 allows additions of employees to the end of the list. Add an option that allows insertions. An insertion should be before the currently selected employee.

7. Modify the case study program of Chapter 3 so that it uses a dynamic array implementation. You should utilize the strategy for minimizing the number of resizings discussed earlier in this section.

5.3 Linked Structures

After arrays, linked structures are probably the most common data structures in programs. In this section, we discuss several characteristics that programmers must keep in mind when using linked structures to implement an ADT.

5.3.1 Singly Linked Structures and Doubly Linked Structures

As the name implies, a linked structure consists of items that are linked to other items. Although there can be many possible links among items, the two simplest linked structures are the *singly linked structure* and the *doubly linked structure.* It is useful to draw diagrams of linked structures using a box and pointer notation. Figure 5.5 uses this notation to show examples of the two kinds of linked structure.

Figure 5.5 **Linked structures**

A singly linked structure

A doubly linked structure

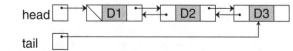

A user of a singly linked structure accesses the first item by following a single privileged *head link*. The user then accesses other items by following the single links (represented by arrows in the figure) that emanate from the items. Thus, in a singly linked structure, it is easy to get to the successor of an item but not so easy to get to an item's predecessor.

A doubly linked structure contains links running in both directions. Thus, it is easy for the user to move to an item's successor or to its predecessor. A second privileged link, called the *tail link,* allows the user of a doubly linked structure to access the last item directly.

The last item in a singly linked structure has no link to the next item. The figure indicates the absence of a link, called a *null link,* by means of a slash instead of an arrow. Note also that the first item in a doubly linked structure has no link to the preceding item.

These linked structures are like arrays in that they are linear sequences of items. However, users of our linked structures cannot immediately access an item by specifying its index position. Instead, a user must start at one end of the structure and follow the links until the desired position (or item) is reached. This property of linked structures has important consequences for several operations, as we see shortly.

The way in which memory is allocated for linked structures is also very unlike that of arrays and has two important consequences for insertion and removal operations:

1. Once we have found an insertion or removal point, the insertion or removal can take place with no shifting of data items.
2. The linked structure can be resized during each insertion or removal with no extra memory cost and no copying of data items.

We now examine the underlying memory support for linked structures that makes these advantages possible.

5.3.2   Noncontiguous Memory and Nodes

Recall that array items must be stored in contiguous memory. This means that the logical sequence of items in the array is tightly coupled to a physical sequence of items in memory. By contrast, a linked structure decouples the logical sequence of items in the structure from any ordering in memory. That is, a given item in a linked structure can be found anywhere in memory as long as the computer can follow a link to its address or location. This kind of memory representation technique is called *noncontiguous memory.*

The basic unit of representation in a linked structure is a *node*. A *singly linked node* contains the following components or fields:

1. A data item.
2. A link to the next node in the structure.

In addition to these components, a *doubly linked node* contains

3. A link to the previous node in the structure.

Figure 5.6 shows a singly linked node and a doubly linked node whose internal links are null.

Figure 5.6   **Nodes with null links**

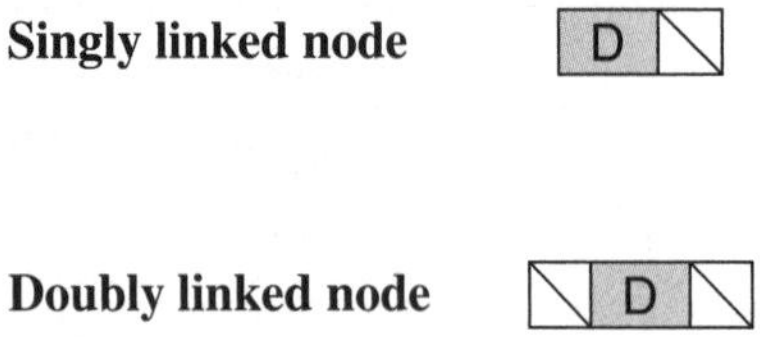

Singly linked node   D

Doubly linked node   D

Depending on the programming language, the programmer can set up nodes to use noncontiguous memory in several ways:

1. In early languages such as FORTRAN, the only built-in data structure was the array. The programmer thus implemented nodes and their noncontiguous memory for a singly linked structure by using two parallel arrays. One array contained the data items. The other array contained the index positions, for corresponding items in the data array, of their successor items in the data array. Thus, following a link meant using a data item's index in the first array to access a value in the second array and then using that value as an index into another data item in the first array. The null link was represented by the value −1. Figure 5.7 shows a linked structure and its array representation. As you can see, this setup effectively decouples the logical position of a data item in the linked structure from its physical position in the array.

Figure 5.7   **An array representation of a linked structure**

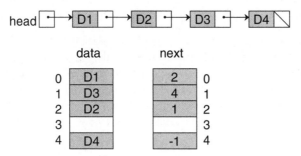

2. In more modern languages such as Pascal and C++, the programmer has direct access to the addresses of data in the form of *pointers*. In these languages, a node in a singly linked structure contains a data item and a pointer value. A special value null or nil represents the null link as a pointer value. The programmer does not use an array to set up the noncontiguous memory but simply asks the computer for a pointer to a new node from a built-in area of noncontiguous memory called the ***object heap***. The programmer then sets the pointer within this node to another node, thus establishing a link to other data in the structure. The use of explicit pointers and a built-in heap represents an advance over the FORTRAN-style technique because the programmer is no longer responsible for managing the underlying array representation of noncontiguous memory (after all, the memory of any computer—RAM—is ultimately just a big array). However, Pascal and C++ still require the programmer to manage the heap insofar as the programmer has to return unused nodes to it with a special `dispose` or `delete` operation.

3. Java programmers set up nodes and linked structures by using ***references*** to objects. As you know from CS1 (or from Appendix A of this book), Java classes are reference types, and a variable of any of these types actually contains a pointer to the object to which it refers or the `null` value if the variable has not yet been initialized. Thus, a Java programmer defines a singly linked node by defining an object that contains two fields: a data item and another node (actually, a reference to the next node). Java provides dynamic allocation of noncontiguous memory for each new node object, as well as automatic return of this memory to the system when the object can no longer be referenced by the application.

In the discussion that follows, we use the terms ***link, pointer,*** and ***reference*** interchangeably.

5.3.3   Defining a Singly Linked Node Class

Node classes are fairly simple and thus are usually defined as ***private inner classes*** within the classes they support. Flexibility and ease of use are critical, so the variables of a node object are usually made visible to the user, and constructors allow the user to set a node's link(s) when the node is created. As mentioned earlier, a singly linked node contains just a data item and a reference to the next node. We assume for generality that the data item is of the class `Object`. Here is the code for a simple singly linked node class:

```
 1 private class Node extends Object{
 2
 3    private Object value;     //Value stored in this node
 4    private Node   next;      //Reference to next node
 5
 6    private Node(){
 7       value = null;
 8       next = null;
 9    }
10
11    private Node(Object value, Node next){
12       this.value = value;
13       this.next = next;
14    }
15 }
```

5.3.4   Using the Singly Linked Node Class

Node variables are declared and initialized to either the null value or a new node object. The next code segment shows some variations on these two options:

```
// Just a null link
Node node1 = null;

// A node containing data and a null link
Node node2 = new Node("A", null);

// A node containing data and a link to node2
Node node3 = new Node("B", node2);
```

Figure 5.8 shows the state of the three variables after this code is run. Note that

- node1 points to no node object yet (is null).
- node2 and node3 point to objects that are linked together.
- node2 points to an object whose next pointer is null.

Figure 5.8   **Nodes with null links**

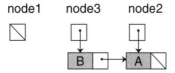

Now suppose we attempt to place the first node at the beginning of the linked structure that already contains node2 and node3 by running the statement

```
node1.next = node3;
```

Java responds by throwing a ***null pointer exception***. The reason is that the variable node1 contains the null value and thus does not reference a node object containing a next field. To accomplish the desired linkage, we could run either

```
node1 = new Node("C", node3);
```

or

```
node1 = new Node("C", null);
node1.next = node3;
```

In general, one can guard against null pointer exceptions by asking whether or not a given node variable is null before attempting to access its fields:

```
if (nodeVariable != null)
   <access a field in nodeVariable>
```

Like arrays, linked structures are processed with loops. Loops can be used to create a linked structure and visit each node in it. The next tester program uses our Node class to create a singly linked structure and print its contents:

```
 1 public class NodeTester{
 2
 3     // Run the test during the construction of the NodeTester object
 4     public NodeTester(){
 5        Node head = null;
 6
 7        // Add five nodes to the beginning of the linked structure
 8        for (int i = 1; i <= 5; i++){
 9           String str = String.valueOf(i);
10           head = new Node(str, head);
11        }
12
13        // Print the contents of the structure
14        while (head != null){
15           System.out.println(head.value);
16           head = head.next;
17        }
18     }
19
20     // Instantiate the NodeTester class so the test runs
21     public static void main(String[] args){
22        new NodeTester();
23     }
24
25     private class Node extends Object{
26
27        private Object value;    //Value stored in this node
28        private Node   next;     //Reference to next node
29
30        private Node(){
31           value = null;
32           next = null;
33        }
34
35        private Node(Object value, Node next){
36           this.value = value;
37           this.next =next;
38        }
39     }
40 }
```

Note the following points about this program:

1. Unlike other tester classes, this one has the test code in a constructor method *(lines 4–18)*. The reason is that the tester class defines a private inner class, which can only be used within an instance of the enclosing class.

2. One pointer, head, is used to generate the linked structure. This pointer is manipulated in such a way that the most recently inserted item is always at the beginning of the structure *(lines 8–11)*.

3. Thus, when the data are displayed, they appear in the reverse order of their insertion *(lines 14–17)*.

4. Also, when the data are displayed, the head pointer is reset to the next node, until the head pointer becomes `null`. Thus, at the end of this process, the nodes are effectively deleted from the linked structure. They are no longer available to the program and are recycled during the next garbage collection.

Exercises 5.3

1. Using box and pointer notation, draw a picture of the nodes created by the first loop in the tester program.

2. Explain why one would implement a private inner class.

3. What is a null pointer exception? How does one guard against it?

4. Write a code segment that transfers items from a full array to a singly linked list. The operation should preserve the ordering of the items.

5. Write a code segment that transfers items from a singly linked list to an array. The operation should preserve the ordering of the items and return an array that is full of items.

5.4 Operations on Singly Linked Structures

5.4.1 Traversal

The second loop in the last tester program effectively removed each node from the linked structure after printing that node's data. However, many applications simply need to visit each node without deleting it. This operation, called a ***traversal,*** makes use of a temporary pointer. This pointer is initialized to the linked structure's `head` pointer and then controls the loop as follows:

```
Node probe = head;
while (probe != null){
    <use or modify probe.value>
    probe = probe.next;
}
```

Figure 5.9 shows the state of the pointer variables `probe` and `head` during each pass of the loop. Note that at the end of the process, the `probe` pointer is `null`, but the `head` pointer still references the first node.

In general, a traversal of a singly linked structure visits every node and terminates when a `null` pointer is reached. Thus, the `null` pointer serves as a ***sentinel*** that stops the process.

Traversals are obviously linear in time and require no extra memory.

Figure 5.9 **Traversing a linked structure**

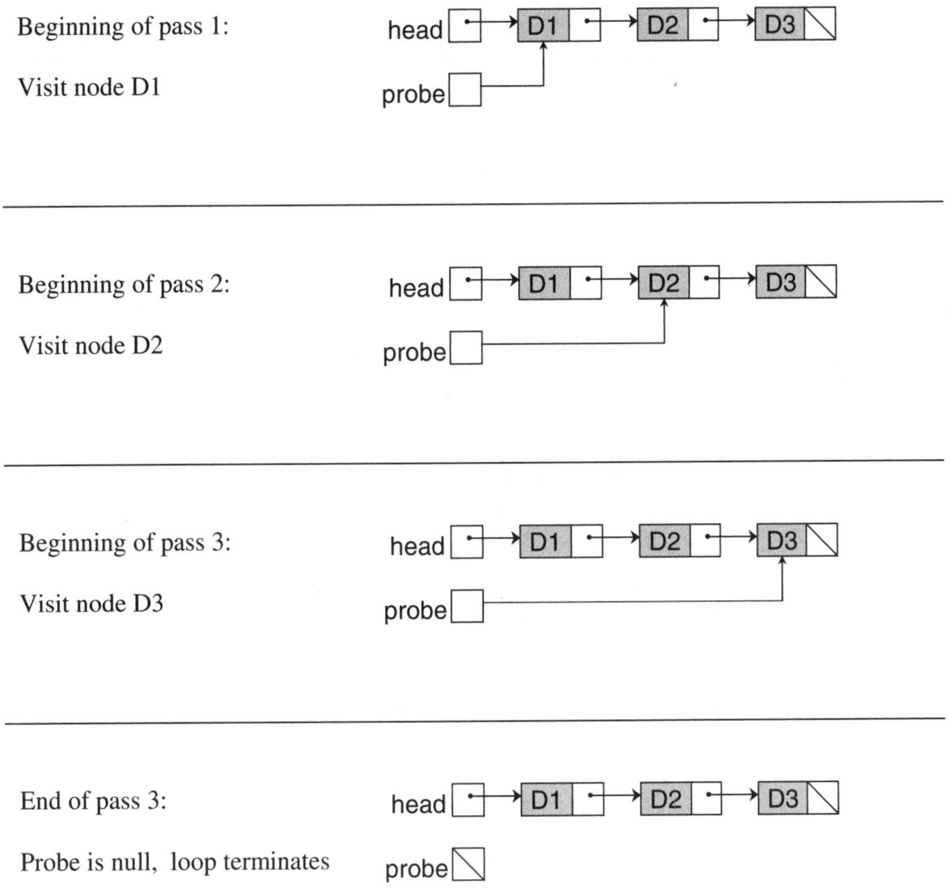
Beginning of pass 1:
Visit node D1
head
probe
D1
D2
D3
Beginning of pass 2:
Visit node D2
head
probe
D1
D2
D3
Beginning of pass 3:
Visit node D3
head
probe
D1
D2
D3
End of pass 3:
Probe is null, loop terminates
head
probe
D1
D2
D3

5.4.2 Searching (Object or *i*th)

We discussed the search for a given item in an array in Chapter 4. The search for a given item in a linked structure resembles a traversal in that we must start at the first node and follow the links until a sentinel is reached. However, in this case, there are two possible sentinels:

1. The `null` pointer, indicating that there are no more data items to examine.
2. A data item that equals the target item, indicating a successful search.

Here is the form of the search for a given item:

```
Node probe = head;
while (probe != null && ! targetItem.equals(probe.value))
   probe = probe.next;
if (probe != null)
   <targetItem has been found>
else
   <targetItem is not in the linked structure>
```

Like a traversal, the search for a given item is linear on the average for singly linked structures.

Unfortunately, accessing the *i*th item is also a linear search operation. The reason is that we must start at the first node and count the number of links until the *i*th node is reached. We assume that $0 <= i < n$, where *n* is the number of nodes in the linked structure. Here is the form for accessing the *i*th item:

```
// Assumes 0 <= index < n
Node probe = head;
while (index > 0){
   probe = probe.next;
   index—;
}
return probe.value;
```

A singly linked structure, even one whose data are in sorted order, is not as efficiently searched as a sorted array using binary search. However, as we see in Chapter 12, there are other ways of organizing linked structures so as to support binary search.

5.4.3   Relacement (Object or *i*th)

The replacement operations in a singly linked structure also employ the traversal pattern. In these cases, we search for a given item or a given position in the linked structure and replace the item with a new item. The first operation, replacing a given item, need not assume that the target item is in the linked structure. If the target item is not present, no replacement occurs and the operation returns `false`. If the target is present, the new item replaces it and the operation returns `true`. Here is the form of the operation:

```
Node probe = head;
while (probe != null && ! targetItem.equals(probe.value))
   probe = probe.next;
if (probe != null){
   probe.value = newItem;
   return true;
}else
   return false;
```

The operation to replace the *i*th item assumes that $0 <= i < n$. Here is the form:

```
// Assumes 0 <= index < n
Node probe = head;
while (index > 0){
   probe = probe.next;
   index—;
}
probe.value = newItem;
```

Both replacement operations are linear on the average.

5.4.4 Inserting at the Beginning

By now, you are probably wondering whether there is a better than linear operation on a linked structure. We are about to see such an operation, and we learn why one might prefer linked structures to arrays in some cases. The first such case is the insertion of an item at the beginning of the structure. This is just what we did repeatedly in the tester program of the previous section. Here is the form:

```
head = new Node(newItem, head);
```

Figure 5.10 traces this operation for two cases. The head pointer is `null` in the first case, so the first item is being inserted into the structure. In the second case, the second item is inserted at the beginning of the same structure.

Figure 5.10   **The two cases of inserting an item at the beginning of a linked structure**

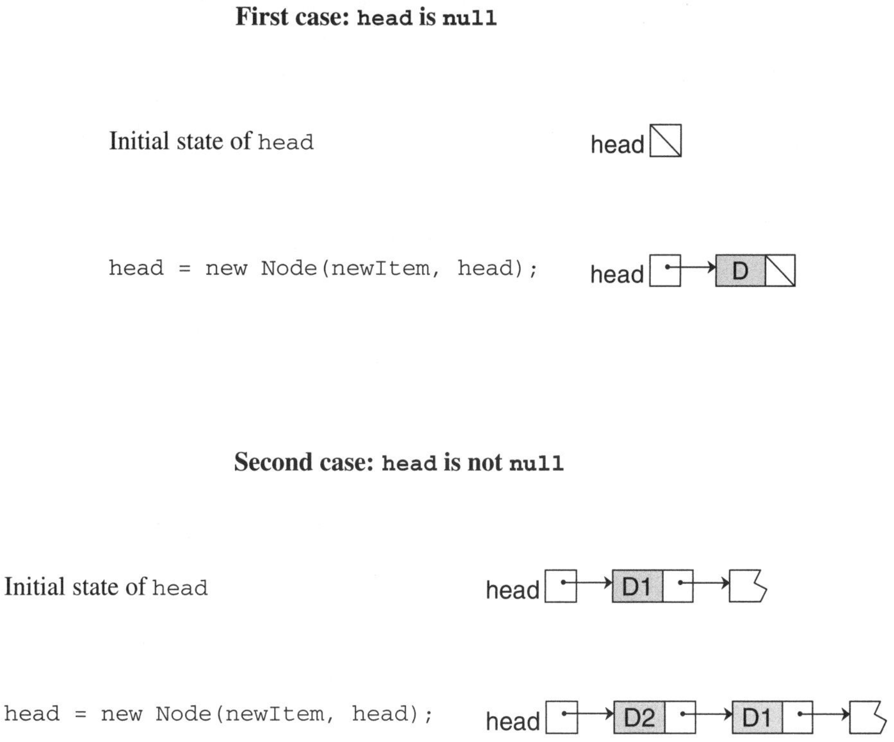

Note that in the second case, no copying of data to shift them down is necessary, so no extra memory is needed. Thus, insertion at the beginning of a linked structure uses constant time and memory, unlike the same operation with arrays.

5.4.5   Inserting at the End

Inserting an item at the end of an array (the add operation in the case study of Chapter 3) requires constant time and memory, unless the array must be resized. The same process for a singly linked structure must consider two cases:

1. The head pointer is null, so we set the head pointer to the new node.

2. The head pointer is not null, so we must search for the last node and aim its next pointer at the new node.

Case 2 returns us to the traversal pattern. Here is the form:

```
Node newNode = new Node(newItem, null);
if (head == null)
```

Continued

Figure 5.11   **Inserting an item at the end of a linked structure**

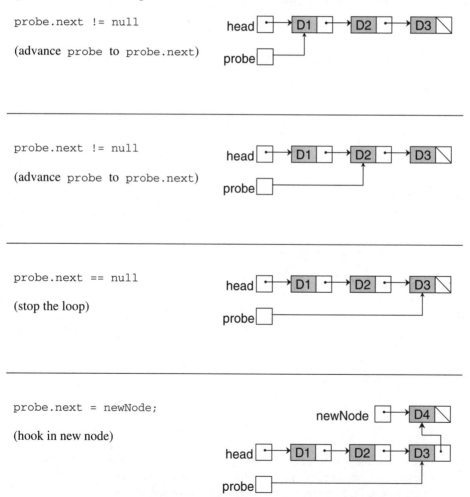

Continued

```
      head = newNode;
else{
   Node probe = head;
   while (probe.next != null)
      probe = probe.next;
   probe.next = newNode;
}
```

Figure 5.11 traces the insertion of a new item at the end of a linked structure of three items. This operation is linear in time and constant in memory.

5.4.6   Removing at the Beginning

In the tester program of the previous section, we repeatedly removed the item at the beginning of the linked structure. A standard removal from the beginning operation assumes that there is at least one node in the structure and returns the item removed. Here is the form:

```
// Assumes at least one node in the structure
Object removedItem = head.value;
head = head.next;
return removedItem;
```

Figure 5.12 traces the removal of the first node. As you can see, the operation uses constant time and memory, unlike the same operation for arrays.

Figure 5.12   **Removing an item at the beginning of a linked structure**

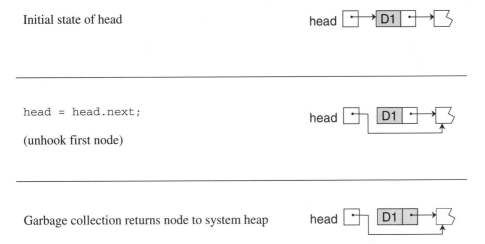

Initial state of head

head = head.next;

(unhook first node)

Garbage collection returns node to system heap

5.4.7   Removing at the End

Removing an item at the end of an array requires constant time and memory, unless the array must be resized. The same process for a singly linked structure assumes at least one node in the structure. There are then two cases to consider:

1. There is just one node. We set the `head` pointer to `null`.

2. There is a node before the last node. We search for this second to last node and set its next pointer to `null`.

In either case, we return the data item contained in the deleted node. Here is the form:

```
// Assumes at least one node in structure
Object removedItem = head.value;
if (head.next == null)
    head = null;
else{
    Node probe = head;
    while (probe.next.next != null)
        probe = probe.next;
    removedItem = probe.next.value;
    probe.next = null;
}
return removedItem;
```

Figure 5.13 shows the removal of the last node from a linked structure of three items. This operation is linear in time and constant in memory.

Figure 5.13   **Removing an item at the end of a linked structure**

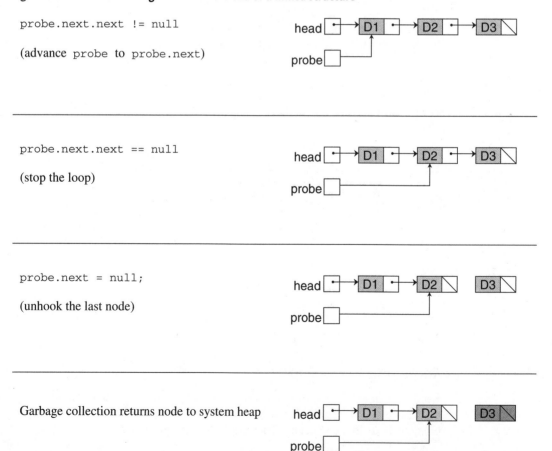

5.4.8   Insertions (Object or *i*th)

The insertion of an item at the *i*th position in an array requires shifting items from position *i* down to position *n* − 1. Thus, we actually insert the item before the item currently at position *i* so that the new item occupies position *i* and the old item occupies position *i* + 1. What about the cases of an empty array or an index that is greater than *n* − 1? If the array is empty, the new item goes at the beginning, whereas if the index is greater than or equal to *n*, the item goes at the end.

The insertion of an item at the *i*th position in a linked structure must deal with the same cases. The case of insertion at the beginning uses the code presented earlier. In the case of an insertion at some other position *i*, however, the operation must first find the node at position *i* − 1 (if *i* < *n*) or the node at position *n* − 1 (if *i* >= *n*). Then there are two cases to consider:

1. That node's next pointer is `null`. This means that *i* >= *n*, so the new item should go at the end of the linked structure.

2. That node's next pointer is not `null`. This means that 0 < *i* < *n*, so the new item must go between the node at position *i* − 1 and the node at position *i*.

As with a search for the *i*th item, the insertion operation must count nodes until the desired position is reached. However, because the target index might be greater than or equal to the number of nodes, we must be careful to avoid going off the end of the linked structure in the search. Thus, the loop has an additional condition that tests the current node's next pointer to see if it is the final node. Here is the form:

```
if (head == null || index <= 0)
   head = new Node(newItem, head);
else{
   // Search for node at position index - 1 or the last position
   Node probe = head;
   while (index > 1 && probe.next != null){
      probe = probe.next;
      index--;
   }
   // Insert new node after node at position index - 1 or last position
   probe.next = new Node(newItem, probe.next);
```

Figure 5.14 shows a trace of the insertion of an item at position 2 in a linked structure containing three items. As with any singly linked structure operation that uses a traversal pattern, this operation has a linear time performance. However, the use of memory is constant. The insertion of an item before a given item in a linked structure uses elements of this pattern and is left as an exercise.

Figure 5.14 **Inserting an item between two items in a linked structure**

`index > 1 && probe.next != null`

(advance `probe` to `probe.next` and

decrement index)

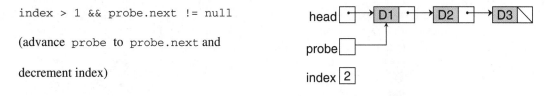

`index == 1`

(stop the loop)

`probe.next = new Node(newItem,`

                    `probe.next);`

(hook in the new node)

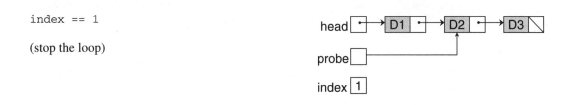

5.4.9   Removals (Object or *i*th)

The removal of the *i*th item from a linked structure has three cases:

1. $i <= 0$. We use the code to remove the first item.

2. $0 < i < n$. We search for the node at position $i - 1$, as in insertion, and remove the following node.

3. $i >= n$. We remove the last node.

We assume that the linked structure has at least one item. The pattern is similar to the one used for insertion in that we must guard against going off the end of the linked structure. However, we must allow the `probe` pointer to go no further than the second node from the end of the structure. Here is the form:

```
// Assumes that the linked structure has at least one item
Object removedItem;
if (index <= 0 || head.next == null) {
   removedItem = head.value;
   head = head.next;
```

Continued

Continued

```
    return removedItem;
}else{
    // Search for node at position index - 1 or the next to last position
    Node probe = head;
    while (index > 1 && probe.next.next != null){
        probe = probe.next;
        index--;
    }
    removedItem = probe.next.value;
    probe.next = probe.next.next;
    return removedItem;
}
```

Figure 5.15 shows a trace of the removal of the item at position 2 in a linked structure containing four items.

Figure 5.15   **Removing an item between two items in a linked structure**

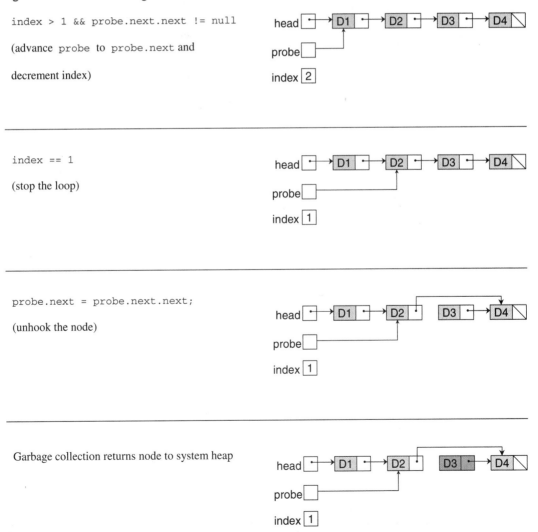

5.4.10   Complexity Trade-off: Time, Space, and Singly Linked Structures

Surprisingly, a tally reveals that the only two linked structure operations that are not linear in time are the insertion and removal of the first item. You might be wondering why we use a linked structure instead of an array if so many of a linked structure's methods have linear behavior. Well, suppose we wish to implement an ADT that just inserts or removes the first item. We will see such an ADT, the stack, in Chapter 7. Of course, one might also choose an array implementation that inserts or removes the last item with similar time performance. Later in the book, we look at linked structures that support logarithmic insertions and searches.

The main advantage of the singly linked structure over the array is not time performance but memory performance. Resizing an array is linear in time and memory. Resizing a linked structure is constant in time and memory. Moreover, no memory ever goes to waste in a linked structure: The physical size of the structure never exceeds the logical size. Linked structures do have an extra memory cost in that a singly linked structure must use n cells of memory for the pointers. This cost increases for doubly linked structures, whose nodes have two links.

A complete comparison of the space requirements must consider an array's **load factor.** The load factor equals the number of items stored in the array divided by the array's capacity. The load factor is 1 when an array is full and 0 when the array is empty. A static array implementation is more space efficient than a linked implementation whenever the load factor is greater than .5. The load factor for a dynamic array implementation normally varies between .25 and 1, although it can obviously sink to 0. Programmers who understand this analysis can pick the implementation that best suits their needs.

5.5   Variations on a Link

5.5.1   A Circular Linked Structure with a Dummy Header Node

The insertion and the removal of the first node are special cases of the insert ith and remove ith operations on singly linked structures. These cases are special because the head pointer must be reset. We can simplify these operations by using a *circular linked structure* with a *dummy header node.* There is always at least one node in this implementation. This node contains no data but serves as a marker for the beginning and the end of the linked structure. Initially, in an empty linked structure, the head variable points to this node, and this node's next pointer points back to the node itself, as shown in Figure 5.16.

Figure 5.16   **An empty circular linked structure with a dummy header node**

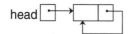

The first node to contain data goes after the header node. Its next pointer then points back to the header in a circular fashion, as shown in Figure 5.17.

Figure 5.17   **A circular linked structure after inserting the first node**

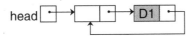

The search for the *i*th node begins with the node after the header node. Assume that the empty linked structure is initialized as follows:

```
head = new Node(null, null);
head.next = head;
```

Here is the code for insertions at the *i*th position using this new representation of a linked structure:

```
// Search for node at position index - 1 or the last position
Node probe = head;
while (index > 0 && probe.next != head){
   probe = probe.next;
   index--;
}
// Insert new node after node at position index - 1 or last position
probe.next = new Node(newItem, probe.next);
```

The advantage of this implementation is that the insertion and removal operations have only one case to consider: the case where the *i*th node lies between a prior node and the current *i*th node. When the *i*th node is the first node, the prior node is the header node. When $i >= n$, the last node is the prior node and the header node is the next node.

5.5.2   Doubly Linked Structures

A doubly linked structure has the advantages of a singly linked structure, and in addition, it allows the user to

1. Move to the previous node from a given node.

2. Move immediately to the last node.

Figure 5.18 shows a doubly linked structure that contains three nodes. Note the presence of two pointers, conventionally known as next and previous, in each node.

Figure 5.18   **A doubly linked structure with three nodes**

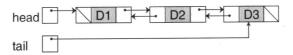

Note also the presence of a second external `tail` pointer that allows direct access to the last node in the structure.

The Java implementation of a node class for doubly linked structures adds a field for the `previous` pointer to the node class discussed earlier. Here is the code for the class, called `TwoWayNode`:

```
 1 private class TwoWayNode extends Object{
 2
 3     private Object      value;      //Value stored in this node
 4     private TwoWayNode next;        //Reference to next node
 5     private TwoWayNode previous;    //Reference to previous node
 6
 7     private TwoWayNode(){
 8         value = null;
 9         previous = null;
10         next = null;
11     }
12
13     private TwoWayNode(Object value){
14         this.value = value;
15         previous = null;
16         next = null;
17     }
18
19     private TwoWayNode(Object value,
20                         TwoWayNode previous,
21                         TwoWayNode next){
22         this.value = value;
23         this.previous = previous;
24         this.next = next;
25     }
26 }
```

The following tester program creates a doubly linked structure by adding items to the end. The program then displays the linked structure's contents by starting at the last item and working backward to the first item:

```
 1 public class TwoWayNodeTester{
 2
 3     // Run the test during the construction of the TwoWayNodeTester object
 4     public TwoWayNodeTester(){
 5
 6         // Create a doubly linked structure with one node
 7         TwoWayNode head = new TwoWayNode("1", null, null);
 8         TwoWayNode tail = head;
 9
10         // Add four nodes to the end of the doubly linked structure
11         for (int i = 2; i <= 5; i++){
12             String str = i + "";
13             tail.next = new TwoWayNode(str, tail, null);
14             tail = tail.next;
15         }
16
17         // Print the contents of the linked structure in reverse order
```

Continued

```
18       TwoWayNode probe = tail;
19       while (probe != null){
20           System.out.println(probe.value);
21           probe = probe.previous;
22       }
23
24   }
25
26   // Main method and definition of TwoWayNode class go here
27 }
```

Consider the following two statements in the first loop of the program:

```
tail.next = new TwoWayNode(str, tail, null);
tail = tail.next;
```

The purpose of these statements is to insert a new item at the end of the linked structure. We assume that there is at least one node in the linked structure and that the
`tail` pointer always points to the last node in the nonempty linked structure. Three
pointers must be set:

1. The previous pointer of the new node must be aimed at the current tail node.

2. The next pointer of the current tail node must be aimed at the new node.

3. The tail pointer must be aimed at the new node.

Figure 5.19 shows the insertion of a new node at the end of a doubly linked structure. As you can see, insertions in the middle of a doubly linked structure would require the redirection of still more pointers. However, the number of redirected pointers is always constant no matter where the target position is.

Figure 5.19.   **Inserting an item at the end of a doubly linked structure**

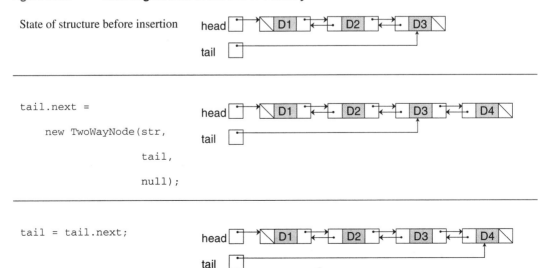

The more general insertion and removal operations for doubly linked structures also have two special cases, as they did with singly linked structures. It is possible to simplify these operations by resorting to a circular list with a dummy header node. We leave this as an exercise.

The run-time complexities of the operations on a doubly linked structure are the same as the corresponding operations on the singly linked structure. However, a linear amount of extra memory is required for the extra pointers of a doubly linked structure.

Exercises 5.5

1. Write a code segment that inserts an item before a given item in a singly linked structure. You should develop and state the preconditions and postconditions of this operation.

2. Write a code segment that inserts an item after a given item in a singly linked structure. You should develop and state the preconditions and postconditions of this operation.

3. Write a code segment that inserts the ith item in a doubly linked structure. You should develop and state the preconditions and postconditions of this operation.

4. Modify the operation of Exercise 3 so that it assumes the presence of a circular structure with a dummy header node.

KEY TERMS

circular linked structure	link	physical size
contiguous memory	linked structure	random access memory (RAM)
data structure	logical size	
doubly linked structure	node	reference
dummy header node	noncontiguous memory	singly linked structure
dynamic array	null pointer exception	static array
garbage	object heap	tail link
head link	pointer	

CHAPTER SUMMARY

Arrays and linked structures are useful data structures for implementing a wide range of collections. There are many trade-offs to consider when using arrays and linked structures. Arrays allow constant-time access to data items by their positions because these items are stored in contiguous memory locations. However, insertions and removals of items require a linear-time shift of items in memory. Because an array is fixed in size when created, some space may be wasted when the array is not full, and some data may be lost when the array becomes full. An array's logical size (the number of items stored in it) may be different from its physical size (the number of positions available for items). Assuming that the available items are at the beginning of an array, the programmer must maintain a separate variable to track the position of the last available item. Finally, the process of resizing a full array to accommodate more items requires a brand new array and a copying process. Resizing an array is thus linear in memory and in time.

Linked structures require extra memory for the links, but no more memory than is necessary to accommodate the available data items. A linked structure's logical size is always the same as its physical size. Insertions and removals require a constant-time adjustment of links and a constant-memory allocation or deallocation of space. However, linked structures require a linear process to access a data item by position.

Doubly linked structures allow more convenient and efficient implementation of some operations than singly linked structures at the cost of using extra memory for the links.

REVIEW QUESTIONS

1. Assume that an array contains spots for 1,000 data items. Explain why the computer can access the 1,000th item just as quickly as the 1st item.

2. What is the difference between the logical size of a data structure and its physical size?

3. Why does the programmer have to track the number of items currently stored in an array?

4. Describe the process of inserting an item into an array at a given position.

5. What must be done when an array becomes full and an item is waiting to be inserted?

6. Why do arrays support binary search?

7. How much memory is required for an empty linked structure?

8. Describe the component parts of a node.

9. How do you locate the last item in a linked structure?

10. What is a null pointer exception? Explain how one can occur in the context of manipulating a linked structure.

11. Describe the process of inserting an item into a linked structure at a given position.

12. Explain why its takes more time to access the last item in a singly linked structure than it takes to access the first item.

13. Assume that you have accessed an item in a singly linked structure and in an array. Compare the times for accessing the previous item in both structures.

14. Repeat Question 12 but assume that each node in the linked structure also has a pointer to the previous node.

15. Describe how you can improve the access time to the last item in a doubly linked structure.

CHAPTER 6

Overview of Collections

OBJECTIVES   Upon completion of this chapter, you should be able to

- Understand the use of interfaces in specifying collections

- Show how a given collection can have several implementations and provide criteria for choosing among them

- Explain how a collection's implementing classes can fit into a hierarchy to exploit abstraction and inheritance

- Give an account of the types of methods typically supported by collections

- Explain the role of iterators in processing collections

- Describe the purpose of a collection-view

- Implement a simple iterator and a collection-view for a collection

There are many kinds of collections, and it is helpful to begin with an overview. In this chapter, we do not present the specific features of any particular collection but instead provide broad background material to help you make sense of the many details that come later. We begin by summarizing the various collections discussed in the book. From there, we introduce a number of issues common to most types of collections: multiple implementations, casting, serialization, iterators, and collection-views. At the end of the chapter, we explain how and why we distinguish between prototypes and professional versions of collections. Throughout the chapter, we illustrate important concepts using a simple collection class called `Tiny`.

6.1   Introduction

As mentioned in Chapter 1, there are four broad categories of collections: linear, hierarchical, graph, and unordered. Common linear collections are strings, lists, stacks, and queues. The hierarchical collections comprise various kinds of trees. The graph collections consist of directed, undirected, weighted, and unweighted graphs.

Among the unordered collections, one usually finds sets, bags, and maps.

The collections just mentioned are widely used. However, there are no standards defining their behavior and few standard names for the implementing classes and methods. This is not to say that all is chaos; far from it, and most libraries of collection classes adhere to recognizable conventions. For convenience, we treat the conventions established in the Java Development Kit (JDK) as our standard. The JDK includes the collections considered most useful by Java's developers. However, important collections have been omitted, and we provide them in a package called `lamborne`. Taken together, the JDK and `lamborne` provide a comprehensive and high-quality collections library that you should find useful throughout your computer science curriculum. For a road map of the JDK and `lamborne` collections, see Section 6.8.

Most collections include an interface and one or more implementations. This arrangement establishes a collection's behavior independently of its implementation. However, the JDK does not consistently adhere to this arrangement. Java defines some collections in terms of a single implementing class and no interface. This lack of uniformity has its roots in Java's history. There have been numerous releases of the JDK. Early releases did not use interfaces widely, and as each new release tried to improve on its predecessors while preserving backward compatibility, inconsistencies arose.

When designing a collection, developers think first about the behavior expected by users. Once a standard has been established, the methods are codified in a Java interface. As you saw in Chapter 2, a Java interface specifies the methods that must be included in any class that implements the interface. For example, if the class library contains several different list implementations, their behavior is codified in a single list interface. Users are guaranteed that all list implementations satisfy a common standard, although the implementations may differ with respect to run-time resource usage.

Given the seeming plethora of collections, how does a programmer choose the right one? The different types of collections organize and access data in markedly different ways. Programmers can usually make a sensible selection if they understand the processing requirements of a problem and the capabilities and uses of the various collections. Choosing the best implementation for the selected collection, on the other hand, can be more difficult, and we deal with this issue shortly.

6.1.1   Summary of the Book's Collections

We now give a short summary of the collections, or ADTs, discussed in this book. Remember as you read about these different types of collections that a collection holds references to objects and not the objects themselves. The same is true for arrays, and just as an array can hold several different references to the same object, a collection can too. For convenience, we usually speak of an object being in a collection, but what we really mean is that a reference to the object is in the collection.

The following collections are in the packages `java.lang`, `java.util`, and `lamborne`. The first two packages are part of the JDK, and `lamborne` was developed by the book's authors. Most of the names listed are those of interfaces, but some are those of concrete classes. At this point, we do not need to know which are which.

Linear Collections

All linear collections share the characteristic that each item, except the first and last, has a unique predecessor and successor. The items in a linear collection can be thought of as laid out along a line. They are ordered but not necessarily sorted. Here are the names of linear collections we will be studying, together with their major distinguishing characteristics.

List	java.util	Items can be accessed at any position within a list. Lists are also called sequences and vectors.
SortedCollection	lamborne	The items are sorted according to some criteria. For instance, a collection of employee objects might be sorted alphabetically by employee name.
BitSet	java.util	The items in a bit set are restricted to 0s and 1s. Bit sets typically support logical operations on strings of bits.
String	java.lang	In Java, a string is an immutable sequence of characters. Some other languages permit manipulations that change the contents or length of a string, but Java does not.
StringBuffer	java.util	When a mutable string is needed in Java, a string buffer is used. Characters in a string buffer can be replaced, added, or removed.
Stack	lamborne	Items in a stack can be accessed from one end only using operations called push and pop. A stack of trays in a cafeteria provides an everyday example.
Queue	lamborne	In a queue, items are inserted at one end, using the operation enqueue, and removed at the other end, using the operation dequeue. We wait in queues at banks, movie theaters, and grocery stores.
PriorityQueue	lamborne	A priority queue is like a queue except that items with a higher priority can jump ahead of those with a lower priority.
Heap	lamborne	A heap is a collection in which the largest item is always at what is called the top, and frequently, this is the only item that is accessible. A sequence of removals from a heap returns items in order from largest to smallest. Items of the same size may or may not be allowed, and if allowed, they are in no particular order with respect to each other. In this context, when we speak of largest and size, we refer to any attribute that might be used to compare the items in a heap.

Hierarchical Collections

In a hierarchical collection, all items, except one, have a unique predecessor and zero or more successors. The exceptional item is called the *root,* and it has no predecessor. Hierarchical collections are also called trees, and they are categorized according to how many successors an item is allowed to have. Here are names and descriptions of the two hierarchical collections discussed in this book:

Tree lamborne A tree, or general tree as it can be called, allows an item to have any number of successors.

Binary Tree lamborne In a binary tree, an item can have at most two successors. Neither the JDK nor lamborne provides a binary tree ADT; however, binary trees are used in the implementation of several other structures and processes.

Graph Collections

In a graph, each item can have many predecessors and many successors. This book includes just one graph interface but several implementations.

Graph lamborne Graphs consist of nodes and connecting edges. Edges can be weighted, unweighted, directed, or undirected. Examples of graphs are as diverse as road maps and circuit board layouts. A normal road map is unweighted and undirected. The towns and cities represent the nodes, and the interconnecting roads are the edges. Adding mileage figures to each road segment yields a weighted graph. If all roads are one-way, the graph is directed.

Unordered Collections

The items in an unordered collection are, as the name suggests, in no particular order; however, there are mechanisms for inserting items in and retrieving items from an unordered collection. Although it makes no sense to speak of the fourth item in an unordered collection, one can retrieve an item according to a distinguishing characteristic, such as an employee's social security number. This book presents several unordered collections, as described next:

Set java.util The distinguishing characteristic of a set is that no matter how many times you add an item to a set, it never contains more than one reference to the item.

Bag lamborne If the same item is added to a bag repeatedly, the bag keeps track of how many times this has happened. For instance, if we read a text file and add each word encountered to a bag, then when we have finished reading the file, the bag contains all the distinct words in the file and a count of how many times each word occurred.

Map java.util A map stores and retrieves by means of unique keys. For instance, a map could be used to store a collection of employee objects using social security numbers as keys. Maps are also called tables and dictionaries.

`Collection`	`java.util`	`Collection` is the name of an interface that captures behavior common to `List`, `SortedCollection`, and `Set`. This allows objects of these types to be used interchangeably in some contexts. In addition, objects from many other ADTs are able to masquerade as `Collection` objects.

6.1.2 The `Tiny` Collection

In this chapter, we focus on the basic features of collections, not on their applications. As our only example, we use a type of collection that is quite simple called `Tiny`. Its sole purpose is to illustrate the features that most collections have in common. Table 6.1 lists the methods in the `Tiny` interface. A `Tiny` collection is linear and closely resembles a stack, but more on that in Chapter 7.

Table 6.1 The `Tiny` Interface

Tiny Method	Description
`public boolean add(Object obj)`	Adds `obj` to the collection provided there is room to do so. Returns `true` if `obj` is added and `false` otherwise.
`public Object removeLast()`	If the collection is empty, returns `null`, else removes and returns the object added to the collection most recently.
`public int size()`	Returns the number of objects in the collection.
`public Iterator iterator()`	Returns an `Iterator` on the collection (see Section 6.5 for details).
`public Collection collectionView()`	Returns a `Collection` object whose backing store is the `Tiny` object, allowing the `Tiny` object to masquerade as a `Collection` (see Section 6.6 for details).

6.2 Multiple Implementations

A major concern of the computer scientist is how best to implement different types of collections. There are usually numerous possibilities; however, many of these take so much space or run so slowly that they can be dismissed as pointless. Those that remain tend to be based on four underlying approaches to organizing and accessing memory:

1. arrays
2. linear linked structures
3. other linked structures
4. hashing into an array

We discussed the first two approaches in Chapter 5, and we encounter the other two later in the book when we study hierarchical and unordered collections.

Arrays and linked structures complement each other. Operations that are fast for arrays are often slow for linked structures, and vice versa. This means that some collections have two equally good but competing implementation strategies. The programmer must then pick the implementation that best fits the demands of the application. The following questions articulate these demands:

- Does the application involve a nearly fixed number of items or does the number vary widely?
- Is computer memory at a premium?
- Are items accessed randomly or is the next item required usually next to the last one processed?
- Which property is more important, fast access or fast insertion and deletion?
- In short, what are the space/time trade-offs of various implementations for a given range of tasks?

To answer these questions, programmers need to know an implementation's overall space requirements and the run-time complexity of its methods. The actual implementation details are not required. Unfortunately, collection libraries are rarely accompanied by the needed information. Consequently, throughout the book, as we introduce each type of collection, we present its major implementations and discuss its space and time complexity. This gives you a general understanding that will allow you to choose appropriate implementations when given a choice.

There are two implementing classes of the `Tiny` interface: `ArrayTiny` and `LinkedTiny`. One would choose `ArrayTiny` if an array-based implementation is preferred or `LinkedTiny` if a linked structure is preferred. When there is more than one way to implement a collection, programmers define a variable of an interface type and assign to it an object that uses the desired implementation. For example, the following code segment creates an instance of `ArrayTiny` and assigns it to a variable of type `Tiny`:

```
Tiny t = new ArrayTiny();
```

The object `t` now can receive any of the messages specified in the `Tiny` interface, and the programmer need no longer be concerned with the fact that `t` refers to an instance of `ArrayTiny`. To select a different implementation, the programmer just substitutes `LinkedTiny()` for `ArrayTiny()` in this code.

6.3 Collections and Casting

With the exception of strings, string buffers, and bit sets, collections can contain any kind of object and nothing but objects. These constraints have several consequences:

1. Primitive types, such as `int`, must be placed in a wrapper (see Appendix A) before being added to a collection.

2. It is impossible to declare a collection that is restricted to just one type of object.

3. Items coming out of a collection are, from the compiler's perspective, instances of `Object`, and they cannot be sent type-specific messages until they have been cast.

Because the third point causes the most difficulty, we devote this section to showing how to cast objects when they are removed from collections. There are two code snippets. The first code snippet begins by adding `Employee` objects (see Chapter 2) to an instance of `Tiny`. Later, the snippet removes the objects and casts them back to `Employee` before trying to send them `Employee`-type messages. The programmer has no difficulty deciding how to cast the objects. They were employees when they went in, and they are still employees when they come out.

```
Tiny cllctn = new ArrayTiny();
Employee emp;
int[] hoursArray1 = {8, 8, 10, 8, 8};
int[] hoursArray2 = {8, 6, 8, 8, 10};

//Add employees to the collection
emp = new Employee("Bill", 8.50, hoursArray1);
cllctn.add(emp);
emp = new Employee("Sue", 8.50, hoursArray2);
cllctn.add(emp);
...
//Remove the last employee added and display his/her name
emp = (Employee)cllctn.removeLast();              //Cast before further use
System.out.println (emp.getName());
...
```

The second code snippet adds a mixture of `Employee` objects and `String` objects to a `Tiny` collection. When an item is removed from the collection, its type must be tested before it is cast.

```
Tiny cllctn = new ArrayTiny();
int[] hoursArray1 = {8, 8, 10, 8, 8};
int[] hoursArray2 = {8, 6, 8, 8, 10};

//Add objects of different types to the collection
cllctn.add ("Shall I compare thee to a summer's day?" 1);
cllctn.add (new Employee ("Ken", 8.50, hoursArray1));
cllctn.add (new Employee ("Sue", 8.50, hoursArray2));
cllctn.add ("My heart leaps up when I behold a rainbow in the sky." 2);

//Remove the objects from the collection and process them differently
//depending on their types.
//Display a string's length and an employee's name.
while (cllctn.size() != 0){
   String message;
   Object obj = cllctn.removeLast();
```

Continued

[1]William Shakespeare, *Eternal Summer.*
[2]William Wordsworth, *My Heart Leaps Up When I Behold.*

Continued

```
    if (obj instanceof String){
        String str = (String)obj;
        message = "The length of the string is: " + str.length();
    }else if (obj instanceof Employee){
        Employee emp = (Employee)obj;
        message = "The employee is called: " + emp.getName();
    }else{
        message = "The type of the object is unknown";
    }
    System.out.println (message);
}
```

The output from this snippet of code is:

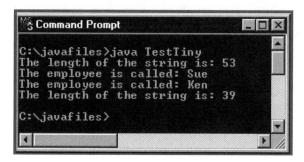

Exercises 6.3

1. Why do software engineers like to distinguish an interface of a given collection from its implementations?

2. Can you think of files as a kind of collection? If so, where do they belong in our classification scheme and why?

3. Return to the segment of code that adds employees and strings to the same collection and explain what would happen if the multiway `if` statement was replaced by the code `System.out.println(obj)`. Why does this code work without casting and without the use of the `instanceof` operator?

4. What features do most collections have in common?

6.4   Collections and Serialization

The collections in this book deal with data stored in memory rather than on disk. Data on disk are manipulated using file and database systems. Although disk-based systems are founded on principles we discuss later, their study is beyond the book's scope. However, there is one aspect of the subject that we must consider: how to save collections to disk and retrieve them later. Many common desktop applications depend on this capability. Image how limited word processors and spreadsheet applications would be if their data were irretrievably lost at the end of every session. Fortunately, Java's serialization mechanism makes it easy to move a collection to and from a disk file. A collection is just an object, and a collection class is made ready for serialization in much the same manner as the `Employee` class discussed in Chapter 2. There are three requirements:

1. The phrase `implements Serializable` must be included in the declaration of the class or one of its superclasses. (Any file that includes `implements Serializable` needs to import `java.io.Serializable`.)

2. All instance variables in the class must represent either primitive types or serializable objects.

3. All items in the collection must be serializable. This last requirement restricts users of collections. If they plan to serialize a collection, they must place in it only serializable objects.

Later in the chapter, when we present an array-based implementation of the `Tiny` collection, we make it serializable. For now, here are two code snippets that use serialization. The first writes a `Tiny` collection to disk, and the second reads it back in.

```
//Write a collection to disk

//Declare the collection and add items to it
Tiny cllctn = new ArrayTiny();
cllctn.add ("A widow bird sat mourning for her love"³);
cllctn.add ("Upon a wintry bough;");
cllctn.add ("The frozen wind crept on above,");
cllctn.add ("The freezing stream below.");
cllctn.add ("There was no leaf upon the forest bare,");
cllctn.add ("No flower upon the ground,");
cllctn.add ("And little motion in the air");
cllctn.add ("Except the mill-wheel's sound.");

//Declare the output stream and write the collection to disk
try{
    FileOutputStream foStream = new FileOutputStream ("testSerial.dat");
    ObjectOutputStream ooStream = new ObjectOutputStream (foStream);
    ooStream.writeObject (cllctn);
    foStream.flush();
    foStream.close();
}catch (Exception e){
    System.out.println ("Error during output: " + e.toString());
}

//Read a collection from disk

//Declare the collection
Tiny cllctn;

//Declare the input stream and read the collection from disk
try{
    FileInputStream fiStream = new FileInputStream ("testSerial.dat");
    ObjectInputStream oiStream = new ObjectInputStream (fiStream);
```

Continued

---

³Percy Bysshe Shelley, *Winter.*

Continued

```
    cllctn = (Tiny) oiStream.readObject();
    fiStream.close();
}catch (Exception e){
    System.out.println ("Error during input: " + e.toString());
}
```

Note that the collection read from the input stream in the second code segment is cast to `Tiny`. The programmer at this point may have no idea that the collection is actually an instance of `ArrayTiny`.

6.5 Iterators

Programmers frequently need to traverse collections sequentially. There are many ways to do this, and they may vary from collection to collection. In many collection libraries, *iterators* make this process as uniform and as simple as possible. Despite the fact that collections differ greatly in how they organize and access data, iterators allow the same patterns of code to traverse collections as diverse as lists, trees, and maps. An iterator is an object attached to a collection. It allows items in the collection to be accessed sequentially, one at a time. The collection is referred to as the iterator's ***backing collection.*** The order in which an iterator traverses its backing collection varies depending on the collection's type.

Early versions of Java supported an iterator in the form of the `Enumeration` interface, but in Java 2, `Iterator` replaces `Enumeration` in the collection framework. Java's online documentation encourages programmers who use `Enumeration` to switch to `Iterator`. Later in the book, we encounter two generalizations of `Iterator` called `ListIterator` and `TreeIterator`.

All iterators implement the three public methods defined in the `Iterator` interface (see `java.util`):

`boolean hasNext()`

Returns `true` if the iterator has more items and `false` otherwise.

`Object next()`

If there is a next item in the sequence, returns that item and advances to the next position; otherwise, throws an exception.

`void remove()`

Removes from the underlying collection the last item returned by the iterator. Throws an exception if the immediately preceding operation was not `next`. (*Warning:* Some iterators do not support this method and throw an exception when the method is called.)

6.5.1 Using an Iterator

We now show how to use an iterator. The first step consists of obtaining an iterator from a collection. We do this by sending the `iterator` message to the collection, which must then create and return an iterator object. The creation of iterators is discussed in the next subsection. After obtaining the iterator, we send it the `hasNext`, `next`, and `remove` messages in whatever combination suits our requirements.

For example, consider the following snippet of code that involves the use of an iterator over our previously introduced `Tiny` collection:

```
Tiny cllctn = new ArrayTiny();
Iterator iter = cllctn.iterator();          //Declare and instantiate an iterator
                                            //tied to the backing collection cllctn

while (iter.hasNext()){
   Object obj = iter.next();
   ... manipulate obj in a manner appropriate to the problem ...
}
```

There is one major problem inherent in the use of iterators. What happens if code unrelated to an iterator changes the structure of a backing collection? The change might not matter if the iterator has already passed the point at which the change occurred. However, at other times, the iterator might, for instance, follow an invalid pointer and return items no longer in the collection. The problem is compounded by the fact that multiple iterators can exist and function simultaneously over a single collection object. Iterators in `java.util` and `lamborne` respond to this problem by throwing exceptions as soon as they detect unexpected structural changes in a backing collection. The approach is called *fail-fast,* and it guarantees that iterators cannot return erroneous information. Here is a snippet of code that illustrates the fail-fast feature:

```
Tiny cllctn = new ArrayTiny();

Iterator iter1 = cllctn.iterator();      //Declare and instantiate two iterators
Iterator iter2 = cllctn.iterator();

... = iter1.next();                      //We use iter1 and iter2 simultaneously.
... = iter2.next();

iter1.remove();                   //Change the structure of the backing collection.
... = iter1.next();                      //iter1 can still be used to access the
                                                       //backing collection.
... = iter2.next();              //fail-fast exception thrown at this point
```

6.5.2.   Implementing `Tiny` and the `iterator` Method

Implementation of the `iterator` method varies depending on the type of collection involved. Nevertheless, the basic approach is similar in most situations. We illustrate by writing an `iterator` method for the `ArrayTiny` class. In the process, we must also implement the rest of the class.

We assume that the `ArrayTiny` class is implemented using an array whose maximum capacity is 100 items. We already know that the class must support the public methods `add`, `removeLast`, `size`, and `iterator`. Let us now agree that items are added in the array's next available slot and removed from the last slot occupied. The method `iterator` creates an instance of the inner class `TinyIterator`. This class in turn supports the public methods `hasNext`, `next`, and `remove`. Here is the listing:

```
 1 import java.util.*;              //java.util contains the Iterator interface
 2                                  // and the Collection interface
 3 import java.io.Serializable;
 4
 5 public class ArrayTiny implements Tiny, Serializable {
 6
 7    public static int DEFAULT_CAPACITY = 100;      // Maximum size of array
 8    private Object items[];                            //An array of items
 9    private int size;                          //Number of items in the array
10    private int modCount;      //Number of times the array has been modified
11
12    public Tiny()
13    {
14      items = new Object[DEFAULT_CAPACITY];//Array's maximum capacity is 100
15      size = modCount = 0;
16    }
17
18    public boolean add (Object item)    //Add a new item at the array's first
19    {                                            //unused location if possible
20      if (size == items.length)
21         return false;
22      else{
23         items[size] = item;
24         size++;
25         modCount++;
26         return true;
27       }
28    }
29
30    public Object removeLast()                 //Remove the most recently added
31    {                                                       //item if possible
32      if (size == 0)
33         return null;
34      else{
35         size--;
36         modCount++;
37         return items[size];
38       }
39    }
40
41    public int size()          //This method helps the user keep track of the
42    {                                            //number of items in the array
43      return size;
44    }
45
46    public Collection collectionView()                      //See Section 6.6
47    {
48      return null;
49    }
50
51    public Iterator iterator()      //Returns an iterator for this collection
52    {
53      return new TinyIterator();
54    }
```

Continued

Continued

```
55
56 //================= inner class TinyIterator =============================
57
58    //We implement iterators as inner classes. Iterators must implement the
59    //Iterator interface defined in java.util.
60    private class TinyIterator implements Iterator{
61
62        private int curPos;               //Current position of the iterator with
63                                          //respect to the backing array.
64        private int expectedModCount;     //This iterator's notion of modCount
65        private boolean removeIsOK;       //True whenever it is OK to use
66                                          //the remove method.
67        private TinyIterator()
68        {
69           curPos = 0;
70           expectedModCount = modCount;
71           removeIsOK = false;     //The remove method cannot be called until
72        }                          //next has been called.
73
74        public boolean hasNext()        //Returns true if some items in the
75        {                               //backing collection have not yet
76           return curPos < size;             //been encountered.
77        }
78
79        public Object next() {                        //Returns the next item.
80           if (modCount != expectedModCount)
81              throw new ConcurrentModificationException();
82           if (!hasNext())
83              throw new NoSuchElementException("There are no more elements");
84
85           removeIsOK = true;        //It is now OK to use the remove method.
86           curPos++;
87           return items[curPos - 1];
88        }
89
90        public void remove()      //Removes the most recently retrieved item.
91        {
92           if (modCount != expectedModCount)
93              throw new ConcurrentModificationException();
94           if (!removeIsOK)
95              throw new IllegalStateException
96              ("Remove must be preceded by next");
97           removeIsOK = false;      //The remove method cannot be called again
98           modCount++;                            //until next is called again.
99           expectedModCount++;
100          //The rest of this method's code is left as an exercise
101       }
102    }
103 }
```

We would like to make a few observations about the code:

1. The class `ArrayTiny` is serializable.

2. The implementation of `ArrayTiny`'s public methods is straightforward. We manage items in the array using the strategy discussed in Chapter 5. The array is

static, but the implementation could be modified to resize the array when it becomes full.

3. The class `TinyIterator` is defined as a `private` inner class.

4. The class `TinyIterator` implements the `Iterator` interface. Thus, this class must implement the public methods `hasNext`, `next`, and `remove`.

5. The method `iterator` returns an instance of the class `TinyIterator`. Because this class implements the `Iterator` interface, the return type of the `iterator` method is also declared as `Iterator`. This allows clients to declare a variable of type `Iterator` (as in the earlier example) and store in it a `TinyIterator` object.

6. One precondition of `remove` and `next` is that no one has illicitly modified the backing collection. The variable `modCount`, defined in the `ArrayTiny` class, and the variable `expectedModCount`, defined in the `TinyIterator` class, track this precondition. These values are the same when an iterator is created. Whenever a `Tiny` or `TinyIterator` method mutates the backing collection, `modCount` is incremented. Whenever a `TinyIterator` method mutates the backing collection, `expectedModCount` is also incremented. Thus, if these values are not equal when a `TinyIterator` method is called, the precondition is violated and a `ConcurrentModificationException` is thrown.

7. The variable `removeIsOK` governs the other precondition of the `remove` operation. This method should be called only after the `next` method is called (thus preventing consecutive removals). The `next` method sets this variable to `true` and `remove` sets it to `false`. Thus, if `remove` finds that the variable is `false`, an `IllegalStateException` is thrown.

Exercises 6.5

1. Complete the `ArrayTiny` class and write a driver program that tests it thoroughly. Be sure to test the fail-fast features.

2. Add the method `boolean equals(Object obj)` to the `ArrayTiny` class. The method returns `true` if `obj`

    a. is an instance of `Tiny`

    b. contains the same number of items as the receiver

    c. has equal items in the same order as the receiver

    Tip: Use an iterator to traverse the items in the collection.

3. Modify `ArrayTiny` so that the user can choose the array size. Continue to use 100 as the default size.

4. Modify `ArrayTiny` further so that the size of the array grows and shrinks dynamically in the manner suggested in Chapter 5.

5. Describe three different ways to trigger a fail-fast situation.

6. Discuss the advantages and disadvantages of implementing the `remove` method in an iterator.

6.6   `Collection` and `collectionView`

When working with collections, programmers occasionally must perform high-level operations, such as transferring all items from one collection to another, removing all items contained in one collection from another, and so forth. A special interface called `Collection` specifies these operations as simple methods. `Collection` is an interface supported in one way or another by most of the collections presented in this book. Some collections, such as sets and lists, support the interface by implementing an interface that extends `Collection`, but they are in the minority. Others return a *collection-view* object when sent the `collectionView` message. A collection-view object satisfies the `Collection` interface and uses the original collection as a backing collection, a characteristic it shares with iterators. Changes made to a collection-view object pass through to the backing collection; for instance, removing an item from a collection-view in fact removes the item from the backing collection.

6.6.1   Two Examples

Now we look at two examples that illustrate the use of collection-view objects. Most collections include a constructor that accepts a `Collection` object as a parameter, thus making it easy to create one type of collection from another. For instance, here is a code snippet that creates a `List` collection from a `Tiny` collection.

```
Tiny cllctn = new ArrayTiny();

cllctn.add("When"⁴);
cllctn.add("in");
cllctn.add("the");
cllctn.add("gold");
cllctn.add("October");
cllctn.add("dusk");

List lst = new LinkedList(cllctn.collectionView());
```

Obviously, the code depends on our implementing a `collectionView` method in `ArrayTiny`, but before considering that challenge, let us look at another application of collection-views.

Any collection that provides a collection-view automatically increases its repertoire of methods to include those in the `Collection` interface. Soon we will list all of the methods in the `Collection` interface, but for now, we focus on just one:

> boolean removeAll (Collection c)
>
> > Removes all of this collection's elements that are also contained in the specified collection.

We now apply this operation to a `Tiny` collection. In the code snippet that follows, we define two `Tiny` collections. We then remove from the first collection all of the items that are also in the second collection:

---

[4]Sara Teasdale, *Arcturus in Autumn*.

```
//Create two Tiny collection objects
Tiny t1 = new ArrayTiny();
Tiny t2 = new ArrayTiny();

//Add five objects to the first collection
t1.add ("A child said, What is the grass?"⁵);
t1.add ("When I am dead, my dearest, sing no sad songs for me;"⁶);
t1.add ("I saw eternity the other night"⁷);
t1.add ("Hark! hark! the lark at heaven's gate sings"⁸);
t1.add ("When I am dead, my dearest, sing no sad songs for me;");

// Add three objects to the second collection
t2.add ("I saw eternity the other night");
t2.add ("Dead hangs the fruit on that tall tree"⁹);
t2.add ("When I am dead, my dearest, sing no sad songs for me;");

//Create a collection-view of each
Collection cv1 = t1.collectionView();
Collection cv2 = t2.collectionView();

//Display the size of t1
System.out.println ("Initially t1 contains " + t1.size() + " objects.");
//Remove from t1 all items that also appear in t2
c1.removeAll (c2);
//Display the size of t1 again
System.out.println ("After removal of all items in t2, t1 contains " +
                    t1.size() + " objects.");
```

The output from this snippet of code is:

```
Initially t1 contains 5 objects.
After removal of all items in t2, t1 contains 2 objects.
```

6.6.2   Summary of Methods in the Collection Interface

Table 6.2 presents a summary of the methods in the Collection interface, as described in Java's online documentation. We ignore the hashCode method for now, which is discussed in Chapter 13. All methods that change the collection's structure are optional. These include add, addAll, clear, remove, removeAll, and retainAll. The word *optional* is misleading in the present context because even optional methods are present and must do something. When optional methods are not fully implemented, they usually throw an UnsupportedOperation Exception. Thus, programmers must be careful when using the Collection interface. They must be certain the implementation supports the methods they intend to use.

---

[5]Walt Whitman, *Song of Myself.*
[6]Christina Georgina Rossetti, *Song.*
[7]Henry Vaughan, *The World.*
[8]William Shakespeare, *Mourning Song.*
[9]Richard Hughes, *Burial of the Spirit of a Young Poet.*

Table 6.2   **The `Collection` Interface**

boolean	**add(Object o)** Ensures that this collection contains the specified element (optional operation).
boolean	**addAll(Collection c)** Adds all of the elements in the specified collection to this collection (optional operation).
void	**clear()** Removes all of the elements from this collection (optional operation).
boolean	**contains(Object o)** Returns true if this collection contains the specified element.
boolean	**containsAll(Collection c)** Returns true if this collection contains all of the elements in the specified collection.
boolean	**equals(Object o)** Compares the specified object with this collection for equality.
int	**hashCode()** Returns the hash code value for this collection. (Please ignore this method for now. We discuss hashing in Chapter 13.)
boolean	**isEmpty()** Returns true if this collection contains no elements.
Iterator	**iterator()** Returns an iterator over the elements in this collection.
boolean	**remove(Object o)** Removes a single instance of the specified element from this collection if it is present (optional operation).
boolean	**removeAll(Collection c)** Removes all of this collection's elements that are also contained in the specified collection (optional operation).
boolean	**retainAll(Collection c)** Retains only the elements in this collection that are contained in the specified collection (optional operation).
int	**size()** Returns the number of elements in this collection.
Object[]	**toArray()** Returns an array containing all of the elements in this collection.
Object[]	**toArray(Object[] a)** Returns an array containing all of the elements in this collection whose run-time type is that of the specified array.

6.6.3   Implementation of the `collectionView` Method (optional pv)

This section is optional. Whether or not you read this and other sections labeled "optional pv" depends on your objectives. If you are only interested in the theory and use of collections, you can skip the section without loss of continuity. However, if you wish to learn techniques for organizing hierarchies of classes, read on. (The abbreviation "pv" stands for "professional version." In the next section, we make a distinction between prototypes and professional versions of collection classes.) The material in this section is presented because of its relationship to professional versions. There are sections labeled "optional pv" in later chapters as well. If you plan to read those, be sure to read this one first.

The implementation of the `collectionView` method is stunningly simple, perplexingly subtle, and remarkably similar from collection to collection. Here is how it is done for the `Tiny` class.

```
private transient Collection col = null;
  //By declaring the variable col transient, we are indicating that we
  //do not want it to be transferred to or from the disk during serialization

public Collection collectionView()
{
   if (col != null) return col;

   col = new AbstractCollection()
       {
           public Iterator iterator(){
               return Tiny.this.iterator();
           }

           public int size() {
               return Tiny.this.size();
           }

           public boolean add (Object obj){
               return Tiny.this.add (obj);
           }
       };
   return col;
}
```

As you can see from the code, the `collectionView` method returns an instance of `AbstractCollection`, which in turn implements the `Collection` interface. Normally, abstract classes cannot be instantiated; however, as this code illustrates, there is a way. An inner class can be defined that provides definitions for all of the abstract methods in the abstract class. In `AbstractCollection`, there are two abstract methods—`iterator` and `size`—and the foregoing inner class provides definitions for both of them. In addition, other methods in the abstract class can be overridden, perhaps to provide a more efficient implementation or to replace an optional method. In `AbstractCollection`, the `add` method is optional and throws an `UnsupportedOperationException`. Here we have provided an overriding `add` method. Notice that all three methods shown accomplish their mission by calling methods in the backing collection via the mechanism `Tiny.this`.

6.6.4 Implementation of **AbstractCollection** (optional pv)

To complete our understanding of collection views, we now examine `Abstract Collection`. There are many methods in `AbstractCollection`, and all but three—`iterator`, `size`, and `add`—do their work indirectly via an iterator over the backing collection. The capabilities of the iterator, therefore, determine the capabilities of methods in `AbstractCollection`. For example, all iterators support `hasNext` and `next`, but many intentionally do not support `remove`. If the iterator does not support `remove`, then `AbstractCollection` does not support `remove`, `removeAll`, and `retainAll`. To illustrate, here is code for `AbstractCollection` taken directly from the JDK. We have added some explanatory comments:

```
public boolean remove(Object o) {          //This method depends on the iterator's
   Iterator e = iterator();                      //remove method. If the iterator's
   if (o == null) {                     //remove method throws an exception, then
      while (e.hasNext()) {                           //so will this method.
         if (e.next() == null) {
            e.remove();
            return true;
         }
      }
   } else {
      while (e.hasNext()) {
         if (o.equals(e.next())) {
            e.remove();
            return true;
         }
      }
   }
   return false;
}
```

```
public boolean removeAll(Collection c) {         //This method depends on the
   boolean modified = false;                    //remove method listed above.
   Iterator e = iterator();
   while (e.hasNext()) {
      if(c.contains(e.next())) {
         e.remove();
         modified = true;
      }
   }
   return modified;
}
```

The code for `add` and `addAll` follows. Overriding the `add` method enables both it and the `addAll` method. Again, we have added our comments to the source code provided in the JDK:

```
public boolean add(Object o)                //An inner class or subclass can
{                                                  //override this method.
   throw new UnsupportedOperationException();
}
```

```
public boolean addAll(Collection c)    //This method depends on an iterator that
{                                          //supports hasNext and next. All
```

Continued

```
   boolean modified = false;          //iterators do. It also depends on the
   Iterator e = c.iterator();             //add method, which needs to be
   while (e.hasNext()) {                               //overridden.
      if (add(e.next()))
         modified = true;
   }
   return modified;
}
```

As you can see, iterators are a very powerful glue for connecting various collection classes in the framework.

Table 6.3 lists the maximum run time for the methods in AbstractCollection. Confirmation of these run times is left as an exercise. Note the following points concerning the table:

1. *m* indicates the number of items in the parameter Collection c.

2. *n* indicates the number of items in this collection, the receiver of the message.

3. We assume that an iterator's remove method has a maximum run time less than or equal to O(n).

Table 6.3 **The Run Times of the Collection Class Methods**

Maximum Run Times for Methods in AbstractCollection

boolean add(Object o)	Throws an UnsupportedOperationException
boolean addAll(Collection c)	O(m)*O (add method)
void clear()	O(n) * O(iterator's remove method)
boolean contains(Object o)	O(n)
boolean containsAll(Collection c)	O(m) * O(contains method) → O(mn)
boolean equals(Object o)	Uses the default implementation in Object → O(1)
int hashCode()	Uses the default implementation in Object → O(1)
boolean isEmpty()	O(1)
Iterator iterator()	abstract
boolean remove(Object o)	O(n) * O(iterator's remove method)
boolean removeAll(Collection c)	O(n) * (O(contains method) + O(iterator's remove method)) → O(mn)
boolean retainAll(Collection c)	O(n) * (O(contains method) + O(iterator's remove method)) → O(mn)
int size()	abstract
Object[] toArray()	O(n)
Object[] toArray(Object[] a)	O(n)
String toString()	O(n) (this method is not in the Collection interface)

Exercises 6.6

1. Explain why most collections should either implement the `Collection` interface or support a `collectionView` method.

2. Write code segments that use `Collection` methods to perform the following tasks with the `Tiny` collections A and B (be sure not to modify A and B):

   a. Create a new `Tiny` collection C that contains the items in both A and B.

   b. Create a new `Tiny` collection C that contains only the items in A that are also in B.

   c. Create a new `Tiny` collection C that contains only the items in A that are not also in B.

3. The inner class defined in the `collectionView` method includes just the methods `iterator`, `add`, and `size`. Explain how this is enough information to describe an object that satisfies the entire `Collection` interface.

4. Add the `collectionView` method to the `ArrayTiny` class. Test the collection-view features and confirm that all of the methods listed in the `Collection` interface are supported. Confirm that the `equals` method only considers two collections equal if they are identical. In Chapter 9, you will have an opportunity to fix this problem.

5. Examine the source code for `AbstractCollection`, which is part of `java.util`, and confirm the run times shown in Table 6.3.

6. Determine why an operation accomplished via a collection-view often runs more slowly, by a factor of *n,* than the same operation applied directly to the backing collection. (*Tip:* Consider the `collectionView` method for the `Tiny` collection and examine the source code for `java.util`'s `AbstractCollection` class.)

6.7 Prototypes and Professional Versions

When we develop a collection, we have four concerns:

1. What are the fundamental operations that characterize the collection and make it a useful tool for organizing and manipulating data?

2. What are the principal strategies for implementing the collection?

3. How can the collection be integrated into a larger framework of collections such that the whole is greater than the sum of its parts?

4. How do we design a hierarchy of collection classes that maximizes code sharing?

The first two questions involve theoretical issues central to the study of collections. The second two concern practical problems of software design. Dealing with all four aspects of collections simultaneously would be difficult and confusing. Therefore, throughout the book, we first discuss the theoretical aspects of a new collection in the context of a stand-alone prototype. Later, we show how the prototype can be extended and integrated into a professional package.

An important difference between a collection's prototype and professional version lies in the methods they each support. For the sake of this discussion, we divide methods into three categories:

Fundamental methods support accessing, inserting, and removing items from a collection. They define the fundamental operations that distinguish one type of collection from another and are implemented using major data manipulation algorithms.

Supporting methods furnish a minimal set of basic support services needed whenever one works with any collection. An example is the `size` method.

General methods support a range of advanced services such as iterators and collection-views.

Prototypes include only the fundamental and supporting methods. Professional versions add methods in the general category.

6.7.1 Overview of the `Tiny` Professional Version (optional pv)

We now develop a professional version of `Tiny`, not because a professional version of `Tiny` is useful, but because the approach and techniques involved are used later and are most easily understood in a simple context. For `Tiny`, as for classes presented later, we separate the interface from the implementation. As in the prototype version, `Tiny` is the name of the interface and `ArrayTiny` is the name of the implementation. Later, as an exercise, you will develop an implementation called `LinkedTiny`.

Figure 6.1 shows how `ArrayTiny` and `LinkedTiny` can be integrated into `lamborne`'s class hierarchy. The class `AbstractContainer`, at the root of this hierarchy, is a subclass of `Object`. The general implementation strategy pushes code as high in the hierarchy as possible, thus maximizing code sharing.

Figure 6.1   **A portion of the `lamborne` class hierarchy**

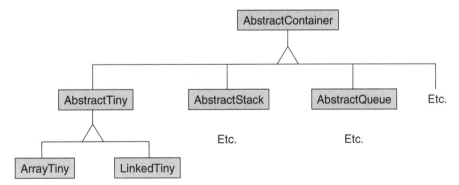

In addition to understanding the class hierarchy, we need to consider the relationship between classes and interfaces. When implementing `Tiny`, there are three interfaces of interest—`Serializable`, `Cloneable`, and of course, `Tiny`. As we discussed earlier in the chapter, any class that adds the phrase `implements Serializable` to its declaration automatically supports serialization of its objects and the objects of any subclass. This capability comes without the necessity of writing any additional methods. Thus, AbstractContainer is the most convenient class in which to implement Serializable.

Cloneable classes implement the clone method and can thereby be copied. Implementing the clone method in an abstract class entails techniques that are beyond this book's scope; hence, we do so in the concrete classes ArrayTiny and LinkedArray. The remaining interface, Tiny, is also implemented in ArrayTiny and LinkedTiny. Table 6.4 summarizes the relationships between the classes and interfaces.

Table 6.4   **The Relationship between Tiny Classes and the Interfaces They Implement**

Name of Class	Interfaces Implemented
AbstractContainer	Serializable
AbstractTiny	
ArrayTiny	Cloneable, Tiny
LinkedTiny	Cloneable, Tiny

6.7.2   Expanding the Tiny Interface (optional pv)

We now expand the Tiny interface presented in Section 6.1. Table 6.5 presents the interface for the professional version of Tiny. It has two fundamental methods—add and removeLast. The one supporting method is size. The general methods include iterator, collectionView, and several others.

Table 6.5   **The Tiny Interface**

Fundamental Methods

boolean	**add(Object o)** Adds obj to this collection provided there is room to do so. Returns true if obj is added and false otherwise.
Object	**removeLast()** If this collection is empty, returns null, else removes and returns the object added to the collection most recently.

Supporting Methods

int	**size()** Returns the number of items in this collection.

General Methods

void	**clear()** Removes all items from this collection.

Table 6.5   **The Tiny Interface** *(Continued)*

object	clone() Returns a shallow copy of this collection. (Does not need to be included here because it will be inherited from Object.)
Collection	collectionView() Returns a collection view of the items contained in this collection.
boolean	equals(Object other) Returns true if the other object is a Tiny collection that equals this Tiny collection. To be equal, two Tiny collections must contain equal items appearing in the same order.
int	hashCode() Returns the hash code value for this collection. (Please ignore this method for now. We discuss it in Chapter 13.)
Iterator	iterator() Returns an iterator over the items contained in this collection. The iterator provides the items in order from oldest to youngest, where the oldest item is the one in the collection longest.
Object[]	toArray() Returns an array containing all of the items in this collection. The oldest item in the collection corresponds to the first item in the array, where the oldest item is the one in the collection longest.
String	toString() Returns a string that lists the items in this collection. The oldest item in the collection corresponds to the first item in the string, where the oldest item is the one that has been in the collection longest. (*Note:* Does not need to be included here because it will be inherited from Object.)

6.7.3   Assigning the Tiny Methods to Classes (optional pv)

Before writing code, we need to decide where in the hierarchy each method will be implemented. A method can appear in more than one place. The version of a method that appears in a subclass can either override or extend the version in the superclass. Table 6.6 shows where each method is implemented. In the table, the first two columns specify the method signatures. The last three columns indicated the point of implementation. Each method's maximum run time is shown. Several general methods are implemented by means of iterators, so their run times depend on the run time of the iterator's operations. Frequently, iterator operations, including instantiation, are O(1).

Note the following points about Table 6.6:

1. For entries marked by a asterisk, the maximum run time is based on the assumption that the method is implemented via an iterator whose hasNext and next methods are O(1). This assumption usually holds.

2. The method iterator is declared as abstract in AbstractContainer so that other methods in AbstractContainer can use it.

Table 6.6   **The `Tiny` Methods and Their Run Times**

Tiny Implementation		Abstract Container	Abstract Tiny	Array Tiny
	Constructors			
	`constructor()`	O(1)	O(1)	O(1)
	`constructor(Collection col)`			O(*n*)
	`constructor(Iterator iter)`			O(*n*)
	Fundamental Methods			
`boolean`	`add(Object item)`			O(1)
`Object`	`removeLast()`			O(1)
	Supporting Methods			
`boolean`	`isEmpty()`	O(1)		
`int`	`size()`	O(1)		
	General Methods			
`void`	`clear()`	O(1)		
`Object`	`clone()`			O(n)
`Collection`	`collectionView()`	O(1)*	O(1)*	
`boolean`	`equals(Object other)`		O(*n*)*	
`int`	`hashCode()`	O(*n*)*		
`Iterator`	`iterator()`	abstract		O(1)
`Object []`	`toArray()`	O(*n*)*		
`String`	`toString()`	O(*n*)*		

6.7.4   The Coding Details (optional pv)

We have already written code for many of the methods in the `Tiny` interface. Table 6.6 indicates where the code should be placed in the class hierarchy. Before discussing the remaining methods, we present skeletal outlines of the `Tiny` interface and the three classes involved in the `ArrayTiny` implementation. When looking at these outlines, notice that two of the classes are declared abstract, thus indicating that they cannot be instantiated. By adding the line

```
package lamborne;
```

to each file, we are specifying that they are all part of the `lamborne` package. Notice that `AbstractContainer` implements `Serializable` and thus passes this capability on to its subclasses. The outlines are:

```
// Tiny.java

package lamborne;
```

Continued

Continued

```java
import java.util.*;

public interface Tiny {

    public boolean add(Object obj);
    ... other methods ...
}
```

```java
// AbstractContainer.java

package lamborne;
import java.util.*;
import java.io.Serializable;

public abstract class AbstractContainer implements Serializable {

    protected int size;
    protected transient int modCount;

    ... constructor and other methods ...
}
```

```java
// AsbtractTiny.java

package lamborne;
import java.util.*;

abstract public class AbstractTiny extends AbstractContainer {

    ... constructor and other methods ...

}
```

```java
//ArrayTiny.java

package lamborne;
import java.util.*;

public class ArrayTiny extends AbstractTiny implements Tiny, Cloneable {

    static public int DEFAULT_CAPACITY = 100;
    private Object items[];                          //The array of items

    ... constructor and other methods ...

}
```

Implementing the Default Constructor

We are now ready to show some additional coding details. At the top level, the default constructor initializes the variables `size` and `modCount`.

```
public AbstractContainer()
{
    size = 0;
    modCount = 0;
}
```

At the next level, the default constructor does nothing other than pass initialization up a level.

```
public AbstractTiny()
{
    super();
}
```

At the bottom level, the default constructor first calls the constructor in the super-class and then initializes the array.

```
public ArrayTiny()
{
    super();
    items = new Object[DEFAULT_CAPACITY];
}
```

Implementing the Iterator-Based Constructor

The iterator-based constructor uses an iterator to initialize the array of items. If the iterator contains more items than the array can hold, we allow an array indexing exception to occur. There are other options, and we ask you to describe them in an exercise.

```
public ArrayTiny (Iterator iter)
{
    super();
    items = new Object[DEFAULT_CAPACITY];
    int size = 0;
    while (iter.hasNext)
        items[size++] = iter.next(); //An index out-of-range error can occur here
}
```

Implementing the `equals` Method

Two `Tiny` collections are equal if they are the same size and contain equal items at comparable locations; however, they do not need to be the same concrete type. One could be an `ArrayTiny` and the other a `LinkedTiny`. Thus, to compare two `Tiny` collections, we establish an iterator on each and traverse the iterators simultaneously, comparing elements from each as we go. The method is implemented in the class `AbstractTiny`.

```
public boolean equals (Object other)

    AbstractTiny otherColl;

    if (other == this) return true;
```

Continued

Continued

```
    if (!(other instanceof Tiny)) return false;

    otherColl = (AbstractTiny)other;
    if (size() != otherColl.size()) return false;

    Iterator thisIter = iterator();
    Iterator otherIter = otherColl.iterator();
    while (thisIter.hasNext()){
       if (!thisIter.next().equals (otherIter.next()))
          return false;
    }

    return true;
}
```

Notice in this code that `other` is cast to `AbstractTiny` and assigned to `otherColl` before being sent the messages `size` and `iterator`. These two messages are not recognized by instances of `Object`.

Implementing the `clone` Method

The `clone` method is implemented by passing an iterator over the current collection to an iterator-based constructor:

```
public Object clone()
{
    return new ArrayTiny (iterator());
}
```

Implementing the `collectionView` Method

Earlier in the chapter, we showed an implementation of the `collectionView` method. This implementation should go in the class `AbstractTiny`. There is also an implementation in `AbstractContainer` that is identical except that the `add` method is omitted. When the `add` method is omitted, the resulting collection-view does not support operations that add items to the underlying collection.

Remaining Methods

The remaining methods are straightforward and are left as exercises. Table 6.6 shows where each should be implemented. Several of the methods involve iterators and use techniques already presented.

Exercises 6.7

1. Complete the implementation of `Tiny`, `AbstractTiny`, and `ArrayTiny` and add them to your copy of the `lamborne` package.

2. Describe other ways to write the iterator-based constructor for `ArrayTiny`. Be sure to handle any error conditions that might arise.

3. Modify `ArrayTiny` so that the array is dynamic. Calculate maximum, minimum, and average run times for methods that are affected by the switch to a dynamic array.

4. Show how the methods `toArray` and `toString`, located in `Abstract Container`, can be implemented via an iterator.

5. What implementation difficulties would be encountered if `equals` were pushed higher in the hierarchy?

6. Generally, fundamental methods are implemented at the bottom of the hierarchy. Why?

7. Generally, the iterator method is implemented at the bottom of the hierarchy. Why?

8. Justify the run time values shown in Table 6.6.

9. Write a linked implementation of `Tiny`. Call it `LinkedTiny` and add it to the `lamborne` package. Provide run time values in code comments. A skeleton of the code follows. Notice that the inner class `OneWayNode` implements `Serializable`. (*Tip:* If you get stuck, peek at the next chapter and see the linked implementation of stacks.)

```java
package lamborne;
import java.util.*;
import java.io.Serializable;

public class LinkedTiny extends AbstractTiny
                        implements Tiny, Cloneable {

    private OneWayNode last;        //last node added

    . . .

    public Iterator iterator()
    {
        return new InnerIter();
    }

    private class InnerIter implements Iterator{

        private OneWayNode curPos;
        private int        expectedModCount = modCount;

        . . .
    }

    private class OneWayNode implements Serializable{
        private Object     value;    //Value stored in this node
        private OneWayNode next;      //Reference to next node

        private OneWayNode()
        {
            value = null;
            next = null;
        }

        private OneWayNode(Object value)
        {
            this.value = value;
            next = null;
        }
```

Continued

Continued

```
        private OneWayNode(Object value, OneWayNode next)
        {
            this.value = value;
            this.next = next;
        }
    }
```

10. AbstractContainer includes the abstract method iterator. Why not simply omit iterator from the class?

6.8   Location Guide

We close the chapter with Table 6.7, which shows where in the book (chapter numbers and appendix letters) different collections are discussed, how they are implemented, whether or not they have prototypes, and the packages containing them.

Table 6.7   **The Locations of the Collection Classes in This Book**

ADT	Discussed in Ch.	Prototypes Based On	Professional Versions Based On	Found in Package
Linear				
List	9	Array & Linked List	Array & Linked List	java.util
SortedCollection	12		Linked Binary Tree	lamborne
String	A		Array	java.lang
StringBuffer	A		Array	java.lang
Stack	7	Array & Linked List	Linked	lamborne
Queue	8	Array & Linked List	Linked	lamborne
PriorityQueue	8, 12	Array of Linked Lists	Array of Linked Lists and Heap	lamborne
Heap	12		Array	lamborne
Hierarchical				
Tree	11		Linked General Tree	lamborne
BinaryTree	11, 12	Linked Binary Tree		lamborne
Graph				
Graph	14	Adjacency List	Adjacency List	lamborne
Unordered				
Collection	6			java.util
Set	13	Hashed	Hashed	java.util
Bag	13	Hashed	Hashed	lamborne
Map	13	Hashed	Hashed	java.util

KEY TERMS

bit set   iterator   string buffer

collection-view

CHAPTER SUMMARY

There are four broad categories of collections—linear, hierarchical, graph, and unordered—and many more subtypes under these. The object-oriented framework provides a way to organize collections so they are easy to use and maintain. The use of an interface to specify a collection enforces the distinction between interface and implementation and allows multiple implementations. Clients can then choose the appropriate implementation based on performance criteria without modifying their own code.

The common features of different implementations of collections can be factored into abstract classes. This strategy exploits inheritance and polymorphism to reuse code without disturbing existing clients of the collections.

Collections support several standard methods. Some of these return the collection's size, test it for emptiness, insert a given item, and remove a given item.

In Java, items stored in collections can be any objects. When an item is examined or removed from a collection, the item returned masquerades as an instance of the class `Object`. The item must therefore be cast down to its actual class before sending it class-specific messages.

An iterator is an object that allows a client to visit the items in a collection in a predetermined order. An iterator is particularly useful for traversing a collection or locating an item in a collection that does not otherwise allow access to it.

Java's `Collection` interface specifies a range of high-level methods that allow clients to do such things as insert or remove multiple items from implementing collections. A programmer-defined collection can acquire this capability without implementing the `Collection` interface. All that is needed is a method called `collectionView`, which returns an object that allows the implementing collection to masquerade as an instance of `Collection`.

REVIEW QUESTIONS

1. Name the four broad categories of collections and give a real-world example of each.
2. Explain how interfaces help to organize collections for users and implementers.
3. Explain how abstract classes help to organize collections for implementers.
4. What are the three methods provided by a simple iterator and which two require implementations?
5. Give an example of the use of an iterator with a collection.
6. Assume that more than one iterator is attached to a single collection. Can any of the iterators remove an item? Why or why not?
7. Give three examples of the methods in the `Collection` interface and describe what they do.
8. Assume that a programmer wants to provide some of the methods specified in the `Collection` interface without implementing that interface. Describe how this could be done.

CHAPTER 7

Stacks

OBJECTIVES   Upon completion of this chapter, you should be able to

- Describe the formal properties of stacks

- Give examples of applications of stacks

- Discuss at least two common ways in which stacks are implemented and the criteria for choosing between them

This chapter introduces the stack, a collection that has widespread use in computer science. The stack is the simplest collection to describe and implement. Yet it has fascinating applications, three of which we discuss later in the chapter. In conformance with the plan proposed in Chapter 6, we consider both a prototype and a professional version of stacks, and we present two standard implementations, one based on arrays and the other on linked lists. The chapter closes with a Case Study in which stacks play a central role: the evaluation of postfix arithmetic expressions.

7.1 Overview of Stacks

Stacks are linear collections in which access is completely restricted to just one end, called the *top.* The classical example is the stack of clean trays found in every cafeteria. Whenever a tray is needed, it is removed from the top of the stack, and whenever clean ones come back from the scullery, they are again placed on the top. No one ever takes some particularly fine tray from the middle of the stack, and it is even possible that trays near the bottom are never used. Stacks are said to adhere to a last-in, first-out protocol (LIFO). The last tray brought back from the scullery is the first one taken by a customer.

The operations for putting items on and removing items from a stack are called *push* and *pop,* respectively. Figure 7.1 shows a stack as it might appear at various stages. Initially, the stack is empty, and then an item called **a** is pushed. Next, three more items called **b, c,** and **d** are pushed, after which the stack is popped, and so forth.

Figure 7.1   **Some states in the lifetime of a stack**

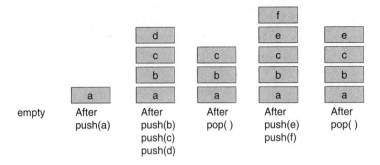

Other everyday examples of stacks include plates and bowls in our kitchen cupboards and PEZ® dispensers. Although we continually add more papers to the top of the piles on our desks, these piles do not quite qualify because we often need to remove a long-lost paper from the middle. With a genuine stack, the item we want next is always the one added most recently.

Applications of stacks in computer science are numerous. Here are just a few, including three we discuss in more detail later in the chapter:

- Parsing expressions in context-free programming languages—a problem in compiler design.
- Translating infix expressions to postfix form and evaluating postfix expressions—discussed later in the chapter.
- Backtracking algorithms—discussed later in the chapter and occurring in problems such as automated theorem proving and game playing.
- Managing computer memory in support of method calls—discussed later in the chapter.
- Supporting the "undo" feature in text editors, word processors, spreadsheet programs, drawing programs, and similar applications.
- Maintaining a history of the links visited by a Web browser.

7.2   A Stack Prototype

We now consider a stack prototype. Following the plan outlined in Chapter 6, we distinguish between fundamental and supporting operations. We have already introduced the fundamental operations `push` and `pop`. The supporting operations include:

`peek`   Returns the top item on a stack without removing it.

`isEmpty`   Returns `true` if there are no more items on a stack.

`isFull`   Returns `true` if a stack can hold no more items.

`size`   Returns the number of items on a stack.

In certain situations, some of these operations are invalid. For instance, attempting to pop an empty stack is an undefined operation that is best handled by throwing an exception. Users of stacks accordingly have three options when using the pop operation:

1. Whenever there is a possibility of an empty stack, send the message isEmpty before sending pop.

2. Catch the exception if it occurs.

3. Ignore the possibility of the error and run the risk of having the program terminate abnormally.

Either of the first two options is reasonable, and a programmer can choose the one that best fits the circumstances. Here is a list of the exceptions thrown by the stack prototype:

peek and pop   Throw an IllegalStateException if the stack is empty.

push   Throws an IllegalStateException if the stack is full and an IllegalArgumentException if the item is null.

Table 7.1 defines the interface for the stack prototype.

Table 7.1   **The Interface for the Stack Prototype**

	Fundamental Methods
void	**push(Object item)**
	Pushes an item onto the top of this stack. Throws an exception if the item is null or the stack is full.
Object	**pop()**
	Returns the item at the top of this stack and removes it from the stack. Throws an exception if the stack is empty.
	Supporting Methods
Object	**peek()**
	Returns the item at the top of this stack without removing it from the stack. Throws an exception if the stack is empty.
boolean	**isEmpty()**
	Returns true if this stack contains no items.
boolean	**isFull()**
	Returns true if this stack is full and can accept no more items.
int	**size()**
	Returns the number of items in this stack.

7.3   Using a Stack

Now that we have defined a stack, we demonstrate how to use one. Table 7.2 shows how the operations listed earlier affect a stack.

Table 7.2   **The Effects of Stack Operations**

Operation	State of the Stack after the Operation	Value Returned	Comment
			Initially, the stack is empty.
push (a)	a		The stack contains the single item **a**.
push(b)	a b		**b** is the top item on the stack.
push(c)	a b c		**c** is the top item.
isEmpty()	a b c	false	The stack is not empty.
size()	a b c	3	The stack contains three items.
peek()	a b c	c	Return the top item on the stack without removing it.
pop()	a b	c	Remove the top item from the stack and return it. **b** is now the top item.
pop()	a	b	Remove and return **b**.
pop()		a	Remove and return **a**.
isEmpty()		true	The stack is empty.
peek()		exception	Peeking at an empty stack throws an exception.
pop()		exception	Popping an empty stack throws an exception.
push(d)	d		**d** is the top item.

Before using a stack in a program, we declare a variable of the interface type and instantiate an object of an implementation type. For instance:

```
StackPT stk1 = new ArrayStackPT();      //Declare and instantiate two stacks
StackPT stk2 = new LinkedStackPT();
```

The classes `ArrayStackPT` and `LinkedStackPT` are implementations of the `StackPT` interface and are described in Section 7.4. But before getting there, let us look at a simple application.

7.3.1   Matching Parentheses

Compilers need to determine if the bracketing symbols in expressions are balanced correctly. For example, every opening [should be followed by a properly positioned closing] and every (by a). Here are some examples:

(. . .) . . . (. . .)	Balanced	
(. . .) . . . (. . .	Unbalanced	Missing a closing) at the end
) . . .(. . .(. . .)	Unbalanced	The closing) at the beginning has no matching opening (

and one of the opening (s has no closing)

[. . . (. . .) . . . .]   Balanced

[. . . (. . .] . . .)   Unbalanced   The bracketed sections are not nested properly

In these examples, three dots represent arbitrary strings that contain no bracketing symbols. As a first attempt at solving the problem of whether brackets balance, we might simply count the number of left and right parentheses. If the expression balances, the two counts are equal. However, the converse is not true. If the counts are equal, the brackets do not necessarily balance. The third example provides a counterexample.

A more complex approach, using a stack, does work. To check an expression,

1. We scan across it, pushing opening brackets onto a stack.

2. On encountering a closing bracket, if the stack is empty or if the item on the top of the stack is not an opening bracket of the same type, we know the brackets do not balance.

3. Pop an item off the top of the stack and, if it is of the right type, continue scanning the expression.

4. When we reach the end of the expression, the stack should be empty, and if it is not, we know the brackets do not balance.

A Java method that implements this strategy is:

```
boolean bracketsBalance (String exp){        //exp represents the expression
   StackPT stk = new LinkedStackPT();                   //Create a new stack
   for (int i = 0; i < exp.length(); I++){   //Scan across the expression
      char ch = exp.charAt(i);
      if (ch == '[' || ch == '('){     //Push an opening bracket onto the stack
         stk.push (new Character(ch));
      }else if (ch == ']' || ch == ')'){            //Process a closing bracket
         if (stk.isEmpty())             //If the stack is empty, then not balanced
            return false;
         char charFromStack = ((Character)stk.pop()).charValue();
         if (ch == ']' && charFromStack != '[' || //If the opening and closing
            (ch == ')' && charFromStack != '('))   //brackets are of different
            return false;                           //types, then not balanced
      }
   }
   return stk.isEmpty();                   //If the stack is empty, then balanced,
}                                          //else not balanced
```

Exercises 7.3

1. Using the format of Table 7.2 on p. 214, complete a table that involves the following sequence of stack operations:

Operation
create stack
push(a)
push(b)
push(c)
pop()
pop()
peek()
push(x)
pop()
pop()
pop()

Figure 7.2   **The user interface for the bracket checker program**

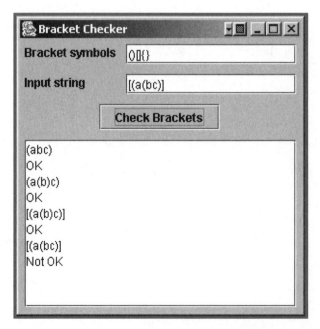

The other columns are labeled **State of the Stack after the Operation, Value Returned,** and **Comment.**

2. Modify the method `bracketsBalance` so that the pair { and } and the pair \ * and * / are included.

3. Write a program that checks the balance of bracketing symbols. The interface appears in Figure 7.2. In the first input field, the user enters the bracketing symbols in pairs. In the second input field, the user enters an expression involving the symbols. In the output area, the program indicates whether the bracketing symbols balance. Notice that the output area displays the results of several tests simultaneously. What is the complexity of the process that is initiated when the user clicks the Check Brackets button?

7.4 Implementations of the Stack Prototype

Because of their simple behavior and linear structure, stacks are implemented easily using arrays or linked structures. Our two implementations of the stack prototype illustrate the typical trade-offs involved in using these two recurring approaches.

7.4.1 Array Implementation

Our first implementation is built around an array called `stack` and a variable called `top`. Initially, the array is empty and `top` equals -1. To push an item onto the stack, we increment `top` and store the item at location `stack[top]`. To pop the stack, we return `stack[top]` and decrement `top`. For example, Figure 7.3 shows how `stack` and `top` appear when four items are on the stack.

Figure 7.3   **An array representation of a stack with four items**

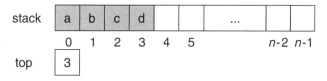

The array, as shown, has a maximum capacity of n items. Herein lies a problem. How do we avoid the problem of stack overflow? There are two obvious solutions:

1. We can force the programmer to specify the array's size when first instantiating a stack. The programmer must then declare a size that allows for the worst case situation but at the cost of perhaps wasting space much of the time. We call this the *static array implementation.*

2. Alternatively, at the cost of additional computation, we can change the size of the array dynamically when it is about to overflow or when it becomes underutilized. Following the analysis in Chapter 5, we double the array's size when push fills it and halve it when pop leaves it three-quarters empty. We call this the *dynamic array implementation.*

These two alternatives illustrate a frequently encountered trade-off: extra computer memory versus extra computation.

In the implementation that follows, we take the first approach, a static array implementation, and leave the second approach as an exercise. We call the class ArrayStackPT. Here is the code:

```
1  // This implementation is based on a static array. Thus, the stack can
2  // become full, and then no more items can be pushed.
3  // The user can specify the stack's capacity when it is created.
4
5  import java.io.Serializable;
6
7  public class ArrayStackPT implements StackPT, Serializable {
8
9      public final static int DEFAULT_CAPACITY = 100;
10     private Object stack[];                    // The array that holds the stack
11     private int top;                           // Index of top item on the stack
12
13     // Creates a stack with the default capacity
14     public ArrayStackPT (){
15        this (DEFAULT_CAPACITY);
16     }
17
18     // Creates a stack with a user-specified capacity
19     public ArrayStackPT (int capacity){
20        if (capacity < 1)
21           throw new IllegalArgumentException ("Capacity must be > O");
22        stack = new Object[capacity];
23        top = -1;
24     }
25
26     public boolean isEmpty(){
27        return top == -1;
28     }
29
30     public boolean isFull(){
31        return size() == stack.length;
32     }
33
34     public Object peek(){
35        if (isEmpty ())
36           throw new IllegalStateException ("Stack is empty");
37        return stack[top];
38     }
39
40     public Object pop(){
41        is (isEmpty())
42           throw new IllegalStateException ("Stack is empty");
43        Object topItem = stack[top];
44        stack[top] = null;
45        top--;
46        return topItem;
```

Continued

Continued

```
47    }
48
49    public void push(Object item){
50        if (item == null)
51            throw new IllegalArgumentException ("Item is null");
52        if (isFull())
53            throw new IllegalStateException ("Stack is full");
54        top++;
55        stack[top] = item;
56    }
57
58    public int size(){
59        return top + 1;
60    }
61 }
```

Note the following points about the implementation:

1. We chose the somewhat arbitrary value of 100 as the default size for the array, but a programmer can choose a different value provided it is greater than 0.

2. The code throws exceptions as specified by the interface.

3. When an item is popped, the corresponding array entry is set to null; otherwise, a reference to the item persists within the stack, and Java's automatic garbage collector will not recognize that the object can be swept away when the popped item is no longer needed by the user.

7.4.2   Linked Implementation

The linked implementation of a stack uses a singly linked list of nodes with a variable top pointing at the list's head. Pushing and popping are accomplished by adding and removing nodes at the head of the list. Figure 7.4 illustrates a stack containing three items.

Figure 7.4   **A linked representation of a stack with three items**

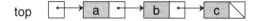

top

The linked implementation requires two classes: the public class LinkedStackPT and a private inner class Node. The class Node contains two fields:

value   an item on the stack

next   a pointer to the next node

Because new items are added to and removed from just one end of the linked list, the methods pop and push are easy to implement, as shown in the next two figures. Figure 7.5 shows the sequence of steps required to push an item onto a linked stack. Figure 7.6 shows the single step necessary to pop an item from a linked stack.

Figure 7.5   **Pushing an item onto a linked stack**

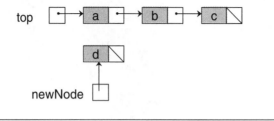

Step 1: get a new node

Step 2: set newNode.next to top

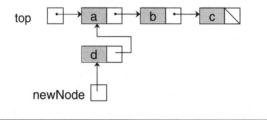

Step 3: set top to new node

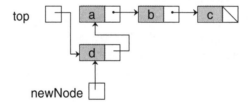

Figure 7.6   **Popping an item from a linked stack**

set top to top.next

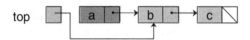

The implementation of `LinkedStackPT` is now straightforward, so without further comment, here is the code:

```
1 // LinkedStackPT
2
3 import java.io.Serializable;
```

Continued

Continued

```
 4
 5 public class LinkStackPT implements StackPT, Serializable {
 6
 7     private int count;
 8     private Node top;
 9
10     public LinkedStackPT(){
11         top = null;
12         count = 0;
13     }
14
15     public boolean isEmpty(){
16         return count == 0;
17     }
18
19     public boolean isFull(){
20         return false;
21     }
22
23     public Object peek(){
24         if (isEmpty())
25             throw new IllegalStateException ("Stack is empty");
26         return top.value;
27     }
28
29     public Object pop(){
30         if (isEmpty())
31             throw new IllegalStateException ("Stack is empty");
32         count--;
33         Object item = top.value;
34         top = top.next;
35         return item;
36     }
37
38     public void push(Object item){
39         if (item == null)
40             throw new IllegalArgumentException ("Item is null");
41         count++;
42         Node n = new Node (item, top);
43         top = n
44     }
45
46     public int size(){
47         return count;
48     }
49
50     // Private inner class to represent a node
51     // Must implement Serializable to allow serialization of the stack
52     private class Node implements Serializable {
53
54         private Object value;     // Value stored in this node
55         private Node   next;      // Reference to next node
56
57         private Node(){
58             value = null;
```

Continued

```
59              next = null;
60          }
61
62      private Node(Object value, Node next){
63          this.value = value;
64          this.next = next;
65      }
66  }
67 }
```

In the code, notice that a linked stack is never considered full, so unless the JVM runs out of memory, we can always push one more item onto a stack. Exceptions are still thrown if we attempt to peek at or pop an empty stack.

7.4.3   Time and Space Analysis for the Two Implementations

An analysis of the time complexity of the two implementations is straightforward. All the methods are very simple and have a maximum run time of $O(1)$. In the dynamic array implementation, the analysis becomes more complex. At the moment of doubling, the `push` method's run time jumps to $O(n)$, but the rest of the time, it remains at $O(1)$. Similar remarks can be made about the pop method. On average, both are still $O(1)$, as shown in Chapter 5; however, the programmer must decide if a fluctuating response time is acceptable and choose an implementation accordingly.

A collection of n objects requires at least enough space to hold the n object references. Let us now see how our two stack implementations compare to this ideal. A linked stack of n items requires n nodes, each containing two references, one to an item and the other to the next node. In addition, there must be a variable that points to the top node, yielding a total space requirement of $2n + 1$ references.

For a static array implementation, a stack's total space requirement is fixed when the stack is instantiated. The space consists of an array with `capacity` elements and an integer variable that indicates the stack's top. Assuming that an integer and a reference occupy the same amount of space, then the total space requirement is `capacity + 1`. As discussed in Chapter 5, a static array implementation is more space efficient than a linked implementation whenever the load factor is greater than .5. The load factor for a dynamic array implementation normally varies between .25 and 1, although it can obviously sink to 0.

Exercises 7.4

1. Modify `ArrayStackPT` to incorporate a dynamic array. Show that the average complexity for `push` is $O(1)$.

2. The following exercises involve implementing a stack iterator:

   a. Add the `iterator` method to `StackPT` and implement it in `ArrayStackPT` and `LinkedStackPT`. A stack iterator returns items in order from youngest to oldest, where the youngest item is the one pushed most recently. We do not want to allow users of a stack to remove any item except the topmost. Therefore, the iterator's `remove` method should throw an exception:

```
throw new UnsupportedOperationException("Remove not allowed");
```

b. How will the iterator's unsupported `remove` method affect a stack's collection-view?

c. Although the iterator's `remove` method throws an exception rather than modifying the structure of the underlying stack, the iterator can still throw a `ConcurrentModificationException`. Explain why.

3. Add an abstract class `AbstractStackPT` as a superclass of `ArrayStackPT` and `LinkedStackPT`. In this class, declare the `iterator` method as abstract. Then use the iterator to implement each of the following methods:

```
toString
toArray
collectionView
equals
```

4. Rewrite the `toString` method using `StringBuffer` instead of `String`. How does this affect the method's run time?

7.5   Three Applications of Stacks

We now discuss three applications of stacks. First, we present algorithms for evaluating arithmetic expressions. These algorithms apply to problems in compiler design, and we will use them in the chapter's case study and in one of the exercises. Second, we describe a general technique for using stacks to solve backtracking problems. The exercises explore applications of the technique. Third, we examine the role of stacks in computer memory management. Not only is this topic interesting in its own right, but it provides a foundation for understanding recursion (see Chapter 10).

7.5.1   Evaluating Arithmetic Expressions

We are so accustomed to evaluating simple arithmetic expressions that we give little conscious thought to the rules involved, and we are surprised by the difficulty of writing an algorithm to do the same thing. It turns out that an indirect approach to the problem works best. First, we transform an expression from its familiar *infix form* to a *postfix form*, and then we evaluate the postfix form. In the infix form, each operator is located between its operands, whereas in the postfix form, an operator immediately follows its operands. Table 7.3 gives several simple examples.

There are similarities and differences between the two forms. In both, operands appear in the same order; however, the operators do not. The infix form sometimes requires parentheses; the postfix form never does. Infix evaluation involves rules of precedence; postfix evaluation applies operators as soon as they are encountered. For

Table 7.3   **Some Infix and Postfix Expressions**

Infix Form	Postfix Form	Value
34	34	34
34 + 22	34 22 +	56
34 + 22 * 2	34 22 2 * +	78
34 * 22 + 2	34 22 * 2 +	750
(34 + 22) * 2	34 22 + 2 *	112

instance, consider the steps in evaluating the infix expression 34 + 22 * 2 and the equivalent postfix expression 34 22 2 * +.

Infix evaluation: 34 + 22 * 2 → 34 + 44 → 78

Postfix evaluation: 34 22 2 * + → 34 44 + → 78

We now present stack-based algorithms for transforming infix expressions to postfix and for evaluating the resulting postfix expressions. In combination, these algorithms allow us to evaluate an infix expression. In presenting the algorithms, we ignore the effects of syntax errors but return to the issue in the case study and the exercises.

Evaluating Postfix Expressions

Evaluation is the simpler process and consists of three steps:

1. Scan across the expression from left to right.

2. On encountering an operator, apply it to the two preceding operands and replace all three by the result.

3. Continue scanning until reaching the expression's end, at which point only the expression's value remains.

To express this procedure as a computer algorithm, we use a stack of operands. In the algorithm, the term *token* refers to either an operand or an operator:

```
create a new stack
while there are more tokens in the expression
   get the next token
   if the token is an operand
      push the operand onto the stack
   else if the token is an operator
      pop the top two operands from the stack
      use the operator to evaluate the two operands just popped
      push the resulting operand onto the stack
   end if
end while
return the value at the top of the stack
```

The time complexity of the algorithm is O(n), where n is the number of tokens in the expression (see the exercises). Table 7.4 shows a trace of the algorithm as it is applies to the expression 4 5 6 * + 3 −.

Table 7.4

Tracing the Evaluation of a Postfix Expression

Postfix Expression: 4 5 6 * + 3 −   **Resulting Value:** 31

Portion of Postfix Expression Scanned So Far	Operand Stack	Comment
		No tokens have been seen yet. The stack is empty.
4	4	Push the operand 4.
4 5	4 5	Push the operand 5.
4 5 6	4 5 6	Push the operand 6.
4 5 6 *	4 30	Replace the top two operands by their product.
4 5 6 * +	34	Replace the top two operands by their sum.
4 5 6 * + 3	34 3	Push the operand 3.
4 5 6 * + 3 −	31	Replace the top two operands by their difference. Pop the final value.

Transforming Infix to Postfix

We now show how to translate expressions from infix to postfix. For the sake of simplicity, we restrict our attention to expressions involving the operators *, /, +, and − (an exercise at the end of the chapter enlarges the set of operators). As usual, multiplication and division have higher precedence than addition and subtraction, except when parentheses override the default order of evaluation.

In broad terms, the algorithm scans, from left to right, a string containing an infix expression and simultaneously builds a string containing the equivalent postfix expression. Operands are copied from the infix string to the postfix string as soon as they are encountered. However, operators must be held back on a stack until operators of greater precedence have been copied to the postfix string ahead of them. Here is a more detailed statement of the process:

1. Start with an empty postfix expression and an empty stack, which will hold operators and left parentheses.
2. Scan across the infix expression from left to right.
3. On encountering an operand, append it to the postfix expression.
4. On encountering an operator, pop off the stack all operators that have equal or higher precedence and append them to the postfix expression. Then push the scanned operator onto the stack.

5. On encountering a left parenthesis, push it onto the stack.

6. On encountering a right parenthesis, shift operators from the stack to the postfix expression until meeting the matching left parenthesis, which is discarded.

7. On encountering the end of the infix expression, transfer the remaining operators from the stack to the postfix expression.

Examples in Tables 7.5 and 7.6 illustrate the procedure. We leave it to the reader to determine the time complexity of the process in the tables and to incorporate the process into a programming project that extends the case study (see the exercises).

Table 7.5   **Tracing the Conversion of an Infix Expression to a Postfix Expression**

Infix Expression: 4 + 5 * 6 − 3   **Equivalent Postfix Expression:** 4 5 6 * + 3 −

Portion of Infix Expression Scanned So Far	Operator Stack	Postfix Expression	Comment
			No characters have been seen yet. The stack and PE are empty.
4		4	Append 4 to the PE.
4 +	+	4	Push + onto the stack.
4 + 5	+	4 5	Append 5 to the PE.
4 + 5 *	+ *	4 5	Push * onto the stack.
4 + 5 * 6	+ *	4 5 6	Append 6 to the PE.
4 + 5 * 6 −	−	4 5 6 * +	Pop * and +, append them to the PE, and push −.
4 + 5 * 6 − 3	−	4 5 6 * + 3	Append 3 to the PE.
		4 5 6 * + 3 −	Pop the remaining operators off the stack and append them to the PE.

Table 7.6   **Tracing the Conversion of an Infix Expression to a Postfix Expression**

Infix Expression: (4 + 5) * (6 − 3)   **Equivalent Postfix Expression:** 4 5 + 6 3 − *

Portion of Infix Expression Scanned So Far	Operator Stack	Postfix Expression	Comment
			No characters have been seen yet. The stack and PE are empty.
(	(		Push (onto the stack.
(4	(	4	Append 4 to the PE.
(4 +	(+	4	Push + onto the stack.
(4 + 5	(+	4 5	Append 5 to the PE.
(4 + 5)	(+	4 5 +	Pop the stack until (is encountered and append operators to the PE.
(4 + 5) *	*	4 5 +	Push * onto the stack.
(4 + 5) * (	* (	4 5 +	Push (onto the stack.
(4 + 5) * (6	* (	4 5 + 6	Append 6 to the PE.
(4 + 5) * (6 −	* (−	4 5 + 6	Push − onto the stack.
(4 + 5) * (6 − 3	* (−	4 5 + 6 3	Append 3 to the PE.
(4 + 5) * (6 − 3	*	4 5 + 6 3 −	Pop stack until (is encountered and append items to the PE.
		4 5 + 6 3 − *	Pop the remaining operators off the stack and append them to the PE.

7.5.2   Backtracking

There are two principal techniques for implementing backtracking algorithms: One uses stacks and the other recursion. Here we explore the use of stacks; in Chapter 10, we consider recursion. To rephrase what was said in Chapter 1, a backtracking algorithm begins in a predefined starting state and then moves from state to state in search of a desired ending state. At any point along the way, when there is a choice between several alternative states, the algorithm picks one, possibly at random, and continues. If the algorithm reaches a state representing an undesirable outcome, it backs up to the last point at which there was an unexplored alternative and tries it. In this way, the algorithm either exhaustively searches all states, or it reaches the desired ending state.

The role of a stack in the process is to remember the alternative states that occur at each juncture. To be more precise:

```
create an empty stack
push the starting state onto the stack
while the stack is not empty
    pop the stack and examine the state
```

Continued

Continued

```
    if the state represents an ending state
        return SUCCESSFUL CONCLUSION
    else if the state has not been visited previously
        mark the state as visited
        push onto the stack all unvisited adjacent states
    end if
end while
return UNSUCCESSFUL CONCLUSION
```

Later in the book, when we encounter trees and graphs, we will recognize this algorithm as a depth-first search. Although short, the algorithm is subtle, and an illustration is needed to elucidate its workings.

Suppose there are just five states, as shown in Figure 7.7, with states 1 and 5 representing the start and end, respectively. Lines between states indicate adjacency. Start-

Figure 7.7

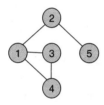

Table 7.7 **The Trace of the Backtracking Algorithm**

Next Step in Algorithm	Stack	Current State	Visited States
Push 1.	1	none yet	
Pop the stack and note the state.		1	
Mark the state as visited.		1	1
Push unvisited adjacent states.	2 3 4	1	1
Pop the stack and note the state.	2 3	4	1
Mark the state as visited.	2 3	4	1 4
Push unvisited adjacent states.	2 3 3	4	1 4
Pop the stack and note the state.	2 3	3	1 4
Mark the state as visited.	2 3	3	1 4 3
All adjacent states already visited.	2 3	3	1 4 3
Pop the stack and note the state.	2	3	1 4 3
Do nothing; location already visited.	2	3	1 4 3
Pop the stack and note the state.		2	1 4 3
Mark the state as visited.		2	1 4 3 2
Push unvisited adjacent states.	5	2	1 4 3 2
Pop the stack and note the state.		5	1 4 3 2
SUCCESS: This is the ending state.		5	1 4 3 2

ing in state 1, the algorithm proceeds to state 4 and then to 3. In state 3, the algorithm recognizes that all adjacent states have been visited and resumes the search in state 2, which leads directly to state 5 and the end. Table 7.7 contains a detailed trace of the algorithm.

Notice in the trace that the algorithm goes directly from state 3 to state 2 without having to back up through states 4 and 1 first. This is a beneficial side effect of using a stack.

It would be interesting to calculate the time complexity of the foregoing algorithm. However, two crucial pieces of information are missing:

1. The complexity of deciding if a state has been visited.

2. The complexity of listing states adjacent to a given state.

If, for the sake of argument, we assume that both of these processes are $O(1)$, then the algorithm as a whole is $O(n)$, where n represents the total number of states (see the exercises).

This discussion has been a little abstract, but at the end of the section, there are several exercises involving the application of backtracking to maze problems.

7.5.3   Memory Management

During a program's execution, both its code and data occupy computer memory. Although the exact manner in which a computer manages memory depends on the programming language and operating system involved, we can present the following simplified, yet reasonably realistic, overview. The emphasis must be on the word *simplified* because a detailed discussion is beyond the book's scope.

As you probably know, a Java compiler translates a Java program into bytecodes. A complex program called the Java Virtual Machine (JVM) then executes these. The memory or ***run-time environment*** controlled by the JVM is divided into six regions, as shown on the left of Figure 7.8. Working up from the bottom, these regions contain:

■   The ***Java Virtual Machine,*** which executes a Java program. Internal to the JVM are two variables, which we call **locationCounter** and **basePtr.** The **location-Counter** points at the instruction the JVM will execute next. The **basePtr** points at the top activation record's base. More is said about these variables soon.

■   Bytecodes for all the methods of our ***program.***

■   The program's ***static variables.***

■   The ***call stack.*** Every time a method is called, an ***activation record*** is created and pushed onto the call stack. When a method finishes execution and returns control to the method that called it, the activation record is popped off the stack. The total number of activation records on the stack equals the number of method calls currently in various stages of execution. At the bottom of the stack is the activation record for the method `main`. Above it is the activation record for the method currently called by `main` and so forth. More will be said about activation records in a moment.

Figure 7.8   **The architecture of a run-time environment**

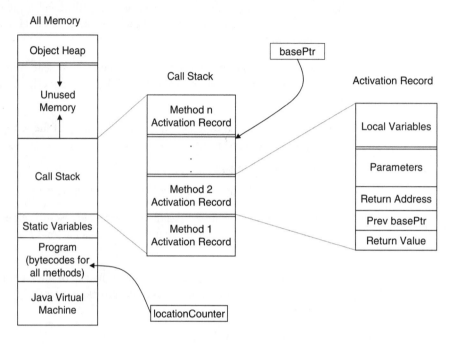

- *Unused memory.* This region's size grows and shrinks in response to the demands of the call stack and the object heap.

- *Object heap.* In Java, all objects exist in a region of memory called the heap. When an object is instantiated, the JVM must find space for the object on the heap, and when the object is no longer needed, the JVM's garbage collector recovers the space for future use. When low on space, the heap extends further into the region marked **unused memory.**

The activation records shown in the figure contain two types of information. The regions labeled **local variables** and **parameters** hold data needed by the executing method. The remaining regions hold data that allow the JVM to pass control backward from the currently executing method to the method that called it.

When a method is called, the JVM

1. Creates the method's activation record and pushes it onto the call stack (the activation record's bottom three regions are fixed in size, and the top two vary depending on the number of parameters and local variables used by the method).

2. Saves the **basePtr**'s current value in the region labeled **Prev basePtr** and sets the **basePtr** to the new activation record's base.

3. Saves the **locationCounter**'s current value in the region labeled **return address** and sets the **locationCounter** to the first instruction of the called method.

4. Copies the calling parameters into the region labeled **parameters.**

5. Initializes local variables as required.

6. Starts executing the called method at the location indicated by the **location-Counter.**

While a method is executing, local variables and parameters in the activation record are referenced by adding an offset to the **basePtr.** Thus, no matter where an activation record is located in memory, the local variables and parameters can be accessed correctly, provided the **basePtr** has been initialized properly.

Just before returning, a method stores its return value in the location labeled **return value.** The value can be a reference to an object, or it can be a primitive such as an integer or character. Because the return value always resides at the bottom of the activation record, the calling method knows exactly where to find it.

When a method has finished executing, the JVM

1. Reestablishes the settings needed by the calling method by restoring the values of the **locationCounter** and the **basePtr** from values stored in the activation record.

2. Pops the activation record from the call stack.

3. Resumes execution of the calling method at the location indicated by the **locationCounter.**

Exercises 7.5

1. Translate by hand the following infix expressions to postfix form:

   a. 33 – 15 * 6

   b. 11 * (6 + 2)

   c. 17 + 3 – 5

   d. 22 – 6 + 33 / 4

2. Evaluate by hand the following postfix expressions:

   a. 10 5 4 + *

   b. 10 5 * 6 –

   c. 22 2 4 * /

   d. 33 6 + 3 4 / +

3. Perform a complexity analysis for postfix evaluation.

4. Perform a complexity analysis for infix to postfix conversion.

5. Compute the complexity of the depth-first search algorithm given that the processes for determining adjacent states and whether or not a state has been visited are both O(1). (*Tip:* Consider the maximum number of times each state gets pushed onto the stack.)

6. Write a program that solves a maze problem. In this particular version of the problem, a hiker must find a path to the top of a mountain. Assume that the hiker leaves a parking lot, marked P, and explores the maze until she reaches the top of a mountain, marked T. Figure 7.9 shows what this particular maze looks like.

Figure 7.9   **A maze problem**

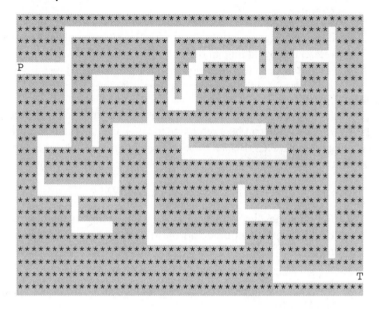

Java source code for the program's interface can be found on the book's CD together with executable code for the program as a whole. You should run the program a few times before writing your solution. The interface allows the user to enter a picture of the maze as a grid of characters. The character * marks a barrier, and P and T mark the parking lot and mountaintop, respectively. A blank space marks a step along a path. The interface includes a Solve button, and when the user selects it, the view should send a message to the model with the contents of the grid as a string parameter. The model then attempts to find a path through the maze and returns "solved" or "unsolved" to the view depending on the outcome. In the model, begin by representing the maze as a matrix of characters (P, T, *, or space), and during the search, mark each visited cell with a dot. Redisplay the grid at the end with the dots included. Here is the backtracking algorithm that is at the core of the solution:

```
instantiate a stack
locate the character 'P' in the matrix
push its location onto the stack
while the stack is not empty
    pop a location, loc, off the stack
    if the matrix contains 'T' at position loc then
       a path has been found
       break
    end if
    store a dot in the matrix at position loc
    examine the cells of the matrix adjacent to loc and for each one that
      contains a space, push its location onto the stack
end while
there is no solution
```

7. Animate the grid of the maze program in the following ways. You should add these features incrementally, testing each one before moving to the next:

    a. Redisplay the grid each time it changes.

    b. Indicate the current location with an X.

    c. Add a button to restore the map and run the algorithm again.

    d. Add buttons to speed up or slow down the animation.

    e. Add a button for single stepping through the animation.

8. Extend the problem as follows:

    a. Display the route to the top of the mountain as a string in the form F4RF2LF15 (meaning "forward 4 spaces, turn right, forward 2 spaces, turn left, forward 15 spaces") and so forth.

    b. Erase all dots except those on the final route.

    c. Allow the user to place Ms at various points along the paths, where M stands for a mushroom. The program should find all the mushrooms, pick them, and retrace its steps back to the parking lot. Animate the program so that the user can follow the course of the program.

9. Compute the time complexity of all algorithms involved in the maze program.

7.6   Interface for a Professional Version

We now develop a professional version of stacks. The package `java.util` includes a stack class, but we do not like it because it extends `Vector`, another class in the same package, and inherits many methods at odds with the behavior of a stack. Therefore, we have added our own stack collection to the `lamborne` package. The presence of two classes called `Stack`, one in `lamborne` and the other in `java.util`, causes a potential naming conflict when both `lamborne` and `java.util` are imported into the same file; however, programmers can resolve the conflict by qualifying the class name with the package name (see Chapter 2).

The interface is listed in Table 7.8 and follows our convention of dividing the methods into three categories: fundamental, supporting, and general. In the table, notice that we no longer consider the possibility of a stack becoming full. Hence, every im-

Table 7.8   **The Interface for `lamborne.Stack`**

	Fundamental Methods
`Object`	`pop()` Returns the item at the top of this stack and removes it from the stack. Throws an exception if the stack is empty.
`void`	`push(Object item)` Pushes an item onto the top of this stack. Throws an exception if the item is `null`.

continued

Table 7.8   **The Interface for `lamborne.Stack` *(Continued)***

Supporting Methods

boolean	**isEmpty()**
	Returns `true` if this stack contains no items.
Object	**peek()**
	Returns the item at the top of this stack without removing it from the stack. Throws an exception if the stack is empty.
int	**size()**
	Returns the number of items in this stack.

General Methods

void	**clear()**
	Removes all items from this stack.
Object	**clone()**
	Returns a shallow copy of this stack. (Does not need to be included here because it will be inherited from `Object`.)
Collection	**collectionView()**
	Returns a collection-view of the items contained in this stack. This collection-view should support none of the optional methods— `add`, `addAll`, `remove`, `removeAll`, `retainAll`—as they violate a stack's basic contract.
boolean	**equals(Object other)**
	Returns `true` if the other object is a stack that equals this stack. To be equal, two stacks must contain equal items appearing in the same order.
int	**hashCode()**
	Returns the hash code value for this stack. (Please ignore this method for now. We discuss hashing in Chapter 13.)
Iterator	**iterator()**
	Returns an iterator over the items contained in this stack. The iterator provides the items in their stack order (that is, from top to bottom). The iterator's `remove` method is not supported because it violates a stack's basic contract. The `remove` method should throw an `UnsupportedOperationException`.
Object[]	**toArray()**
	Returns an array containing all of the items in this stack. The top of the stack corresponds to the first item in the array.
String	**toString()**
	Returns a string that lists the items in this stack. The top of the stack corresponds to the first item in the string. (Does not need to be included here because it will be inherited from `Object`.)

plementation must take steps to avoid that condition. Array implementations do so by using dynamic arrays, whereas linked implementations are free of the problem in the first place. Note that the methods in a stack's general category are the same as those listed for `Tiny` in Chapter 6.

7.7 **Implementation of the Professional Version (optional pv)**

The `lamborne` package provides only one implementation of `Stack`, namely, `LinkedStack`. An array implementation is left as an exercise. Although it is possible to implement `LinkedStack` from scratch, it makes more sense to incorporate the class into `lamborne`'s class hierarchy, following the technique we used for class `Tiny` in Chapter 6. The hierarchy of the stack classes is shown in Figure 7.10. (Note that `ArrayStack` is not actually implemented in `lamborne` but is left as an exercise.)

Table 7.9 shows where each method is implemented together with its maximum run time. The relationships between the classes and the interfaces are shown in Table 7.10.

Figure 7.10   **The stack class hierarchy in `lamborne`**

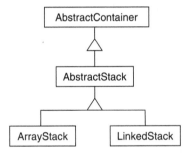

Table 7.9   **The Methods of the Stack Implementation and Their Run Times**

	Stack Implementation	Abstract Container	Abstract Stack	Linked Stack
Constructors				
constructor	()	O(1)	O(1)	O(1)
constructor	(Collection col)			O(n)
constructor	(Iterator iter)			O(n)
Fundamental Methods				
Object	pop()			O(1)
Void	push(Object item)			O(1)
Supporting Methods				
boolean	IsEmpty()	O(1)		
Object	peek ()			O(1)
int	size()	O(1)		

continued

Table 7.9   **The Methods of the Stack Implementation and Their Run Times** *(Continued)*

Stack Implementation		Abstract Container	Abstract Stack	Linked Stack
General Methods				
void	clear()	O(1)		O(1)
Object	clone()			O(n)
Collection	collectionView()	O(1)		
boolean	equals (Object other)		O(n)	
int	hashCode()	O(n)		
Iterator	iterator()	abstract		O(1)
Object []	toArray()	O(n)		
String	toString()	O(n)		

Table 7.10   **The Relationship between Stack Classes and the Interfaces They Implement**

Name of Class	Interfaces Implemented
AbstractContainer	Serializable
AbstractStack	
ArrayStack	Cloneable, Stack
LinkedStacked	Cloneable, Stack

Most of the implementation details for the professional stack now follow easily; however, two points are worth mentioning:

1. The iterator must not support the remove method.

2. The collectionView method must return a collection-view object that does not override the add method.

These restrictions protect a stack from operations that could violate a stack's contract. If an iterator allowed removals, then internal items could be removed from a stack using either an iterator's remove method or a collection-view's remove, removeAll, or retainAll methods. If a collection-view object supported add, then internal items could be added to a stack using a collection-view's add or addAll methods.

Of course, some might argue that giving a stack additional capabilities would be advantageous. If that perspective is accepted, then it should apply equally to queues, and both stacks and queues become indistinguishable from lists, which allow addition and removal of items at arbitrary locations within a linear structure.

We close the section by showing two snippets of code. The first snippet lists the `collectionView` method in `AbstractContainer`. The `add` method is not overridden. The second shows `LinkedStack`'s `iterator` method and supporting inner class. The `remove` method is not supported. The two other public methods have a maximum run time of O(1).

```
//collectionView method in AbstractContainer

private transient Collection col = null;
   //By declaring the variable col transient, we are indicating that we
   //do not want it to be transferred to or from the disk during serialization

public Collection collectionView()
{
   if (col != null) return col;

   col = new AbstractCollection()
        {
            public Iterator iterator(){
               return AbstractContainer.this.iterator();
            }

            public int size() {
               return AbstractContainer.this.size();
            }
        };
   return col;
}
```

```
//iterator method in LinkedStack together with the supporting inner class

   public Iterator iterator()
   {
      return new InnerIter();
   }

   private class InnerIter implements Iterator{

      private OneWayNode curPos;
      private int        expectedModCount = modCount;

      private InnerIter()
      {
         curPos = top;
      }

      public boolean hasNext()
      {
         return curPos != null;
      }
```

Continued

Continued

```
    public Object next()
    {
        if (modCount != expectedModCount)
            throw new ConcurrentModificationException();
        if (!hasNext())
            throw new NoSuchElementException("There are no more elements");

        Object item = curPos.value;
        curPos = curPos.next;
        return item;
    }

    // Not supported by stacks, so throws exception
    public void remove()
    {
        throw new UnsupportedOperationException("Remove not allowed");
    }
  }
}
```

Exercises 7.7

1. The stack iterator does not support removal. Write a test program that confirms a stack's collection-view object does not support removal either. Explain why. (*Tip:* Look at the source code for `AbstractCollection`.)

2. Implement your own versions of `AbstractStack` and `LinkedStack`. To do so, import `lamborne.Stack` and `lamborne.AbstractContainer` but no other classes from `lamborne`. Your versions of `AbstractStack` and `LinkedStack` are not part of `lamborne`, so do not include the line

```
package lamborne;
```

at the beginning of each file.

3. In Chapter 6, the clear method for class `Tiny` involved only `AbstractContainer`, yet for stacks, the method also involves `LinkedStack`. Explain why.

4. Even if the methods in `Tiny` were renamed to conform to those used in `Stack`, a `Tiny` collection would still differ in some significant ways from a `Stack` collection. Explain.

5. Add a column to the stack implementation in Table 7.8. This column is for a dynamic array implementation and should be labeled **Array Stack.** You should be able to compute the run time information in the column without actually doing the implementation. Remember that the values shown are for maximum run times.

6. Implement a professional version of `ArrayStack` using a dynamic array and add it to your copy of `lamborne`. The iterator-based constructor should include an integer parameter indicating the initial capacity of the array.

7.8   Case Study: Evaluating Postfix Expressions

For the case study, we present a program that evaluates postfix expressions. The program allows the user to enter an arbitrary postfix expression and then displays the expression's value or an error message if the expression is invalid. The stack-based algorithm for evaluating postfix expressions is at the heart of the program.

7.8.1   Request

Write an interactive program for evaluating postfix expressions.

7.8.2   Analysis

As always, a careful analysis gets us off to a good start.

The Interface

There are many possibilities for the user interface. Considering the educational setting, we would like the user to experiment with numerous expressions while retaining a transcript of the results. Errors in an expression should not stop the program but should generate messages that give insight into where the evaluation process breaks down. With these requirements in mind, we propose the interface in Figure 7.11.

The user enters an expression in the first text area, and the program displays the results in the second. The expression, as entered, can be spread across any number of lines, with arbitrary spacing between tokens, provided adjacent operands have some

Figure 7.11   **The user interface for the postfix expression evaluator**

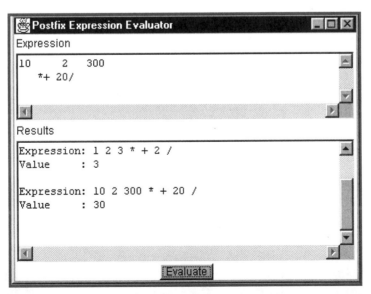

white space between them. After the user selects Evaluate, the expression is redisplayed in the results area with exactly one space between each token and is followed on the next line by its value or an error message. The results area is scrollable, and at any time, the user can review the expressions entered so far.

Error Detection

The program should detect and report all input errors, be they intentional or unintentional. The errors that come to mind are:

- The user selects the Evaluate button before entering an expression.
- The expression contains too many operands; in other words, there is more than one operand left on the stack when the end of the expression is encountered.
- The expression contains too few operands; in other words, an operator is encountered when there are fewer than two operands on the stack.
- The expression contains unrecognizable tokens. The program expects the expression to be composed of integers, four arithmetic operators ($+$, $-$, $*$, $/$), and white space (space, tab, and newline). Anything else is unrecognizable.
- The expression includes division by 0.

Here are examples that illustrate each type of error with an appropriate error message:

Expression:

Error: *Expression contains no tokens*

Portion of expression processed: *None*

The stack is empty

Expression: *1 2 3 +*

Error: *Too many operands on the stack*

Portion of expression processed: *1 2 3 +*

Operands on the stack: *1 5*

Expression: *1 + 2 3 4 ***

Error: *Too few operands on the stack*

Portion of expression processed: *1 +*

Operands on the stack: *1*

Expression: *1 2 % 3 +*

Error: *Unknown token type*

Portion of expression processed: *1 2 %*

Operands on the stack: *1 2*

Expression: *1 2 0 / +*

Error: *Divide by 0*

Portion of expression processed: *1 2 0 /*

Operands on the stack: *1*

Classes and Responsibilities

As always, we assume the existence of a view or interface and a model. In what follows, the prefix PF is short for the word *postfix*.

PFExpressionInterface. The interface is simple. When the user clicks the Command button, the interface sends three messages to the model:

1. The interface asks the model to format the expression string with exactly one space between each token, and then it displays the formatted string.
2. The interface asks the model to evaluate the expression, and then it displays the value returned.
3. The interface catches any exceptions thrown by the model, asks the model for the conditions that pertained when the error was detected, and displays appropriate error messages.

PFExpressionModel. The responsibilities of the model are now clear. It must be able to format and evaluate an expression string, throw exceptions in response to syntax errors in the string, and report on its internal state. To meet these responsibilities, the model can divide its work between two major processes:

1. Scan a string and extract the tokens.
2. Evaluate a sequence of tokens.

The output of the first process becomes the input to the second. These processes are complex, and they recur in other problems. For both reasons, they are worth encapsulating in separate classes, which we call `Scanner` and `PFEvaluator`.

Scanner. Considering the manner in which it will be used, the scanner takes a string as input and returns a sequence of tokens as output. Rather than return these tokens all at once, the scanner implements an iterator and responds to the messages `hasNext` and `next`.

PFEvaluator. The evaluator takes a scanner as input, iterates across the scanner's tokens, and either returns an expression's value or throws an exception. In the process, the evaluator uses the stack-based algorithm described earlier in the chapter. At any time, the evaluator can provide information about its internal state.

Token. If the scanner is to return tokens, then a token class is needed. A token has a value and a type. The possible types are represented by arbitrarily chosen integer constants with the names PLUS, MINUS, MUL, DIV, and INT. The values of the first four are the corresponding characters +, −, *, and /. The value of an INT is found by converting a substring of numeric characters, such as 534, to its internal integer representation. A token can provide a string representation of itself by converting its value to a string.

The Object Diagram

Figure 7.12 is an object diagram that shows the relationships between the proposed classes. Notice that both the model and the evaluator use the scanner. We have already discussed why the evaluator needs the scanner. The model uses the scanner to format the expression string. Although this task could be accomplished by manipulating the expression string directly, it is easier to use the scanner, and the performance penalty is negligible. Normally, predefined classes are not included in the object model, but showing the classes String and Stack gives us a better overview of how the system works.

Figure 7.12   **An object model diagram for the expression evaluator**

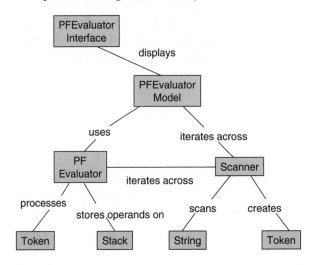

7.8.3   Design

We now look more closely at the inner workings of each class. Figure 7.13 is a message diagram that summarizes the messages sent between classes. Next we list each class's instance variables and methods.

Instance Variables and Methods for Class
PFEvaluatorInterface

The attributes include the obvious window objects. The reference to the model can be local to the buttonClicked method. The public methods are:

Figure 7.13 **A message diagram for the expression evaluator**

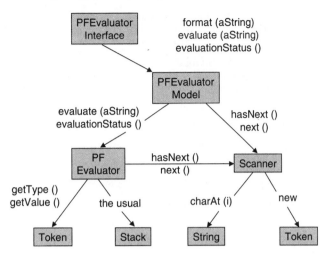

```
PFEvaluatorInterface ()
```
Set the window's title.
```
void buttonClicked (Button buttonObj)
```
Retrieve the expression string from the interface.

Send it to the model for formatting.

Send it to the model for evaluation.

And either display the value or catch exceptions thrown by the evaluator, ask the model for the associated details, and display error messages.

Instance Variables and Methods for Class `PFEvaluatorModel`

The model communicates with the scanner and the evaluator, so it needs references to both. The evaluator must be an instance variable because it is referenced in more than one method; however, the scanner can be local to the `format` method. The public methods are:

```
String format(String expressionStr)
```
Instantiate a scanner on the expression string.

Build a response string by iterating across the scanner and appending a string representation of each token to the response string.

Return the response string.
```
int evaluate(String expressionStr)
```
Ask the evaluator to evaluate the expression string.

Return the value.
```
String evaluationStatus()
```
Ask the evaluator for its status.

Return the status.

Instance Variables and Methods for Class **PFEvaluator**

The evaluator's attributes include a stack, a scanner, and a string variable called `expressionSoFar`, which holds the portion of the expression string processed so far. The stack is a `lamborne Stack` and is instantiated as a `lamborne LinkedStack`. The public methods are:

`PFEvaluator(Iterator scanner)`

  Initialize `expressionSoFar`.

  Instantiate a `LinkedStack`.

  Save a reference to the scanner.

`int evaluate()`

  Iterate across the scanner and evaluate the expression.

  Throw exceptions in the following situations:

    1. The scanner is null or empty.

    2. There are too many operands.

    3. There are too few operands.

    4. There are unrecognizable tokens.

    5. A divide by 0 exception is thrown by the JVM.

`String evaluationStatus()`

  Return a multipart string that contains the portion of the expression processed and the contents of the stack.

Instance Variables and Methods for Class **Scanner (implements Iterator)**

Let us suppose that a third party has provided the scanner. Consequently, we do not need to consider its inner workings, and its public methods are just those of any iterator. For those who are interested, the book's CD contains the complete source code.

`Scanner (String str)`

  Save a reference to the string that will be scanned and tokenized.

`boolean hasNext()`

  Return `true` if the string contains another token and `false` otherwise.

`Object next()`

  Return the next token.

`void remove()`

  This method is a required part of the `Iterator` interface; however, removal is not supported, and the method throws an `UnsupportedOperationException` when called.

Instance Variables and Methods for Class **Token**

A token's attributes are `type` and `value`. Both are integers. The type is one of the following:

```
public  static  final  int  UNKNOWN   = 0;         // unknown
public  static  final  int  INT       = 4;         // integer
public  static  final  int  MINUS     = 5;         // minus     operator
public  static  final  int  PLUS      = 6;         // plus      operator
public  static  final  int  MUL       = 7;         // multiply  operator
public  static  final  int  DIV       = 8;         // divide    operator
```

The actual values of the symbolic constants are arbitrary. A token's value is

- a binary number for integer operands
- a character code for operators; for instance, `(int)` `'*'` corresponds to the multiplication operator

The public methods are:

`Token (int value)`

Construct a new integer token with the specified value.

`Token (char ch)`

If ch is an operator (+, −, *, /), then construct a new operator token; otherwise, construct a token of unknown type.

`int getType()`

Return a token's type.

`int getValue()`

Return a token's value.

`boolean isOperator()`

Return `true` if the token is an operator and `false` otherwise.

`String toString()`

Return the token's numeric value as a string if the token is an integer; otherwise, return the token's character representation.

7.8.4   Implementation

All the code can be found on the book's CD. The code for the interface is routine, except for the minor complication of using a `try-catch` statement. The code for the model is trivial. Neither is worth listing here, and the internal workings of the scanner are not presented. That leaves the token and the evaluator classes, which we now present:

```
1 public class Token {
2
3    // Values of token types
4    public static final int UNKNOWN   = 0         // unknown
5
6    public static final int INT       = 4;        // integer
7
8    public static final int MINUS     = 5;        // minus     operator
```

Continued

Continued

```
 9    public static final int PLUS    = 6;        // plus      operator
10    public static final int MUL     = 7;        // multiply operator
11    public static final int DIV     = 8;        // divide    operator
12
13    // Helper to determine if type is among the operators
14    private static final int FIRST_OP = 5;       // first operator code
15
16    private int type;                            // The type of token
17    private int value;                           // The token's value
18
19    public Token (int value)
20    {
21       type = INT;
22       this.value = value;
23    }
24
25    public Token (char ch)
26    {
27       type = type (ch);
28       value = (int) ch;
29    }
30
31    public boolean isOperator()
32    {
33       return type >= FIRST_OP;
34    }
35
36    public String toString()
37    {
38       if (type == INT)
39          return "" + value;
40       else
41          return "" + (char)value;
42    }
43
44    public int getType()
45    {
46       return type;
47    }
48
49    public int getValue()
50    {
51       return value;
52    }
53
54    // Generates the type of token from the source character
55    private static int type (char ch)
56    {
57       int type;
58       switch (ch){
59          case '*':
60             type = MUL
61             break;
62          case '/':
63             type = DIV;
64             break;
```

Continued

```
65          case '+':
66              type = PLUS;
67              break;
68          case '-':
69              type = MINUS;
70              break;
71          default:
72              type = UNKNOWN;
73          }
74      return type;
75      }
76 }
```

```java
 1 import java.util.Iterator;
 2 import lamborne.*;
 3
 4 public class PFEvaluator {
 5
 6    private String expressionSoFar;  // Portion of the source scanned so far
 7    private String operandStack;     // Stack of operands
 8    private Iterator scanner;        // Reference to this expression's scanner
 9
10    public PFEvaluator()
11    {
12        this (null);
13    }
14
15    public PFEvaluator (Iterator scanner)
16    {
17        expressionSoFar = "";
18        operandStack = new LinkedStack();
19        this.scanner = scanner;
20    }
21
22    // Implements evaluation algorithm using a stack of operands
23    public int evaluate(){
24        if (scanner == null || !scanner.hasNext()){
25            throw new IllegalArgumentException ("Expression contains no tokens");
26        }
27
28        Token t1, t2, currentToken, result;
29        while (scanner.hasNext()){
30            currentToken = (Token) scanner.next();
31            expressionSoFar += currentToken + " ";
32            if(currentToken.getType() == Token.INT){
33                operandStack.push(currentToken);
34            }else if (currentToken.isOperator()){
35                if (operandStack.size() < 2)
36                    throw new RuntimeException ("Too few operands on the stack");
37                t2 = (Token) operandStack.pop();   // Right operand went on last
38                t1 = (Token) operandStack.pop();
39                result =
40                    new Token (computeValue)currentToken, t1.getValue(),
```

Continued

```
41                                                      t2.getValue())));
42                operandStack.push(result);
43          }else.
44             throw new RuntimeException ("Unknown token type");
45       }
46
47     if (operandStack.size() > 1)
48        throw new RuntimeException ("Too many operands on the stack");
49
50     result = (Token) operandStack.pop();
51     return result.getValue();
52   }
53
54   // Returns the current state of the evaluator, consisting of
55   //    - The portion of the expression scanned thus far
56   //    - The current contents of the operand stack
57   public String evaluationStatus()
58   {
59     String str = "";
60     if (expressionSoFar == "")
61        str += "Portion of expression processed: none\n";
62     else
63        str += "Portion of expression processed: " + expressionSoFAR + "\n";
64     if (operandStack.isEmpty())
65        str += "The stack is empty";
66     else{
67        Iterator iter = operandStack.iterator();   // Notice use of iterator
68        String operands = "";
69        while (iter.hasNext ())
70           operands = iter.next() + " " + operands;
71        str += "Operands on the stack          : " + operands;
72     }
73     return str;
74   }
75
76   // Returns the result of evaluating a binary expression
77   // Divide by zero exceptions are caught by the JVM
78   private int computeValue(Token op, int value1, int value2){
79     int result = 0;
80     switch (op.getType()){
81        case Token.PLUS:
82           result = value1 + value2;
83           break;
84        case Token.MINUS:
85           result = value1 - value2;
86           break;
87        case Token.MUL:
88           result = value1 * value2;
89           break;
90        case Token.DIV:
91           result = value1 / value2;
92           break;
93        default:
94           throw new RuntimeException ("Unknown operator");
95     }
96     return result
97   }
98 }
```

Exercises 7.8

1. Run the case study with several different input expressions, some of which are syntactically incorrect.

2. What is the run-time complexity of the process initiated when the user clicks the Evaluate button?

3. Modify the evaluator program to allow exponentiation using ^ as the symbol for exponentiation. In infix form, exponentiation operations associate from right to left. For example, 2^2^3 (infix notation) evaluates to 2^8, or 256, not 4^3, or 64.

4. Modify the evaluator program so that it accepts infix instead of postfix expressions. (*Tip:* Implement a method that converts the input expressions to postfix form.)

5. Modify the evaluator program so that it accepts a series of assignment statements instead of a single expression. Expressions can include previously defined variables, where a variable is defined once it appears on the left side of an assignment statement. For the sake of simplicity, assume that variable names consist of a single letter. A semicolon terminates each assignment statement.

6. Extend Exercise 5 so that the series of assignment statements can be located in a text file. The user should be able to select an Open command from a File menu, at which point the program should transfer the contents of the named file to the input text area. See Appendix A for details on text files and file dialogs.

KEY TERMS

activation record

backtracking

call stack

dynamic array
    implementation

infix

pop

postfix

prefix

push

run-time environment

static array
    implementation

top

CHAPTER SUMMARY

The stack collection has a wide range of applications in computer science. Most of these, such as parsing expressions, evaluating expressions, and providing run-time support for method calls, involve backtracking.

A stack enforces last-in, first-out processing of items. That is, the item most recently inserted is always the next item to be removed.

A stack is a linear collection with access to one end, called the top. The push operation adds an item to the top, whereas the pop operation removes an item from the top. The only other operations return a stack's size, test it for emptiness, and return the item at the top.

A stack can support an iterator, but the iterator should not support a method to remove items.

The two common implementations of a stack use an array and a singly linked structure.

REVIEW QUESTIONS

1. Name five common applications of stacks.
2. What happens when you attempt to pop an item from an empty stack?
3. Compare the run-time efficiency of an array implementation of a stack with a linked implementation.
4. Why can you not use an iterator to remove items from a stack?
5. Would it be wise to provide a collection-view for a stack? If not, why not?

CHAPTER 8

Queues

OBJECTIVES   Upon completion of this chapter, you should be able to

- Describe the formal properties of queues

- Give examples of applications of queues

- Discuss at least two common ways in which queues are implemented and the criteria for choosing between them

- Explain the differences between a queue and a priority queue

In this chapter, we explore the queue, another ADT that has widespread use in computer science. We consider both a prototype and a professional version of the queue ADT. There are several implementation strategies for queues, some based on arrays and others based on linked structures. To illustrate the application of a queue, we develop a case study that simulates a supermarket checkout line. We close the chapter with an examination of a special kind of queue, known as a ***priority queue,*** and show how it is used in a second case study.

8.1   Overview of Queues

Like stacks, queues are linear collections. However, insertions are restricted to one end, called the ***rear,*** and removals to the other end, called the ***front.*** A queue thus supports a first-in, first-out protocol (FIFO). Queues are omnipresent in everyday life and occur in any situation where people or things are lined up for processing on a first-come, first-served basis. Checkout lines in stores, highway tollbooth lines, and airport baggage check-in lines are familiar examples of queues.

Queues have two fundamental operations: ***enqueue,*** which adds an item to the rear of a queue, and ***dequeue,*** which removes an item from the front. Figure 8.1 shows a queue as it might appear at various stages in its lifetime. In the figure, the queue's front is on the left and its rear is on the right. Initially, the queue is empty. Then an

Figure 8.1   **The states in the lifetime of a queue**

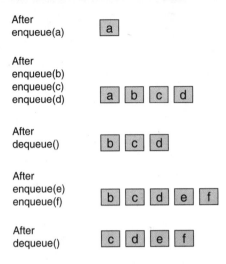

After
enqueue(a)

After
enqueue(b)
enqueue(c)
enqueue(d)

After
dequeue()

After
enqueue(e)
enqueue(f)

After
dequeue()

item called **a** is enqueued. Next three more items called **b, c,** and **d** are enqueued, after which an item is dequeued, and so forth.

Related to queues is an ADT called a *priority queue.* In a queue, the item dequeued or served next is always the item that has been waiting the longest. But in some circumstances, this restriction is too rigid, and we would like to combine the idea of waiting with a notion of priority. The result is a priority queue, in which higher priority items are dequeued before those of lower priority, and items of equal priority are dequeued in FIFO order. Consider, for example, the manner in which passengers board an aircraft. The first-class passengers line up and board first, and the lower priority coach-class passengers line up and board second. However, this is not a true priority queue because once the first-class queue has emptied and the coach-class queue starts boarding, late arriving first-class passengers usually go to the end of the second queue. In a true priority queue, they would immediately jump ahead of all the coach-class passengers.

Most examples of queues in computer science involve scheduling access to shared resources. For instance:

CPU access   Processes are queued for access to a shared CPU.

Disk access   Processes are queued for access to a shared secondary storage device.

Printer access   Print jobs are queued for access to a shared laser printer.

Process scheduling can use either simple queues or priority queues. For example, processes involving keyboard and screen outputs are often given higher priority access to the CPU than those that are computationally intensive. The result is that users, who tend to judge a computer's speed by its response time, are given the impression that the computer is fast.

Processes waiting for a shared resource can also be prioritized by their expected duration, with short processes given higher priority than longer ones, again with the intent of improving the apparent response time of a system. Imagine 20 print jobs queued up for access to a printer. If 19 jobs are 1 page long and 1 job is 200 pages long, more users will be happy if the short jobs are given higher priority and printed first.

8.2 A Queue Prototype

The fundamental operations of the queue ADT are `enqueue` and `dequeue`. The supporting operations are

`peek`   Returns the front item on a queue without removing it.

`isEmpty`   Returns `true` if there are no more items on a queue.

`isFull`   Returns `true` if a queue can hold no more items.

`size`   Returns the number of items on a queue.

As with stack operations, certain queue operations have preconditions which, if violated, result in exceptions. Here is a list of the exceptions thrown by the queue prototype:

`peek` and `dequeue`   Throw an `IllegalStateException` if the queue is empty.

`enqueue`   Throws an `IllegalStateException` if the queue is full and an `IllegalArgumentException` if the item is `null`.

Table 8.1 defines the queue prototype's interface. We then close the section with Table 8.2, a short illustration of the queue operations in action.

Table 8.1   **The Interface for the Queue Prototype**

	Fundamental Methods
void	**enqueue(Object item)** Adds an item to the rear of this queue. Throws an exception if the item is `null` or the queue is full.
Object	**dequeue()** Returns the item at the front of this queue and removes it from the queue. Throws an exception if the queue is empty.
	Supporting Methods
object	**peek()** Returns the item at the front of this queue without removing it from the queue. Throws an exception if the queue is empty.

continued

Table 8.1 **The Interface for the Queue Prototype** *(Continued)*

boolean   **isEmpty()**
Returns `true` if this queue contains no items.

boolean   **isFull()**
Returns `true` if this queue is full and can accept no more items.

int   **size()**
Returns the number of items in this queue.

Table 8.2 **The Effects of Queue Operations**

Operation	State of the Queue after the Operation	Value Returned	Comment
			Initially, the queue is empty.
enqueue(a)	a		The queue contains the single item **a**.
enqueue (b)	a b		**a** is at the front of the queue and **b** is at the rear.
enqueue (c)	a b c		**c** is added at the rear.
isEmpty()	a b c	false	The queue is not empty.
size()	a b c	3	The queue contains three items.
peek()	a b c	a	Return the front item on the queue without removing it.
dequeue ()	b c	a	Remove the front item from the queue and return it. **b** is now the front item.
dequeue ()	c	b	Remove and `return` **b**.
dequeue ()		c	Remove and return **c**.
isEmpty()		true	The queue is empty.
peek()		exception	Peeking at an empty queue throws an exception.
dequeue()		exception	Trying to dequeue an empty queue throws an exception.
enqueue(d)	d		**d** is the front item.

Exercises 8.2

1. Substitute a queue for a stack in the maze exercise in Section 7.5. How does this change the manner in which a path through the maze is found?

2. Write a **.java** file for QueuePT. You will need it in the exercises at the end of the next section. Be sure to include complete preconditions and postconditions for each method in the file.

8.3   Implementations of the Queue Prototype

Our approach to the implementation of queues is similar to the one we used for stacks. The structure of a queue lends itself to either an array implementation or a linked implementation. Because the linked implementation is somewhat more straightforward, we consider it first.

8.3.1   Linked Implementation

The linked implementations of stacks and queues have much in common. Both classes, `LinkedStackPT` and `LinkedQueuePT`, use a singly linked `Node` class to implement nodes. The operation `dequeue` is similar to `pop` in that it removes the first node from a linked list. However, `enqueue` and `push` differ. The operation `push` adds a node at the beginning of a linked list, whereas `enqueue` adds a node at the end. To provide fast access to both ends of a queue's linked list, there are pointers to both ends. Figure 8.2 shows a linked queue containing four items.

Figure 8.2   **A linked queue with four items**

Here is the code for the declarations of the instance variables `front` and `rear`:

```
private Node front;     // head node in the linked structure
private Node rear;      // tail node in the linked structure
```

During an `enqueue` operation, we create a new node, set the next pointer of the last node to the new node, and finally set the variable `rear` to the new node, as shown in Figure 8.3.

Here is code for the `enqueue` method:

```
public void enqueue(Object item){
    if (item == null)
        throw new IllegalArgumentException
                ("Trying to enqueue null onto the queue");

    Node node = new Node (item, null);
    if (isEmpty())
        front = node;
    else
        rear.next = node;
    rear = node;
    count++;
}
```

Figure 8.3   **Adding an item to a linked queue**

Step 1: get a new node

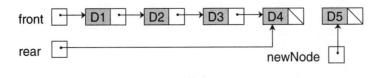

Step 2: set rear.next to the new node

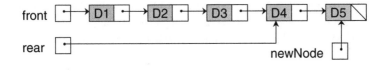

Step 3: set rear to the new node

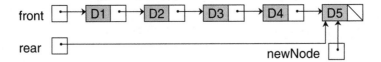

As mentioned earlier, dequeue is similar to pop. However, if the queue becomes empty after a dequeue operation, the front and rear pointers must both be set to null. Here is the code:

```
public Object dequeue(){
    if (isEmpty())
        throw new IllegalStateException ("Trying to dequeue an empty queue");

    Object item = front.value;
    front = front.next;
    if (front == null)
        rear = null;
    count--;
    return item;
}
```

Completion of the LinkedQueuePT is left as an exercise.

8.3.2   Array Implementation

The array implementations of stacks and queues have less in common than the linked implementations. The array implementation of a stack needs to access items at only the logical end of the array. However, the array implementation of a queue must access items at the logical beginning and the logical end. Doing this in a computationally effective manner is complex, so we approach the problem in a sequence of three attempts.

A First Attempt

Our first attempt at implementing a queue fixes the front of the queue at index position 0 and maintains an index variable, called rear, that points to the last item at position $n - 1$, where n is the number of items in the queue. A picture of such a queue, with four items in an array of six cells, is shown in Figure 8.4. For this implementation, enqueue operations are efficient; however, dequeue operations entail shifting all but the first item in the array to the left, which is an O(n) process.

Figure 8.4   **An array implementation of a queue with four items**

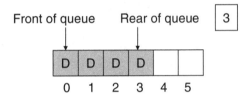

A Second Attempt

We can avoid dequeue's linear behavior by not shifting items left each time the operation is applied. The modified implementation maintains a second index, called front, that points to the item at the front of the queue. The front pointer starts at 0 and advances through the array as items are dequeued. Figure 8.5 shows such a queue after five enqueue and two dequeue operations.

Figure 8.5   **An array implementation of a queue with a front pointer**

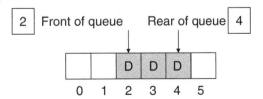

Notice that, in this precedure, cells to the left of the queue's front pointer are unused until we shift all elements left, which we do whenever the rear pointer is about to run off the end. Now the maximum run time of dequeue is O(1), but at the cost of boosting the maximum run time of enqueue from O(1) to O(n).

A Third Attempt

By using a *circular array implementation,* we can simultaneously achieve good run times for both `enqueue` and `dequeue`. The implementation resembles the previous one in two respects:

1. The rear pointer starts at –1 and the front pointer starts at 0.

2. The front pointer chases the rear pointer through the array. During `enqueue`, the rear pointer moves further ahead of the front pointer, and during `dequeue`, the front pointer catches up by one position.

However, when either pointer is about to run off the end of the array, it is reset to 0. This has the effect of wrapping the queue around to the beginning of the array without the cost of moving any items.

As an example, let us assume that an array implementation uses six cells, that six items have been enqueued, and that two items have then been dequeued. According to this procedure, the next enqueue resets the rear pointer to 0. Figure 8.6 shows the state of the array before and after the rear pointer is reset to 0 by the last enqueue operation.

Figure 8.6   **Wrapping data around a circular array implementation of a queue**

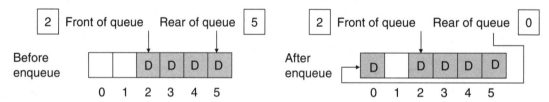

The rear pointer now appears to chase the front pointer until the front pointer reaches the end of the array, at which point it too is reset to 0. As you can readily see, the maximum run times of both `enqueue` and `dequeue` are now O(1).

The alert reader will naturally wonder what happens when the queue becomes full and how the implementation can detect this condition. By maintaining a count of the items in the queue, we can determine if the queue is full or empty. When this count equals the size of the array, we know it's time to resize, assuming that we are using a dynamic array implementation.

After resizing, we would like the queue to occupy the initial segment of the array, with the front pointer set to 0. To achieve this, we consider two cases at the beginning of the resizing process:

1. The front pointer is less than the rear pointer. In this case, we loop from `front` to `rear` in the original array and copy to positions 0 through count - 1 in the new array.

2. The rear pointer is less than the front pointer. In this case, we loop from `front` to count - 1 in the original array and copy to positions 0 through count -

front - 1 in the new array. We then loop from 0 to rear in the original array and copy to positions count - front to count - 1 in the new array.

The resizing code for enqueue and dequeue is more complicated than the code for push and pop, but the process is still linear. Completion of the various implementations of class ArrayQueuePT is left as an exercise.

8.3.3 Time and Space Analysis for the Two Implementations

The time and space analysis for the two queue prototypes parallels that for the corresponding stack prototypes, so we do not dwell on the details. Consider first the linked implementation of queues. The maximum run time of all methods is O(1), and the total space requirement is $2n + 2$, where n is the size of the queue.

For the circular array implementation of queues, if the array is static, then the maximum run time of all methods is O(1). If the array is dynamic, enqueue and dequeue jump to O(n) anytime the array is resized but retain an average run time of O(1). Space utilization for the array implementation again depends on the load factor. For load factors above .5, an array implementation makes more efficient use of memory than a linked implementation, and for load factors below .5, use is less efficient.

Exercises 8.3

1. Discuss the pros and cons of using doubly rather than singly linked lists to implement queues.

2. Implement and test the class LinkedQueuePT. Remember that this class implements QueuePT and Serializable.

3. Implement the class ArrayQueuePT using the circular array strategy discussed in this section. The enqueue method should throw an exception if the array is full. Remember that this class implements QueuePT and Serializable.

4. Modify your implementation of ArrayQueuePT from Exercise 3 so that the array is resized when its load factor reaches a critical point. Show that maximum run times for enqueue and dequeue are now O(n), but that the average run times are still O(1).

5. This exercise involves implementing a queue iterator. (Skip this exercise if you have already done its counterpart in Section 7.4.)

   a. Add an iterator method to QueuePT and implement it in Array QueuePT and LinkedQueuePT. A queue iterator returns items in order from oldest to youngest, where the oldest item is the one enqueued least recently. We do not want to allow users of a queue to remove any item except the first; therefore, the iterator's remove method should throw an exception.

   ```
   throw new UnsupportedOperationException("Remove not allowed");
   ```

   b. How will this restriction affect the behavior of a queue's collection-view?

c. Although an iterator's `remove` method throws an exception rather than modifying the structure of the underlying queue, the iterator can still throw a `ConcurrentModificationException`. Explain why.

6. Add an abstract class `AbstractQueuePT` as a superclass of `ArrayQueuePT` and `LinkedQueuePT`. In this class, declare the `iterator` method as abstract. Then use the iterator to implement each of the following methods:

```
toString
toArray
collectionView
equals
```

(Skip this question if you have already done its counterpart in Section 7.4.)

7. Rewrite the `toString` method using `StringBuffer` instead of `String`. How does this affect the method's run time? (Skip this question if you have already done its counterpart in Section 7.4.)

8.4   Two Applications of Queues

We now look briefly at two applications of queues: one involving computer simulations and the other round-robin CPU scheduling.

8.4.1   Simulations

Computer simulations are used to study the behavior of real-world systems, especially when it is impractical or dangerous to experiment with these systems directly. For example, a computer simulation could mimic traffic flows on a busy highway. Urban planners could then experiment with factors affecting traffic flows, such as the number and types of vehicles on the highway, the speed limits for different types of vehicles, the number of lanes in the highway, the frequency of tollbooths, and so forth. Outputs from such a simulation might include the total number of vehicles able to move between designated points in a designated period and the average duration of a trip. By running the simulation with many combinations of inputs, the planners could determine how best to upgrade sections of the highway, subject to the ever-present constraints of time, space, and money.

As a second example, consider the problem faced by the manager of a supermarket when trying to determine the number of checkout clerks to schedule at various times of the day. Some important factors in this situation are:

■ the frequency with which new customers arrive

■ the number of checkout clerks available

■ the number of items in a customer's shopping cart

■ the period of time considered

These factors could be inputs to a simulation program, which would then determine the total number of customers processed, the average time each customer waits for service, and the number of customers left standing in line at the end of the simulated time period. By varying the inputs, particularly the frequency of customer arrivals and the number of available checkout clerks, a simulation program could help the manager make effective staffing decisions for busy and slow times of the day. By adding an input that quantifies the efficiency of different checkout equipment, the manager can even decide whether it is cheaper to add more clerks or buy better equipment.

A common characteristic of both examples, and of simulation problems in general, is the moment-by-moment variability of essential factors. Consider the frequency of customer arrivals at checkout stations. If customers arrived at precise intervals, each with exactly the same number of items, it would be easy to determine how many clerks to have on duty. However, such regularity does not reflect the reality of a supermarket. Sometimes several customers show up at practically the same instant, and at other times no new customers arrive for several minutes. In addition, the number of items varies from customer to customer, and therefore, so does the amount of service required by each customer. All this variability makes it impossible to devise formulas to answer simple questions about the system, such as how customer waiting time varies with the number of clerks on duty. A simulation program, on the other hand, avoids the need for formulas by imitating the actual situation and collecting pertinent statistics.

Simulation programs use a simple technique to mimic variability. For instance, suppose new customers are expected to arrive on average once every 4 minutes. Then during each minute of simulated time, a program can generate a random number between 0 and 1. If the number is less than .25, the program adds a new customer to a checkout line; otherwise, it does not. More sophisticated techniques based on probability distribution functions produce even more realistic results. Obviously, each time the program runs, the results change slightly, but this only adds to the realism of the simulation.

Now let us discuss the common role played by queues in these examples. Both examples involve service providers and service consumers. In the first example, service providers include tollbooths and traffic lanes, and service consumers are the vehicles waiting at the tollbooths and driving in the traffic lanes. In the second example, clerks provide a service that is consumed by waiting customers. To emulate these conditions in a program, we associate each service provider with a queue of service consumers.

Simulations operate by manipulating these queues. At each tick of an imaginary clock, a simulation adds varying numbers of consumers to the queues and gives consumers at the head of each queue another unit of service. Once a consumer has received the needed quantity of service, it leaves the queue and the next consumer steps forward. During the simulation, the program accumulates statistics such as how many ticks each consumer waited in a queue and the percentage of time each provider is busy. The duration of a tick is chosen to match the problem being simulated. It could represent a millisecond, a minute, or a decade. In the program itself, a tick probably corresponds to one pass through the program's major processing loop.

Object-oriented languages are well suited to implementing simulation programs. For instance, in a supermarket simulation, each customer is an instance of a `Customer` class. A customer object keeps track of when the customer starts standing in line, when service is first received, and how much service is required. Likewise, a clerk is an instance of a `Clerk` class, and each clerk object contains a queue of customer objects. A simulator class coordinates the activities of the customers and clerks. At each clock tick, the simulation object

- generates new customer objects as appropriate
- assigns customers to cashiers
- tells each cashier to provide one unit of service to the customer at the head of the queue

We develop a program based on these ideas in the chapter's first case study, and we will ask you to extend the program in a series of exercises.

8.4.2   Round-Robin CPU Scheduling

Most modern computers allow multiple processes to share a single CPU. There are various techniques for scheduling these processes. The most common, **round-robin scheduling,** adds new processes to the end of a **ready queue,** which consists of processes waiting to use the CPU. Each process on the ready queue is dequeued in turn and given a slice of CPU time. When the time slice runs out, the process is returned to the rear of the queue, as shown in Figure 8.7.

Figure 8.7   **Scheduling processes for a CPU**

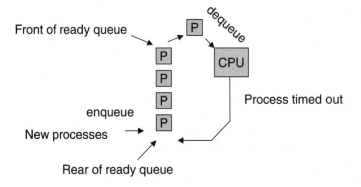

Generally, not all processes need the CPU with equal urgency. For instance, user satisfaction with a computer is greatly influenced by the computer's response time to keyboard and mouse inputs; thus, it makes sense to give precedence to processes handling these inputs. Round-robin scheduling adapts to this requirement by using a priority queue and assigning each process an appropriate priority. As a follow-up to this discussion, the chapter's second case study shows how a priority queue can be used to schedule patients in an emergency room.

Exercise 8.4

Suppose customers in a 24-hour supermarket are ready to be checked out at the precise rate of one every 2 minutes. Suppose also that it takes exactly 5 minutes for one clerk to process one customer. How many clerks need to be on duty to meet the demand? Will customers need to wait in line? How much idle time will each clerk experience per hour? Now suppose that the rates—one customer every 2 minutes and 5 minutes per customer—represent averages. Describe in a qualitative manner how this will affect customer waiting time. Will this change affect the average amount of idle time per clerk? For both situations, describe what happens if the number of clerks is decreased or increased.

8.5   Interface for a Professional Version

The JDK does not include a queue abstract data type, a shortcoming that programmers can surmount by using lists (see Chapter 9) in a restricted manner. However, to provide a more appealing alternative, we have added a queue ADT to `lamborne`. The professional versions of queues and stacks have much in common, differing only in their fundamental methods. The supporting and general methods are the same for both. The queue interface is listed in Table 8.3. As with stacks, we expect implementations to avoid the possibility of queues becoming full.

Table 8.3   **The Interface for `lamborne.Queue`**

Fundamental Methods	
`Object`	`dequeue()` Returns the item at the head of this queue and removes it from the queue. Throws an exception if the queue is empty.
`void`	`enqueue(Object item)` Adds an item to the tail of this queue. Throws an exception if the item is `null`.
Supporting Methods	
`boolean`	`isEmpty()` Returns `true` if this queue contains no items.
`Object`	`peek()` Returns the item at the head of this queue without removing it from the queue. Throws an exception if the queue is empty.
`int`	`size()` Returns the number of items in this queue.
General Methods	
`void`	`clear()` Removes all items from this queue.
`Object`	`clone()` Returns a shallow copy of this queue. (Does not need to be included here because it will be inherited from `Object`.)
`Collection`	`collectionView()` Returns a collection-view of the items contained in this queue. This collection-view should support none of the optional methods—`add`, `addAll`, `remove`, `removeAll`, `retainAll`—as they violate a stack's basic contract.

continued

Table 8.3	The Interface for `lamborne.Queue` *(Continued)*	
`boolean`	`equals(Object other)`	Returns `true` if the other object is a queue that equals this queue. To be equal, two queues must contain equal items appearing in the same order.
`int`	`hashCode()`	Returns the hash code value for this queue. (Please ignore this method for now. We discuss hashing in Chapter 13.)
`Iterator`	`iterator()`	Returns an iterator over the items contained in this queue. The iterator provides the items in their queue order (from first to last). The iterator's `remove` method is not supported because it violates a queue's basic contract. The `remove` method should throw an `UnsupportedOperationException`.
`Object[]`	`toArray()`	Returns an array containing all of the items in this queue. The head of the queue corresponds to the first item in the array.
`String`	`toString()`	Returns a string that lists the items in this queue. The head of the queue corresponds to the first item in the string. (Does not need to be included here because it will be inherited from `Object`.)

8.6 Implementation of the Professional Version (optional pv)

The professional implementations of queues and stacks are so similar in their general structure that we forgo a discussion in this section; however, Figure 8.8 shows the relevant hierarchy diagram, followed by Tables 8.4 and 8.5 and a listing of the interface and class headers. (Note that `ArrayQueue` is not actually implemented in `lamborne` but is left as an exercise.)

Figure 8.8   The queue class hierarchy in `lamborne`

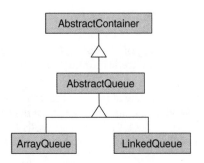

Table 8.4

The Methods of the Queue Implementation and Their Run Times

Queue Implementation		Abstract Container	Abstract Queue	Linked Queue
Constructors				
constructor	()	O(1)	O(1)	O(1)
constructor	(Collection col)			O(n)
constructor	(Iterator iter)			O(n)
Fundamental Methods				
void	enqueue (Object item)			O(1)
Object	dequeue ()			O(1)
Supporting Methods				
boolean	isEmpty()	O(1)		
Object	peek ()			O(1)
int	size ()	O(1)		
General Methods				
void	clear ()	O(1)		O(1)
Object	clone ()			O(n)
Collection	collectionView ()	O(1)		
boolean	equals (Object other)		O(n)	
int	hashCode ()	O(n)		
Iterator	iterator ()	abstract		O(1)
Object []	toArray ()	O(n)		
String	toString ()	O(n)		

Table 8.5

The Relationship between Queue Classes and the Interfaces They Implement

Name of Class	Interfaces Implemented
AbstractContainer	Serializable
AbstractQueue	
ArrayQueue	Cloneable, Queue
LinkedQueue	Cloneable, Queue

```
public interface Queue

abstract public class AbstractContainer implements Serializable

abstract public class AbstractQueue extends AbstractContainer

public class LinkedQueue extends AbstractQueue implements Queue, Cloneable
```

Exercises 8.6

1. The queue iterator does not support removal. Write a test program that confirms a queue's collection-view object does not support removal either. Explain why this is the case. (*Tip:* Look at the source code for `AbstractCollection`.) (Skip this exercise if you have already done its counterpart in Section 7.7.)

2. Implement your own version of `AbstractQueue` and `LinkedQueue`. To do so, import `lamborne.Queue` and `lamborne.AbstractContainer` but no other classes from `lamborne`. Your versions of `AbstractQueue` and `LinkedQueue` are not part of `lamborne`, so do not include the line

```
package lamborne;
```

at the beginning of each file. (Skip this exercise if you have already done its counterpart in Section 7.7.)

3. In Chapter 6, the `clear` method for class `Tiny` involved only `Abstract Container`, yet for queues the method also involves `LinkedQueue`. Explain why. (Skip this exercise if you have already done its counterpart in Section 7.7.)

4. Add a column to the queue implementation in Table 8.4. This column is for a dynamic array implementation, and it should be labeled **Array Queue.** You should be able to complete the run-time information in the column without actually doing the implementation.

5. Implement a professional version of `ArrayQueue` using a dynamic array and add it to your copy of `lamborne`. The iterator-based constructor should include an integer parameter indicating the initial capacity of the array.

8.7   Case Study 1: Simulating a Supermarket Checkout Line

In this case study, we develop a program to simulate supermarket checkout stations. To keep the program simple, we omit some important factors and ask the reader to add them as part of the exercises.

8.7.1   Request

Write a program that allows the user to predict the behavior of a supermarket checkout line under various conditions.

8.7.2   Analysis

For the sake of simplicity, we impose the following restrictions:

■ There is just one checkout line, staffed by one cashier.

■ Each customer has the same number of items to check out and requires the same processing time.

■ The probability that a new customer will arrive at the checkout does not vary over time.

The inputs to our simulation program are:

■ The total time, in abstract minutes, that the simulation is supposed to run.

■ The number of minutes required to serve an individual customer.

■ The probability that a new customer will arrive at the checkout line during the next minute. This probability should be a floating-point number greater than 0 and less than or equal to 1.

The program's outputs are the total number of customers processed, the number of customers left in the line when time runs out, and the average waiting time for a customer. Table 8.6 summarizes the inputs and outputs.

Table 8.6   **The Inputs and Outputs of the Supermarket Checkout Simulator**

Inputs	Ranges of Values for Inputs	Outputs
Total minutes	$0 < \text{total} <= 1{,}000$	Total customers processed
Average minutes per customer	$0 < \text{average} <= \text{total}$	Customers left in line
Probability of a new customer arrival in the next minute	$0 < \text{probability} <= 1$	Average waiting time

The Interface

We propose the interface in Figure 8.9 for the system.

Figure 8.9   **The user interface for the supermarket checkout simulator**

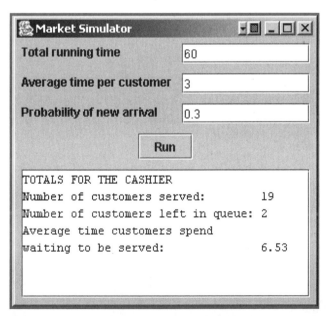

Classes and Responsibilities

As far as classes and their overall responsibilities are concerned, we divide the system into a view class and several model classes. The view class, called `Market View`, is responsible for interacting with the user, validating the three input values, and communicating with the model. The design and implementation of the class `MarketView` are straightforward, and its code can be found on the book's CD. The classes in the model are in Table 8.7.

Table 8.7	**The Classes in the Model**
Class	*Responsibilities*
`MarketModel`	A market model object:
	1. Runs the simulation.
	2. Creates a cashier object.
	3. Sends new customer objects to the cashier.
	4. Maintains an abstract clock.
	5. During each tick of the clock, tells the cashier to provide another unit of service to a customer.
`Cashier`	A cashier object:
	1. Contains a queue of customer objects.
	2. Adds new customers to this queue when directed to do so.
	3. Removes customers from the queue in turn.
	4. Gives the current customer a unit of service when directed to do so and releases the customer when service has been completed.
`Customer`	A customer object:
	1. Knows the customer's arrival time and how much service the customer needs.
	2. Knows when the cashier has provided enough service.
	The class as a whole generates new customers when directed to do so according to the probability of a new customer arriving.
`Queue`	Used by a cashier to represent a line of customers.

The Object Diagram

The relationships among these classes are shown Figure 8.10.

Figure 8.10   **An object model diagram of the supermarket checkout simulator**

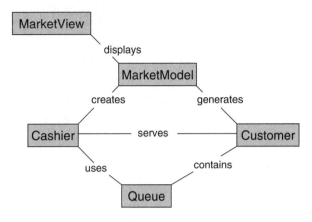

8.7.3   Overall Design

The overall design of the system is reflected in the following message diagram:

Figure 8.11   **A message diagram of the supermarket checkout simulator**

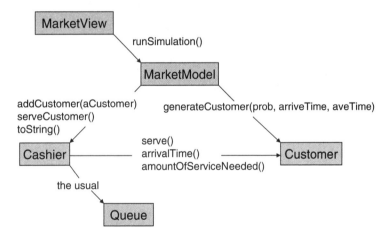

We now design and implement each class in turn.

8.7.4   Design of `MarketModel`

Because we have restricted the checkout situation, design of the class `Market Model` is fairly simple. The constructor

1. Saves the inputs—probability of new arrival, length of simulation, and average time per customer.

2. Creates the single cashier.

The only other method needed is runSimulation. This method runs the abstract clock that drives the checkout process. On each tick of the clock, the method does three things:

1. Asks the Customer class to generate a new customer, which it may or may not do depending on the probability of a new arrival and the output of a random number generator.

2. If a new customer is generated, sends the new customer to the cashier.

3. Tells the cashier to provide a unit of service to the current customer.

When the simulation ends, the runSimulation method returns the cashier's results to the view. Here is the pseudocode for the method:

```
for each minute of the simulation
    ask the Customer class to generate a new customer
    if a customer is generated
        cashier.addCustomer (customer)
    cashier.serveCustomers (current time)
return cashier's results
```

8.7.5   Implementation of **MarketModel**

Here is a complete listing of the class MarketModel:

```
1 public class MarketModel {
2
3    private Cashier cashier;
4    private double  probabilityOfNewArrival;
5    private int     lengthOfSimulation, averageTimePerCus;
6
7    public MarketModel(int lengthOfSimulation,
8                       int averageTimePerCus,
9                       double probabilityOfNewArrival)
10   {
11       this.probabilityOfNewArrival = probabilityOfNewArrival;
12       this.lengthOfSimulation = lengthOfSimulation;
13       this.averageTimePerCus = averageTimePerCus;
14       cashier = new Cashier();
15   }
16
17   public String runSimulation()
18   {
19       // Run the clock for n ticks, where n = lengthOfSimulation
20       for (int currentTime = 0; currentTime < lengthOfSimulation;
21            currentTime++) {
22
23           // Ask the Customer class to generate a new customer
24           Customer customer =
25                   Customer.generateCustomer (probabilityOfNewArrival,
26                                              currentTime,
27                                              averageTimePerCus);
28
```

Continued

Continued

```
29              // Send customer to cashier if successfully generated
30              if (customer != null)
31                  cashier.addCustomer (customer);
32
33              // Tell cashier to provide another unit of service
34              cashier.serveCustomers (currentTime);
35          }
36          return cashier.toString();
37      }
38 }
```

Note that the `Customer` method `generateCustomer` receives from the model the probability of a new customer arriving, the current time, and the average time needed per customer. The `Customer` class uses this information to determine whether to create a customer and, if it does, how to initialize the customer.

8.7.6   Design of `Cashier`

A cashier is responsible for serving a queue of customers. During this process, the cashier tallies the customers served and the minutes they spend waiting in line. At the end of the simulation, the class's `toString` method returns these totals as well as the number of customers remaining in the queue. The class has the instance variables

`totalCustomerWaitTime`

`customersServed`

`queue`

`currentCustomer`

The last variable holds the customer currently being processed.

To allow the market model to send a new customer to a cashier, the class implements the method `addCustomer`. This method expects a customer as a parameter and adds the customer to the cashier's queue.

The method `serveCustomers` handles the cashier's activity during one clock tick. The method expects the current time as a parameter and responds in one of several different ways, as listed in Table 8.8.

Here is pseudocode for the method `serveCustomers`:

```
if currentCustomer is null
    if queue is empty
        return
    else
        currentCustomer = queue.dequeue()
        totalCustomerWaitTime = totalCustomerWaitTime +
                                currentTime -
                                currentCustomer.arrivalTime()
        customersServed++
currentCustomer.serve()
if currentCustomer.amountOfServiceNeeded() == 0
    currentCustomer = null
```

Table 8.8 **Responses of a Cashier during a Clock Tick**

Condition	What It Means	Action to Perform
The current customer is `null` and the queue is empty.	There are no customers to serve.	None; just return.
The current customer is `null` and the queue is not empty.	There is a customer waiting at the front of the queue.	• Dequeue a customer and make him the current customer. • Ask him when he was instantiated, determine how long he has been waiting, and add that time to the total waiting time for all customers. • Increment the number of customers served. • Give the customer one unit of service and dismiss him if he is finished.
The current customer is not `null`.	Serve the current customer.	Give the customer one unit of service and dismiss him if he is finished.

8.7.7 Implementation of `Cashier`

Here is the code for the `Cashier` class:

```
1 import lamborne.*;
2 public class Cashier {
3
4     private int       totalCustomerWaitTime, customersServed;
5
6     private Customer currentCustomer;
7     private Queue     queue;
8
9     public Cashier(String name)
10     {
11        totalCustomerWaitTime = 0;
12        customersServed = 0;
13        currentCustomer = null;
14        queue = new LinkedQueue();
15     }
16
17     public void addCustomer(Customer c)
18     {
19        queue.enqueue(c);
20     }
21
22     public void serveCustomers(int currentTime)
23     {
24        if (currentCustomer == null){
25           // No customers yet
26           if (queue.isEmpty())
27              return;
```

Continued

Continued

```
28              else{
29                  // Dequeue first waiting customer and tally results
30                  currentCustomer = (Customer) queue.dequeue();
31                  totalCustomerWaitTime = totalCustomerWaitTime +
32                                          currentTime -
33                                          currentCustomer.arrivalTime();
34              customersServed++;
35          }
36      }
37
38      // Give a unit of service
39      currentCustomer.serve();
40
41      // If current customer is finished, send him away
42      if (currentCustomer.amountOfServiceNeeded() == 0)
43          currentCustomer = null;
44  }
45
46  public String toString()
47  {
48      String str = "TOTALS FOR THE CASHIER\n" +
49                   "Number of customers served:        " +
50                   customersServed + "\n";
51      if (customersServed != 0){
52          double aveWaitTime = (double)totalCustomerWaitTime /
53                               customersServed;
54          str += "Number of customers left in queue: " +
55                 queue.size() + "\n" +
56                 "Average time customers spend\n" +
57                 "waiting to be served:        " +
58                 Format.justify('l', aveWaitTime, 5, 2);
59      }
60      return str;
61  }
62 }
```

8.7.8 Design of `Customer`

The `Customer` class maintains a customer's arrival time and the amount of service needed. The constructor initializes these with data provided by the market model. The instance methods include:

- `arrivalTime()`: Returns the time at which the customer arrived at a cashier's queue.
- `amountOfServiceNeeded()`: Returns the number of service units left.
- `serve()`: Decrements the number of service units by one.

The remaining method, `generateCustomer`, is `static`. This method expects the parameters probability of a new customer arriving, current time, and number of service units per customer. The method returns a new instance of Customer with the given time and service units provided the probability is greater than or equal to a random number between 0 and 1. Otherwise, the method returns `null`, indicating that no customer was generated.

8.7.9   Implementation of `Customer`

Here is the code for the `Customer` class:

```
1 public class Customer {
2
3    private int arrivalTime;
4    private int amountOfServiceNeeded;
5
6    // Returns a Customer object if the probability of arrival is
7    // greater than or equal to a random number between 0 and 1
8    // Otherwise, returns null, indicating no new customer
9    public static Customer generateCustomer(double probabilityOfNewArrival,
10                                            int arrivalTime,
11                                            int averageTimePerCustomer)
12    {
13       if (Math.random() <= probabilityOfNewArrival)
14          return new Customer(arrivalTime, averageTimePerCustomer);
15       else
16          return null;
17    }
18
19    public Customer(int arrivalTime, int serviceNeeded)
20    {
21       this.arrivalTime = arrivalTime;
22       this.amountOfServiceNeeded = serviceNeeded;
23    }
24
25    public int arrivalTime()
26    {
27       return arrivalTime;
28    }
29
30    public int amountOfServiceNeeded()
31    {
32       return amountOfServiceNeeded;
33    }
34
35    // Accepts a unit of service from the cashier
36    public void serve()
37    {
38       amountOfServiceNeeded--;
39    }
40 }
```

Exercises 8.7

1. The simulator's interface asks the user to enter the average number of minutes required to process a customer; however, as written, the simulation assigns the same processing time to each customer. In real life, processing times vary around the average. Modify the `Customer` class's constructor so that it randomly generates service times between 1 and (average * 2 + 1).

2. Observe that results can vary considerably for the same set of inputs from run to run. Explain why. Does this diminish the usefulness of the results or change the manner in which one should interpret the results? Now modify the simulation so that it accepts another input, namely, the number of times the simulation should be repeated before returning the results. When the results are returned, they should reflect all of these repetitions. Determine how increasing the number of repetitions affects the variability of the results.

3. Run the simulator with the run time equal to 1,000, the probability of new arrivals equal to .25, and the average service time per customer varying from 1 to 10. Make two graphs, the first showing the average service time per customer versus the number of customers served and the second showing the average service time per customer versus the number of customers left in line. Explain the observed results.

4. Modify the simulator's interface so that it accepts the number of cashiers as input. At the beginning of a simulation, the model should create this number of cashiers. During the simulation, pass each new customer to the cashier with the fewest customers. For a slightly more complex variant, pass each new customer to the cashier who has the least work remaining. To compute the work remaining, a cashier considers the service requirements of the customers.

5. Design and implement a simulation that would help city planners determine the best settings for a traffic light at a four-way intersection. In the first version, assume that left turns are forbidden. Later, you can consider left turns with and without the presence of a turning lane. Remember that when a light turns green, all cars are not the same distance from the intersection, and they do not all surge forward simultaneously.

8.8   Priority Queues

As mentioned earlier, the queue ADT can be extended to the notion of a priority queue. When items are added to a priority queue, they are assigned a rank order. When they are dequeued, items of higher priority are removed before those of lower priority. Items of equal priority are dequeued in the usual FIFO order. The `lamborne` package includes a `PriorityQueue` interface that extends the `Queue` interface through the addition of a single method

```
void enqueue(Object item, int priority)
```

where `priority` is a positive integer representing the priority of the item being enqueued. Items can still be enqueued using the method

```
void enqueue(Object item)
```

and they are assigned a default priority of 1.

The `lamborne` package includes two implementation of `PriorityQueue`. These are called `HeapPriorityQueue` and `LinkedPriorityQueue`. The first is discussed in Chapter 12, and the second is examined shortly. The constructor for `LinkedPriorityQueue` has the form

```
LinkedPriorityQueue(int maxPriority)
```

where `maxPriority` is a positive integer indicating the highest priority to be used with this priority queue.

The next code segment shows how to declare and use a priority queue.

```
// Create a new priority queue to hold items with priorities 1 and 2
PriorityQueue q = new LinkedPriorityQueue (2);

// Add the integers 1,2,3 to the queue with a priority of 1
for (int i = 1; i <= 3; i++)
    q.enqueue(new Integer(i), 1);

// Add the integers 10,11,12 to the queue with a priority of 2
for (i = 10; i <= 12; i++)
    q.enqueue(new Integer(i), 2);

// Dequeue and display all integers in the queue
while (! q.isEmpty())
    System.out.println(((Integer)q.dequeue()).intValue());
```

In this example, integers go onto the priority queue in the order 1, 2, 3, 10, 11, 12, but leave in the order 10, 11, 12, 1, 2, 3, thus demonstrating the role played by priorities.

8.8.1 Implementation of a Linked Priority Queue

We now discuss the implementation of a linked priority queue. For the sake of simplicity, we will do so in the context of a prototype. Table 8.9 gives the interface.

Table 8.9   **The Interface for the Priority Queue Prototype**

PriorityQueuePT Interface Extends QueuePT

void   **enqueue(Object item)**
Adds an item to the tail of the subqueue with priority 1. Throws an exception if the item is `null`.

void   **enqueue(Object item, int priority)**
Adds an item to the tail of the subqueue with the specified priority. Throws an exception if the item is `null` or the priority is not between 1 and the maximum priority allowed for this priority queue.

The linked implementation is based on an array of subqueues, and an item with priority n goes on the queue at index position $n - 1$. Figure 8.12 shows a priority queue with four priorities. We call this a linked implementation because each array element contains a reference to a queue. The completion of the linked implementation of priority queues is left as an exercise.

Figure 8.12   **A linked priority queue with four priorities**

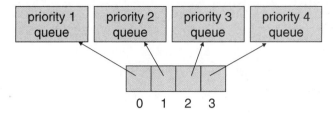

Exercises 8.8

1. Implement a linked priority queue and call it `LinkedPriorityQueuePT`. Do not forget to include the clause

```
implements PriorityQueuePT, Serializable
```

The class has two constructors. The default constructor throws an exception because this constructor should never be used. The second constructor expects an integer that specifies the number of priorities to be used in the queue.

2. Perform a complexity analysis of the linked priority queue's methods. Be sure to analyze the use of memory as well as the run time.

3. One drawback to the suggested implementation of priority queues is that the number of priorities must be fixed when the priority queue is instantiated.

   a. Devise a remedy for this problem.

   b. Implement your solution.

8.9   Case Study 2: An Emergency Room Scheduler

8.9.1   Request

Write a program that allows a supervisor to schedule treatments for patients coming into a hospital's emergency room. Because some patients are in more critical condition than others, they are not treated on a strictly first-come, first-served basis but are assigned a priority when admitted. Patients with a high priority receive attention before those with a lower priority.

8.9.2   Analysis

Patients come into the emergency room in one of three conditions, which in ascending order of priority are:

1. fair

2. critical

3. serious

The program allows the user to enter a patient's name and condition. When the user selects the Schedule button, the patient is placed in line for treatment according to the severity of his or her condition. When the user selects the Treat Next Patient button, the program removes and displays the patient first in line with the most serious condition. When the user selects the Treat All Patients button, the program removes and displays all patients in order from patient to serve first to patient to serve last.

Each command button produces an appropriate message in the output area. Table 8.10 lists the interface's responses to the commands:

Table 8.10 **The Commands of the Emergency Room Program**

Command	Response
Schedule	`<patient name>` is added to the `<condition>` list
Treat Next Patient	`<patient name>` is being treated
Treat All Patients	`<patient name>` is being treated
	. . .
	`<patient name>` is being treated

8.9.3 Proposed Interface

We now propose the interface in Figure 8.13 for the system. The application is divided into a view class, called ERView, and a model class, called ERModel. As usual, view interacts with the user and sends messages to the model. The model maintains a priority queue of patients. The development of the system is left as a programming project.

Figure 8.13   **The user interface for the emergency room program**

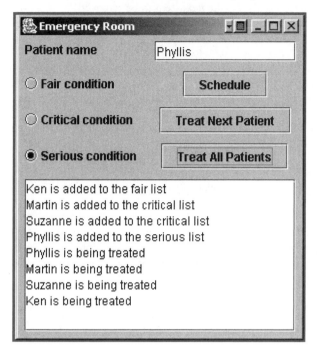

Exercise 8.9

Design and implement the emergency room scheduler. Do not forget to include an object model diagram and a message diagram.

circular array implementation	front	round-robin scheduling
dequeue	priority queue	simluation
enqueue	ready queue	
	rear	

CHAPTER SUMMARY

The queue collection has a wide range of applications in computer science. Most of these, such as simulations and resource allocation in operating systems, involve scheduling.

A queue enforces first-in, first-out processing of items. That is, the item least recently inserted is always the next item to be removed.

A queue is a linear collection. The item most recently inserted is at the rear of the queue, whereas the next item to be removed is at the front of the queue. The enqueue operation adds an item to the rear, whereas the dequeue operation removes an item from the front. The only other operations return a queue's size, test it for emptiness, and return the item at the front.

A queue can support an iterator, but the iterator should not support a method to remove items.

There are several array-based implementations of a queue. The best linked implementation uses a doubly linked structure.

A priority queue is collection that attaches a priority to each item when it is inserted. The higher its priority, the closer an item is to the front of the queue. Items with the same priority are processed in a first-in, first-out manner. A linked implementation of a priority queue uses a single queue of items for each priority value.

REVIEW QUESTIONS

1. Name three common applications of queues.

2. Name one application that should not use a queue.

3. Why does an array implementation of a queue require more effort and planning than an array implementation of a stack?

4. Describe three different strategies for using an array to implement a queue.

5. Why would you use a doubly linked structure rather than a singly linked structure to implement a queue?

6. What is the difference between a queue and a priority queue?

7. Name two applications of priority queues.

8. What is the difference between a priority queue and a sorted array?

CHAPTER 9

Lists

OBJECTIVES Upon completion of this chapter, you should be able to

- Describe the formal properties of lists
- Give examples of applications of lists
- Discuss at least two common ways in which lists are implemented and the criteria for choosing between them

This chapter covers lists, the last of the three major linear ADTs discussed in the book, the other two being stacks and queues. Lists support a much wider range of operations than stacks and queues and, consequently, are both more widely used and more difficult to implement. To make sense of a list's profusion of fundamental operations, we classify them into three groups: index-based, content-based, and position-based operations. We present prototypes that illustrate the two most common list implementations: arrays and linked structures. The package `java.util` includes professional versions based on both approaches, and we examine these. The chapter's case study shows how to implement a common desktop tool: a personal to-do list.

9.1   Overview of Lists

A list supports manipulation of items at any point within a linear collection and is unlike stacks and queues, which restrict access only to the ends. Some common examples of lists include:

- a *recipe,* which is a list of instructions
- a *string,* which is a list of characters
- a *document,* which is a list of words
- a *file,* which is a list of data blocks on disk

In all these examples, order is critically important, and shuffling the items renders the collections meaningless; however, the items in a list are not necessarily sorted.

Words in a dictionary and names in a phone book are examples of sorted lists, but the words in this paragraph equally form a list and are unsorted. In Chapter 12, we discuss sorted lists in detail. While the items in a list are always logically contiguous, they need not be physically contiguous. Array implementations of lists use physical position to represent logical order, but linked implementations do not.

We say that the first item in a list is at the **head** and the last is at the **tail.** Using this terminology, we can characterize a stack as a list in which manipulations are restricted to the head and a queue as a list in which insertions are made at the tail and removals from the head. If we relax these restrictions slightly and allow insertions and deletions to occur at both the head and the tail, we have what is called a **deque,** or **double-ended queue.**

In a list, items retain position relative to each other over time, and additions and deletions affect predecessor/successor relationships only at the point of modification. Figure 9.1 shows how a list changes in response to a succession of operations. The operations are:

add(o)   Adds object o to a list's tail.

add(i, o)   Inserts object o at the *i*th index in a list, where the first item is at index 0.

remove(o)   Removes the first instance of object o from a list.

remove(i)   Removes the object at the *i*th index in a list.

set(i, o)   Replaces the object at the *i*th index with object o.

Figure 9.1   **The states in the lifetime of a list**

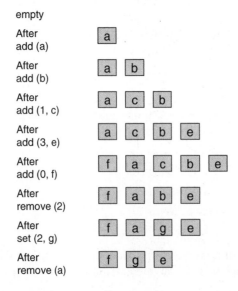

empty

After
add (a)

After
add (b)

After
add (1, c)

After
add (3, e)

After
add (0, f)

After
remove (2)

After
set (2, g)

After
remove (a)

9.2   A List Prototype

The fundamental operations for stacks and queues are universally agreed on—push and pop for stacks and enqueue and dequeue for queues—but for lists, there are no such standards. For instance, the operation of putting a new item in a list is sometimes called "add" and sometimes "insert." However, if we look at most textbooks on data structures and at the list ADT provided in Java, we can discern several broad categories of operations, which we call index-based operations, content-based operations, and position-based operations. Before trying to write list prototypes, we present these categories, and to avoid confusion later, we proceed in a manner that is consistent with the approach taken in the interfaces `java.util.List` and `java.util.ListIterator`.

Index-based operations manipulate items at designated indexes within a list and provide the convenience of random access. Suppose a list contains n items. Because a list is linearly ordered, we can unambiguously refer to an item in a list via its relative position from the head of the list using an index that runs from 0 to $n - 1$. Thus, the head is at index 0 and the tail is at index $n - 1$. Here are some fundamental index-based operations:

`add(i, o)` Opens up a slot in the list at index `i` and inserts object `o` in this slot.

`get(i)`   Returns the object at index `i`.

`remove(i)` Removes and returns the object at index `i`.

`set(i, o)` Replaces the object at index `i` with the object `o` and returns the original object.

When viewed from this perspective, lists are sometimes called *vectors* or *sequences,* and in their use of indexes, they are reminiscent of arrays. However, an array is a concrete data type with a specific and unvarying implementation based on a single block of physical memory, whereas a list is an abstract data type that can be represented in a variety of different ways, among which are array implementations. In addition, a list has a much larger repertoire of basic operations than an array, even though all list operations can be mimicked by suitable sequences of array operations.

Content-based operations are based on the content of a list, not on an index. Most of these operations search for an object equal to a given object before taking further action. Here are some basic content-based operations:

`add(o)`   Adds object `o` at a list's tail.

`contains(o)` Returns `true` if a list contains an object equal to object `o`.

`indexOf(o)`   Returns the index of the first instance of object `o` in a list.

`remove(o)`   Removes the first instance of object `o` from a list and returns `true` if `o` is removed, else returns `false`.

Position-based operations are performed relative to a currently established position within a list, and in `java.util`, they are provided via an extended iterator called a *list iterator.* A list iterator uses the underlying list as a backing collection, and the iterator's current position is always in one of three places:

1. just before the first item

2. between two adjacent items

3. just after the last item

Initially, when a list iterator is first instantiated, the position is immediately before the first item. From this position, the user can either navigate to another position or modify the list in some way. Here are the navigational operations:

`hasNext()`	Returns `true` if there are any items following the current position.
`next()`	Returns the next item and advances the position.
`hasPrevious()`	Returns `true` if there are any items preceding the current position.
`previous()`	Returns the previous item and moves the position backward.
`nextIndex()`	Returns the index of the next item or −1 if none.
`previousIndex()`	Returns the index of the previous item or −1 if none.

Conspicuously absent from this roster of operations are ones for moving directly to either the beginning or end of a list. The authors of `java.util` omitted these operations for reasons best known to themselves. The lack of an operation for returning to the head of a list is not critical because instantiating a new list iterator has the same effect; however, a succession of next operations is the only way to move to a list's tail. We will endure this defect, but in the exercises at the end of Sections 9.4 and 9.6, we ask you to remedy the problem.

The remaining position-based operations are used to modify the backing list. These operations work at the currently established position in the list:

`add(o)`	Inserts object o at the current position.
`remove()`	Removes the last item returned by next or previous.
`set(o)`	Replaces the last item returned by next or previous.

Although there are many list operations, our classification system reduces the potential confusion. Table 9.1 gives a recap.

Based on the foregoing discussion of list operations, we now propose two list prototypes. Bear in mind that these are just prototypes and include only those operations needed to illustrate the basic issues involved in implementing lists. The first prototype, `ListPT`, includes several index-based and content-based operations. The second prototype, `ListIteratorPT`, contains position-based operations.

Table 9.1　　**Summary of Basic List Operations**

Index-Based	Content-Based	Position-Based
add(i, o)	add(o)	hasNext()
get(i)	contains(o)	next()
remove(i)	indexOf(o)	hasPrevious()
set(i, o)	remove(o)	previous()
		nextIndex()
		previousIndex()
		add(o)
		remove()
		set(o)

This split of the list ADT into two components is consistent with the design decisions made in `java.util`. The split has the major advantage that one can have several list iterators going at once over the same underlying list. However, there is an accompanying disadvantage. A list iterator can be invalidated if changes are made to the underlying list by any means other than through the list iterator in question. To deal with the problem, list iterators follow the same fail-fast policy as regular iterators. As soon as a list iterator detects an unexpected change in the backing list, it throws an exception. List iterators are created by sending the `listIterator` message to a list. This is analogous to the manner in which we create regular iterators for stacks and queues. Tables 9.2 and 9.3 formalize our definitions of `ListPT` and `ListIteratorPT`.

Table 9.2　　**The `ListPT` Interface**

Fundamental Methods

void	**add(int i, Object o)** Adds the object o to the list at index i. Throws an exception if the object o is null or the list is full or if i is out of range (i < 0 || i > size()).
boolean	**contains(Object o)** Returns true if the object o is in the list, else returns false.
Object	**get(int i)** Returns the object at index i. Throws an exception if i is out of range (i < 0 || i >= size()).
int	**indexOf(Object o)** Returns the index of the first object equal to object o or –1 if there is none.

continued

Table 9.2	**The `ListPT` Interface (Continued)**

`Object`	`remove(int i)` Removes and returns the object at index `i`. Throws an exception if `i` is out of range (`i < 0 or i >= size()`).
`Object`	`set(int i, Object o)` Returns the object at index `i` after replacing it with the object `o`. Throws an exception if the object `o` is `null` or if `i` is out of range (`i < 0 or i >= size()`).

Supporting Methods

`boolean`	`isEmpty()` Returns `true` if this list contains no items.
`boolean`	`isFull()` Returns `true` if this list is full and can accept no more items.
`int`	`size()` Returns the number of items in this list.

General Methods

`ListIteratorPT`	`listIterator()` Returns a list iterator over this list.

Table 9.3	**The `ListIteratorPT` Interface**

Navigation Methods

`boolean`	`hasNext()` Returns `true` if there are any items after the current position, else returns `false`.
`boolean`	`hasPrevious()` Returns `true` if there are any items preceding the current position, else returns `false`.
`Object`	`next()` Returns the item following the current position and advances the current position. Throws an exception if `hasNext` would return `false`.
`Object`	`previous()` Returns the item preceding the current position and moves the current position back. Throws an exception if `hasPrevious` would return `false`.

Modification Methods

`void`	`add(Object o)` Inserts the object `o` at the current position. After insertion, the current position is located immediately after the newly inserted item. Throws an exception if the object `o` is `null` or the list is full.

Table 9.3	**The `ListIteratorPT` Interface (Continued)**

`void`	`remove()` Removes the last object returned by `next` or `previous`. Throws an exception if `add` or `remove` has occurred since the last `next` or `previous`.
`void`	`set(Object o)` Replaces the last object returned by `next` or `previous` with object o. Throws an exception if `add` or `remove` has occurred since the last `next` or `previous`.

Exercises 9.2

1. Which of the list operations discussed in this section should be include in a sorted list ADT and which new operations, if any, should be added? Do any of the operations behave differently in lists and sorted lists? Give reasons for your answers.

2. Write the code for the interfaces `ListPT` and `ListIteratorPT`. For each method, include comments that state the preconditions and postconditions.

3. Extend `ListPT` and `ListIteratorPT` to include all of the list operations discussed in this section.

9.3   Using Lists

To make certain there are no ambiguities in the meaning of the operations that have been given, we now present two examples that show sequences of these operations in action. First, in Table 9.4, we present a sequence of list operations.

Table 9.4	**Effects of Operations on a List**		
List Operation	*State of the List after the Operation*	*Value Returned*	*Comment*
			Initially, the list is empty.
`add(0,a)`	a		The list contains the single item **a**.
`add(1,b)`	a b		**a** is the head, **b** is the tail.
`add(1,c)`	a c b		**c** is at index 1.
`isEmpty()`	a c b	`false`	The list is not empty.
`size()`	a c b	3	The list contains three items.
`indexOf(b)`	a c b	2	The index of **b** is 2.
`indexOf(q)`	a c b	−1	**q** is not in the list.

continued

Table 9.4   **Effects of Operations on a List** *(Continued)*

List Operation	State of the List after the Operation	Value Returned	Comment
`contains(c)`	a c b	true	**c** is in the list.
`get(1)`	a c b	c	Return c, which is at index 1.
`get(3)`	a c b	exception	The index is out of range, so throw an exception.
`set(2,e)`	a c e	b	Replace **b** at index 2 with **e** and return **b**.
`remove(0)`	c e	a	Remove **a** at position 0 and return it. **b** is now at the head of the list.
`remove(2)`	c e	exception	The index is out of range, so throw an exception.
`remove(1)`	c	e	Remove and return **e**.
`remove(0)`		c	Remove and return **c**.
`isEmpty()`		true	The list is empty.
`remove(0)`		exception	The index is out of range, so throw an exception.
`set(0,a)`		exception	The index is out of range, so throw an exception.

Second, in the Table 9.5, we present a sequence of list iterator operations and indicate the state of the underlying list after each operation. Remember that a list iterator's current position is located before the first item, after the last item, or between two items. In the table, the current position is indicated by a comma and by an integer variable called current position. Suppose the list contains n items. Then

current position $= i$ if it is located before the item at index i, where $i = 0, 1, 2, \ldots, n - 1$

current position $= n$ if it is located after the last item

Table 9.5   **The Effects of Iterator Operations on a List**

List Iterator Operation	Current Position after the Operation	State of the List after the Operation	Value Returned	Comment
instantiate a new list iterator over a list that contains the items a b c	0	,a b c	a list iterator object	Initially, the list contains **a**, **b**, and **c**, and the current position equals 0. The following operations use this iterator object, and some change the state of the underlying list.

Table 9.5　　　**The Effects of Iterator Operations on a List** *(Continued)*

List Iterator Operation	Current Position after the Operation	State of the List after the Operation	Value Returned	Comment
hasNext()	0	,a b, c	true	There are items following the current position.
next()	1	**a,** b, c	a	Return **a** and advance the current position.
next()	2	a, **b,** c	b	Return **b** and advance the current position.
remove()	1	a, c	void	Remove **b,** the last item returned by previous or next. Note the location of the current position.
add(b)	2	a b, c	void	Insert **b** immediately to the left of the current position indicator.
next()	3	a b **c,**	c	Return **c** and advance the current position.
next()	3	a b c,	exception	The current position is at the end of the list; therefore, it is impossible to retrieve a next item.
hasNext()	3	a b c,	false	The current position is at the end of the list; therefore, there is no next item.
hasPrevious()	3	a b c,	true	There are items preceding the current position.
previous()	2	a b, **c**	c	Return **c** and move the current position backward.
remove()	2	a b,	void	Remove **c,** the last item returned by previous or next. Note the location of the current position.
previous()	1	a, **b**	b	Return **b** and move the current position backward.
set(e)	1	a, **e**	void	Replace **b**, the last item returned by previous or next. The item **e** is now considered the last item returned.
add(b)	2	a b, e	void	Insert **b** immediately to the left of the current position indicator.

continued

Table 9.5   **The Effects of Iterator Operations on a List** *(Continued)*

List Iterator Operation	Current Position after the Operation	State of the List after the Operation	Value Returned	Comment
add(c)	3	a b c, e	void	Insert **c** immediately to the left of the current position indicator.
remove()	3	a b c, e	exception	add has occurred since the last next or previous.
previous()	2	a b, **c** e	c	Return **c** and move the current position backward.
previous()	2	a, **b** c e	c	Return **b** and move the current position backward.

Notice in Table 9.5 that there is always a current position. From the specification for the list iterator interface, we know that remove and set operate on the last item returned by a successful next or previous operation, provided there have been no intervening add or remove operations. In the table, we highlight this last item returned in boldface. If no item is highlighted, then remove and set are invalid. The highlighted item, when present, can be on either side of the current position indicator—on the left after a next operation or on the right after a previous operation.

Exercises 9.3

1. Assume you are given the list (a, b, c), which contains the three items a, b, and c in the indicated order. Construct a table similar to Table 9.5 that shows the state of the list after the following sequence of list iterator operations:
```
next()
next()
remove()
previous()
add(d)
next()
hasNext()
```

2. Write a code segment that creates a new list, adds three items to it, and uses index-based operations to print the items in reverse order.

3. Write a code segment that creates a new list, adds three items to it, and uses an iterator to print the items in reverse order.

4. Write a short tester program that runs some of the methods in the list prototype. You will use this program in the next section.

9.4 Implementations of the List Prototype

In this section, we develop two implementations of the list prototype. The first uses a static array, and the second uses a doubly linked structure. In each case, we provide a partial implementation and tips on how to complete it. The completion of both implementations, as well as the development of alternative implementations, are left as exercises.

9.4.1 Static Array Implementation

The static array implementation stores the list's items in an array whose size remains fixed. We assume that the list can hold no more than, say, 100 items. After the 100th item is added, the method `isFull` returns `true`.

The implementation, `ArrayListPT`, has the following components:

- a class header
- variable declarations
- a constructor definition
- other method definitions
- a private inner class for the list iterator called `ListIter`

The listing follows after a few preliminary remarks. First, some methods are shown in their entirety, but for others, only their position is indicated. Second, insertions in and deletions from a list are accomplished using array manipulation algorithms described in Chapter 5. Third, as you read the code for the inner class `ListIter`, refer to Table 9.5. Pay particular attention to the current position indicator and the last item returned by `next` and `previous`. In the code, the iterator's `add` operation is done relative to the iterator's current position as recorded in the variable `curPos`. The iterator's `set` and `remove` operations are applied to the item returned by the most recent call to `next` or `previous`. The position of this returned item is indicated by the variable `lastItemPos`, and this variable is set to −1 whenever there is no valid item to `set` or `remove`.

```
1  import java.util.*;                        //Contains exception classes
2  import java.io.Serializable;               //The Serializable interface
3
4  public class ArrayListPT implements ListPT, Serializable {
5
6      private static int DEFAULT_CAPACITY = 100;      //Maximum size of list
7      private Object items[];                         //The array of items
8      private int size;                        // Number of items in the list
9      private int modCount;        //Number of times the list has been modified
10
11     public ArrayListPT()                             //Default constructor
12     {
13         items = new Object[DEFAULT_CAPACITY];
14         size = 0;
```

Continued

Continued

```
15        modCount = 0;
16     }
17
18     public void add (int index, Object item) {        //Adds a new item at the
19                                                       //given index if possible
20        if (item == null)
21           throw new IllegalArgumentException ("Cannot insert null");
22        if (isFull())                        //If list full, throw an exception
23           throw new IllegalStateException ("List is full");
24        if (index < 0 || index > size)  //If out of range, throw an exception
25           throw new IndexOutOfBoundsException
26           ("Index " + index + " out of range");
27
28        for (int i = size; i > index; i—)              //Shift items to right
29              items[i] = items[i - 1];
30        items[index] = item;                           //Insert new item
31        size++;
32        modCount++;
33     }
34
35     public ListIteratorPT listIterator()
36     {
37        return new ListIter();
38     }
39
40     //Other ListPT methods go here and are left as an exercise
41     //Note 1: the remove method increments modCount
42     //Note 2: the set method does not change modCount
43     .........
44     .........
45     .........
46
47 //================= inner class ListIter =========================
48
49     private class ListIter implements ListIteratorPT, Serializable{
50
51        private int curPos;
52           //Current position indicator with respect to the backing list
53           //Equals i if immediately before the item at index i
54           //Equals size() if after the last item
55
56        private int lastItemPos;
57           //Equals index of last item returned by next or previous
58           //Equals -1 initially and after add and remove
59
60        private int expectedModCount;
61           //This iterator's notion of modCount
62
63        private ListIter()                                        //Constructor
64        {
65           curPos = 0;
66           lastItemPos = -1;
67           expectedModCount = modCount;
68        }
69
70        // Methods for navigation
```

Continued

```
71
72      public boolean hasNext()        //Returns true if there are items after
73      {                                          //the current position
74         return curPos < size;
75      }
76
77      public boolean hasPrevious() //Returns true if there are items before
78      {                                          //the current position
79         return curPos > 0;
80      }
81
82      public Object next(){                      //Returns the next item
83         if (modCount != expectedModCount)
84            throw new ConcurrentModificationException();
85         if (!hasNext())
86            throw new NoSuchElementException("There are no more elements");
87
88         lastItemPos = curPos;    //Remember index of the last item returned
89         curPos++;                       //Advance the current position
90         return items[lastItemPos];
91      }
92
93      public Object previous(){                  //Returns the previous item
94         if (modCount != expectedModCount)
95            throw new ConcurrentModificationException();
96         if (!hasPrevious())
97            throw new NoSuchElementException("There are no more elements");
98
99         lastItemPos = curPos - 1;    //Remember the index of the last item
100                                                 //returned
101         curPos--;                       //Move the current position backward
102         return items[lastItemPos];
103      }
104
105     // Methods for modifications
106
107      public void add(Object o)        //Adds object o at the current position
108      {
109     //This is left as an exercise.
110     //Throw an exception if expectedModCount != modCount
111     //Make the addition at curPos via the backing list's add method, which
112     //    will increment modCount or
113     //    will throw an exception if object o is null or the list is full
114     //Increment curPos and expectedModCount
115     //Set lastItemPos equal -1
116      }
117
118      public void remove()          //Removes the most recently retrieved item
119      {
120         if (modCount != expectedModCount)
121            throw new ConcurrentModificationException();
122         if (lastItemPos == -1)
123            throw new IllegalStateException
124            ("There is no established item to remove.");
125
```

Continued

Continued

```
126            ArrayListPT.this.remove(lastItemPos);    //Call the backing list's
127                              //remove method, which will increment modCount
128            expectedModCount++;          //Increment expectedModCount as well
129            if (lastItemPos < curPos)   //If the item removed was obtained via
130              curPos--;          //next, then move the current position back
131            lastItemPos = -1;  //Block remove and set until after a successful
132                                            //next or previous
133          }
134
135       public void set(Object o) //Replaces the most recently retrieved item
136       {
137          //This is left as an exercise
138          //Throw an exception if expectedModCount != modCount
139          //Throw an exception if lastItemPos == -1
140          //Make the replacement via backing list's set method, which
141          //    will throw an exception if the object o is null but
142          //    will not change modCount
143          //Do not change modCount, expectedModCount, lastItemPos, curPos
144       }
145     }
146 }
```

The completion of the code is left as an exercise.

9.4.2 Doubly Linked Implementation

The implementation consists of a doubly linked structure with sentinel node, and the algorithms for insertion and deletion of items come from Chapter 5. The implementation uses two private inner classes: one for the iterator and the other for a two-way node. As you will see, the linked and array implementations are very similar in organization, and the variables curPos and lastItemPos play the same role in each. Here is the code:

```
1 import java.util.*;                         //Contains exception classes
2 import java.io.Serializable;                //The Serializable interface
3
4 public class LinkedListPT implements ListPT, Serializable {
5
6    private TwoWayNode head;                             //Sentinel node
7    private int size;                        //Number of items in the list
8    private int modCount;        //Number of times the list has been modified
9
10
11 //Constructor — sets up circular linked structure with a dummy header node
12    public LinkedListPT()
13    {
14       head = new TwoWayNode(null, null, null);
15       head.next = head;
16       head.previous = head;
17       size = 0;
18       modCount = 0;
19    }
20
```

Continued

Continued

```
21      //Adds item to list at index
22      public void add (int index, Object item)
23      {
24         if (item == null)
25            throw new IllegalArgumentException ("Cannot insert null");
26         if (index < 0 || index > size)
27            throw new IndexOutOfBoundsException
28            ("Index " + index + " out of range");
29
30         //Locate node before insertion point
31         TwoWayNode nodeBefore = getNode (index - 1);
32
33         //Create new node and link it into the list
34         TwoWayNode newNode = new TwoWayNode (item, nodeBefore,
35                                              nodeBefore.next);
36         nodeBefore.next.previous = newNode;
37         nodeBefore.next = newNode;
38
39         size++;
40         modCount++;
41      }
42
43      public boolean contains (Object item){
44         // Traverse the links looking for item
45         // and return true if it is found
46         TwoWayNode probe = head.next;
47         while (probe != head)
48            if (item.equals (probe.value))
49               return true;
50            else
51               probe = probe.next;
52
53         // Item not found so return false
54         return false;
55       }
56
57      public boolean isEmpty(){
58         return size() == 0;
59      }
60
61      public boolean isFull(){
62         return false;
63      }
64
65      public Object get(int index){
66         if (index < 0 || index >= size)
67            throw new IllegalArgumentException ("Index " + index +
68                                                " out of range");
69         return getNode(index).value;
70      }
71
72      // Helper method that returns the ith node
73      private TwoWayNode getNode (int i){
74         TwoWayNode ithNode = head;
75         for (int k = -1; k < i; k++)
```

Continued

Continued

```
 76            ithNode = ithNode.next;
 77        return ithNode;
 78    }
 79
 80    public ListIteratorPT iterator()//Returns iterator for this collection
 81    {
 82        return new ListIter();
 83    }
 84
 85    public Object peek(){
 86        if (isEmpty())
 87            throw new IllegalStateException ("Peeking at an empty list");
 88        return head.next.value;
 89    }
 90
 91    //Removes the node and item at the indicated index
 92    public Object remove(int index){
 93        if (index < 0 || index >= size)
 94            throw new IndexOutOfBoundsException
 95            ("Index " + index + " out of range");
 96
 97        //Locate the node before the one that is being deleted
 98        TwoWayNode nodeBefore = getNode(index - 1);
 99
100        //Remember the node being removed
101        TwoWayNode nodeRemoved = nodeBefore.next;
102
103        //Link around the removed node
104        nodeRemoved.next.previous = nodeBefore;
105        nodeBefore.next = nodeRemoved.next;
106
107        size--;
108        modCount++;
109        return nodeRemoved.value;
110    }
111
112    public Object set(int index, Object newItem){
113        if (index < 0 || index >= size)
114            throw new IllegalArgumentException ("Index " + index +
115                                              " out of range");
116        if (newItem == null)
117            throw new IllegalArgumentException("Cannot insert null");
118        TwoWayNode ithNode = getNode(index);
119        Object oldItem = ithNode.value;
120        ithNode.value = newItem;
121        return oldItem;
122    }
123
124    public int size(){
125        return size;
126    }
127
128    public String toString(){
129        String str = "";
130
131        // Traverse the array concatenating the string
```

Continued

Continued

```
132        // representations of the items
133        for (TwoWayNode probe = head.next; probe != head; probe = probe.next)
134            str += probe.value.toString() + " ";
135
136        return str;
137    }
138
139 //================= inner class TwoWayNode =========================
140
141    private class TwoWayNode extends Object{
142
143        private Object     value;     //Value stored in this node
144        private TwoWayNode next;       //Reference to next node
145        private TwoWayNode previous; //Reference to previous node
146
147        private TwoWayNode(){
148            value = null;
149            previous = null;
150            next = null;
151        }
152
153        private TwoWayNode(Object value){
154            this.value = value;
155            previous = null;
156            next = null;
157        }
158
159        private TwoWayNode(Object value,
160                           TwoWayNode previous,
161                           TwoWayNode next){
162            this.value = value;
163            this.previous = previous;
165            this.next = next;
165        }
166    }
167
168 //================= inner class ListIter =========================
169
170    private class ListIter implements ListIteratorPT, Serializable{
171
172        private TwoWayNode curPos;
173    //Current position indicator with respect to the backing store
174    //Points at the node which would be returned by next
175    //The current position is considered to be immediately before this node
176    //If curPos == head then at end of list
177    //If curPos.previous == head then at beginning of list
178
179        private TwoWayNode lastItemPos;
180          //Points at the last item returned by next or previous
181          //Equals null initially and after add and remove
182
183        private int expectedModCount;
184          //This iterator's notion of modCount
185
186        private ListIter()                                      //Constructor
```

Continued

Continued

```
187        {
188            curPos = head.next;          //Points at first item if there is one
189            lastItemPos = null;
190            expectedModCount = modCount;
191        }
192
193        // Methods for navigation
194
195        public boolean hasNext()      //Returns true if there are items after
196        {                                             //the current position
197            return curPos != head;
198        }
199
200        public boolean hasPrevious() //Returns true if there are items before
201        {                                             //the current position
202            return curPos.previous != head;
203        }
204
205        public Object next(){                    //Returns the next item.
206            if (modCount != expectedModCount)
207                throw new ConcurrentModificationException();
208            if (!hasNext())
209                throw new NoSuchElementException("There are no more elements");
210
211          lastItemPos = curPos;//Remember the index of the last item returned
212            curPos = curPos.next;              //Advance the current position
213            return lastItemPos.value;
214        }
215
216        public Object previous(){                //Returns the previous item
217            if (modCount != expectedModCount)
218                throw new ConcurrentModificationException();
219            if (!hasNext())
220                throw new NoSuchElementException("There are no more elements");
221
222          lastItemPos = curPos.previous;//Remember the index of the last item
223
224            curPos = curPos.previous;      //Move the current position backward
225            return lastItemPos.value;
226        }
227
228        // Methods for modifications
229
230        public void add(Object o)      //Adds object o at the current position
231        {
232            if (modCount != expectedModCount)
233                throw new ConcurrentModificationException();
234            if (o == null)
235                throw new IllegalArgumentException("Cannot insert null");
236
237            //Create new node for object o
238            TwoWayNode newNode = new TwoWayNode(o, curPos.previous, curPos);
239
240            //Link the new node into the list
241            curPos.previous.next = newNode;
242            curPos.previous = newNode;
```

Continued

Continued

```
243
244          //curPos does not change
245
246          size++;
247          modCount++;
248          expectedModCount++;
249          lastItemPos = null;//Block remove and set until after a successful
250                                              //next or previous
251      }
252
253      public void remove()        //Removes the most recently retrieved item
254      {
255          if (modCount != expectedModCount)
256              throw new ConcurrentModificationException();
257          if (lastItemPos == null)
258              throw new IllegalStateException
259              ("There is no established item to remove.");
260
261          if (lastItemPos == curPos)  //If item being removed is the same as
262              curPos = curPos.next;              //curPos, then advance curPos
263
264          //Link around the item being removed
265          lastItemPos.previous.next = lastItemPos.next;
266          lastItemPos.next.previous = lastItemPos.previous;
267
268          size--;
269          modCount++;
270          expectedModCount++;
271          lastItemPos = null;//Block remove and set until after a successful
272                                              //next or previous
273      }
274
275
276      public void set(Object o)// Replaces the most recently retrieved item
277      {
278          //This is left as an exercise
279          //Throw an exception if expectedModCount != modCount
280          //Throw an exception if lastItemPos == null
281          //Throw an exception if object o is null
282          //Replace the value of the node at lastItemPos
283          //Do not change modCount, expectedModCount, lastItemPos, curPos
284      }
285  }
286 }
```

Again, completion of the code is left as an exercise.

9.4.3 Time and Space Analysis for the Two Implementations

The run times of the list methods can be determined in two different ways:

1. We can examine the code and do the usual sort of analysis.

2. We can reason from more general principles.

Here we take the second approach. As a starting point, we consider three basic manipulations involving lists. The manipulations are locating the *i*th item, searching for a specified item, and either inserting or deleting an item at a preestablished position. Run times for these manipulations were established in Chapter 5, and for convenience, we list them again in Table 9.6.

Table 9.6

Average and Maximum Run Times for Three Basic Manipulations

	Locate the ith Item	Search for a Specified Item	Insert or Delete an Item at a Preestablished Position
Array	O(1)	O(n)	O(n)
Doubly Linked List	O(n)	O(n)	O(1)

Using the information in Table 9.6, we now estimate the complexity of the list's get(i) method to be O(1) for an array implementation and O(n) for a doubly linked implementation. The list's remove(o) method involves first locating a specified object and then removing it from a now established position. For both implementations, the operation is O(n)—array implementation locate O(n) + remove O(n), linked implementation locate O(n) + remove O(1). As a final example, consider the list iterator's remove() method, which removes an item at a preestablished position. The operation is O(n) for an array implementation and O(1) for a list implementation. Table 9.7 lists the complexity of the methods just discussed. Filling in the empty slots is left as an exercise.

Table 9.7

Average and Maximum Run Times for List Operations

ListPT *Method*	ArrayListPT	LinkedListPT
add(i, o)		
contains(o)		
get(i)	O(1)	O(n)
indexOf(o)		
isEmpty()		
isFull()		
listIterator()		
remove(i)	O(n)	O(n)
set(i, o)		
size()		
ListIteratorPT Method		
add(o)		
hasNext()		

Table 9.7 **Average and Maximum Run Times for List Operations** *(Continued)*

`ListIteratorPT` *Method*	`ArrayListPT`	`LinkedListPT`
`hasPrevious()`		
`next()`		
`previous()`		
`remove()`	$O(n)$	$O(n)$
`set(o)`		

A space analysis for list implementations follows the pattern already established for stacks and queues. The array implementation requires memory for the following items:

■ an array that can hold `capacity` references
■ a reference to the array
■ a variable called `size`
■ a variable called `modCount`

Thus, the total space requirement for the array implementation is `capacity` + 3. The linked implementation requires memory for the following items:

■ *n* data nodes plus one sentinel node, where each node contains three references
■ a variable called head that points to the sentinel
■ a variable called `size`
■ a variable called `modCount`

Thus, the total space requirement for the linked implementation is $3(n + 1) + 3 = 3n + 6$.

When comparing the memory requirements of the two implementations, one must remember that the space utilization for the array implementation depends on the load factor. For load factors above .33, an array implementation makes more efficient use of memory than a linked implementation, and for load factors below .33, use is less efficient.

Exercises 9.4

1. Complete Table 9.7, which shows average and maximum run times for list operations.
2. Complete the static array implementation of the list prototype.
3. Complete the doubly linked implementation of the list prototype.
4. Modify the array implementation to use a dynamic rather than a static array. How does this change affect the run time of the methods?

5. Modify the linked implementation so that it uses singly linked rather than doubly linked nodes. How does this change affect the run time of the methods?

6. In the linked implementation, modify the private method `getNode` so that it locates the *i*th node by moving in the direction that is most efficient, rather than always forward from the head toward the tail of the list. How does this change affect the run time of methods that use the `getNode` method?

7. Add operations `moveToHead()` and `moveToTail()` to the `ListIteratorPT` and to the implementations of this interface. For each implementation, what is the maximum run time for these operations?

8. Suppose you wanted to traverse a linked list to print its items. Give analyses of the complexity of a traversal that uses the method `get` with a loop. Then suggest a more efficient way to traverse a linked list.

9. Define and implement a sorted list ADT. As a starting point, refer to Exercise 1 in Section 9.2. Use either an array or a doubly linked implementations.

9.5   Three Applications of Lists

Lists have many applications. In this section, we look briefly at three: Java's object heap, organization of files on a disk, and implementation of other ADTs.

9.5.1   Heap Storage Management

In Section 7.5, we discussed one aspect of Java memory management, the call stack. Now we complete that discussion by showing how free space in the **object heap** can be managed using a linked list. Heap management techniques can have a significant impact on an application's overall performance, especially if the application creates and abandons many objects during the course of its execution. Implementers of Java Virtual machines are therefore willing to spend a great deal of effort to organize the heap in the most efficient manner possible. Their elaborate solutions are beyond this book's scope, so we present a simplified technique here.

In our technique, contiguous blocks of free space on the heap are linked together in a *free list*. When an application instantiates a new object, the JVM searches the free list for the first block large enough to hold the object and returns any excess space to the free list. When the object is no longer needed, the garbage collector returns the object's space to the free list. This technique as stated has two defects. Over time, large blocks on the free list become fragmented into many smaller blocks, and searching the free list for blocks of sufficient size can take $O(n)$ run time, where n is the number of blocks in the list. To counteract fragmentation, the garbage collector periodically reorganizes the free list by recombining physically adjacent blocks. To reduce search time, multiple free lists can be used. For instance, if an object reference requires 4 bytes, then list 1 could consist of blocks of size 4; list 2, blocks of size 8; list 3, blocks of size 16; list 4, blocks of size 32; and so forth. The last list would contain all blocks over some designated size. In this way, space is always allocated in units of 4 bytes, and space for a new object is taken from the head of the first nonempty list containing blocks of sufficient size. Allocating space for a new object now takes $O(1)$ time unless the object requires more space than is available in the first block of the last list. At that point, the last list must be searched, giving the operation a maximum run time of $O(n)$, where n is the size of the last list.

In this discussion, we have completely ignored two difficult problems. The first has to do with deciding when to run the garbage collector. Running the garbage collector takes time away from the application, but not running it means the free lists are never replenished. The second problem concerns how the garbage collector identifies objects that are no longer referenced and, consequently, no long needed.

9.5.2 Organization of Files on a Disk

A computer's file system has three major components: a directory of files, the files themselves, and free space. To understand how these work together to create a file system, we first consider a disk's physical format. Figure 9.2 shows the standard arrangement. The disk's surface is divided into concentric tracks, and each track is further subdivided into sectors. The numbers of these vary depending on the disk's capacity and physical size; however, all tracks contain the same number of sectors, and all sectors contain the same number of bytes. For the sake of this discussion, let us suppose that a sector contains 8K bytes of data plus a few additional bytes reserved for a pointer. A sector is the smallest unit of information transferred to and from the disk, regardless of its actual size, and a pair of numbers *(t, s)* specifies a sector's location on the disk, where t is the track number and s the sector number. Figure 9.2 shows a disk with n tracks. The k sectors in track 0 are labeled from 0 to $k - 1$.

Figure 9.2   **Tracks and sectors on the surface of a disk**

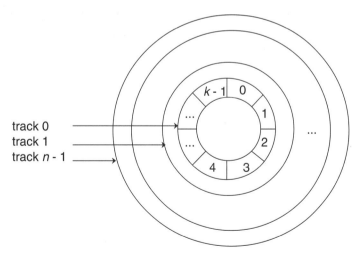

A file system's directory is organized as a hierarchical collection. The directory's internal structure is not a suitable topic for this chapter; however, let us suppose that it occupies the first few tracks on the disk and contains an entry for each file. This entry holds the file's name, creation date, size, and so forth. In addition, it holds the address of the sector containing the first bytes in the file. Depending on its size, a file might be completely contained within a single sector or it might span several. Usually, the last sector is only partially full, and no attempt is made to recover the unused space. The sectors that make up a file do not need to be physically adjacent because each sector, except the last, ends with a pointer to the sector containing the next portion of the file. Finally, sectors that are not in use are linked together in a free list. When new files are created, they are allocated space from this list, and when old files are deleted, their space is returned to the list.

Because all sectors are the same size and because space is allocated in sectors, a file system does not experience the same fragmentation problem encountered in Java's object heap. Nonetheless, there is still a difficulty. To transfer data to or from the disk, read/write heads must first be positioned to the correct track, the disk must rotate until the desired sector is under the heads, and then the transfer of data takes place. Of these three steps, the transfer of data takes the least time. Fortunately, data can be transferred to or from several adjacent sectors during a single rotation without the need to reposition the heads. Thus, a disk system's performance is optimized when multisector files are not scattered across the disk. However, over time, as files of varying sizes are created and destroyed, this sort of scattering becomes frequent, and the file system's performance degrades. As a countermeasure, file systems include a utility, run either automatically or at the explicit request of the user, that reorganizes the file system so that the sectors in each file are contiguous and have the same physical and logical order.

9.5.3 Implementation of Other ADTs

Lists are frequently used to implement other ADTs, such as stacks and queues. There are two ways to do this:

1. Extend the list class, making the new class a subclass of the list class.
2. Use an instance of the list class within the new class and let the list contain the data items.

For example, `java.util` implements a `Stack` class by extending a list class called `Vector`. However, extension is not a wise choice in this case because this version of `Stack` inherits the methods from `Vector` that allow users to access items at positions other than the top, thus violating the spirit of the stack ADT. In the case of stacks and queues, a better design decision is to contain a list within the stack or queue. In that case, all of the list operations are available to the implementer, but only the essential stack or queue operations are available to the user.

ADTs that use lists inherit their performance characteristics. For example, a stack that uses an array-based list has the performance characteristics of an array-based stack, whereas a stack that uses a link-based list has characteristics of a link-based stack.

The primary advantage of using a list ADT to implement another ADT is that coding becomes easier. Instead of operating on a concrete array or linked structure, the implementer of a stack need only call the appropriate list methods. The main disadvantage is that some additional space overhead can occur—for instance, when a stack is implemented using a list that in turn is based on doubly linked nodes. We saw in Chapter 7 that a singly linked list works well for the link-based implementation of a stack.

In Chapter 11 (trees), Chapter 13 (unordered collections), and Chapter 14 (graphs), we will see other situations in which lists can be used in the implementation of ADTs, although in the interest of optimizing performance, we do not always do so.

Exercises 9.5

1. Why do large blocks of memory on the heap's free list become fragmented over time?

2. Draw diagrams that illustrate the multilist technique of heap management and justify the run times given in the text. If there are n lists, assume each is referenced by an entry in an array of n items. Further, assume that initially all of the free space is contained in a single block in the last list.

3. How much unused space goes to waste when a file of 30,000 bytes is stored on a disk whose sector size is 8K bytes? Repeat the exercise for a file of 100 bytes.

4. Draw a diagram of a disk that shows how a file of 30,000 bytes might be stored in several noncontiguous sectors. Assume each sector contains 8K bytes plus a pointer in the form of *(t, s)*, where t is a track number and s is a sector number.

5. Assume a hard disk has the following performance characteristics:

time to move the read/write heads between any two tracks	10 msecs
sector size	8K bytes
sectors per track	63
rotational speed	10,000 rpm

   In addition, assume that you are working with a 10-sector file and the read/write heads are not already positioned on the track containing the first sector.

   a. What is the minimum time needed to read the file, assuming all sectors are contiguous and in matching physical and logical order?

   b. What is the maximum time needed to read the file if the sectors are all on the same track? How must the sectors be arranged on the track to achieve this maximum?

   c. What is the maximum time needed to read the file if the sectors are spread across 10 tracks?

6. Implement `StackPT` using an instance variable of type `ListPT`. Call the result `ListBasedStackPT`.

7. Demonstrate that the instance variable within the class `ListBasedStackPT` can be instantiated as either `ArrayListPT` or `LinkedListPT`.

9.6   Interface for a Professional Version

The package `java.util` includes a professional version of list and list iterator, and Tables 9.8 and 9.9 list the methods in their interfaces. There are an intimidating number of methods, but fortunately, we have already encountered the most important ones

Table 9.8 **The List Interface**

List Interface Extends Collection

Fundamental Methods

void	**add(int index, Object element)** Inserts the specified element at the specified position in this list (optional operation).
boolean	**add(Object o)** Appends the specified element to the end of this list (optional operation).
boolean	**contains(Object o)** Returns true if this list contains the specified element.
Object	**get(int index)** Returns the element at the specified position in this list.
int	**indexOf(Object o)** Returns the index in this list of the first occurrence of the specified element or –1 if this list does not contain this element.
int	**lastIndexOf(Object o)** Returns the index in this list of the last occurrence of the specified element or –1 if this list does not contain this element.
Object	**remove(int index)** Removes the element at the specified position in this list (optional operation).
boolean	**remove(Object o)** Removes the first occurrence in this list of the specified element (optional operation).
Object	**set(int index, Object element)** Replaces the element at the specified position in this list with the specified element (optional operation).

Supporting Methods

boolean	**isEmpty()** Returns true if this list contains no elements.
int	**size()** Returns the number of elements in this list.

General Methods

boolean	**addAll(Collection c)** Appends all of the elements in the specified collection to the end of this list, in the order that they are returned by the specified collection's iterator (optional operation).
boolean	**addAll(int index, Collection c)** Inserts all of the elements in the specified collection into this list at the specified position (optional operation).

Table 9.8 **The List Interface** *(Continued)*

List Interface Extends Collection

void	**clear()** Removes all of the elements from this list (optional operation).
Object	**clone()** Not officially listed here because it is inherited from Object.
boolean	**containsAll(Collection c)** Returns true if this list contains all of the elements of the specified collection.
boolean	**equals(Object o)** Compares the specified object with this list for equality.
int	**hashCode()** Returns the hash code value for this list. (Please ignore this method for now. We will discuss hashing in Chapter 13.)
Iterator	**iterator()** Returns an iterator over the elements in this list in proper sequence.
ListIterator	**listIterator()** Returns a list iterator of the elements in this list in proper sequence.
ListIterator	**listIterator(int index)** Returns a list iterator of the elements in this list in proper sequence, starting at the specified position in this list.
boolean	**removeAll(Collection c)** Removes from this list all of the elements that are contained in the specified collection (optional operation).
boolean	**retainAll(Collection c)** Retains only the elements in this list that are contained in the specified collection (optional operation).
List	**subList(int fromIndex, int toIndex)** Returns a view of the portion of this list between the specified fromIndex, inclusive, and toIndex, exclusive.
Object	**toArray()** Returns an array containing all of the elements in this list in proper sequence.
Object[]	**toArray(Object[] a)** Returns an array containing all of the elements in this list in proper sequence; the run-time type of the returned array is that of the specified array.
String	**toString()** Not officially listed here because it is inherited from Object.

Table 9.9   **The `ListIterator` Interface**

ListIterator Interface Extends Iterator

Navigation Methods

boolean	**hasNext()**
	Returns `true` if there are any items after the current position, else returns `false`.
boolean	**hasPrevious()**
	Returns `true` if there are any items preceding the current position, else returns `false`.
Object	**next()**
	Returns the item following the current position and advances the current position. Throws an exception if `hasNext` would return `false`.
Object	**previous()**
	Returns the item preceding the current position and moves the current position back. Throws an exception if `hasPrevious` would return `false`.

Modification Methods

void	**add(Object o)**
	Inserts the object `o` at the current position. After insertion, the current position is located immediately after the newly inserted item. Throws an exception if the object `o` is `null` or the list is full.
void	**remove()**
	Removes the last object returned by `next` or `previous`. Throws an exception if `add` or `remove` has occurred since the last `next` or `previous`.
void	**set(Object o)**
	Replaces the last object returned by `next` or `previous` with object `o`. Throws an exception if `add` or `remove` has occurred since the last `next` or `previous`.

Index Methods

int	**nextIndex()**
	Returns the index of the element that would be returned by a subsequent call to `next`.
int	**previousIndex()**
	Returns the index of the element that would be returned by a subsequent call to `previous`.

in our list prototype. The interfaces `List` and `ListIterator` extend `Collection` and `Iterator`, respectively. The descriptions for many of the methods are quoted directly from Java's online documentation.

The package `java.util` provides two principal implementations of `List`. These are `ArrayList` and `LinkedList`, and their performance characteristics match those of the corresponding implementations of `ListPT`. The class `Vector` also implements `List`, but it should probably be ignored because it seems to be included for the sake of maintaining backward compatibility with earlier versions of the JDK.

9.7 Implementation of the Professional Version (optional pv)

The implementation classes for lists in `java.util` are numerous and complex and were written without any consideration for making them easy to read. In contrast, the classes for stacks and queues were written to be easily understood while still being professional. Instead of a detailed discussion in this section, we present an overview followed by an extended set of exercises.

The list implementation classes are organized in a hierarchy that is similar to the one for stacks and queues discussed in Chapters 7 and 8 (Figure 9.3). The interfaces implemented by each class are shown in Table 9.10.

Figure 9.3   **The hierarchy of list classes**

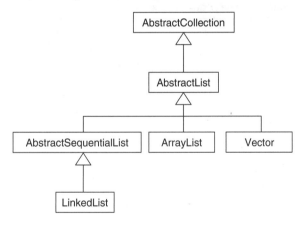

Table 9.10   **The Relationship between List Classes and the Interfaces They Implement**

Name of Class	Interfaces Implemented
AbstractCollection	Collection
AbstractList	List
AbstractSequentialList	
LinkedList	List, Cloneable, Serializable
ArrayList	List, Cloneable, Serializable
Vector	List, Cloneable, Serializable

As usual, the abstract classes make heavy use of iterators to implement general methods such as toArray and methods that map other collections into lists such as addAll and removeAll. Table 9.11 lists, with the exception of Vector, all of the list implementation classes, their methods, and their complexities. Note the following points about Table 9.11:

1. m indicates the number of items in the Collection c parameter.
2. n indicates the number of items in this collection, the receiver of the message.
3. We assume that an iterator's remove method has a maximum run time less than or equal to O(n).
4. UOE indicates that the method throws an UnsupportedOperationException.
5. *irm* is short for "iterator's remove method."
6. *am* is short for "add method."
7. i' means min (1, i, $n - i$).

Table 9.11   Implementation Scheme for the List Classes

List Implementation		Abstract Collection	Abstract List	Abstract Sequential List	Linked Array	Array List
		Constructors				
constructor()		O(1)	O(1)	O(1)	O(1)	O(1)
constructor(initCapacity)		O(m)				O(1)
constructor(Collection c)		O(am)			O(m)	O(m)
		Fundamental Methods				
void	add(int i, object o)		UOE	O(n)	O(i')	O($n - i$)
boolean	add(Object o)	UOE-	O(n)		O(1)	O(n)
boolean	contains(Object o)	O(n)			O(n)	O(n)
Object	get(int i)		abstract	O(i)	O(i')	O(1)
int	indexOf(Object o)		O(n)		O(n)	O(n)
int	lastindexOf(Object o)		O(n)		O(n)	O(n)
Object	remove(int i)		UOE	O(n)	O(i')	O($n - i$)
boolean	remove(Object o)	O(n) O(irm)			O(n)	
Object	set(int i, Object o)		UOE	O(n)	O(i')	O(1)
		Supporting Methods				
boolean	isEmpty()	O(1)				
int	size()	abstract			O(1)	O(1)

Table 9.11   **Implementation Scheme for the List Classes *(Continued)***

List Implementation		Abstract Collection	Abstract List	Abstract Sequential List	Linked Array	Array List
General Methods						
boolean	addAll (Collection c)	$O(m)$			$O(m)$	$O(m + n)$
boolean	addAll(int i, Collection c)	$O(am)$	$O(m)$	$O(mn)$	$O(m + i')$	$O(m + n)$
void	clear()	$O(n)$ $O(irm)$	$O(n^2)$		$O(1)$	$O(n)$
Object	clone()				$O(n)$	$O(n)$
boolean	containsAll(Collection c)	$O(mn)$				
boolean	equals (Object o)	$O(1)$	$O(n)$			
int	hashcode()	$O(1)$	$O(n)$			
Iterator	iterator()	abstract	$O(1)$	$O(1)$		
ListIterator			listIterator()		$O(1)$	
ListIterator $O(1)$	int index)		listIterator(		$O(1)$	abstract
boolean	removeAll(Collection c)	$O(mn)$				
boolean	retainAll(Collection c)	$O(mn)$				
List	subList(int from, int to)		$O(n)$			
Object[]	toArray()	$O(n)$			$O(n)$	$O(n)$
Object[]	toArray (Object[] a)	$O(n)$			$O(n)$	$O(n)$
String	toString()	$O(n)$				

Table 9.12 lists the classes and methods involved in the implementation of the list iterator. Note the following points about Table 9.12:

1. The maximum run times are shown.

2. The second entry shown for `AbstractList` indicates the value if the underlying concrete class is `ArrayList`.

We now provide an extended set of exercises that allows you to explore these implementations.

Table 9.12   **Implementation Scheme for the List Iterator**

ListIterator Implementation		In Abstract List	In Linked List
Constructors			
`constructor`	`(int i)`	O(1)	O(i')
Navigation Methods			
`boolean`	`hasNext()`	O(1)	O(1)
`boolean`	`hasPrevious()`	O(1)	O(1)
`Object`	`next()`	O(n) or O(1)	O(1)
`Object`	`previous()`	O(n) or O(1)	O(1)
Modification Methods			
`void`	`add(Object o)`	O(n)	O(1)
`void`	`remove()`	O(n)	O(1)
`void`	`set(Object o)`	O(n) or O(1)	O(1)
Index Methods			
`int`	`nextIndex()`	O(1)	O(1)
`int`	`previousIndex()`	O(1)	O(1)

Exercises 9.7

1. Consider some rows in Table 9.11 in which there are multiple implementations all with the same maximum run time. What advantages, if any, do the redundant implementations provide? To what extent are the advantages worth the extra effort?

2. Identify all methods that are implemented via the services of an iterator or list iterator.

3. One might argue that some of the run times shown in abstract classes are overly pessimistic, as they do not take into account the run times in the underlying concrete class. Replace each run-time value in the abstract classes by a pair of values—one based on the assumption that the underlying concrete class is `ArrayList` and the other based on the assumption that it is `LinkedList`. When doing this exercise, if one method is implemented via another, then for the other method, use the version at the concrete level or as close to it as possible.

4. In abstract classes, why bother to provide an implementation for methods that are implemented in the concrete classes?

5. In abstract classes, some methods are UOE and others are abstract. What is the basis for this distinction?

6. The `listIterator` method is implemented in `AbstractList`, is abstract in `AbstractSequentialList`, is implemented in `LinkedList`, and is not listed in `ArrayList`. Discover the rationale for this arrangement and/or suggest improving modifications.

7. The linked version of lists includes the methods getFirst, getLast, removeFirst, removeLast, addFirst, and addLast; all are O(1). Explain how these methods can be used to mimic stacks and queues.

8. The linked version of lists uses doubly linked nodes with a sentinel. Under what circumstances would it be worthwhile to have a singly linked version?

9. Should a singly linked version have a tail pointer as well as a head pointer?

10. What are the minimum, average, and maximum run times for getFirst, get Last, and other such methods for a singly linked version?

11. Implement a singly linked version of lists.

12. Why are all single item index-based operations O(*n*) in the linked version of lists?

13. Is there any point in implementing the remove method in the array version of lists? If yes, do so.

14. Notice the differences in maximum run times for methods in the linked version and methods in the array version. Explain these differences. In what sense are they complementary?

15. Compute minimum and average run times for the list methods, especially in the last two columns. Also explain the maximum run times shown.

16. Which operations involve searching? Why are they all O(*n*) regardless of implementation?

17. Consider the manner in which serialization is implemented in the array version (see the Java 2 source code and documentation for details). The array of objects is transient, and the implementation provides the methods readObject and writeObject. Explain why this is the case, and then go back and do the same thing for ArrayTiny, ArrayStack, and ArrayQueue.

18. Consider the manner in which serialization is implemented in the linked version. Why are the instance variables transient? Why not use default serialization rather than implement readObject and writeObject? Now redo serialization for LinkedTiny, LinkedStack, and LinkedQueue in a similar manner.

19. In the array version, consider the way in which the array is resized. Explain why Java 2 uses a different resizing strategy than the one used in earlier chapters of this book and compare the performance of the two strategies.

20. The array version uses System.arrayCopy for copying arrays and opening up space in arrays. This method could also be used for closing up space in arrays. This method is O(*n*), but faster than using a for loop. Modify methods in Utilities to use System.arrayCopy.

21. Add to lamborne an interface called ExtendedListIterator. This interface extends ListIterator by adding two new operations:

void moveToHead ()   Establishes the iterator's position just before the first item in the list.

void moveToTail ()   Establishes the iterator's position just before the last item in the list.

To support ExtendedListIterator, extend the appropriate list classes in java.util and add these extensions to lamborne as well.

9.8 Case Study: Maintain a List of Tasks (a To-Do List)

This case study consists of a program that maintains a to-do list. We are going to present one solution and then suggest several variations in the exercises at the end of the section. In one of the exercises, you are asked to support the standard File menu options New, Open, and Save, which you can do by means of serialization. Without serialization, to-do lists disappear when the computer shuts down, which limits the application in a most unrealistic manner.

The case study is divided into a view and model. Within the model, the to-do list itself is implemented as an `ArrayList`. The code in the model is written to take maximum advantage of the performance characteristics of an `ArrayList`. The exercises ask you to explore the performance consequences of using other approaches.

In the exercises, we also ask you to change the interface in a significant manner and then to choose the most efficient implementation for that interface. You will see that the implementation that is best for one interface is not necessarily the best for another.

9.8.1 Request

Write a program that allows the user to maintain a list of tasks, commonly known as a to-do list.

9.8.2 Analysis

Each task in the list consists of a name and a description. The name is a single line of text. The description consists of a multiline chunk of text. Thus, the interface should display separate areas for entering or displaying the two parts of a task. We use a text field for the name and a text area for the task. Figure 9.4 shows a task displayed in the proposed interface.

Figure 9.4   **Interface for a to-do list application**

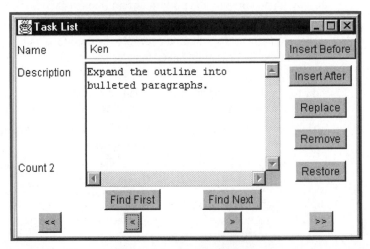

The interface provides a window on the currently selected task in the list. The user navigates the list of tasks by selecting one of the movement buttons in the bottom row or by entering a target name in the Name field and selecting one of the two buttons in the next row up. The user enters, removes, or replaces a task by selecting a button from the column at the right of the interface. Table 9.13 summarizes the functions of the buttons.

Table 9.13   **Description of the Interface's Command Buttons**

Button Label	Effect
Insert Before	Creates a new task object with the data displayed and inserts it before the current task. The new task becomes the current task. Displays an error message if • the task has no name • the list is not empty and no task is current
Insert After	Creates a new task object with the data displayed and inserts it after the current task. The new task becomes the current task. Displays an error message if • the task has no name • the list is not empty and no task is current
Replace	Replaces the current task's name and description with the data displayed. Displays an error message if • the task has no name • no task is current
Remove	Removes the current task from the list. If the list becomes empty or the deleted task was the last task, the data fields are cleared; otherwise, the next task becomes the current task. Displays an error message if no task is current.
Restore	Undoes changes the user has made to data on the screen since the last command.
Find First	Starting at the beginning of the list, searches for a task whose name is the one in the name field. Displays the first instance of a task with this name and makes it current or displays a message that no task with this name exists, after which no task is current. Displays an error message if no name is provided.
Find Next	Starting from the current task in the list, searches for a task whose name is the one in the name field. Displays the next instance of a task with this name and makes it current or displays a message that no task with this name exists, after which no task is current. Displays an error message if no name is provided.
<<	Moves to the first task in the list, makes it current, and displays its data. If the list is empty, this command does nothing. Displays an error message if there are unprocessed data on the screen.
<	Moves to the previous task in the list, makes it current, and displays its data. If the first task is already displayed, this command does nothing. Displays an error message if there are unprocessed data on the screen.

continued

Table 9.13	Description of the Interface's Command Buttons *(Continued)*

Button Label	Effect
>	Moves to the next task in the list, makes it current, and displays its data. If the last task is already displayed, this command does nothing. Displays an error message if there are unprocessed data on the screen.
>>	Moves to the last task in the list, makes it current, and displays its data. If the list is empty, this command does nothing. Displays an error message if there are unprocessed data on the screen.

Classes

The implementation is based on the three classes `TaskListView`, `TaskList Model`, and `Task`, whose responsibilities are as follows:

`TaskListView`   Responds to user requests and interacts with the model.

`TaskListModel`   Maintains the to-do list in response to requests from the view and keeps track of the current task.

`Task`   Stores the name and description of one task and provides these on demand.

Because of the familiar structure and simplicity of the application, we omit the object and message diagrams.

9.8.3   Design

The design of the `TaskListView` class is straightforward, and we let the listing speak for itself. The `Task` class is trivial, and we leave both its design and implementation as an exercise. That leaves only the `TaskListModel` class to consider. This class has two instance variables. One is the to-do list and the other is an indicator of which task is current. Table 9.14 summarizes the methods. There is a close correspondence between methods in this class and the command buttons in the interface.

Table 9.14	Summary of the Methods in the `TaskListModel` Class

Method	What It Does
`boolean hasCurrentPosition()`	Returns `true` if the model has a current position; otherwise, returns `false`.
`Task get()`	Returns the current task or `null` if there is none.
`int size()`	Returns the number of tasks in the to-do list.
`String insertBefore(Task task)`	Inserts the new task before the current task. The new task becomes current. Returns an error message if the new task does not have a name or if there was no current task in a nonempty list; otherwise, returns `null`.

Table 9.14 **Summary of the Methods in the `TaskListModel` Class** *(Continued)*

Method	What It Does
String insertAfter(Task task)	Inserts the new task after the current task. The new task becomes current. Returns an error message if the new task does not have a name or if there was no current task in a nonempty list; otherwise, returns `null`.
String replace(Task task)	Replaces the current task with `task` with the new task. The new task becomes current. Returns an error message if the new task does not have a name or if there was no current task; otherwise, returns `null`.
String remove()	Removes the current task. If the list becomes empty or the deleted task was the last task, no task is current; otherwise, the next task becomes the current task. Returns an error message if there was no current task; otherwise, returns `null`.
String getFirst()	Makes the first task current if there is one. Always returns `null`.
String getPrevious()	Makes the previous task current if there is one, else no change. Always returns `null`.
String getNext()	Makes the next task current if there is one, else no change. Always returns `null`.
String getLast()	Makes the last task current if there is one. Always returns `null`.
String findFirst(Task task)	Starting at the beginning of the list, searches for a task whose name is the same as the one in the specified task. Makes current the first instance of a task with this name or leaves no task current if the search fails. Returns an error message if the specified task has no name; otherwise, returns `null`.
String findNext(Task task)	Starting at the current task, searches for a task whose name is the same as the one in the specified task. Makes current the first instance of a task with this name or leaves no task current if the search fails. Returns an error message if the specified task has no name; otherwise, returns `null`.

9.8.4 Implementation

Here is the code for the class `TaskListView`:

```
1 import java.awt.*;
2 import javax.swing.*;
3 import java.awt.event.*;
4
5 public class TaskListView extends JFrame{
```

Continued

Continued

```
6
7      ///////////////////////////////////////////////////// main
8
9      public static void main (String[] args){
10         JFrame theFrame = new TaskListView();
11         theFrame.setSize (400, 300);
12         theFrame.setVisible (true);
13     }
14
15     ///////////////////////////////////////////////////// Model
16
17     private TaskListModel model = new TaskListModel();
18     private String oldName = "";
19     private String oldDescription = "";
20
21     ///////////////////////////////////////////////////// View
22
23     // Create controls
24     private JButton    btFindFirst    = new JButton("Find First");
25     private JButton    btFindNext     = new JButton("Find Next ");
26     private JButton    btInsertBefore = new JButton("Insert Before");
27     private JButton    btInsertAfter  = new JButton("Insert After");
28     private JButton    brReplace      = new JButton("Replace");
29     private JButton    btRemove       = new JButton("Remove");
30     private JButton    btRestore      = new JButton("Restore");
31
32     private JButton    btFirst        = new JButton("<<");
33     private JButton    btPrevious     = new JButton("<");
34     private JButton    btNext         = new JButton(">");
35     private JButton    btLast         = new JButton(">>");
36
37     private JLabel     lbName         = new JLabel("Name");
38     private JLabel     lbDescription  = new JLabel("Description");
39     private JLabel     lbCount        = new JLabel("Count 0");
40
41     private JTextField tfname         = new JTextField("");
42     private JTextArea  taDescription  = new JTextArea("");
43
44     public TaskListView(){
45
46         // Set title
47         setTitle ("Task List");
48
49         // Create container and layout
50         Container contentPane = getContentPane();
51         EasyGridLayout layout = new EasyGridLayout();
52         contentPane.setLayout (layout);
53
54         // Set constraints
55         JScrollPane spDescription = new JScrollPane(taDescription);
56         layout.setConstraints(btFindFirst     ,6,2,1,1);
57         layout.setConstraints(btFindNext      ,6,3,1,1);
58         layout.setConstraints(btInsertBefore  ,1,4,1,1);
59         layout.setConstraints(btInsertAfter   ,2,4,1,1);
60         layout.setConstraints(brReplace       ,3,4,1,1);
61         layout.setConstraints(btRemove        ,4,4,1,1);
```

Continued

Continued

```
 62          layout.setConstraints(btRestore         ,5,4,1,1);
 63
 64          layout.setConstraints(btFirst           ,7,1,1,1);
 65          layout.setConstraints(btPrevious        ,7,2,1,1);
 66          layout.setConstraints(btNext            ,7,3,1,1);
 67          layout.setConstraints(btLast            ,7,4,1,1);
 68
 69          layout.setConstraints(lbName            ,1,1,1,1);
 70          layout.setConstraints(lbDescription     ,2,1,1,1);
 71          layout.setConstraints(lbCount           ,5,1,1,1);
 72
 73          layout.setConstraints(tfname            ,1,2,2,1);
 74          layout.setConstraints(spDescription     ,2,2,2,4);
 75
 76          // Add controls to container
 77          contentPane.add(btFindFirst);
 78          contentPane.add(btFindNext);
 79          contentPane.add(btInsertBefore);
 80          contentPane.add(btInsertAfter);
 81          contentPane.add(brReplace);
 82          contentPane.add(btRemove);
 83          contentPane.add(btRestore);
 84
 85          contentPane.add(btFirst);
 86          contentPane.add(btPrevious);
 87          contentPane.add(btNext);
 88          contentPane.add(btLast);
 89
 90          contentPane.add(lbName);
 91          contentPane.add(lbDescription);
 92          contentPane.add(lbCount);
 93
 94          contentPane.add(tfname);
 95          contentPane.add(spDescription);
 96
 97
 98          // Specify listeners
 99          btFindFirst.addActionListener(new MyButtonListener());
100          btFindNext.addActionListener(new MyButtonListener());
101          btInsertBefore.addActionListener(new MyButtonListener());
102          btInsertAfter.addActionListener(new MyButtonListener());
103          brReplace.addActionListener(new MyButtonListener());
104          btRemove.addActionListener(new MyButtonListener());
105          btRestore.addActionListener(new MyButtonListener());
106          btFirst.addActionListener(new MyButtonListener());
107          btPrevious.addActionListener(new MyButtonListener());
108          btNext.addActionListener(new MyButtonListener());
109          btLast.addActionListener(new MyButtonListener());
110
111          addWindowListener(new MyWindowAdapter());
112      }
113
114      //////////////////////////////////////////////////////////// Controller
115
116      private Task getDataOnScreen(){
```

Continued

Continued

```
117         String name = tfname.getText().trim();
118         String description = taDescription.getText();
119
120         Task task = new Task (name, description);
121         return task;
122      }
123
124   private boolean unprocessedDataOnScreen(){
125         if (oldName. equals (tfname.getText().trim()) &&
126              oldDescription.equals (taDescription.getText()))
127           return false;
128         else{
129           new MessageBox (this, "Unprocessed data on screen!", 250, 100);
130           return true;
131         }
132      }
133
134   private boolean unprocessedDescriptionOnScreen(){
135         if (oldDescription.equals (taDescription.getText()))
136           return false;
137         else{
138           new MessageBox(this,"Unprocessed description on screen!", 250, 100);
139           return true;
140         }
141      }
142
143   private void displayResultsOf (String str){
144         if (str != null)
145           new MessageBox (this, str, 250, 100);
146         else{
147           if (!model.hasCurrentPosition()){
148             tfname.setText ("");
149             taDescription.setText ("");
150           }else{
151             Task task = model.get();
152             tfname.setText (task.getName());
153             taDescription.setText (task.getDescription());
154           }
155           oldName = tfname.getText();
156           oldDescription = taDescription.getText();
157           lbCount.setText ("Count " + model.size() + "       ");
158         }
159      }
160
161   // Button action listener
162   private class MyButtonListener implements ActionListener{
163      public void actionPerformed (ActionEvent event){
164         Object buttonObj = event.getSource();
165         if      (buttonObj == btInsertBefore)
166           displayResultsOf (model.insertBefore (getDataOnScreen()));
167
168         else if (buttonObj == btInsertAfter)
169           displayResultsOf (model.insertAfter (getDataOnScreen()));
170
171         else if (buttonObj == brReplace)
172           displayResultsOf (model.replace (getDataOnScreen()));
```

Continued

Continued

```
173
174            else if (buttonObj == btRemove){
175                if (unprocessedDataOnScreen()) return;
176                displayResultsOf (model.remove());
177
178            }else if (buttonObj == btRestore){
179                tfname.setText (oldName);
180                taDescription.setText (oldDescription);
181
182            }else if (buttonObj == btFirst){
183                if (unprocessedDataOnScreen()) return;
184                displayResultsOf (model.getFirst());
185
186            }else if (buttonObj == btPrevious){
187                if (unprocessedDataOnScreen()) return;
188                displayResultsOf (model.getPrevious());
189
190            }else if (buttonObj == btNext){
191                if (unprocessedDataOnScreen()) return;
192                displayResultsOf (model.getNext());
193
194            }else if (buttonObj == btLast){
195                if (unprocessedDataOnScreen()) return;
196                displayResultsOf (model.getLast());
197
198            }else if (buttonObj == btFindFirst){
199                if (unprocessedDescriptionOnScreen()) return;
200                displayResultsOf (model.findFirst (getDataOnScreen()));
201
202            }else if (buttonObj == btFindNext){
203                if (unprocessedDescriptionOnScreen()) return;
204                displayResultsOf (model.findNext (getDataOnScreen()));
205            }
206        }
207    }
208
209    // Window listener
210    private class MyWindowAdapter extends WindowAdapter{
211        public void windowClosing (WindowEvent e){
212            System.exit(0);
213        }
214    }
215 }
```

Here is a partial listing for the `TaskListModel` class. We leave the missing portions as an exercise that can be completed by reviewing the method descriptions given in Table 9.14:

```
1 import java.util.*;
2
3 public class TaskListModel extends Object {
4
5    // Instance variables --------------------------------
6
```

Continued

Continued

```
 7      private List list;
 8      private int currentPosition;
 9
10      // Constructor------------------------------------------
11
12      public TaskListModel(){
13   // Choose one of the following list implementations
14          list = new ArrayList();
15          // list = new LinkedList();
16
17      currentPosition = -1;
18      }
19
20      // Public methods--------------------------------------
21
22      public boolean hasCurrentPosition(){
23         return currentPosition != -1;
24      }
25
26      public Task get(){
27         if (! list.isEmpty() && hasCurrentPosition())
28            return (Task) list.get(currentPosition);
29         else
30            return null;
31      }
32
33      public int size() ...
34
35      public String insertBefore (Task task){
36         if (list.isEmpty() || hasCurrentPosition()){
37            if (task.getName().equals(""))
38               return "Enter a name before inserting";
39            else{
40               if (currentPosition == -1)
41                  currentPosition++;
42               list.add (currentPosition, task);
43               return null;
44            }
45         }else
46            return "Establish a current position before inserting";
47      }
48
49      public String insertAfter (Task task) ...
50
51      public String replace(Task task) ...
52
53      public String remove()...
54
55      public String getFirst(){
56         if (! list.isEmpty())
57            currentPosition = 0;
58         return null;
59      }
60
61      public String getPrevious(){
```

Continued

Continued

```
62        if (currentPosition > 0 && hasCurrentPosition())
63           currentPosition--;
64        return null;
65     }
66
67     public String getNext() ...
68
69     public String getLast() ...
70
71     public String findFirst(Task task){
72        currentPosition = -1;
73        return findNext (task);
74     }
75
76     public String findNext(Task task) ...
77
78 }
```

Exercises 9.8

1. Complete the implementation of the case study. An executable version of the case study plus source code for the interface and parts of the model are available on the book's CD.

2. What are the run times of the processes triggered when the user clicks the various command buttons? What would these times be if a `LinkedList` were used in place of an `ArrayList`, assuming no changes are made in the code? Are there any places where the code could be rewritten to improve the performance when a `LinkedList` is used?

3. Redo the model using a list iterator to the greatest advantage possible. You will need to decide whether to use an `ArrayList` or a `LinkedList`. What are the run times of the user-initiated processes now?

4. Add a File menu with options New, Open, and Save.

5. Modify the Find commands so that they allow wild card searches.

6. Currently, the interface displays the number of items in the list. Modify the application so that the interface also displays the index of the currently displayed task, where the first task has an index of 1.

7. The application's Restore command can undo only the user's most recent change to the to-do list. Replace the Restore command by Undo and Redo commands supported by a stack of all the changes made to the list. This is a feature common to many applications.

8. Redo the case study with a new interface that has a list control on the left containing all the task names in their list order. Display the name and description of the currently selected task name to the right of the list control in a text field and text area, respectively. The text field and text area are also used for data input. Add command buttons labeled Up and Down that allow the user to move a selected task up or down in the list. Add other command buttons to the interface as

needed to provide full maintenance capabilities for the to-do list. You may need to add some other methods to the model. Implement the model in the most efficient manner possible by making suitable use of the list interface, the list iterator interface, or a combination of both. Finally, determine the average and maximum run times of each user-initiated operation and discuss which interface is better from a user's perspective, the only one that really matters, this one or the one used in the case study.

9. Most word processors have a feature called wordwrap, which automatically moves the user's next word down a line when the right margin is reached. To illustrate how this feature works, write a program that allows the user to format text typed into a Java text area. This program will be fairly crude in that the user must first enter the text to be formatted and then format it by selecting a button. The interface should consist of a button labeled Format, a text area, and an integer field labeled Line Length. The number entered into this field specifies the maximum number of characters allowed on a line. When the user selects the Format button, the view should send a message with the text area's string and the integer field's value (the line length) to the model. The model should then

   a. Open a string tokenizer (see Appendix A) on the string.

   b. Create a list of lists. Each sublist within the top-level list will represent a line of formatted text.

   c. While there are more words in the tokenizer, add them to the next available sublist in the list. Be careful not to exceed the user's line length for each line.

   d. At the end of the process, traverse sublists, add their contents to a new string, and return this string.

   The view should then refresh the contents of the text area with the model's results. You should decide what to do about newlines, white space other than the space character, and so forth. Options might include justification, which would require a more sophisticated program.

KEY TERMS

content-based operation	index-based operation	tail
deque	list iterator	vector
free list	position-based operation	
head	sequence	

CHAPTER SUMMARY

The list is the most general-purpose and commonly used collection. Aside from its direct use to model a list of items, a list frequently implements other collections, such as stacks and queues.

A list is a linear collection that allows access to each item. Although there is no universally agreed upon set of operations for lists, a list implementation usually provides a large number of them. List operations commonly belong to three categories that provide index-based access, content-based access, and position-based access. An index-based operation inserts, removes, accesses, or replaces an item at a given index position, usually counting from 0 to the size of the list minus 1. A content-based operation does the same after a search for a given item. A position-based operation does the same after moving to the next or the previous item using a position pointer.

Position-based operations are commonly packaged in a list iterator, which extends the capabilities of a simple iterator to include moving to the previous item, insertions, and replacements.

The most common implementations of lists are with arrays and doubly linked structures. A doubly linked structure is preferred to a singly linked one to allow a more efficient implementation of a list iterator.

Java provides a `List` interface and two implementations, `ArrayList` and `LinkedList`, as well as a `ListIterator` interface. The `List` interface extends the `Collection` interface, so Java's lists support all of the high-level `Collection` methods.

REVIEW QUESTIONS

1. Name three common applications of lists.
2. Describe an application for which an array-based implementation of a list should be preferred to a link-based implementation.
3. What are the restrictions on the use of a list iterator?
4. Why does Java use a doubly linked structure to implement the `LinkedList` class?
5. Is there a limit to the number of items that can be inserted into an array-based list, and if so, how can it be overcome?

CHAPTER 10

Recursion, Searching, Sorting, and Backtracking

OBJECTIVES   Upon completion of this chapter, you should be able to

- Describe the basic features of a recursive algorithm

- Discuss the differences between the use of recursion and the use of loops to solve similar problems

- Explain the way in which recursion supports a divide-and-conquer strategy of problem solving

- Give an account of the common uses of recursion in searching and sorting problems

- Explain how recursive methods can support a backtracking strategy of problem solving

This chapter introduces recursion, a topic you may have already encountered in your first programming course. Recursion is used widely in divide-and-conquer, backtracking, and recursive descent algorithms. As examples of divide and conquer, we consider several highly efficient algorithms for searching and sorting. Our example of backtracking involves a maze solving program, and for recursive descent algorithms we present a recursive descent parser. We also discuss the close relationship between recursion and stacks. Finally, this chapter serves as an essential precursor to later chapters on trees and graphs, both of which involve recursive processes.

10.1   Overview of Recursion

When asked to add the integers from 1 to n, we usually think of the process as iterative. We start with 0, add 1, then 2, then 3, and so forth until we reach n, or expressed differently

```
sum(n) = 1 + 2 + 3 + . . . + n, where n >= 1
```

Java's looping constructs make implementing the process easy. There is, however, a completely different way to look at the problem that at first seems very strange:

```
sum(1) = 1
sum(n) = n + sum(n - 1) if n > 1
```

At first glance, expressing `sum(n)` in terms of `sum(n - 1)` seems to yield a circular definition; however, it does not. Consider, for example, what happens when the definition is applied to the problem of calculating `sum(4)`:

```
sum(4) = 4 + sum(3)
       = 4 + 3 + sum(2)
       = 4 + 3 + 2 + sum(1)
       = 4 + 3 + 2 + 1
```

The fact that `sum(1)` is defined to be 1, without making reference to further invocations of `sum`, saves the process from going on forever and the definition from being circular. A function defined in terms of itself in this way is called ***recursive.***

As a second example, we give two definitions of the factorial function: the first is iterative and the second recursive:

```
factorial(n) = 1 * 2 * 3 * . . . * n, where n >= 1     //Iterative

factorial(1) = 1                                       //Recursive
factorial(n) = n * factorial(n - 1) if n > 1
```

From these examples, we might incorrectly conclude that recursive definitions are more complex than iterative ones; however, such is not always the case. Consider, for example, Fibonacci numbers, which have applications in several areas of science. The first and second Fibonacci numbers are defined to be 1. Thereafter, each Fibonacci number is defined to be the sum of its two immediate predecessors, thus yielding the following sequence of numbers:

1 1 2 3 5 8 13 21 34 55 89 144 233 . . .

This is a recursive definition, as becomes obvious when we express it more formally:

```
fibonacci(1) = 1
fibonacci(2) = 1
fibonacci(n) = fibonacci(n - 1) + fibonacci(n - 2) if n > 2
```

You cannot rewrite the definition nonrecursively.

The preceding recursive functions conform to a common pattern:

■ For small values of *n*, the function has predefined values. These are called the ***base cases.***

■ For all other values of *n*, the function is defined in terms of itself at lower values of *n*. This is the ***recursive step.***

If a recursive function is defined correctly, repeated application of the recursive rule eventually leads to the base cases and termination of the recursive process.

10.1.1   Implementing Recursion

Given a recursive definition of some process, it is usually easy to write a ***recursive method*** that implements the function. A method is said to be recursive if it calls itself. Let us start with a method that computes factorials.

```
int factorial (int n){
   if (n <= 1)
      return 1;
   else
      return n * factorial (n - 1);
}
```

Notice that the method begins with the test n <= 1 rather than n == 1 even though no one should call the method with a value of *n* less than 1; however, it seems prudent to write the method in a robust manner that can withstand accidental abuse. For comparison, here is an iterative version of the method. As you can see, it is longer and slightly more difficult to understand.

```
int factorial (int n){
   int i, product;
   product = 1;
   for (i = 2; i <= n; i++)
      product = product * i;
   }
   return product;
}
```

As a second example, here is a recursive method for calculating Fibonacci numbers:

```
int fibonacci (int n){
   if (n <= 2)
      return 1;
   else
      return fibonacci (n - 1) + fibonacci (n - 2);
}
```

In both the recursive methods that have been shown, notice how closely the code follows the original recursive definitions, making it easy to write a recursive method when a recursive definition can be used as a starting point. In the preceding discussion, we have not considered whether recursive methods are more or less computationally efficient than their iterative counterparts, but we return to this subject later in the chapter.

10.1.2 Tracing Recursive Calls

A diagram known as a ***call tree*** provides a conceptual overview of the relationship between the multiple invocations of a recursive method. Suppose we want to compute the factorial of 4.

We begin by calling `factorial(4)`,

  which in turn calls `factorial(3)`,

    which in turn calls `factorial(2)`,

      which in turn calls `factorial(1)`,

      which returns 1 to `factorial(2)`,

    which returns 2 to `factorial(3)`,

  which returns 6 to `factorial(4)`,

which returns 24, as illustrated in Figure 10.1.

Figure 10.1   **Call tree for computing 4!**

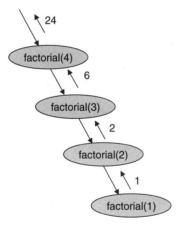

At first, it may seem strange to have all these invocations of the `factorial` method, each in a state of suspended animation, waiting for the completion of the ones further down the line. However, when the last invocation completes its work, it returns to its predecessor, which completes its work, and so forth up the line, until eventually the original invocation reactivates and finishes the job. Fortunately, we do not have to repeat this dizzying mental exercise every time we use recursion.

A call tree for the `fibonacci` method (Figure 10.2) is more complex because the method makes two calls to itself, but again, the call tree illustrates clearly the relationship between the multiple invocations of the method. The figure shows the calls involved when we compute the fifth Fibonacci number. To keep the diagram

Figure 10.2   **Call tree for computing the fifth Fibonacci number**

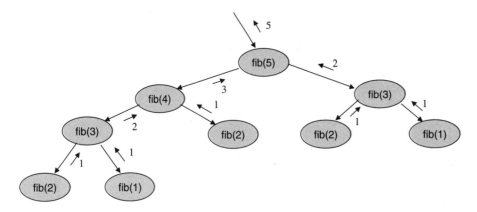

reasonably compact, we write fib(5) instead of fibonacci(5). The veritable explosion of method calls suggests that the method has poor performance characteristics, a fact that we will confirm shortly.

10.1.3   Guidelines for Writing Recursive Methods

The most important guideline for writing recursive methods is to start with a clearly stated recursive definition of the process to be implemented, after which the writing of a recursive method is fairly automatic; however, there are several pitfalls to avoid. First, just as we must guard against writing infinite loops, so too we must avoid recursions that never end. A recursive method must have well-defined termination or *stopping states.* For the factorial method, this was expressed in the lines:

```
if (n <= 1)
    return 1;
```

Second, the *recursive steps,* in which the method calls itself, must eventually lead to the stopping states. For the factorial method, the recursive step was expressed in the lines:

```
else
    return n * factorial(n - 1);
```

Because each invocation of the factorial method is passed a smaller value, the stopping state must be reached eventually. Had we accidentally written

```
else
    return n * factorial(n + 1);     // Error
```

the method would describe an *infinite recursion.* Eventually, the user would notice and terminate the program, or else the Java interpreter would run out of memory, at which point the program would crash with a stack overflow error.

Here is a subtler example of a malformed recursive method:

```
int badMethod (int n){
   if (n == 1)
      return 1;
   else
      return n * badMethod(n - 2);
}
```

This method works well if n is odd, but when n is even, the method passes through the stopping state and keeps on going. For instance,

```
badMethod(4)
  calls badMethod(2)
    calls badMethod(0)
      calls badMethod(-2)
        calls badMethod(-4)
          calls badMethod(-6)
              . . .
```

As with loops, *off-by-one errors* can occur in recursive algorithms. A common example is an incorrect test for a base case. For instance, if the range of values should include a lower bound, the termination condition should be

```
if (n >= lowerBound)
```

instead of

```
if (n > lowerBound)
```

Finally, if you have any doubts about the relationships between the recursive method calls, draw a call tree for the method.

10.1.4   Run-Time Support for Recursive Methods

As discussed in Chapter 7, computers can use a call stack to support method calls. Recall that

■ A large storage area known as a call stack is created at program startup.

■ When a method is called, an activation record is pushed onto the call stack.

■ The activation record contains, among other things, parameters passed to the method, the method's local variables, and the value returned by the method.

■ When a method returns, its activation record is popped off the stack.

To understand how a recursive method uses the call stack, we ignore, for the sake of simplicity, all parts of the activation record except for the parameters and the return value. The method `factorial` has one of each:

```
int factorial (int n){
   if (n <= 1)
```

Continued

Continued

```
            return 1;
        else
            return n * factorial (n - 1);
    }
```

Thus, an activation record for this method requires cells for the following items:

■ the value of the parameter n

■ the return value of `factorial`

Suppose we call `factorial(4)`. A trace of the state of the call stack during calls to `factorial` down to `factorial(1)` is shown in Figure 10.3.

Figure 10.3   **Activation records on the call stack during recursive calls to** `factorial`

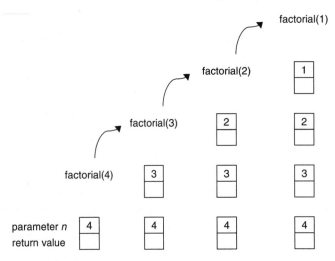

When the recursion unwinds, the return value from each call is multiplied by the parameter n in the record below and the top record is popped, as shown in the trace in Figure 10.4.

Figure 10.4   **Activation records on the call stack during returns from recursive calls to** `factorial`

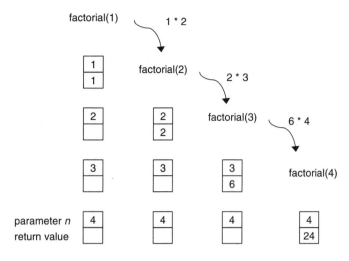

10.1.5   Time Analysis for Two Recursive Methods

Calculating the run time of recursive and nonrecursive methods is done in much the same way. We illustrate with the `factorial` method:

```
int factorial (int n){
    if (n <= 1)                        // Comparison: t1
        return 1;                      // Return: t2
    else
        return n * factorial (n - 1);  // Call, multiply, and return: t3
}
```

One activation of the method takes time

```
t1 + t2 if n <= 1
t1 + t3 if n > 1
```

The first case occurs once, and the second case occurs the $n - 1$ times the method calls itself recursively. Thus:

```
executionTime
    = t1 + t2 + (n - 1)*(t1 + t3)
    = k1 + n * k2
    = O(n)
```

where k1 and k2 are method-dependent constants. It should be obvious that the run time of the nonrecursive iterative version of the method is also $O(n)$.

From this, we should not draw the mistaken conclusion that the run times of recursive and nonrecursive versions of a method are always going to be the same. As a dramatic counterexample, the recursive fibonacci method is $O(r^n)$, where $r \approx 1.62$. In fact, the call tree in Figure 10.2 suggests that the method's order is going to be exponential. In contrast, the iterative version of the method is $O(n)$. It is beyond the book's scope to prove that the recursive algorithm is $O(r^n)$, but it is easy to demonstrate that the number of recursive calls increases rapidly with n, as shown in Table 10.1.

Table 10.1   **Growth of Recursive Calls to Compute the nth Fibonacci Number**

n	Number of Recursive Calls
2	1
4	5
8	41
16	1,973
32	4,356,617

The values in the table were obtained by running the following program:

```
 1 public class Tester{
 2
 3     static int count;
 4
 5     public static void main (String[] args){
 6         KeyboardReader reader = new KeyboardReader();
 7         int i, fibn, n;
 8         for (i = 1; i <= 5; i++){
 9             count = 0;
10             n = (int) Math.pow (2, i);
11             fibn = fibonacci (n);
12             System.out.println ("" + n + ":" + count);
13             reader.pause();
14         }
15     }
16
17     static int fibonacci (int n){
18         count++;
19         if (n <= 2)
20             return 1;
21         else
22             return fibonacci (n - 1) + fibonacci (n - 2);
23     }
24 }
```

Programs such as this are frequently useful for gaining an empirical sense of an algorithm's efficiency.

10.1.6   Space Analysis for Two Recursive Methods

Previously, our space analysis was limited to the memory requirements of data structures; however, when dealing with recursion, we must also consider the space needed for a method's multiple activation records. For instance, the recursive computation of $n!$ requires n activation records on the call stack immediately before the recursive calls begin to unwind (see Figure 10.3). Thus, even though this method does not directly manipulate any large data structures, its space requirements are $O(n)$.

The space requirements of the recursive fibonacci method are less obvious. Consider the line of code containing the two recursive calls:

```
return fibonacci(n - 1) + fibonacci(n - 2);
```

The Java Virtual Machine will have returned from the first call before embarking on the second, so in the call tree for the fibonacci method (see Figure 10.2), we need to consider only the longest string of calls, which for n would be $n - 1$. Thus, the method's space requirements are $O(n)$.

Exercises 10.1

In each of the following exercises, you are asked to write a recursive method in the context of an appropriate tester program. For each, begin by attempting to write a recursive definition of the process if one is not already given. Also draw a call tree and compute the time and space complexity of the method. Not all of the exercises are chosen because they illustrate particularly good applications of recursion but rather because they provide some useful practice.

1. Java's Math class implements a method called pow(base, exponent) that returns the base raised to the given exponent. Write a recursive method to do the same thing. The methods should expect nonnegative integer parameters and return an integer.

2. Write a recursive method to sum the numbers in an integer array.

3. Use a Tester program to implement and test a recursive method to compute the greatest common divisor (gcd) of two integers. The recursive definition of gcd is

```
gcd(a, b) = b, when a = 0
gcd(a, b) = gcd(b, a % b), when a > 0
```

4. The expression *N choose K* means the number of ways of choosing *K* items from *N* items, where $K <= N$. For example, 52 choose 13 is the number of ways one could deal a bridge hand (13 of 52 cards). The recursive definition of *N choose K*, where *K* and *N* are nonnegative integers and $K <= N$, is

```
choose(n, k) = 1, when k = 0 or k = n
choose(n, k) = choose(n - 1, k) + choose(n - 1, k - 1), otherwise.
```

Write a recursive Java method that computes *N choose K*. Draw a call tree for choose(4, 2). Is the run-time behavior of choose more complex than that of fibonacci? Modify choose to count the number of times that it is called. Then display the count where n is fixed at 10 and k ranges from 10 down to 1. Try to come up with a generalization about the number of calls of choose as a function of k.

5. According to an old legend, monks were given the task of moving *n* stone disks from one pillar, called A, to another pillar, called C. As the monks moved the disks, they had to maintain the relative ordering of the disks, with the largest disk at the bottom and the smallest disk at the top. The monks also had to follow two other rules when moving disks:

■ Move only one disk at a time.

■ A third pillar, called B, could be used as an intermediate place to store disks.

Here is an informal description of a recursive solution to this problem, known as the Towers of Hanoi problem:

1. If *n* = 1, move the disk from A to C.

2. If *n* = 2, move the first disk from A to B, move the second disk from A to C, and move the first disk from B to C.

3. If *n* = 3, use the method of step 2 to move the first two disks from A to B using C, move one disk from A to C, and then use this method to move the first two disks from B to C using A.

.

.

.

n. For any *n*, use the method of the previous step to move *n* − 1 disks from A to B using C, move one disk from A to C, and move *n* − 1 disks from B to C using A.

Use this description to develop a recursive method for solving the Towers of Hanoi problem. The program should accept *n* as an input and display the moves as it runs.

10.2   Recursion and Searching

In Chapter 4, we introduced linear and binary search algorithms for arrays. These algorithms were implemented using iteration, but as we show in this section, they can be rewritten using recursion. Implementing a linear search as a recursive method is rather unnatural because we normally think of linear search as an iterative rather than a recursive process; however, the same is not true of a binary search. Both recursive methods are based on a divide-and-conquer approach, as is often, but not always, the case when recursion is used. The methods are declared public static, so they can be included in a utility class such as Java's Math class.

We illustrate the recursive search methods using arrays of integers, but the methods can easily be rewritten for other primitive types, for generic objects, and for linked lists instead of arrays. Some of these different possibilities are explored in the exercises at the end of the section.

10.2.1　Linear Search of an Array

Assuming that the items in an array are in random order, we usually think of a linear search in the following terms:

■ Scan down the array until the target item is found and return its position.

■ If the target item is not found, return -1.

Such a description suggests an iterative rather than a recursive solution, so we try again:

■ Search for the target item in the first location of the array.

■ If it is found, return its position.

■ Else repeat the process using the smaller array obtained by ignoring the first item (divide and conquer).

Here is a corresponding recursive method:

```
public static int linearSearch(int target, int[] array, int pos){
   if (pos >= array.length)                            //Stopping state
      return -1;
   else if (array[pos] == target)                      //Stopping state
       return pos;
   else
       return linearSearch(target, array, pos + 1);    //Recursive call

}
```

Note that the method uses a current position parameter, `pos`, that is incremented before each recursive call. The first time the method is called, the parameter must be set to 0, as follows:

```
int result = linearSearch(target, array, 0);           //Initial call
```

We leave it as an exercise to show that the method's maximum run time is $O(n)$, as is the average run time when target items are in the array. These are the same performance figures established in Chapter 4 for the iterative version of the method. We also leave it as an exercise to show that the method's maximum space requirements are $O(n)$.

From a user's perspective, the `pos` parameter introduces an unnecessary complexity that can be avoided by using a common stratagem. We replace the method by two others as follows:

```
public static int linearSearch(int target, int[] array){
   return linearSearchHelper (target, array, 0);
}

private static int linearSearchHelper(int target, int[] array, int pos){
   if (pos >= array.length)                            //Stopping state
```

Continued

Continued

```
      return -1;
   else if (array[pos] == target)              //Stopping state
      return pos;
   else
      return linearSearchHelper(target, array, pos + 1); //Recursive call

}
```

Users call the public method, which in turn calls the recursive helper method.

10.2.2   Binary Search of an Array

If the elements in an array are sorted, a binary search can quickly determine if a target item is present. The process can be stated informally as follows:

■ If the item in the middle of the array equals the target item, return its index.

■ Else repeat the process on either the first or second half of the array.

In more detail, given a contiguous segment of an array:

■ If the segment is empty, return −1.

■ If the item in the middle of the segment equals the target item, return the index of the item.

■ Else if the item in the middle of the segment is less than the target item, halve the segment and repeat the process on the upper half; else repeat the process on the lower half (divide and conquer).

■ Initially perform the process with a segment composed of the whole array.

Here is code for the binary search method:

```
public static int binarySearch (int target, int[] array){
   return binarySearchHelper(target, array, 0, array.length - 1);
}

private static int binarySearchHelper(int target, int[] array,
                                      int low, int high){
   if (low > high)                              //Stopping state
      return -1;
   else{
      int middle = (low + high) / 2;
      if (array[middle] == target)              //Stopping state
         return middle;
      else if (array[middle] < target)          //Recursive call
         return binarySearchHelper (target, array, middle + 1, high);
      else                                      //Recursive call
         return binarySearchHelper (target, array, low, middle - 1);
   }
}
```

Note that the search method now expects two position parameters, `low` and `high`, indicating the lower and upper bounds of the portion of the array being examined on each call. These parameters converge during successive recursive calls, until either the target is found or they cross, indicating a futile search.

Figures 10.5 and 10.6 provide a visual representation of how the method behaves during a successful and an unsuccessful search. During a successful search, recursion continues until the midvalue of a segment equals the target. During an unsuccessful search, recursion continues until an empty segment is encountered.

Figure 10.5

A successful search for the number 5

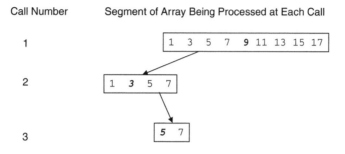

Figure 10.6

An unsuccessful search for the number 6

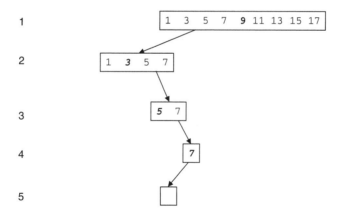

We would now like to determine the method's maximum run time. The worst case occurs when the target item is not in the array. In this situation, the number of recursive calls is limited by the number of times the array is subdivided in arriving at an empty segment. For an array of size n, this equals the number of times n must be divided by 2, using integer arithmetic, in order to reach 0.

$$n\,/\,2\,/\,2\ldots/\,2 \rightarrow 0$$

From Chapter 4, we know that this value is bounded above by $1 + \log_2 n$. Considering the initial call to the search method, we see that the method is never called more than $2 + \log_2 n$ times when searching an array of n items.

On each call, the method either encounters a stopping condition or does exactly one recursive call. If we let k represent the most time-consuming of these activities, we can see that the maximum run time for the method is:

```
maximum running time ≤ k(2 + log₂ n)
                     = O(log n)
```

The average run time for target items that are in the array is also $O(\log n)$, but establishing this fact is beyond the book's scope.

The space requirements of the method are now easy to determine. As the method is never called more than $2 + \log_2 n$ times, the maximum number of activation records on the call stack is $O(\log n)$.

Exercises 10.2

1. Compute the maximum and average run times for the iterative recursive search method. Also determine the maximum number of activation records required.

2. Suppose an array contains the values

```
20 44 48 55 62 66 74 88 93 99
```

at index positions 0 through 9. Trace the values of the variables `low`, `high`, and `middle` in a recursive binary search of this array for the target value 90. Repeat for the target value 44.

3. Write a small simulation program that does a large number of recursive binary searches and use it to estimate the run time of the search method as a function of n, the number of items in the array. Consider separately the case of searching for numbers in the array and not in the array. Part of the challenge of the problem is to devise a simulation that is simple yet convincing. Are the results consistent with the run times discussed in the text?

4. The next two exercises extend this section's discussion of searching to arrays and linked lists of objects. The exercises are done in the context of the classes `ArrayListPT` and `LinkedListPT` (see Chapter 9).

   a. Rewrite the `indexOf` methods in the two classes so that they use recursion instead of iteration. Compare the time and space complexity of the new methods with those of the originals. Is there any point to this exercise other than as an opportunity to increase your skill in writing recursive methods?

   b. Add a method called `binaryIndexOf` to `ListPT` that should be called only when the list is known to be in ascending order. Implement the method in `ArrayListPT` and `LinkedListPT` using a recursive binary search strategy. For this to work, the items in the list and the item being searched for must implement the `Comparable` interface. Compute the time and space complexity of these methods. Is a binary search of a linked list more or less efficient than a linear search?

10.3 Recursion and Sorting

The $O(n^2)$ sort algorithms discussed in Chapter 4 were simple but slow; however, sorting is of such overwhelming importance in many applications that it is often essential to perform sorts in the most efficient manner possible. Computer scientists have responded by developing several $O(n\log n)$ algorithms. The algorithms achieve greater efficiency at the cost of greater program complexity. We now present two of these: quicksort and mergesort. Both use a divide-and-conquer recursive approach. As with searching, we discuss these algorithms in the context of integer arrays and extend them to other settings in the exercises.

10.3.1 Quicksort

Quicksort is an algorithm devised by C. A. R. Hoare. Here is an outline of the process:

- Begin by selecting the item at an array's midpoint and call it the ***pivot.*** (Later, we discuss alternative ways of choosing the pivot.)

- Partition items in the array so that all items less than the pivot end up to the pivot's left, with the rest to its right. The final position of the pivot itself varies depending on the actual items involved. For instance, the pivot ends up being rightmost in the array if it is the largest item and leftmost if it is the smallest. But wherever the pivot ends up, this is its final position in the fully sorted array.

- Reapply the process recursively to the subarrays formed by splitting the array at the pivot. One subarray consists of all items to the left of the pivot, and the other has all items to the right (divide and conquer).

- The process terminates each time it encounters a subarray with fewer than two items.

Partitioning

The most complicated part of the algorithm from the programmer's perspective is the operation of partitioning the items in a subarray. There are two principal ways of doing this. Here is an informal description of the easier method as it applies to any subarray:

- Interchange the pivot with the last item in the subarray.

- Establish a boundary between the items known to be less than the pivot and the rest of the items. Initially, this boundary is positioned immediately before the first item.

- Starting with the first item in the subarray, scan across the subarray. Every time an item less than the pivot is encountered, swap it with the first item after the boundary and advance the boundary.

- Finish by swapping the pivot with the first item after the boundary.

Figure 10.7   **Partitioning a subarray so that all numbers less than the pivot are to its left, and the rest are to its right**

1. Let the subarray consist of the numbers shown

   with a pivot of 14.

   12 19 17 18 `14` 11 15 13 16

   Swap the pivot with the last item.

   12 19 17 18 `16` 11 15 13 `14`

2. Establish the boundary before the first item.

   `:` 12 19 17 18 16 11 15 13 14

3. Scan for the first item less than the pivot.

   `:` `12` 19 17 18 16 11 15 13 14

   Swap this item with the first item after the

   boundary. In this example, the item gets swapped

   with itself.

   `:` `12` 19 17 18 16 11 15 13 14

   Advance the boundary.

   12 `:` 19 17 18 16 11 15 13 14

4. Scan for the next item less than the pivot.

   12 `:` 19 17 18 16 `11` 15 13 14

   Swap this item with the first item after the

   boundary.

   12 `:` `11` 17 18 16 `19` 15 13 14

   Advance the boundary.

   12 11 `:` 17 18 16 19 15 13 14

5. Scan for the next item less than the pivot.

   12 11 `:` 17 18 16 19 15 `13` 14

   Swap this item with the first item after the

   boundary.

   12 11 `:` `13` 18 16 19 15 `17` 14

   Advance the boundary.

   12 11 13 `:` 18 16 19 15 17 14

6. Scan for the next item less than the pivot;

   12 11 13 `:` 18 16 19 15 17 14

   however, there is not one.

7. Interchange the pivot with the first item after the

   12 11 13 `:` `14` 16 19 15 17 `18`

   boundary. At this point, all items less than the

   pivot are to the pivot's left and the rest are to its

   right.

Figure 10.7 illustrates these steps as applied to the numbers 12 19 17 18 14 11 15 13 16. In step 1, the pivot is established and interchanged with the last item. In step 2, the boundary is established before the first item. In steps 3–6, the subarray is scanned for items less than the pivot, these are swapped with the first item after the boundary, and the boundary is advanced. Notice that items to the left of the boundary are less than the pivot at all times. Finally, in step 7, the pivot is swapped with the first item after the boundary, and the subarray has been successfully partitioned.

Figure 10.8 presents another view of a subarray at various stages during the partitioning process. The correspondences between Figures 10.7 and 10.8 are as follows:

Figure 10.7	**Figure 10.8**
Step 1	Initial
Step 2	Start Scanning
Steps 3–5	During Scanning
Step 6	Done Scanning
Step 7	Final

Figure 10.8   **States of a subarray at various stages during the partitioning process**

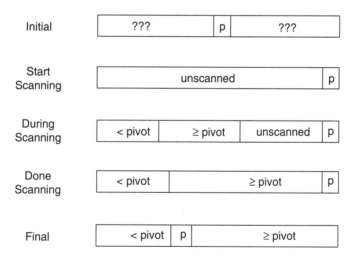

We are now ready to implement the foregoing process with a method called `partition`:

```
1 private static int partition (int[] a, int low, int high){
2    //a      The whole array
```

Continued

Continued

```
 3    //low        Index of the first item in the subarray
 4    //high       Index of the last item in the subarray
 5
 6    int i;          //Used to scan across the subarray
 7    int boundary;   //Marks the boundary between numbers less than pivot and
 8                    //add the rest
 9    int middle;     //Location of pivot
10    int pivot;      //The pivot value
11    int temp;       //A temporary variable used during swaps
12
13    //Locate the pivot
14    middle = (low + high) / 2;
15    pivot = a[middle];
16
17    //Swap the pivot with the last item
18    a[middle] = a[high]; a[high] = pivot;
19
20    boundary = low;
21       //At this point all items in subarray to left of boundary are less
22       //than the pivot, which must be true as there are none.
23
24    //Scan for items less than the pivot using i
25    for (i = low; i < high; i++){
26
27       if (a[i] < pivot){
28
29          //If the item is less than the pivot, swap it with the first
30          //item after the boundary.
31          temp = a[boundary]; a[boundary] = a[i]; a[i] = temp;
32
33          //Advance the boundary
34          boundary++;
35
36       }
37
38       //At this point all items in subarray to left of boundary are still
39       //less than the pivot, which is true because only items less than
40       //the pivot were swapped after which the boundary was advanced.
41    }
42
43    //At this point the subarray has been completely scanned and all items
44    //less than the pivot have been moved left of the boundary.
45
46    //Swap the pivot with the first item after the boundary.
47    temp = a[high]; a[high] = a[boundary]; a[boundary] = temp;
48
49    //Return the final location of the pivot to the calling method in order
50    //to facilitate partitioning.
51    return boundary;
52 }
```

Completing the Algorithm

Having written the `partition` method, we can complete the implementation of the `quickSort` method:

```java
public static void quickSort (int[] a){
   quickSortHelper(a, 0, a.length - 1);
}

private static void quickSortHelper (int[] a, int low, int high){
   if (low < high){
      int pivotLocation = partition(a, low, high);
      quickSortHelper(a, low, pivotLocation - 1);
      quickSortHelper(a, pivotLocation + 1, high);
   }
}
```

Figure 10.9 illustrates the results of applying the `quickSort` method to an array containing the integers 12 19 17 18 14 11 15 13 16. All of the recursive stages are shown. Stage 1 shows the full array before and after partitioning. The pivot is marked. Stage 2 shows the two subarrays generated when the array in stage 1 is subdivided. Again, each of these subarrays is shown twice and so forth. Notice that recursion stops whenever a subarray with fewer than two items is generated.

Figure 10.9   **Subarrays generated at each recursive stage of the quicksort algorithm**

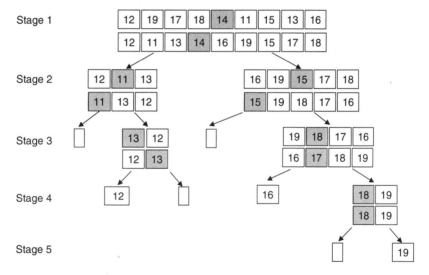

Quicksort's Run Time

We now present an informal analysis of quicksort's run time. First, consider the process of swapping items as implemented in the `partition` method. The run time of this method is clearly O(length of the subarray). Second, at each stage (see Figure 10.9), the combined length of all subarrays is less than or equal to n, the length of the original array, so that the combined run time for all activations of the `partition` method at any single stage is at most O(n). Thus, the total run time for the algorithm is at most O(n * number of stages).

All that remains is to compute the number of stages; however, that number varies depending on the circumstances. In the best case, each pivot ends up, after partitioning, at the middle of its subarray, thus assuring that the subarray is subdivided as evenly as possible. As we know from our analysis of the binary search algorithm, the number of stages is then bound above $2 + \log_2 n$. Thus, in this best case, the maximum run time of quicksort is O($n\log n$).

Unfortunately, we cannot guarantee this best case behavior. In fact, in some situations, the maximum run time is O(n^2). Suppose, for example, that at each stage the pivot just happens to be the smallest item in its subarray. Then the result of each partitioning is an empty subarray and a subarray that has one less item than its parent. This yields a sequence of subarrays of length $n, n - 1, n - 2, \ldots 2, 1$. The run time at stage i is then O($n - i$), so as shown in Chapter 4, the run time for all stages is:

$$O(n + n - 1 + n - 2 + \ldots + 2 + 1) = O(n^2)$$

Fortunately, on average, quicksort is O($n\log n$), a fact that we will not attempt to establish in this book.

Quicksort's Space Requirements

On average, quicksort stops after O($\log n$) recursive stages. Consequently, as only one recursive thread needs to be followed at a time, the space demands on the call stack also average O($\log n$), but in the worst case, they expand to O(n).

Improving Quicksort

Quicksort performs best when the number of recursive stages is reduced to a minimum, which in turn depends on the effectiveness of the partitioning process. We would like each partition to divide its subarray in two pieces of nearly equal length. The best way to achieve this goal is to choose a pivot equal to the subarray's median value. Then, after partitioning, half the items are probably to its left and half to its right. Unfortunately, the computational cost of finding the median value outweighs the benefit of doing so. As a compromise, the pivot is sometimes chosen as the median of the subarray's first, middle, and last values.

Another way to improve quicksort is to reduce the number of swaps required during partitioning. For instance, a technique that is on average more efficient can be stated as follows:

> After selecting a pivot value, move two index pointers from the opposite ends of the subarray toward the middle. As these pointers converge, items are swapped whenever an item on the left is greater than or equal to the pivot and an item on the right is less than or equal to the pivot. This process terminates when the pointers meet.

This technique does not require swapping the pivot at the beginning and end of the process, although the pivot might, of course, be moved at some point during the process. In this method, every time a swap occurs, it moves the items involved to their final positions within the partition. In contrast, the method presented earlier is less efficient because it swaps the smaller item to its final position while the larger item might be swapped several times.

There is a completely different approach to improving the efficiency of quicksort. Even though quicksort is on average O($n\log n$), the O(n^2) sorting algorithms of Chapter 4 can still be faster than quicksort for small values of n. Thus, it is advantageous to combine two different sorting algorithms. When the subarrays are large, we use quicksort, but once they become small, we switch to one of the nonrecursive algorithms. Alternatively, we could partially sort the array using quicksort, stopping each recursive descent when a subarray falls below some predefined size, say, 10 items. After this, we could sort the whole array, not just individual subarrays, using insertion sort, which is known to perform well on arrays that are nearly in order.

We explore some of these suggestions in the exercises.

10.3.2   Mergesort

Mergesort also employs a divide-and-conquer strategy to break the O(n^2) barrier. Here is an outline of the algorithm:

■ Compute the middle position of an array and recursively sort its left and right subarrays (divide and conquer).

■ Merge the two sorted subarrays back into a single sorted array.

■ Stop the process when subarrays can no longer be subdivided.

This top-level design strategy can be implemented as three Java methods:

■ mergeSort—the public method called by clients

■ mergeSortHelper—a private helper method that hides the extra parameter required by recursive calls

■ merge—a private method that implements the merging process

The merging process uses an extra array, which we call copyBuffer. To avoid the overhead of allocating and deallocating the copyBuffer each time merge is called, the buffer is allocated once in mergeSort and subsequently passed to mergeSortHelper and merge. Each time mergeSortHelper is called, it needs to know the bounds of the subarray with which it is working. These bounds are provided by two parameters: low and high. Here is the code for mergeSort:

```
public static void mergeSort(int[] a){
    // a            array being sorted
    // copyBuffer   temp space needed during merge

    int[] copyBuffer = new int[a.length];
    mergeSortHelper(a, copyBuffer, 0, a.length - 1);
}
```

After checking that it has been passed a subarray of at least two items, merge SortHelper computes the midpoint of the subarray, recursively sorts the portions below and above the midpoint, and calls `merge` to merge the results. Here is the code for `mergeSortHelper`:

```
private static void mergeSortHelper(int[] a, int[] copyBuffer,
                                    int low, int high){
    // a           array being sorted
    // copyBuffer  temp space needed during merge
    // low, high   bounds of subarray
    // middle      midpoint of subarray

    if (low < high){
        int middle = (low + high) / 2;
        mergeSortHelper(a, copyBuffer, low, middle);
        mergeSortHelper(a, copyBuffer, middle + 1, high);
        merge(a, copyBuffer, low, middle, high);
    }
}
```

Figure 10.10 shows the subarrays generated during recursive calls to `merge SortHelper`, starting from an array of eight items. Note that in this example the subarrays are evenly subdivided at each stage and there are 2^{k-1} subarrays to be merged at stage k. Had the length of the initial array not been a power of 2, then an exactly even subdivision would not have been achieved at each stage and the last stage would not have contained a full complement of subarrays. Figure 10.11 traces the process of merging the subarrays generated in Figure 10.10.

Figure 10.10   **Subarrays generated during a mergesort**

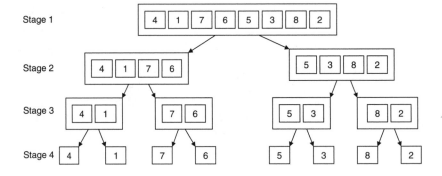

Figure 10.11   **Merging the subarrays generated during a mergesort**

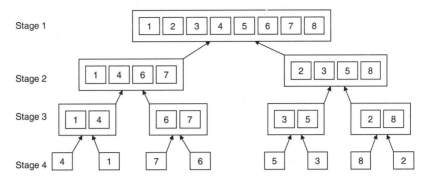

Finally, here is the code for the merge method:

```
1 private static void merge(int[] a, int[] copyBuffer,
2                           int low, int middle, int high){
3     // a           array that is being sorted
4     // copyBuffer  temp space needed during the merge process
5     // low         beginning of first sorted subarray
6     // middle      end of first sorted subarray
7     // middle + 1  beginning of second sorted subarray
8     // high        end of second sorted subarray
9
10    //Initialize i1 and i2 to the first items in each subarray
11    int i1 = low, i2 = middle + 1;
12
13    //Interleave items from the subarrays into the copyBuffer in such a
14    //way that order is maintained.
15    for (int i = low; i <= high; i++){
16        if (i1 > middle)
17            copyBuffer[i] = a[i2++];        //First subarray exhausted
18        else if (i2 > high)
19            copyBuffer[i] = a[i1++];        //Second subarray exhausted
20        else if (a[i1] < a[i2])
21            copyBuffer[i] = a[i1++];        //Item in first subarray is less
22        else
23            copyBuffer[i] = a[i2++];        //Item in second subarray is less
24    }
25
26    for (int i = low; i <= high; i++)       //Copy sorted items back into
27        a[i] = copyBuffer[i];               //proper position in a
28 }
```

The merge method combines two sorted subarrays into a larger sorted subarray. The first subarray lies between low and middle, and the second is between middle + 1 and high. The process consists of three steps:

1. Set up index pointers to the first items in each subarray *(line 11)*. These are at positions low and middle + 1.

2. Starting with the first item in each subarray, repeatedly compare items. Copy the smaller item from its subarray to the copy buffer and advance to the next item in the subarray. Repeat until all items have been copied from both subarrays. If the end of one subarray is reached before the other's, finish by copying the remaining items from the other subarray *(lines 15–24)*.

3. Copy the portion of `copyBuffer` between `low` and `high` back to the corresponding positions in the array `a` *(lines 26–27)*.

Time and Space Analysis for Mergesort

The run time of the `merge` method is dominated by the two `for` statements, each of which loop (`high` - `low` + 1) times. Consequently, the method's run time is O(high − low), and all the merges at a single stage take O(*n*) time. Because mergesort splits subarrays as evenly as possible at each stage, the number of stages is O(log*n*), and the maximum run time for mergesort is O(*n*log*n*) in all cases.

Mergesort has two space requirements that depend on the array's size. First, O(log*n*) space is required on the call stack to support recursive calls. Second, O(*n*) space is used by the copy buffer.

Improving Mergesort

Mergesort can be improved in two ways. First, the `merge` method can be modified so that the first `for` statement makes a single comparison on each iteration (see Exercises 10.3). Second, there exists a complex process that allows one to merge two subarrays without using a copy buffer and without changing the order of the method; however, it is beyond this book's scope. Third, subarrays below a certain size can be sorted using an alternative approach.

Exercises 10.3

1. Assume that the data in an array are arranged in the following order:
   ```
   44 39 12 26 38 66 10
   ```
   a. Draw a diagram that shows the subarrays generated when quicksort is applied to this array. For the pivot, choose the value at a subarray's midpoint.
   b. Repeat the exercise for mergesort.

2. Create two arrays using the integers 1–7 that demonstrate the best and the worst case behavior of quicksort as it is implemented in this section.

3. Devise a simulation that will allow you to determine the array sizes above which quicksort and mergesort become more efficient than insertion sort, bubble sort, and selection sort.

4. Following the suggestions in the section titled Improving Quicksort, make the following three modifications to quicksort:
   a. Let the pivot be the median of the first, middle, and last value in the subarray.
   b. Conduct swaps by moving two index pointers from the opposite ends of the subarray toward the middle. As these pointers converge, swap items whenever an item on the left is greater than or equal to the pivot and an item on the right is less than or equal to the pivot. End this process when the pointers meet.
   c. Stop recursion when a subarray of 10 or fewer items is encountered and complete the sorting process by calling insertion sort on the complete array.

5. Devise a simulation that compares the sorting algorithm in Exercise 4 with the quicksort method presented in the book. Attempt to determine if 10 is the optimal subarray size at which to stop recursion.

6. Determine the maximum run time of insertion sort when it is called in step c of Exercise 4.

7. Devise a simulation that generates performance figures for quicksort and mergesort, thus allowing you to decide which, if either, of these two sort algorithms is on average faster.

8. Modify the `merge` method in mergesort so that the number of comparisons on each iteration is reduced to one. Proceed as follows:

   ■ Copy the first subarray into `copyBuffer` from position `low` to `middle`.

   ■ Copy the second subarray in reverse order into `copyBuffer` from position `middle + 1` to `high`.

   ■ Compare the items `copyBuffer[low..middle]` to `copyBuffer [high..middle + 1]`. In this process, it is not necessary to test if either subarray has reached its end because the other subarray provides a sentinel value. Thus, `copyBuffer[middle + 1]` is a sentinel for all values in `copyBuffer[low..middle]`, and `copyBuffer[middle]` is a sentinel for all values in `copyBuffer[high..middle + 1]`.

9. Add `public` methods `quickSort` and `mergeSort` to `ListPT`. Implement the methods in `ArrayListPT` and `LinkedListPT`. For this to work, the items in the list must implement the `Comparable` interface. Compute the time and space complexity of these methods. When quicksort is applied to a linked list, is it more efficient to choose the last item as the pivot rather than the item at the list's midpoint? Why? Are there any drawbacks to doing so?

10.4   Recursion and Backtracking

In Chapter 7, we examined one approach to solving backtracking problems, namely, by using stacks. Now we show how recursion can be used instead. As stated in Chapter 7, a backtracking algorithm begins in a predefined starting state and then moves from state to state in search of a desired ending state. At every point along the way, when there is a choice between several alternative states, the algorithm picks one, possibly at random, and continues. If the algorithm reaches a state representing an undesirable outcome, it backs up to the last point at which there was an unexplored alternative and tries it. In this way, the algorithm either exhaustively searches all states or reaches the desired ending state.

Recursion is applied to backtracking by calling a recursive method each time an alternative state is considered. The recursive method tests the current state, and if it is an ending state, success is reported all the way back up the line; otherwise, there are two possibilities. One, the recursive method calls itself on an untried adjacent state. Two, all adjacent states have been tried, and the recursive method reports failure to the method that called it. In this procedure, the activation records on the call stack serve as the memory of the system so that, when control returns to a recursive method, it can resume where it left off. To be more precise:

```
SUCCESS = true
FAILURE = false
outcome = testState(starting state)
. . .
. . .
. . .
boolean testState (state)
   if state == ending state then
      return SUCCESS
   else
      mark state as visited
      for all adjacent unvisited states
         if testState(adjacentState) == SUCCESS then
            return SUCCESS
         end if
      end for
      return FAILURE
   end if
end testState
```

We now illustrate the process with a simple example. Suppose there are only five states, as shown in the following diagram, with states 1 and 5 representing the starting and ending states, respectively, and lines between states indicating adjacency. The succession of calls and returns then proceeds as follows:

```
call testState (state1)
   call testState(state2)
      call testState(state3)
      return FAILURE
   return FAILURE
   call testState(4)
      call testState(5)
      return SUCCESS
   return SUCCESS
return SUCCESS
```

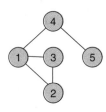

Keep in mind that we are presenting a generic application of recursion to backtracking. In a specific situation, the problem details can lead to minor variations; however, the general approach remains valid. To give you some practice with recursive backtracking, Exercise 10.4 includes an application to the Eight Queens problem. In addition, the chapter's first case study employs recursive backtracking.

Exercise 10.4

The Eight Queens problem requires determining the various ways in which eight queens can be placed on a chessboard so that none of them attack any of the others. The rules of chess allow a queen to move an arbitrary number of squares in a horizontal, vertical, or diagonal direction. Figure 10.12 shows one solution to the problem.

Backtracking is the best approach that anyone has found to solving this problem, and we illustrate how it works in Figure 10.13.

Figure 10.12   **One solution to the Eight Queens problem**

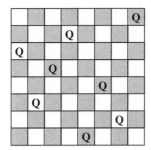

Figure 10.13   **Using backtracking to find a solution to the Eight Queens problem**

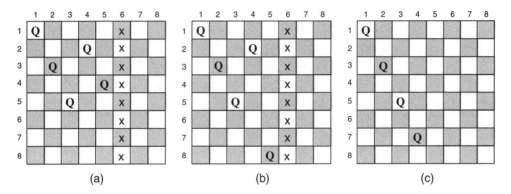

(a)   (b)   (c)

- Figure 10.13 (a): We place the first queen in square (1, 1) of column one. We place the second queen in column two in the first square not under attack, namely (3, 2). Applying the same strategy to columns three, four, and five, we place queens in squares (5, 3), (2, 4), and (4, 5).

- Figure 10.13 (b): When we attempt to place a queen in column six, we discover that all of the squares are under attack, so we backtrack to column five and place the queen in the next square not under attack, which is (8, 5).

- Figure 10.13 (c): However, all squares in column six are still under attack, and we must backtrack to column five again. There are no untried squares left in column five, and we backtrack to column four, where we try the next square not under attack at (7, 4). Now we can go forward again to column five and so on. In this way, we will find a solution if there is one.

Here is a recursive algorithm based on the preceding strategy that lists not just one but all the possible solutions. Initially, the algorithm is called with the value of c equal to 1.

```
void tryQueen(int c)
   for r = 1 to 8
      if square (r, c) is not under attack then
```

Continued

Continued

```
        place queen in square (r, c)
        if c == 8 then
            display configuration
        else
            tryQueen(c + 1)
        end if
        remove queen from square (r, c)
      end if
    end for
end tryQueen
```

a. Write a complete program that solves the Eight Queens problem.

b. What is the maximum run time of this program?

10.5   Why Recursion?

As we discuss in more detail soon, recursive methods can always be rewritten to remove recursion, thus raising the question: Why use recursion in the first place? When writing a method, we should balance several, sometimes conflicting, considerations. Prominent among these are efficiency, simplicity, and maintainability. First and foremost, we must meet the performance requirements of our application, after which we should strive to write code that is as easy to develop and maintain as possible. Because of the time and space overhead associated with method calls, recursive methods usually are not as efficient as their nonrecursive counterparts; however, their elegance and simplicity sometimes make them the preferred choice. To put these remarks in perspective, we consider examples of process which we feel should not be recursive, others which might be recursive, and finally those which should be recursive.

Summing the numbers in an array should never be done recursively, except as an exercise (see Exercise 2, Section 10.1). The result is awkward and inefficient. The recursive `fibonacci` method discussed in Section 10.1 affords another poor application of recursion. Although the method is simple and follows the definition closely, it is very inefficient and should be replaced by the equivalent $O(n)$ iterative method.

Binary search is implemented equally well with or without recursion. We presented an iterative version in Chapter 4 and a recursive one earlier in this chapter. Both methods are straightforward and clear, and both have a maximum run time of $O(\log n)$. Although the overhead associated with method calls makes the recursive method slower and more space intensive, this consideration is relatively unimportant considering the fact that searching an array of even 1 million items takes no more than 20 recursive calls.

Quicksort, we feel, is implemented best using recursion. We will soon see an iterative version, which is marginally faster but considerably more complex. While the iterative version might be worth considering if we were developing a utilities library for commercial distribution, the added development and maintenance costs normally outweigh the slight performance advantage.

10.5.1 Getting Rid of Recursion

The fact that Java implements recursion by means of a call stack suggests that every recursive method can be emulated as an iterative method operating on a stack, and in fact, this is the case. However, the general manner of making this conversion produces results that are so awkward that we say no more about it. Instead, we suggest approaching each conversion on an individual basis. Frequently, recursion can be replaced by iteration alone, as is the case when computing factorials or Fibonacci numbers. Sometimes a stack is also needed, as illustrated in the following nonrecursive version of quicksort:

```java
public class Entry {
   public int low;
   public int high;

   public Entry (int low, int high){
      this.low = low;
      this.high = high;
   }
}
   . . .
   . . .
public static void quickSort (int[] a){
   lamborne.Stack stack = new LinkedStack();
   stack.push(Entry (0, a.length - 1));

   while (! stack.isEmpty()){
      Entry entry = stack.pop();
      if (entry.low < entry.high){
         int pivotLocation = partition(a, entry.low, entry.high);
         stack.push (new StackEntry (entry.low, pivotLocation - 1));
         stack.push (new StackEntry (pivotLocation + 1, entry.high));
      }
   }
}
```

Here recursive calls have been replaced by pushing subarray limits onto a stack. Notice that the `partition` method is used unchanged.

10.5.2 Tail-Recursion

We have seen that recursion has two costs: extra time and extra memory. However, as Guy Steele has shown (see "Debunking the 'Expensive Procedure Call' Myth," *Proceedings of the National Conference of the ACM,* 1977), it is possible to run certain types of recursive algorithms as if they were iterative ones without the overhead associated with recursion. The essential requirement is that the algorithms must be *tail-recursive.* An algorithm is tail-recursive if no work is done in the algorithm after a recursive call. For example, according to this criterion, the factorial method presented earlier is not tail-recursive because a multiplication is performed after each recursive call. We can convert this version of the factorial method to a tail-recursive version by performing the multiplication before the recursive call. To do so, we need an additional parameter that passes down the accumulated value of the factorial on each recursive call. In the last call to the method, this value is returned as the result:

```
int factIter (int n, int result){
   if (n <= 1)
      return result;
   else
      return factIter (n - 1, n * result);
}
```

Note that the multiplication is performed before the recursive call when the parameters are evaluated. On the first call to `factIter`, the `result` parameter should be 1:

```
int factorial (int n){
   return factIter (n, 1);
}
```

Steele showed that compilers can translate tail-recursive code written in a high-level language to a loop in machine language. The machine code treats the method's parameters as variables associated with the loop and generates an iterative process rather than a recursive one. Thus, these methods incur none of the costs usually associated with recursion.

There are, however, two catches. The programmer must be able to convert a recursive method to a tail-recursive method, and the compiler must be one that generates iterative machine code from tail-recursive methods. Unfortunately, some methods are difficult or impossible to convert to tail-recursion, and few compilers perform the needed optimization. If you find that your Java compiler supports this optimization, you should convert some methods to tail-recursion and see if they run faster than the originals.

Exercises 10.5

1. Redo Exercises 10.1 without using recursion and compare the results to the recursive versions.

2. Redo mergesort without using recursion and compare the result to the recursive version.

3. Redo the Eight Queens problem without using recursion and compare the result to the recursive version.

4. Write a tail-recursive implementation of the exponentiation method in Exercise 1 of Section 10.1.

5. Write a tail-recursive implementation of the Fibonacci method.

10.6   Case Study 1: A Maze Solver

In Chapter 7, we discussed the role of stacks in backtracking and presented an exercise involving a program to solve a maze problem. Earlier in this chapter, we showed how backtracking algorithms can be implemented with recursion. Now, in this case study, we develop a recursive solution to a maze problem.

10.6.1   Request

Write a program that allows the user to draw a maze and then have the computer find a path out of it.

10.6.2   Analysis

As was discussed in Chapter 7, we can represent the maze as a two-dimensional array of characters. With two exceptions, each character at position (row, column) in this grid is initially either a space, indicating a path, or a star (*), indicating a wall. The exceptions, the letters P and T, mark the single start (a parking lot) and exit (a mountaintop) positions, respectively.

Recall from the discussion in Chapter 7 that the algorithm leaves a period in each cell that it visits so that cells will not be visited again. At the end of the search process, the solution path contains the periods, but they are also in other paths explored but which lead to dead ends. In the new version of the program, we can discriminate between the solution path and cells visited but not on the path by using two marking characters: the period and X. The algorithm initially leaves an X in each cell that it visits. If the algorithm cannot find a solution path from this cell, it is marked with a period. Thus, at the end of the process, the solution path consists of cells with an X, whereas cells visited but on dead-end paths contain a period.

We now develop the recursive algorithm, called getOut, that attempts to find a path through this maze. This algorithm

- Expects the index positions of a cell in the grid as parameters
- Can observe or modify cells in the grid
- Returns true if the cell marked T is found or false if a dead end is reached

We assume that someone has defined the successive integer constants NORTH, SOUTH, EAST, WEST, and FAILED to represent the four directions and a dead-end condition, respectively. getOut begins by examining the state of the cell at position (row, column). Here are the possible states and the algorithm's actions:

1. If this cell contains T, then getOut returns true (the player exits the maze).
2. If this cell contains * (a wall) or a period (a mark left on a branch of the same path), then getOut returns false, indicating a dead end.
3. If this cell contains a space (an untried path), then getOut
   - puts an X into the cell
   - uses recursion in each of the four directions from the current cell, breaking and returning true if one of these calls returns true

Here is the pseudocode for getOut:

```
If row < 0 or row >= ROW_ MAX or col < 0 or col >= COL_MAX
   return false
If maze[row][col] = 'T'
   return true
```

Continued

Continued

```
Else if maze[row][col] = '*' or
       maze[row][col] = 'X' or
       maze[row][col] = '.' or
   return false
Else
   Set maze[row][col] to 'X'
   Set found to false
   Set direction to NORTH
   While not found and direction != FAILED
      If direction = NORTH
         Set found to getOut(row - 1, column)
      Else if direction = SOUTH
         Set found to getOut(row + 1, column)
      Else if direction = EAST
         Set found to getOut(row, column + 1)
      Else if direction = WEST
         Set found to getOut(row, column - 1)
      Increment direction
If not found
   Set maze[row][col] to "."
Return found
```

The interface displays the maze in a text area. The maze initially consists of a 15 by 30 grid of * characters, as shown in the Figure 10.14.

Figure 10.14   **The user interface for the maze program**

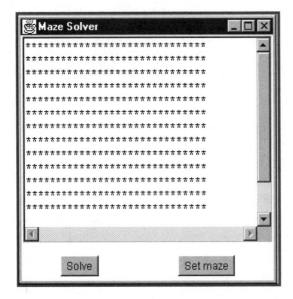

The user creates a path by deleting the * character and replacing it with a space character. The P character indicates the start position and the T character indicates the exit position. The program assumes that the user will not alter the original dimensions of the grid. The user selects the Set maze button to signal that the editing process is finished. Figure 10.15 shows a maze after the user has edited it and selected the Set maze button.

Figure 10.15 **The maze interface after the user has indicated the possible paths**

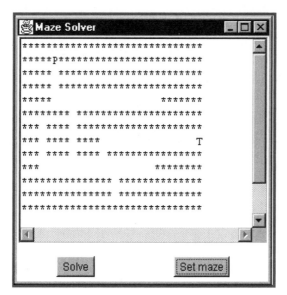

The user then selects the Solve button to attempt to find a path from the start symbol to the exit symbol. Whether or not a solution path exists, the program responds with a message box and a display of the positions visited with a period and X, as shown in Figure 10.16.

Figure 10.16   **The maze interface after the user has selected Solve**

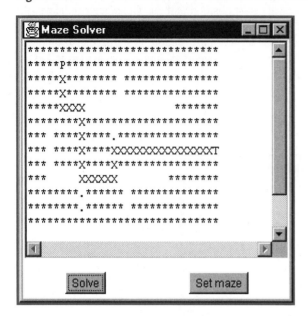

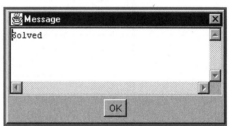

10.6.3   Classes

We divide the responsibilities between a view class called `MazeView` and a model class called `MazeModel`. `MazeView` is responsible for interacting with the user and updating the display of the maze. `MazeModel` maintains the data model of the maze and carries out the search for a path.

10.6.4   Implementation of `MazeView`

When the view needs to update the model with a new maze, it sends the model the message `setMaze(aString)`. The string parameter is the text currently in the text area. When the view needs to obtain the maze from the model, it sends the message `getMaze` to the model. This message returns a string that can be displayed in the text area. The method `printMaze` is provided for the model to request that the current state of the maze be displayed. Here is a listing of `MazeView`:

```
 1 import java.awt.*;
 2 import javax.swing.*;
 3 import java.awt.event.*;
 4
 5 public class MazeView extends JFrame {
 6
 7    /////////////////////////////////////////////////////// main
 8
 9    public static void main (String[] args) {
10       JFrame theFrame = new MazeView ();
11       theFrame.setSize (300, 300);
```

Continued

Continued

```
12          theFrame.setVisible (true);
13      }
14
15      //////////////////////////////////////////////////////// Model
16
17      private MazeModel model;
18
19      //////////////////////////////////////////////////////// View
20
21      // Create controls
22      private JTextArea taMaze  = new JTextArea("");
23      private JButton    btSolve = new JButton("Solve");
24      private JButton    btSet   = new JButton("Set maze");
25
26      public MazeView() {
27          // Set title and initialize
28          setTitle("Maze Solver");
29          model = new MazeModel(this);
30          taMaze.setText(model.getMaze());
31          taMaze.setFont(new Font ("Courier", Font.PLAIN, 10));
32
33          // Create container and layout
34          Container contentPane = getContentPane();
35          EasyGridLayout layout = new EasyGridLayout();
36          contentPane.setLayout (layout);
37
38          // Set constraints
39          JScrollPane spMaze = new JScrollPane(taMaze);
40          layout.setConstraints(spMaze ,1,1,2,1);
41          layout.setConstraints(btSolve,5,1,1,1);
42          layout.setConstraints(btSet   ,5,2,1,1);
43
44          // Add controls to container
45          contentPane.add(spMaze);
46          contentPane.add(btSolve);
47          contentPane.add(btSet);
48
49          //Specify listeners
50          btSolve.addActionListener(new MyButtonListener());
51          btSet.addActionListener(new MyButtonListener());
52          addWindowListener(new MyWindowAdapter());
53      }
54
55      public void printMaze(){
56          taMaze.setText(model.getMaze());
57      }
58
59      //////////////////////////////////////////////////////// Controller
60
61      // Button action listener
62      private class MyButtonListener implements ActionListener{
63          public void actionPerformed (ActionEvent event){
64              Object buttonObj = event.getSource();
65              if (buttonObj == btSolve)
66                  if (model.solveMaze())
```

Continued

Continued

```
67                    new MessageBox(MazeView.this, "Solved", 150, 100);
68              else
69                    new MessageBox(MazeView.this, "No path out", 150, 100);
70          else if (buttonObj == betSet)
71              model.setMaze(taMaze.getText());
72      }
73    }
74
75    // Window listener
76    private class MyWindowAdapter extends WindowAdapter{
77      public void windowClosing (WindowEvent e){
78          System.exit(0);
79      }
80    }
81 }
```

10.6.5   Implementation of `MazeModel`

`MazeModel` uses the recursive search algorithm discussed earlier. Most of the `MazeModel` methods manipulate a two-dimensional array of characters. Here is a listing of `MazeModel`:

```
 1 public class MazeModel extends Object{
 2
 3    static private int NORTH = 0
 4                       SOUTH = 1,
 5                       EAST = 2,
 6                       WEST = 3,
 7                       FAILED = 4;
 8
 9    static private int ROW_MAX = 15, COL_MAX = 30;
10    private char[][] maze;
11    private int startRow, startCol;
12    private MazeView view;
13
14    public MazeModel (MazeView mv){
15      view = mv;
16      maze = new char[ROW_MAX][COL_MAX];
17      initMaze();
18    }
19
20    public boolean solveMaze(){
21
22      findStartPos();
23      maze[startRow][startCol] = ' ';
24      boolean solved = getOut (startRow, startCol);
25      maze[startRow][startCol] = 'p';
26      view.printMaze();
27      return solved;
28    }
29
30    private void initMaze(){
```

Continued

```
31          for (int row = 0; row < ROW_MAX; row++)
32              for (int col = 0; col < COL_MAX; col++)
33                  maze[row][col] = '*''
34      }
35
36      public void setMaze (String mazeStr){
37
38
39          for (int row = 0; row < ROW_MAX; row++){
40              int StrPos = row * COL_MAX + row;
41              for (int col = 0; col < COL_MAX; col++){
42                  maze[row][col] = mazeStr.charAt(strPos);
43                  strPos++;
44              }
45          }
46      }
47
48      public String getMaze(){
49          String str = "";
50          for (int row = 0; row < ROW_MAX; row++){
51              for (int col = 0; col < COL_MAX; col++)
52                  str = str + maze[row][col];
53              str = str + "\n";
54          }
55          return str;
56      }
57
58      private void findStartPos (){
59          for (int row = 0; row < ROW_MAX; row++)
60              for (int col = 0; col < COL_MAX; col++)
61                  if (maze[row][col] = = 'P'){
62                      startRow = row;
63                      startCol = col;
64                      return;
65                  }
66      }
67
68      private boolean getOut(int row, int col){
69          // Check for the border of the maze
70          if (row < 0 || row >= ROW_MAX || col < 0 || col >= COL_MAX)
71              return false;
72
73          // Check for the exit position
74          else if (maze[row][col] == 'T')
75              return true;
76
77          // Check for a wall or a position already visited
78          else if (maze[row][col] == '*' ||
79                  maze[row][col] == 'X' ||
80                  maze[row][col] == '.')
81              return false;
82          else{
83              maze[row][col] = 'X';                    // Mark position as visited
84              view.printMaze();
85              bollean found = false;
```

Continued

Continued

```
 86                     int direction = NORTH;
 87                     while (! Found && direction != FAILED){    // Try all directions
 88                        if (direction == NORTH)
 89                           found = getOut(row - 1, col);
 90                        else if (direction == SOUTH)
 91                           found - getOut(row + 1, col);
 92                        else if (direction == EAST)
 93                           found = getOut(row, col + 1);
 94                        else if (direction == WEST)
 95                           found = getOut(row, col - 1);
 96                        direction++;
 97                     }
 98                     if (! found){                     // Mark cell as on dead end path
 99                        maze[row][col] = '.';
100                        view.printMaze();
101                     }
102                     return found;
103                  }
104            }
105 }
```

Exercises 10.6

1. Modify the maze program of the case study to count and display the number of calls of the getOut method for each solution. Test the program with mazes that have one, two, and three intersections and explain any patterns that you see in the numbers.

2. Return to the stack version of the maze program of Chapter 7 and explain how one might modify the program to display just the solution path.

10.7   Recursive Descent and Programming Languages

In Chapter 7, we discussed methods that use a stack to convert expressions from infix to postfix and then evaluate the postfix form. Recursive methods are also used in processing languages, whether they are programming languages such as Java or natural languages such as English. In this section, we give a brief overview of grammars, parsing, and a recursive descent parsing strategy, followed in the next section by a related case study.

10.7.1   Introduction to Grammars

Most programming languages, no matter how small or large, have a precise and complete definition called a grammar. A grammar consists of several parts:

1. A *vocabulary* (or *dictionary* or *lexicon*) consisting of words and symbols allowed in sentences in the language.

2. A set of *syntax rules* that specify how symbols in the language are combined to form sentences.

3. A set of *semantic rules* that specify how sentences in the language should be interpreted. For example, the statement "x = y" might mean "copy the value of y to the variable x."

Computer scientists have developed several notations for expressing grammars. For example, suppose we would like to define a language for representing simple arithmetic expressions such as

```
4 + 2
3 * 5
6 - 3
10 / 2
(4 + 5) * 10
```

but we don't want to allow expressions such as 4 + 3 - 2 or 4 * 3 / 2. The following Extended Backus-Naur Form (EBNF) grammar defines the syntax and vocabulary of this little language:

```
expression = term [ addingOperator  term ]

term = factor [ multiplyOperator factor ]

factor = number | "(" expression ")"

number = digit { digit }

digit = "0" | "1" | "2" | "3" | "4" | "5" | "6" | "7" | "8" | "9"

addingOperator = "+" | "-"

multiplyingOperator = "*" | "/"
```

This grammar uses three kinds of symbols:

1. *Terminal symbols.* These symbols are in the vocabulary of the language and literally appear in programs in the language—for instance, + and * in the preceding examples.

2. *Nonterminal symbols.* These symbols name phrases in the language, such as `expression` or `factor` in the preceding examples. A phrase usually consists of one or more terminal symbols and/or the names of other phrases.

3. *Metasymbols.* These symbols are used to organize the rules in the grammar. Table 10.2 lists the metasymbols used in EBNF.

Thus, the rule

```
expression = term [ addingOperator term ]
```

means "an `expression` is defined as a `term`, which might or might not be followed by an `addingOperator` and another `term`." The symbol to the left of the = in a rule is called the *left side of the rule;* the set of items to the right of the = is called the *right side of the rule.*

Table 10.2   **The Metasymbols in EBNF**

Metasymbols	Use
**	Enclose literal items
=	Means "is defined as"
[ ]	Enclose optional items
{ }	Enclose zero or more items
( )	Group together required choices
|	Indicates a choice

The grammar just discussed does not allow expressions such as 45 * 22 + 14 / 2, forcing programmers to use parentheses if they want to form an equivalent expression, such as (45 * 22) + (14 / 2). The next grammar solves this problem by allowing iteration over terms and factors:

```
expression = term { addingOperator  term }

term = factor { multiplyOperator factor }

factor = number | "(" expression ")"

number = digit { digit }

digit = "0" | "1" | "2" | "3" | "4" | "5" | "6" | "7" | "8" | "9"

addingOperator = "+" | "-"

multiplyingOperator = "*" | "/"
```

In any grammar, there is one privileged symbol known as the **start symbol.** In our two example grammars, the start symbol is expression. The use of this symbol is discussed shortly.

You might have noticed that the foregoing grammars have a **recursive** quality. For instance, an expression consists of terms, a term consists of factors, and a factor can be a number or an expression within parentheses. Thus, an expression can contain another expression.

10.7.2   Recognizing, Parsing, and Interpreting Sentences in a Language

To process the sentences in a language, we use recognizers, parsers, and interpreters. A **recognizer** analyzes a string to determine if it is a sentence in a given language. The inputs to the recognizer are the grammar and a string. The outputs are "Yes" or "No" and appropriate syntax error messages. Obviously, if there are one or more syntax errors, we get "No," and the string is not a sentence.

A *parser* has all of the features of a recognizer and in addition returns information about the syntactic and semantic structure of the sentence. This information is used in further processing and might be contained in a *parse tree* (see Chapter 11) or in some other representation.

An *interpreter* carries out the actions specified by a sentence. In other words, an interpreter runs the program. Occasionally, parsing and interpreting occur at the same time; otherwise, the input to the interpreter is the data structure that results from parsing.

From now on, we don't distinguish between a recognizer and a parser, but use "parser" to refer to both.

10.7.3 Lexical Analysis and the Scanner

When developing a parser, it is convenient to assign the task of recognizing symbols in a string to a lower level module called a *scanner.* The scanner performs *lexical analysis* in which individual words are picked out of a stream of characters. The scanner also outputs lexical error messages as needed. Examples of lexical errors are inappropriate characters in a number and unrecognized symbols (ones not in the vocabulary).

The output of the scanner is a stream of words called *tokens.* These become the input to another module called the *syntax analyzer.* This module uses the tokens and the grammar rules to determine whether or not the program is syntactically correct. Thus, the lexical analyzer determines if characters go together to form correct words, while the syntax analyzer determines if words go together to form correct sentences. For simplicity, we refer to the lexical analyzer as the scanner and to the syntax analyzer as the parser. The connection between the scanner and parser is shown in Figure 10.17.

Figure 10.17   **A scanner and parser working in tandem**

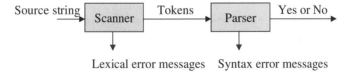

10.7.4 Parsing Strategies

There are several strategies for parsing. One of the simplest is called *recursive descent parsing.* A recursive descent parser defines a method for each rule in the grammar. Each method processes the phrase or portion of the input sentence covered by its rule. The top-level method corresponds to the rule that has the start symbol on its left side. When this method is called, it calls the methods corresponding to the nonterminal symbols on the right side of its rule. For example, here is the top-level rule and the associated parsing method for the first grammar:

```
expression = term [ addingOperator term ]              //Rule

private void expression(){                              //Parsing method
    term();
    Token token = scanner.get();
    if (token.type == Token.PLUS || token.type == Token.MINUS){
        scanner.next();
        term();
        token = scanner.get();
    }
}
```

Note the following points:

1. Each nonterminal symbol in the grammar becomes the name of a method in the parser.

2. The body of a method processes the phrases on the right side of the rule.

3. To process a nonterminal symbol, we just invoke a method.

4. To process an optional item, we use an `if` statement.

5. We observe the current token by sending the message `get` to the scanner object.

6. We scan to the next token by sending the message `next` to the scanner object.

Our parser descends through the grammar rules, starting with the top-level method and working its way down to lower level methods, which can then recursively call methods at a higher level.

Recursive descent parsers can easily be extended to interpret as well as parse programs. In the case of our languages, for example, each parsing method could compute and return the value represented by the associated phrase in the expression. The value returned by the top method would be the value of the entire expression. Alternatively, as we show in Chapter 11, a recursive descent parser can build and return a parse tree. Another module then traverses this tree to compute the value of the expression.

10.8   Case Study 2: A Recursive Descent Parser

In case study of Chapter 7, we developed a program that used a stack to evaluate postfix expressions. That program assumed the user entered syntactically correct postfix expressions and made no attempt to parse them. We also presented an algorithm in Chapter 7 to convert infix expressions to postfix expressions. If one added error handling to this algorithm, one would have a parser. In this case study, we develop a recursive descent parser using the methods described earlier in this chapter.

10.8.1   Request

Write a program that parses arithmetic expressions.

10.8.2 Analysis

The interface provides an input text area into which the user can type an expression. When the user selects the Parse button, the program parses the expression and displays the following information in an output text area:

- the message "No errors" if the expression is syntactically correct
- a message containing the kind of error, the offending token, and the input string up to the point of error, if a syntax error occurs

10.8.3 Proposed Interface

In a GUI-based system, we would also like to have a module to manage the user interface. We called this the *parser interface module.* It sets up buttons and data display areas and handles button options. Figure 10.18 shows the complete structure of a parsing system. Figures 10.19 and 10.20 give the interfaces.

Figure 10.18   **Modules in a GUI-based parser**

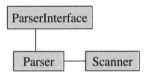

Figure 10.19   **The user interface for the parser program**

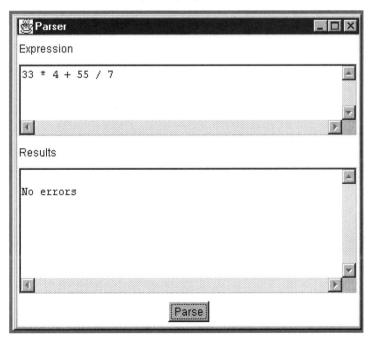

Figure 10.20   **Reporting syntax errors**

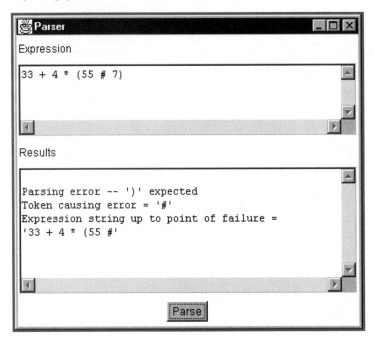

Classes

We developed the Scanner and Token classes for evaluating expressions in the case study of Chapter 7. To these we add the classes Parser and ParserInter face. The code for the interface is on the book's CD.

10.8.4   Implementation of **Parser**

The class Parser implements the recursive descent strategy discussed earlier. There is one parsing method for each rule in the grammar. Here is the code:

```
 1 public class Parser extends Object {
 2
 3    private Scanner scanner;
 4    private String  completionMessage;
 5    private boolean parseSuccessful;
 6
 7
//==============================================================================
 8
 9    public Parser (){
10       parseSuccessful = false;
11       completionMessage = "Parsing error -- nothing has been parsed yet";
12    }
13
14
```

Continued

Continued

```
//==============================================================================
15
16      public boolean successful (){
17          return parseSuccessful;
18      }
19
20
//==============================================================================
21
22      public String toString(){
23          return completionMessage;
23      }
25
26
//==============================================================================
27
28      public void parse (String str){
29          if (str == null || str.length() == 0){
30              parseSuccessful = false;
31              completionMessage = "Parsing error -- expression null or empty";
32              throw new RuntimeException (completionMessage);
33          }
34          completionMessage = "No errors";
35          parseSuccessful = true;
36          scanner = new Scanner (str);
37          scanner.first();
38          expression();
39          accept (scanner.get(), Token.EOE, "symbol after end of expression");
40      }
41
42      private void accept (Token token, int expected, String errorMessage){
43          if (token.type != expected)
44              fatalError (token, errorMessage);
45      }
46
47      private void fatalError (Token token, String errorMessage){
48          parseSuccessful = false;
49          completionMessage = "Parsing error --" + errorMessage +
50                              "\nToken causing error = '" + token + "'" +
51                              "\nExpression string up to point of failure = " +
52                              "\n'" + scanner.stringUpToCurrentToken() + "'";
53          throw new RuntimeException (completionMessage);
54      }
55
56      private void expression(){
57          term();
58          Token token = scanner.get();
59          while (token.type == Token.PLUS || token.type == Token.MINUS){
60              scanner.next();
61              term();
62              token = scanner.get();
63          }
64      }
65
66      private void term(){
```

Continued

```
67          primary();
68          Token token = scanner.get();
69          while (token.type == Token.MUL || token.type == Token.DIV){
70              scanner.next();
71              primary();
72              token = scanner.get();
73          }
74      }
75
76      private void primary(){
77          Token token = scanner.get();
78          switch (token.type){
79              case Token.INT;
80                  scanner.next();
81                  break;
82              case Token.L_PAR;
83                  scanner.next();
84                  expression();
85                  accept (scanner.get(), Token.R_PAR, "')' expected");
86                  scanner.next();
87                  break;
88              default;
89                  fatalError (token, "bad primary");
90          }
91      }
92 }
```

The methods `accept` and `fatalError` *(lines 42–54)* handle the bulk of the possible syntax errors. `accept` expects three parameters: the expected token type, the type of the current token, and an error message. If the current token's type is not the expected one, `accept` calls `fatalError` with the message. `fatalError` builds the appropriate completion message and then throws a new `RunTimeException`. As we saw earlier, this exception is caught in the parser interface module.

Exercise 10.8

An interpreter not only parses expressions for their syntax but also evaluates them to determine their values. Extend the parser of Case Study 2 so that it both parses and evaluates expressions. The only change to the interface is that the output contains the value of the expression if that expression is syntactically correct. The program also detects as a semantic error the attempt to divide by 0. Make each parsing method responsible for computing and returning the value of that portion of the expression that it parses. For example, the method `primary` has the following options:

■ The current token is an integer literal, so return that token's integer value.

■ The current token is a left parenthesis, consume it, call `expression`, and return that method's value.

■ The current token is something else, so there is a syntax error. Return a default value of 0.

KEY TERMS

base case	parser	scanner
infinite recursion	partition	stack overflow
interpreter	pivot	stopping state
lexical analysis	quicksort	syntax analyzer
mergesort	recognizer	tail-recursive
metasymbol	recursive descent	terminal symbol
nonterminal symbol	recursive step	token

CHAPTER SUMMARY

A recursive algorithm sometimes provides a more natural, elegant, and simple solution to a given problem than a loop. Recursive problem solving is a special case of the divide-and-conquer strategy. A problem that lends itself to a recursive solution typically can be broken into smaller subproblems of exactly the same form as the original problem. During decomposition, a recursive algorithm runs itself with a smaller instance of the problem (usually a data parameter). The decomposition continues until one or more base cases of the problem are reached, at which point the algorithm stops the recursion and returns a simple value. When the algorithm returns from a recursive decomposition, it may combine the value returned with another value to form a more complex solution.

Some recursive methods require a run-time stack to track the recursive calls. Each time a recursive method is called, a new stack frame is pushed onto the stack. When each call returns, its stack frame is popped. A stack frame records information about a single method call, such as the values of its parameters, its return value, and the address of the next instruction in the calling method.

Any recursive algorithm can be translated to an equivalent algorithm that uses a loop. Because some recursive algorithms require a stack at run time to track the recursive calls, their iterative counterparts also require the use of an explicit stack collection.

The use of recursion does not always incur substantially more overhead than the use of loops. Tail-recursive algorithms do not use their returned values for further computation when recursive calls return. Thus, optimizing compilers can translate these recursive algorithms to iterative machine code. Programmers looking for elegant solutions at no extra performance cost should translate their non-tail-recursive algorithms to tail-recursive algorithms. When this translation cannot be accomplished and performance is an issue, the programmer would do better to use a loop with an explicit stack.

Quicksort and mergesort are two common, efficient sorting algorithms that use recursion. Quicksort selects a pivot element, rearranges the items around this element, and recursively sorts the items that are smaller and the items that are larger than the pivot. Mergesort recursively sorts the lower half and the upper half of a list and merges the results.

REVIEW QUESTIONS

1. Describe two common applications of recursive methods.

2. Describe the difference between a base case and a recursive step in a recursive method.

3. What type of control statement is typically used in a recursive method?

4. What is the role of the parameter(s) in a recursive method?

5. What is the role of the return value in a recursive method?

6. Describe the features of a run-time environment that are needed to support the execution of a recursive method.

7. Are recursive methods slower than the equivalent methods that use loops? Why or why not?

8. Describe what happens when the base case of a recursive method is never reached.

9. What is the difference between tail-recursion and non-tail-recursion?

10. Which two common sorting algorithms use recursion?

CHAPTER 11

Introduction to Trees

OBJECTIVES   Upon completion of this chapter, you should be able to

- Use the appropriate vocabulary to describe trees

- State the differences between a binary tree and a general tree

- Understand the difference between linked and array implementations of trees and state the criteria for choosing between them

- Discuss the common ways in which trees are traversed

- Write recursive methods for processing trees

This chapter provides the conceptual framework for working with the hierarchical collections known as trees. We begin with an overview of the terminology used to talk about trees and examine representations of the two most common: binary trees and general trees. To explore the representation of binary trees, we then develop a prototype binary tree class. A case study illustrates the use of a variant of a binary tree called an expression tree for evaluating arithmetic expressions. We then show how to add a tree collection that represents general trees to the Java collection framework. Chapter 12 continues our examination of trees by looking at some special-purpose variations, such as heaps, binary search trees, and other kinds of search trees.

11.1   Overview of Trees

To this point, we have been discussing linear collections; however, many applications require collections in which there is a hierarchical relationship between items. In computer science, we call these collections trees. They are characterized by the fact that each item can have multiple successors, and all items, except a privileged item called the *root,* have exactly one predecessor.

For example, consider Figure 11.1, which is the parse tree for the sentence, "The girl hit the ball with a bat." In this, and in all diagrams of trees, the items are called *nodes.* Trees

Figure 11.1 **Parse tree for a sentence**

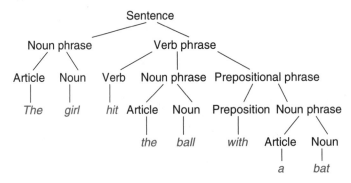

are drawn with the root at the top. Immediately below a node and connected to it by lines are its successors, or ***children.*** A node without children (in blue italic in the figure) is a ***leaf.*** Immediately above a node is its predecessor, or ***parent.*** Thus, the root node "Sentence" has two children but no parent. In contrast, the leaf node "ball" has a parent but no children. A node, such as "Noun phrase," that has children is an ***interior node.***

A book's table of contents is another familiar example of a hierarchical collection or tree. Here, however, each node is on a single line, and indentation indicates parent-child relationships (Figure 11.2). The ellipses (. . .) indicate omitted entries. In addition, trees are used to organize a computer's file system (Figure 11.3) as we are reminded every time we view the files on our hard drive.

These examples barely scratch the surface because the applications of trees are truly multitudinous. In this and the next chapter, we encounter a few more: expression trees, search trees, and heaps.

Figure 11.2 **Partial Table of Contents for *The Albatross Book of Living Verse,* published by W. Collins Sons and Co. Ltd., London**

The Albatross Book of Living Verse
  Early Ballads of Unknown Date and Authorship
    Childe Maurice 5
    The Douglas Tragedy 8
    True Thomas 10
    . . .
  Early Songs of Unknown Date and Authorship
    Cuccu Song 43
    . . .
  The Fourteenth to Sixteenth Centuries Chaucer to the Elizabethans
    Geoffrey Chaucer (1340?-1400)
      Prologue (from "The Canterbury Tales") 62
      Five Pilgrims (from "The Canterbury Tales") 62
      The Freres Tale 73
      . . .
    John Skelton (1460?-1529)
      The Prelates (from "Colin Clout") 92
      . . .

Figure 11.3   **A partial directory tree of the files on the disorganized home computer of one of the authors**

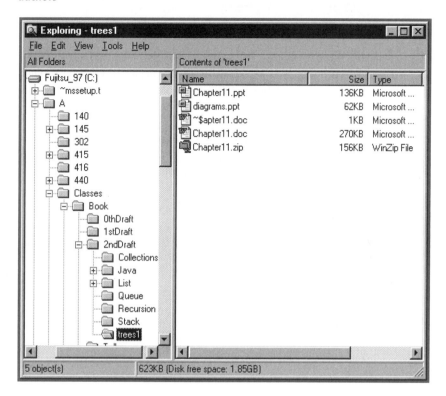

11.1.1   Talking about Trees

We have already introduced some of the terminology associated with trees, but there is more. The terminology is a peculiar mix of biological, genealogical, and geometric terms. Table 11.1 provides a quick summary with the earlier terms repeated. Figure 11.4 shows a tree and some of its properties.

Table 11.1   **A Summary of Terms Used to Describe Trees**

Term	Definition
Node	An item stored in a tree.
Root	The topmost node in a tree. It is the only node without a predecessor.
Child	A successor of a node. A node can have more than one child, and its children are viewed as organized in left to right order. The leftmost child is called the first child, and the rightmost is the last child.
Parent	The predecessor of a node. A node can have only one parent.

continued

Table 11.1   **A Summary of Terms Used to Describe Trees** *(Continued)*

Term	Definition
Siblings	The children of a common parent.
Edge/Branch	The line that connects a parent to its child.
Descendant	A node's descendants include its children, its children's children, etc., down to the leaves.
Ancestor	A node's ancestors include its parent, its parent's parent, etc., up to the root.
Path	The sequence of edges that connects a node and one of its descendants.
Path length	The number of edges in a path.
Leaf	A node that has no children.
Interior node	A node that has at least one child.
Depth or level	The depth or level of a node equals the length of the path connecting it to the root. Thus, the root depth or level of the root is 0. Its children are at level 1 and so on.
Height	The height of a tree equals the length of the longest path in the tree, or put differently, the maximum level number among leaves in the tree.
Subtree	The tree formed by considering a node and all its descendants. We exclude the root when forming subtrees.

Figure 11.4   **A tree and some of its properties**

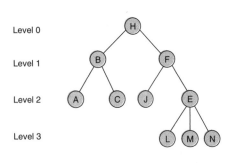

Property	Value
Number of nodes	10
Height	3
Root node	H
Leaves	A, C, J, L, M, N
Interior nodes	H, B, F, E
Nodes at level 2	A, C, J, E
Ancestors of E	F, H
Descendants of F	J, E, L, M, N
Nodes in right subtree of F	E, L, M, N

The trees we have been discussing are sometimes called *general trees* to distinguish them from a special category called *binary trees.* In a binary tree, each node has at most two children, referred to as the *left child* and the *right child.* In a binary tree, when a node has only one child, we distinguish between it being a left child and a right child. Thus, the two trees shown in Figure 11.5 are not the same when considered as binary trees, although they are the same when considered as general trees.

Figure 11.5 **Two unequal binary trees that just happen to have equal sets of nodes**

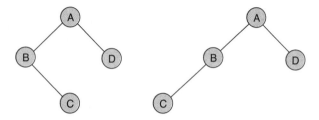

11.1.2 Formal Definitions of General and Binary Trees

Although at this point you probably have a clear understanding of what a tree is, we now give a more formal definition. As is often the case, one cannot understand the formal definition without an intuitive grasp of the concept being defined; however, the formal definition is important because it provides an unambiguous and precise basis for further discussion. For the sake of comparison, we present recursive and nonrecursive definitions. The recursive definitions are particularly important because they suggest the basic pattern for the many algorithms that process trees recursively.

Nonrecursive definition of a general tree: A *general tree* is either empty or consists of a finite set of *nodes* and a finite set of *edges* that connect pairs of nodes. The node at one end of an edge is called the *parent* and at the other the *child.* One node is distinguished from all others and is called the *root.* All nodes except the root are connected by an edge to exactly one parent.

Recursive definition of a general tree: A *general tree* is either empty or consists of a finite set of nodes T. One node r is distinguished from all others and is called the *root.* In addition, the set $T - \{r\}$ is partitioned into disjoint subsets, each of which is a general tree.

Recursive definition of a binary tree: A *binary tree* is either empty or consists of a root plus a *left subtree* and a *right subtree,* each of which are binary trees.

11.2 Representations of Trees

As we have grown to expect from previous chapters, there are two general approaches to representing trees: one using linked nodes and the other using arrays. However, the use of arrays is usually limited to complete binary trees (we define this term shortly).

11.2.1   Linked Representations

To begin, Figure 11.6 shows a rather obvious linked representation of a general tree. Here each node contains a data item and pointers to the node's children. The child pointers are usually stored in a list, which grows and shrinks as children are added and removed. A list also accommodates the fact that not all nodes have the same number of children. Occasionally, pointers are added to each node. These can include a pointer to a node's parent and sometimes to its left and right siblings. The extra pointers can speed certain operations on trees but at the cost of increasing the size of each node.

Figure 11.6   **A general tree and its linked representation**

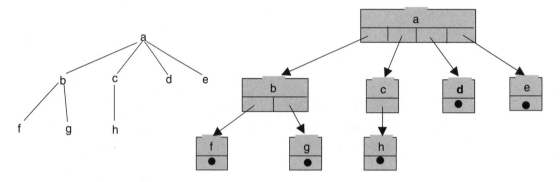

The linked representation of a binary tree is similar to that of a general tree except that each node always has exactly two pointers, one to each child (Figure 11.7). Here there is no need to store the pointers in a list.

Figure 11.7   **A binary tree with its linked representation**

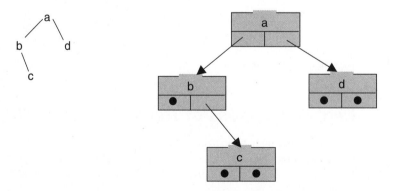

Somewhat surprisingly, it is often advantageous to represent a general tree in terms of a binary tree. For the tree shown in Figure 11.6, this apparent impossibility is achieved as illustrated in Figure 11.8. How is it done? For each node, the left link points to a node's first child, if any, and the right link points to the node's right sibling, if any. The drawback to the representation is that we lose the direct links between a node and each of its children; however, the representation's simplicity makes it popular.

Figure 11.8   **A binary tree representation of a general tree**

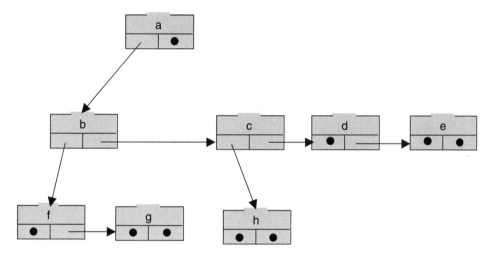

Figure 11.8 rather obscures the fact that a binary tree is being used to represent the general tree, but it can be redrawn to make it look more like a binary tree at the cost of looking less like a general tree, as illustrated in Figure 11.9.

Figure 11.9   **Redrawing a general tree to emphasize its binary implementation**

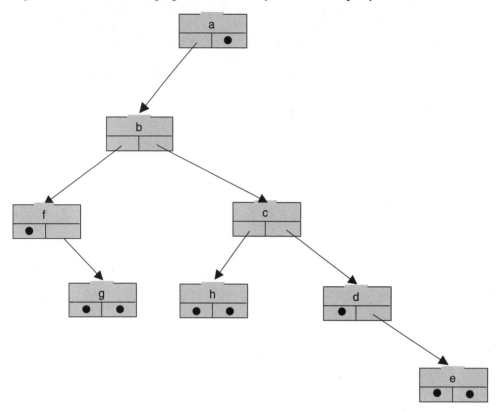

11.2.2   Array Representation of a Complete Binary Tree

A binary tree is ***complete*** if each level except the last has a complete complement of nodes and if the nodes on the last level are filled in from the left (Figure 11.10). An array-based implementation of a binary tree is also possible but is difficult to define and practical only in some special situations. Mapping stacks, queues, and lists to arrays is straightforward because all are linear and support the same notion of adjacency, with each element having an obvious predecessor and successor. But given a node in a tree, what would be its immediate predecessor in an array? Is it the parent or a left sibling? What is its immediate successor? Is it a child or a right sibling? Trees are hierarchical and resist being flattened. Nevertheless, for complete binary trees, there is an elegant and efficient array-based representation.

Consider the complete binary tree in Figure 11.10.

In an array-based implementation, the elements are stored by level, as shown in Figure 11.11.

Figure 11.10 **A complete binary tree**

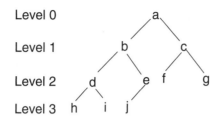

Level 0

Level 1

Level 2

Level 3

Figure 11.11 **An array representation of a complete binary tree**

0	1	2	3	4	5	6	7	8	9
a	b	c	d	e	f	g	h	i	j

Given an arbitrary item at position i in the array, it is easy to determine the location of related items, as shown in the Table 11.2.

Table 11.2 **The Locations of Given Items in an Array Representation of a Complete Binary Tree**

Parent	$(i-1)/2$
Left sibling, if there is one	$i-1$
Right sibling, if there is one	$i+1$
Left child, if there is one	$i*2+1$
Right child, if there is one	$i*2+2$

Thus, for item d at location 3, we get the results shown in Table 11.3.

Table 11.3 **The Relatives of a Given Item in an Array Representation of a Complete Binary Tree**

Parent	b at 1
Left sibling, if there is one	Not applicable
Right sibling, if there is one	e at 4
Left child, if there is one	h at 7
Right child, if there is one	i at 8

One might naturally ask why the array representation does not work for incomplete binary trees. The reason is not hard to see. In an incomplete binary tree, some levels are not filled above others. But the calculation of a node's relatives in an array is based on being able to multiply or divide its index by 2, which cannot be done when levels are not filled in a top-down manner.

Needless to say, the array representation is pretty rare and is used mainly to implement a special-purpose binary tree called a *heap,* which is discussed in Chapter 12.

11.3   Binary Tree Operations

We now turn our attention to the operations that we might want to perform on a binary tree. Despite a truly overwhelming array of uses, there is no agreed on generic binary tree class, although one could easily be defined. Instead, each application of trees seems to start over from scratch. The reason is that the insertion and deletion algorithms tend to be tailored very specifically to the demands of particular applications. In contrast, generic stack and queue classes are immensely useful and find application in a wide range of situations without any need for modification or fine-tuning.

11.3.1   A Binary Tree Prototype

Let us begin with a binary tree prototype based on a linked representation. The purpose of the prototype, called `BinaryTreePT`, is to illustrate some of the algorithms commonly encountered when working with classes that use binary trees in their internal representation. Thus, we do not provide some operations usually associated with collections, such as insertion or removal of items at arbitrary positions. We organize the binary tree prototype operations as follows:

Constructor methods: There are three of these. The default constructor creates an empty binary tree. The second constructor allows the client to create a binary tree whose root node contains a given item. The third constructor allows the user to specify the item at the root as well as the left and the right subtrees. The last two constructors are intended to take the place of a general insertion operation.

Property examination methods: There are three of these—isEmpty, size, and equals—with the usual meanings.

Cloning method: The binary tree class implements the Cloneable interface. Thus, the prototype must implement a clone method, which returns a copy of the structure of the tree. Objects within the two trees are shared, however.

Iterator methods: There are four types of iterators. Each type of iterator traverses a particular path and direction as it visits the nodes in the tree.

1. **Preorder traversal:** The preorder traversal algorithm visits the root node, traverses the left subtree, and traverses the right subtree. The path traveled by a preorder traversal is illustrated in Figure 11.12.

2. **Inorder traversal:** The inorder traversal algorithm traverses the left subtree, visits the root node, and traverses the right subtree. The path traveled by an inorder traversal is illustrated in Figure 11.13.

Figure 11.12   **A preorder traversal**

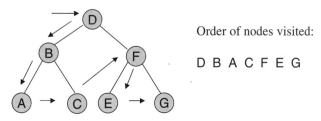

Order of nodes visited:

D B A C F E G

Figure 11.13   **An inorder traversal**

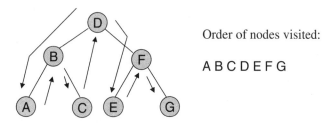

Order of nodes visited:

A B C D E F G

3. Postorder traversal: The postorder traversal algorithm traverses the left subtree, traverses the right subtree, and visits the root node. The path traveled by a postorder traversal is illustrated in Figure 11.14.

Figure 11.14   **A postorder traversal**

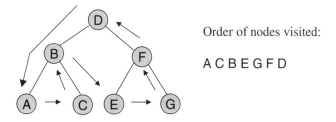

Order of nodes visited:

A C B E G F D

4. Level order traversal: Beginning with level 0, the level order traversal algorithm visits the nodes at each level in left-to-right order. The path traveled by a level order traversal is illustrated in Figure 11.15.

`toString` **methods:** There are five of these methods, and each returns a string representation of a binary tree. The string is formed by concatenating string representations of the node values. The methods differ in the order in which they visit the nodes: preorder, inorder, postorder, and level order. The fifth method, the one that is actually called `toString`, is based on a preorder traversal and

Figure 11.15   **A level order traversal**

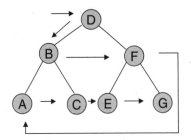

Order of nodes visited:

D B F A C E G

includes parentheses and commas inserted in a manner that indicates the tree's structure. For instance, `toString` applied to the tree in Figure 11.12 yields the string "D(B(A,C),F(E,G))." The other four methods omit information that describes the tree's structure and are implemented by using the iterators described above. For instance, `toStringPreorder` applied to the tree in Figure 11.12 yields the string "DBACFEG."

The binary tree prototype does not support changes to the tree structure, such as insertions or removals of nodes. Furthermore, the iterators do not support removals. We illustrate these kinds of operations when we develop a general tree ADT later in the chapter.

Table 11.4 provides a detailed specification of the public methods in the class `BinaryTreePT`. Unlike earlier prototypes, there is only one implementing class, so there is no need for an interface. Also, we make no attempt to state or enforce preconditions and postconditions.

Table 11.4   **The Interface for the Binary Tree Prototype**

<table>
<tr><td colspan="2" align="center">***Constructors***</td></tr>
<tr><td colspan="2">`BinaryTreePT()`
Creates an empty binary tree.</td></tr>
<tr><td colspan="2">`BinaryTreePT(Object item)`
Creates a binary tree with item in the root node.</td></tr>
<tr><td colspan="2">`BinaryTreePT(Object item, BinaryTreePT leftTree,`
        `BinaryTreePT rightTree)`
Creates a binary tree with item in the root node and `leftTree` and `rightTree` as the root node's left and right subtrees, respectively.</td></tr>
<tr><td colspan="2" align="center">***Supporting Methods***</td></tr>
<tr><td>`boolean`</td><td>`isEmpty()`
Returns `true` if this binary tree contains no items.</td></tr>
<tr><td>`int`</td><td>`size()`
Returns the number of items in this binary tree.</td></tr>
</table>

continued

Table 11.4   **The Interface for the Binary Tree Prototype *(Continued)***

General Methods

Object   **clone()**
Returns a shallow copy of this binary tree.

boolean   **equals(Object other)**
Returns `true` if the other object is a binary tree that equals this binary tree. To be equal, two binary trees must contain equal items appearing in the same positions.

Iterator   **iterator()**
Returns an iterator consisting of the items resulting from a preorder traversal. The iterator's `remove` method is not supported.

Iterator   **iteratorInorder ()**
Returns an iterator consisting of the items resulting from an inorder traversal. The iterator's `remove` method is not supported.

Iterator   **iteratorLevelorder ()**
Returns an iterator consisting of the items resulting from a level order traversal. The iterator's `remove` method is not supported.

Iterator   **iteratorPostorder ()**
Returns an iterator consisting of the items resulting from a postorder traversal. The iterator's `remove` method is not supported.

Iterator   **iteratorPreorder ()**
Returns an iterator consisting of the items resulting from a preorder traversal. The iterator's `remove` method is not supported.

String   **toString()**
Returns a string consisting of the string representations of the items resulting from a preorder traversal. Parentheses and commas are inserted in such a manner as to indicate the tree's structure.

String   **toStringInorder()**
Returns a string consisting of the string representations of the items resulting from an inorder traversal.

String   **toStringLevelorder()**
Returns a string consisting of the string representations of the items resulting from a level order traversal.

String   **toStringPostorder()**
Returns a string consisting of the string representations of the items resulting from a postorder traversal.

String   **toStringPreorder()**
Returns a string consisting of the string representations of the items resulting from a preorder traversal.

11.3.2   A Tester Program for **BinaryTreePT**

To illustrate the use and behavior of a binary tree, we now display a listing of a tester program. The program tests all the `BinaryTreePT` methods directly except for the iterator methods. These are tested indirectly by way of the `toString` methods that use them.

```
 1 import lamborne.*;
 2 import java.util.*;
 3 import ioutil.*;
 4
 5 public class TestBTPT{
 6
 7    public static void main (String[] args){
 8       BinaryTreePT a, b, c;
 9       KeyboardReader reader = new KeyboardReader();
10
11       System.out.println ("#1<<<<<<<<<<<<<<<<<<<<<<<<<");
12
13       a = new BinaryTreePT();
14       System.out.println ("Expect empty string        : " + a);
15       a = new BinaryTreePT("5");
16       System.out.println ("Expect 5                   : " + a);
17       b = new BinaryTreePT ("+", new BinaryTreePT ("3"),
18                                  new BinaryTreePT ("4"));
19       System.out.println ("Expect +(3,4)              : " + b);
20       c = new BinaryTreePT ("*", a, b);
21       System.out.println ("Expect *(5,+(3,4))         : " + c);
22       c = new BinaryTreePT ("-", c, b);
23       System.out.println ("Expect -(*(5,+(3,4)),+(3,4)) : " + c);
24       System.out.println ("Expect 9                   : " + c.size());
25
26       System.out.println ("#2<<<<<<<<<<<<<<<<<<<<<<<<<");
27
28       System.out.println ("Expect -*5+34+34           : " +
29                            c.toStringPreorder());
30       System.out.println ("Expect 5*3+4-3+4           : " +
31                            c.toStringInorder());
32       System.out.println ("Expect 534+*34+-           : " +
33                            c.toStringPostorder());
34       System.out.println ("Expect -*+5+3434           : " +
35                            c.toStringLevelorder());
36
37       System.out.println ("#3<<<<<<<<<<<<<<<<<<<<<<<<<");
38
39       BinaryTreePT d = (BinaryTreePT)c.clone();
40       BinaryTreePT e = new BinaryTreePT ("*", a, b);
41       e = new BinaryTreePT ("-", e, b);
42       BinaryTreePT f = new BinaryTreePT ("*", a, b);
43       f = new BinaryTreePT ("-", b, f);
44       System.out.println ("Expect equal trees : " + c + "\n" +
45                            "                   : " + d + "\n" +
46                            "                   : " + e);
47       System.out.println ("Expect tt ff ft f: " +
48                            c.equals(c) + c.equals(d)   + " " +
49                            c.equals(b)   + c.equals("x") + " "  +
50                            c.equals(null) + c.equals(e) +  " " +
51                            c.equals(f) );
52    }
53 }
```

Figure 11.16 shows a snapshot of the tester program's output:

Figure 11.16   **The output of the binary tree tester program**

```
#1<<<<<<<<<<<<<<<<<<<<<<<<
Expect empty string      :
Expect 5                 : 5
Expect +(3,4)            : +(3,4)
Expect *(5,+(3,4))       : *(5,+(3,4))
Expect -(*(5,+(3,4)),+(3,4)) : -(*(5,+(3,4)),+(3,4))
Expect 9                 : 9
#2<<<<<<<<<<<<<<<<<<<<<<<<
Expect -*5+34+34         : -*5+34+34
Expect 5*3+4-3+4         : 5*3+4-3+4
Expect 534+*34+-         : 534+*34+-
Expect -*+5+3434         : -*+5+3434
#3<<<<<<<<<<<<<<<<<<<<<<<<
Expect equal trees : -(*(5,+(3,4)),+(3,4))
                   : -(*(5,+(3,4)),+(3,4))
                   : -(*(5,+(3,4)),+(3,4))
Expect tt ff ft f: truetrue falsefalse falsetrue false
```

11.3.3   Implementation of the Class `BinaryTreePT`

In this section, we show how to implement much of the `BinaryTreePT` class; however, some methods are left as exercises. These methods are either quite simple or are similar in structure to others that we do present. To begin, the class `BinaryTreePT` uses two instance variables: one for the size and one to point to the root node:

```
1 import java.util.*;
2 import lamborne.*;
3
4 public class BinaryTreePT extends Object implements Cloneable{
5
6     private BTNode root;
7     private int    size;
```

Each node in a tree is of class `BTNode`, which is implemented as a private class within `BinaryTreePT`.

```
246     private class BTNode {
247
248         public Object value;      // Value stored in this node
249         public BTNode left;       // Reference to left child
250         public BTNode right;      // Reference to right child
251
252         public BTNode()
253         {
254             value = null;
255             left = null;
256             right = null;
257         }
258
259         public BTNode(Object value)
260         {
261             this.value = value;
262             left = null;
263             right = null;
264         }
265
266         public BTNode(Object value, BTNode left, BTNode right)
267         {
268             this.value = value;
269             this.left = left;
270             this.right = right;
271         }
272     }
```

The first two constructors are trivial, and we show only the third. A defect of the third constructor is to cause a sharing of items and structure among several trees. If the programmer uses this constructor with care, no problems occur. However, it is possible to create trees whose left and right subtrees are the same set of nodes or to create trees whose structure contains cycles that could throw the traversal algorithms into infinite loops. For now, we do not worry about these problems in the context of the binary tree prototype. Suggestions for solutions are in the exercises.

```
25     public BinaryTreePT(Object item, BinaryTreePT leftTree,
26                                       BinaryTreePT rightTree)
27     {
28         int     leftSize = 0,
29                 rightSize = 0;
30         BTNode leftNode = null,
31                 rightNode = null;
32
33         if (leftTree != null){
34             leftSize = leftTree.size();
35             leftNode = leftTree.root;
36         }
37
```

Continued

Continued

```
38              if (rightTree != null){
39                  rightSize = rightTree.size();
40                  rightNode = rightTree.root;
41              }
42
43              root = new BTNode (item, leftNode, rightNode);
44              size = 1 + leftSize + rightSize;
45      }
```

Many of the methods involve traversing a binary tree in some order (preorder, inorder, postorder, and sometimes level order) and share a common structure. Here is a typical structure involving an inorder traversal:

```
public <return type> myMethod()
{
    myMethodHelper(root);
    return something;
}

private <return type> myMethodHelper(BTNode node)
{
    if (node == null)
        return something;
    else{
        myMethodHelper(node.left);
        do something with node;     // Line X
        myMethodHelper(node.right);
        return something;
    }
}
```

Methods based on preorder and postorder traversals are obtained by moving *line X* before the first recursive call or after the second recursively call, respectively. To be specific, here is the code needed to generate a preorder iterator. In the code, we first build a queue containing the node values and then return an iterator based on the queue. We could have used a list instead; however, a list iterator allows removals, and at the moment, we are not prepared to deal with the complexities this would cause.

```
137     public Iterator iteratorInorder()
138     {
139         Queue nodes = new LinkedQueue();
140         iteratorInorder (root, nodes);
141         return nodes.iterator();
142     }
143     private void iteratorInorder (BTNode currentNode, Queue nodes)
144     {
145         if (currentNode == null) return;
146         iteratorInorder (currentNode.left, nodes);
147         nodes.enqueue (currentNode.value);
148         iteratorInorder (currentNode.right, nodes);
149     }
```

The method `clone` is based on a preorder traversal, meaning that a node is processed before processing passes to its children:

```
65      public Object clone()
66      {
67          BinaryTreePT cloneTree = new BinaryTreePT();
68          cloneTree.root = clone(root);
69          cloneTree.size = size;
70          return cloneTree;
71      }
72
73      private BTNode clone(BTNode source)
74      {
75          if (source == null)
76              return null;
77          else{
78              BTNode target = new BTNode(source.value,
79                                          clone(source.left),
80                                          clone(source.right));
81              return target;
82          }
83      }
```

The method `toString` is also based on a preorder traversal:

```
199     public String toString()
200     {
201         return toString(root);
202     }
203
204     private String toString(BTNode node)
205     {
206         String str = "";
207         if (node != null){
208             str += node.value.toString();
209             if (node.left != null || node.right != null)
210                 str += "(" + toString(node.left) + "," +
211                                 toString(node.right) + ")";
212         }
213         return str;
214     }
```

Some methods do a traversal indirectly by means of an appropriate iterator as illustrated by the code for `toStringLevelorder`:

```
231     public String toStringLevelorder()
232     {
233         return toString(iteratorLevelorder());
234     }
235
236     private String toString(Iterator iter)
237     {
238         String str = "";
239         while (iter.hasNext())
```

Continued

Continued

```
240                     str += iter.next().toString();
241                 return str;
242         }
```

The last binary tree method we present is `iteratorLevelorder`. The method starts
with level 0 and visits each node from left to right at that level. The method then repeats
the process for the next level and so on, until all the nodes have been visited. Clearly,
the method needs some way of constraining the recursive process to march across a tree
at each level. It does this by scheduling the nodes to be visited on a second queue. In
the present example, the top-level public method `iteratorLevelorder` creates
two queues: one for scheduling and the other to build the backing store for the iterator.
The method places the root node at the front of the scheduling queue and passes the two
queues to the helper method, which is also called `iteratorLevelorder`:

```
170     public Iterator iteratorLevelorder()
171     {
172         Queue nodes = new LinkedQueue();       // Backing store
173         Queue levelsQu = new LinkedQueue();    // Scheduling queue
174
175         if (!isEmpty()){
176             levelsQu.enqueue (root);
177             iteratorLevelorder (levelsQu, nodes);
178         }
179         return nodes.iterator();
180     }
```

The recursive pattern for a level order traversal dequeues a node for processing and
then enqueues the left and right subtrees before the recursive call:

```
182     private void iteratorLevelorder(Queue levelsQu, Queue nodes)
183     {
184         BTNode node;
185
186         if (levelsQu.isEmpty()) return;
187
188         node = (BTNode)(levelsQu.dequeue());
189         nodes.enqueue (node.value);
190         if (node.left  != null) levelsQu.enqueue (node.left);
191         if (node.right != null) levelsQu.enqueue (node.right);
192         iteratorLevelorder (levelsQu, nodes);
193     }
```

The order in which the subtrees are enqueued determines the order in which the
process moves across each level of the tree. At any given time, the scheduling queue
contains the nodes remaining to be visited.

Exercises 11.3

1. Complete the implementation of the class `BinaryTreePT` and run it with the
tester program shown in this section.

2. Determine the complexities of the various `BinaryTreePT` methods.

3. Modify the third `BinaryTreePT` constructor so that the problems associated with it, such as the sharing of structure among multiple trees, are avoided. (*Tip:* Use the `clone` method.) Compare the complexity of the new version with the complexity of the original version.

4. Add a method called `height` to the `BinaryTreePT` class. This method should return the number of levels in the tree less one. You can implement this method either by updating an additional instance variable every time a tree's height changes or by traversing the tree each time the method is called. Implement the method using both strategies and compare the complexity of the two approaches.

5. Add a method called `frontier` to the `BinaryTreePT` class. This method should return a queue-based iterator that gives access to the leaf nodes of the tree in order from left to right. What is the method's complexity?

6. Add a method called `path` to the `BinaryTreePT` class. This method expects an object as a parameter and does a preorder search for the given object. The method stops when it encounters the first instance of the target object during the search. It then returns a stack-based iterator that gives access to the items on the path from the root node to the target item's node. Obviously, if the target object does not exist, the method should return an empty iterator. The first object in the iterator should be the target object, and the last item in the iterator should be the root object. What is the method's complexity?

7. Repeat with Exercise 6, but return a queue-based iterator. The root object should be at the queue's head.

11.4   Case Study 1: Parsing and Expression Trees

In Chapter 10, we developed a recursive descent parser for a language of arithmetic expressions. In Chapter 7, we showed how to use a stack to convert infix expressions to postfix form. We also showed in Chapter 7 how to use a stack to evaluate postfix expressions. Yet another way to process expressions is to build a data structure called a ***parse tree*** during parsing. For a language of expressions, this structure is also called an ***expression tree.*** Figure 11.17 shows several expression trees that result from parsing infix expressions. Note the following points:

1. An expression tree is never empty.

2. Each interior node represents an operator.

3. Each leaf node represents a numeric operand.

If we assume that an expression tree represents the structure of an infix expression, then we can make the following requests of an expression tree:

■ Ask for the expression's value.

■ Ask for the expression in postfix form.

■ Ask for the expression in prefix form.

■ Ask for the expression in infix form.

These operations involve traversals of an expression tree similar to those discussed for a binary tree earlier in this chapter. For example, to compute an expression's

Figure 11.17   **Some expression trees**

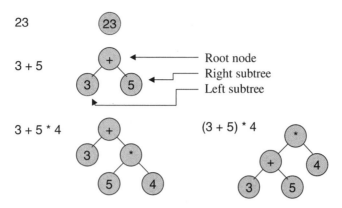

value, we perform an inorder traversal. Here is the algorithm for evaluating an expression tree:

```
If the root node is a number
   Return the number
Else
   Evaluate the left subtree
   Evaluate the right subtree
   Return the result of applying the operator in the root to these values
```

We now develop an expression tree in the context of a case study.

11.4.1   Request

Write a program that uses an expression tree to evaluate expressions or convert them to alternative forms.

11.4.2   Interface

We add to the user interface of Case Study 7.1 a button to display the expression in prefix form. Figure 11.18 shows the proposed interface.

Figure 11.18 **The interface for the parser program**

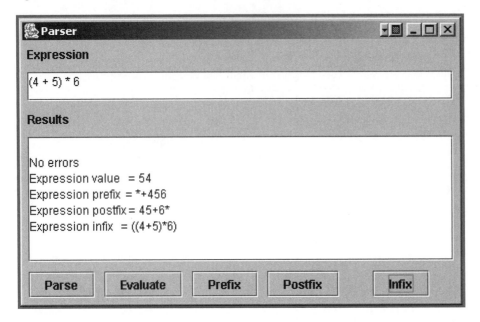

11.4.3 Analysis and Design of the Class `ExpressionTree`

The parser builds an expression tree in two ways:

1. Build a leaf node containing a number.

2. Build an interior node whose value is an operator and whose left and right subtrees are other expression trees.

Thus, ExpressionTree needs constructors similar to those of BinaryTreePT discussed earlier.

In response to user commands, the parser interface asks the expression tree to evaluate itself or to return the original expression in prefix, infix, or postfix form. Table 11.5 summarizes these operations.

Table 11.5 **The `ExpressionTree` Methods**

Method	What It Does
ExpressionTree()	Throws an exception warning that the user is trying to instantiate an empty tree.
ExpressionTree(Token token)	Creates a root node whose value is the token. Throws an exception if the token does not represent an integer.

continued

Table 11.5   The `ExpressionTree` Methods *(Continued)*

Method	What It Does
`ExpressionTree(Token token, ExpressionTree leftTree, ExpressionTree rightTree)`	Creates a root node whose value is the token and whose left and right subtrees are the other expression trees. Throws an exception if the token is not an operator or if the left and rigt subtrees are `null`.
`String prefix()`	Returns the string representation of the expression in prefix form. Parentheses are not needed to specify the order of evaluation.
`String infix()`	Returns the string representation of the expression in infix form. Parentheses are not needed to specify the order of evaluation.
`String postfix()`	Returns the string representation of the expression in postfix form. Parentheses are not needed to specify the order of evaluation.
`String toString()`	Returns a prefix representation of the tree with parentheses and commas inserted to indicate the tree's structure.
`int evaluate()`	Returns the value of the expression.

Here is a short tester program that illustrates the use of the `ExpressionTree` methods:

```
 1 import java.util.*;
 2
 3 public class TestET{
 4
 5    public static void main (String[] args){
 6       ExpressionTree a, b, c;
 7
 8       a = new ExpressionTree (new Token(4));
 9       b = new ExpressionTree (new Token('+'),
10                               new ExpressionTree (new Token(2)),
11                               new ExpressionTree (new Token(3)));
12       c = new ExpressionTree (new Token('*'), a, b);
13       c = new ExpressionTree (new Token('-'), c, b);
14
15       System.out.println ("Expect ((4*(2+3))-(2+3))     : " + c.infix());
16       System.out.println ("Expect -*4+23+23             : " + c.prefix());
17       System.out.println ("Expect 423+*23+-             : " + c.postfix());
18       System.out.println ("Expect -(*(4,+(2,3)),+(2,3)) : " + c.toString());
19       System.out.println ("Expect 15                    : " + c.evaluate());
20       System.out.println ("Expect exception");
21       a = new ExpressionTree();
22    }
23 }
```

The `ExpressionTree` class uses the class `BTNode` to implement a node. The constructors throw exceptions with appropriate error messages as indicated in Table 11.5.

We now develop the traversal method `postfix` and leave all the others methods as exercises. The public method `postfix` returns the string representation of the expression tree in postfix form. The method simply passes the root node to a private helper method that performs the traversal. The private helper method, also called `postfix`, implements a postorder traversal similar to the one for `BinaryTreePT` discussed earlier. The method returns an empty string when the node is `null`. Otherwise, the method concatenates the postfix representations of the operands (the left stubtree and the right subtree, in that order) and the operator and returns this string. Here is the code:

```
113     public String postfix(){
114         return postfix (root);
115     }
116
117     private String postfix (BTNode node){
118         String str;
119         if (node == null)
120             return "";
121         else
122             return postfix (node.left) +
123                     postfix (node.right) +
124                     node.value.toString();
125     }
```

11.4.4   Analysis, Design, and Implementation of the Class `Parser`

It is easiest to build an expression tree with a parser that uses a recursive descent strategy, and fortunately, we already have such a parser from Case Study 10.2. Thus, we borrow that parser and modify it.

The method `parse` now returns an expression tree to the parser interface, which uses that tree to obtain information about the expression. Each parsing method that handles a syntactic form in the language builds and returns an expression tree. That tree represents the phrase of the expression parsed by the method. We develop two of these methods and leave the other as an exercise.

The method `primary` processes either a number or an expression nested in parentheses. When the token is a number, the method creates a leaf node containing the number and returns it. Otherwise, if the token is a left parenthesis, the method calls the method `expression` to parse the nested expression. This method returns a tree representing the results, and `primary` passes this tree back to its caller. Here is the revised code for `primary`:

```
82      private ExpressionTree primary(){
83          ExpressionTree tree;
84          Token token = scanner.get();
85          switch (token.type){
86              case Token.INT:
87                  tree = new ExpressionTree(token);
```

```
 88                scanner.next();
 89                break;
 90            case Token.L_PAR:
 91                scanner.next();
 92                tree = expression();
 93                accept (scanner.get(), Token.R_PAR, "')' expected");
 94                scanner.next();
 95                break;
 96        default:
 97                tree = null;
 98                fatalError (token, "unexpected token");
 99        }
100        return tree;
101    }
```

The method `expression` processes a term followed by zero or more adding operators and terms. The method `expression` begins by calling the method `term`, which returns a tree representing the term. If the current token is not an adding operator, then `expression` passes the tree back to its caller. Otherwise, `expression` enters a loop. In this loop, `expression` builds an interior node whose value is the adding operator, whose left subtree is the tree just received from the last call to `term`, and whose right substree is the tree received from a new call to `term`. This process ends when `expression` does not see an adding operator. At this point, a fairly complex tree might be built up, and `expression` returns it. Here is the code for `expression`:

```
60    private ExpressionTree expression(){
61        ExpressionTree tree = term();
62        Token token = scanner.get();
63        while (token.type == Token.PLUS || token.type == Token.MINUS){
64            scanner.next();
65            tree = new ExpressionTree(token, tree, term());
66            token = scanner.get();
67        }
68        return tree;
69    }
```

The analysis and design of the class `ParserInterface` are straightforward and left as an exercise.

Exercise 11.4

Complete the program developed in Case Study 1 and test it with a variety of expressions.

11.5   General Tree Operations

As with a binary tree, there is no standard general tree ADT. Nevertheless, in this section, we develop an ADT that supports many of the operations one might want for general trees. Unlike the class `BinaryTreePT`, the general tree class that we present is a professional class, not a prototype. Hence, this class supports several operations, such as replacement and insertion, which we associate with other collections. As usual for collection classes, we enforce preconditions on several operations. The general tree class developed here also supports two kinds of iterators:

1. **A simple iterator.** The iterator supports the standard operations hasNext and next but not remove. The iterator is not directly connected to the tree as a backing store but instead is connected to a queue that results from a preorder traversal of the tree.

2. **A tree iterator.** The tree iterator is connected to the tree as a backing store and allows a wide range of operations, including removals and treelike movements to given nodes in the hierarchy.

The implementation class is called LinkedTree and uses the binary tree representation discussed earlier. Each node has a first child and a right sibling. The first child is actually the leftmost child. The right sibling is the next child to the right. That node's right sibling is considered the next child to the right in this sequence and so on. We now turn to the two interfaces for the general tree ADT: Tree and TreeIterator.

11.5.1   The **Tree** Interface

The Tree interface contains the three types of methods found in professional classes developed earlier in this book. A complete list of methods appears in Table 11.6 at the end of this section. The supporting and general methods are familiar from our discussion of other collection ADTs and require no comment. The fundamental methods of trees, like those of lists, are of two subtypes: content-based and index-based.

Content-Based Methods

These methods are quite easy to understand and use. They are contains, get, and remove. Each method expects an Object as a parameter. contains searches the tree for the given object and returns true or false. get and remove perform a preorder traversal of the tree in search of the given object. get returns the first instance of the given object encountered or returns null if the object does not exist. remove deletes the given object and returns true or returns false if the object does not exist.

Index-Based Methods

The index-based methods addFirstChild, addRightSibling, get, set, and remove expect an array of int as a parameter. This array allows a client to specify a given node in the tree in terms of its index position. The index position of a node is indicated by the sequence of integers in the index array. This sequence specifies the path from the root node to the target node. The root node is indicated by the empty array {} or any array whose first value is 0, such as {0} or {0,1,2}. Otherwise, if a value in the index array is positive, it specifies the ith child of a node at a given level, where i ranges from 1 to the number of siblings at that level. The level is the index of the value plus 1 (where the root is at level 0) in the array. To summarize, here is the form of a tree index that specifies a node, other than the root node, at level n:

```
{<ith child at level 1>, . . . ,<ith child at level n>}
```

For example, the array {2,3,1} specifies the first child of the third child of the second child of the root if one reads the numbers from right to left. The following illustrates several example positions:

```
root
    child 1             <<<<<< this node is at index {1}
    child 2
        child 1
        child 2         <<<<<< this node is at index {2,2}
        child 3
            child 1     <<<<<< this node is at index {2,3,1}
```

In general, processing stops when the first 0 is encountered in an index array. In the case of an invalid index, the methods get, set, and remove return null, whereas the methods addFirstChild and addRightSibling return false. The method indexOf returns the index array of the first instance of a given item encountered during a preorder traversal or {−1} if the item does not exist in the tree.

To illustrate the use and effects of some of the fundamental tree operations, here is a short tester program that builds and examines a general tree. Figure 11.19 shows the program's output.

Figure 11.19   **Output of the tester program for a general tree**

```
(a(b(c,d,e)))  :  a(b(c,d,e))

Hierarchical list:

a

        b

                c

                d

                e

    b  :  b

    c  :  c

    d  :  d

    e  :  e

    a  :  a

    null  :  null
```

```
1  import lamborne.*;
2  import java.util.*;
3
4  public class TestTree{
5
6      public static void main (String[] args){
7          Tree a = new LinkedTree();
8
9          a.clear();
10         a.addRoot ("x");
11         a.set(new int[]{0}, "a");
12         a.addFirstChild (new int[]{}, "x");
13         a.set(new int[] {1}, "b");
14         a.addFirstChild (new int[] {1},"c");
15         a.addRightSibling (new int[] {1,1},"d");
16         a.addRightSibling (new int[] {1,2}, "x");
17         a.set(new int[] {1,3}, "e");
18
19         System.out.println("(a(b(c,d,e)) : " + a);
20
21         System.out.println("Hierarchical list: \n" + a.hierarchicalList());
22
23         System.out.println("b : " + a.get(new int[]{1}));
24         System.out.println("c : " + a.get(new int[]{1,1}));
25         System.out.println("d : " + a.get(new int[]{1,2}));
26         System.out.println("e : " + a.get(new int[]{1,3}));
27         System.out.println("a : " + a.get(new int[]{0}));
28
29         System.out.println("null : " + a.get(new int[]{2}));
30      }
31 }
```

Table 11.6 lists the methods of the Tree interface.

Table 11.6	The **Tree** Interface

	Fundamental Methods
boolean	**addFirstChild(int index[], Object item)** Adds the item to this tree as the first child of the node at the specified index. If the index is invalid, returns false, else returns true. Throws an exception if the item is null. Some implementations might choose not to allow duplicates.
boolean	**addRoot(Object item)** Adds the item as the root of this tree. Throws an exception if the item is null or the tree is nonempty, else returns true.
boolean	**addRightSibling(int index[], Object item)** Adds the item to this tree as the right sibling of the node at the specified index. If the index is invalid, returns false, else returns true. Throws an exception if the item is null. Some implementations might choose not to allow duplicates.
boolean	**contains(Object item)** Returns true if the specified item is in this tree. Throws an exception if the item is null.

continued

Table 11.6 **The Tree Interface (Continued)**

Object	**get(Object item)** Returns the first item encountered during a preorder traversal that is equal to the specified item or null if there is none. Throws an exception if the specified item is null.
Object	**get(int index[])** Returns the item at the specified index or null if the index is invalid.
int[]	**indexOf(Object item)** Returns the index of the first item encountered during a preorder traversal that is equal to the specified item or {−1} if there is none. Throws an exception if the specified item is null.
Object	**remove(int index[])** Removes and returns the item at the specified index position. Returns null if the index is invalid. All of the item's children are removed also.
boolean	**remove(Object item)** Removes the first item encountered during a preorder traversal that is equal to the specified item. Returns true if the tree changes. Throws an exception if the item is null. All of the item's children are removed also.
Object	**set(int index[], Object item)** Stores the specified item at the specified location. Returns the item previously stored at the location or null if the location is invalid. Throws an exception if the specified item is null.

Supporting Methods

boolean	**isEmpty()** Returns true if this tree contains no elements.
int	**size()** Returns the number of items in this tree.

General Methods

void	**clear()** Removes all items from this tree.
Object	**clone()** Returns a shallow copy of this tree.
Collection	**collectionView()** Returns a collection-view of the items in this tree.
boolean	**equals(Object other)** Returns true if the specified item is a tree that equals this tree. Two trees are considered equal if they have the same structure and equal items at each position within this structure.
int	**hashCode()** Returns the hash code value for this sorted collection.
String	**hierarchicalList()** Returns a multiline string that lists the items in this tree in preorder with one node per line and with children indented more than their parent. The result looks similar to a book's table of contents.

continued

Table 11.6	The `Tree` Interface *(Continued)*
`Iterator`	`iterator()` Returns an iterator over the items contained in this tree. The iterator provides the items in preorder. The iterator could support removal depending on the implementation.
`Object[]`	`toArray()` Returns an array containing all of the items in this tree. The items are stored in the array in preorder.
`String`	`toString()` Returns a string that contains a nested parenthesized list of the items in this tree.
`TreeIterator`	`treeIterator()` Returns a tree iterator on this tree.

11.5.2   The `TreeIterator` Interface

An iterator for a general tree provides a wide range of navigation operations, as well as operations for modifying the contents and structure of the tree. To support navigation, a tree iterator must maintain a slightly larger state than a list iterator. Obviously, the iterator must track the current node. To allow the client to back up from the current node along the path to the root, the iterator must also maintain a stack of parent nodes. Table 11.7 describes the methods in the `TreeIterator` interface.

Table 11.7	The `TreeIterator` Interface
`boolean`	**addRoot (Object item)** Adds the specified item as the root of this tree. Throws an exception if the item is `null` or the tree in nonempty, else returns `true`. The current node equals the root, and there is no current parent.
`boolean`	**addFirstChild (Object item)** Adds the specified item as the first child of the current node. Throws an exception if the item is `null` or if there is no current node, else returns `true`. The current parent now equals the old current node, and the current node now equals the new node.
`boolean`	**addRightSibling (Object item)** Adds the specified item as the right sibling of the current node. Throws an exception if the item is `null` or if there is no current node or if the root is current, else returns `true`. The current parent does not change, and the current node now equals the new node.
`Object`	**getCurrent ( )** Returns the item in the current node or `null` if there is no current node.

`Object`	**getFirstChild ( )**
	If there is no current node, then
	    returns `null`
	Else
	    current parent = current node

continued

Table 11.7   **The `TreeIterator` Interface *(Continued)***

	returns item in first child or `null` if there is none current node = first child or undefined if there is none Endif

`Object`	**getParent ( )**
	If there is no current parent, then
	   returns `null`
	Else
	   returns item in current parent
	   current node = current parent
	   current parent = current node's parent or undefined if now at root
	Endif

`Object`	**getRightSibling ( )**
	If there is no current node, then
	   returns `null`
	Else
	   returns item in right sibling or `null` if there is none
	   current node = right sibling or undefined if there is none
	Endif

`Object`	**getRoot ( )** Returns the item in the root or `null` if the tree is empty.
`boolean`	**hasChild ( )** Returns `true` if the current node has a child, else returns `false`. Throws an exception if there is no current node.
`boolean`	**hasCurrentPosition ( )** Returns `true` if there is a current node
`boolean`	**hasParent ( )** Returns `true` if there is a current parent
`boolean`	**hasRightSibling ( )** Returns `true` if the current node has a right sibling. Throws an exception if there is no current node.

`boolean`	**moveTo (int index[ ])**
	If the index is invalid, then
	   returns true
	   current node = specified node
	   current parent = current node's parent or undefined if there is none
	Else
	   returns `false`
	   current node and current parent are now undefined
	Endif

`boolean`	**moveTo (Object item)**
	If the item is `null`, then
	   throws an exception
	Else if the item is not found, then
	   returns `false`
	   current node and current parent are now undefined
	Else
	   returns `true`

continued

Table 11.7   **The `TreeIterator` Interface *(Continued)***

---

	current node = first node in preorder traversal that contains specified item current parent = current node's parent or undefined if there is none Endif

`boolean`	**removeCurrent ( )**
	If there is no current node, then
	    throws an exception
	Else
	    returns item in current node
	    removes current node and its children
	    current node = current node's right sibling or undefined if there is none
	Endif

`Object`	**setCurrent (Object item)** Returns the item in the current node and sets the content of the current node to the specified item. Throws an exception if the specified item is `null` or if there is no current node.

The following tester program uses an iterator to load a tree with the same items as in the previous tester program. The program displays the tree itself and then uses the iterator to access and display the items:

```
1 import lamborne.*;
2 import java.util.*;
3
4 public class TestTreeIterator{
5
6   public static void main (String[] args){
7        Tree a = new LinkedTree();
8        TreeIterator c = a.treeIterator();
9
10        c.addRoot ("x");
11        c.setCurrent("a");
12        c.addFirstChild ("x");
13        c.setCurrent("b");
14        c.addFirstChild ("c");
15        c.addRightSibling ("d");
16        c.addRightSibling ("x");
17        c.setCurrent("e");
18
19        System.out.println("(a(b(c,d,e)) : " + a);
20
21        // Now use iterator to access nodes
22        System.out.println("a     : " + c.getRoot());
23        System.out.println("b     : " + c.getFirstChild());
24        System.out.println("c     : " + c.getFirstChild());
25        System.out.println("d     : " + c.getRightSibling());
26        System.out.println("e     : " + c.getRightSibling());
27        System.out.println("null  : " + c.getRightSibling());
28        System.out.println("b     : " + c.getParent());
29        System.out.println("a     : " + c.getParent());
30    }
31 }
```

Note that the last call to getRightSibling in *line 27* leaves the current position undefined and returns null. However, the binary tree of parent nodes is still valid, so the first call to getParent returns the node above the three siblings, as expected.

11.6 Implementation of the General Tree Class (optional pv)

11.6.1 Responsibilities of the Classes in the Implementation

Our implementation of a general tree consists of the classes AbstractTree and LinkedTree. As with stacks and queues, the abstract tree class extends the AbstractContainer class. Table 11.8 shows the division of the responsibilities for the public methods and their complexity.

Table 11.8   **The Tree Implementation Classes**

Tree Implementation		Abstract Container	Abstract Tree	Linked Tree
	constructor()	O(1)	O(1)	O(1)
boolean	addFirstChild(int index[], Object item)		uses moveTo (index)	
boolean	addRoot(Object item)		X	
boolean	addRightSibling (int index[], Object item)		uses moveTo (index)	
void	clear()	O(1)		O(1)
Object	clone()			exercise
Collection	collectionView()	based on iterator		
boolean	contains(Object item)		uses get (item)	
boolean	equals(Object other)		exercise	
Object	get(Object item)		exercise	
Object	get(int index[])		uses moveTo (index)	
int	hashCode()	traverses iterator		
String	hierarchicalList()			O(n)
int[]	indexOf(Object item)		exercise	
boolean	IsEmpty()	uses size method		

continued

Table 11.8   **The Tree Implementation Classes (Continued**

Tree Implementation		Abstract Container	Abstract Tree	Linked Tree
Iterator	iterator()	abstract		O(n)
boolean	remove(Object item)		exercise	
Object	remove(int index[])		uses moveTo (index)	
Object	set(int index[], Object item)		uses moveTo (index)	
int	size()	O(1)		O(1) or O(n)
object[]	toArray()	traverses iterator		
String	toString()	traverses iterator		O(n)
TreeIterator	treeIterator()		abstract	O(1)

11.6.2   Design and Implementation of the Class `AbstractTree`

Note from Table 11.8 that the `AbstractTree` class implements almost twice as many methods as the concrete `LinkedTree` class. We are able to achieve this by making liberal use of the tree iterator. Most methods create an iterator on the tree and call an iterator method to accomplish their tasks. As an example, consider the strategy for the method `addFirstChild`. We

1. Create a tree iterator.

2. Use the iterator to move to the index.

3. If the move operation returns `true`, then return the result using the iterator to add the first child.

4. Otherwise, return `false`.

Here is the code for this method:

```
public boolean addFirstChild (int index[], Object item){
   TreeIterator treeIter = treeIterator();
   if (treeIter.moveTo (index))
      return treeIter.addFirstChild (item);
   else
      return false;
}
```

Here is a complete listing of `AbstractTree`, with some methods left as exercises:

```
1 package lamborne;
2
3 import java.util.*;
```

Continued

Continued

```
 4
 5  abstract public class AbstractTree extends AbstractContainer {
 6
 7      public AbstractTree()
 8      {
 9         super();
10      }
11
12      public boolean addFirstChild (int index[], Object item)
13      {
14         TreeIterator treeIter = treeIterator();
15         if (treeIter.moveTo (index))
16            return treeIter.addFirstChild (item);
17         else
18            return false;
19      }
20
21      public boolean addRoot (Object item)
22      {
23         return treeIterator().addRoot (item);
24      }
25
26      public boolean addRightSibling (int index[], Object item)
27      {
28         TreeIterator treeIter = treeIterator();
29         if (treeIter.moveTo (index))
30            return treeIter.addRightSibling (item);
31         else
32            return false;
33      }
34
35      public boolean contains (Object item)
36      {
37         return (get (item) != null);
38      }
39
40      public boolean equals (Object other)
41      {
42         throw new UnsupportedOperationException
43             ("This is left as an exercise");
44      }
45
46      public Object get (Object item)
47      {
48         throw new UnsupportedOperationException
49             ("This is left as an exercise");
50      }
51
52      public Object get (int index[])
53      {
54         TreeIterator treeIter = treeIterator();
55         treeIter.moveTo (index);
56         return treeIter.getCurrent();
57      }
58
```

Continued

Continued

```
59      public int[] indexOf (Object item)
60      {
61         throw new UnsupportedOperationException
62              ("This is left as an exercise");
63      }
64
65      public Object remove (int index[]){
66         TreeIterator treeIter = treeIterator();
67         if (treeIter.moveTo (index))
68            return treeIter.removeCurrent();
69         else
70            return null;
71      }
72
73      public boolean remove (Object item){
74         throw new UnsupportedOperationException
75              ("This is left as an exercise");
76      }
77
78      public Object set (int index[], Object item)
79      {
80         TreeIterator treeIter = treeIterator();
81         if (treeIter.moveTo (index))
82            return treeIter.setCurrent (item);
83         else
84            return null;
85      }
86
87      public abstract TreeIterator treeIterator();
88
89 }
```

11.6.3　Design and Implementation of the Class `LinkedTree`

The class LinkedTree uses the class TreeNode. Because we use a binary tree representation, TreeNode is similar to BTNode but renames the subtree pointers to child and sibling.

Although most of the public tree methods are implemented in the AbstractTree class, they use the tree iterator methods that are implemented in the inner class InnerTreeIterator. The implementation of this class in turn is the responsibility of the LinkedTree class. We discuss the implementation of the tree iterator in Section 11.6.4.

Here is a listing of the portion of the LinkedTree class that does not involve the tree iterator:

```
1 package lamborne;
2
3 import java.util.*;
4
5 public class LinkedTree extends AbstractTree
```

Continued

Continued

```
 6                              implements Tree, Cloneable {
 7
 8  // ============================== Tree ==============================
 9
10     private TreeNode root;
11
12     public LinkedTree()
13     {
14        super();
15        root = null;
16     }
17
18     public void clear()
19     {
20        super.clear();
21        root = null:
22     }
23
24     public Object clone()
25     {
26        throw new UnsupportedOperationException
27              ("This is left as an exercise");
28     }
29
30     public String hierarchicalList()
31     {
32        return hierarchicalList (root, 0);
33     }
34
35     private String hierarchicalList (TreeNode curNode, int level)
36     {
37        if (curNode == null) return "";
38        String str = "";
39        for (int i = 0; i < level; i++) str += " ";
40        str += curNode.value.toString();
41        if (curNode.child != null)
42           str += "\n" + hierarchicalList (curNode.child, level + 4);
43        if (curNode.sibling != null)
44           str += "\n" + hierarchicalList (curNode.sibling, level);
45        return str;
46     }
47
48     public Iterator iterator()
49       // The iterator returns items in preorder
50     {
51        Queue qu = new LinkedQueue();
52        preorderTraverse (root, qu);
53        return qu.iterator();
54     }
55
56     private void preorderTraverse (TreeNode curNode, Queue qu)
57     /*
58      *Creates a queue of items from an preorder traversal of the tree
59      *
60      *Pre: none
```

Continued

Continued

```
 61        *Post: no change
 62        *Ret: a queue containing the results of an inorder traversal
 63        *     of the tree
 64        */
 65      {
 66          if (curNode == null) return;
 67          qu.enqueue (curNode.value);
 68
 69          if (curNode.child != null)
 70              preorderTraverse (curNode.child, qu);
 71          if (curNode.subling != null)
 72              preorderTraverse (curNode.sibling, qu);
 73          return;
 74      }
 75
 76      public int size()
 77      {
 78          if (size == -1)
 79              size = size (root);
 80          return size;
 81      }
 82
 83      private int size (TreeNode node)
 84      {
 85          if (node == null)
 86              return 0;
 87          else
 88              return 1 + size (node.child) + size (node.sibling);
 89      }
 90
 91      public String toString()
 92      {
 93           return toString (root);
 94      }
 95
 96      private String toString (TreeNode curNode)
 97      {
 98          if (curNode == null) return "";
 99          String str = curNode.value.toString();
100          if (curNode.child != null)
101              str += "(" + toString (curNode.child) + ")";
102          if (curNode.sibling != null)
103              str += "," + toString (curNode.sibling);
104          return str;
105      }
106
107 }
```

Note the following points about this code:

1. The `iterator` method builds a queue as a backing store. This requires a performance hit of $O(n)$ and does not allow removals from the tree. An alternative approach, which is left as an exercise, is to keep the iterator in continuous touch with the tree so as to allow removals and to avoid the performance cost.

2. The `size` method is usually $O(1)$. However, after a node has just been deleted, the size information is invalidated and requires $O(n)$ to recalculate.

11.6.4 Design and Implementation of the Tree Iterator

The tree iterator is implemented in the class `InnerTreeIter`, which defines the methods listed in Table 11.9.

Table 11.9 **The `TreeIterator` Methods**

TreeIterator Implementation		*Linked Tree*
	`constructor()`	O(1)
`boolean`	`addRoot(Object item)`	O(1)
`boolean`	`addFirstChild(Object item)`	O(1)
`boolean`	`addRightSibling(Object item)`	O(1)
`Object`	`getCurrent()`	O(1)
`Object`	`getFirstChild()`	O(1)
`Object`	`getParent()`	O(1)
`Object`	`getRightSibling()`	O(1)
`Object`	`getRoot()`	O(1)
`boolean`	`hasChild()`	O(1)
`boolean`	`hasCurrentPosition()`	O(1)
`boolean`	`hasParent()`	O(1)
`boolean`	`hasRightSibling()`	O(1)
`boolean`	`moveTo(int index[])`	O($\log n$) if balanced
`boolean`	`moveTo(Object item)`	exercise
`Object`	`removeCurrent()`	O(1)
`Object`	`setCurrent(Object item)`	O(1)

The `Binary tree` variable `parents` is used to support the `getParent` method. This method allows the client to navigate back up the tree from the current node to its ancestors. Figure 11.20 shows the manner in which the `parents` binary tree maintains pointers to the ancestors of the current node in a general tree.

Figure 11.20   **The parents stack for a general tree**

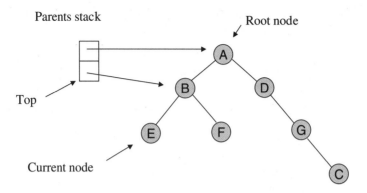

When the client moves to a parent node, the tree pops a node from the `parents` binary tree and makes this node the current node. This method works even when the current pointer is invalid. Here is the code for the method `getParent`:

```
public Object getParent()
{
    if (parents.isEmpty()) return null;

    currentNode = (TreeNode)(parents.pop());
    return currentNode.value;
}
```

The `parents` variable is set to a new empty binary tree when

■ The tree is instantiated.
■ The tree is cleared.
■ The user moves to the root.
■ The user inserts an item at the root.

The current node is pushed onto the `parents` binary tree when

■ The client moves to a first child.
■ The client adds a first child.

Here is the code for the methods `getFirstChild` and `addFirstChild`:

```
public Object getFirstChild()
{
    if (currentNode == null) return null;

    parents.push (currentNode);
    currentNode = currentNode.child;
    if (currentNode == null)
        return null;
```

Continued

Continued

```
      else
         return currentNode.value;
   }

   public boolean addFirstChild (Object item)
   {
      if (item == null)
         throw new IllegalArgumentException
                     ("Trying to add null item to tree");
      if (!hasCurrentPosition())
         throw new IllegalStateException
                     ("Trying to add when no node is current");

      TreeNode newChild = new TreeNode (item, null, currentNode.child);
      currentNode.child = newChild;
      parents.push (currentNode);
      currentNode = newChild;
      size++;
      return true;
   }
```

The rest of the code for the tree iterator implementation can be found on the book's CD.

Exercises 11.6

1. Complete the methods left as exercises in the tree implementation.

2. Rewrite Iterator so that it doesn't first build a queue and then return an iterator on that queue. Instead, it should stay in continuous contact with the underlying tree.

3. Design and implement a postorder iterator for the tree ADT.

4. All manipulation of the modCount variable has been omitted from the LinkedTree class. Correct this deficiency and check the results.

5. Rewrite LinkedTree using parent pointers in the nodes rather than using a binary tree of parents. What are the advantages and disadvantages of this approach?

11.7   Case Study 2: A Skills Database

11.7.1   Request

Write a program to keep track of skills by person and department.

11.7.2   Analysis

The application suggests a general tree structure as shown in Figure 11.21. There are three departments. The Finance Department has two employees. Sue Jones has three skills. The employees in other departments and their skills are not shown.

Figure 11.21   **A typical collection of skills data**

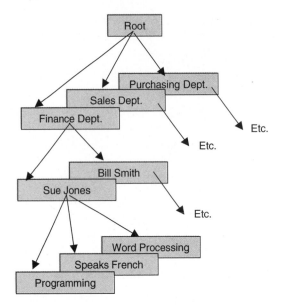

Many interfaces are possible. Figure 11.22 shows a typical one. Here is how the interface works:

- The items in the tree are displayed in hierarchical form in the list box on the left. When the program starts, only the root node is displayed.

- To enter a new item, the user selects an existing item, enters a name and a description in the corresponding fields, and selects one of the following buttons:

  Insert Child inserts the new item in the next level in the tree. Thus, in this application, if the user inserts a child when a department name is selected, the new item is inserted at the level of personnel.

  Insert Sibling inserts the new item in the current level in the tree. Thus, in this application, if the user inserts a child when a department name is selected, the new item is inserted at the level of departments.

- To navigate to an item, the user selects it in the list box. When the user selects an item, its information is displayed in the Name and Description fields.

- The user can also modify the display of items in the list box by double-clicking an item. This has the effect of either expanding or contracting the number of items displayed.

- The user can edit or delete an existing item by selecting it and selecting the button Modify or Remove.

- The result of selecting List All With Skill (where the skill is programming) is displayed in Figure 11.22. When the user selects List All, the contents of the entire database are displayed in hierarchical format in the text area, as shown in Figure 11.23.

Figure 11.22   **The user interface for the skills program**

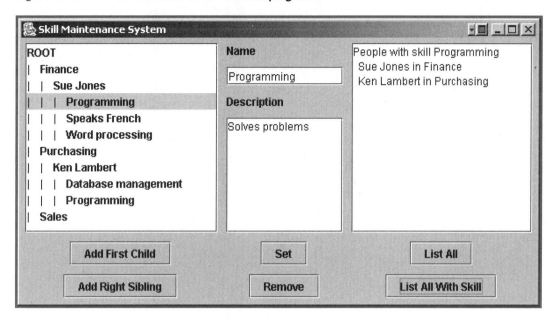

Figure 11.23   **The result of selecting List All in the skills program**

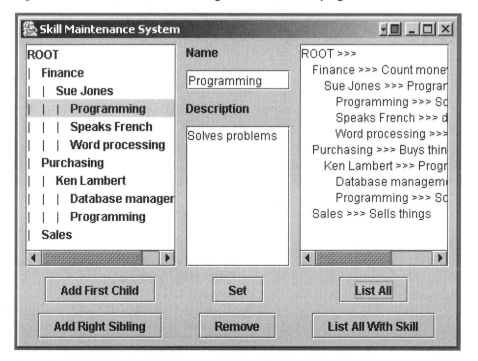

11.7.3   Design and Implementation of the Model Classes

In this application, we are restricting ourselves to just a name and description for each item. Be it a department, employee, or class, we use an Item class for all three. Figure 11.24 is a summary of the class Item:

Figure 11.24   **A summary of the class Item**

```
Class:
    Item extends Object
Private Instance Variables:
    String name
    String description
Public Methods:
    Item (String name,
          String description
    String toString( )
    boolean equals (Object item)
```

The class SkillsModel maintains the database in a general tree. Table 11.10 lists its public methods.

Table 11.10   **The public Methods of the Class SkillsModel**

Method	What It Does
SkillsModel()	Creates a new skills model that contains a new general tree.
Item get(int treeIndex[])	Returns the item specified by treeIndex.
void moveTo(int treeIndex[])	Moves to the item specified by treeIndex.
void insertChild(Item item, int treeIndex[])	Inserts item as the child of the item specified by treeIndex.
void insertSibling(Item item, int treeIndex[])	Inserts item as the right sibling of the item specified by treeIndex.
void modify(Item item, int treeIndex[])	Modifies the item specified by treeIndex with the contents of item.
void remove(int treeIndex[])	Removes the item specified by treeIndex.
List getNamesOfChildren(int treeIndex[])	Returns a list containing the names of the children of the item specified by treeIndex.
String getStringOfAllItems()	Returns a string representing a hierarchical traversal of the tree.
String getStringOfAllWithSkill(String targetSkill)	Returns a string of all the names of persons having targetSkill.

Note that several methods receive an array named `treeIndex` from the interface. As discussed earlier in this chapter, the data in this array specify the position of the currently selected item in the tree. For example, suppose the tree has a root and three levels below that. Then a tree index of (0, 0, 0) indicates the root, and a tree index of (2, 4, 1) indicates an item reached by navigating to the second child of the root, and then from there to the fourth child, and from there to the first child. The details of how the interface builds a tree index are discussed shortly. Here is a complete listing of the class `SkillsModel`:

```
1  // SkillsModel
2  import lamborne.*;
3  import java.util.*;
4
5  public class SkillsModel extends Object{
6
7      private Tree tree;
8
9      public SkillsModel()
10     {
11         tree = new LinkedTree();
12         tree.addRoot(new Item("ROOT", ""));
13     }
14
15     public Item get (int treeIndex[])
16     {
17         return (Item)(tree.get(treeIndex));
18     }
19
20     public void addFirstChild (int treeIndex[], Item item)
21     {
22         tree.addFirstChild (treeIndex, item);
23     }
24
25     public void addRightSibling (int treeIndex[], Item item)
26     {
27         tree.addRightSibling (treeIndex, item);
28     }
29
30     public void set (int treeIndex[], Item item)
31     {
32         tree.set (treeIndex, item);
33     }
34
35     public void remove (int treeIndex[])
36     {
37         tree.remove(treeIndex);
38     }
39
40     public List getNamesOfChildren (int treeIndex[])
41     {
42         TreeIterator treeIter = tree.treeIterator();
43         treeIter.moveTo (treeIndex);
44         List list = new LinkedList();
45         Object obj = treeIter.getFirstChild();
46         while (obj != null) {
```

Continued

Continued

```
47              String name = ((Item(obj)).name;
48              list.add (name);
49              obj = treeIter.getRightSibling();
50          }
51          return list;
52      }
53
54      public String getStringOfAllItems()
55      {
56          return tree.hierarchicalList();
57      }
58
59      public String getStringOfAllWithSkill (String targetSkill)
60      {
61          Item department, employee, skill;
62          TreeIterator treeIter = tree.treeIterator();
63
64          String result = "People with skill " + targetSkill;
65
66          treeIter.getRoot();
67          department = (Item)(treeIter.getFirstChild());
68          while (department != null){
69              employee = (Item)(treeIter.getFirstChild());
70              while (employee != null){
71                  skill = (Item)(treeIter.getFirstChild());
72                  while (skill != null){
73                      if (skill.name.equals (targetSkill)){
74                          result += "\n  " + employee.name +
75                                  " in " + department.name;
76                          break;
77                      }else{
78                          skill = (Item)(treeIter.getRightSibling());
79                      }
80                  }
81                  treeIter.getParent();
82                  employee = (Item)(treeIter.getRightSibling());
83              }
84              treeIter.getParent();
85              department = (Item)(treeIter.getRightSibling());
86          }
87
88          return result;
89      }
90 }
```

11.7.4   Design and Implementation of the View Classes

The primary challenge in the design of the view class, `SkillsInterface`, is to display a view of the tree as a hierarchical list in a scrolling list box. To facilitate this task, we implement a helper class called `TreeList`. Instead of communicating directly with the scrolling list, the view sends messages to a tree list. The tree list returns information about events in the scrolling list to the view and converts information received from the view into a form that can be displayed in the scrolling list.

The tree list stores items in the scrolling list with multiple prefixes of "|". The root item has no prefix. A child of the root has one prefix. A grandchild of the root has two prefixes and so on.

Table 11.11 lists the public methods for the class `TreeList`.

Table 11.11   The Methods of the Class `TreeList`

Method	What It Does
`TreeList(java.awt.List list, int maxLevel)`	Constructs a tree list that tracks the scrolling list `list` and maintains `maxLevel` levels in its hierarchy.
`int getSelectedIndex()`	Returns the index of the selected item in the list.
`void select (int pos)`	Selects the item at position `pos` in the list.
`public void add (String str, int pos, int level)`	Inserts a string at position `pos` with level `level`.
`int[] getTreeIndex (int pos)`	Returns the tree index of the selected item in the list.
`int getLevel (int pos)`	Returns the level of the item at position `pos` in the list. The level associated with an item in the list equals the number of | characters in the string + 1.
`boolean isExpanded (int pos)`	Returns `true` if the item at position `pos` is expanded or `false` otherwise. The following items are considered to be expanded: a leaf an item followed by an item at a higher level in the tree
`void contract (int pos)`	From the list remove all successors of the selected item until one with the same or lower level is encountered.
`public void expand (int pos, java.util.List listOfStrings)`	To the list add all successors of the selected item.
`void addFirstChild (String str, int pos)`	Adds the first child to the item at position `pos`.
`void addRightSibling (String str, int pos)`	Add a right sibling to the item at position `pos`.
`void set (String str, int pos)`	Replaces the item at position `pos` with `str`.
`void remove (int pos)`	From the list remove the selected item and all successors until one with the same or lower level is encountered.

To illustrate how view uses the tree list, consider what should happen when the user double-clicks an item in the scrolling list. The method `listDoubleClicked`, as defined in the class `SkillsInterface`, should respond in one of three ways:

1. Do nothing if the item selected is at the bottom level in the hierarchy.

2. Expand the hierarchy of items under the selected item if that hierarchy is already contracted.

3. Contract the hierarchy of items under the selected item if that hierarchy is already expanded.

The algorithm for handling a double-click in a list begins by asking the tree list for the position of the selected item, its tree index, and its level. Because there are only four possible levels in the data model, the class `SkillsInterface` maintains these as constants. Thus, the algorithm handles the first possibility by comparing the level of the selected item to the largest level. The algorithm chooses one of the other two possibilities by asking the tree list whether or not the item at the selected position is expanded. If the item is expanded, the tree list is told to contract it. Otherwise, the algorithm asks the model for a list of names of the children of the node at the tree index and tells the tree list to expand the selected item with that list of names. Here is the code as embedded in the class `ListMouseListener`:

```
// List mouse listener
private class ListMouseListener extends MouseAdapter{
    public void mouseClicked(MouseEvent e) {
        int selection = treeList.getSelectedIndex();
        int treeIndex[] = treeList.getTreeIndex(selection);

        if (e.getClickCount() == 2){
            if (treeList.getLevel (selection) == kSkillLevel)
                return;

            if (treeList.isExpanded (selection))
                treeList.contract (selection);
            else{
                java.util.List listOfNames =
                        model.getNamesOfChildren (treeIndex);
                treeList.expand (selection, listOfNames);
            }
        }else if (e.getClickCount() == 1){
            Item item = model.get (treeIndex);
            displayItem (item);
        }
    }
}
```

Complete listings of the classes `SkillsInterface` and `TreeList` are on the book's CD.

KEY TERMS

binary tree	interior node	postorder traversal
children	leaf	preorder traversal
complete binary tree	left subtree	right subtree
expression tree	level order traversal	root
general tree	parent	tree iterator
inorder traversal	parse tree	

CHAPTER SUMMARY

Trees are hierarchical collections. Each item in a tree, with the exception of the root item, has a unique predecessor and zero or more successors. The root item has only successors. An item in a binary tree has at most two successors. Trees with more than two successors are sometimes called general trees. The successors of an item are also called its children, and all of the items below a given item and reachable from it are its descendants. The predecessor of a given item is called its parent, and all of the items above a given item and reachable from it are its ancestors. A item with no successors is called a leaf.

Binary trees can also be defined recursively. According to this definition, a binary tree is either empty or consists of three parts: an item and a left subtree and a right subtree, where each subtree is itself a binary tree.

The level of an item within a binary tree is the distance from that item to the root item. A binary tree is complete if each level but the last one has a complete set of items and the last level is occupied from left to right.

The structure of a binary tree supports several standard traversal operations. Each traversal starts at the root item. A preorder traversal visits an item, then traverses the left subtree, and then traverses the right subtree. An inorder traversal traverses the left subtree, then visits an item, and then traverses the right subtree. A postorder traversal traverses the left subtree, then traverses the right subtree, and then visits an item. A level order traversal visits each node in a level, from left to right, before descending to the next level.

Two common implementations of trees use arrays and linked structures. A complete binary tree lends itself nicely to an array implementation, whereas other types of trees are best represented with linked structures.

REVIEW QUESTIONS

1. Describe the difference between a binary tree and a general tree.
2. What is the root item?
3. What is a leaf?
4. Describe the order in which items are visited in the preorder, inorder, postorder, and level order traversals of a binary tree.
5. Which type of tree is suitable for an array implementation?

CHAPTER 12

Special-Purpose Trees

OBJECTIVES Upon completion of this chapter, you should be able to

■ Describe the basic features of heaps

■ Explain the use of an array to implement a heap

■ Provide a description and a complexity analysis of heap sort

■ Give an account of the basic features of binary search trees

■ Show how a binary search tree can represent a priority queue

In this chapter, we examine some trees with particular properties that make them useful in specific applications. These applications include searching, sorting, and implementing priority queues.

12.1 Heaps

A *heap* is an ordered collection in which the objects are stored in order from greatest to smallest. A common implementation of a heap uses a binary tree in which the item in each node is greater than or equal to the items in both of its children. This constraint on the order of the nodes is called the *heap property*. You should not confuse this kind of heap with the heap that a computer uses to manage dynamic memory. Figure 12.1 shows two examples of heaps.

As the figure shows, the largest item is in the root node, and the smallest items are in the leaves. The arrangement of data in a heap supports an efficient sorting method called the *heap sort*. Heaps are also used to implement priority queues. Before we discuss these applications, let us develop a heap ADT using the approach of the professional ADTs as found in the `lamborne` package.

Figure 12.1   **Examples of heaps**

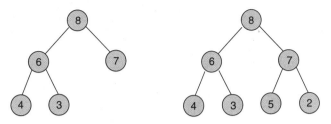

12.1.1   The Shapes of Binary Trees

As you can see in Figure 12.1, a heap is a binary tree. When storing data in and re-trieving data from binary trees, the shape of the tree often affects the efficiency of these operations. We now introduce some terminology that allows us to talk about a binary tree's shape:

Full binary tree: A binary tree is *full* if it contains the maximum number of nodes for its height. Each node in a full binary tree is either an interior node with two non-empty children or a leaf. The number of leaves in a nonempty full binary tree is one greater than the number of interior nodes. A full binary tree has the minimum height necessary to accommodate a given number of nodes. Such a tree is *fully balanced*. A fully balanced tree of height d can accommodate up to $2^{d+1} - 1$ nodes. In a fully balanced binary tree, there can be up to 2^n nodes in level n. The height of a fully balanced tree of n nodes is $\log_2 n$.

Complete binary tree: A binary tree is *complete* if its shape is restricted by starting at the root node and filling the tree by levels from left to right. Thus, all full trees are complete, but not all complete trees are full. A complete binary tree of height d has filled all of the levels except possibly level d.

Figure 12.2 shows some examples of tree that have these properties. The examples are a complete but not full binary tree, a binary tree that is not complete, and a full binary tree.

Figure 12.2   **Different types of binary trees**

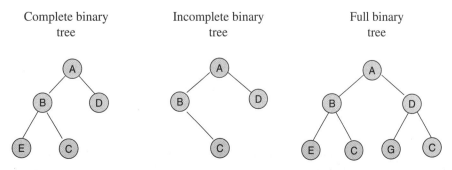

In Chapter 11, we discussed the array representation of a binary tree. The array representation assumes that the tree is complete. We also assume that a heap is a complete binary tree.

12.1.2 Comparable Objects Revisited

The items in a heap must be comparable. As discussed in Chapter 3, two items A and B are comparable if A is less than, greater than, or equal to B. Comparable items also submit to the usual test for equality of any items. Some Java classes, such as String, already implement the Java Comparable interface, which guarantees that their instances can be used as items in a heap. The Java programmer is required to implement this interface for any other classes of objects that might be stored in a heap.

The Comparable interface specifies a single method, compareTo, which any comparable class must implement. When we wish to compare two of these objects, we first cast them to class Comparable and use the compareTo method, as in the following code segment:

```
Comparable item1 = (Comparable) <get object from wherever>;
Comparable item2 = (Comparable) <get object from wherever>;
if (item1.compareTo(item2) <a comparison operator> 0)
    <some code>
```

12.1.3 The Heap Interface

The heap ADT is a kind of collection, so a heap should recognize messages to return its size, to return its string representation, to test for emptiness, to return an iterator, and so forth.

The two most critical heap operations are add and pop. add expects a comparable object as a parameter and inserts the object into its proper place in the heap. That place is generally at a level below an object that is larger and above an object that is smaller. pop deletes the topmost node in the heap, returns the object contained there, and maintains the heap property. It is also useful to provide a peek operation, which returns but does not remove the topmost object in a heap.

Two sorting operations are provided in the interface to the heap ADT. The first one expects an array of objects and returns an array of objects. The second expects a Java collection and returns an array of objects. Both arrays returned contain the objects in ascending order. Both operations use a heap sort, to be discussed shortly, and for convenience, are defined as static methods.

The heap iterator allows a client to visit the nodes in the heap in descending order, but it does not support removals. The toArray method likewise returns an array of items in descending order.

Table 12.1 summarizes these operations and others, which are specified in the interface Heap.

Table 12.1   The **Heap** Interface

boolean	**add(Object item)** Adds an item to the top of this heap. Throws an exception if the item is noncomparable. Returns `true` if the item is actually added. Some implementations might choose not to allow duplicates.
void	**clear()** Removes all items from this heap.
Object	**clone()** Returns a shallow copy of this heap.
Collection	**collectionView()** Returns a collection-view of the items in this heap.
boolean	**equals(Object other)** Returns `true` if the specified item is a heap that equals this heap. Two heaps are considered equal if their items are equal when taken in descending order.
int	**hashCode()** Returns the hash code value for this heap.
boolean	**isEmpty()** Returns `true` if this heap contains no elements.
Iterator	**iterator()** Returns an iterator over the items in this heap. The iterator provides the items sorted in descending order. The iterator should not support removal.
Object	**peek()** Returns the item at the head of this heap without removing it from the heap. Throws an exception if the heap is empty.
Object	**pop()** Returns the item at the head of this heap and removes it from the heap. Throws an exception if the heap is empty.
int	**size()** Returns the number of items in this heap.
static Object []	**sort(Object a[])** Returns an array of items sorted in ascending order. The items are taken from the specified input array. Throws an exception if the specified array is `null` or has length zero or if the array contains noncomparable items. (Actually, static methods cannot be placed in an interface. Therefore, this merely acts as a reminder. The user must cast the heap to an abstract heap before using this method.)
static Object []	**sort(Collection col)** Returns an array of items sorted in ascending order. The items are taken from the specified input collection. Throws an exception if the specified collection is `null` or has size zero or if the collection contains noncomparable items. (Actually, static methods cannot be placed in an interface. Therefore, this merely acts as a reminder. The user must cast the heap to an abstract heap before using this method.)

continued

Table 12.1   The `Heap` Interface *(Continued)*

`Object[]`	`toArray()` Returns an array containing all the items in this heap. The array is sorted in descending order.
`String`	`toString()` Returns a string that lists the items in this heap sorted in descending order.

12.1.4   The Heap Implementation

There are various ways to implement a heap. Because of the nature of the add and pop operations, it is very convenient to use the array representation of a binary tree discussed in Chapter 11. The responsibilities for the heap implementation are divided in the usual manner among the classes AbstractContainer, AbstractHeap, and ArrayHeap. Table 12.2 lists the methods and their complexity.

As usual, we develop some of the critical methods and refer the reader to the complete code listings on the book's CD for the other methods.

Table 12.2   The Methods in the `Heap` Implementation and Their Complexity

	Heap Implementation	Abstract Container	Abstract Heap	Array Heap
	`constructor()`	O(1)	O(1)	O(1)
	`constructor(Collection col)`			O($n\log n$)
	`constructor(Iterator iter)`			O($n\log n$)
	`constructor(Iterator iter,` `int initialCapacity)`			O($n\log n$)
	`constructor(int` `initialCapacity)`			O(1)
`boolean`	`add(Object item)`			O($\log n$)
`void`	`clear()`	O(1)		O(1)
`Object`	`clone()`			O(n)
`Collection`	`collectionView()`	based on iterator		
`boolean`	`equals(Object other)`		traverses iterator	
`int`	`hashCode()`	traverses iterator		
`boolean`	`isEmpty`	uses **size** method		
`Iterator`	`iterator()`	abstract		O($n\log n$)

Table 12.2   **The Methods in the `Heap` Implementation and Their Complexity (Continued)**

	Heap Implementation	Abstract Container	Abstract Heap	Array Heap
`Object`	`peek()`			O(1)
`Object`	`pop()`			O(log$n$)
`int`	`size()`	O(1)		
`static Object []`	`sort(Object a[])`		O($n$log$n$)	
`static Object []`	`sort(Collection col)`		O($n$log$n$)	
`Object []`	`toArray()`	traverses iterator		
`String`	`toString()`	traverses iterator		

12.1.5   Implementing the Heap Sort

The two static heap sort methods are implemented in the class `AbstractHeap`. The heap sort is surprisingly simple. To return an array of items in ascending order, we perform two steps:

1. Build a heap from the input array.

2. Beginning with the last cell in the output array, remove an item from the heap, insert it into the cell, and repeat this process for the remaining cells in the array, moving from the last position down to the first position.

The implementation must also check for items that are not comparable or for an input array that is `null` or empty and throw the appropriate exceptions if necessary. Here is the code for the heap sort method that sorts an array:

```
// Sort in ascending order
public static Object[] sort (Object in[]){
   if (in == null)
      throw new IllegalArgumentException
          ("Trying to sort when the array is null");
   if (in.length == 0)
      throw new IllegalArgumentException
          ("Trying to sort when array has length 0");

   int i;
   Heap heap = new ArrayHeap (in.length);
   Object out[] = new Object[in.length];
   for (i = 0; i < in.length; i++){
      if (!(in[i] instanceof Comparable))
         throw new IllegalArgumentException
            ("Trying to sort when the array contains a non-comparable item");

      heap.add (in[i]);
```

Continued

Continued

```
    }
    for (i = out.length - 1 ; i >= 0; i--)
        out[i] = heap.pop();
    return out;
}
```

The implementation of the second heap sort method, which expects a Java collection and returns an array, is similar but uses an iterator to traverse the collection.

Note that the array returned by the static sort method contains the items provided by the input parameter instead of copies of these items. In this regard, the sort method is similar to the methods `clone` and `toArray`. They are "shallow copiers" and thus allow the client to access and modify the heap's items by using more than one reference. The danger here, in the case of `clone` and `toArray`, is that a client might alter the attribute of an item used to compare it to others and thus violate the heap property of the tree. More robust versions of these methods perform a deep copy of the items as well.

12.1.6   Implementing **add** and **pop**

The methods `add` (insertion) and `pop` (removal), which are used throughout the heap implementation, are defined in the class `ArrayHeap`. In the array implementation, both methods need to maintain the structure of the heap within the array. This structure is similar to the array representation of a binary tree discussed in Chapter 11, with the constraint that each node is greater than either of its children.

Let us consider insertion first. The goal is to find the new item's proper place in the heap and insert it there. Here is our strategy for insertions:

1. Insert the item at the bottom of the heap. In the array implementation, this will be in the cell after the last item currently in the array.

2. Enter a loop that "walks" the new item up the heap, while the new item's value is greater than that of its parent. Each time this relationship is true, we swap the new item with its parent. When this process stops (either the new item is less than or equal to its parent or we will have reached the top node), the new item is in its proper place.

Recall that the position of an item's parent in the array is computed by subtracting 1 from the item's position and dividing the result by 2. The top of the heap is at position 0 in the array. Here is the code for the method `add`:

```
public boolean add (Object item){
    if (!(item instanceof Comparable))
        throw new IllegalArgumentException
            ("Trying to add a non-comparable item to heap");
    int curPos, parent;

    heap = Utilities.expandArrayIfNeeded (heap, size);
    heap[size] = item;
```

Continued

Continued

```
    size++;
    modCount++;
    curPos = size - 1;
    while (curPos > 0){
        parent = (curPos - 1) / 2;
        Comparable parentItem = (Comparable)(heap[parent]);
        if (parentItem.compareTo ((Comparable)item) >= 0)
            return true;
        else{
            heap[curPos] = heap[parent];
            heap[parent] = item;
            curPos = parent;
        }
    }
    return true;
}
```

A quick analysis of this method reveals that at most $\log_2 n$ comparisons must be made to walk up the tree from the bottom, so the add operation is O($\log n$). The method occasionally triggers a doubling in the size of the underlying array. When it occurs, this operation is O(n), but amortized over all additions, the operation is O(1) per addition.

The goal of a removal is to return the item in the root node after deleting this node and adjusting the positions of other nodes so as to maintain the heap property. Here is our strategy for removals:

1. Save pointers to the top item and the bottom item in the heap and move the item from the bottom of the heap to the top.

2. Walk down the heap from the top, moving the largest child up one level, until the bottom of the heap is reached.

Here is the code for the method pop:

```
public Object pop(){
    if (size == 0)
        throw new NoSuchElementException
            ("Trying to remove from an empty heap");

    int curPos, leftChild, rightChild, maxChild, lastIndex;
    Object topItem = heap[0];
    Comparable bottomItem = (Comparable)(heap[size - 1]);

    heap = Utilities.shrinkArrayIfNeeded (heap, size, initCapacity);

    heap[0] = bottomItem;
    size--;
    modCount++;
    lastIndex = size - 1;
    curPos = 0;
    while (true){
        leftChild = 2 * curPos + 1 ;
```

Continued

Continued

```
        rightChild = 2 * curPos + 2;
        if (leftChild > lastIndex) break;
        if (rightChild > lastIndex)
           maxChild = leftChild;
        else{
           Comparable leftItem  = (Comparable)(heap[leftChild]);
           Comparable rightItem = (Comparable)(heap[rightChild]);
           if (leftItem.compareTo (rightItem) > 0)
              maxChild = leftChild;
           else
              maxChild = rightChild;
        }
        Comparable maxItem = (Comparable)(heap[maxChild]);
        if (bottomItem.compareTo (maxItem) >= 0)
           break;
        else{
           heap[curPos] = heap[maxChild];
           heap[maxChild]= bottomItem;
           curPos = maxChild;
        }
     }
     return topItem;
}
```

Once again, analysis shows that the number of comparisons required for a removal is at most $\log_2 n$, so the pop operation is $O(\log n)$. The method pop occasionally triggers a halving in the size of the underlying array. When it occurs, this operation is $O(n)$, but amortized over all removals, the operation is $O(1)$ per removal.

12.1.7   Analysis of the Heap Sort

Now we are in a position to analyze the heap sort. In general, two steps are required for a heap sort:

1. Build a heap from a collection.

2. Remove the items from the heap and place them in order in an array.

The first step requires n insertions, each with a complexity of $O(\log n)$. Thus, the overall complexity of the first step is $O(n\log n)$. The second step requires n removals, each with a complexity of $O(\log n)$, so its overall complexity is also $O(n\log n)$. Thus, the overall time complexity of heap sort is $2n\log n$, or $O(n\log n)$. Heap sort has a space complexity of $O(n)$ due to the extra memory required for the heap.

12.1.8   Implementation of the Iterator

The strategy for creating the iterator for the array representation of a heap requires two steps:

1. Transfer the items from the heap's array to a new array.

2. Sort the new array.

The next code segment shows the data, the constructor, and the method `next` for the class `InnerIter`, which implements the iterator for the array representation of a heap:

```
private class InnerIter implements Iterator{

    private int    curPos;
    private Object sortedItems[];
    private int    expectedModCount = modCount;

    protected InnerIter(){
        curPos = size - 1;
        if (size > 0){
            sortedItems = new Object[size];
            for (int i = 0; i < size; i++){
                sortedItems[i] = heap[i];
            }
            sortedItems = AbstractHeap.sort (sortedItems);
        }
    }

    public Object next(){
        if (modCount != expectedModCount)
            throw new ConcurrentModificationException();
        if (!hasNext())
            throw new NoSuchElementException("There are no more elements");

        Object item = sortedItems[curPos];
        curPos--;
        return item;
    }
```

Note that the iterator's backing store is not the heap's array, but a copy whose items are in ascending order. However, the current position index in the iterator starts at size − 1 and works its way back to 0 as each item is visited. Thus, the iterator returns a traversable sequence of items in descending order. Because the heap has the largest item on top, the "natural order" for a heap iterator is descending order on the items. This can be done at an initial cost of O($n$log$n$). The other choice is for the iterator to serve up items in the physical order in which they are stored in the heap, using the heap's array as a backing store. The cost is then O(1) per item, but the iterator is less useful.

12.1.9 Using a Heap to Implement a Priority Queue

You will recall the discussion of priority queues in Chapter 9, where we implemented a priority queue ADT with an array of queues. Another common implementation of priority queues uses a heap. Items with the highest priority are located near the top of the heap. The `enqueue` operation wraps the item and its priority number in an object called a priority node before inserting the node into the heap. The `dequeue` operation removes the topmost node from the heap, extracts the item, and returns it. The next code segment shows the public methods of the concrete class HeapPriorityQueue and the implementation of the class PriorityNode:

```
1 // HeapPriorityQueue
2
3 package lamborne;
4
5 import java.util.*;
6
7 public class HeapPriorityQueue extends AbstractPriorityQueue
8                                implements PriorityQueue, Cloneable {
9
10    private ArrayHeap heap;      // A heap of items
11
12    public HeapPriorityQueue(){
13       super();
14       heap = new ArrayHeap();
15    }
16
17    public void clear(){
18       super.clear();
19       heap = new ArrayHeap();
20    }
21
22    public Object clone(){
23       HeapPriorityQueue clone = new HeapPriorityQueue();
24       clone.heap = (ArrayHeap)(heap.clone());
25       clone.size = size;
26       return clone;
27    }
28
29    public String debugString(){
30       return heap.debugString();
31    }
32
33    public Object dequeue(){
34       if (size == 0)
35          throw new NoSuchElementException
36                ("Trying to dequeue an empty priority queue");
37
38       size--;
39       modCount++;
40       return ((PriorityNode)(heap.pop())).value;
41    }
42
43    public void enqueue (Object item, int priority){
44       if (item == null)
45          throw new IllegalArgumentException
46                ("Trying to enqueue a null item");
47       if (priority < 1)
48          throw new IllegalArgumentException
49                ("Priority must be >= 1 ");
50
51       size++;
52       modCount++;
53       heap.add (new PriorityNode (item, priority));
54    }
```

Continued

Continued

```
55
56    public Iterator iterator()
57    // The iterator returns the items in their queued order
58    {
59        return new InnerIter();
60    }
61
62    public Object peek(){
63        if (size == 0)
64            throw new NoSuchElementException
65                    ("Trying to peek at an empty priority queue");
66
67        return (PriorityNode)(heap.peek())).value;
68    }
69
70    public String toString(){
71        if (size == 0) return "[]";
72
73        Iterator iter = heap.iterator();
74        String str = "";
75        PriorityNode next;
76        int currentPriority = -1;
77        while (iter.hasNext()){
78            next = (PriorityNode)(iter.next());
79            if (currentPriority == next.priority)
80                str += ", " + next.value;
81            else{
82                if (currentPriority != -1)
83                    str += "]\n";
84                currentPriority = next.priority;
85                str += "Priority " + currentPriority + ": [" + next.value;
86            }
87        }
88        return str + "]";
89    }
90
91 private class PriorityNode implements Comparable {
92
93    private Object      value;        // Value stored in this item
94    private int         priority;     // Priority of item
95    private int         subpriority   // Subpriority of item, assigned
96                                      // by constructor
97
98    private PriorityNode(){
99        throw new IllegalArgumentException
100                   ("Trying to create a null priority item");
101    }
102
103    private PriorityNode (Object value, int priority){
104        this.value = value;
105        this.priority = priority;
106        subpriority = subpriorityCounter;
107        subpriorityCounter++;                  // Warning: Jumps from +2G to -2G
108    }
109
```

Continued

Continued

```
110     public int compareTo (Object item){
111         int prior   = ((PriorityNode)item).priority;
112         int subprior = ((PriorityNode)item).subpriority;
113         if (priority != prior)
114             return priority - prior;
115         else
116             return subprior - subpriority
117     }
118
119     public String toString(){
120         return "(" + value + "," +
121             priority + "," + subpriority + ")";
122     }
123 }
124 }
```

Although heap implementation of priority queues is simple and widely discussed in the literature, it loses out to the linked implementation in the efficiency department. Table 12.3 shows how badly.

Table 12.3   Comparing Priority Queue Implementations

	PriorityQueue Implementation	Abstract Container	Abstract Priority Queue	Linked Priority Queue	Heap Priority Queue
	constructor()	O(1)	O(1)	O(1)	O(1)
	constructor(int maxPriority)			O(1)	
void	clear()	O(1)		O(1)	O(1)
Object	clone()			O(n)	O(n)
Collection	collectionView()	based on iterator			
Object	dequeue()			O(1)	O(logn)
void	enqueue(Object item)		uses enqueue (i, I)		
void	enqueue(Object item, int priority)		abstract	O(1)	O(logn)
boolean	equals(Object other)		traverses iterator		
int	hashCode()	traverses iterator			
boolean	isEmpty()	uses size method			
Iterator	iterator()	abstract		O(1)	O(nlogn)
Object	peek()			O(1)	O(1)

Table 12.3 **Comparing Priority Queue Implementations *(Continued)***

	PriorityQueue Implementation	*Abstract Container*	*Abstract Priority Queue*	*Linked Priority Queue*	*Heap Priority Queue*
`int`	`size()`	O(1)			
`Object[]`	`toArray()`	traverses iterator			
`String`	`toString()`	traverses iterator		O(n)	O($n$log$n$)

`HeapPriorityQueue` does have a compensating space advantage if the range of priorities is large compared to the number of items being queued. One other point that might be made in its favor is that the number of priorities does not have to be fixed ahead of time. However, `LinkedPriorityQueue` could be modified to avoid this restriction by allowing it to grow.

Exercise 12.1

An O(n) `equals` method could be implemented in `ArrayHeap`. This is better than the O($n$log$n$) `equals` method currently implemented in `AbstractHeap`, which is based on an iterator that takes O($n$log$n$) to create in `ArrayHeap`. Explain why this is a bad idea.

12.2   Binary Search Trees

The storing and retrieving of objects are a requirement in many systems. The underlying data structure has an enormous influence on the efficiency of these operations. For instance, suppose one is working with an array of integers. Storing a new integer in the array can be done in O(1) time by adding the new integer immediately after the last number currently stored in the array. However, searching the array for an integer is much less efficient. One must begin at the top of the array and search down until one either encounters the integer or the end of the numbers. This is an O(n) operation. Keeping the integers in ascending order within the array allows one to do a binary search, which is O(log$n$), but changes the complexity of insertions to O(n). In this section, we examine a technique for storing objects that has the potential to be O(log$n$) for searches, insertions, and deletions. We say "potential" because in some situations the efficiency of all three operations degenerates to O(n).

12.2.1   The Sorted Collection ADT and Its Interface

To illustrate the concept of a data structure that supports efficient searches, insertions, and deletions, we first develop an ADT called a ***sorted collection***. From the client's point of view, a sorted collection appears to be a linear sequence of items that are automatically maintained in ascending order. Thus, the sorted collection supports many of the index-based and object-based operations associated with a list. However, there is only one way to add an item to a sorted collection, and that is by placing the item in its proper position in relation to the other comparable items in the collection. Table 12.4 lists the methods in the interface `SortedCollection`.

Table 12.4   **The `SortedCollection` Interface**

`boolean`	`add(Object item)` Adds an item to this sorted collection in the last possible position while still retaining the collection's sorted character. Throws an exception if the item is noncomparable, else returns `true`.
`Boolean`	`addUnique(Object item)` Adds an item to this sorted collection provided the item is not equal to one already in this collection. Returns `true` if the collection changes. Throws an exception if the item is noncomparable.
`void`	`clear()` Removes all items from this sorted collection.
`Object`	`clone()` Returns a shallow copy of this sorted collection.
`Collection`	`collectionView()` Returns a collection-view of the items in this sorted collection.
`boolean`	`contains(Object item)` Returns `true` if this sorted collection contains an item equal to the specified item. Throws an exception if the item is noncomparable.
`boolean`	`equals(Object other)` Returns `true` if the other object is a sorted collection that equals this sorted collection. Two sorted collections are considered equal if their items are equal when taken in ascending order.
`int`	`indexOf(Object item)` Returns the index of the first item equal to the specified item or −1 if there is none. Throws an exception if the specified item is noncomparable.
`Object`	`get(int i)` Returns the ith item in this collection. Throws an exception if the index i is out of the range 0 to size − 1.
`Object`	`get(Object item)` Returns the first item equal to the specified item or `null` if there is none. Throws an exception if the specified item is noncomparable.
`int`	`hashCode()` Returns the hash code value for this sorted collection.
`boolean`	`isEmpty()` Returns `true` if this sorted collection contains no elements.

Table 12.4   The `SortedCollection` Interface *(Continued)*

`Iterator`	`iterator()` Returns an iterator over the items contained in this sorted collection. The iterator provides the items sorted in ascending order. The iterator could support removal depending on the implementation.
`Object`	`remove(int i)` Removes and returns the *i*th item in this collection. Throws an exception if the index *i* is out of the range 0 to size − 1.
`boolean`	`remove(Object item)` Removes the first item equal to the specified item from the collection. Returns `true` if the collection changes. Throws an exception if the item is noncomparable.
`int`	`size()` Returns the number of items in this sorted collection.
`Object[]`	`toArray()` Returns an array containing all the items in this sorted collection. The array is sorted in ascending order.
`String`	`toString()` Returns a string that lists the items in this collection sorted in ascending order.

Note that whenever an item is a parameter in one of these methods, the item must be comparable, as discussed earlier.

12.2.2   Implementation of the Sorted Collection ADT

The organization of the classes used in the implementation of the sorted collection ADT follows the usual pattern. They consist of the classes `AbstractContainer` and `AbstractSortedCollection` and the concrete class `LinkedBST SortedCollection`. The concrete class is a ***binary search tree*** representation, which we discuss later. For now, note the complexity of the insertions, removals, and searches, which is $O(\log_2 n)$ if the tree is balanced. Table 12.5 lists the methods in the implementation.

Table 12.5   **The Methods of the `SortedCollection` Implementation and Their Complexity**

	SortedCollection Implementation	Abstract Container	Abstract Sorted Collection	LinkedBST Sorted Collection
	constructor()	O(1)	O(1)	O(1)
	constructor(Collection col, boolean addUnique)			O($n \log n$) if balanced
boolean	add(Object item)		abstract	O($\log n$) if balanced
boolean	addUnique(Object item)		uses add method	
void	clear()	O(1)		O(1)
Object	clone()			O($n \log n$) if balanced
Collection	collectionView()	based on iterator		
boolean	contains(Object item)		uses get method	
boolean	equals(Object other)		traverses iterator	
int	indexOf(Object item)		exercise	
Object	get(int i)		abstract	O(n)
Object	get(Object item)		abstract	O($\log n$) if balanced
int	hashCode()	traverses iterator		
boolean	isEmpty()	uses size method		
Iterator	iterator()	abstract		O(n)
Object	remove(int i)		uses get (i) and remove (item)	
boolean	remove(Object item)		abstract	O($\log n$) if balanced
int	size()	O(1)		
Object[]	toArray()	traverses iterator		
String	toString()	traverses iterator		

Actually, a sorted collection can be instantiated with any number of concrete classes, but we examine only one here: the binary search tree. But before we develop a binary search tree, we digress for a moment to the general topic of binary search.

12.2.3 Binary Search Revisited

The call tree for a binary search of a typical array is shown in Figure 12.3. The items visited for comparison are shaded. As the figure shows, it requires at most four comparisons to search the entire array of eight items. Because the array is sorted, the search algorithm can reduce the search space by one-half after each comparison.

Figure 12.3 **A call tree for the binary search of an array**

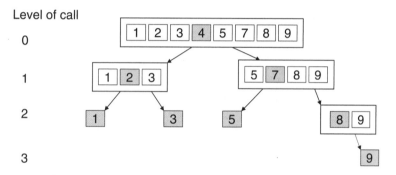

Now, let us transfer the items that are shaded in the call tree for the binary search to an explicit binary tree structure, as shown in Figure 12.4. This tree is a binary search tree. Note each node in the tree is greater than or equal to its left child and less than or equal to its right child.

Figure 12.4 **A binary search tree**

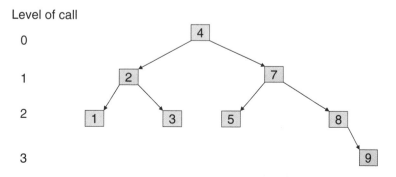

Now, consider the following recursive search process using this tree:

```
If the tree is empty
   Return false
Else if the item in the root equals the target
   Return true
Else if the item in the root is greater than the target
   Return the result of searching the root's left subtree
Else
   Return the result of searching the root's right subtree
```

Like the binary search of a sorted array, the search of a binary search tree can potentially throw away one-half of the search space after each comparison. We say "potentially" because the efficiency of the search depends in part on the shape of the tree. Figure 12.5 shows three binary search trees that contain the same items but have different shapes.

Figure 12.5   **Three binary tree shapes with the same data**

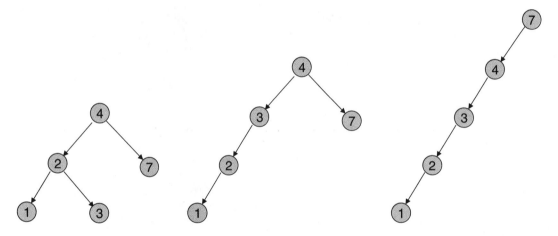

The trees degrade in their support for efficient search from left to right. The leftmost tree is full and is said to be balanced. Hence, it supports the most efficient searches. The rightmost tree looks just like a one-way linked list and as such supports only a linear search. Thus, everything depends on how the data come into the tree. In particular, data coming into the tree in close to sorted order produce a tree whose shape is not optimal for searching. But let us first develop a binary search tree implementation and discuss some of its basic operations before considering how to fix its shape.

12.2.4   The Binary Search Tree Implementation

The class LinkedBSTSortedCollection is a concrete subclass of the class AbstractSortedCollection. We choose a linked implementation that is similar to the one used for binary trees in Chapter 11, although an array implementation is also possible. Thus, LinkedBSTSortedCollection uses the class BTNode to represent nodes in the tree.

The method get implements the binary search process discussed earlier, except that we now use a loop instead of a recursive method:

```
public Object get (Object item){
    if (!(item instanceof Comparable))
        throw new IllegalArgumentException
            ("Trying to get a non-comparable item from collection");

    BTNode currentNode;
    int comparison;

    currentNode = root;
    while (currentNode != null){
        comparison =
        ((Comparable)(currentNode.value)).compareTo ((Comparable)item);
        if (comparison == 0)
            return currentNode.value;
        else if (comparison > 0)
            currentNode = currentNode.left;
        else
            currentNode = currentNode.right;
    }
    return null;
}
```

The method add always places a new item in a leaf node of the tree. For a nonempty tree, this method probes down the tree from the root until it finds a node at the bottom whose left or right pointer is empty and is the logical place for the new node. add maintains two pointers, currentNode and parent, for this search. The parent pointer trails the currentNode so that, when the search ends, parent points at the node whose left or right pointer is the target of the assignment. Figure 12.6 shows the state of these pointers immediately before the insertion of a new item into a tree.

Figure 12.6   **Inserting an item into a binary search tree**

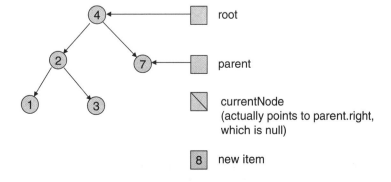

Here is the code for the method `add`:

```
public boolean add (Object item){
   if (!(item instanceof Comparable))
      throw new IllegalArgumentException
            ("Cannot add a non-comparable item");

   BTNode currentNode, parent;
   int comparison = 0;
   modCount++;

   if (size == 0){
      root = new BTNode (item);
      size++;
      return true;
   }

   parent = null;
   currentNode = root;
   while (currentNode != null){
      comparison =
      ((Comparable)(currentNode.value)).compareTo ((Comparable)item);
      parent = currentNode;
      if (comparison > 0)
         currentNode = currentNode.left;
      else
         currentNode = currentNode.right;
   }

   if (comparison > 0)
      parent.left = new BTNode (item);
   else
      parent.right = new BTNode (item);

   size++;
   return true;
}
```

Because the insertion process uses a binary search to locate the insertion point, the process is potentially O(log$n$).

The `remove(Object obj)` method also uses a binary search to locate the target item, so removals are also potentially O(log$n$). A bit of extra work is usually involved in adjusting the tree after a removal, but this work is also no more complex than O(log$n$). The development of the `remove` method is left as an exercise.

The index-based method `get(int i)` returns the item at a given position in the binary search tree. The method must locate in the tree the item that would be at the ith position in a sorted array of the same items. `get` calls a helper method, which implements a simple recursive algorithm. The helper method requires a node parameter and the following two parameters:

■ A counter, which is decremented between the two recursive calls and indicates that the target node has been reached when it becomes 0

■ A basket, which eventually contains the item when it is found

Because Java does not support reference parameters, we must pass instances of two helper classes, Counter and Basket, to the recursive get method. These objects are containers for an int and an Object, respectively. Here is the code for the two methods:

```
public Object get (int i){
    if (i < 0 || i >= size)
        throw new IllegalArgumentException
            ("Index with value " + i + " out of range 0 to " +
            (size - 1));

    Counter count = new Counter (i + 1);
    Basket basket = new Basket();
    get (root, count,  basket);
    return basket.value;
}

private void get (BTNode currentNode, Counter count, Basket basket){
    if (currentNode == null)
        return;

    get (currentNode.left, count, basket);
    count.value--;
    if (count.value == 0)
        basket.value = currentNode.value;
    else if (count.value > 0)
        get (currentNode.right, count, basket);
    return;
}
```

12.2.5 Analysis of Binary Search Trees

As we have seen, the complexity of the get, add, and remove operations is O($\log n$) when the tree is balanced. As the tree becomes less balanced, the constant of proportionality in these operations increases until, in the worst case of a totally "linear" tree, they become O(n).

Surprisingly, binary search trees tend to be close to balanced if items are inserted or removed in random order. Thus, we need not worry about their performance in those cases. However, to guarantee optimal performance in all cases, we must rely on methods of keeping a tree balanced during insertions and removals. We consider a few of these methods in the next section.

Exercises 12.2

1. Using the current implementation of iterator in BinarySearchTree, what is the impact on the iterator if the structure of the underlying Binary SearchTree changes? How does this differ from the relationship that exists between other iterators and their underlying backing store? What are the advantages and disadvantages of the difference?

2. Support the iterator method in BinarySearchTree by adding an Inner Iter class. Calls to next on this iterator should provide an inorder traversal;

however, this must be done without the support of recursion. Instead `Inner Iter` keeps a stack that allows backing up the tree structure when necessary. See the `BinaryTreePT` class for sample code.

3. Redo `BinarySearchTree` with parent pointers. This makes several methods more efficient and/or easier to code.

4. Explain why a `SortedCollection` that only uses "unique adds" is conceptually similar to a `SortedSet`.

5. Rewrite method `clone` in `LinkedBSTSortedCollection` so that it is O(n) rather than O($n$log$n$).

12.3   "Better" Binary Search Trees (optional)

The degenerate O(n) performance of a binary tree search tree occurs when the tree becomes unbalanced. There are various ingenious techniques for coping with the problem, all of which have the common goal of trying to keep the tree balanced, thus assuring O(log$n$) behavior for searches, insertions, and deletions. The price of these techniques is greater programming complexity. The algorithms for insertion and deletion become more difficult to write, but the reward of better performance justifies the extra effort.

One way of keeping a binary search tree balanced is to run a rebalancing algorithm on the tree after every insertion or deletion. However, because the best rebalancing algorithm is linear, this strategy degrades insertions and deletions to linear operations.

The methods for squeezing optimal performance out of search trees are usually encapsulated in one of the following data structures:

splay trees   2-3-4 trees

AVL trees   red-black trees

2-3 trees   B-trees

Here we discuss 2-3 and AVL trees. We won't write code for either of these but use diagrams to illustrate the basic operations.

12.3.1   2-3 Trees

A 2-3 tree is a special kind of tree in which each node contains either one or two comparable items. When there is one item in an interior node, that node can have at most two children. When there are two items in an interior node, that node can have up to three children. These children are called the left, the middle, and the right. The right child must be absent when the parent node contains just one item.

If there is just one item in a node, then a 2-3 tree is organized like a binary search tree in that a left child must be less than its parent and a middle child must be greater than its parent. However, when a node contains two items, the following are true:

■   The left child must be less than the smaller item in the parent.

■ The middle child must be in between the two items in the parent.

■ The right child must be greater than the larger item in the parent.

Figure 12.7 shows a 2-3 tree with several nodes of this kind.

Figure 12.7   **A 2-3 tree**

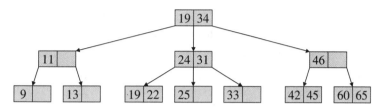

One point you will note from the examples in the figure is that the leaf nodes of a 2-3 tree are all at the same level. This is true of any 2-3 tree. This also guarantees that the height of a 2-3 tree is always less than or equal to the height of the equivalent fully balanced binary search tree. This in turn guarantees O(log$n$) behavior for searches, insertions, and deletions.

The recursive search of a 2-3 tree proceeds as follows:

```
If the root is empty
   Return false
Else if the target equals the first item in the root
   Return true
Else if there is a second item in the root and the target equals it
   Return true
Else if the target is less than the first item in the root
   Return the result of searching the left subtree
Else if there is no second item in the root
      or the target is less than that item
   Return the result of searching the middle subtree
Else
   Return the result of searching the right subtree
```

Insertions into a 2-3 tree place new items in leaf nodes. There are three cases:

1. The tree is empty. Make a new node and insert the item as the first item.

2. A leaf node is found that would contain the item if it were in the tree, and this node contains only one item. Insert the item into this node. For example, suppose the value 15 were being inserted into the tree of Figure 12.7. Then it would go into the node that already contains 13, in the right slot. If the value were 11 instead, 13 would be moved to the right in this node and 11 inserted in the left slot.

3. The item must be inserted into a node that already contains two items. Create new space by splitting the node into two nodes. The old node receives the smallest item, and the new node receives the largest item. We pass the middle item back up to the parent node with a pointer to the new node. If the parent node contains one item, the middle item and the pointer to the node are added to the parent node. If the parent has two items, the process of splitting and passing the middle item up is repeated. A new level is added to the tree if the root node is slit during this process.

The development of the algorithm for insertion and its complexity analysis are left as exercises.

Removal of an item from a 2-3 tree is more or less the inverse of insertion, and it involves combining rather than splitting nodes. Once again, we leave the development of a removal algorithm as an exercise.

12.3.2   AVL Trees

The AVL tree is named for its designers, the Russian mathematicians G.M. Adelson-Velsky and E.M. Landis. An AVL tree is like a binary search tree, except that heights of the left and the right subtrees of any given node differ by at most 1. Thus, an AVL tree is very nearly balanced, and the performance of insertions, deletions, and searches is guaranteed to be O(log$n$).

Figure 12.8 shows several AVL trees. Each node is labeled with the difference between the heights of its left and right subtrees. Note that the absolute value of this difference is at most 1.

Figure 12.8   **Some AVL trees**

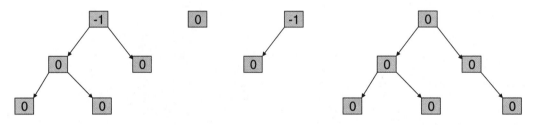

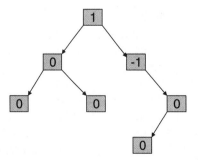

Figure 12.9 shows two binary search trees that cannot be AVL trees. As in the previous figure, each node is labeled with the difference between the heights of its left and right subtrees, so you can spot where the trees violate the AVL property.

Figure 12.9   **Some non-AVL trees**

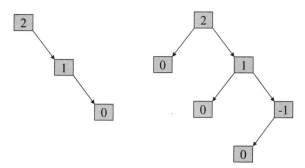

Clearly, searches proceed just as in the case of binary search trees and have a similar, though optimal, performance.

Insertions must preserve the AVL property. Here is the overall strategy for an insertion:

1. Insert as in a binary search tree. This places a node on the frontier of the tree.

2. Walk back on the path from the new node to the root of the tree and compute the difference of the heights of the left subtree and right subtree of each node on this path.

3. If the root is reached without any difference exceeding 1, do nothing.

4. Otherwise, stop at the first node whose difference value exceeds 1 and rebalance the tree by performing a *rotation* operation. Rotations are discussed shortly.

The process of computing the heights of each subtree on the path back to the root is expensive. To mitigate this cost, we can store the difference factor as a datum in each node. Then, we keep a list of nodes on the insertion path for use during the rebalancing process.

The rotation operation starts with the offending node (whose difference factor is greater than 1) and examines the nodes in the two layers on the path down to the inserted node. Based on the shape of these layers, the rotation operation takes two possible forms:

1. A *single rotation*. We use this when the path from the offending node to the inserted node has a linear shape, as shown in Figure 12.10.

Figure 12.10

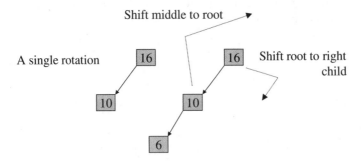

2. A *double rotation*. We use this when the path from the offending node to the inserted node has a dogleg shape, as shown in Figure 12.11.

Figure 12.11

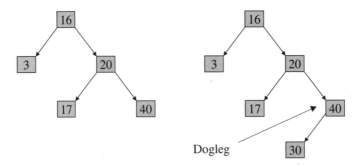

A single rotation is fairly simple. We shift the node with the middle value to the top and shift the node formerly at the top to the right or left, as appropriate. A double rotation consists of two single rotations:

1. We move the highest node to the top and shift the previous node to the left or right. This step always moves into the bend of the dogleg.

2. We then shift the top node to the right and the previous right node to the top.

A rotation operation is constant, so the insertion operation remains O(log*n*). Removals of items from an AVL tree are complicated but remain O(log*n*).

Exercises 12.3

1. In this exercise, you will develop a professional version of the sorted collection ADT. To begin, redo SortedCollection so that it now extends Collection and is tied into the Java collection hierarchy. AbstractSortedCollection should now be a subclass of `AbstractCollection` rather than `Abstract Container`. In other words, it is joined into the main Java collection hierarchy. Methods in `AbstractSortedCollection` should override methods in `AbstractCollection` if doing so improves efficiency and/or clarity. Methods have been added to the interface as needed to retain consistency with `Collec tion` and to reflect the conventions established by `SortedSet` and `List`.

To complete this exercise, you need to understand the concept of subcollection as it is used in the Java collection suite. The critical point here is that the subcollection is not a separate collection but only a restricted view of the backing store.

Here is a suggested interface for a professional version of sorted collection:

SortedCollection Interface

boolean	add(Object item)
boolean	addAll(Collection col)
boolean	addAllUnique(Collection col)
boolean	addUnique(Object item)
void	clear()
Object	clone()
boolean	contains(Object item)
boolean	containsAll(Collection col)
boolean	equals(Object other)
Object	first()
int	indexOf(Object item)
Object	get(Object item)
Object	get(int i)
int	hashCode()
SortedCollection	headCollection(Object to)
boolean	isEmpty()
Iterator	iterator()
Object	last()
Object	remove(int i)
boolean	remove(Object item)
boolean	removeAll(Collection col)
boolean	retainAll(Collection coll)
int	size()
SortedCollection	subCollection(int from, int to)
SortedCollection	subCollection(Object from, Object to)
SortedCollection	tailCollection(Object from)
Object[]	toArray()
Object[]	toArray(Object a[])
String	toString()

2. Develop a prototype 2-3 tree class that illustrates the features of that representation of binary search trees.

3. Develop a prototype AVL tree class that illustrates the features of that representation of binary search trees.

KEY TERMS

2-3 tree	binary search tree	heap
AVL tree	full binary tree	sorted collection

CHAPTER SUMMARY

Certain special types of trees make them useful in particular applications. A heap is a complete binary tree in which each item is greater than or equal to its children. It is possible to insert an item into a heap and access it in logarthmic time. The heap sort uses these two processes, insertion and access, to generate a sorting algorithm that runs in $n\log n$ time.

A heap can also be used to implement a priority queue. Each item is added to a heap, in which the position of the item is determined by its priority.

A binary search tree positions items in such a manner that smaller items are to the left and larger items are to the right of a given item. A given target item can then be inserted and accessed in logarithmic time, provided that the tree is balanced. A balanced tree has a full shape, in which each item except the leaves usually has two successors.

2-3 trees are set up to maintain balancing as items are inserted, thereby guaranteeing logarithmic searches.

REVIEW QUESTIONS

1. Explain the difference between a heap and a plain old binary tree.
2. How does the heap sort work?
3. What is the run-time complexity of the heap sort?
4. Explain the difference between a binary search tree and a plain old binary tree.
5. Under what conditions can the run-time performance of a binary search tree degenerate?

CHAPTER 13

Unordered Collections: Sets, Maps, and Bags

OBJECTIVES   Upon completion of this chapter, you should be able to

- Describe the basic features of unordered collections

- Discuss the differences among sets, maps, and bags

- Explain the basic ideas related to hashing

- Give an account of the collision problem

- Describe several ways of resolving the collision problem

- Discuss the factors involved in the complexity analysis of hashing

The collection ADTs we have covered thus far are all ordered. That is, each item in an ordered collection has a position at which the client can locate it. Another category contains the unordered collections. From the client's perspective, the items in an unordered collection are in no particular positions. Thus, none of the operations on an unordered collection are position-based. Clients can insert, retrieve, or remove objects from unordered collections, but they cannot access the *i*th item, the next item, or the previous item. Some examples of unordered collections are sets, maps, and bags. We begin this chapter with an overview of these collections. We then introduce hashing, a common implementation strategy for unordered collections, and illustrate this strategy by developing prototype classes for map, set, and bag. After a brief discussion of the classes provided for maps and sets in Java's collections framework, we show how to add a bag class to this framework. The two case studies make use of these classes.

13.1   Overview of Sets, Maps, and Bags

13.1.1   Sets

The concept of a set should be familiar from mathematics. A set is a collection of items that from the client's perspective are unique. That is, there are no duplicate items in a set. There are many operations on sets in mathematics. Some of the most typical are

- Test for the empty set.
- Return the number of items in the set.
- Add an item to the set.
- Remove an item from the set.
- Test for set membership (whether or not a given item is in the set).
- Return the **union** of two sets. The union of two sets A and B is a set that contains all of the items in A and all of the items in B.
- Return the **intersection** of two sets. The intersection of two sets A and B is the set of items in A that are also items in B.
- Return the **difference** of two sets. The difference of two sets A and B is the set of items in A that are not also items in B.
- Test a set to determine whether or not another set is its **subset.** The set B is a subset of set A if and only if B is an empty set or all of the items in B are also in A.

Table 13.1 shows the results of some of these operations for example sets.

Table 13.1   **Results of Some Typical Set Operations**

Sets **A** and **B**	`A.union(B)`	`A.intersection(B)`	`A.difference(B)`	`A.subset(B)`
{12 5 17 6} {42 17 6}	{12 5 42 17 6}	{17 6}	{12 5}	false
{21 76 10 3 9} {}	{21 76 10 3 9}	{}	{21 76 10 3 9}	true
{87} {22 87 23}	{22 87 23}	{87}	{}	false
{22 87 23} {87}	{22 87 23}	{87}	{22 23}	true

Aside from their role in mathematics, sets have many applications in data processing. For example, in the field of database management, the answer to a query that contains the conjunction of two keys could be constructed from the intersection of the sets of items containing these keys.

13.1.2   Maps

A map is a collection in which each item, or **value,** is associated with a unique **key.** Users add, remove, and retrieve items from a map by specifying their keys. One occasionally sees a map referred to as a **table, keyed list, dictionary,** or **association list.**

The package `java.util` defines several classes, `Dictionary`, `Hashtable`, and `Map`, which represent maps. Another way to think of a map is as a collection of unique items called *entries* or *associations.* Each entry contains a key and a value (the item).

Table 13.2 shows the data in two maps. The first map is keyed by strings, and the second is keyed by integers. Note the following points about the two example maps:

1. The keys are in no particular order.

2. The keys are unique. That is, the keys for a given map form a set.

3. The values need not be unique. That is, the same value can be associated with more than one key.

Table 13.2 **A Map Keyed by Strings and a Map Keyed by Integers**

Map 1		Map 2	
Key	Value	Key	Value
"occupation"	"teacher"	80	"Mary"
"hair color"	"brown"	39	"Joe"
"height"	72	21	"Sam"
"age"	72	95	"Renee"
"name"	"Bill"	40	"Lily"

There are many operations that one could perform on maps. At a bare minimum, a client should be able to

- Test a map for emptiness.
- Determine a map's size.
- Insert a value at a given key.
- Remove a given key.
- Retrieve a value at a given key.
- Determine whether or not a map contains a key.
- Determine whether or not a map contains a value.
- Iterate through all of the keys.
- Iterate through all of the values.

Maps have a wide range of applications. For example, interpreters and compilers of programming languages make use of symbol tables. Each key in a symbol table corresponds to an identifier in a program. The value associated with a key contains the attributes of the identifier—a name, a data type, and other information. Perhaps the most prevalent application of maps is in database management.

13.1.3 Bags

A bag is an unordered collection that allows the insertion of duplicate items. That is, we can throw anything we want into a bag and eventually find it there. Thus, a bag is a kind of poor person's set: You can put things into it, take things out of it, and find out how many of a thing are in it, but you cannot compute the union, intersection, or difference of two bags.

To get a bag, we subtract from a set the union, intersection, difference, and subset operations and add the proviso that the bag counts duplicate items. For convenience, we also add one operation that returns a count of the occurrences of a given item. Bags serve primarily as utility structures in data processing.

13.1.4 Iterators for Unordered Collections

It is possible to obtain iterators of sets, bags, and maps. A map actually returns two iterators: one of the keys and the other of the values. However, the items in all of these iterators reflect no particular order in the collections, even though one item now follows another.

13.1.5 A Brief Example

Assume that someone wants to display a table of the frequencies of the words in a file. The table should have two columns. The first column is a sorted list of the unique words. The second column is a list containing the corresponding frequencies of the words in the first column. Figure 13.1 shows a sample output for a file that contains the text, "This file contains several words and three words in this file appear twice."

Figure 13.1 **The output of a word frequency program**

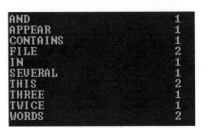

One could implement an algorithm to solve this problem using arrays, vectors, linked lists, or several other collections discussed in this book. But such an algorithm is very complicated. A simpler algorithm uses a bag, a set, and a sorted collection (as discussed in Chapter 12) as follows:

1. Transfer all of the words from the file to the bag.

2. Obtain the unique words by converting the bag to a set.

3. Obtain a sorted list of these words by converting the set to a sorted collection.

4. Print the words in the sorted collection and use these words to look up the associated frequencies in the bag and print these frequencies.

Here is the pseudocode:

```
Create a bag called wordBag

While there are more words in the file
    Read the next word and convert it to uppercase
    Insert the word into wordBag

Convert wordBag to a set called wordSet
Convert wordSet to a sorted collection called uniqueWords

For each word in uniqueWords
    Print the word
    Print the number of occurrences of that word in wordBag
    Print a newline
```

Now assume that we have at our disposal the classes `LinkedBSTSortedCollection`, `HashSet`, and `HashBag` with the operations discussed earlier. Here is a further refinement of our algorithm that is closer to Java code:

```
Bag wordBag = new HashBag();

While there are more words in the file
    String word = read the next word
    wordBag.add(word.toUppercase());

Set wordSet = new HashSet(wordBag.iterator());
SortedCollection uniqueWords = new LinkedBSTSortedCollection(wordSet);

for (int i = 0; i < uniqueWords.size(); ++i){
    String word = (String)uniqueWords.get(i);
    int frequency = wordBag.getCount(word);
    System.out.println(Format.justify('l', word, 20) +
                      Format.justify('r', frequency, 5));
}
```

Most of the actual processing occurs behind the scenes in the conversion operations. As you can see, a wide array of ADTs with conversion operations is a powerful tool for organizing computation.

Exercise 13.1

Use the Java 2 collection `HashSet` and the `lamborne` collections `HashBag` and `LinkedBSTSortedCollection` to implement the word frequency program discussed in this section. (*Tip:* Also use a `StreamTokenizer` to obtain words from a text file; see Case Study 1 for details.)

13.2   Implementation Considerations

Most clients who use sets, maps, and bags want to build higher level, more domain-specific operations with the primitives provided. These operations likely employ many insertions and retrievals. Thus, the paramount consideration from the implementer's perspective is the speed of insertion and retrieval in sets, maps, and bags.

Unordered collections can be implemented using several of the collections already presented. For example, one might use a list to implement a set. However, this is not a wise choice because a list supports only linear searches and insertions.

One consideration is that we want sets, maps, and bags to contain any objects, not just comparable objects. This implies that we cannot use sorted collections, whose items must be comparables, to implement general unordered collections. It seems that this restriction does not bode well for the implementation of more efficient (better than linear) searches and insertions, which, as far as we have seen, require a special ordering of the data. However, we can overcome this restriction and obtain optimal performance by using a new access technique called ***hashing.*** Hashing can potentially achieve O(1) efficiency for insertion and retrieval operations.

13.2.1   Hashing

Hashing is a technique of storing and retrieving data in which each item is associated with a ***hash code.*** This code is based on some property of the item and can be computed in constant time by a function known as a ***hash function.*** The same hash function is run when an item is inserted, retrieved, or removed, so these operations are potentially O(1).

We now give a brief overview of one of many possible hashing strategies to illustrate how hashing works. In this strategy, known as ***chaining,*** the items are stored in an array of linked lists, or ***chains.*** Each item's hash code locates the ***bucket,*** or index of the chain in which the item already resides or is to be inserted. The `get` and `remove` operations each perform the following steps:

1.   Compute the item's hash code, or index in the array.

2.   Search the linked list at that index for the item.

If the item is found, it can be returned (method `get`) or removed (method `remove`). Figure 13.2 shows an array of linked lists with five buckets and eight items. The hash code of each item is the index of its linked list in the array. For example, the items D7, D3, and D1 have the hash code 4.

Figure 13.2   **A hash table with five buckets**

index

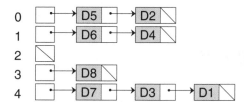

To insert an item into this structure, the `add` method performs the following steps:

1. Compute the item's hash code, or index in the array.
2. If the array cell is empty, then insert the item into this cell.
3. Otherwise, if an item already exists at this position, then a ***collision*** occurs. There are a number of ways to process a collision, some of which we discuss shortly. The simplest one, which is used here, is to view the existing item as the head of a linked list or chain of items at that position. When a collision occurs, the new item is inserted at the head of this list.

Our discussion has left open the question of how to compute an item's hash code. In this implementation, the code of an item should be an index in the array. Java provides a standard `hashcode` method for any object. This method returns the object's hash code (a large integer) in the JVM. Thus, we can compute a valid index in our array by taking the modulus of the absolute value of the item's Java hash code and the size of the array.

13.2.2   Analysis of the Chaining Method of Hashing

Analysis shows that the location of an item using this strategy consists of two parts:

1. Computing the index
2. Searching a linked list when collisions occur

The first part has constant time behavior. The second part has linear behavior. The amount of work is O(n) in the worst case. In this case, all of the items are in one chain, which is a linked list. However, if the lists are evenly distributed throughout the array and the array is fairly large, the second part can be close to constant as well. In the best case, each array cell is occupied by a chain of length 1, so the performance is exactly O(1). As with a binary search tree, random insertion of items tends to result in an even distribution. However, as the number of items increases, the lengths of the chains also increase, resulting in degraded performance.

The trade-offs and optimizations of various hashing strategies are the subject of later courses in computer science. For now, we merely mention the load factor of the array of buckets. We introduced the concept of a load factor in Chapter 5. In the context of hashing, the load factor is the result of dividing the number of entries by the array's capacity. For example, let E be 100 entries and let A be 30 array cells. Then the load factor of the structure, E/A, is 100/30 or 3.33. As the load factor increases, there is a greater chance that some chains are fairly long and add to the complexity of access. A load factor of less than 1 reduces this complexity but at the cost of additional memory for the array. We now consider some strategies to mitigate these problems.

13.2.3   Other Hashing Strategies

The primary factor that causes a hashing strategy to degrade in performance is the frequency of collisions. Thus, any mechanism that reduces the likelihood of collisions improves performance. Suppose we are willing to tolerate collisions until the load factor reaches a maximum value, say, 0.75. Then we might employ one of two common strategies, called ***rehashing*** and ***quadratic hashing,*** to try to locate an empty bucket.

Rehashing

The method of rehashing attempts to find an empty bucket by applying a different hashing function when a collision occurs. This process is repeated until an empty bucket is found or the method runs out of hashing functions to apply. In the latter case, the rehashing method resorts to adding the new item to the front of the bucket's chain. When using this method, one obviously needs to have on hand several hashing functions that are likely to generate different hash values. In addition to the function that uses Java's Hashcode method mentioned earlier, here are two other hashing functions:

1. In cases of a key such as a social security number, add the parts to generate a number and then use the modulus technique mentioned earlier. For example, the social security number 104-31-2000 produces the code $104 + 31 + 2000$, or 2135.

2. Pass the code generated from method 1 as a seed to a random number generator. This method assumes that the random number generated from a given seed is always the same.

Hashing functions 1 and 2 are likely to generate different hash values, but collisions might still occur as the array fills up. In his book *Searching and Sorting,* Volume 3 of *The Art of Computer Programming* (Menlo Park, CA: Addison-Wesley, 1973), Knuth found that the average search complexity for rehashing is

$$- (1 / D) + \log_e(1 - D)$$

for a successful search and

$$1 / (1 - D)$$

for an unsuccessful search, where D = number of active items / array size.

Quadratic Hashing

The quadratic method of hashing uses a single hashing function. This method repeatedly attempts to locate an empty bucket by probing the position $k + r^2$. k is the original hash value that caused the collision, and r is incremented by 1 after each unsuccessful attempt. Of course, this method works effectively only if the maximum load factor is less than 1 and the search for the position wraps around the array. According to Knuth, the average search complexity for the quadratic method is

$$1 - \log_e(1 - D) - (D / 2)$$

for the successful case and

$$1 / (1 - D) - D - \log_e(1 - D)$$

for the unsuccessful case.

13.3   A Prototype Class for Maps

We now use a hashing strategy to implement a simple prototype class for maps. As usual, we provide just the minimum number of operations necessary to develop and illustrate the implementation, and we make no attempt to handle exceptional conditions.

13.3.1   The Interface for the Class `HashMapPT`

We begin with the class HashMapPT, a prototype class for maps. The operations for this class appear in the Table 13.3.

Table 13.3   **The Methods of the Map Prototype**

Method	What It Does
public HashMapPT()	Constructor.
public void clear()	Removes all of the entries from the map.
public boolean containsKey (Object key)	Returns true if the map contains key; otherwise, returns false.
public boolean containsValue (Object value)	Returns true if the map contains at least one instance of value; otherwise, returns false.
public Object get(Object key)	If the map contains key, returns the associated value; otherwise, returns null.
public boolean isEmpty()	Returns true if the map is empty; otherwise, returns false.
public Object put(Object key, Object value)	If the map contains key, replaces the associated value with value and returns the old value; otherwise, associates and inserts key and value.
public Object remove(Object key)	If the map contains key, removes and returns the associated value; otherwise, returns null.
public int size()	Returns the number of items in the map.
public String toString()	Returns a string representation of the items in the map.

13.3.2 Design of `HashMapPT`

Our prototype map class uses the bucket/chaining method described earlier. Thus, the implementation must maintain an array and represent entries in such a manner as to allow chaining. To manage the array, we declare three instance variables: `table` (the array), `size` (the number of entries in the map), and `capacity` (the number of cells in the array). To represent an entry, we define the private inner class `Entry`. The attributes of an entry are similar to those of the node classes of earlier chapters: a key, a value, and a pointer to the next entry in a chain. The value of `capacity` is by default a constant, which we define as 3 to ensure frequent collisions. Other settings for the capacity of the array are possible and are left as exercises.

Because the same technique is used to locate the position of an entry for insertions, retrievals, and removals, we implement it in one method, `containsKey`. From the client's perspective, this method searches for a given key and returns `true` or `false`. From the implementer's perspective, this method also sets the values of some instance variables to information that can be used during insertions, retrievals, and removals. Table 13.4 gives the variables and their roles in the implementation:

Table 13.4   **The Variables Used for Accessing Entries in the Class `HashMapPT`**

Temporary Instance Variable	*Purpose*
`Entry foundEntry`	Contains the entry just located or is undefined otherwise.
`Entry priorEntry`	Contains the entry prior to the one just located or is undefined otherwise.
`int index`	Contains the index of the chain in which the entry was just located or is undefined otherwise.

We now examine how `containsKey` locates an entry's position and sets these variables. Here is the pseudocode for this process:

```
containsKey(key)
Set index to the hash code of the key (using the method described earlier)
Set priorEntry to null
Set foundEntry to table[index]
while (foundEntry != null)
   if (foundEntry.key equals key)
      return true
   else
      Set priorEntry to foundEntry
      Set foundEntry to foundEntry.next
return false;
```

As you can see, the algorithm uses `index`, `foundEntry`, and `priorEntry` during the search. If the algorithm hashes to an empty array cell, then no entry was found, but `index` contains the bucket for a subsequent insertion of its first entry. If the algorithm hashes to a nonempty array cell, then the algorithm loops down the chain of entries until it finds a matching entry or runs off the chain. In either case, the algorithm leaves `foundEntry` and `priorEntry` set to the appropriate values for a subsequent retrieval, insertion, or removal of the entry.

The method `get` calls `containsKey` and returns the value contained in `foundEntry` if the key was found or returns `null` otherwise:

```
get(key)
If containsKey(key)
    return foundEntry.value
Else
    return null
```

The method `put` calls `containsKey` to determine whether or not an entry exists at the target key's position. If the entry is found, `put` replaces its value with the new value and returns the old value. Otherwise, `put`

1. Creates a new entry whose next pointer is the entry at the head of the chain.

2. Sets the head of the chain to the new entry.

3. Increments the size.

4. Returns `null`.

Here is the pseudocode for `put`:

```
put(key, value)
if (!containsKey (key))
    Entry newEntry = new Entry (key, value, table[index])
    table[index] = newEntry
    size++
    return null
else
    Object returnValue = foundEntry.value
    foundEntry.value = value
    return returnValue
```

The strategy of the method `remove` is similar, although `remove` uses the variable `priorEntry` when the entry to be removed comes after the head of the chain. Here is a complete listing of the class `HashMapPT`:

```
1  // HashMapPT
2
3  public class HashMapPT {
4
5      private static final int DEFAULT_CAPACITY = 3;
6                                    // Purposely set to a small value in order
7                                    // to ensure collisions
8
9      // Temporary variables
10     private Entry foundEntry;   // entry just located
```

Continued

Continued

```
11                                  // undefined if not found
12    private Entry priorEntry;    // entry prior to one just located
13                                  // undefined if not found
14    private int    index;        // index of chain in which entry located
15                                  // undefined if not found
16
17    // Instance variables
18    private int    capacity;     // size of table[]
19    private Entry table[];       // the table of collision lists
20    private int    size;         // number of entries in the map
21
22    public HashMapPT(){
23        capacity = DEFAULT_CAPACITY;
24        clear();
25    }
26
27    public void clear(){
28        size = 0;
29        table = new Entry[capacity];
30    }
31
32    public boolean containsKey (Object key){
33        index = Math.abs(key.hashCode()) % capacity;
34        priorEntry = null;
35        foundEntry = table[index];
36        while (foundEntry != null){
37            if (foundEntry.key.equals (key))
38                return true;
39            else{
40                priorEntry = foundEntry;
41                foundEntry = foundEntry.next;
42            }
43        }
44        return false;
45    }
46
47    public boolean containsValue (Object value){
48        for (int i = 0; i < table.length; i++){
49            for (Entry entry = table[i]; entry != null; entry = entry.next)
50                if (entry.value.equals (value))
51                    return true;
52        }
53        return false;
54    }
55
56    public Object get(Object key){
57        if (containsKey (key))
58            return foundEntry.value;
59        else
60            return null;
61    }
62
63    public boolean isEmpty(){
64      return size == 0;
65    }
66
```

Continued

Continued

```
67    public Object put(Object key, Object value){
68       if (!containsKey (key)){
69          Entry newEntry = new Entry (key, value, table[index]);
70          table[index] = newEntry;
71          size++;
72          return null;
73       }else{
74          Object returnValue = foundEntry.value;
75          foundEntry.value = value;
76          return returnValue;
77       }
78    }
79
80    public Object remove(Object key){
81       if (!containsKey (key))
82          return null;
83       else{
84          if (priorEntry == null)
85             table[index] = foundEntry.next;
86          else
87             priorEntry.next = foundEntry.next;
88          size--;
89          return foundEntry.value;
90       }
91    }
92
93    public int size(){
94       return size;
95    }
96
97    public String toString(){
98       String rowStr;
99       String str = "HashMapPT: capacity = " +  capacity
100                 + " load factor = " + ((double)size() / capacity);
101       for (int i = 0; i < table.length; i++){
102          rowStr = "";
103          for (Entry entry = table[i]; entry != null; entry = entry.next)
104             rowStr += entry + " ";
105          if (rowStr != "")
106             str += "\nRow " + i + ": " + rowStr;
107       }
108       return str;
109    }
110
111    private class Entry {
112
113       private Object key;       //Key for this entry
114       private Object value;     //Value for this entry
115       private Entry  next;      //Reference to next entry
116
117       private Entry(){
118          key = null;
119          value = null;
120          next = null;
121       }
```

Continued

```
122
123        private Entry(Object key, Object value, Entry next){
124            this.key = key;
125            this.value = value;
126            this.next =next;
127        }
128
129        public String toString(){
130            return "(" + key + ", " + value + ")";
131        }
132    }
133 }
```

Note that the method `toString` returns not only the string representations of each key/value pair but also the current capacity and load factor of the map. This information allows the client to examine the complexity of the map at run time.

Exercises 13.3

1. Develop a tester program that allows the client to examine how the load factor changes when the number of entries in the map increases. The keys should be randomly generated numbers. The interface should allow the client to enter the number of keys and should display the map.

2. Implement a constructor that allows the client to specify the capacity of the array. Modify the tester program of Exercise 1 so that the client can enter the capacity as an input value.

3. Implement the quadratic rehashing method and test it with the tester program.

4. Update the tester program to allow the client to specify the maximum load factor, so as to test the rehashing method of Exercise 3.

5. The `add` method can be modified to take advantage of the map's knowledge of the current load factor. Whenever a new item pushes the map over the maximum load factor, `add` regenerates the map with a capacity equal to 2 * capacity + 1. Make this change to `add` and test it with the tester program.

13.4   A Prototype Class for Sets

The prototype class for sets is similar to the prototype class for maps. We provide a brief discussion of the interface, design, and implementation.

13.4.1   The Interface for the Class `HashSetPT`

The clients of a set deal with items and no keys. Thus, the interface for the prototype class `HashSetPT` is somewhat simpler than the interface for the class `HashMapPT`. In particular,

1. A set has no `get` method for retrievals.

2. A set does not distinguish `containsKey` and `containsValue` but instead provides the single method `contains`.

3. A single object, an item, is the parameter in all cases.

Table 13.5 lists the methods in the interface for the class `HashSetPT`.

Table 13.5   **The Methods of the Set Prototype**

Method	What It Does
`public HashMapPT()`	Constructor.
`public boolean add(Object item)`	If the set contains `item`, returns `false`; otherwise, adds `item` to the set and returns `true`.
`public void clear()`	Removes all the entries from the set.
`public boolean contains (Object item)`	Returns `true` if the set contains `item`; otherwise, returns `false`.
`public boolean isEmpty()`	Returns `true` if the set is empty; otherwise, returns `false`.
`public boolean remove(Object item)`	If the set contains `item`, removes and returns `true`; otherwise, returns `false`.
`public int size()`	Returns the number of items in the set.
`public String toString()`	Returns a string representation of the items in the set.

13.4.2   Design and Implementation

The design of the class `HashSetPT` is also quite similar to the design of the class `HashMapPT`. Because we use the same hashing strategy, the instance variables are the same. However, each object of class `Entry` now consists of just an item and a pointer to the next entry in the chain.

The design of the methods for `HashSetPT` is also virtually the same as the corresponding methods in `HashMapPT`. Here are the differences:

1. The method `contains` now searches for an item in an entry instead of a key.

2. The method `add` inserts an item only if it is not already present in the set.

3. The methods `add` and `remove` return a Boolean value to indicate the success or failure of an addition or removal.

Here is a partial listing of the class `HashSetPT`, omitting the code that is the same for `HashMapPT`:

```
1 // HashSetPT
2
3 public class HashSetPT {
4
5     // Same data as in HashMapPT
6
```

Continued

Continued

```
 7    public HashSetPT(){
 8        capacity = DEFAULT_CAPACITY;
 9        clear();
10    }
11
12    public boolean add(Object item){
13        if (!contains (item)){
14            Entry newEntry = new Entry (item, table[index]);
15            table[index] = newEntry;
16            size++;
17            return true;
18        }else
19            return false;
20    }
21
22    public boolean contains (Object item){
23        index = Math.abs(item.hashCode()) % capacity;
24        priorEntry = null;
25        foundEntry = table[index];
26        while (foundEntry != null){
27            if (foundEntry.item.equals (item))
28                return true;
29            else{
30                priorEntry = foundEntry;
31                foundEntry = foundEntry.next;
32            }
33        }
34        return false;
35    }
36
37    public boolean remove(Object item){
38        if (!contains (item))
39            return false;
40        else{
41            if (priorEntry == null)
42                table[index] = foundEntry.next;
43            else
44                priorEntry.next = foundEntry.next;
45            size--;
46            return true;
47        }
48    }
49
50    public String toString(){
51        String rowStr;
52        String str = "HashSetPT: capacity = " +  capacity
53                    + " load factor = " + ((double)size() / capacity);
54        for (int i = 0; i < table.length; i++){
55            rowStr = "";
56            for (Entry entry = table[i]; entry != null; entry = entry.next)
57                rowStr += entry + " ";
58            if (rowStr != "")
59                str += "\nRow " + i + ": " + rowStr;
60        }
61        return str;
62    }
63
```

Continued

```
64    private class Entry {
65
66        private Object item;        //Item for this entry
67        private Entry  next;        //Reference to next entry
68
69        private Entry(){
70            item = null;
71            next = null;
72        }
73
74        private Entry(Object item, Entry next){
75            this.item = item;
76            this.next =next;
77        }
78
79        public String toString(){
80            return "" + item;
81        }
82    }
83 }
```

Exercises 13.4

1. Write a short tester program that allows the user to enter data into a set. The input should be a string. The program should extract each character from the string, add it to the set, and update the display with the contents of the set.

2. Add the methods `union`, `intersection`, and `difference` to the class `HashSetPT`. Each method should expect a set as a parameter and return a new set that contains the results of performing the operation with the receiver set and the parameter set.

3. Add the method `subset` to the class `HashSetPT`. This method expects a set as a parameter. The method should return `true` if this set is a subset of the receiver set or `false` otherwise.

4. Update the tester program of Exercise 1 to allow the client to test the methods written for Exercises 2 and 3.

5. Analyze the complexity of the methods of Exercises 2 and 3.

6. Explain how it is possible to implement a map with a set. Discuss alternative implementations that make use of the "has-a" and "is-a" relations among classes.

13.5   A Prototype Class for Bags

The prototype class for bags is similar to the prototype class for sets. We provide a brief discussion of the interface, design, and implementation.

13.5.1   The Interface for Class **HashBagPT**

The primary difference between a bag and a set is that a bag can contain multiple instances of an item. Thus, the interface to the prototype class HashBagPT is almost the same as the interface to the class `HashSetPT`, as shown in Table 13.6. Note, however, the following differences:

1. A new method, `getCount`, returns a count of the number of instances of a given item in the bag.

2. The methods `add` and `remove` now return an `int` instead of a `boolean`. This value gives the client an immediate update of the count of instances following an addition or removal.

Table 13.6   **The Methods of the Bag Prototype**

Method	What It Does
`public HashMapPT()`	Constructor.
`public int add(Object item)`	Adds `item` to the bag and returns a count of the instances of `item`. After the first instance of `item` is added, just increments that item's count.
`public void clear()`	Removes all the entries from the set.
`public boolean contains (Object item)`	Returns `true` if the set contains `item`; otherwise, returns `false`.
`public int getCount(Object item)`	Returns a count of the number of instances of `item`.
`public boolean isEmpty()`	Returns `true` if the set is empty; otherwise, returns `false`.
`public int remove(Object item)`	If the set does not contain `item`, returns −1; otherwise, returns the count of the instances of `item`. Until the last instance of `item` is removed, just decrements the item's count.
`public int size()`	Returns the number of items in the set.
`public String toString()`	Returns a string representation of the items in the set.

13.5.2   Design and Implementation

The design of the class `HashBagPT` involves some simple modifications of the class `HashSetPT`. First, we add a field in the `Entry` class to count the instances of a given entry. Second, the method `add` merely increments this count when the target entry is found. Third, the method `remove` decrements this count when more than one instance of the target entry is found. Here is the code for methods `add`, `getCount`, and `remove` in class `HashBagPT`:

```
public int add(Object item){
    size++;
    if (!contains (item)){
        Entry newEntry = new Entry (item, table[index]);
```

Continued

Continued

```
      table[index] = newEntry;
      return 1;
   }else{
      foundEntry.count++ ;
      return foundEntry.count;
   }
}

public int getCount(Object item){
   if (contains (item))
      return foundEntry.count;
   else
      return 0;
}

public int remove(Object item){
   if (!contains (item))
      return -1;
   else if (foundEntry.count == 1){
      if (priorEntry == null)
         table[index] = foundEntry.next;
      else
         priorEntry.next = foundEntry.next;
   }
   size--;
   foundEntry.count--;
   return foundEntry.count;
}
```

Exercises 13.5

1. Add a method `keys` to the class `HashMapPT`. This method should build and re-turn an object of class `HashSetPT` that contains the keys in the map.

2. Add a method `values` to the class `HashMapPT`. This method should build and return an object of class `HashBagPT` that contains the values in the map.

3. The implementations of the three prototype classes are done from scratch, although they all could be based on a similar class. For example, one might base a set implementation on a map or the other way around. Discuss the advantages and disadvantages of basing the implementations in either direction.

13.6   The Map and Set Classes in the Java Collections Framework

As mentioned in Chapter 6, the Java collections framework provides several classes for maps and sets. They implement four interfaces:

Interface	Type of Collection
Map	Like our prototype map but with some extra methods.
Set	Like our prototype set but with some extra methods.

SortedMap   Like a map but with an iterator that allows clients to view the items in sorted order.

SortedSet   Like a set but with an iterator that allows clients to view the items in sorted order.

The collections framework omits a bag class. A possible implementation of this is developed in the next section. We now give a brief overview of each type of the map and set classes and discuss some implementation issues.

13.6.1   Maps

Table 13.7, which is taken from Sun's JDK1.4 documentation, lists the methods in Java's Map interface. Note that this interface has all of the methods we developed in the prototype as well as some of those suggested in the exercises. One method not in the prototype is entrySet. This method returns a Set of the *entries* in the map. As was discussed in the context of our prototype, an entry associates a key and a value. Java defines an interface for map entries, as shown in Table 13.8.

Table 13.7   **The Methods of Java's Map Interface**

void	**clear()** Removes all mappings from this map (optional operation). An implementation that does not support the operation should throw an exception.
boolean	**containsKey(Object key)** Returns true if this map contains a mapping for the specified key. Throws an exception if key is an inappropriate type for this map (which includes the situation in which the key is null and null is not allowed).
boolean	**containsValue(Object value)** Returns true if this map maps one or more keys to the specified value. The value could be null.
Set	**entrySet()** Returns a set view of the mappings in this map. Because the set is backed by the map, changes in one affect the other.
boolean	**equals(Object other)** Compares the specified object with this map for equality. Two maps are considered equal if they contain equal (key/value) pairs. The physical order of the pairs does not matter.
Object	**get(Object key)** Returns the value to which this map maps the specified key. Throws an exception if the key is an inappropriate type for this map (which includes the situation in which the key is null and null is not allowed).
int	**hashCode()** Returns the hash code value for this map.

Table 13.7   **The Methods of Java's Map Interface** *(Continued)*

`boolean`	`isEmpty()` Returns `true` if this map contains no key/value mappings.
`Set`	`keySet()` Returns a set view of the keys in this map. Because the set is backed by the map, changes in one affect the other.
`Object`	`put(Object key, Object value)` Associates the specified value with the specified key in this map (optional operation). Returns the previous value associated with this key or `null` if the key was not previously present. Throws an exception if the operation is not supported by the implementation or if the type of the key or map is inappropriate for the implementation (which includes the situation in which the key or value is `null` and `null` is not allowed).
`void`	`putAll(Map t)` Copies all of the mappings from the specified map to this map (optional operation). Throws an exception if the operation is not supported by the implementation or if the type of the key or map is inappropriate for the implementation (which includes the situation in which the key or value is `null` and `null` is not allowed).
`Object`	`remove(Object key)` Removes the mapping for this key from this map if present (optional operation). Throws an exception if the operation is not supported by the implementation.
`int`	`size()` Returns the number of key/value mappings in this map.
`Collection`	`values()` Returns a collection view of the values in this map. The collection is backed by the map, so changes in one affect the other.

Table 13.8   **The Methods of Java's Map.Entry Interface**

Map.Entry Interface		Inner Class in HashMap
	`constructor()`	O(1)
`boolean`	`equals(Object obj)`	O(1)
`Object`	`getKey()`	O(1)
`Object`	`getValue()`	O(1)
`int`	`hashCode()`	O(1)
`Object`	`setValue(Object value)`	O(1)
`String`	`toString()`	O(1)

Because Map is not a proper extension of the Java Collection interface, some methods normally provided for collections, such as addAll, containsAll, retainAll, removeAll, and toArray, are omitted.

The implementation of the map classes makes widespread use of the method entrySet. As Table 13.9 shows, the complexity of this method is O(1), whereas the complexity of the methods that use it to traverse a map is at least O(*n*). The implementation classes for ordinary maps are AbstractMap and HashMap, whose methods are shown in the table.

Table 13.9   **Java's HashMap Implementation**

Map Implementation		Abstract Map	Hash Map
	constructor()	O(1)	
	constructor(int initialCapacity, float loadFactor		O(1)
	constructor(int initialCapacity,		O(1)
	constructor(Map t)		O(*n*)
void	clear()	uses entry set clear	O(*n*)
Object	clone()		O(*n*)
boolean	containsKey(Object key)	traverses entry set iterator	O(1)
boolean	containsValue(Object value)	traverses entry set iterator	O(*n*)
Set	entrySet()	abstract	O(1)
boolean	equals(Object other)	traverses entry set iterator	
Object	get(Object key)	traverses entry set iterator	O(1)
int	hashCode()	traverses entry set iterator	
boolean	isEmpty()	uses size method	O(1)
Set	keySet()	based on iterator on entry set	O(1)
Object	put(Object key, Object value)	UOE	O(1)
void	putAll(Map t)	traverses entry set iterator on Map t and uses put method	O(*n*)
Object	remove(Object key)	traverses entry set iterator	O(1)
int	size()	uses entry set size	O(1)
String	toString()	traverses entry set iterator	
Collection	values()	based on iterator on entry set	O(1)

The implementation chains entries that collide. The methods `containsKey`, `get`, `put`, and `remove` are O(1), assuming the chains remain short.

A ***sorted map*** allows clients to visit the items in a map in sorted order. The implementations of a sorted map must guarantee that the methods `keySet`, `entrySet`, and `values` return collections of items in sorted order. The `SortedMap` interface extends the `Map` interface. Table 13.10 lists the methods not already provided by the `Map` interface.

Table 13.10   **Java's `SortedMap` Interface**

SortedMap Interface Extends Map

`Comparator`	`comparator()` Returns the comparator associated with this sorted map or `null` if it uses its keys' natural ordering.
`Object`	`firstKey()` Returns the first (lowest) key currently in this sorted map.
`SortedMap`	`headMap(Object toKey)` Returns a view of the portion of this sorted map whose keys are strictly less than `toKey`.
`Object`	`lastKey()` Returns the last (highest) key currently in this sorted map.
`SortedMap`	`subMap(Object fromKey, Object toKey)` Returns a view of the portion of this sorted map whose keys range from `fromKey`, inclusive, to `toKey`, exclusive.
`SortedMap`	`tailMap(Object fromKey)` Returns a view of the portion of this sorted map whose keys are greater than or equal to `fromKey`.

13.6.2   Sets

The interface for Java sets provides a superset of the methods in our prototype. Because the `Set` interface extends the `Collection` interface, the collection-based methods that are omitted from `Map` appear here. Table 13.11, which is taken from Java's documents, lists the `Set` methods. Note that Java omits the set combiners `union`, `intersection`, and `difference` and the predicate `subset`.

Table 13.11   **Java's `Set` Interface**

`boolean`	`add(Object o)` Adds the specified element to this set if it is not already present (optional operation).

continued

Table 13.11   **Java's Set Interface *(Continued)***

boolean	**addAll(Collection c)** Adds all of the elements in the specified collection to this set if they're not already present (optional operation).
void	**clear()** Removes all of the elements from this set (optional operation).
boolean	**contains(Object o)** Returns true if this set contains the specified element.
boolean	**containsAll(Collection c)** Returns true if this set contains all of the elements of the specified collection.
boolean	**equals(Object o)** Compares the specified object with this set for equality.
int	**hashCode()** Returns the hash code value for this set.
boolean	**isEmpty()** Returns true if this set contains no elements.
Iterator	**iterator()** Returns an iterator over the elements in this set.
boolean	**remove(Object o)** Removes the specified element from this set if it is present (optional operation).
boolean	**removeAll(Collection c)** Removes from this set all of its elements that are contained in the specified collection (optional operation).
boolean	**retainAll(Collection c)** Retains only the elements in this set that are contained in the specified collection (optional operation).
int	**size()** Returns the number of elements in this set (its cardinality).
Object[]	**toArray()** Returns an array containing all of the elements in this set.
Object[]	**toArray(Object[] a)** Returns an array containing all of the elements in this set whose run-time type is that of the specified array.

Java's sorted set allows clients to visit the elements of a set in sorted order. The interface for sorted sets is similar to that of sorted maps.

Exercises 13.6

1. Consult Java's documentation and draw a table of the implementation classes for sorted maps that is similar to Table 13.7.

2. Consult Java's documentation and draw a table of Java's `Set` implementation classes.

3. Consult Java's documentation and draw a table for the `SortedSet` implementation classes.

4. According to the Java documentation, the `Set` classes are based on `Map` classes. Discuss this design decision and compare it with a decision to base the implementation the other way—using a set to implement a map.

13.7 Adding a Bag ADT to the Collections Framework (optional pv)

As mentioned earlier, Java omits the bag ADT from its collections framework. We now develop an interface and a set of classes to remedy this omission.

13.7.1 The `Bag` Interface

The interface for the bag ADT is a simple extension of the interface for the prototype developed earlier. To the list of prototype methods we add the methods `clone`, `collectionView`, `equals`, `hashCode`, and `iterator`. These methods make the bag ADT consistent with the other collection ADTs. Table 13.12 descibes the methods in the `Bag` interface. Note the following points:

1. The methods that connect bags to other collections, `collectionView` and `iterator`, return collections without duplicate items, even though there may be duplicates in the bag. Another way to do this might be to return collections with duplicates.

2. If the implementer of the iterator provides a `remove` method, this method should remove all instances of the item at once.

Table 13.12   **The Methods of the `Bag` Interface**

`int`	`add(Object item)` Adds the specified item to this bag and returns the number of instances of the item now in the bag. Throws an exception if the item is `null`.
`void`	`clear()` Removes all items from this bag.
`Object`	`clone()` Returns a shallow copy of this bag.
`Collection`	`collectionView()` Returns a collection view of the items in this bag. *Each item appears only once, even if the bag contains multiple instances of it.*
`boolean`	`contains(Object item)` Returns `true` if the item is in this bag. Throws an exception if the item is `null`.

continued

Table 13.12   **The Methods of the `Bag` Interface** *(Continued)*

`boolean`	`equals(Object other)` Returns `true` if the other object is a bag that equals this bag. To be equal, two bags must contain equal items with equal frequencies. Order does not matter.
`int`	`getCount(Object item)` Returns the number of instances of the specified item in this bag. Throws an exception if the item is `null`.
`int`	`hashCode()` Returns the hash code value for this bag.
`boolean`	`isEmpty()` Returns `true` if the bag is empty.
`Iterator`	`iterator()` Returns an iterator over the items in this bag. *Each item appears only once, even if the bag contains multiple instances of it.* The items appear in no particular order. If the iterator supports removal, it should remove all instances of an item at once.
`int`	`remove(Object item)` Tries to remove one instance of the specified item from this bag. If the item is present, returns the number of instances remaining, else returns –1. Throws an exception if the item is `null`.
`int`	`size()` Returns the number of items in this bag. Each instance of an item counts toward the total.
`String`	`toString()` Returns a string that lists the items in the bag plus the count for each. The list is not sorted.

13.7.2   The `Bag` Implementation

As usual, we place the bag classes beneath the `AbstractContainer` class. `AbstractBag` implements `equals`, to no surprise. The concrete class `HashBag` uses the hashing method developed earlier for the prototype. Table 13.13 lists the methods and their complexity.

Table 13.13   **The Methods of the `Bag` Implementation and Their Complexity**

Bag Implementation	Abstract Container	Abstract Bag	Hash Bag
`constructor()`	O(1)	O(1)	O(1)
`constructor(int capacity)`			O(1)
`constructor(Collection col, int capacity)`			O(n)

Table 13.13   **The Methods of the Bag Implementation and Their Complexity** *(Continued)*

	Bag Implementation	Abstract Container	Abstract Bag	Hash Bag
	`constructor(Iterator iter, int capacity)`			$O(n)$
`int`	`add(Object item)`			$O(1)$
`void`	`clear()`	$O(1)$		$O(1)$
`Object`	`clone()`			$O(n)$
`Collection`	`collectionView()`	based on iterator		
`boolean`	`contains(Object item)`			$O(1)$
`boolean`	`equals(Object other)`		traverses iterator $O(n^2)$	
`int`	`getCount(Object item)`		abstract	$O(1)$
`int`	`hashCode()`	traverses iterator		
`boolean`	`isEmpty()`	uses size method		
`Iterator`	`iterator()`	abstract		$O(1)$
`int`	`remove(Object item)`			$O(1)$
`int`	`size()`	$O(1)$		
`Object[]`	`toArray()`	traverses iterator		
`String`	`toString()`	traverses iterator		

The implementation of the class `HashBag` is quite similar to that of `HashBagPT` discussed earlier. The next listing shows the methods of class `HashBag` that are not in the prototype:

```
1    public HashBag (Collection col, int capacity){
2        super();
3
4        if (col == null)
5            throw new IllegalArgumentException("Collection is null");
6
7        buildBag (col.iterator(), capacity);
8    }
9
10   public HashBag (Iterator iter, int capacity){
11       super();
12
13       if (iter == null)
14           throw new IllegalArgumentException("Iterator is null");
15
16       buildBag (iter, capacity);
```

Continued

Continued

```
17      }
18
19      private void buildBag (Iterator iter, int capacity){
20          this.capacity = capacity;
21          table = new Entry[capacity];
22          while (iter.hasNext())
23              add (iter.next());
24      }
25
26      public Object clone(){
27          Iterator iter = iterator();
28          HashBag clone = new HashBag (capacity);
29          while (iter.hasNext()){
30              Object nextItem = iter.next();
31              for (int i = 1; i <= getCount (nextItem); i++)
32                  clone.add (nextItem);
33          }
34          return clone;
35      }
36
37      public boolean isEmpty(){
38          return size == 0;
39      }
40
41      public Iterator iterator(){
42          return new InnerIter();
43      }
44
45      private class InnerIter implements Iterator{
46
47          private int        expectedModCount = modCount;
48          private int        index;      // Current index into table[]
49          private Entry      nextEntry;  // Next node in the set
50          private int        left;       // Number of items left
51
52          protected InnerIter () {
53              left = size();
54              getFirst();
55          }
56
57          public boolean hasNext() {
58              return left > 0;
59          }
60
61          public Object next() {
62              if (modCount != expectedModCount)
63                  throw new ConcurrentModificationException();
64              if (!hasNext())
65                  throw new NoSuchElementException("There are no more elements");
66
67              Object returnValue = nextEntry.item;
68              left -= nextEntry.count;
69              getNext();
70              return returnValue;
71          }
72
```

Continued

Continued

```
 73          private void getFirst(){
 74              if (left <= 0) return;
 75
 76              for (index = 0; index < table.length; index++){
 77                  nextEntry = table[index];
 78                  if (nextEntry != null)
 79                      return;
 80              }
 81          }
 82
 83          private void getNext(){
 84              if (left <= 0) return;
 85              nextEntry = nextEntry.next;
 86              if (nextEntry != null) return;
 87              for (index = index + 1; index < table.length; index++){
 88                  nextEntry = table[index];
 89                  if (nextEntry != null)
 90                      return;
 91              }
 92          }
 93
 94          public void remove()
 95          {
 96              throw new UnsupportedOperationException("Remove not allowed");
 97          }
 98      }
 99
100 }
```

Exercises 13.7

1. Implement the `remove` method in private class `InnerIter`. What capabilities does this add for users of `HashBag`? Remember to include in your answer the effect on `collectionView`.

2. Add rehashing to the implementation using the strategy discussed in the sections on prototypes. This involves adding load factor considerations starting with the constructors.

3. Rewrite the `clone` method so that it does not use an iterator. Instead, it should build the clone by manipulating the underlying array and entry objects directly. Compare the computational complexity of the new version with the original. Under what circumstances is the effort of doing the new version justified?

4. Add the following two methods:

Method	What It Does
`int add (Object item, int count)`	Adds count instances of item to the bag.
`int remove (Object item, int count)`	Removes count instances of item from the bag.

Are these methods worthwhile improvements? Explain.

5. Suppose that `oldBag` is a `HashBag`. What is the difference between each of the following statements?

```
HashBag newBag = oldBag.clone();
HashBag newBag = new HashBag (oldBag.collectionView());
HashBag newBag = new HashBag (oldBag.iterator());
```

13.8 Case Study 1: A File Concordance System

A *concordance* is a list of words from a text file, wherein each word is followed by the lines in which the word occurs. Variations on the information in a concordance include the words that several files share, the number of words unique to one among several files, and the frequency of each word in a file.

Suppose the files 1.dat and 2.dat contain the following words:

1.dat   **2.dat**

aaa aaa aaa xxx yyy zzz   aaa bbb bbb bbb xxx yyy zzz

These files have four words in common. 1.dat has no words unique to it, whereas 2.dat has one word (bbb) unique to it. In addition, each file has several instances of some words.

13.8.1 Request

Write a program that implements a file concordance system.

13.8.2 Analysis

The interface is shown in Figure 13.3. Note that the files being analyzed are 1.dat and 2.dat from our earlier discussion. When the user selects Add, the program pops up a file dialog. If the user opens a file, the name of that file is added to the end of the list. The user can remove a file from the list by selecting the file and selecting Remove. The user can obtain statistics on a file by selecting the file and selecting Statistics or by double-clicking an item in the list. The program then displays

Figure 13.3 **The user interface for the concordance program**

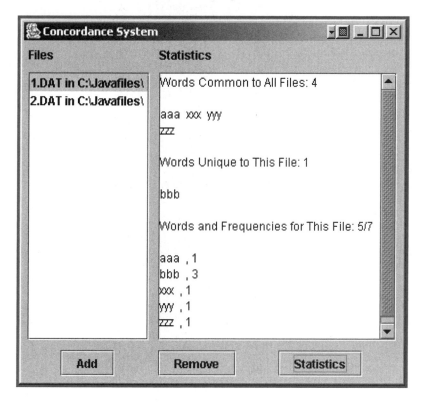

- the words common to all files in the list
- the words unique to the selected file
- a table of words and their frequencies in the selected file

The responsibilities are divided between two classes: `ConcordanceInterface` and `ConcordanceModel`.

13.8.3   Design and Implementation

The design of class `ConcordanceInterface` is straightforward. The only new wrinkle is the use of a file dialog to obtain a file from the user. Java's `FileDia log` class makes this task easy. Here is a listing of the implementation:

```
1 import java.awt.*;
2 import javax.swing.*;
3 import java.awt.event.*;
4 import ioutil.*;
5
```

Continued

Continued

```
 6  public class ConcordanceInterface extends JFrame{
 7
 8     ///////////////////////////////////////////////////// main
 9
10     public static void main (String[] args){
11        JFrame theFrame = new ConcordanceInterface();
12        theFrame.setSize (400, 400);
13        theFrame.setVisible (true);
14     }
15
16     ///////////////////////////////////////////////////// Model
17
18     private ConcordanceModel model  = new ConcordanceModel();
19
20     ///////////////////////////////////////////////////// View
21
22     // Create controls
23     private DefaultListModel   lmFiles  = new DefaultListModel();
24     private JLabel             lbFiles  = new JLabel     ("Files");
25     private JList              ltFiles  = new JList      (lmFiles);
26     private JLabel             lbStats  = new JLabel     ("Statistics");
27     private JTextArea          taStats  = new JTextArea ("");
28     private JButton            btAdd    = new JButton    ("Add");
29     private JButton            btRemove = new JButton    ("Remove");
30     private JButton            btStats  = new JButton    ("Statistics");
31
32     public ConcordanceInterface(){
33
34        // Set title
35        setTitle ("Concordance System");
36
37        // Create container and layout
38        Container contentPane = getContentPane();
39        EasyGridLayout layout = new EasyGridLayout();
40        contentPane.setLayout (layout);
41
42        // Set constraints
43        JScrollPane spFiles = new JScrollPane(ltFiles);
44        JScrollPane spStats = new JScrollPane(taStats);
45
46        layout.setConstraints(lbFiles  , 1,1,1,1);
47        layout.setConstraints(spFiles  , 2,1,1,1);
48        layout.setConstraints(lbStats  , 1,2,1,1);
49        layout.setConstraints(spStats  , 2,2,2,1);
50        layout.setConstraints(btAdd    , 3,1,1,1);
51        layout.setConstraints(btRemove , 3,2,1,1);
52        layout.setConstraints(btStats  , 3,3,1,1);
53
54        // Add controls to container
55        contentPane.add(lbFiles);
56        contentPane.add(spFiles);
57        contentPane.add(lbStats);
58        contentPane.add(spStats);
59        contentPane.add(btAdd);
60        contentPane.add(btRemove);
61        contentPane.add(btStats);
```

Continued

Continued

```
62
63        // Specify listeners
64        btAdd.addActionListener(new MyButtonListener());
65        btRemove.addActionListener(new MyButtonListener());
66        btStats.addActionListener(new MyButtonListener());
67        ltFiles.addMouseListener(new ListMouseListener());
68        addWindowListener(new MyWindowAdapter());
69      }
70
71      //////////////////////////////////////////////////////// Controller
72
73      private void messageBox(String str){
74        new MessageBox(this, str, 350, 100);
75      }
76
77      private void addFile(){
78        String searchStr = "";
79        int i;
80        FileDialog fileDialog = new FileDialog (this, "Input file",
81                                        FileDialog.LOAD);
82        fileDialog.setSize(450, 300);
83        fileDialog.setVisible (true);
84        String fileName = fileDialog.getFile();
85        String dirName = fileDialog.getDirectory();
86        searchStr = fileName + " in " + dirName;
87        if (fileName != null && dirName != null){
88          for (i = 0; i < lmFiles.size(); i++){
89            if (searchStr.equals (lmFiles.get(i)))
90              break;
91          }
92          if (i >= lmFiles.size()){
93            lmFiles.add (0, searchStr);
94            model.addFile (dirName, fileName);
95          }else
96            messageBox ("This file name is already present");
97        }
98      }
99
100     private void removeFile(){
101       int index = ltFiles.getSelectedIndex();
102       if (index == -1)
103         messageBox ("You must select a file name first");
104       else{
105         model.removeFile (index);
106         lmFiles.remove (index);
107       }
108     }
109
110     private void computeStatistics(){
111       int index = ltFiles.getSelectedIndex();
112       if (index == -1)
113         messageBox ("You must select a file name first");
114       else{
115         String str = model.computeStatistics(index);
116         taStats.setText (str);
```

Continued

Continued

```
117        }
118    }
119
120    // List mouse listener
121    private class ListMouseListener extends MouseAdapter{
122        public void mouseClicked(MouseEvent e) {
123            if (e.getClickCount() == 2)         .
124                computeStatistics();
125        }
126    }
127
128    // Button action listener
129    private class MyButtonListener implements ActionListener{
130        public void actionPerformed (ActionEvent event){
131            Object buttonObj = event.getSource();
132            if (buttonObj == btAdd)
133                addFile();
134            else if (buttonObj == btRemove)
135                removeFile();
136            else
137                computeStatistics();
138        }
139    }
140
141    // Window listener
142    private class MyWindowAdapter extends WindowAdapter{
143        public void windowClosing (WindowEvent e){
144            System.exit(0);
145        }
146    }
147 }
148
```

The class `ConcordanceModel` stores the words from the files in a list of bags.
The model uses the Java class `StreamTokenizer` to input words from the files.
Here is the code:

```
 1 import java.io.*;
 2 import java.util.*;
 3 import lamborne.*;
 4 import ioutil.Format;
 5
 6 public class ConcordanceModel extends Object{
 7
 8     private static int CAPACITY = 3;
 9
10     private List      wordBags;
11     private Object    commonWords[];
12
13     public ConcordanceModel()
14     {
15         wordBags    = new LinkedList();
16         commonWords = null;
17     }
```

Continued

```
18
19      public void addFile (String dirName, String fileName)
20      {
21          System.out.println ("Adding Directory " + dirName +
22                              " File " + fileName);
23
24        try{
25              // Open the file and establish a tokenizer on it
26              File file = new File (dirName, fileName);
27              FileInputStream stream = new FileInputStream (file);
28              InputStreamReader isReader = new InputStreamReader (stream);
29              BufferedReader bufReader = new BufferedReader (isReader);
30              StreamTokenizer tokenizer = new StreamTokenizer (bufReader);
31
32              // Declare quote and period to be whitespace
33              tokenizer.whitespaceChars ((int)'"', (int)'"');
34              tokenizer.whitespaceChars ((int)'.', (int)'.');
35
36              // Read the words from the file and put each one in a set and
37              // in a bag
38              Bag bag = new HashBag(CAPACITY);
39              Set set = new HashSet();
40              String word = "";
41
42              tokenizer.nextToken();
43              while (tokenizer.ttype != StreamTokenizer.TT_EOF){
44                  if (tokenizer.ttype == StreamTokenizer.TT_WORD){
45                      word = tokenizer.sval;
46                      bag.add (word);
47                      set.add (word);
48                  }
49                  tokenizer.nextToken();
50              }
51
52              // Add the bag to the end of the list of bags
53              wordBags.add (bag);
54
55              // We no longer know which words are common to all files
56              commonWords = null;
57
58
59        }catch(IOException e){
60              System.out.println ("Error in file input:\n" + e);
61        }
62      }
63
64      public void removeFile (int index)
65      {
66          wordBags.remove (index);
67
68          // We no longer know which words are common to all files
69          commonWords = null;
70      }
71
72      public String computeStatistics (int index)
```

Continued

Continued

```
73    {
74         int maxWordWidth;
75         int wordsPerLine = 3;
76         int sortedArrayLength = 0;
77         Set commonSet, tempSet, uniqueSet;
78         Bag tempBag;
79         Object uniqueWords[] = null, theseWords[] = null;
80         int i;
81         String str = "";
82
83         // Determine maxWordWidth
84         // Needed so that we can format user output in a readable format
85         maxWordWidth = 1;
86         tempBag = (Bag)(wordBags.get(index));
87         Iterator iter = tempBag.iterator();
88         while (iter.hasNext()){
89             String word = (String)(iter.next());
90             if (word.length() > maxWordWidth)
91                 maxWordWidth = word.length();
92         }
93         maxWordWidth += 2;
94
95         // Determine the words common to all files
96         if (commonWords == null){
97             tempBag = (Bag)(wordBags.get(0));
98             commonSet = new HashSet (tempBag.collectionView());
99             for (i = 1; i < wordBags.size(); i++){
100                tempBag =  (Bag)(wordBags.get(i));
101                tempSet = new HashSet (tempBag.collectionView());
102                commonSet.retainAll (tempSet);
103            }
104            sortedArrayLength = commonSet.size();
105            if (sortedArrayLength != 0)
106                commonWords = AbstractHeap.sort ((Collection)commonSet);
107            else
108                commonWords = new Object[0];
109        }
110        str += "Words Common to All Files: " + commonWords.length + "\n";
111        for (i = 0; i < commonWords.length; i++){
112            if (i%wordsPerLine == 0) str += "\n";
113            str +=
114              Format.justify ('l', commonWords[i].toString(), maxWordWidth);
115        }
116        str += "\n";
117
118        // Determine the words unique to this file
119        tempBag = (Bag)(wordBags.get(index));
120        uniqueSet = new HashSet (tempBag.collectionView());
121        for (i = 0; i < wordBags.size(); i++){
122            if (i == index) continue;
123            tempBag = (Bag)(wordBags.get(i));
124            tempSet = new HashSet (tempBag.collectionView());
125            uniqueSet.removeAll (tempSet);
126        }
127        sortedArrayLength = uniqueSet.size();
```

Continued

Continued

```
128          if (sortedArrayLength != 0)
129              uniqueWords = AbstractHeap.sort ((Collection)uniqueSet);
130          str += "\nWords Unique to This File: " + sortedArrayLength + "\n";
131          for (i = 0; i < sortedArrayLength; i++){
132              if (i%wordsPerLine == 0) str += "\n";
133              str +=
134                 Format.justify ('l', uniqueWords[i].toString(), maxWordWidth);
135          }
136          str += "\n";
137
138          // Determine the words and frequencies for this file
139          tempBag = (Bag)(wordBags.get(index));
140          tempSet = new HashSet (tempBag.collectionView());
141          str += "\nWords and Frequencies for This File: "
142             + tempSet.size() + "/" + tempBag.size() + "\n\n";
143          sortedArrayLength = tempSet.size();
144          if (sortedArrayLength != 0)
145              theseWords = AbstractHeap.sort (tempBag.collectionView());
146          for (i = 0; i < sortedArrayLength; i++)
147              str +=
148                 Format.justify ('l', theseWords[i].toString(), maxWordWidth)
149                 + ", "
150                 + tempBag.getCount (theseWords[i]) + "\n";
151
152          // Return the string
153          return str;
154      }
155 }
```

Exercise 13.8

In this case study, words are put into bags. When statistics are computed, many sets must be generated from these bags. Answer the following questions:

a. How computationally expensive is this operation?

b. As an alternative, the words could be put into sets and into bags. How computationally expensive would this be?

c. How much computation would be saved when statistics are being computed?

d. What is the cost in terms of additional space required?

e. Under what circumstances would this modification be worthwhile versus not worthwhile?

13.9   Case Study 2: A Credit Approval System

13.9.1   Request

Write a program that implements a credit approval system.

13.9.2 Analysis

The program allows the user to enter new accounts, remove them, list them all, make deposits to accounts, and approve purchases on these accounts. When the program approves a purchase, the amount is deducted from the client's account. The interface consists of one window for creating and managing accounts and two other windows for approving purchases. Figure 13.4 shows the three program windows. The manager has just entered a new account for Ken with a balance of $100. Ken then requests purchase approval for $50, and the request is approved.

Figure 13.4 The user interface for the credit approval program

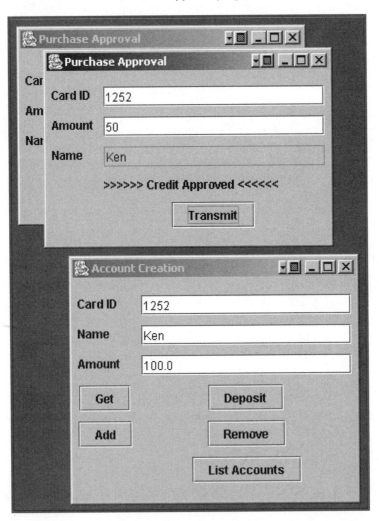

13.9.3　Classes

The program consists of the following classes and their responsibilities:

Class	Responsibility
CreditAccountsApplication	The main method module. Creates the models and the views and opens the views.
AccountCreationView	Handles the window for creating and managing accounts.
CreditApprovalView	Handles the window for approving purchases.
CreditAccountsModel	Represents the database of accounts.
Account	Represents an individual account.

13.9.4　Design and Implementation

The model classes are simple. We use a table to represent the database of accounts. Here is a complete listing of the class CreditAccountsModel:

```
 1 import java.util.*;
 2
 3 public class CreditAccountsModel extends Object{
 4
 5     private Map map;
 6
 7     public CreditAccountsModel()
 8     {
 9         map = new HashMap();
10     }
11
12     public Account getAccount (String accountId)
13     {
14         return (Account)(map.get (accountId));
15     }
16
17     public boolean insertAccount (Account account)
18     {
19         if (map.containsKey (account.getCardId()))
20             return false;
21         else{
22             map.put (account.getCardId(), account);
23             return true;
24         }
25     }
26
27     public void removeAccount (Account account)
28     {
29         map.remove (account.getCardId());
```

Continued

Continued

```
30        }
31
32        public String toString()
33        {
34            Iterator iter = map.values().iterator();
35            String str = "";
36            while (iter.hasNext())
37                str += iter.next() + "\n";
38            return str;
39        }
40 }
```

The view classes each access the model either for information about an account or to modify an account. The approval process is the simplest of the two views. The class `CreditApprovalView` displays one button. The action for this button examines the data in the fields, looks up the account in the model, and responds according to the results. Here is the code for the class `CreditApprovalView`:

```
1 // CreditApprovalView
2 import java.awt.*;
3 import javax.swing.*;
4 import java.awt.event.*;
5 import ioutil.*;
6
7 public class CreditApprovalView extends JFrame{
8
9     /////////////////////////////////////////////////////////// Model
10
11    private CreditAccountsModel model;
12
13    /////////////////////////////////////////////////////////// View
14
15    // Create controls
16    private JLabel       lbCardId         = new JLabel      ("Card ID");
17    private JLabel       lbPurchaseAmount = new JLabel      ("Amount");
18    private JLabel       lbName           = new JLabel      ("Name");
19    private JTextField   tfCardId         = new JTextField  ("");
20    private DoubleField  dfPurchaseAmount = new DoubleField (0);
21    private JTextField   tfName           = new JTextField  ("");
22    private JLabel       lbApproval       = new JLabel      ("");
23    private JButton      btTransmit       = new JButton     ("Transmit");
24
25    public CreditApprovalView(CreditAccountsModel model){
26
27        // Set title and model. Disable name and approval fields
28        setTitle ("Purchase Approval");
29        this.model = model;
30        tfName.setEditable (false);
31
32        // Create container and layout
33        Container contentPane = getContentPane();
34        EasyGridLayout layout = new EasyGridLayout();
35        contentPane.setLayout (layout);
36
```

Continued

Continued

```
37        // Set constraints
38        layout.setConstraints(lbCardId         ,1,1,1,1);
39        layout.setConstraints(lbPurchaseAmount ,2,1,1,1);
40        layout.setConstraints(lbName           ,3,1,1,1);
41        layout.setConstraints(tfCardId         ,1,2,1,1);
42        layout.setConstraints(dfPurchaseAmount ,2,2,1,1);
43        layout.setConstraints(tfName           ,3,2,1,1);
44        layout.setConstraints(lbApproval       ,4,2,1,1);
45        layout.setConstraints(btTransmit       ,5,2,1,1);
46
47        // Add controls to container
48        contentPane.add(lbCardId);
49        contentPane.add(lbPurchaseAmount);
50        contentPane.add(lbName);
51        contentPane.add(tfCardId);
52        contentPane.add(dfPurchaseAmount);
53        contentPane.add(tfName);
54        contentPane.add(btTransmit);
55        contentPane.add(lbApproval);
56
57        // Specify listeners
58        btTransmit.addActionListener(new MyButtonListener());
59        addWindowListener(new MyWindowAdapter());
60    }
61
62    ////////////////////////////////////////////////////// Controller
63
64    // Button action listener
65    private class MyButtonListener implements ActionListener{
66        public void actionPerformed (ActionEvent event){
67            String cardId = tfCardId.getText().trim();
68            double amount = dfPurchaseAmount.getNumber();
69            Account account;
70
71            if (cardId.equals ("") || amount <= 0){
72                new MessageBox(CreditApprovalView.this,
73                               "Enter the card id and a positive amount",
74                               300, 100);
75                return;
76            }
77
78            account = model.getAccount (cardId);
79
80            if (account == null){
81                new MessageBox(CreditApprovalView.this, "Invalid card id",
82                               250, 100);
83                return;
84            }
85
86            tfName.setText (account.getName());
87
88            if (account.withdraw (amount))
89                lbApproval.setText (">>>>>> Credit Approved <<<<<<");
90            else
91                lbApproval.setText (">>>>>> CREDIT DENIED <<<<<<");
```

Continued

Continued

```
 92        }
 93    }
 94
 95    // Window listener
 96    private class MyWindowAdapter extends WindowAdapter{
 97        public void windowClosing (WindowEvent e){
 98            System.exit(0);
 99        }
100    }
101 }
```

The class `AccountCreationView` builds an account or an account's key from the screen data and handles the specific user requests to create, get, or remove the account. Here is the code for class `AccountCreationView`:

```
 1 import java.awt.*;
 2 import javax.swing.*;
 3 import java.awt.event.*;
 4 import ioutil.*;
 5
 6 public class AccountCreationView extends JFrame{
 7
 8     //////////////////////////////////////////////////////// Model
 9
10     private CreditAccountsModel model;
11
12     //////////////////////////////////////////////////////// View
13
14     // Create controls
15     private JLabel       lbCardId   = new JLabel       ("Card ID");
16     private JLabel       lbName     = new JLabel       ("Name");
17     private JLabel       lbAmount   = new JLabel       ("Amount");
18     private JTextField   tfCardId   = new JTextField   ("");
19     private JTextField   flName     = new JTextField   ("");
20     private DoubleField  dfAmount   = new DoubleField  (0);
21     private JButton      btGet      = new JButton      ("Get");
22     private JButton      btAdd      = new JButton      ("Add");
23     private JButton      btDeposit  = new JButton      ("Deposit");
24     private JButton      btRemove   = new JButton      ("Remove");
25     private JButton      btList     = new JButton      ("List Accounts");
26
27     public AccountCreationView(CreditAccountsModel model)
28     {
29         // Set title and model
30         setTitle ("Account Creation");
31         this.model = model;
32
33          // Create container and layout
34         Container contentPane = getContentPane();
35         EasyGridLayout layout = new EasyGridLayout();
36         contentPane.setLayout (layout);
37
38         // Set constraints
39         layout.setConstraints(lbCardId  ,1,1,1,1);
```

Continued

Continued

```
40        layout.setConstraints(lbName    ,2,1,1,1);
41        layout.setConstraints(lbAmount  ,3,1,1,1);
42        layout.setConstraints(tfCardId  ,1,2,1,1);
43        layout.setConstraints(flName    ,2,2,1,1);
44        layout.setConstraints(dfAmount  ,3,2,1,1);
45        layout.setConstraints(btGet      ,4,1,1,1);
46        layout.setConstraints(btAdd      ,5,1,1,1);
47        layout.setConstraints(btDeposit ,4,2,1,1);
48        layout.setConstraints(btRemove  ,5,2,1,1);
49        layout.setConstraints(btList     ,6,2,1,1);
50
51        // Add controls to container
52        contentPane.add(lbCardId);
53        contentPane.add(lbName);
54        contentPane.add(lbAmount);
55        contentPane.add(tfCardId);
56        contentPane.add(flName);
57        contentPane.add(dfAmount);
58        contentPane.add(btGet);
59        contentPane.add(btAdd);
60        contentPane.add(btDeposit);
61        contentPane.add(btRemove);
62        contentPane.add(btList);
63
64        // Specify listeners
65        btGet.addActionListener(new MyButtonListener());
66        btAdd.addActionListener(new MyButtonListener());
67        btDeposit.addActionListener(new MyButtonListener());
68        btRemove.addActionListener(new MyButtonListener());
69        btList.addActionListener(new MyButtonListener());
70        addWindowListener(new MyWindowAdapter());
71    }
72
73    ///////////////////////////////////////////////////// Controller
74
75    private void messageBox(String str){
76        new MessageBox(this, str, 300, 150);
77    }
78
79    private void get(){
80        Account account = getAccount();
81        if (account == null)
82            return;
83        else
84            display (account);
85    }
86
87    private Account getAccount(){
88        String id = tfCardId.getText().trim();
89
90        if (id.equals ("")){
91            messageBox ("Enter the card id first");
92            return null;
93        }
94
```

Continued

Continued

```
 95        Account account = model.getAccount (id);
 96
 97        if (account == null){
 98            messageBox ("There is no such account");
 99            return null;
100        }
101
102        return account;
103    }
104
105    private void display (Account account){
106        if (account == null){
107            tfCardId.setText ("");
108            flName.setText ("");
109            dfAmount.setNumber (0);
110        }else{
111            tfCardId.setText (account.getCardId());
112            flName.setText (account.getName());
113            dfAmount.setNumber (account.getBalance());
114        }
115    }
116
117    private void add (){
118        Account account = buildAccountFromScreenData();
119
120        if (account == null)
121            return;
122
123        if (!model.insertAccount (account)){
124            messageBox ("The account is already present");
125            return;
126        }
127    }
128
129    private Account buildAccountFromScreenData(){
130        String id = tfCardId.getText().trim();
131        String name = flName.getText().trim();
132        double amount = dfAmount.getNumber();
133
134        if (id.equals ("") || name.equals ("")){
135            messageBox ("Card id and name are both required");
136            return null;
137        }
138
139        if (amount < 0){
140            messageBox ("The amount must be nonnegative");
141            return null;
142        }
143
144        return new Account (id, name, amount);
145    }
146
147    private void deposit(){
148        Account account = getAccount();
149
150        if (account == null)
151            return;
152
```

Continued

```
153        double amount = dfAmount.getNumber();
154
155     if (amount <= 0){
156        new MessageBox(AccountCreationView.this,
157                      "The deposit amount must be positive",
158                      300, 400);
159        return;
160     }
161
162     account.deposit (amount);
163     dfAmount.setNumber (account.getBalance());
164  }
165
166  private void remove(){
167     Account account = getAccount();
168
169     if (account == null)
170        return;
171
172     model.removeAccount (account);
173     display (null);
174  }
175
176  private void listAccounts(){
177     messageBox ("Here is a list of all the accounts\n" + model);
178  }
179
180  // Button action listener
181  private class MyButtonListener implements ActionListener{
182     public void actionPerformed (ActionEvent event){
183        Object buttonObj = event.getSource();
184        if      (buttonObj == btGet)
185           get();
186        else if (buttonObj == btAdd)
187           add();
188        else if (buttonObj == btDeposit)
189           deposit();
190        else if (buttonObj == btRemove)
191           remove();
192        else
193           listAccounts();
194     }
195  }
196
197  // Window listener
198  private class MyWindowAdapter extends WindowAdapter{
199     public void windowClosing (WindowEvent e){
200        System.exit(0);
201     }
202  }
203 }
```

Exercise 13.9

In this case study, when a purchaser quits the window, the application also quits, thus closing all the other windows. Modify the program so that only the creator of accounts can quit the application by closing the window.

KEY TERMS

association	concordance	key
association list	dictionary	keyed list
bucket	hash code	load factor
chaining	hash function	quadratic hashing
collision	hashing	rehashing

CHAPTER SUMMARY

Sets, bags, and maps are unordered collections. A set contains unique items. A bag is like a set but allows duplicate items. A map associates a set of keys with values. Sets and bags are used primarily to keep items without a need for ordering them. Maps are used to represent tables of information that is associated with other information.

The operations to insert, remove, and access items in an unordered collection are content-based. One can use an iterator to visit each item in an unordered collection, but the visitation is not necessarily position-based.

Java's `Set` interface extends `Collection`, so all of the high-level `Collection` methods are available to users of sets. Java also provides the interfaces `SortedSet` and `SortedMap`, which extend `Set` and `Map`, respectively, and allow the user to visit the items in a sorted order.

Because access times are critical, unordered collections are commonly implemented using a hashing technique. Hashing involves the use of a constant-time function to determine the position of an item in an array. Thus, a hashing implementation can lead to constant access, insertion, and removal times for unordered collections.

The load factor in a hashing technique is the number of items divided by the array's capacity. When this factor becomes large, collisions can occur. A collision results when two items hash to the same position in the array.

There are many ways to resolve collisions. One can start with a large array, at the cost of wasted memory. One can rehash to a different position, at the cost of extra processing time. Or one can keep the colliding items in buckets, which consist of linked structures, at the cost of a potential increase to linear access times.

REVIEW QUESTIONS

1. How does a bag differ from a set?
2. Describe the structure of a map from the client's perspective.
3. Suppose you want to access all of the items in an unordered collection. How do you go about this?

4. Describe two ways in which you can transfer all of the items in a list to a set.

5. Explain what will happen to the items in Question 4 if some of them are duplicates.

6. Why is hashing such an efficient way of implementing unordered collections?

7. What is a load factor in the context of hashing?

8. What are collisions?

9. How does rehashing resolve collisions?

10. Describe how the bucket/chaining method resolves collisions.

CHAPTER 14

Graphs

OBJECTIVES Upon completion of this chapter, you should be able to

- Use the appropriate vocabulary to describe graphs

- Discuss the differences among common types of graphs such as undirected, directed, and directed acyclic graphs

- List several appropriate applications of graphs

- Explain the differences between the adjacency matrix and adjacency list representations of graphs and state the criteria for choosing between them

- Describe the breadth-first and depth-first traversal algorithms

- Understand the basic features of the shortest path problem and the topological sort problem

This chapter covers one of the most general and useful collections, the graph. We begin by introducing some terms used to talk about graphs. We then consider two common representations of graphs: the adjacency matrix representation and the adjacency list representation. We next discuss some widely used and well-known graph-based algorithms. The algorithms of principal interest deal with minimal spanning trees, topological sorting, and shortest path problems. Finally, we introduce a prototype class for graphs, a professional class for graphs, and conclude with a case study.

14.1   Introduction

A graph is a kind of ordered collection in that each item can have successors and predecessors. However, it is more general than a list, wherein each item has at most one successor and one predecessor, or a tree, wherein each item can have just one predecessor and several successors. In a graph, each item can have several predecessors as well. Actually, lists and trees are special cases of graphs.

Informally, we can think of a graph as a set of points connected by line segments. Each point can be labeled, each line segment can also be labeled, or points and line segments can be unlabeled. Figure 14.1 shows some graphs that illustrate these possibilities.

Figure 14.1 **Possibilities for labeling graphs**

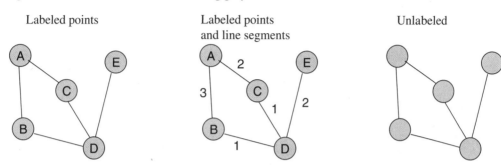

Labeled points   Labeled points and line segments   Unlabeled

Graphs serve as models of a wide range of objects. Among them are

- a road map
- a map of airline routes
- a layout of an adventure game world
- a schematic of the computers and connections that make up the Internet
- the links between pages using hypertext
- the relationship between students and courses
- the prerequisite structure of courses in a computer science department
- the well-known puzzle of connecting three houses to three utilities with crossing line segments (planar vs. nonplanar)
- a diagram of the flow capacities in a communications or transportation network
- a finite state diagram
- a critical path analysis

14.2 Terminology

We now introduce some terms for talking about graphs. Mathematically, a graph is a set V of *vertices* and a set E of *edges,* such that each edge in E connects two of the vertices in V. We also use the term *node* as a synonym for vertex. Vertices and edges can be labeled or unlabeled. When the edges are labeled with numbers, the numbers can be viewed as *weights,* and the graph is said to be a *weighted graph.* Figure 14.1 shows examples of unlabeled, labeled, and weighted graphs.

One vertex is *adjacent* to another vertex if there is an edge connecting the two vertices. These two vertices are also called *neighbors.* A *path* is a sequence of edges that allows one vertex to be reached from another vertex in a graph. Thus, a vertex is ***reachable*** from another vertex if and only if there is a path between the two. The ***length of a path*** is the number of edges on the path. A graph is ***connected*** if there is a path from each vertex to every other vertex. A graph is ***complete*** if there is an edge from each vertex to every other vertex. Figure 14.2 shows graphs that are disconnected, connected but not complete, and complete.

Figure 14.2   **Disconnected, connected, and complete graphs**

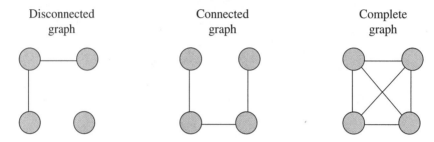

A ***subgraph*** consists of a subset of a graph's vertices and a subset of its edges. A ***connected component*** is a subgraph consisting of the set of vertices that are reachable from a given vertex. Figure 14.3 shows a disconnected graph with vertices A, B, C, D, and E and the connected component that contains the vertex B.

Figure 14.3   **A connected component of a graph**

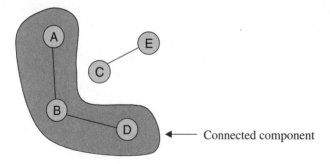

A ***simple path*** is a path that does not pass through the same vertex more than once. By contrast, a ***cycle*** is a path that begins and ends at the same vertex. Figure 14.4 shows a graph with a simple path and a graph with a cycle.

Figure 14.4   **A simple path and a cycle**

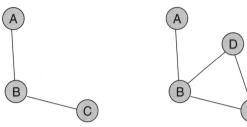

Simple path: ABC   Cycle: BCD

Graphs such as those in the figures thus far are **undirected** in that their edges indicate no direction. This implies that one can move in either direction along an edge that connects two vertices. There can be at most one edge connecting any two vertices in an undirected graph. By contrast, the edges in a **directed graph,** or **digraph**, specify an explicit direction, as shown in Figure 14.5.

Figure 14.5   **Directed graphs (digraphs)**

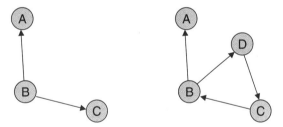

Each edge in a digraph is a **directed edge.** Such an edge has a **source vertex** and a **destination vertex.** When there is only one directed edge connecting two vertices, the vertices are in the relation of predecessor and successor. However, the relation of adjacency between them is asymmetric; that is, the source vertex is adjacent to the destination vertex, but not conversely. One can convert an undirected graph to the equivalent directed graph by replacing each undirected edge with two directed edges that point in opposite directions.

A special case of a digraph that contains no cycles is known as a **directed acyclic graph,** or **DAG.** The second directed graph in Figure 14.5 contains a cycle. Figure 14.6 reverses the direction of one edge to produce a DAG.

Figure 14.6   **A directed graph and a directed acyclic graph (DAG)**

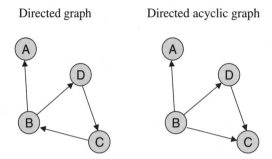

To convert an undirected graph to an equivalent directed graph, we replace each edge in the undirected graph with a pair of edges pointing in opposite directions, as shown in Figure 14.7.

Figure 14.7   **Converting an undirected graph to a directed graph**

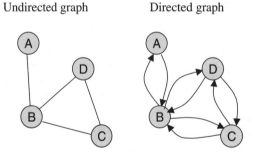

A graph that has relatively many edges is a ***dense graph,*** whereas one that has relatively few edges is a ***sparse graph.***

Hereafter, when we say "graph," we mean an undirected graph, unless we explicitly state otherwise. Also, when we say "component," we mean a connected component in an undirected graph.

14.3   Representations of Graphs

To represent graphs, we need a convenient way to store the vertices and the edges that connect them. The two common representations of graphs are the ***adjacency matrix*** and the ***adjacency list.***

14.3.1 Adjacency Matrix

The adjacency matrix representation stores the information about a graph in a matrix or two-dimensional array. Assume that a graph has N vertices labeled 0, 1, . . . , $N-1$. Then,

■ The adjacency matrix for the graph is a two-dimensional array A with N rows and N columns.

■ The cell $A[i][j]$ contains 1 if there is an edge from vertex i to vertex j in the graph. Otherwise, there is no edge and that cell contains 0.

Figure 14.8 shows a directed graph. Each node is labeled with a letter. Next to each node is its row number in the adjacency matrix.

Figure 14.8 **Labeling graph nodes with their rows in an adjacency matrix**

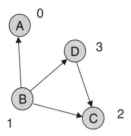

Table 14.1 describes the adjacency matrix for this graph. The matrix itself is the 4 by 4 group of boxed cells containing 1s and 0s. The two columns of numbers and letters to the left of the matrix contain the row positions and the labels of the vertices, respectively. The vertices represented in these two columns are considered the source vertices of potential edges. The numbers and letters above the matrix represent the destination vertices of potential edges.

Table 14.1 **The Adjacency Matrix for the Graph in Figure 14.8**

		0	1	2	3
		A	B	C	D
0	A	0	0	0	0
1	B	1	0	1	1
2	C	0	0	0	0
3	D	0	0	1	0

Note that there are four edges in this graph, so only 4 of the 16 matrix cells are occupied by 1: cells (1,0), (1,2), (1,3), and (3,2). This is an example of a sparse graph, which produces a sparse adjacency matrix. If the graph is undirected, then four more cells are occupied by 1 to account for the bidirectional character of each edge.

If the edges have weights, the weight values can occupy the matrix cells. The cells that indicate no edges must then have some value not within the range of the allowable weights. If the vertices are labeled, then the labels can be stored in a separate one-dimensional array.

14.3.2 Adjacency List

The adjacency list representation stores the information about a graph in an array of linked lists. Assume that a graph has N vertices labeled 0, 1, . . . , $N - 1$. Then,

- The adjacency list for the graph is an array of N linked lists.
- The ith linked list contains a node for vertex j if and only if there is an edge from vertex i to vertex j.

Figure 14.9 shows a directed graph and its adjacency list representation. Note that the labels of the vertices are included in the nodes for each edge. When the edges have weights, the weights can also be included in the nodes. If the graph is undirected, there are two nodes for each edge in the adjacency list.

Figure 14.9   **A directed graph and its adjacency list**

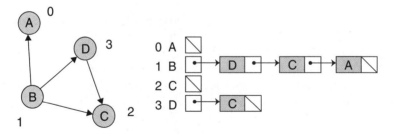

14.3.3 Analysis of the Two Representations

As far as run time is concerned, the behavior of two common graph operations illustrates the differences between the adjacency matrix and the adjacency list. These operations are:

1. Determine whether or not there is an edge between two given vertices.
2. Find all of the vertices adjacent to a given vertex.

The adjacency matrix supports the first operation in constant time because it requires just an index operation into a two-dimensional array. By contrast, the adjacency list supports the first operation in linear time because it requires an index into an array of linked lists and then a search of a linked list for a target vertex.

The adjacency list tends to support the second operation more efficiently. In the adjacency list, the set of adjacent vertices for a given vertex is the linked list for that vertex, which can be located with one index operation. By contrast, the set of adjacent vertices for a given vertex in the adjacency matrix must be computed by traversing that vertex's row in the matrix and accumulating just those positions that contain 1. In other words, the operation must always visit N cells in the adjacency matrix, whereas the operation typically visits much fewer than N nodes in an adjacency list. The limiting case is that of a complete graph. In this case, each cell in the matrix is occupied by 1, each linked list has N nodes, and the performance is a tossup.

As far as memory usage is concerned, the adjacency matrix always requires N^2 cells, no matter how many edges connect the vertices. Thus, the only case in which no cells are wasted is that of a complete graph. By contrast, the adjacency list requires an array of N pointers and a number of nodes equal to twice the number of edges in the case of an undirected graph. The number of edges typically is much smaller than N, although as the number of edges increases, the extra memory required for the pointers in the adjacency list becomes a significant factor.

14.3.4 Further Run-Time Considerations

The number of edges in a complete directed graph with N vertices is $N * (N - 1)$, and the number of edges in a complete undirected graph is $N * (N - 1) / 2$.

Another commonly performed operation in graph algorithms is to iterate across all the neighbors of a given vertex. Let n = number of vertices and m = number of edges. Then

- Using an adjacency matrix to iterate across all neighbors, one must traverse a row in a time that is $O(n)$. To repeat this for all vertices is $O(n^2)$.
- Using an adjacency list, the time to traverse across all neighbors depends on the number of neighbors. On the average, this time is $O(m/n)$. To repeat this for all vertices is $O(m)$, which for a dense graph is $O(n^2)$ and for a sparse graph is $O(n)$. Thus, adjacency lists can provide a run-time advantage when working with sparse graphs.

14.4 Graph Traversals

Central to many graph-based processes is the need to traverse or search a graph. One starts at a given vertex and from it visits all vertices to which it connects. Graph traversals are thus different from tree traversals, which always visit all of the nodes in a given tree.

14.4.1   A Generic Traversal Algorithm for a Connected Graph

Here is a generic method for doing a graph traversal starting at an arbitrary vertex v:

```
void traverseFromVertex (Graph g, Vertex startVertex) {
   mark all vertices in the graph as unvisited
   insert the startVertex into an empty collection
   while (the collection is not empty) {
      remove a vertex from the collection
      if (the vertex has not been visited) {
         mark the vertex as visited
         process the vertex in whatever manner is suitable to the situation
         insert all adjacent unvisited vertices into the collection
      }
   .}
}
```

In the foregoing method

1. All vertices reachable from v are processed exactly once.
2. Determining all vertices adjacent to a given vertex is straightforward:
   a. When an adjacency matrix is used, we iterate across the row corresponding to the vertex.
      ■ This is an O(n) operation.
      ■ Repeating this for all vertices is O(n^2).
   b. When an adjacency list is used, we traverse the vertex's linked list.
      ■ Performance depends on how many vertices are adjacent to the given vertex.
      ■ Repeating this for all vertices is O(m), where m is the number of edges.

14.4.2   Breadth-First and Depth-First Traversals

There are two common orders in which vertices can be visited during a graph traversal. The first, a ***depth-first traversal (DFS),*** uses a stack as the collection in the generic algorithm. The use of a stack forces the traversal process to go deeply into the graph before backtracking to another path. Put another way, the use of a stack constrains the algorithm to begin its traversal from the most recently visited vertex.

The second kind of traversal, a ***breadth-first traversal (BFS),*** uses a queue as the collection in the generic algorithm. The use of a queue forces the traversal process to visit every vertex adjacent to a given vertex before it moves deeper into the graph. Thus, the algorithm is constrained to begin its traversal with the least recently visited vertex. In this respect, a breadth-first traversal of a graph is similar to a level order traversal of a tree as discussed in Chapter 11.

In Figure 14.10, the nodes of a graph are numbered in the order in which they are visited during these two kinds of traversals.

Figure 14.10   **Depth-first and breadth-first traversals of a given graph**

Depth-first traversal

Breadth-first traversal

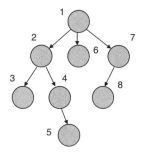
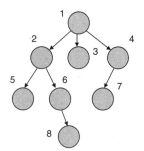

A depth-first traversal can also be implemented recursively. This fact should not be too surprising; remember the relationship between stacks and recursion established earlier in the text. Here is a method for recursive depth-first traversal. It uses an auxiliary method called dfs:

```
void traverseFromVertex (Graph g, Vertex startVertex) {
    mark all vertices in the graph as unvisited
    dfs (startVertex)
}

void dfs (Graph g, Vertex v) {
    mark v as visited
    process v in whatever manner is suitable to the situation
    for (each vertex, w, adjacent to v)
    if (w has not been visited)
    dfs (g, w)
}
```

As just presented, a traversal starting at a vertex v is limited to the vertices reachable from v, which in an undirected graph is the component containing v. If we desire to traverse all the vertices of an undirected graph component by component, these methods can be extended, as illustrated next:

```
void traverseAll (Graph g) {
    mark all vertices in the graph as unvisited
    instantiate an empty collection
    for (each vertex in the graph) {
        if (the vertex has not been visited)
            insert the vertex in the collection
        while (the collection is not empty) {
            remove a vertex from the collection
            if (the vertex has not been visited) {
                mark the vertex as visited
                process the vertex
```

Continued

Continued

```
                    insert all adjacent unvisited vertices in the collection
            }
        }
    }
}
void traverseAll (Graph g) {
    mark all vertices in the graph as unvisited
    for (each vertex, v, in the graph)
        if (v unvisited)
            dfs (g, v)
}

void dfs (Graph g, Vertex v) {
    mark v as visited
    process v in whatever manner is suitable to the situation
    for (each vertex, w, adjacent to v)
    if (w unvisited)
    dfs (g, w)
}
```

Performance for the basic traversal algorithm, ignoring the processing of a vertex, is $O(m)$ or $O(n^2)$, depending on the representation, as illustrated below. We assume that inserting and deleting from the collection are $O(1)$, which they can be with list-based stacks and queues.

```
void traverseFromVertex (Graph g, Vertex startVertex) {
    mark all vertices in the graph as unvisited          O(n)
    insert the startVertex into an empty collection       O(1)
    while (the collection is not empty) {           loop O(n) times
        remove a vertex from the collection               O(1)
        if (the vertex has not been visited) {            O(1)
            mark the vertex as visited                    O(1)
            process the vertex                            O(?)
            insert all adjacent unvisited vertices into the collection
                                                    O(n) or O(m/n)

        }
    }
}
```

14.4.3   Graph Components

The traversal algorithms that we have discussed can be used to partition the vertices of a graph into disjoint components. Here, by way of example, each component is stored in a set, and the sets are stored in a list:

```
List partitionIntoComponents (Graph g) {
    List list = new List ()
    Set set
    mark all vertices in the graph as unvisited
    for (each vertex, v, in the graph) {
    if (v unvisited) {
    set = new Set ()
    list.insert (set, 0)
    dfs (g, v, set)
```

Continued

Continued

```
    }
    return list
}

void dfs (Graph g, Vertex v, Set set) {
    mark v as visited
    set.insert (v)
    for (each vertex, w, adjacent to v)
       if (w unvisited)
          dfs (g, w, set)
}
```

14.5   Trees within Graphs

The method `traverseFromVertex` implicitly yields a tree rooted at the vertex from which the traversal starts and includes all the vertices reached during the traversal. This tree is a subgraph of the graph being traversed. Consider, for instance, the depth-first search variant of the method. Suppose `dfs` has just been called using vertex `v`. If a recursive call using vertex `w` now occurs, then we consider `w` to be a child of `v`. The edge (`v`, `w`) corresponds to the parent-child relationship, or edge, between `v` and `w`. The starting vertex is the root of this tree. The tree is called a ***depth-first search tree.***

It is also possible to build a breadth-first search tree. Figure 14.10 showed these two kinds of trees within a graph that was traversed from a given vertex.

14.5.1   Spanning Trees and Forests

A *spanning tree* is of interest because it has the fewest number of edges possible and still retains a connection between all the vertices in the component. If the component contains n vertices, the spanning tree contains $n - 1$ edges. When we traverse all the vertices of an undirected graph, not just those in a single component, we generate a *spanning forest.*

14.5.2   Minimum Spanning Tree

When the edges in a graph are weighted, we can sum the weights for all edges in a spanning tree and attempt to find a spanning tree that minimizes this sum. There are several algorithms for finding a ***minimum spanning tree*** for a component. Repeated application to all the components in a graph yields a ***minimum spanning forest*** for a graph. For example, consider the map of air miles between cities. It is very useful to determine how an airline can service all cities while minimizing the total length of the routes it needs to support. To accomplish this, one could treat the map as a weighted graph and generate its minimum spanning forest.

14.5.3   Algorithms for Minimum Spanning Trees

There are two well-known algorithms for finding a minimum spanning tree, one by Prim and the other by Kruskal. Both are examples of greedy algorithms. Here is Prim's algorithm. Without loss of generality, we assume the graph is connected.

```
void minimumSpanningTree (Graph g) {
    mark all vertices and edges as unvisited
    mark some vertex, say v, as visited
    for (k = 1; k < number of vertices; k++) {
        find the least weight edge from a visited vertex to
            an unvisited vertex, say w
        mark the edge and w as visited
    }
}
```

At the end of this process, the marked edges are the branches in a minimum spanning tree. Here is a proof by contradiction:

1. Suppose G is a graph for which Prim's algorithm yields a spanning tree that is not minimum.

2. Number the vertices in the order in which they are added to the spanning tree by Prim's algorithm, giving $v_1, v_2, \ldots, v_n$. In this numbering scheme, v_1 represents the arbitrary vertex at which the algorithm starts.

3. Number each edge in the spanning tree according to the vertex it leads into; for instance, e_i leads into vertex i.

4. Because we are assuming that Prim's algorithm does not yield a minimum spanning tree for G, there is a first edge, call it e_i, such that the set of edges $E_i = \{e_2, e_3, \ldots, e_i\}$ cannot be extended into a mininum spanning tree, whereas the set of edges $E_{i-1} = \{e_2, e_3, \ldots, e_{i-1}\}$ can be. The set E_{i-1} could even be empty, meaning that Prim's algorithm goes wrong with the first edge added.

5. Let $V_i = \{v_1, v_2, \ldots, v_{i-1}\}$. This set contains at least v_1.

6. Let T be any spanning tree that extends E_{i-1}. T does not include e_i.

7. Adding any more edges to T creates a cycle, so let us create a cycle by adding edge e_i.

8. This cycle includes two edges that cross the boundary between V_i and the rest of the vertices in the graph. One of these edges is e_i. Call the other e. Because of the manner in which e_i was chosen, $e_i <= e$.

9. Remove e from T. Again we have a spanning tree, and because $e_i <= e$, it too is minimum. But this contradicts our earlier assumption that E_i could not be extended into a minimum spanning tree. So if we have reasoned correctly, the only way to escape this apparent contradiction is to suppose that there is no graph to which Prim's algorithm does not apply.

Maximum run time is $O(m * n)$. Solution:

Suppose n = number of vertices and m = number of edges, then

step 2. $O(n + m)$ time

step 3. $O(1)$ time

step 4. the loop executes $O(n)$ times

step 5. if this is done in a straightforward manner, then

        look at m edges—$O(m)$ time

        for each edge, determine if the endpoints are visited or unvisited—$O(1)$ time

step 6. O(1) time

Max Time = $O(n + m + n * m)$

but $n + m + n * m < 1 + n + m + n * m = (n + 1) * (m + 1)$

implies $O(m * n)$

A better result can be obtained by modifying the algorithm slightly. Central to the modified algorithm is a heap of edges. The heap is coded so that the edge with the smallest weight is on top. This is in contrast to the heaps discussed earlier in the text, which kept the largest element on top. Because the graph is connected, $n - 1 <= m$.

```
1.  void minimumSpanningTree (Graph g) {
2.      mark all edges as unvisited
3.      mark all vertices as unvisited
4.      mark some vertex, say v, as visited
5.      for (all edges leading from v)
6.          add the edge to the heap
7.      k = 1
8.      while (k < number of vertices) {
9.          remove an edge from the heap
10.         if (one end of this edge, say vertex w, has not been visited) {
11.             mark the edge and w as visited
12.             for (all edges leading from w)
13.                 add the edge to the heap
14.             k++
15.         }
16.     }
17. }
```

The maximum run time is O($m\log n$) for the adjacency list representation. Solution:

Suppose n = number of vertices and m = number of edges; then, ignoring lines that O(1), we get:

step 2. O(m)

step 3. O(n)

step 5. O(n) loops

step 6. O($\log m$)

steps 5 & 6. O($n\log m$)

step 8. O(n)

step 9. O($\log m$), which can happen at most m times; therefore, O($m\log m$)

step 12. all executions of this inner loop are bounded by m

step 13. O($\log m$)

steps 12 & 13. O($m\log m$)

Total

= O($m + n + \log m + n\log m + m\log m$)

= O($m\log m$)

= O($m\log n$) because $m <= n * n$ and $\log n * n = 2\log n$

14.6   Topological Sort

A directed acyclic graph (DAG) has an order among the vertices. For example, in a graph of courses for an academic major, such as computer science, some courses are prerequisites for others. A natural question to ask in these cases is: To take a given course, in what order should I take all of its prerequisites? The answer lies in a ***topological order*** of vertices in this graph. Figure 14.11(a) shows a graph of courses P, Q, R, S, and T. Figures 14.11(b) and 14.11(c) show two possible topological orderings of the courses in this graph.

Figure 14.11(a)   A graph of courses

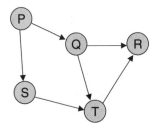

Figure 14.11(b)   The first topological ordering of the graph

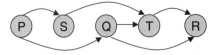

Figure 14.11(c)   The second topological ordering of the graph

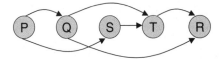

The process of finding and returning a topological order of vertices in a graph is called a ***topological sort.*** One topological sort algorithm is based on a graph traversal. One can use either a depth-first traversal or a breadth-first traversal. We use a depth-first traversal. The vertices are returned in a list in ascending order (topologically speaking):

```
List topologicalSort (Graph g) {
   List list = new List ()
```

Continued

Continued

```
    mark all vertices in the graph as unvisited
    for (each vertex, v, in the graph)
       if (v unvisited)
          dfs (g, v, list)
    return list
}

void dfs (Graph g, Vertex v, List list) {
    mark v as visited
    for (each vertex, w, adjacent to v)
       if (w unvisited)
          dfs (g, w, list)
    list.insert (v, 0)     // insert at beginning of list
}
```

The performance of this algorithm is O(m) if list insertions are O(1), which is doable.

14.7 The Shortest Path Problem

It is often useful to determine the shortest path between two vertices in a graph. Consider an airline map, represented as a weighted directed graph whose weights represent miles between airports. The shortest path between two airports is the path that has the smallest sum of edge weights.

The *single-source shortest path problem* asks for a solution that contains the shortest paths from a given vertex to all of the other vertices. This problem has a widely used solution by Dijkstra. His solution is O(n^2) and assumes that all weights must be positive.

Another problem, known as the *all-pairs shortest path problem,* asks for the set of all the shortest paths in a graph. A widely used solution by Floyd is O(n^3).

14.7.1 Dijkstra's Algorithm

We now develop Dijkstra's algorithm for computing the single-source shortest path. The inputs to this algorithm are a directed acyclic graph with edge weights > 0 and a single vertex that represents the source vertex. The algorithm computes the distances of the shortest paths from the source vertex to all of the other vertices in the graph. The output of the algorithm is a two-dimensional array, `results`. This array has N rows, where N is the number of vertices in the graph. The first column in each row contains a vertex. The second column contains the distance from the source vertex to this vertex. The third column contains the immediate predecessor vertex on this path.

In addition to this array, the algorithm uses a temporary array, `included`, of N Booleans to track whether or not a given vertex has been included in the set of vertices for which we already have determined the shortest path. The algorithm consists of two major steps: an initialization step and a computation step.

14.7.2 The Initialization Step

In this step, we initialize all of the columns in the `results` array and all of the cells in the `included` array according to the following algorithm:

```
For each vertex in the graph
    Store vertex in the current row of the results array
    If vertex = source vertex
        Set the row's distance cell to 0
        Set the row's path cell to undefined
        Set included[row] to true
    Else if there is an edge from source vertex to vertex
        Set the row's distance cell to the edge's weight
        Set the row's path cell to source vertex
        Set included[row] to false
    Else
        Set the row's distance cell to infinity
        Set the row's path cell to undefined
        Set included[row] to false
    Go to the next row in the results array
```

At the end of this process, the following are true:

- The cells in the `included` array are all `false`, except for the cell that corresponds to the row of the source vertex in the `results` array.
- The distance in a row's distance cell is either 0 (for the source vertex), infinity (for a vertex without a direct edge from the source), or a positive number (for a vertex without a direct edge from the source). We represent infinity in the implementation with a large number, such as `Double.MAX_VALUE`.
- The vertex in a row's path cell is either the source vertex or undefined. We represent undefined in the implementation with the `null` value.

Figure 14.12 shows the state of the two arrays after the initialization step has been run with a given graph.

Figure 14.12   **The data structures used to compute the shortest path of a given graph**

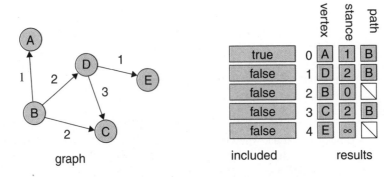

graph   included   results

14.7.3   The Computation Step

In the computation step, Dijkstra's algorithm finds a shortest path from the source to a vertex, marks this vertex's cell in the `included` array, and continues this process until all of these cells are marked. Here is the algorithm for this step:

```
Do
   Find the vertex F that is not yet included and has the minimal distance
   Mark F as included
   For each other vertex T not included
      If there is an edge from F to T
         Set new distance to F's distance + edge's weight
         If new distance < T's distance in the results array
            Set T's distance to new distance
            Set T's path in the results array to F
While all vertices are not included
```

As you can see, the algorithm repeatedly selects the vertex with the shortest path distance that has not yet been included and marks it as included before entering the nested `for` loop. In the body of this loop, the process runs through any edges from the included vertex to unincluded vertices and determines the smallest possible distance from the source vertex to any of these other vertices. The critical step in this process is the nested `if` statement, which resets the distance and predecessor cells for an unincluded vertex if a new minimal distance has been found to it through the included vertex.

14.7.4   Analysis

The initialization step must process every vertex, so it is $O(n)$. The outer loop of the computation step also iterates through every vertex. The inner loop of this step iterates through every vertex not included thus far. Hence, the overall behavior of the computation step resembles that of the $O(n^2)$ sorting algorithms, so Dijkstra's algorithm is $O(n^2)$.

14.8   A Graph Prototype

To develop a graph ADT, we need to consider various factors:

- the requirements of clients
- the mathematical nature of graphs
- the commonly used representations: adjacency matrix and adjacency list

All graphs, whether they are directed, undirected, weighted, or unweighted, are collections of vertices connected by edges. A quite general graph allows the labels of vertices and edges to be any kind of objects, although they typically are strings or numbers. Clients should be able to insert and remove vertices, insert or remove an edge between a source vertex and a destination vertex, and retrieve all of the vertices and edges. It is also useful to obtain the neighboring vertices and the incident edges of a given vertex in a graph and to set and clear marks on the vertices and edges. Finally, clients should be able to choose, as their needs dictate, between an adjacency matrix representation and an adjacency list representation.

The graph prototype shown here allows clients to create undirected graphs. The vertices are labeled with strings, and the edges are weighted with doubles. The prototype uses an adjacency list representation and consists of the classes `LinkedGraphPT`, `LinkedVertexPT`, and `LinkedEdgePT`.

14.8.1 Example Use of the Graph Prototype

Assume that we want to create the undirected graph is Figure 14.13. The following code segment does this and displays the graph's string representation in the terminal window:

```
LinkedGraphPT g = new LinkedGraphPT();

// Insert vertices
g.addVertex ("A");
g.addVertex ("B");
g.addVertex ("C");
g.addVertex ("D");
g.addVertex ("E");

// Insert weighted edges
g.addEdge ("A", "B", 3);
g.addEdge ("A", "C", 2);
g.addEdge ("B", "D", 1);
g.addEdge ("C", "D", 1);
g.addEdge ("D", "E", 2);

System.out.println (g);
```

Figure 14.13   **An undirected graph**

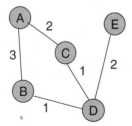

The next code segment displays the neighboring vertices and the incident edges of the vertex labeled "D" in our example graph:

```
System.out.println("Neighboring vertices of D:");
Iterator vertices = g.neighboringVertices("D");
```

Continued

Continued

```
while (vertices.hasNext())
    System.out.println(vertices.next());

System.out.println("Incident edges of D:");
Iterator edges = g.incidentEdges("D");
while (edges.hasNext())
    System.out.println(edges.next());
```

The implementation of the graph prototype is straightforward but somewhat tedious. In what follows, we present the interfaces and code for the three classes without discussion.

14.8.2   The Class `LinkedGraphPT`

Table 14.2 lists the methods in the class `LinkedGraphPT`.

Table 14.2   **The Methods for the Graph Prototype and Their Complexity**

LinkedGraphPT for an Undirected Graph

	`constructor()`	O(1)
	`constructor (Iterator iter)`	O(*n*)
void	`addEdge(String fromLabel, String toLabel, double weight)` Adds an edge with the specified weight between the specified vertices. The `fromLabel` and `toLabel` can be switched without changing the meaning.	O(1)
void	`addVertex(String label)` Adds a vertex with the specified label.	O(1)
void	`clear()` Removes all vertices and edges from this graph.	O(1)
void	`clearEdgeMarks()` Clears all edge marks.	O(*m*)
void	`clearVertexMarks()` Clears all vertex marks.	O(*n*)
boolean	`containsEdge(String fromLabel, String toLabel)` Returns `true` if the graph contains an edge from a vertex with `fromLabel` to a vertex with `toLabel`, else returns `false`. The `fromLabel` and `toLabel` can be switched without changing the meaning.	O(*m/n*)
boolean	`containsVertex(String label)` Returns `true` if the graph contains a vertex with the specified label, else returns `false`.	O(1)
Iterator	`edges()` Returns an iterator over the edges.	O(1)

continued

Table 14.2   **The Methods for the Graph Prototype and Their Complexity** *(Continued)*

LinkedGraphPT for an Undirected Graph

EdgePT	`getEdge(String fromLabel, String toLabel)` Returns the edge connecting vertices with the specified labels or `null` if there is no such edge. The `fromLabel` and `toLabel` can be switched without changing the meaning.	$O(m/n)$
LinkedVertexPT	`getVertex(String label)` Returns the vertex with the specified label or `null` if there is no such vertex.	$O(1)$
Iterator	`incidentEdges(LinkedVertexPT vertex)` Returns an iterator over edges incident to the specified vertex. Throws an exception if the specified vertex is `null` or absent.	$O(1)$
boolean	`isEmpty()` Returns `true` if the graph contains no vertices.	$O(1)$
Iterator	`neighboringVertices(LinkedVertexPT vertex)` Returns an iterator over the vertices adjacent to the specified vertex.	$O(1)$
boolean	`removeEdge(String fromLabel, String toLabel)` If the graph contains an edge between the specified vertices, then removes the edge and returns `true`, else returns `false`. The `fromLabel` and `toLabel` can be switched without changing the meaning.	$O(m/n)$
boolean	`removeVertex(String label)` If this graph contains a vertex with the specified label, then removes the vertex and all edges involving this vertex and returns `true`, else returns `false`.	$O(\max(m, n))$
int	`sizeEdges()` Returns the number of edges in this graph.	$O(1)$
int	`sizeVertices()` Returns the number of vertices in this graph.	$O(1)$
String	`toString()` Returns a string representation of this graph.	$O(\max(m, n))$
Iterator	`vertices()` Returns an iterator over the vertices.	$O(1)$

Here is a complete listing of this class, which uses a hash map to contain the vertices:

```
1 import java.util.*;
2
3 public class LinkedGraphPT {
4
5     protected int vertexCount;
6     protected int edgeCount;
7     protected Map vertices;
8
```

Continued

Continued

```
 9      public LinkedGraphPT()
10      {
11          vertexCount = 0;
12          edgeCount = 0;
13          vertices = new HashMap();
14      }
15
16      public LinkedGraphPT (Iterator iter)
17      {
18          vertexCount = 0;
19          edgeCount = 0;
20          vertices = new HashMap();
21          while (iter.hasNext()){
22              String str = (String)(iter.next());
23              addVertex (str);
24          }
25      }
26
27      public void addEdge
28          (String fromLabel, String toLabel,double weight)
29      {
30          LinkedVertexPT fromVertex, toVertex;
31
32          fromVertex = getVertex (fromLabel);
33          toVertex   = getVertex (toLabel);
34          fromVertex.addEdgeTo (toVertex, weight);
35          edgeCount++;
36      }
37
38      public void addVertex (String label)
39      {
40          vertices.put (label, new LinkedVertexPT (label));
41          vertexCount++;
42      }
43
44      public void clear()
45      {
46          vertexCount = 0;
47          edgeCount = 0;
48          vertices = new HashMap();
49      }
50
51      public void clearEdgeMarks()
52      {
53          LinkedEdgePT edge;
54          Iterator iter = edges();
55          while (iter.hasNext()){
56              edge = (LinkedEdgePT)(iter.next());
57              edge.clearMark();
58          }
59      }
60
61      public void clearVertexMarks()
62      {
63          LinkedVertexPT vertex;
```

Continued

Continued

```
64          Iterator iter = vertices();
65          while (iter.hasNext()){
66              vertex = (LinkedVertexPT)(iter.next());
67              vertex.clearMark();
68          }
69      }
70
71      public boolean containsEdge (String fromLabel, String toLabel)
72      {
73          return getEdge (fromLabel, toLabel) != null;
74      }
75
76      public boolean containsVertex (Object label)
77      {
78          return vertices.containsKey (label);
79      }
80
81      public Iterator edges()
82      {
83          return new InnerEdgeIterator();
84      }
85
86      public LinkedEdgePT getEdge (String fromLabel, String toLabel)
87      {
88          LinkedVertexPT fromVertex, toVertex;
89
90          fromVertex = (LinkedVertexPT)(vertices.get (fromLabel));
91          toVertex   = (LinkedVertexPT)(vertices.get (toLabel));
92          return fromVertex.getEdgeTo (toVertex);
93      }
94
95      public LinkedVertexPT getVertex (String label)
96      {
97          return (LinkedVertexPT)(vertices.get(label));
98      }
99
100     public Iterator incidentEdges (LinkedVertexPT vertex)
101     {
102         return vertex.incidentEdges();
103     }
104
105     public boolean isEmpty()
106     {
107         return vertexCount == 0;
108     }
109
110     public Iterator neighboringVertices (LinkedVertexPT vertex)
111     {
112         return vertex.neighboringVertices();
113     }
114
115     public boolean removeEdge (String fromLabel, String toLabel)
116     {
117         LinkedVertexPT fromVertex, toVertex;
118         boolean edgeRemovedFlg;
119         fromVertex = (LinkedVertexPT)(getVertex (fromLabel));
```

Continued

Continued

```
120          toVertex   = (LinkedVertexPT)(getVertex (toLabel));
121          edgeRemovedFlg = fromVertex.removeEdgeTo (toVertex);
122
123          if (edgeRemovedFlg)
124              edgeCount--;
125
126          return edgeRemovedFlg;
127     }
128
129     public boolean removeVertex (String label)
130     {
131          LinkedVertexPT removedVertex, nextVertex;
132
133          removedVertex = (LinkedVertexPT)(vertices.remove (label));
134
135          if (removedVertex == null)
136              return false;
137
138          // Examine all vertices
139          Iterator iter = vertices();
140          while (iter.hasNext()){
141              nextVertex = (LinkedVertexPT)(iter.next());
142              if (nextVertex.removeEdgeTo (removedVertex))
143                  edgeCount--;
144          }
145          vertexCount--;
146
147          return true;
148     }
149
150     public int sizeEdges()
151     {
152          return edgeCount;
153     }
154
155     public int sizeVertices()
156     {
157          return vertexCount;
158     }
159
160     public String toString()
161     {
162          Iterator iter;
163          String str;
164
165          iter = vertices();
166          str = sizeVertices() + " Vertices: ";
167          while (iter.hasNext())
168              str += " " + iter.next();
169          str += "\n";
170          iter = edges();
171          str += sizeEdges() + " Edges: ";
172          while (iter.hasNext())
173              str += " " + iter.next();
174
```

Continued

Continued

```
175              return str;
176      }
177
178      public Iterator vertices()
179      {
180          return vertices.values().iterator();
181      }
182
183 //===============================================================
184
185      private class InnerEdgeIterator implements Iterator
186      {
187          private Iterator vertexIter;
188          private Iterator edgeIter;
189          private Object   nextEdge;
190          private Set      edgesToSkip;
191
192          private InnerEdgeIterator()
193          {
194              vertexIter = vertices();
195              getFirstEdgeFromNextVertex();
196              edgesToSkip = new HashSet();
197          }
198
199          private void getFirstEdgeFromNextVertex()
200          {
201              nextEdge = null;
202              while (vertexIter.hasNext()){
203                  LinkedVertexPT vertex = (LinkedVertexPT)(vertexIter.next());
204                  edgeIter = incidentEdges (vertex);
205                  if (edgeIter.hasNext()){
206                      nextEdge = edgeIter.next();
207                      break;
208                  }
209              }
210          }
211
212          public boolean hasNext()
213          {
214              return nextEdge != null;
215          }
216
217          public Object next()
218          {
219              edgesToSkip.add (nextEdge);
220              Object returnedEdge = nextEdge;
221              do {
222                  getNextEdge();
223              }while (nextEdge != null && edgesToSkip.contains (nextEdge));
224
225              return returnedEdge;
226          }
227
228          private void getNextEdge()
229          {
230              if (edgeIter.hasNext())
```

Continued

Continued

```
231                    nextEdge = edgeIter.next();
232               else
233                    getFirstEdgeFromNextVertex();
234          }
235
236     public void remove()
237     {
238          throw new UnsupportedOperationException("Remove not allowed");
239     }
240
241    }
242
243 }
```

14.8.3 The Class `LinkedVertexPT`

Table 14.3 lists the methods in the class `LinkedVertexPT`.

Table 14.3 **The Methods for the Class `LinkedVertexPT` and Their Complexity**

LinkedVertexPT for an Undirected Graph

	Public Methods	
void	**clearMark()** Unmarks the vertex.	O(1)
String	**getLabel()** Returns the vertex's label.	O(1)
boolean	**isMarked()** Returns `true` if the vertex is marked, else returns `false`.	O(1)
void	**setLabel(String label, LinkedGraphPT g)** Changes the vertex's label to the specified label. The graph should not already contain a vertex with the specified label.	O(1)
void	**setMark()** Marks the vertex.	O(1)
String	**toString()** Returns a string representation of this vertex.	O(1)
	Protected Methods	
	constructor (String label)	O(1)
void	**addEdgeTo (LinkedVertexPT toVertex, double weight)** Adds an edge, with the specified weight, that connects this vertex to the specified vertex.	O(1)
LinkedEdgePT	**getEdgeTo(LinkedVertexPT toVertex)** Returns the edge that connects this vertex and the specified vertex or `null` if there is none.	O(m/n)

continued

Table 14.3   **The Methods for the Class `LinkedVertexPT` and Their Complexity** *(Continued)*

LinkedVertexPT for an Undirected Graph

Iterator	`incidentEdges()` Returns an iterator over the edges incident to this vertex.	O(1)
Iterator	`neighboringVertices()` Returns an iterator over the vertices neighboring this vertex.	O(1)
boolean	`removeEdgeTo(LinkedVertexPT toVertex)` Returns `true` and removes the edge between this vertex and the specified vertex, or returns `false` if there is no such edge.	O(*m/n*)

Here is a listing of the implementation of `LinkedVertexPT`, which maintains a list of edges:

```
1  import java.util.*;
2
3  class LinkedVertexPT {
4
5      protected String  label;    // Label associated with this vertex
6      protected boolean mark;     // Indicates if the vertex is marked
7      private   List    edgeList; // List of edges leaving this vertex
8
9  // ===================== public methods =========================
10
11     public void clearMark()
12     {
13         mark = false;
14     }
15
16     public String getLabel()
17     {
18         return label;
19     }
20
21     public boolean isMarked()
22     {
23         return mark;
24     }
25
26     public void setLabel (String lbl, LinkedGraphPT g)
27     {
28         g.vertices.remove (label);
29         g.vertices.put (lbl, this);
30         label = lbl;
31     }
32
33     public void setMark()
```

Continued

Continued

```
34      {
35          mark = true;
36      }
37
38      public String toString()
39      {
40          return label.toString();
41      }
42
43  // ===================== protected methods =========================
44
45      protected LinkedVertexPT (String label)
46      {
47          this.label = label;
48          mark = false;
49          edgeList = new LinkedList();
50      }
51
52      protected void addEdgeTo (LinkedVertexPT toVertex, double weight)
53      {
54          LinkedEdgePT edge = new LinkedEdgePT (this, toVertex, weight);
55          edgeList.add (0, edge);
56          toVertex.edgeList.add (0,edge);
57      }
58
59      protected LinkedEdgePT getEdgeTo (LinkedVertexPT toVertex)
60      {
61          int index = edgeList.indexOf (new LinkedEdgePT (this, toVertex));
62          if (index == -1)
63              return null;
64          else
65              return (LinkedEdgePT)(edgeList.get (index));
66      }
67
68      protected Iterator incidentEdges()
69      {
70          return edgeList.iterator();
71      }
72
73      protected Iterator neighboringVertices()
74      {
75          return new InnerNeighboringVerticesIterator(this);
76      }
77
78      protected boolean removeEdgeTo (LinkedVertexPT toVertex)
79      {
80          LinkedEdgePT edge = new LinkedEdgePT (this, toVertex);
81          toVertex.edgeList.remove  (edge);
82          return edgeList.remove (edge);
83      }
84
85
86  //****************** InnerNeighboringVerticesEnumeration ********************
87
88      private class InnerNeighboringVerticesIterator implements Iterator
```

Continued

Continued

```
 89      {
 90          private Iterator iter;
 91          private LinkedVertexPT thisVertex;
 92
 93          protected InnerNeighboringVerticesIterator(LinkedVertexPT v)
 94          {
 95              iter = edgeList.iterator();
 96              thisVertex = v;
 97          }
 98
 99          public boolean hasNext()
100          {
101              return iter.hasNext();
102          }
103
104          public Object next()
105          {
106            if (!iter.hasNext())
107                throw new NoSuchElementException
108                ("There are no more elements");
109
110            return ((LinkedEdgePT)(iter.next())).getOtherVertex (thisVertex);
111          }
112
113          public void remove()
114          {
115              throw new UnsupportedOperationException("Remove not allowed");
116          }
117      }
118
119 }
```

14.8.4   The Class `LinkedEdgePT`

Table 14.4 lists the methods in the class `LinkedEdgePT`.

Table 14.4   **The Methods for the Class `LinkedEdgePT` and Their Complexity**

LinkedEdgePT for an Undirected Graph

	constructor(LinkedVertexPT from, LinkedVertexPT to) The from and to vertices can be switched without changing the meaning.	O(1)
	constructor(LinkedVertexPT from, LinkedVertexPT to, double weight) The from and to vertices can be switched without changing the meaning.	O(1)
void	**clearMark()** Unmarks the edge.	O(1)

Table 14.4 **The Methods for the Class `LinkedEdgePT` and Their Complexity** *(Continued)*

LinkedEdgePT for an Undirected Graph

boolean	**equals(Object obj)**	O(1)
	Returns `true` if the specified object is an edge between the same vertices as this edge, else returns `false`. (*Note:* This method is useful when edges are stored in collections such as lists.)	
LinkedVertexPT	**getOtherVertex(LinkedVertexPT thisVertex)**	O(1)
	Returns this edge's other vertex. If this vertex is `null`, then returns either vertex for this edge.	
double	**getWeight()**	O(1)
	Returns the edge's weight.	
boolean	**isMarked()**	O(1)
	Returns `true` if the edge is marked, else returns `false`.	
void	**setMark()**	O(1)
	Marks the edge.	
void	**setWeight(double weight)**	O(1)
	Sets the edge's weight to the specified value.	
String	**toString()**	O(1)
	Returns a string representation of this edge.	

Here is a listing of the class `LinkedEdgePT`:

```
1 public class LinkedEdgePT {
2
3     private double          weight;
4     private boolean         mark;
5     private LinkedVertexPT  vertex1;
6     private LinkedVertexPT  vertex2;
7
8     protected LinkedEdgePT (LinkedVertexPT from, LinkedVertexPT to)
9     {
10          vertex1 = from;
11          vertex2 = to;
12          weight = 0;
13          mark = false;
14     }
15
16     protected LinkedEdgePT (LinkedVertexPT from, LinkedVertexPT to,
17                      double weight)
18     {
19          vertex1 = from;
20          vertex2 = to;
21          this.weight = weight;
22          mark = false;
23     }
```

Continued

Continued

```
24
25      public void clearMark()
26      {
27          mark = false;
28      }
29
30      public boolean equals (Object obj)
31      {
32          if (!(obj instanceof LinkedEdgePT))
33              return false;
34
35          LinkedEdgePT edge = (LinkedEdgePT) obj;
36          return (vertex1 == edge.vertex1 && vertex2 == edge.vertex2) ||
37                  (vertex1 == edge.vertex2 && vertex2 == edge.vertex1);
38      }
39
40      public LinkedVertexPT getOtherVertex (LinkedVertexPT thisVertex)
41      {
42          if (thisVertex == null || thisVertex == vertex2)
43              return vertex1;
44          else
45              return vertex2;
46      }
47
48      public double getWeight()
49      {
50          return weight;
51      }
52
53
54      public boolean isMarked()
55      {
56          return mark;
57      }
58
59      public void setMark()
60      {
61          mark = true;
62      }
63
64      public void setWeight (double weight)
65      {
66          this.weight = weight;
67      }
68
69      public String toString()
70      {
71          return "" + vertex1 + ":" + vertex2   + ":" + weight;
72      }
73
74 }
```

14.9 A Professional Graph Implementation (optional pv)

The lamborne package provides a Graph interface and several classes that collaborate to satisfy the requirements of users of graphs. These requirements go beyond those of the prototype, in that

- ▪ vertices and edges can be labeled with any objects
- ▪ clients can use directed graphs as well as undirected graphs
- ▪ clients can choose between adjacency list and adjacency matrix implementations (although lamborne provides only the former)

The lamborne graph classes are shown in the class hierarchy in Figure 14.14. The abstract classes are shaded, whereas the concrete classes are not.

Figure 14.14 **The hierarchy of the lamborne graph classes**

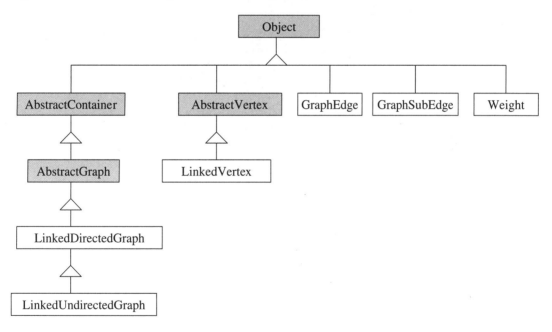

14.9.1 The **Graph** Interface

The Graph interface specifies the basic graph operations for clients of graphs. Table 14.5 lists the methods of this interface. The interfaces Vertex and Edge specify the methods for the classes that represent vertices and edges. Clients do not create instances of these classes directly; that is done when a client inserts a vertex or an edge into a graph.

Table 14.5   **The Methods for the Class** `Graph`

Graph Interface

`void`	`addEdge(Object fromLabel, Object toLabel, Object edgeLabel)` Adds an edge with the specified label between the specified vertices. Throws an exception if (1) any labels are `null`, (2) either vertex is missing, (3) `fromLabel` equals `toLabel`, or (4) the edge is already present.
`void`	`addVertex(Object label)` Adds a vertex with the specified label. Throws an exception if the label is `null` or if this graph already contains a vertex with the specified label.
`void`	`clear()` Removes all vertices and edges from this graph.
`void`	`clearEdgeMarks()` Clears all edge marks.
`void`	`clearVertexMarks()` Clears all vertex marks.
`Object`	`clone()` Returns a shallow copy of this graph.
`Collection`	`collectionView()` Returns a collection-view of the labels of the vertices in this graph.
`boolean`	`containsEdge(Object fromLabel, Object toLabel)` Returns `true` if the graph contains an edge from a vertex with `fromLabel` to a vertex with `toLabel`, else returns `false`. Throws an exception if either label is `null` or either vertex is absent.
`boolean`	`containsVertex(Object label)` Returns `true` if the graph contains a vertex with the specified label, else returns `false`. Throws an exception if the label is `null`.
`Iterator`	`edges()` Returns an iterator over the edges.
`boolean`	`equals(Object other)` Returns `true` if the other object is a graph with the same morphology and labels as this graph.
`Edge`	`getEdge(Object fromLabel, Object toLabel)` Returns the edge connecting vertices with the specified labels or `null` if there is no such edge. Throws an exception if either label is `null` or either vertex is absent.
`Vertex`	`getVertex(Object label)` Returns the vertex with the specified label or `null` if there is no such vertex. Throws an exception if the label is `null`.
`int`	`hashCode()` Returns the hash code value for this graph.
`Iterator`	`incidentEdges(Vertex vertex)` Returns an iterator over edges incident to the specified vertex. Throws an exception if the specified vertex is `null` or absent.
`boolean`	`isEmpty()` Returns `true` if this graph contains no vertices.
`Iterator`	`iterator()` Returns an iterator over the labels of the vertices.

Table 14.5   **The Methods for the Class Graph (Continued)**

Graph Interface

Iterator	**neighboringVertices(Vertex vertex)** Returns an iterator over the vertices adjacent to the specified vertex. Throws an exception if the specified vertex is null or absent.
boolean	**removeEdge(Object fromLabel, Object toLabel)** If the graph contains an edge between the specified vertices, then removes the edge and returns true, else returns false. Throws an exception if either label is null or either vertex is absent.
boolean	**removeVertex(Object label)** If this graph contains a vertex with the specified label, then removes the vertex and all edges involving this vertex and returns true, else returns false. Throws an exception if the label is null.
int	**size()** Returns the number of vertices in this graph.
int	**sizeEdges()** Returns the number of edges in this graph.
int	**sizeVertices()** Returns the number of vertices in this graph.
Object[]	**toArray()** Returns an array containing all the labels of the vertices in this graph.
String	**toString()** Returns a string representation of this graph.
Iterator	**vertices()** Returns an iterator over the vertices.

Table 14.6 lists the Vertex methods and Table 14.7 lists the Edge methods.

Table 14.6   **The Vertex Interface**

void	**clearMark()** Unmarks the vertex.
Object	**getLabel()** Returns the vertex's label.
boolean	**isMarked()** Returns true if the vertex is marked, else returns false.
void	**setLabel(Object label, Graph g)** Changes the vertex's label to the specified label. Throws an exception if (1) either the specified label or graph is null or (2) the specified graph already contains another vertex with the specified label.
void	**setMark()** Marks the vertex.
String	**toString()** Returns a string representation of this vertex.

Table 14.7   **The Edge Interface**

void	**clearMark()** Unmarks the edge.
int	**compareTo(Object that)** Returns -1, 0, or 1 depending on whether this edge's label is less than, equal to, or greater than that edge's label, respectively. Throws an exception if that is not an edge or either edge fails to have a comparable label.
boolean	**equals(Object obj)** Returns true if the specified object is an edge whose from vertex and to vertex equal those of this edge, else returns false. (*Note:* This method is useful when edges are stored in collections such as lists.)
Vertex	**getFromVertex()** Returns the edge's source vertex.
Object	**getLabel()** Returns the edge's label.
Vertex	**getToVertex()** Returns the edge's destination vertex.
double	**getWeight()** Returns the edge's weight. Throws an exception if the edge's label is not a weighable object.
int	**hashCode()** Returns the edge's hash code.
boolean	**isMarked()** Returns true if the edge is marked, else returns false.
void	**setLabel(Object label)** Changes the edges label to the specified label. Throws an exception if the specified label is null.
void	**setMark()** Marks the edge.
void	**setWeight(double weight)** Sets the edge's weight to the specified value.
String	**toString()** Returns a string representation of this edge.

14.9.2   Weights

Because edges can be labeled with any objects, clients must wrap numeric weights in other objects if they wish to weight the edges of a graph. A client can place a weight on an edge as follows:

1. Instantiate a weighable object that contains the desired weight.

2. Use this object as the edge's label when inserting the edge into the graph.

A weight can be either a double or an int. A weighable object must implement the Weighable interface. This interface, defined in the lamborne package, extends the `Comparable` interface with the methods `setWeight` and `getWeight`. Table 14.8 describes these methods.

Table 14.8	The `Weighable` Interface

```
double  getWeight()
          Gets the object's weight.

  void  setWeight (double weight)
          Sets the object's weight.
```

For the convenience of clients, the `lamborne` package also provides a `Weight` class that implements the `Weighable` interface. Here is an example of its use:

```
// Create a graph g with vertices labeled "A" and "B"
<code for that stuff>

// Add an edge with weight 2.5 from vertex "A" to vertex "B"

g.addEdge("A", "B", new Weight(2.5));
```

14.9.3 Implementation

Tables 14.9, 14.10, 14.11, and 14.12 list the responsibilities of the graph classes and the performance of their methods.

Table 14.9	The `Graph` Implementation

	Graph Implementation	Abstract Container	Abstract Graph	Linked Directed Graph	Linked Undirected Graph
	`constructor()`	O(1)	O(1)	O(1)	O(1)
	`constructor(Collection col)`		O(n)	O(n)	O(n)
	`constructor(Iterator iter)`		O(n)	O(n)	O(n)
`void`	`addEdge(Object fromLabel, Object toLabel, Object edgeLabel)`			O(1)	O(1)
`void`	`addVertex(Object label)`		abstract	O(1)	
`void`	`clear()`	O(1)	O(1)		

continued

Table 14.9 The Graph Implementation *(Continued)*

Graph Implementation	Abstract Container	Abstract Graph	Linked Directed Graph	Linked Undirected Graph
void `clearEdgeMarks()`		traverses edges iterator		
void `clearVertexMarks()`		traverses vertices iterator		
Object `clone()`			exercise	
Collection `collectionView()`	based on iterator			
boolean `containsEdge(Object fromLabel, Object toLabel)`		uses `getEdge` method		
boolean `containsVertex(Object label)`		$O(1)$		
Iterator `edges()`		abstract	$O(1)$	$O(1)$
boolean `equals(Object other)`		exercise		
Edge `getEdge(Object fromLabel, Object toLabel)`		abstract	$O(m/n)$	
Vertex `getVertex(Object label)`		$O(1)$		
int `hashCode()`	traverses iterator	exercise		
Iterator `incidentEdges(Vertex vertex)`			$O(1)$	
boolean `isEmpty()`	uses size method			
Iterator `iterator`	abstract	$O(1)$		
Iterator `neighboringVertices(Vertex vertex)`			$O(1)$	
boolean `removeEdge(Object fromLabel, Object toLabel)`			$O(m/n)$	$O(m/n)$
boolean `removeVertex(Object label)`			$O(\max(m,n))$	$O(\max(m,n))$
int `size()`	$O(1)$			
int `sizeEdges()`		$O(1)$		
int `sizeVertices()`		$O(1)$		
Object[] `toArray()`	traverses iterator			
String `toString()`	traverses iterator	traverses vertices and edges iterators		
Iterator `vertices()`		$O(1)$		

Table 14.10 **The `Vertex` Implementation**

Vertex Implementation		Abstract Vertex	Linked Vertex
	constructor (Object label)	O(1)	O(1)
void	clearMark()	O(1)	
Object	getLabel()	O(1)	
boolean	isMarked()	O(1)	
void	setLabel(Object label)	O(1)	
void	setMark()	O(1)	
String	toString()	O(1)	

Protected Methods Needed by LinkedVertex to Support LinkedDirectedGraph

void	addEdgeTo(LinkedVertex toVertex, Object edgeLabel)	O(m/n)
void	addEdgeTo(LinkedVertex toVertex, GraphSubEdge subEdge)	O(m/n)
GraphEdge	getEdgeTo(LinkedVertex toVertex)	O(m/n)
Iterator	incidentEdges()	O(1)
Iterator	neighboringVertices()	O(1)
boolean	removeEdgeTo(LinkedVertex toVertex)	O(m/n)

Table 14.11 **The `Edge` Implementation**

Edge Implementation		GraphEdge
	constructor (Vertex from, Vertex to)	O(1)
	constructor (Vertex from, Vertex to, Object label)	O(1)
	constructor (Vertex from, Vertex to, GraphSubEdge subEdge)	O(1)
void	clearMark()	O(1)
int	compareTo (Object that)	O(1)
boolean	equals (Object obj)	O(1)
Vertex	getFromVertex()	O(1)
Object	getLabel()	O(1)
Vertex	getToVertex()	O(1)
double	getWeight()	O(1)
int	hashCode()	O(1)
boolean	isMarked()	O(1)
void	setLabel(Object label)	O(1)

continued

Table 14.11   **The Edge Implementation** *(Continued)*

Edge Implementation		GraphEdge
void	setMark()	O(1)
void	setWeight(double weight)	O(1)
String	toString	O(1)

Table 14.12   **The Weighable Implementation**

Weighable Implementation		Weight
	constructor()	O(1)
	constructor (double weight)	O(1)
int	compareTo(Object obj)	O(1)
boolean	equals(Object obj)	O(1)
double	getWeight()	O(1)
void	setWeight(double weight)	O(1)
String	toString()	O(1)

Here is a short tester program that illustrates the use of the graph classes:

```
1 import lamborne.*;
2 import java.util*;
3
4 public class GraphTest{
5
6    public static void main(String[] args){
7
8       // Create a directed graph using an adjacency list
9       Graph g = new LinkedDirectedGraph();
10
11      // Add vertices labeled A, B, and C to the graph and print it
12      g.addVertex ("A");
13      g.addVertex ("B");
14      g.addVertex ("C");
15      System.out.println(g);
16
17      // Insert edges with weight 2.5 and print the graph
18      g.addEdge ("A", "B", new Weight(2.5));
19      g.addEdge ("B", "C", new Weight(2.5));
20      g.addEdge ("C", "B", new Weight(2.5));
21      System.out.println(g);
22
23      // Mark all the vertices
24      Iterator vertices = g.vertices();
25      while (vertices.hasNext())
```

Continued

Continued

```
26              ((GraphVertex)vertices.next()).setMark();
27
28         // Print the vertices adjacent to vertex B
29         GraphVertex v = g.getVertex("B");
30         Iterator BNeighbors = g.neighboringVertices(v);
31         while (BNeighbors.hasNext())
32            System.out.println(BNeighbors.next());
33
34         // Print the edges out of vertex B
35         Iterator BEdges = g.incidentEdges(v);
36         while (BEdges.hasNext())
37            System.out.println(BEdges.next());
38      }
39 }
```

14.9.4 A Note on Performance

Specific algorithms can be implemented much more efficiently by ignoring the Graph class and working directly with adjacency lists and adjacency matrices. However, using the Graph class does make life easier for the application programmer, which is often the most important consideration.

14.10 Case Study: Testing Graph Algorithms

14.10.1 Request

Write a program that allows the user to test some graph processing algorithms.

14.10.2 Analysis

The program allows the user to enter a description of the graph's vertices and edges and to select whether the graph is directed or undirected. The program also allows the user to enter the label of a starting vertex for certain tests. The user selects a button to

- Find the minimum spanning tree from the start vertex
- Determine the single-source shortest paths
- Perform a topological sort

When the user selects a button, the program attempts to build a graph with the inputs. If the inputs generate a valid graph, the program computes and displays a result. Otherwise, the program displays an error message and waits for the user's input. Figure 14.15 shows a shot of the interface. The string "a>b:1" means that there is an edge with weight 1 connecting vertices a and b.

Figure 14.15   **The user interface for the graph tester program**

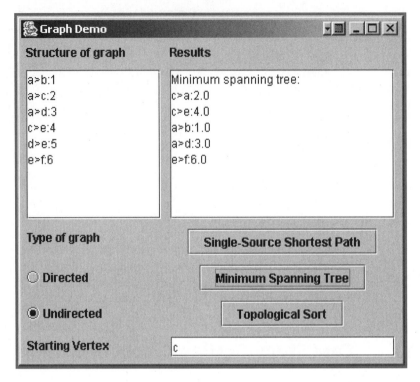

The program consists of two main classes: `GraphDemoView` and `GraphDemo Model`. As usual, the view class handles interaction with the user, whereas the model class represents the data structure and performs the primary computations. We now develop portions of these classes and leave their completion as an exercise.

14.10.3   The Class `GraphDemoView`

The setup of the window objects is straightforward. When the user selects a button, the method `getInputData` sends a message to the model with the text from the input fields. This message returns `true` or `false`, indicating either a legitimate graph or a poorly formed graph.

If the model is able to build a graph from the input, another message is sent to the model to perform the desired task. The interface then displays the results. Table 14.13 presents the public methods that the model provides to the view.

Table 14.13   The Public Methods of the Class `GraphDemoModel`

Method	What It Does
`void createGraph(String rep, boolean directed, String startLabel)`	Attempts to create a graph with string representation `rep`. `directed` indicates whether the graph is directed or undirected. `startLabel` is the label of the starting vertex.
`boolean validGraph()`	Returns `true` if a valid graph and start label exist and `false` otherwise.
`List getMinimumSpanTree()`	*Preconditions:* The graph is valid and is undirected. Returns a list containing the edges in the minimum spanning tree for the graph.
`List getSortedVertices()`	*Preconditions:* The graph is valid. Returns a list of vertices representing a topological order of vertices in the graph.
`public Object[][] getSingleShortestPaths()`	*Preconditions:* The graph is valid. Returns a two-dimensional array of *N* rows and three columns, where *N* is the number of vertices. The first column contains the vertices. The second column contains the distance from the start vertex to this vertex. The third column contains the path from the start vertex to this vertex.

Here is a complete listing of the class `GraphDemoView`:

```
 1 import java.awt.*;
 2 import javax.swing.*;
 3 import java.awt.event.*;
 4 import lamborne.*;
 5 import java.util.*;
 6 import ioutil.*;
 7
 8 /* Format of input in text area
 9    Each line of input should consist of one of the three following:
10       1) blank line
11       2) vertexLabel
12       3) vertexLabel1>vertexLabel2:weight
13    Meaning:
14       1) blank lines are ignored
15       2) a vertex with the indicated label is added to the graph
16          unless one is already present, in which case the line is
17          ignored
18       3) an edge from vertexLabel1 to vertexLabel2, with the indicated
```

Continued

Continued

```
19          weight, is added; vertices with the indicated labels are added
20          unless they are already present; the line is ignored if there is
21          already an edge from vertexLabel1 to vertexLabel2
22  */
23
24  public class GraphDemoView extends JFrame{
25
26     //////////////////////////////////////////////////////// main
27
28     public static void main (String[] args){
29        JFrame theFrame = new GraphDemoView();
30        theFrame.setSize (400, 350);
31        theFrame.setVisible (true);
32     }
33
34     //////////////////////////////////////////////////////// Model
35
36     GraphDemoModel model;
37
38     //////////////////////////////////////////////////////// View
39
40     // Create controls
41     private JLabel        lbStructure     = new JLabel("Structure of graph");
42     private JLabel        lbResults       = new JLabel("Results");
43     private JTextArea     taStructure     = new JTextArea("");
44     private JTextArea     taResults       = new JTextArea("");
45     private JLabel        lbType          = new JLabel("Type of graph");
46     private JRadioButton  rbDirected      = new JRadioButton("Directed");
47     private JRadioButton  rbUndirected    = new JRadioButton("Undirected");
48     private JLabel        lbStartVertex   = new JLabel("Starting Vertex");
49     private JTextField    tfStartVertex   = new JTextField("");
50     private JButton       btShortestPath  = new JButton(
51                                             "Single-Source Shortest Path");
52     private JButton       btMinSpanTree   = new JButton(
53                                             "Minimum Spanning Tree");
54     private JButton       btTopoSort      = new JButton("Topological Sort");
55
56     public GraphDemoView(){
57
58        // Set title and model. Initialize controls.
59        setTitle("Graph Demo");
60        model = new GraphDemoModel();
61        taResults.setEditable(false);
62
63        // Select the default radio button and add buttons to a group
64        rbDirected.setSelected(true);
65        ButtonGroup bgGraphType = new ButtonGroup();
66        bgGraphType.add(rbDirected);
67        bgGraphType.add(rbUndirected);
68
69        // Create container and layout
70        Container contentPane = getContentPane();
71        EasyGridLayout layout = new EasyGridLayout();
72        contentPane.setLayout (layout);
73
74        // Set constraints
```

Continued

Continued

```
 75        JScrollPane spStructure = new JScrollPane(taStructure);
 76        JScrollPane spResults = new JScrollPane(taResults);
 77        layout.setConstraints(lbStructure    ,1,1,1,1);
 78        layout.setConstraints(lbResults      ,1,2,1,1);
 79        layout.setConstraints(spStructure    ,2,1,1,1);
 80        layout.setConstraints(spResults      ,2,2,1,1);
 81        layout.setConstraints(lbType         ,3,1,1,1);
 82        layout.setConstraints(rbDirected     ,4,1,1,1);
 83        layout.setConstraints(rbUndirected   ,5,1,1,1);
 84        layout.setConstraints(lbStartVertex  ,6,1,1,1);
 85        layout.setConstraints(tfStartVertex  ,6,2,1,1);
 86        layout.setConstraints(btShortestPath ,3,2,1,1);
 87        layout.setConstraints(btMinSpanTree  ,4,2,1,1);
 88        layout.setConstraints(btTopoSort     ,5,2,1,1);
 89
 90     // Add controls to container
 91     contentPane.add(lbStructure);
 92     contentPane.add(lbResults);
 93     contentPane.add(spStructure);
 94     contentPane.add(spResults);
 95     contentPane.add(lbType);
 96     contentPane.add(rbDirected);
 97     contentPane.add(rbUndirected);
 98     contentPane.add(lbStartVertex);
 99     contentPane.add(tfStartVertex);
100     contentPane.add(btShortestPath);
101     contentPane.add(btMinSpanTree);
102     contentPane.add(btTopoSort);
103
104     // Specify listeners
105     btShortestPath.addActionListener(new MyButtonListener());
106     btMinSpanTree.addActionListener(new MyButtonListener());
107     btTopoSort.addActionListener(new MyButtonListener());
108     addWindowListener(new MyWindowAdapter());
109   }
110
111   ///////////////////////////////////////////////////// Controller
112
113   private void messageBox(String str){
114     new MessageBox(this, str, 350, 150);
115   }
116
117   private void getInputData(){
118     String graphString = taStructure.getText().trim();
119     model.createGraph(graphString, rbDirected.isSelected());
120   }
121
122   private void findShortestPath(String startLabel){
123     Object[][] paths = model.getSingleShortestPaths(startLabel);
124     if (paths == null){
125       messageBox ("Starting vertex missing or not in graph");
126       return;
127     }
128     taResults.setText("");
129     for (int row = 0; row < paths.length; row++){
```

Continued

Continued

```
130              Vertex toVert = (Vertex)paths[row][0];
131              double distance = ((Double)paths[row][1]).doubleValue();
132              Vertex pred = (Vertex)paths[row][2];
133              String str = toVert.toString() + ":" + distance;
134              if (pred != null)
135                 str = str + " from pred " + pred.toString();
136              str = str + "\n";
137              taResults.append(str);
138          }
139      }
140
141      private void findMinSpanTree(String startLabel){
142          java.util.List edges = model.getMinimumSpanTree(startLabel);
143          if (edges == null){
144              messageBox ("Starting vertex missing or not in graph");
145              return;
146          }
147          taResults.setText("Minimum spanning tree:\n");
148          for (int i = 0; i < edges.size(); i++){
149              GraphEdge e = (GraphEdge)edges.get(i);
150              taResults.append(toString(e) + "\n");
151          }
152      }
153
154      private String toString(GraphEdge e){
155          Vertex fv = e.getFromVertex();
156          Vertex tv = e.getToVertex();
157          double weight = e.getWeight();
158          return fv.toString() + ">" +
159                  tv.toString() + ":" +
160                  weight;
161      }
162
163      private void topologicalSort(){
164          if (!rbDirected.isSelected())
165              messageBox(
166              "Error: topological sorting \nrequires a directed graph");
167          else{
168              java.util.List vertices = model.getSortedVertices();
169              taResults.setText("Topological order of vertices:\n");
170              Iterator iter = vertices.iterator();
171              while (iter.hasNext()){
172                  Vertex v = (Vertex)(iter.next());
173                  taResults.append(v.toString() + "\n");
174              }
175          }
176      }
177
178      // Button action listener
179      private class MyButtonListener implements ActionListener{
180          public void actionPerformed (ActionEvent event){
181              getInputData();
182              if (! model.graphValid())
183                  messageBox (model.graphStatus());
184              else{
185                  String startLabel = tfStartVertex.getText().trim();
```

Continued

```
186                Object buttonObj = event.getSource();
187                if (buttonObj == btShortestPath)
188                    findShortestPath(startLabel);
189                else if (buttonObj == btMinSpanTree)
190                    findMinSpanTree(startLabel);
191                else if (buttonObj == btTopoSort)
192                    topologicalSort();
193            }
194        }
195    }
196
197    // Window listener
198    private class MyWindowAdapter extends WindowAdapter{
199        public void windowClosing (WindowEvent e){
200            System.exit(0);
201        }
202    }
203 }
```

14.10.4   The Class `GraphDemoModel`

The class `GraphDemoModel` maintains three instance variables: a `String` for the start label, a `Graph` for the graph, and a `boolean` for the graph's validity. The method `createGraph` initializes these variables when creating a graph. The method receives a string representation of the graph from the view. In this representation, each edge is on one line and has the form

```
<to label>><from label>:<edge weight>
```

where the labels are strings of letters or digits and the edge weight is a string representing an integer or a double.

The delimiters that separate the words are `">"`, `":"`, and `"\n"`. It is thus convenient to use a `StringTokenizer` to implement the method. The method must check for well-formed representations of the edges, whether or not a vertex or an edge appears twice in the representation, and so forth. Here is the code:

```
public void createGraph(String rep,
                        boolean directed){
    if (directed)
        graph = new LinkedDirectedGraph();
    else
        graph = new LinkedUndirectedGraph();
    if (rep.equals("")){
        graphStatus = "No graph";
        return;
    }
    StringTokenizer lines = new StringTokenizer(rep, "\n");
    while (lines.hasMoreTokens()){
        String line = lines.nextToken().trim();
```

Continued

Continued

```
        if (line.equals("")) continue;
        StringTokenizer words = new StringTokenizer(line, ">:");
        if (words.countTokens() == 1){
           // One token in line, assume it is a vertex
           String label = words.nextToken();
           if (! graph.containsVertex(label))
              graph.addVertex(label);
           continue;
        }else if (words.countTokens() != 3){
           // Wrong number of tokens in line. Out of here
           graphStatus = "Wrong number of tokens in line: '"
                         + line + "'";
           return;
        }
        // Three tokens in line, assume it is vertex>vertex:weight
        String label1 = words.nextToken();
        String label2 = words.nextToken();
        String weightStr = words.nextToken();
        double weight = 0;
        try{
           weight = Double.valueOf(weightStr).doubleValue();
        }
        catch(NumberFormatException e){
           graphStatus = "Third token in line must be a number: '"
                         + line + "'";
           return;
        }
        if (! graph.containsVertex(label1))
           graph.addVertex(label1);
        if (! graph.containsVertex(label2))
           graph.addVertex(label2);
        if (! graph.containsEdge(label1, label2))
           graph.addEdge(label1, label2, new Weight(weight));
     }
     if (graph.isEmpty())
        graphStatus = "No graph";
     else
        graphStatus = "Graph valid";
}
```

The method `getSortedVertices`, which returns a list representing a topological sort of the graph, could be implemented using the pseudocode discussed earlier. However, we perform the actual sort using a `static` method `sort`. This method can then be integrated directly into the graph ADT, which we ask you to do in the exercises. We need two `static` methods, including the `private` helper method `dfs`. Here is the code for all three methods:

```
public List getSortedVertices(){
   return GraphDemoModel.sort(graph);
}

public static List sort (Graph g){
```

Continued

Continued

```
      List list = new LinkedList();
      g.clearVertexMarks();
      Iterator vertices = g.vertices();
      while (vertices.hasNext()){
         Vertex v = (Vertex)vertices.next();
         if (! v.isMarked())
            dfs (g, v, list);
      }
      return list;
   }

   private static void dfs (Graph g, Vertex v, List list) {
      v.setMark();
      Iterator neighbors = g.neighboringVertices(v);
      while (neighbors.hasNext()){
         Vertex w = (Vertex)neighbors.next();
         if (! w.isMarked())
            dfs (g, w, list);
      }
      list.add (0, v);     // insert at beginning of list
   }
```

The methods `getMinimumSpanningTree` and `getSingleShortest Paths` also call `static` methods and are left as exercises.

Exercises 14.10

1. The adjacency matrix representation of a directed graph uses the class `MatrixDirectedGraph`. Implement and test this class.

2. The adjacency matrix representation of an undirected graph uses the class `MatrixUndirectedGraph`. Implement and test this class.

3. Complete the case study program of this chapter.

4. Implement and test a `static` method `sort`, which performs a topological sort of a graph.

5. Implement and test a `static` method for `getMinimumSpanningTree` for directed graphs.

6. Implement and test a `static` method for `getSingleShortestPaths` for directed graphs.

KEY TERMS

adjacency list	depth-first search tree	path
adjacency matrix	depth-first traversal	simple path
all-pairs shortest path	directed graph	single shortest path
breadth-first traversal	directed acyclic graph (DAG)	sparse graph
complete graph		subgraph
connected component	edge	topological sort
connected graph	minimum spanning forest	undirected graph
cycle	minimum spanning tree	vertex
dense graph	neighbor	weighted graph

CHAPTER SUMMARY

A graph is a nonlinear collection in which each item may have zero or more predecessors and successors. Graphs have many applications. They are often used to represent networks of items that can be connected by various paths.

A graph consists of one or more vertices (items) connected by one or more edges. One vertex is adjacent to another vertex if there is an edge connecting the two vertices. These two vertices are also called neighbors. A path is a sequence of edges that allows one vertex to be reached from another vertex in a graph. A vertex is reachable from another vertex if and only if there is a path between the two. The length of a path is the number of edges on the path. A graph is connected if there is a path from each vertex to every other vertex. A graph is complete if there is an edge from each vertex to every other vertex.

A subgraph consists of a subset of a graph's vertices and a subset of its edges. A connected component is a subgraph consisting of the set of vertices that are reachable from a given vertex.

Directed graphs allow travel along an edge in just one direction, whereas undirected graphs allow two-way travel. Edges can be labeled with weights, which indicate the cost of traveling along them.

Graphs have two common implementations. One implementation uses an adjacency matrix. For a graph with N vertices, this matrix is a two-dimensional array A with N rows and N columns. The matrix cell $A[i][j]$ contains 1 if there is an edge from vertex i to vertex j in the graph. Otherwise, there is no edge and that cell contains 0. The adjacency matrix implementation wastes memory if not all the vertices are connected.

Another implementation uses an adjacency list. The adjacency list for the graph with N vertices is an array of N linked lists. The ith linked list contains a node for vertex j if and only if there is an edge from vertex i to vertex j.

The adjacency matrix always requires N^2 cells, no matter how many edges connect the vertices. Thus, the only case in which no cells are wasted is that of a complete graph. By contrast, the adjacency list requires an array of N pointers and a number of nodes equal to twice the number of edges in the case of an undirected graph. There are various trade-offs in the run times of graph operations with the two implementations.

There are many commonly used graph algorithms. Among them are the breadth-first traversal, the depth-first traversal, computing the shortest path between two vertices, computing a minimum spanning tree, and a topological sort.

REVIEW QUESTIONS

1. Describe two common applications of graphs.
2. How does a graph differ from a tree?
3. What is a connected graph?
4. What is a complete graph?
5. Why would you attach weights to edges in a graph?
6. Describe the adjacency matrix implementation of a graph.
7. Describe the adjacency list implementation of a graph.
8. Compare the memory costs of the adjacency matrix implementation and the adjacency list implementation.
9. What are a spanning tree and a spanning forest?

CHAPTER 15

Multithreading, Networks, and Client/Server Programming

Thus far in this book, we have explored ways of structuring programs in terms of multiple cooperating algorithms and data structures. But there is another common strategy for decomposing a program in modern computer systems. This strategy involves the use of multiple *threads.* Threads represent processes that can run concurrently to solve a problem. They can be organized in a system of *clients* and *servers.* Client and server threads can run concurrently on a single computer or can be distributed across several computers that are linked in a network. This chapter offers an introduction to multithreading, networks, and client/server programming. We provide just enough material to get you started with these topics; more complete surveys are available in more advanced computer science courses.

15.1 Threads and Processes

You are well aware that an algorithm describes a computational process that runs to completion. You are also aware that a process consumes resources, such as CPU cycles and memory. Until now, we have associated an algorithm or a program with a single process, and we have assumed that this process runs on a single computer. However, it does not follow from these facts that your program's process is the only one that runs on your computer or that your program could not describe several processes that could run concurrently on your computer or on several networked computers. The following historical summary suggests that the contrary is the case:

Time-sharing systems: In the late 1950s and early 1960s, computer scientists developed the first time-sharing operating systems. These systems allowed several programs to run concurrently on a single computer. Instead of giving their programs to a human scheduler to run one after the other on a single machine, users logged into the computer via remote terminals. They then ran their programs and had the illusion, if the system performed well, of having sole possession of the machine's resources (CPU, disk drives, printer, etc.). Behind the scenes, the operating system created processes for these programs, gave each process a turn at the CPU and other resources, and performed all of the work of scheduling, saving state during context switches, and so forth. Time-sharing systems are still in widespread use in the form of Web servers, file servers, and other kinds of servers on networked systems.

Multiprocessing systems: One feature of most time-sharing systems allows a single user to run one program and then return to the operating system to run another program before the first program is finished. The concept of a single user running several programs at once was extended to desktop microcomputers in the late 1980s, when these machines became more powerful. For example, the Macintosh Multi-Finder allowed a user to run a word processor, a spreadsheet, and the Finder (the file browser) concurrently and to switch from one application to the other by selecting an application's window. Users of stand-alone PCs now take this capability for granted. A related development was the ability of a program to start another program by "forking" or creating a new process. For example, a word processor might do this to print a document in the background, while the user is staring at the window thinking about the next words to type.

Networked systems: The late 1980s and early 1990s saw the rise of networked systems. Now the processes associated with a single program or with several programs were distributed across several CPUs linked by high-speed communication lines. Thus, for example, the Web browser that appears to be running on my machine is actually making requests as a client to a Web server application that runs on a multiuser machine at the local Internet service provider. The problems of scheduling and running processes are more complex on a networked system, but the basic ideas have not changed.

15.1.1 Threads

Whether they are networked or stand-alone machines, most modern computers use threads to represent processes. The Java Virtual Machine already runs several threads even if the programmer does not explicitly implement any. For example, the garbage collector is a thread, and the main application program runs as a thread.

In Java, a thread is an object like any other in that it can hold data, be sent messages, be stored in data structures, and be passed as parameters to methods. However, a thread can also be executed as a process. To do this, the thread's class must implement a `run` method. During its lifetime, a thread can be in various states. Figure 15.1 shows some of the states in the lifetime of a Java thread.

Figure 15.1   **States in the lifetime of a thread**

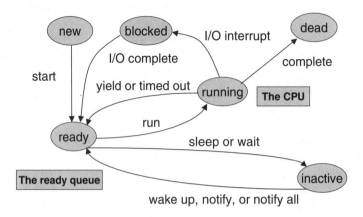

When it is created, a thread remains inactive until someone sends it the `start` message. The receipt of this message makes the thread *ready* and places it on the *ready queue.* The thread's `run` method is also activated, but the thread must wait its turn on the ready queue for access to the CPU. After the thread gets access to the CPU and runs some instructions in its `run` method, the thread can lose the CPU in several ways:

1. **Time-out:** Most computers running Java programs automatically time out a running thread every few milliseconds. This process, also known as *time slicing,* has the effect of sending the running thread to the rear of the ready queue. The thread at the front of the ready queue is then dequeued and given access to the CPU.

2. **Sleep:** A thread can be put to sleep for a given number of milliseconds. When the thread wakes up, it goes to the rear of the ready queue.

3. **Block:** A thread can wait for some event to occur. Examples of such events are user inputs or signals that another thread is done with a critical task. When a blocked thread is notified that an event has occurred, it goes to the rear of the ready queue.

When a thread gives up the CPU, the computer saves its state so that when it returns to the CPU, its `run` method can pick up where it left off. When the run method has executed its last instruction, the thread dies as a process but continues to exist as an object.

There are two common ways to create threads:

1. Extend the `Thread` class and instantiate the new class.

2. Implement the `Runnable` interface and a `run` method. Then instantiate the new class and wrap it in a new instance of the `Thread` class.

The following code segment shows both ways of creating threads and starting them.

```
MyThreadClass process1 = new MyThreadClass();

MyRunnableClass process2 = new Thread(new MyRunnableClass());

process1.start();
process2.start();
```

Table 15.1 lists some important `Thread` methods.

Table 15.1 Some Thread Methods

Thread Method	What It Does
`Thread()`	Constructor.
`Thread(String name)`	Constructor.
`Thread(Runnable target)`	Constructor.
`Thread(Runnable target, String name)`	Constructor.
`static Thread currentThread()`	Returns the currently running thread.
`boolean isAlive()`	Returns `true` if the thread's `run` method has not completed or `false` otherwise.
`String getName()`	Returns the name of the thread (by default, "Thread" + number).
`void run()`	Code for the thread to execute when running.
`void setName(String name)`	Modifies the thread's name.
`void sleep(long millis)`	Tells the thread to become inactive for `millis` milliseconds.
`void start()`	Puts the thread in the ready queue and calls its `run` method.
`static void yield()`	Tells the thread to give up the CPU and go to the ready queue.

We now consider some example programs that illustrate the behavior of threads.

15.1.2 Sleeping Threads

In our first example, we develop a program that allows the user to start several threads. Each thread does not do much when started; it simply goes to sleep for a random number of milliseconds and terminates on waking up. The interface allows the user to specify the number of threads to run and the maximum sleep time. When a thread is started, it sends a message identifying itself and its sleep time to the interface; then it goes to sleep. When a thread wakes up, it sends another message identifying itself to the interface. A snapshot of the interface is shown in Figure 15.2.

Figure 15.2   **The interface for the sleeping threads program**

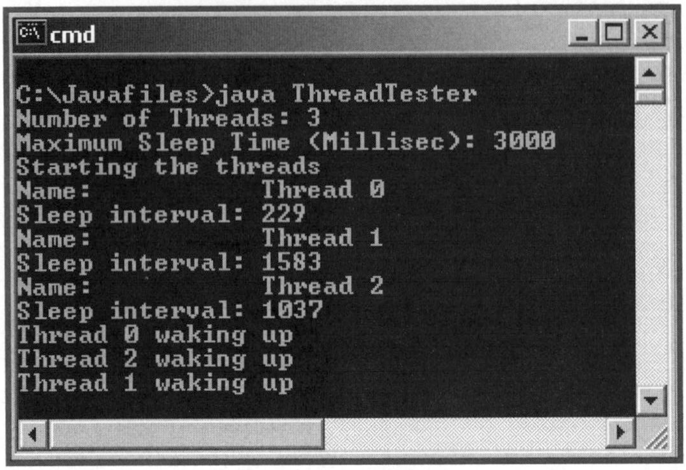

The following points can be concluded from the data in the figure:

1. When a thread goes to sleep, the next thread has an opportunity to acquire the CPU and display its information in the view.

2. The threads do not necessarily wake up in the order in which they were started. The size of the sleep interval determines this order. In Figure 15.2, thread 0 has the shortest sleep time, so it wakes up first. Thread 2 wakes up before thread 1 because thread 2 has a shorter sleep interval.

The program consists of two classes. `ThreadTester` represents the interface. `SleepyThread`, a subclass of `Thread`, represents a thread. Here is the code for the class `ThreadTester`:

```
 1 import ioutil.KeyboardReader;
 2
 3 public class ThreadTester{
 4
 5    public static void main (String args[]){
 6       KeyboardReader reader = new KeyboardReader();
 7       System.out.print("Number of Threads: ");
 8       int numThreads = reader.readInt();                      // Obtain # threads
 9       System.out.print("Maximum Sleep Time (Millisec): ");
10       int sleepMax = reader.readInt();                        // Obtain sleep max
11
12       SleepyThread [] threads = new SleepyThread[numThreads]; // Create array
13       for (int i = 0; i < numThreads; i++)
14          threads[i] = new SleepyThread(i, sleepMax);     // Create the threads
15       System.out.println("Starting the threads");
16
17       for (int i = 0; i < numThreads; i++)                         // Start them up
18          threads[i].start();
19    }
20 }
```

Here is the code for the class `SleepyThread`:

```
 1 public class SleepyThread extends Thread{
 2
 3    private int sleepInterval;
 4
 5    public SleepyThread(int number, int sleepMax){
 6       super ("Thread " + number);
 7       sleepInterval = (int) (Math.random() * sleepMax);
 8    }
 9
10    public void run(){
11       System.out.println("Name:            " +        // Identify myself
12                         getName() +
13                         "\nSleep interval: " +
14                         sleepInterval);
15
16       try{
17          sleep(sleepInterval);                        // I sleep for a bit
18       }
19       catch(InterruptedException e){
20          System.out.println(e.toString());
21       }
22
23       System.out.println(getName() + " waking up");     // I'm awake
24    }
25 }
```

Note that the method `sleep` *(line 17)* must be invoked within a `try-catch` statement.

15.1.3   Producer, Consumer, and Synchronization

In the previous example, the threads ran independently and did not interact. However, there are many applications in which threads interact by sharing data. One of these is the ***producer/consumer relationship.*** Think of an assembly line in a factory. The person (or robot) at the beginning of the line produces an item that is then ready for access by the next person on the line. This person then processes the item in some way until it is ready for the next person and so on. Three requirements must be met for the assembly line to function properly:

1. A producer must produce each item before a consumer consumes it.

2. Each item must be consumed before the producer produces the next item.

3. A consumer must consume each item just once.

Let us now consider a computer simulation of the producer/consumer relationship. In its simplest form, the relationship has only two threads: a producer and a consumer. They share a single data cell that contains an integer. The producer sleeps for a bit, writes an integer to the shared cell, and generates the next integer to be written, until the integer reaches an upper bound. The consumer sleeps for a bit and reads the integer from the shared cell, until the integer reaches the upper bound. Figure 15.3 shows the interface of this program. The user enters the number of accesses (data items produced and consumed). The output announces that the producer and consumer threads have started up and shows when each thread accesses the shared data.

Figure 15.3   **The interface for the producer/consumer program**

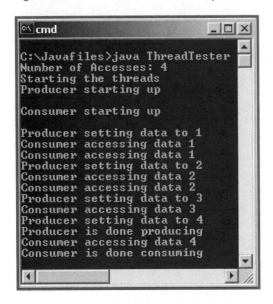 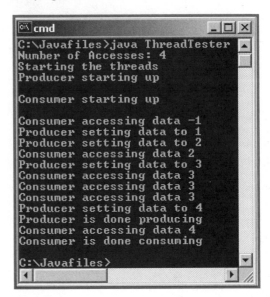

The first run of the program (on the left) shows that data are being produced and consumed in just about the correct order. The only problem is that the consumer makes two accesses to data 1 and data 2. However, some really bad things happen in the second run of the program (on the right):

1. The consumer accesses the shared cell before the producer has written its first datum.

2. The producer then writes two consecutive data (1 and 2) before the consumer has accessed the cell.

3. The consumer accesses data 3 three times.

The producer produces all of its data as expected, but the consumer can access data that are not there, can miss data, and can access the same data more than once. These are known as *synchronization problems.* Before we explain why they occur, we present the essential parts of the program itself, which consists of the four classes in Table 15.2.

Table 15.2   **The Classes in the Producer/Consumer Tester**

Class	Role and Responsibility
ThreadTester	Represents the interface. Creates the shared cell and producer and consumer threads and starts the threads.
SharedCell	Represents the shared data, which is an integer initially -1.
Producer	Represents the producer process. Repeatedly writes an integer to the cell and increments the integer, until it reaches an upper bound.
Consumer	Represents the consumer process. Repeatedly reads an integer from the cell, until it reaches an upper bound.

The code for class `ThreadTester` is similar to the previous example. Here is the code:

```
1 import ioutil.KeyboardReader;
2
3 public class ThreadTester{
4
5    public static final int SLEEP_INTERVAL = 2000;
6
7    public static void main (String args[]){
8       KeyboardReader reader = new KeyboardReader();
9       System.out.print("Number of Accesses: ");
10      int accessCount = reader.readInt();          // Obtain # accesses
11      SharedCell cell = new SharedCell();           // Create shared cell
12      Producer p = new Producer(accessCount, cell); // Create producer
13      Consumer c = new Consumer(accessCount, cell); // Create consumer
14
15      System.out.println("Starting the threads");     // Start 'em up
16      p.start();
17      c.start();
18   }
19 }
```

Here is the code for the class `SharedCell`:

```
1 public class SharedCell{
2
3      private int data;
4
5      public SharedCell(){
6         data = -1;
7      }
8
9      public void setData(int data){
10        System.out.println(Thread.currentThread().getName() +
11                            " setting data to " + data);
12        this.data = data;
13     }
14
15     public int getData(){
16        System.out.println(Thread.currentThread().getName() +
17                            " accessing data " + data);
18        return data;
19     }
20
21 }
```

Here is the code for the classes `Producer` and `Consumer`:

```
1 public class Producer extends Thread{
2
3    private SharedCell cell;
4    private int accessCount;
5
```

Continued

Continued

```
6      public Producer(int accessCount, SharedCell cell){
7         super ("Producer");
8         this.accessCount = accessCount;
9         this.cell = cell;
10     }
11
12     public void run(){
13        System.out.println(getName() + " starting up\n"); // Identify myself
14
15        for (int i = 1; i <= accessCount; i++){
16           try{
17              sleep((int) (Math.random() * ThreadTester.SLEEP_INTERVAL));
18           }
19           catch(InterruptedException e){
20               System.out.println(e.toString());
21           }
22           cell.setData(i);                    // Produce by setting shared cell
23        }
24
25        System.out.println(getName() + " is done producing");      // Done
26     }
27
28 }
```

```
1 public class Consumer extends Thread{
2
3     private SharedCell cell;
4     private int accessCount;
5
6     public Consumer(int accessCount, SharedCell cell){
7         super ("Consumer");
8         this.accessCount = accessCount;
9         this.cell = cell;;
10     }
11
12     public void run(){
13        System.out.println(getName() + " starting up\n"); // Identify myself
14        int value;
15        do{
16           try{
17              sleep((int) (Math.random() * ThreadTester.SLEEP_INTERVAL));
18           }
19           catch(InterrupedException e){
20               System.out.println(e.toString());
21           }
22           value = cell.getData();        // Consume by accessing shared cell
23        }while (value != accessCount);
24
25        System.out.println(getName() + " is done consuming");      // Done
26     }
27
28 }
```

The cause of the synchronization problems is not hard to spot in this code. On each pass through their main loops, the threads sleep for a random interval of time. Thus, if the consumer thread has a shorter interval than the producer thread on a given cycle, the consumer wakes up sooner and accesses the shared cell before the producer has a chance to write the next datum. Conversely, if the producer thread wakes up sooner, it accesses the shared data before the consumer has a chance to read the previous datum.

Obviously, to solve this problem, we need to synchronize the actions of the producer and consumer threads. In addition to holding data, the shared cell must be in one of two states: writeable or not writeable. The cell is writeable if it has not yet been written to (at startup) or if it has just been read from. The cell is not writeable if it has just been written to. These two conditions can now control the callers of the `setData` and `getData` methods in the `SharedCell` class as follows:

1. While the cell is writeable, the caller of `getData` (the consumer) must wait or suspend activity, until the producer writes a datum. When this happens, the cell becomes not writeable, the caller of `getData` is notified to resume activity, and the data are returned (to the consumer).

2. While the cell is not writeable, the caller of `setData` (the producer) must wait or suspend activity, until the consumer reads a datum. When this happens, the cell becomes writeable, the caller of `setData` is notified to resume activity, and the data are modified (by the producer).

Here is the code that shows the changes to the class `SharedCell`:

```
 1 public class SharedCell{
 2
 3     private int data;
 4     private boolean writeable;
 5
 6     public SharedCell(){
 7         data = -1;
 8         writeable = true;
 9     }
10
11     public synchronized void setData(int data){
12         while (! writeable){              // Producer must wait
13             try{                           // until consumer has
14                 wait();                    // accessed cell
15             }
16             catch(InterruptedException e){
17                 System.out.println(e.toString());
18             }
19         }
20
21         System.out.println(Thread.currentThread().getName() +
22                           " setting data to " + data);
23         this.data = data;
24         writeable = false;
25         notify();                          // Tell consumer to become ready
26     }
27
28     public synchronized int getData(){
29         while (writeable){                               // Consumer must wait
```

Continued

Continued

```
30              try{                                    // until producer has
31                  wait();                             // accessed cell
32              }
33              catch(InterruptedException e){
34                  System.out.println(e.toString());
35              }
36          }
37          System.out.println(Thread.currentThread().getName() +
38                              " accessing data " + data);
39          writeable = true;
40          notify();                                   // Tell producer to become ready
41          return data;
42      }
43
44 }
```

The shared cell object has now become what is known as a ***monitor.*** A monitor is an object on which a process can obtain a ***lock.*** This lock prevents another process from accessing data in the monitor until a condition becomes true. Note two other points about this code:

1. The methods `setData` and `getData` are now declared as `synchronized`. The code in a synchronized method runs as an indivisible unit. This means that the calling thread is not timed out until the method finishes, thus preventing synchronization problems due to time slicing.

2. The methods `wait` and `notify`, respectively, suspend and resume the execution of the calling thread. The method `wait` must be invoked within a `try catch` statement and sends the calling thread into an inactive state. The method `notify` sends the least recently entered thread waiting on this monitor object to the end of the ready queue. The method `notifyAll` sends all such threads to the ready queue.

We have only scratched the surface of the kinds of problems that can arise when programs run several threads. For a thorough discussion of multithreading and concurrent programming, see Stephen J. Hartley, *Concurrent Programming: The Java Language* (New York: Oxford University Press, 1998).

Exercises 15.1

1. Write a program that uses threads to demonstrate time slicing (if that exists on your computer).

2. Modify the program of Exercise 1 so that it shows how much time elapses before a thread is timed out.

3. Redo the producer/consumer program to handle multiple producers and a single consumer. Discuss any problems that might arise due to the presence of multiple producers.

4. Revisit the market simulator case study in Chapter 8. Imagine that the cashiers and customers are independent processes looking to access the queues as shared

resources. Discuss the design of a simulator that uses Java threads to represent these processes.

5. Implement the simulator that you designed in Exercise 4.

15.2   Networks, Servers, and Clients

Clients and servers are applications or processes that can run locally on a single computer or remotely across a network of computers. The tools required are threads, IP addresses, sockets, and file streams.

15.2.1   IP Addresses

Every computer on a network has a unique identifier called an ***IP address*** (IP stands for Internet Protocol). This address can be specified either as an ***IP number*** or as an ***IP name.*** An IP number has the form *ddd.ddd.ddd.ddd,* where each *d* is a digit. For example, the IP number of one author's office computer is 137.113.194.106. Because IP numbers can be difficult to remember, people customarily use an IP name to specify an IP address. This author's IP name is lambertk.

Java represents an IP address with the class `InetAddress`, as defined in the package `java.net`. This class includes a static method that allows the programmer to obtain the IP address of the *local host* (the computer on which the program is currently running). For example, the next program and Figure 15.4 show how to obtain and display the IP address information of the local host:

```
1  // Displays IP address of current host
2
3  import java.net.*;
4
5  public class HostInfo{
6
7     public static void main(String[] args){
8        try{
9           InetAddress ipAddress = InetAddress.getLocalHost();
10          System.out.println("IP address:\n" + ipAddress);
11       }
12       catch(UnknownHostException e){
13          System.out.println("Unknown host:\n" + e.toString());
14       }
15    }
16 }
```

Figure 15.4   **The interface for getting the local host**

Note that the call of the `getLocalHost` method is embedded in a `try-catch` statement *(lines 8-14)*. If the host computer does not happen to have an IP address, the `catch` clause displays the information about the unknown host exception.

Now suppose we know a host's IP name but want to obtain the complete IP information, including the IP number. The next program uses the static method `getBy Name` to accomplish this:

```
1 // Gets the IP address of any machine by name
2
3 import java.net.*;
4 import ioutil.KeyboardReader;
5
6 public class Resolver{
7
8     public static void main(String[] args){
9         System.out.print("Name: ");
10        KeyboardReader reader = new KeyboardReader();
11        try{
12            String name = reader.readLine();
13            InetAddress ipAddress = InetAddress.getByName(name);
14            System.out.println("IP address:\n" + ipAddress);
15        }
16        catch (Exception e){
17            System.out.println("Unknown host:\n" + e.toString());
18        }
19    }
20 }
```

If the user enters the IP name "lambert", the output will be the same as in Figure 15.4. Unlike the method `getLocalHost`, the method `getByName` can search the entire Internet for the IP address of the given name.

Table 15.3 lists the most common `InetAddress` methods.

Table 15.3   **Some `InetAddress` Methods**

InetAddress Method	*What It Does*
`static InetAddress getByName (String host)`	Returns the IP address of a host, given the host's name.
`static InetAddress getLocalHost()`	Returns the local host's IP address.
`String getHostName()`	Returns the host name for this IP address.
`String toString()`	Converts this IP address to a string.

15.2.2   Ports, Servers, Clients

Clients connect to servers via objects known as *ports.* A port serves as a channel through which several clients can exchange data with the same server or with different servers. Ports are usually specified by numbers. Some ports are dedicated to special servers or tasks. For example, until recently, almost every computer reserved port number 13 for a day/time server, which allowed clients to obtain the date and time.

15.2.3   Sockets and a Day/Time Client Program

You can also write a Java program that is a client to a server. To do this, you must use a *socket.* A socket is an object that serves as a communication link between a single server process and a single client process. Several sockets can be created on the same port of a host computer. Figure 15.5 shows the relationships between a host computer, ports, servers, clients, and sockets.

Figure 15.5   **Setup of day/time host and clients**

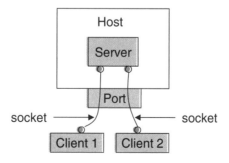

A Java day/time client program uses the class `Socket`, as defined in the package `java.net`. Our example program:

1. Prompts the user for and inputs the IP address of the host *(lines 8–9)*.
2. Opens a socket on port 13 of the host *(line 12)*.
3. Opens a buffered reader on the socket's input stream *(lines 14–15)*.
4. Reads the day/time from the buffered reader *(line 16)*.
5. Displays the day/time *(line 17)*.

Here is a Java program that performs these tasks. Figure 15.6 shows the output.

Figure 15.6   **The interface of the day/time client program**

```
 1 import java.net.*;
 2 import java.io.*;
 3 import ioutil.KeyboardReader;
 4
 5 public class DayTimeClient{
 6
 7    public static void main (String[] args){
 8       KeyboardReader reader = new KeyboardReader();
 9       System.out.print ("Host name or IP number: ");
10       String name = reader.readLine();
11       try{
12          Socket socket = new Socket (name, 13);
13          InputStream is = socket.getInputStream();
14          BufferedReader serverInput = new BufferedReader(
15                                       new InputStreamReader(is));
16          String time = serverInput.readLine();
17          System.out.println ("The time is:\n" + time);
18          socket.close();
19       }catch (Exception e){
20          System.out.println ("Error:\n" + e.toString());
21       }
22    }
23 }
```

The client program assumes that a day/time server is currently running at the given IP address and is attached to the given port. If these assumptions are not satisfied, an exception is thrown and an error message is output.

As you can see, a Java socket is fairly easy to use. It resembles a file object in that the programmer opens it, connects an input stream to it for accessing data, and closes it when finished. Table 15.4 lists several common `Socket` methods.

Table 15.4   **Some `Socket` Methods**

`Socket` *Method*	*What It Does*
`Socket (Strong IPName, int port)`	Creates a stream socket and connects it to the specified port number at the specified IP address.
`void close()`	Closes this socket.
`InetAddress getInetAddress()`	Returns the address to which this socket is connected.
`int getPort()`	Returns the remote port to which this socket is connected.
`InputStream getInputStream()`	Returns an input stream for this socket.
`OutputStream getOutputStream()`	Returns an output stream for this socket.
`String toString()`	Converts this socket to a `String`.

15.2.4   Server Sockets and a Day/Time Server Program

You can also write a day/time server program in Java. A Java day/time server program uses the classes `Socket` and `ServerSocket`, as defined in the package `java.net`. Table 15.5 lists some common methods in this class.

Table 15.5   **Some `ServerSocket` Methods**

`ServerSocket` *Method*	*What It Does*
`ServerSocket (int port)`	Opens a server socket on the specified port.
`Socket accept()`	Listens for a connection to be made to this server socket. When the connection is made, returns the socket for the client.
`void close()`	Closes this server socket.
`InetAddress getInetAddress()`	Returns the local address of this server socket.
`int getLocalPort()`	Returns the port on which this server socket is listening.
`String toString()`	Returns the implementation address and implementation port of this socket as a `String`.

The basic sequence of operations for a day/time server program is:

1. Open a server socket on a port.
2. Wait for a connection from a client.
3. When the connection is made, send the date and time to the client.

A port can be chosen at random or can be specified by a programmer-supplied number. The next program runs a simple day/time server that uses port 13. This server displays information about the host, the port, and the client. Here is the relevant code segment:

```java
1  import java.net.*;
2  import java.io.*;
3  import java.util.*;
4
5  public class DayTimeServer{
6
7      public static void main(String[] args){
8          try{
9              System.out.println ("Start Server");
10             InetAddress localHost = InetAddress.getLocalHost();
11             System.out.println ("Host: " + localHost + "\n");
12             ServerSocket listen = new ServerSocket (13);
13             System.out.println ("Listening on port: " +
14                             listen.getLocalPort() + "\n");
15             Socket client = listen.accept();
16             System.out.println ("Client: " + client.toString() + "\n");
17             PrintStream clientOutput =
18                     new PrintStream(client.getOutputStream(), true);
19             clientOutput.println(new Date());
20             client.close();
21         }catch (Exception e){
22             System.out.println ("Error:\n" + e.toString());
23         }
24     }
25 }
```

Note the following points about this code:

1. The value 13 is passed to the server socket constructor *(line 12)*. This has the effect of opening a server socket on a randomly selected available port. The number of this port is displayed in *lines 13–14*.

2. The `ServerSocket` method `accept` blocks or waits for a client's connection *(line 15)*. This means that the thread in which the code is running (in this case, the main application's thread) becomes inactive until the client connects. When that happens, method `accept` creates and returns a `Socket` object that represents the client's connection, and the server's thread returns to the ready queue. The information about this socket is displayed in *line 16*.

3. The server program then opens a print stream on the client socket's output stream *(lines 17–18)*. These streams support a one-way conversation from server to client.

4. The server writes a `Date` object to the client's output stream and closes the client's socket *(lines 19–20)*.

The server starts when the user clicks its button (Figure 15.7).

Figure 15.7 **Starting the day/time server program**

The client then enters the server's IP name from another window (Figure 15.6). When this happens, the date and time are displayed in the client's window after the server displays the client's information in its own window (Figure 15.8).

Figure 15.8 **The completion of the day/time server program**

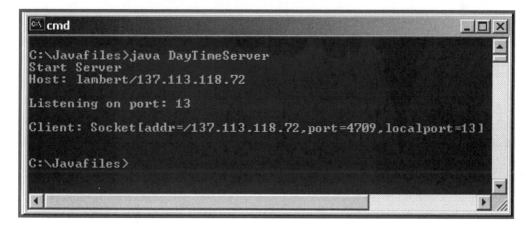

15.2.5 Two-Way Conversations between Clients and Servers

Clients and servers can have two-way conversations using the streams that are connected to sockets. They simply open output streams to "talk" and input streams to "listen." We now modify our example programs to allow the client to reply to the server when it received the day and time.

The day/time client program must now do two extra things:

1. Open an output stream on the server's socket.

2. Send a reply to the server after receiving the day and time.

Here is the code for the modified day/time client:

```
String name = reader.readLine();
int port = portField.getNumber();
try{
    Socket socket = new Socket (name, port);
    InputStream is = socket.getInputStream();
    BufferedReader serverInput =
                new BufferedReader(new InputStreamReader(is));
    PrintStream serverOutput =
                new PrintStream (socket.getOutputStream());
    String time = serverInput.readLine();                    // Get day/time
    System.out.println ("The time is:\n" + time);
    serverOutput.println ("Thanks!");                        // Send reply
    socket.close();
}catch (Exception e){
    System.out.println ("Error:\n" + e.toString());
}
```

The server must create an input stream on the client's socket and read from this stream after writing to its output stream. The client's input is displayed in the server's window as shown in Figure 15.9.

Figure 15.9   **The day/time server displays the client's message**

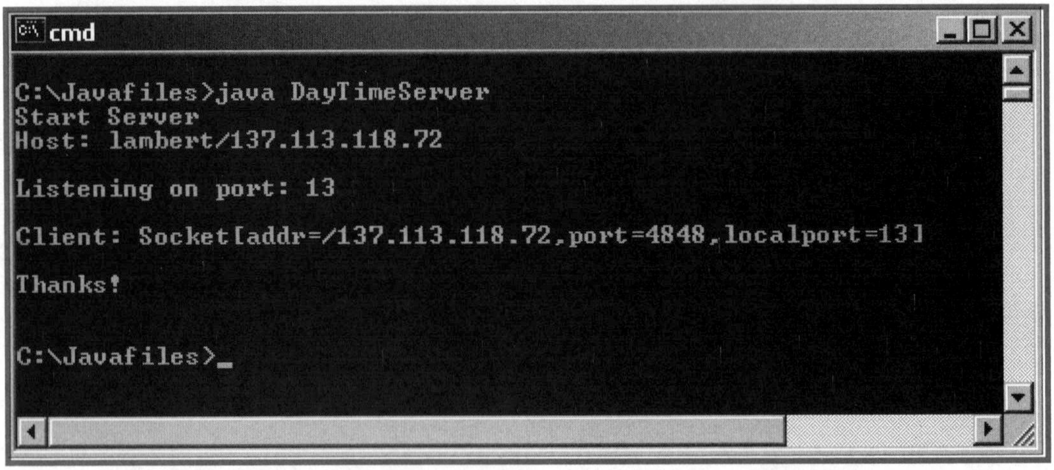

15.2.6   Making the Server Handle Several Clients

Our day/time server opens a server socket and handles a request from just one client. By contrast, most server programs run an infinite command loop to take requests from an arbitrary number of clients. We can modify our code to achieve this by embedding the server's code in a while (true) loop as follows:

```
1 import java.net.*;
2 import java.io.*;
3 import java.util.*;
4
5 public class DayTimeServer{
6
7    public static void main(String[] args){
8       try{
9          System.out.println ("Start Server");
10         InetAddress localHost = InetAddress.getLocalHost();
11         System.out.println ("Host: " + localHost + "\n");
12         ServerSocket listen = new ServerSocket (13);
13         System.out.println ("Listening on port: " +
14                             listen.getLocalPort() + "\n");
15         while (true){
16            Socket client = listen.accept();
17            System.out.println ("Client: " +
18                                client.toString() + "\n");
19            PrintStream clientOutput =
20                    new PrintStream(client.getOutputStream(),
21                                       true);
22            BufferedReader clientInput =
23                    new BufferedReader(new InputStreamReader(
24                                       client.getInputStream()));
25            clientOutput.println(new Date());
26            String s = clientInput.readLine();
27            System.out.println (s + "\n");
28            client.close();
29         }
30      }catch (Exception e){
31         System.out.println ("Error:\n" + e.toString());
32      }
33   }
34 }
```

This modification works nicely to handle multiple requests for the date and time. However, the use of a while (true) loop creates two problems:

1. The main application in which the server runs cannot quit.

2. The main application cannot do anything else but run this server.

15.2.7   Using a Server Daemon

To solve the problems just mentioned, we can package the day/time server in a separate thread that runs concurrently with the main application. This thread, called a *server daemon,* listens for clients and handles their requests. The structure of the modified program is shown in Figure 15.10.

Figure 15.10   **Day/time server daemon**

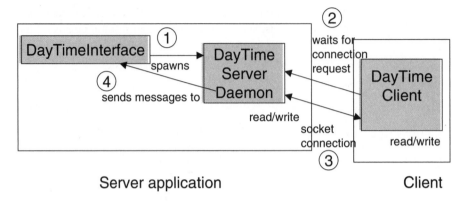

As the figure shows, the main application now (1) spawns a server daemon thread which (2) waits for a connection request from a client. A client then (3) connects to the server via the daemon which (4) sends messages to the application for service.

The main class, `DayTimeInterface`, is now a GUI application. It sets up a text area to display output and starts the server daemon. Here is the code:

```
1 import javax.swing.*;
2 import java.awt.*;
3 import java.awt.event.*;
4
5 public class DayTimeInterface extends JFrame{
6
7     /////////////////////////////////////////// main
8
9     public static void main(String[] args){
10        JFrame frm = new DayTimeInterface();
11        frm.setSize (400, 300);
12        frm.setTitle("Day Time Server");
13        frm.setVisible(true);
14    }
15
16    /////////////////////////////////////////// View
17
18    // Create control
19    private JTextArea output = new JTextArea("");
20
21    public DayTimeInterface(){
22        // Set title
23        setTitle("Main Application");
24
25        // Create container and layout
26        Container contentPane = getContentPane();
27        EasyGridLayout layout = new EasyGridLayout();
28        contentPane.setLayout (layout);
29
30        // Set constraints and add control to container
```

Continued

Continued

```
31            JScrollPane spOutput = new JScrollPane(output);
32            layout.setConstraints(spOutput   , 1,1,1,1);
33            contentPane.add(spOutput);
34
35            // Specify listener
36            addWindowListener(new MyWindowAdapter());
37
38            // Start the server daemon
39            new DayTimeServerDaemon(this);
40        }
41
42    ///////////////////////////////////////////// Controller
43
44    public void println(String text){
45        output.append(text + "\n");
46    }
47
48    // Window listener
49    private class MyWindowAdapter extends WindowAdapter{
50        public void windowClosing (WindowEvent e){
51            System.exit(0);
52        }
53    }
54
55 }
```

Note that this class includes a public method, `println` *(lines 44–46),* which the
server daemon can call to update the view. A reference to the view is passed to the
server daemon when it is instantiated *(line 39).*

The class `DayTimeServerDaemon` extends `Thread` and packages the code
from the previous version of the day/time server in its `run` method. Here is the code:

```
1 import java.net.*;
2 import java.io.*;
3 import java.util.*;
4
5 public class DayTimeServerDaemon extends Thread{
6
7    private DayTimeInterface serverOutput;
8
9    public DayTimeServerDaemon(DayTimeInterface dTI){
10       serverOutput = dTI;
11       start();
12    }
13
14    public void run (){
15       try{
16          serverOutput.println ("Start Server");
17          InetAddress localHost = InetAddress.getLocalHost();
18          serverOutput.println ("Host: " + localHost + "\n");
19          ServerSocket listen = new ServerSocket (13);
20          serverOutput.println ("Listening on port: " +
```

Continued

Continued

```
21                            listen.getLocalPort() + "\n");
22        while (true){
23            Socket client = listen.accept();
24            serverOutput.println ("Client: " +
25                            client.toString() + "\n");
26            PrintStream clientOutput =
27                    new PrintStream(client.getOutputStream(),
28                                    true);
29            BufferedReader clientInput =
30                    new BufferedReader(new InputStreamReader(
31                                    client.getInputStream()));
32            clientOutput.println(new Date());
33            String s = clientInput.readLine();
34            serverOutput.println (s + "\n");
35            client.close();
36        }
37    }catch (Exception e){
38        serverOutput.println ("Error:\n" + e.toString());
39    }
40  }
41
42 }
```

The only remaining issue is that each client still must wait for the daemon to process the request of the current client. For small tasks, such as obtaining the date and time, this delay is not significant. However, for other tasks that might vary in size, many clients might have to wait for one client with a huge task. A means of guaranteeing fair access to the server is described in the next section.

15.2.8   Using a Client Handler

To solve the problem of giving many clients timely access to the server, we relieve the server daemon of the task of handling the client's request and assign it instead to a separate *client handler* thread. Thus, the server daemon simply listens for client connections and dispatches these to new client handler objects. The structure of the modified system is shown in Figure 15.11.

Figure 15.11   **Day/time client handler**

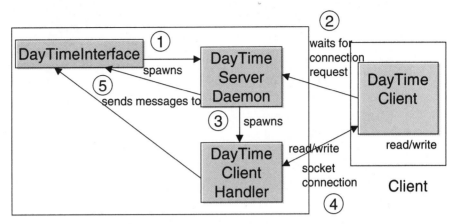

Server application

Here is the code for the classes `DayTimeServerDaemon` and `DayTime ClientHandler`:

```
1 import java.net.*;
2 import java.io.*;
3 import java.util.*;
4
5 public class DayTimeServerDaemon extends Thread{
6
7     private DayTimeInterface serverOutput;
8
9     public DayTimeServerDaemon(DayTimeInterface dTI){
10        serverOutput = dTI;
11        start();
12    }
13
14    public void run (){
15        try{
16            serverOutput.println ("Start Server");
17            InetAddress localHost = InetAddress.getLocalHost();
18            serverOutput.println ("Host: " + localHost + "\n");
19            ServerSocket listen = new ServerSocket (13);
20            serverOutput.println ("Listening on port: " +
21                                    listen.getLocalPort() + "\n");
22            while (true){
23                Socket client = listen.accept();
24                serverOutput.println ("Client: " +
25                                    client.toString() + "\n");
26                new DayTimeClientHandler (serverOutput, client);
27            }
28        }catch (Exception e){
29            serverOutput.println ("Error:\n" + e.toString());
30        }
31    }
32
33 }
```

```
1 import java.net.*;
2 import java.io.*;
3 import java.util.*;
4
5 public class DayTimeClientHandler extends Thread{
6
7    private DayTimeInterface serverOutput;
8    Socket client;
9
10   public DayTimeClientHandler(DayTimeInterface view, Socket clientSocket){
11      serverOutput = view;
12      client = clientSocket;
13      start();
14   }
15
16   public void run (){
17      try{
18         PrintStream clientOutput =
19                     new PrintStream(client.getOutputStream(),
20                                      true);
21         BufferedReader clientInput =
22                     new BufferedReader(new InputStreamReader(
23                                      client.getInputStream()));
24         clientOutput.println(new Date());
25         String s = clientInput.readLine();
26         serverOutput.println (s + "\n");
27         client.close();
28      }catch (Exception e){
29         serverOutput.println ("Error:\n" + e.toString());
30      }
31   }
32
33 }
```

15.2.9   The Model, View, Controller Pattern Revisited

We can generalize from the architecture of the day/time client/server application to the architecture of any client/server application by adding a data model. In this approach, the interface instantiates the model and starts the server daemon. When clients make requests for services, the client handlers send messages to the model to process these requests. This general architecture is shown in Figure 15.12.

Figure 15.12   **The model, view, controller pattern for client/server applications**

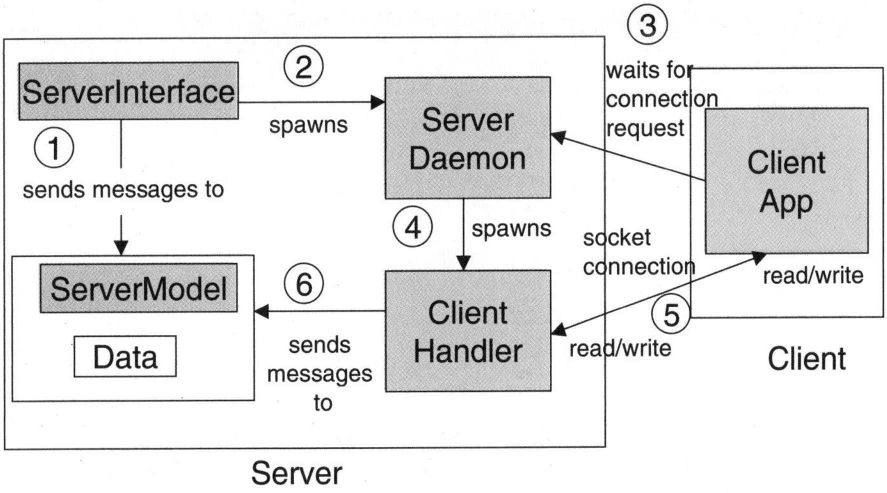

15.3   Case Study: A Campus Directory

In this case study, we implement a simple campus phone directory as a client/server program. The program uses the general architecture discussed earlier.

15.3.1   Request

Write a program that allows several concurrent users to enter names and phone numbers into a directory. The program should also allow users to search the directory by name.

15.3.2   Analysis

There are two interfaces: one for the server and one for the client. The server's interface displays a list of names currently in the directory. A status area displays all of the activity of the client and the server, such as connections, requests for information, and the information returned. The server and clients agree to use port 7777 for their interaction. Figure 15.13 shows the server's interface after a client has connected and added a name and phone number.

Figure 15.13   **The user interface of the directory server**

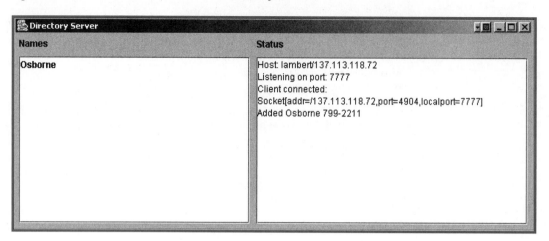

The client's interface has three data entry fields. These fields are for entering the IP name of the server and the name and phone number of a person in the directory. The command buttons of the interface perform the tasks in Table 15.6. Figure 15.14 is a snapshot of the client's interface just after the transaction with the server shown earlier.

Table 15.6   **The Commands in the Directory Client Interface**

Command Button	What It Does
Connect	Attempts to connect to the server using the IP name in the text field.
Find	Attempts to find the number for the person's name in the server's directory.
Add	Adds the name and number to the server's directory.

Figure 15.14   **The interface of a directory client after connecting to the server**

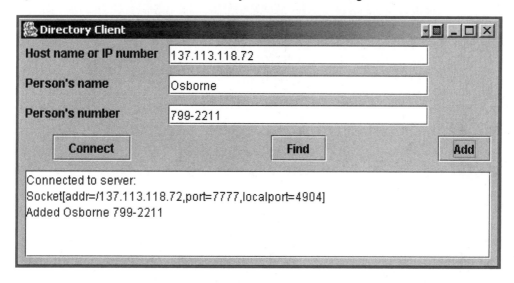

The server application consists of the classes `DirectoryInterface`, `DirectoryModel`, `DirectoryServerDaemon`, and `DirectoryClient Handler`. The client application consists of the class `DirectoryClient`. The responsibilities of these classes are divided in the manner discussed earlier for typical client/server applications.

15.3.3   Design

One important difference between this application and the day/time application discussed earlier is that the day/time client closed its socket as soon as it received the date and time from the server. In the present application, the client might run any number of commands during a session with the server. On the client's side, the command loop is buried in the event-driven interface. On the server's side, the client handler object must now loop for commands until the client has disconnected. This loop takes the form of a `while (true)` loop, whose exits are breaks that run when the input from the client is `null` and when that input equals "EXIT." Here is the pseudocode for this style of client handling:

```
Open the input and output streams on the client's socket
while (true)
    Read the input from the client
    If the input is null or "EXIT"
        break
    else
        Process the input
        Write the output to the client
Close the client's socket
```

Another difference is that the inputs now consist of commands and data. We represent the commands as strings ("ADD," "FIND," and "EXIT"). The data accompanying the "ADD" command are a name and a phone number. The datum accompanying the "FIND" command is only a name. No data accompany the "EXIT" command. The client handler reads these items in the appropriate sequence from the client's input stream, sends messages to the model, and replies to the client with the results.

15.3.4 Implementation

The class `DirectoryInterface` sets up a GUI and passes the model and itself to the server daemon. Here is a complete listing:

```
 1 import java.awt.*;
 2 import javax.swing.*;
 3 import java.awt.event.*;
 4 import ioutil.*;
 5
 6 public class DirectoryInterface extends JFrame{
 7
 8    ///////////////////////////////////////////////////// main
 9
10    public static void main(String[] args){
11       Frame frm = new DirectoryInterface();
12       frm.setSize (500, 300);
13       frm.setVisible(true);
14    }
15
16    ///////////////////////////////////////////////////// Model
17
18    private DirectoryModel model;
19
20    ///////////////////////////////////////////////////// View
21
22    // Create controls
23    private JLabel namesLabel    = new JLabel("Names");
24    private JLabel statusLabel   = new JLabel("Status");
25    private DefaultListModel lmNames = new DefaultListModel();
26    private JList ltNames = new JList(lmNames);
27    private JTextArea statusArea = new JTextArea("");
28
29    public DirectoryInterface(){
30       setTitle("Directory Server");
31
32       // Create container and layout
33       Container contentPane = getContentPane();
34       EasyGridLayout layout = new EasyGridLayout();
35       contentPane.setLayout (layout);
36
37       // Set constraints
38       layout.setConstraints(namesLabel, 1,1,1,1);
39       layout.setConstraints(statusLabel, 1,3,1,1);
40       JScrollPane spName = new JScrollPane(ltNames);
41       layout.setConstraints(spName, 2,1,2,5);
```

Continued

```
42          JScrollPane spStatus = new JScrollPane(statusArea);
43          layout.setConstraints(spStatus, 2,3,4,5);
44
45          // Add controls to container
46          contentPane.add(namesLabel);
47          contentPane.add(statusLabel);
48          contentPane.add(spName);
49          contentPane.add(spStatus);
50
51          // Specify listeners
52          addWindowListener(new MyWindowAdapter());
53
54          model = new DirectoryModel(this);
55          new DirectoryServerDaemon(this, model);
56       }
57
58       public void append(String text){
59          statusArea.append(text);
60       }
61
62       public void displayNames(Object[] names){
63          lmNames.clear();
64          for (int i = 0; i < names.length; i++)
65             lmNames.add(i, (String)names[i]);
66       }
67
68       ///////////////////////////////////////////////////// Controller
69
70       // Window listener
71       private class MyWindowAdapter extends WindowAdapter{
72          public void windowClosing (WindowEvent e){
73             System.exit(0);
74          }
75       }
76
77 }
```

The class `DirectoryServerDaemon` is similar to the server daemon previously developed. One exception is that the daemon receives the model from the interface and passes it onto the client handlers. Another exception is that the daemon opens a server socket on port 7777. The daemon also sends the client's socket information to the interface for display.

The class `DirectoryClient` maintains the input and output streams to the server as instance variables. This allows the client's commands to be decomposed into separate methods that access these variables. Here is the relevant code for `Directory Client` minus the GUI setup and the main method:

```
1    private BufferedReader serverInput;
2    private PrintStream serverOutput;
3
4    ///////////////////////////////////////////////////// Controller
```

Continued

Continued

```
 5
 6    private class ConnectButtonListener implements ActionListener{
 7       public void actionPerformed(ActionEvent event){
 8          String name = ipField.getText();
 9          try{
10             Socket socket = new Socket(name, 7777);
11             serverInput = new BufferedReader(
12                          new InputStreamReader(socket.getInputStream()));
13             serverOutput = new PrintStream(socket.getOutputStream());
14             statusArea.append("Connected to server:\n" + socket + "\n");
15          }catch (Exception e){
16             statusArea.append("Error connecting to server:\n" +
17                               e.toString() + "\n");
18          }
19       }
20    }
21
22    private class AddButtonListener implements ActionListener{
23       public void actionPerformed(ActionEvent event){
24          if (serverInput == null) return;
25          String name = nameField.getText();
26          String number = numberField.getText();
27          try{
28             serverOutput.println("ADD");
29             serverOutput.println(name);
30             serverOutput.println(number);
31             statusArea.append(serverInput.readLine() +
32                               "\n");
33          }catch(Exception e){
34             statusArea.append("Error:\n" +
35                               e.toString() + "\n");
36          }
37       }
38    }
39
40    private class FindButtonListener implements ActionListener{
41       public void actionPerformed(ActionEvent event){
42          if (serverInput == null) return;
43          String name = nameField.getText();
44          try{
45             serverOutput.println("FIND");
46             serverOutput.println(name);
47             statusArea.append(serverInput.readLine() +
48                               "\n");
49          }catch(Exception e){
50             statusArea.append("Error:\n" + e.toString() +
51                               "\n");
52          }
53       }
54    }
55
56    private class MyWindowAdapter extends WindowAdapter{
57       public void windowClosing (WindowEvent event){
58          try{
59             serverOutput.println("EXIT");
60          }catch(Exception e){
61             statusArea.append("Error:\n" + e.toString() +
```

Continued

Continued

```
62                                    "\n");
63             }
64          System.exit(0);
65       }
66    }
```

The class `DirectoryClientHandler` implements the `while (true)` loop discussed in the design. Note that each input should be checked for `null` or "EXIT" to determine whether or not the client has disconnected. Here is a complete listing:

```
 1 import java.net.*;
 2 import java.io.*;
 3 import java.util.*;
 4
 5 public class DirectoryClientHandler extends Thread{
 6
 7    private DirectoryInterface serverOutput;
 8    private DirectoryModel model;
 9    private Socket client;
10
11    public DirectoryClientHandler (DirectoryInterface view,
12                                   DirectoryModel model,
13                                   Socket clientSocket){
14       serverOutput = view;
15       this.model = model;
16       client = clientSocket;
17       start();
18    }
19
20    public void run (){
21       try{
22          PrintStream clientOutput =
23                   new PrintStream(client.getOutputStream(), true);
24          BufferedReader clientInput =
25                   new BufferedReader(new InputStreamReader(
26                                      client.getInputStream()));
27          while (true){
28             String command = clientInput.readLine();
29             if (command == null)
30                break;
31             else if (command.equals("FIND")){
32                String name = clientInput.readLine();
33                if (name == null) break;
34                String number = model.findEntry(name);
35                if (number == null)
36                   clientOutput.println("Sorry, " + name +
37                                        " not in directory");
38                else{
39                   clientOutput.println(number);
40                   serverOutput.append("Accessed " + name + " " +
41                                       number + "\n");
42                }
43             }else if (command.equals("ADD")){
44                String name = clientInput.readLine();
45                if (name == null) break;
```

Continued

```
46              String number = clientInput.readLine();
47              if (name == null) break;
48              model.addEntry(name, number);
49              clientOutput.println("Added " + name + " " + number);
50              serverOutput.append("Added " + name + " " + number + "\n");
51          }else if (command.equals("EXIT")){
52              serverOutput.append("Client " + client + "\nexiting\n");
53              break;
54          }
55        }
56      client.close();
57    }
58    catch (IOException e){
59      serverOutput.append ("Error in i/o:\n" + e.toString() + "\n");
60    }
61  }
62
63 }
```

Exercises 15.3

1. Add operations to delete an entry and modify an entry to the directory program.

2. The directory program does not support synchronization of clients. Discuss the problems that could arise.

3. Develop a solution to the synchronization problems that you discussed in Exercise 2.

KEY TERMS

client	monitor	synchronization
client handler	port	thread
IP address	server	time slicing
IP name	server daemon	
local host	socket	

CHAPTER SUMMARY

Modern computer systems support the running of multiple cooperating processes. These processes may run concurrently on a single processor or on separate processors. In the case of multiple processors, they may inhabit a single machine or be scattered across a network. When the latter is the case, the processes often assume the roles of client and server.

A process may be described by a single program or by a component part of a program. In Java, a thread describes a process. A program can instantiate and start any number of threads. The JVM automatically schedules threads for execution by placing them on a ready queue. Unless they have special priorities, threads receive access to the CPU in an FIFO basis and return to the rear of the ready queue after a slice of execution time. Messages can also be sent to threads to force them to wait for events to occur, to go to sleep, and so forth. When this happens, they leave the CPU or the ready queue and become inactive. When they become active again, they go to the rear of the queue.

Threads and the processes they describe can be used to solve a wide range of problems, such as the producer/consumer problem and various simulation problems. When threads share memory or other critical resources, the programmer must synchronize them to coordinate their activity.

Networked applications also need a way to access the addresses of computers and to route data among them. IP addresses and sockets accomplish this. Given an IP address, a client can open a socket on a server. If the server has a server socket listening for clients, it can allow a connection to be established. Data can then be exchanged through these sockets by attaching input and output streams and using the standard file I/O messages.

REVIEW QUESTIONS

1. Describe the different states in the lifetime of a thread.
2. How does the JVM schedule the execution of multiple threads?
3. Give an example of a thread synchronization problem and its solution.
4. What is an IP address? How is it accessed by a Java program?
5. Explain how two networked computers can communicate via sockets.

Review of Java Language Features

This appendix covers the non-GUI features of Java needed for a typical CS2 course. We make no attempt to provide a complete description of Java. For a full reference, consult the documentation at Sun's Web site.

A.1   Reserved Words

Here are the reserved words in Java:

abstract	do	if	operator	switch
boolean	double	implements	outer	synchronized
break	else	import	package	this
byte	extends	inner	private	throw
case	final	instanceof	protected	throws
catch	finally	int	public	transient
char	float	interface	rest	try
class	for	long	return	var
const	future	native	short	void
continue	generic	new	static	volatile
default	goto	null	super	while

A.2   Data Types

Java supports two kinds of data types: primitive types and reference types. We discuss reference types in Section A.10. Primitive types represent numbers, characters, and Boolean values. The numeric types are listed in Table A.1.

Table A.1   **Java's Primitive Types**

Type	Storage Requirements	Range
byte	1 byte	−128 to 127
short	2 bytes	−32,768 to 32,767
int	4 bytes	−2,147,483,648 to 2,147,483,647
long	8 bytes	−9,223,372,036,854,775,808L to 9,223,372,036,854,775,807L
float	4 bytes	−3.40282347E+38F to 3.40282347E+38F
double	8 bytes	−1.79769313486231570E+308 to 1.79769313486231570E+308

Type char represents the Unicode character set, consisting of 65,536 values. These values include those of the traditional ASCII set and other international characters. Table A.2 shows the ordering of the ASCII character set. The printable characters range from ASCII 33 to ASCII 126. The values from ASCII 0 to ASCII 32 and ASCII 127 are associated with white space characters, such as the horizontal tab (HT), or non-printing control characters, such as the Escape key (ESC). The digits in the left column represent the leftmost digits of the ASCII code, and the digits in the top row are the rightmost digits. Thus, the ASCII code of the character R at row 8, column 2, is 82.

Table A.2   **The ASCII Character Set**

	0	1	2	3	4	5	6	7	8	9
0	NUL	SOH	STX	ETX	EOT	ENQ	ACK	BEL	BS	HT
1	LF	VT	FF	CR	SO	SI	DLE	DC1	DC2	DC3
2	DC4	NAK	SYN	ETB	CAN	EM	SUB	ESC	FS	GS
3	RS	US	SP	!	"	#	$	%	&	'
4	(	)	*	+	,	−	.	/	0	1
5	2	3	4	5	6	7	8	9	:	;
6	<	=	>	?	@	A	B	C	D	E
7	F	G	H	I	J	K	L	M	N	O
8	P	Q	R	S	T	U	V	W	X	Y
9	Z	[	\	]	^	_	'	a	b	c
10	d	e	f	g	h	i	j	k	l	m
11	n	o	p	q	r	s	t	u	v	w
12	x	y	z	{	|	}	~	DEL		

Character literals are enclosed in single quotes (for example, 'a'). Table A.3 lists some commonly used escape sequences for nonprinting characters.

Table A.3   **Some Escape Sequences**

Escape Sequence	Meaning
\b	backspace
\t	tab
\n	newline
\"	double quotation mark
\'	single quotation mark
\\	backslash

The type `boolean` represents the Boolean values `true` and `false`. `boolean` is the type of all expressions that serve as conditions of `if` statements and loops.

Reference types represent objects, such as strings, arrays, other built-in Java objects, and user-defined objects. We consider reference types shortly.

A.3   Variables, Scope, and Lifetime

Variables can be declared just before use. They can be declared with or without initializing assignments. Here are some examples:

```
int x, y;
double z = 45.6;
char ch = 'k', tab = '\t';
```

Variables can play three different roles:

1. **Local variables:** These are declared within a method's block and serve as temporary working storage for an activation of the method.
2. **Instance variables:** These are declared outside any method but within a class definition, and they serve as common storage for an instance of a class.
3. **Class variables:** These are also declared outside any method but within a class definition. They are prefaced with the keyword `static`, and they serve as common storage for all instances of a class. For example, `Math.PI` is a static variable defined in the `Math` class.

Java provides reasonable default values for variables that have not been initialized, except when these variables are local. Uninitialized local variables cause syntax errors.

Java is lexically scoped. This means that the scope of a variable is the block of program text (delimited by {}) within which it is declared.

The visibility of a variable is also controlled by an optional visibility modifier. Here are some examples:

```
// Visible to the entire world
public int visibleToAnyone;

// Visible within this class only
private int visibleJustToMe;

// Visible within this class, its subclasses, and other classes within its
// package
protected int visibleToMyDescendantsAndPackage;

// Visible within this class and other classes within its package
int visibleToMyPackage;
```

The lifetime of a local variable is an activation of the method in which it is declared. The lifetime of a class's instance variable is the lifetime of an instance or object of that class. The lifetime of a class variable is the lifetime of a program that uses the class.

Constants are a special kind of variable in Java, declared by including the reserved word final. Here are some examples:

```
final int MAX_SIZE = 100;          // An instance constant
static final char TAB = '\t';      // A class constant
```

Java identifiers are case sensitive. Java programmers use the following naming conventions:

- Constants are uppercase and use underscores (_) to show separations in multi-word names (MAX_SIZE).
- Variables and methods are lowercase but capitalize any nested words after the first one (degreesFahrenheitLabel).
- Classes are like variables but capitalize the first word too (AreaAndRadius).

A.4   Expressions

Java uses the standard operators for arithmetic, comparison, logic, increment, decrement, and assignment that are found in C++. Operator precedences appear in Table A.4. As usual, parentheses can override the standard precedence.

Table A.4   **Operator Precedences**

Operator	Function	Association
()	Parentheses	Left to right
[]	Array subscript	
.	Object member selection	
++	Increment	Right to left

continued

Table A.4   **Operator Precedences** *(Continued)*

Operator	Function	Association
`--`	Decrement	
`+`	Unary plus	
`-`	Unary minus	
`!`	Boolean negation	
`~`	Bitwise negation	
`(type)`	Type cast	
`*`	Multiplication	Left to right
`/`	Division	
`%`	Modulus	
`+`	Addition or concatenation	Left to right
`-`	Subtraction	
`<<`	Bitwise shift left	Left to right
`>>`	Bitwise shift right	
`>>>`	Bitwise shift right, sign extension	
`<`	Less than	Left to right
`<=`	Less than or equal to	
`>`	Greater than	
`>=`	Greater than or equal to	
`instanceOf`	Class membership	
`==`	Equal to	Left to right
`!=`	Not equal to	
`&`	Boolean AND (complete)	Left to right
	Bitwise AND	
`^`	Boolean exclusive OR	Left to right
	Bitwise OR	
`|`	Boolean OR (complete)	Left to right
	Bitwise OR	
`&&`	Boolean AND (partial)	Left to right
`||`	Boolean OR (partial)	
`?:`	Ternary conditional	Right to left
`=`	Assign	Right to left
`+=`	Add and sign	
`-=`	Subtract and assign	
`*=`	Multiply and assign	
`/=`	Divide and assign	
`%=`	Modulo and assign	
`<<=`	Shift and left assign	
`>>=`	Shift right and assign	

Table A.4	**Operator Precedences** *(Continued)*		
Operator	*Function*		*Association*
>>>=	Shift right, sign extension, and assign		
&=	Boolean or bitwise AND and assign		
|=	Boolean or bitwise OR and assign		
^=	Boolean or bitwise exclusive OR and assign		

Comparison and logical operators return the `boolean` values `true` or `false`. Java evaluates compound Boolean expressions by using short-circuit evaluation.

A.5 Control Statements

A.5.1 Compound Statement

A compound statement consists of a list of zero or more declarations and statements enclosed within {}. A semicolon must terminate each statement, except for the compound statement itself. Here is the form:

```
{
   <declaration or statement-1>
   .
   .
   <declaration or statement-n>
}
```

A.5.2 `if` and `if-else` Statements

`if` and `if-else` statements have the following forms:

```
if (<boolean expression>)
   <statement>
```

```
if (<boolean expression>)
   <statement>
else
   <statement>
```

A.5.3 `while` and `do-while` Statements

`while` statements have the following form:

```
while (<boolean expression>)
   <statement>
```

do-while statements have the following form:

```
do
   <statement>
while (<boolean expression>)
```

A.5.4   **for** Statement

for statements have the following form:

```
for (<initializer list>; <termination list>; <update list>)
   <statement>
```

The initializer list, termination list, and update list are optional. Here are three examples:

```
for (int i = 1; i <= 10; i++)                     // Print in ascending order
   System.out.println(i);

for (int j = 10; j >= 1; j--)                     // Print in descending order
   System.out.println(j);

for (int i = 1, j = 10; i <= 10, j >= 1; i++, j--)     // Print both ways
   System.out.println(i + " " + j);                    // at once
```

When a variable is declared in the header of a for loop, its scope is the body of the loop.

A.5.5   **switch** Statement

The switch statement handles a selection among cases, where each case is a constant of a primitive type. Here is an example:

```
switch (ch){
   case 'a':
   case 'A': doSomthing1();
            break;
   case 'b':
   case 'B': doSomething2();
            break;
   case 'c': doSomething3();
            break;
   default:  doSomething4();
}
```

The break statements are optional, but they are required if the case lists are to be considered mutually exclusive. The default statement is also optional but highly recommended.

A.6   Mixed-Mode Operations and Casting

When an expression's operands are of different primitive types, Java automatically promotes the value of the less inclusive type to a value of the more inclusive type. The value returned by the expression is of the more inclusive type. For example:

```
int i = 6;
double d1, d2 = 3.14;

d1 = d2 * i;                    // Multiplies 3.14 by 3.0 and returns 9.42
```

Two exceptions to this rule are assignment and parameter passing. A value of a less inclusive type is automatically promoted to the variable's type before assignment. However, if the value already is of a more inclusive type than the variable, a syntax error occurs. In this case, the programmer must explicitly convert the value to the variable's type before assignment by using a cast operator. The rule for passing a value as a parameter to a method is similar, as shown in the following example:

```
double dVar = 3.14;

int iVar;

void methodX(int x){
    .
}

iVar = (int)dVar;                 // Cast to an int before using
methodX((int)dVar);
```

The cast operator for each type has the form (`<type name>`).

A.7   Strings

String literals, including the empty string (" "), are sequences of characters enclosed within double quotes. String variables are declared and initialized in the usual manner:

```
String last = "Doe", first = "John";
```

Strings are objects. They are instances of the class String. This class defines many methods that the program can use to manipulate strings. Some of these are listed in Table A.5.

Table A.5   `String` Methods

Method	Description
`charAT (anIndex) returns char`	Ex: `chr = myStr.charAT (4);` Returns the character at the position `anIndex`. Remember the first character is at position 0. An exception is thrown (i.e., an error is generated) if `anIndex` is out of range (i.e., does not indicate a valid position within `myStr`).
`compareTo (aString) returns int`	Ex: `i = myStr.compareTo("abc");` Compares two strings lexicographically. Returns 0 if `myStr` equals `aString`, a value less than 0 if `myStr` is lexicographically less than `aString`, and a value greater than 0 if `myStr` is lexicographically greater than `aString`.
`equals (aString) returns boolean`	Ex: `bool = myStr.equals("abc");` Returns `true` if `myStr` equals `aString`, else returns `false`. Because of implementation peculiarities in Java, never test for equality like this: `myStr == aString`
`equalsIgnoreCase (aString) returns boolean`	Similar to `equals` but ignores case during the comparison.
`indexOf (aCharacter) returns int`	Ex: `i = myStr.indexOf('z')` Returns the index within `myStr` of the first occurrence of `aCharacter` or –1 if `aCharacter` is absent.
`indexOf (aCharacter, beginIndex) returns int`	Ex: `i = myStr.indexOf('z', 6);` Similar to the preceding method except the search starts at position `beginIndex` rather than at the beginning of `myStr`. An exception is thrown (i.e., an error is generated) if `beginIndex` is out of range (i.e., does not indicate a valid position within `myStr`).
`indexOf (aSubstring) returns int`	Ex: `i = myStr.indexOf("abc")` Returns the index within `myStr` of the first occurrence of `aSubstring` or –1 if `aSubstring` is absent.
`indexOf (aSubstring, beginIndex) returns int`	Ex: `i = indexOf("abc", 6)` Similar to the preceding method except the search starts at position `beginIndex` rather than at the beginning of `myStr`. An exception is thrown (i.e., an error is generated) if `beginIndex` is out of range (i.e., does not indicate a valid position within `myStr`).
`length() returns int`	Ex: `i = myStr.length();` Returns the length of `myStr`.
`replace (oldChar, newChar) returns String`	Ex: `str = myStr.replace('z', 'Z');` Returns a new string resulting from replacing all occurrences of `oldChar` in `myStr` with `newChar`. `myStr` is not changed.

continued

Table A.5 **`String` Methods** *(Continued)*

Method	Description
`substring (beginIndex)` `returns String`	Ex: `str = myStr.substring(6);` Returns a new string that is a substring of `myStr`. The substring begins at location `beginIndex` and extends to the end of `myStr`. An exception is thrown (i.e., an error is generated) if `beginIndex` is out of range (i.e., does not indicate a valid position within `myStr`).
`substring (beginIndex, endIndex)` `returns String`	Ex: `str = myStr.substring(4, 8);` Similar to the preceding method except the substring extends to location `endIndex-1` rather than to the end of `myStr`.
`toLowerCase() returns String`	Ex: `str = myStr.toLowerCase();` `str` is the same as `myStr` except that all letters have been converted to lowercase. `myStr` is not changed.
`toUpperCase() returns String`	Ex: `str = myStr.toUpperCase();` `str` is the same as `myStr` except that all letters have been converted to uppercase. `myStr` is not changed.
`trim() returns String`	Ex: `str = myStr.trim();` `str` is the same as `myStr` except that leading and trailing spaces, if any, are absent. `myStr` is not changed.

The programmer runs a method with a string by sending the string the appropriate message. Here are some examples:

```
String str = "Hi there";

System.out.println(str.length());          // Prints 8
System.out.println(str.charAt(3));         // Prints t
System.out.println(str.toUpperCase());     // Prints HI THERE
System.out.println(str + " Bill " + 3);    // Prints Hi there Bill 3
```

None of the `String` methods modifies a string. In fact, neither the contents nor the size of a string can be changed. The class `StringBuffer` allows you to modify a string. The class `StringTokenizer` (defined in `java.util`) allows you to extract words from a string as if it were an iterator. See Sun's Java documentation for details.

A.8 Arrays

Array variables are declared as follows:

```
int[] intArray1, intArray2;        // For an array of integers
String[] stringArray1;             // For an array of strings
double[][] matrix;                 // For a two-dimensional array
                                   // of floating-point numbers
```

or alternatively,

```
int intArray1[], intArray2[];          // For an array of integers
String stringArray1[];                 // For an array of strings
double matrix[][];                     // For a two-dimensional array
                                       // of floating-point numbers
```

Arrays are objects. To initialize an array variable, one must instantiate an array object with the operator `new` as follows:

```
intArray1 = new int[10];               // Array of 10 integers
intarray2 = new int[150];              // Array of 150 integers

stringArray = new String[5];           // Array of 5 strings

matrix = new double[6][8];             // A two-dimensional array with
                                       // 6 rows and 8 columns
```

The form of array instantiation is

```
new <element type>[<int-exp>] . . .[<int-exp>]
```

where the integer dimensions can be any integer expressions, including variables.

Java provides reasonable default values for an array's elements during instantiation. An array cannot be resized. The public variable `length` contains the number of cells in an array. Thus,

```
System.out.println(intArray2.length);      // Prints 150
```

An initializer list can be used to specify an array's elements when an array variable is declared. For example,

```
int[] intArray3 = {34, 45, 56};        // Array containing 34 45 56
String[]stringArray2 = {"Hi", "there"};   // Array containing "Hi" "there"
int[][] matrix2 = {{1,2}, {3,4}, {5,6}};  // A 3 by 2 two-dimensional array
                                          // with the given values
```

Array subscripts have the usual form. Indexing is zero based, meaning that the range of permissible index values runs from 0 to the size of the array minus 1. Java throws a run-time exception if an array index is out of bounds. For example:

```
int[] a = {23, 34, 45};

for (int i = 0; i <= a.length; i++)    // Oops! Find the error!
   System.out.println(a[i];            // Prints the contents and then
                                       // halts the program with a run-time
                                       // error message
```

A.9 Methods and Parameters

Java methods have a fairly conventional form:

```
<optional access modifier> <return type> <name> (<formal parameter list>){
   <local data declarations and statements>
}
```

When the return type is `void`, the method can exit with or without a return statement but does not return a value. When the return type is some other type, the method must return a value of that type or a less inclusive type.

A formal parameter list consists of zero or more formal parameter declarations of the form

```
<type> <parameter name>
```

separated by commas. The number and types of the actual parameters used when the method is called must match those of the formal parameters. Actual parameters of less inclusive types are automatically promoted to more inclusive types.

All parameters are passed by value; that is, Java copies the actual parameter's value into temporary working storage. Thus, the values of variables of primitive types do not change when these variables are passed as parameters to methods. Java handles variables of reference types differently, as we will see shortly.

A method is invoked when a message is sent to an object. Thus, for example, if the parameterless method m is defined in the class C and an object o of class C has been instantiated, then the message `o.m()` results in a call of method m. In the implementation of class C, however, method m can be called directly as `m()`, without the dot notation. This call is actually shorthand for sending a message to the object itself and could be rewritten as `this.m()`. The Java reserved word `this` always stands for the current object in a class implementation.

Instance methods execute when messages are sent to instances of classes. Class methods, which are prefaced with the Java reserved word `static`, are executed when messages are sent to classes. For example, methods `main` and `Math.sqrt` are class methods.

Java methods can be overloaded. That is, more than one method can have the same name, as long as the types or number of the formal parameters is different. For example, there are several different methods with the name `println`, and each of these methods expects a different type of parameter.

A.10 Reference Types

All Java classes are reference types. They are so called because variables of these types refer or point to objects. This idea is most clearly seen when one looks at how Java handles the assignment of objects. For example, consider the following code:

```
int[] a, b;              // Declare array variables

a = new int[5];          // Instantiate an array object and assign to a

b = a;                   // a and b now refer to the same array object

a[0] = 121;              // a[0] and b[0] are both 121
```

The assignment b = a does not create a new array that is a copy of the array referred to by a but instead stores a's pointer to its array in b. The same thing happens during a method call with an array parameter. For example:

```
int[] a;                 // Declare array variable

a = new int[5];          // Instantiate an array object and assign to a

void methodX(int[] b){
   b[0] = 121;
}

methodX(a);              // During the call, a and b point to the same
                         // array object
                         // When the call returns, a[0] will be 121
```

Java passes a copy of the pointer to the array object to methodX. The method then modifies a cell in the object, which changes the state of the object referenced by the parameter b and the variable a.

When an instance variable of a reference type is declared but not initialized, Java gives it a default value of null. An attempt to send a message to the variable at this point causes a run-time error (null pointer exception).

Comparing two objects for equality or inequality can sometimes give unexpected results. When used with reference types, the operators == and != test for pointer equality and inequality, respectively. Thus, two variables are == if they point to the same object. However, if they point to different objects with the same state, == returns false and != returns true. In general, it is best to use the method equals, when it is implemented, to compare two objects for equality. This method compares the contents of the objects rather than pointers to them.

A.11   Wrapper Classes

Occasionally, you need to store values of primitive types in structures that can contain only objects. Java provides wrapper classes to allow the programmer to convert primitive values to the appropriate objects. Here are some examples:

```
Integer i = new Integer(3);          // Wrap 3 in an Integer object
System.out.println(i.intValue());    // Extract 3 and print it
```

Wrapper classes are also used to convert strings to primitive values:

```
byte   b = Byte.valueOf ("12").byteValue();           // String to byte
double d = Double.valueOf ("3.14e4").doubleValue();   // String to double
float  f = Float.valueOf ("3.14e4").floatValue();     // String to float
int    i = Integer.valueOf ("12").intValue();         // String to int
long   l = Long.valueOf ("12").longValue();           // String to long
short  s = Short.valueOf ("12").shortValue();         // String to short
```

Finally, wrapper classes define a few useful methods and constants, such as

```
System.out.println(Integer.MAX_VALUE);          // Print largest integer
System.out.println(Character.digit('A', 16));   // Print 10 (from Hex)
```

A.12 Classes

The features of classes are discussed in Chapter 2.

A.13 Interfaces

An interface is a collection of method headers and constants. When a class implements an interface, that class must implement all of the methods that appear in the interface.

A.14 Adapters

An interface forces the classes implementing it to implement all the methods in the interface whether the client classes need them or not. To alleviate this burden, Java provides adapter classes for some interfaces. An adapter class implements an interface with method stubs. Thus, any class that extends an adapter need only implement those methods in the adapter's interface that really need to be used. Here are the possibilities:

```
public class myClass implements AnInterface{
// All methods in AnInterface must be implemented here
}
```

```
public class myClass extends AnAdapter{
// Zero or more methods in AnAdapter's interface can be implemented here
}
```

Adapter classes are typically used to define listener classes for handling GUI events.

A.15 Exceptions

Java divides run-time errors into two broad categories: errors and exceptions. Errors are serious run-time problems that usually should not be handled by the programmer. For example, if a method gets stuck in an infinite recursion, as described in Chapter

10, Java throws a `StackOverflowError`. Java defines a separate class for each type of error. You can browse through these in Sun's Web site, starting with the class `Error` in the package `java.lang`.

Exceptions come in two varieties: those that Java requires the programmer to handle, such as `IOException`, and those that the programmer may or may not handle, such as `ArithmeticException` and `ArrayIndexOutOfBounds Exception`. To explore Java's `Exception` class hierarchy on Sun's Web site, select the desired package in the package index and scroll to the bottom of the page. Most of the exception classes are defined in `java.lang`, but several important ones are also defined in `java.io` and `java.util`.

The next code segments show how one might handle exceptions in the cases of division and array subscripting:

```
// Catch an attempt to divide by zero

try{
   quotient = dividend / divisor;
   System.out.println("Successful division");
}catch (ArithmeticException e){
   System.out.println("Error1: " + e.toString());
}
```

```
// Catch an attempt to use an array index that is out of range

try{
   a[x] = 0;
   System.out.println("Successful subscripting");
}catch (ArrayIndexOutOfBoundsException e){
   System.out.println("Error2: " + e.toString());
}
```

When Java detects an error and throws an exception, control is immediately transferred from the offending instruction in the `try` statement to the `catch` statement. Thus, the output of the first message would be skipped if an exception occurs in either of the foregoing code segments. If the `try` statement completes successfully, the `catch` statement is not executed.

A `try` statement can be followed by more than one `catch` statement. For example, the next code segment combines the exception handling of the previous two segments:

```
// Catch an attempt to divide by zero and to use an array index
// that is out of bounds

try{
   quotient = dividend / divisor;
   System.out.println("Successful division");
   a[x] = quotient;
   System.out.println("Successful subscripting");
}catch (ArithmeticException e){
```

Continued

Continued

```
    System.out.println("Error1: " + e.toString());
}catch (ArrayIndexOutOfBoundsException e){
    System.out.println("Error2: " + e.toString());
}
```

The same two exceptions are possible in this example, but Java gets to throw only one of them. When this occurs, control shifts to the first `catch` statement following the `try` statement. If the class of the exception thrown is the same as or is a subclass of the class of that `catch` statement's parameter, then the code for the `catch` statement executes. Otherwise, Java compares the exception thrown to the parameter of the next `catch` statement and so on.

It is possible (and often desirable) to define new kinds of exceptions that can be thrown by methods in user-defined classes. The rules for doing this are beyond the scope of this book and can be found on Sun's Web site.

A.16 Packages

A Java package is a name that stands for a set of related classes. For example, the package `java.io` stands for all of the Java file stream classes. Exceptions and interfaces can also be parts of a package.

The package `java.lang` contains many commonly used classes, such as `Math` and `String`. This package is implicitly imported into every Java program file, so no `import` statement is required. To use any other package, such as `java.io`, in a program file, the programmer must explicitly import the package with an `import` statement.

Programs can import all of the classes in a given package, using the form

```
import <package name>.*;
```

It is also possible to import selected classes from a given package and omit others. For example, the following line imports just the `Hashtable` class from the `java.util` package and omits the others:

```
import java.util.Hashtable;
```

This statement has the effect of making the `Hashtable` class visible to the program file but leaves the rest of the classes in the `java.util` package invisible.

Occasionally, a program uses classes that have the same name but are defined in different packages. For example, the `List` class in `java.awt` implements a scrolling list box, whereas the `List` interface in `java.util` specifies operations for Java's list collections. To avoid ambiguity in these programs, you must prefix the class name with its package wherever the class name is used. Here is an example:

```
import java.util.*;
import java.awt.*;
```

Continued

Continued

```
.
.
// Instantiate a scrolling list box to display the data
java.awt.List listView = new java.awt.List();
.
.
// Instantiate an array list to contain the data
java.util.List listModel = new ArrayList();
```

To define and compile a package, perform the following steps:

1. Create three directories on your disk. Name the first directory **testbed** and the second directory **sources.** The third directory should have the name of the package you are defining, such as **mypackage.** The **sources** and **mypackage** directories should be contained as subdirectories in the **testbed** directory.

2. Place a tester program (say, **Tester.java**) for your package in the **testbed** directory.

3. Open a DOS window and move to the **mypackage** directory.

4. Place the Java source files (**.java** extension) for your package in the **mypackage** directory. Each source file in the package should have the line

```
package mypackage;
```

at the beginning of the file.

5. Compile the Java files using the DOS command **javac *.java**. If all goes well, the bytecode files (**.class** extension) should be in the **mypackage** directory.

6. Move up to the **testbed** directory and compile the tester program.

7. Run the tester program using the DOS command **java Tester**. If all goes well, your package is ready for release. Before distributing your package, move the source (**.java**) files to the **sources** directory. A package should have just **.class** files.

8. Go back to step 5 each time you need to modify a source file in the package.

A.17   Text Files

At the lowest level, Java views the data in files as a stream of bytes. A stream of bytes from which data are read is called a *file input stream.* A stream of bytes to which data are written is a *file output stream.* Java provides a set of classes for connecting a program to a file stream and for manipulating data in the stream. These classes are defined in the java.io package.

The classes FileInputStream and FileOutputStream are used to connect programs to files. Terminal output uses the object System.out, which is an instance of the PrintStream class. The class InputStreamReader is used to read character data from a file input stream. The class BufferedReader is used to read input one line at a time. The class PrintWriter takes data of different types (int, double, String, etc.) and writes them as byte-level data to a file output stream. The File class is used to establish connections with the file and directory system on a disk. Several of these classes are typically used in combination to process files.

A standard file input process is described in the following algorithm:

```
Open an input connection to a file
Read the data from the file and process it
Close the input connection to the file
```

We now present a short program that serves as an example of this process. The program prompts the user for a file name. When the user enters a file name, the program opens the file for input, calls the method readAndProcessData, and closes the file. In the first version of the program, readAndProcessData is a simple stub; in later versions, this method reads the text from the file, converts it to uppercase, and displays the results in the terminal window.

```java
import java.io.*;
import ioutil.KeyboardReader;

public class FileTester{

    public static void main (Button buttonObj){
        KeyboardReader reader = new KeyboardReader();
        String fileName = reader.readLine("File name: ");
        try{
            FileInputStream stream = new FileInputStream (fileName);
            readAndProcessData (stream);
            stream.close();
        }
        catch(IOException e){
            System.out.println("Error in opening input file:\n" +
                                e.toString());
        }
        Console.pause();
    }

    private static void readAndProcessData (FileInputStream stream){
        System.out.println("Running readAndProcessData\n" +
                            "File opened successfully");
    }
}
```

After a file input stream has been successfully opened, we can read data from it. We now examine the input of data from text files. A text file contains characters. Java provides several ways to read these characters from a file. We examine just two:

1. Read one character at a time, using the class InputStreamReader
2. Read one line at a time, using the class BufferedReader

The next code segment shows how the method `readAndProcessData` would be completed to read the text from the file one character at a time:

```
private static void readAndProcessData (FileInputStream stream){
    InputStreamReader reader = new InputStreamReader (stream);
    try{
        int data = reader.read();
        while (data != -1){
            char ch = (char) data;
            ch = Character.toUpperCase (ch);
            System.out.print (ch + "");
            data = reader.read();
        }
    }catch(IOException e){
        System.out.println ("Error in file input:\n" + e.toString());
    }
}
```

The first step is to connect an instance of the class `InputStreamReader` to the `FileInputStream` parameter. This is done by passing the file input stream as a parameter to the input stream reader's constructor. The next step is to enter a `try-catch` statement to read data from the stream. The form of the input loop is fairly general:

```
Get the first datum from the stream
While the datum does not indicate that the end of stream has been reached
    Process the datum
    Get the next datum from the stream
```

Note three other points:

1. The value −1 indicates that the end of the stream has been reached.

2. The data returned by `read()` are of type `int`. These are the ASCII values of the characters in the file. Thus, you must cast them to characters for further processing.

3. The `catch` statement should handle an `IOException`, which might occur during the input of a datum.

The next code segment shows how the method `readAndProcessData` is completed to read the text from a file one line at a time:

```
private static void readAndProcessData (FileInputStream stream){
    InputStreamReader iStrReader = new InputStreamReader (stream);
    BufferedReader reader = new BufferedReader (iStrReader);
    try{
        String data = reader.readLine();
        while (data != null){
            data = data.toUpperCase();
            System.out.print (data + "\n");
            data = reader.readLine();
        }
    }catch(IOException e){
        System.out.println ("Error in file input:\n" + e.toString());
    }
}
```

To set up the reader, we proceed as before by first connecting an input stream reader to the file input stream. To the input stream reader we then connect an instance of `BufferedReader`. However, note the following variations:

1. We now call the method `readLine` to obtain a string representing the next line of text in the stream.

2. When this string has the value `null`, we have reached the end of the stream.

3. We use the `String` instance method `toUpperCase` to convert the entire string to uppercase.

4. The newline character is not part of the string obtained from `readLine`. Thus, we have to append a newline before output.

The use of a `BufferedReader` not only allows us to work with whole lines of text but also can improve the speed at which the data are input.

Summary of Hierarchies, Interfaces, and Classes

B.1 Hierarchies

lamborne interfaces and classes are listed in **bold**

java.util interfaces and classes are listed in plain

B.2 Interfaces

Stack
Queue
  PriorityQueue
Collection
  List
  Set
    SortedSet
  SortedCollection (our extension)
Heap
Tree
Map
  SortedMap
Bag
Graph
Vertex
Edge
Comparable
  Weighable
Iterator
  ListIterator
TreeIterator

B.3   Classes

Class	Implements
AbstractContainer	Serializable
AbstractStack	
LinkedStack	**Stack,** Cloneable
AbstractQueue	
LinkedQueue	**Queue,** Cloneable
AbstractPriorityQueue	
LinkedPriorityQueue	**PriorityQueue,** Cloneable
HeapPriorityQueue	**PriorityQueue,** Cloneable
AbstractHeap	
ArrayHeap	**Heap,** Cloneable
AbstractTree	
LinkedTree	**Tree,** Cloneable
AbstractBag	
HashBag	**Bag,** Cloneable
AbstractGraph	
LinkedDirectedGraph	**Graph,** Cloneable
LinkedUndirectedGraph	**Graph,** Cloneable
AbstractVertex	
LinkedVertex	**Vertex**
GraphEdge	**Edge**
Weight	**Weighable**
AbstractCollection	Collection
AbstractList	List
AbstractSequentialList	
LinkedList	List, Cloneable, Serializable
ArrayList	List, Cloneable, Serializable
Vector	List, Cloneable, Serializable
Stack	
AbstractSet	Set
HashSet	Set, Cloneable, Serializable
TreeSet	SortedSet, Cloneable, Serializable
AbstractSortedCollection	
LinkedBSTSortedCollection	**SortedCollection,** Cloneable
AbstractMap	Map
HashMap	Map, Cloneable, Serializable
TreeMap	SortedMap, Cloneable, Serializable

Installation Instructions

The programs and programming projects in this book require that you have a Java Development Kit (JDK) installed on your computer. A free JDK for Windows® and UNIX® users is available from Sun Microsystems. Macintosh users are encouraged to upgrade to OS X, which comes with an integrated JDK. Alternatively, academic users can use JGrasp, a free integrated program development environment from Auburn University. The CD that comes with this book has a copy of JGrasp.

C.1 Working with the JDK

Sun Microsystems maintains an excellent Web site where programmers can find complete documentation for the Java API (Application Programming Interface) and download a free JDK. Here are two of the items that you can access on the Web:

Sun's top-level Java page (www.javasoft.com/): This page contains news about events in the Java world and links to documentation, Java-related products, program examples, and free downloads of the JDK.

Products and APIs (www.javasoft.com/products/): This page allows you to select the version of the JDK that matches your computer and to begin the download process. You can also download the documentation if you do not want to access it on the Web.

Be sure to download the most current version of the JDK for your computer (as of this writing, JDK1.4). After downloading, you install the JDK on your computer by running the installation program. You should print the **Readme** file for further reference. The Windows installation leaves the directory **j2sdk1.4.0** on your disk. To use ioutil and lamborne, you should copy the files **ioutil.jar** and **lambore.jar** from your CD to the directory with the path **j2sdk1.4.0\jre\lib\ext** and also to the directory with the path **Program Files\Java\jre1.4.0\lib\ext**.

Place the following command in the **autoexec.bat** file and restart your machine.

```
path=%path%;c:\;c:\j2sdk1.4.0\bin
SET CLASSPATH=c:\j2sdk1.4.0\classes;.
```

Be sure to terminate CLASSPATH with ";.".

Before you use the JDK, make sure that all of your Java source program (**.java**) files are in the current directory (this can be any directory on your computer). You can define more than one class in a source file, but the usual procedure is to have one source file for each class. Each source file should begin with the same name as the class that it contains and should end with **.java**. Remember that Java class names and file names are case sensitive. If you want to run an applet, the appropriate **html** file should also be in this directory.

You can then do the following at the system command prompt:

Compile a program: The basic syntax is `javac <filename>`, where `<file name>` is a Java source file name (ending in **.java**). Java locates and compiles all of the files required by your program. Any syntax error messages are displayed in the command window, and a bytecode (**.class**) file is generated for each class defined in your program.

Run an application: The basic syntax is `java <filename>`, where `<file name>` is the name of the class that defines the `main` method of your program. Note that the **.class** extension must be omitted. Run-time error messages are displayed in the command window.

Run an applet: The basic syntax is `appletviewer <filename>`, where `<filename>` is the name of an **html** file that links to your applet.

In addition to these Web resources, Sun's Java development team has published a number of useful reference books on various features of Java programming. Here are a few:

Arnold & Gosling, *The Java Programming Language* (2nd ed.) (Reading, MA: Addison-Wesley, 1998).

Gosling & Yellin, *The Java Application Programming Interface, Volume 1: Core Packages* (Reading, MA: Addison-Wesley, 1996).

Gosling & Yellin, *The Java Application Programming Interface, Volume 2: Window Toolkit and Applets* (Reading, MA: Addison-Wesley, 1996).

Gosling, Joy, & Steele, *The Java Language Specification* (Reading, MA: Addison-Wesley, 1996).

C.2   Working with JGrasp

JGrasp is a powerful IDE but is incredibly easy to use. To get started, just follow these steps:

1. Install the JDK on your computer as directed above.
2. Place the jar files for `lamborne` and `ioutil` in the appropriate directories as directed above.
3. Install JGrasp from the CD.
4. Place the Java source program files for your application in a single directory.
5. Launch the Java source program file that contains the `main` method. This will launch JGrasp and display the file in a window.
6. Select the compiler tool (marked +) in the JGrasp toolbar. All of the needed source files will be compiled to bytecode.
7. Select the execute tool to the right of the compile tool to run the program.

abstract Simplified or partial, hiding detail.

abstract class A class that defines attributes and methods for subclasses but is never instantiated.

abstract data type (ADT) A class of objects, a defined set of properties of those objects, and a set of operations for processing the objects.

abstract method A method specified but not implemented in an abstract class. The subclasses must implement this method.

Abstract Window Toolkit (AWT) The Java package that contains the definitions of all the classes used to set up graphical user interfaces.

acceptance testing The final phase of testing, during which a program runs in conditions similar to its eventual use.

accessor A method used to examine an attribute of an object without changing it.

activation record An area of computer memory that keeps track of a method call's parameters, local values, return value, and the caller's return address. *See also* **run-time stack**.

actual parameter A variable or expression contained in a method call and passed to that method. *See also* **formal parameter.**

adapter class A Java class that allows another class to implement an interface without implementing all of its methods. *See also* **interface.**

adjacency list An implementation of a graph that contains an array of linked lists for each vertex. A node in a list represents an edge from the list's vertex to the node's vertex.

adjacency matrix An implementation of a graph that contains a two-dimensional array. Each dimension is the number of vertices, and the cell at position

$[i][j]$ is occupied if there is an edge connecting vertices i and j.

adjacent The property of being connected by an edge.

algorithm A finite sequence of effective statements that, when applied to a problem, solves it.

alias A situation in which two or more names in a program can refer to the same memory location. An alias can cause subtle side effects.

all-pairs shortest path problem A problem that asks for the set of all the shortest paths in a graph.

analysis The phase of the software life cycle in which the programmer describes what the program will do. *See also* **user requirements.**

applet A Java program that can be downloaded and run on a Web browser.

argument A value or expression passed in a method call.

array A data structure whose elements are randomly accessed by means of index positions. *See also* **random access data structure.**

array index The relative position of the components of an array.

assembly language A programming language that uses mnemonic symbols but has the structure of machine language. *See also* **machine language.**

assignment statement A method of putting values into memory locations.

association A pair consisting of a key and a value. *See also* **association list.**

association list A collection whose items are accessed by specifying unique keys. *See also* **dictionary, hash table, keyed list,** and **map.**

attribute A property that a computational object models, such as the balance in a bank account.

AVL tree A special type of search tree that supports O(log*n*) operations in the worst cases.

backing collection The collection on which an iterator has been opened. *See also* **iterator.**

backtracking algorithm A type of algorithm that explores possible paths to a solution and returns to alternative paths when a given path fails.

bag An unordered collection that allows duplicate items. *See also* **unordered collection.**

base address The location of an array object in memory. *See also* **offset.**

behavior The set of actions that a class of objects supports.

big-O notation A formal notation used to express the amount of work done by an algorithm or the amount of memory used by an algorithm. *See also* **complexity.**

binary search The process of examining a middle value of a sorted array to see which half contains the value in question and halving until the value is located.

binary search tree A binary tree in which each node is greater than its left child and less than its right child.

binary tree A tree in which each node has at most two children.

black box testing A method of testing in which the range of test data is limited and is made without knowledge of the program's inner workings. *See also* **white box testing.**

block An area of program text, enclosed in Java by the symbols { }, that contains statements and data declarations.

bottom-up implementation A method of coding a program that starts with lower level modules and a test driver module.

breadth-first traversal A graph traversal that visits each node at a given level before moving to the next level.

bubble sort A sorting algorithm that repeatedly shifts the larger of two items down to the end of a list.

bucket A data structure used to resolve collisions during hashing. *See also* **chaining.**

bytecode The kind of object code generated by a Java compiler and interpreted by a Java virtual machine. Bytecode is platform independent.

call Any reference to a method by an executable statement. Also referred to as *invoke.*

call stack *See* **run-time stack.**

call tree A diagram that traces the calls of a recursive method.

cast An operator used to convert a value of one type to a value of a different type, for example, `double` to `int`.

chaining A method of resolving collisions during hashing. Items with the same hash value are placed in a linked list. *See also* **bucket.**

child A successor of a given node in a tree. *See also* **parent** and **tree.**

class A description of the attributes and behavior of a set of computational objects.

class constant A constant that is visible to all instances of a class and, if public, is accessed by specifying the class name. For example, `Math.PI` is a class constant.

class constructor A method used to create and initialize an instance of a class.

class method A method invoked when a message is sent to a class. For example, `Math.sqrt` is a class method. *See also* **message.**

class variable A variable that is visible to all instances of a class and, if public, is accessed by specifying the class name.

client A computational object that receives a service from another computational object. *See also* **client/server relationship.**

client handler A thread that processes requests from clients.

client/server relationship A means of describing the organization of computing resources in which one resource provides a service to another resource.

cloning The process of copying an object. *See also* **deep copy** and **shallow copy.**

code coverage The process of selecting test data that exercise every branch of an `if` statement. *See also* **whitebox testing.**

coding The process of writing executable statements that are part of a program to solve a problem. *See also* **implementation.**

cohesive method A method designed to accomplish a single task.

collection A group of items that can be accessed individually or treated as a unit.

collection-view A method that allows objects to satisfy the `Collection` interface and is used to convert objects to specific types of collections.

collision An event that occurs when two items hash to the same key. *See also* **hashing.**

complete binary tree A binary tree whose shape is restricted by starting at the root node and filling the tree by levels from left to right.

complete graph A graph in which there is an edge from each vertex to every other vertex.

complexity For algorithms, the formula that expresses the rate of growth of work or memory as a function of the size of the data or problem that it solves. *See also* **big-O notation.**

concatenation An operation in which the contents of one data structure are placed after the contents of another data structure.

concordance A list of words from a text file, wherein each word is followed by the lines in which the words occur.

concrete class A class that can be instantiated. *See also* **abstract class.**

connected component A subgraph consisting of the set of vertices that are reachable from a given vertex.

connected graph A graph in which there is a path from each vertex to every other vertex.

constant behavior The property of an algorithm whose run time or memory usage remains the same regardless of the size of its data set.

constant of proportionality The measure of the amount of work of an algorithm that never varies with the size of its data set.

contained class A class that is used to define a data object within another class.

container A Java class that allows the programmer to group window objects for placement in a window.

contiguous memory Computer memory organized so the data are accessible in adjacent cells.

control structure A structure that controls the flow of execution of program statements.

cycle A path that begins and ends at the same vertex.

data abstraction The separation between the conceptual definition of a data structure and its eventual implementation.

data structure The representation chosen to implement an abstract data type.

data type A formal description of the set of values that a variable can have.

data validation The process of examining data prior to their use in a program.

debugging The process of eliminating errors or "bugs" from a program.

deep copy The process whereby copies are made of the individual components of a data structure. *See also* **cloning** and **shallow copy.**

default constructor A method that Java provides for creating objects of a class. The programmer can override this method to do extra things.

dense graph A graph that has many edges relative to its vertices. *See also* **sparse graph.**

depth-first traversal A graph traversal that visits the successors of each node before moving to other nodes at the same level.

design The phase of the software life cycle in which the programmer describes how the program will accomplish its tasks.

design error An error such that a program runs but unexpected results are produced. Also referred to as a *logic error.*

dictionary A data structure that allows the programmer to access items by specifying key values. *See also* **association list, hash table, keyed list,** and **map.**

directed acyclic graph (DAG) A directed graph without cycles.

directed graph (digraph) A graph whose edges specify explicit directions.

divide-and-conquer algorithms A class of algorithms that solves problems by repeatedly dividing them into simpler problems. *See also* **recursion.**

double A Java data type used to represent numbers with a decimal point.

doubly linked list A linked list in which each node has a pointer to the previous node and a pointer to the next node.

driver A method that is used to test other methods.

dynamic array An array whose memory is allocated from the object heap. *See also* **object heap** and **static array.**

dynamic memory Memory allocated under program control from the object heap and accessed by means of pointers. *See also* **object heap** and **pointer.**

dynamic structure A data structure that may expand or contract during execution of a program. *See also* **dynamic memory.**

edge A link between two vertices in a graph.

empty link *See* **null value.**

encapsulation The process of hiding and restricting access to the implementation details of a data structure.

enumeration A Java interface that allows the programmer to process a sequence of objects.

event An occurrence, such as a button click or a mouse motion, that can be detected and processed by a program.

event-driven loop A process, usually hidden in the operating system, that waits for an event, notifies a program that an event has occurred, and returns to wait for more events.

exception An abnormal state or error that occurs during run time and is signaled by the operating system.

expanding capabilities implementation A coding strategy that begins with a running but incomplete program and gradually adds features until the program is complete.

explicit type conversion The use of an operation by a programmer to convert the type of a data object.

exponential behavior The property of an algorithm whose run time or memory usage grows exponentially with the size of its data set.

expression tree A tree used to represent expressions during parsing and evaluation.

external pointer A special pointer that allows users to access the nodes in a linked list.

fail-fast An approach to error conditions in which exceptions are thrown as soon as the errors are encountered.

Fibonacci numbers A series of numbers generated by taking the sum of the previous two numbers in the series. The series begins with the numbers 1 and 2.

final method A method that cannot be implemented by a subclass.

flowchart A diagram that displays the flow of control of a program. *See also* **control structure.**

formal parameter A name, introduced in a method definition, that is replaced by an actual parameter when the method is called.

formal specification The set of preconditions and postconditions of a method.

free list A collection of nodes available for use in linked structures. *See also* **object heap.**

full binary tree A binary tree that contains the maximum number of nodes for its height.

garbage collection The automatic process of reclaiming memory when the data of a program no longer need it.

general tree A tree in which each node can have an arbitrary number of children.

global identifier A name that can be used by all of the methods of a class.

global variable *See* **global identifier.**

grammar The set of rules for constructing sentences in a language.

graph A collection whose items can have an arbitrary number of predecessors and successors.

graphical user interface (GUI) A means of communication between human beings and computers that uses a pointing device for input and a bitmapped screen for output. The bitmap displays images of windows and window objects such as buttons, text fields, and pull-down menus. The user interacts with the interface by using the mouse to manipulate the window objects directly. *See also* **window object.**

greedy algorithm An algorithm that does what is most profitable, urgent, or gratifying at any given instant without regard to future consequences.

hash table A data structure that allows the programmer to access items by specifying key values and supports very fast lookups. *See also* **association list, dictionary, keyed list,** and **map.**

hashing The method of determining the location of a given item in a hash table. *See also* **hash table.**

heap A complete binary tree wherein each item is greater than either of its children.

heap property The feature of a binary tree that makes it a heap. *See also* **heap.**

heap sort A sorting algorithm that builds a heap from a list of items and then transfers them from the heap back to the list in sorted order.

heap underflow A condition in which memory leakage causes dynamic memory to become unavailable.

hierarchical collection A collection whose items have at most one predecessor and zero or more successors.

high-level language Any programming language that uses words and symbols to make it relatively easy to read and write a program. *See also* **assembly language** and **machine language.**

identity The property of an object that it is the same thing at different points in time, even though the values of its attributes might change.

implementation The phase of the software life cycle in which the program is coded in a programming language.

index *See* **array index.**

infinite recursion A recursive process that does not halt because the stopping state has been incorrectly specified.

infix A notation for writing expressions in which the operator lies between the operands.

information hiding A condition in which the user of a module does not know the details of how it is implemented, and the implementer of a module does not know the details of how it is used.

inheritance The process by which a subclass can reuse attributes and behavior defined in a superclass. *See also* **subclass** and **superclass.**

initializer list A means of expressing a set of data that can be assigned to the cells of an array in one statement.

inner class A class that is defined within another class.

inorder traversal A tree traversal that visits the left child, visits the item, and visits the right child of each node.

insertion sort A sorting algorithm that inserts the ith item into its proper place among the first i items in an array on the ith pass through the array.

instance A computational object bearing the attributes and behavior specified by a class.

instance method A method that is called when a message is sent to an instance of a class. *See also* **message.**

instance variable Storage for data in an instance of a class.

instantiation The process of creating a new object or instance of a class.

integration testing The phase of testing in which software components are brought together and tested for their interaction. *See also* **unit testing.**

interface A formal statement of how communication occurs between the user of a module (class or method) and its implementer. In Java, a software component that simply specifies the methods to be implemented by a class. A class that implements several interfaces can thus adopt the behavior of several classes.

IP address The unique location of an individual computer on the Internet.

IP name A representation of an IP address that uses letters and periods.

IP number A representation of an IP address that uses digits and periods.

iterator A software component that allows the client to access a collection's items in a given sequence.

key The value used to access data in a keyed list.

keyed list A data structure that allows the programmer to access items by using key values. *See also* **association list, dictionary, hash table,** and **map.**

leaf A node in a tree that has no children.

level order traversal A tree traversal that visits each node, from left to right, at a given level before moving to the next level.

lexical analysis The phase of parsing that involves recognizing words in a given expression. *See also* **scanning.**

linear behavior An increase of work or memory in direct proportion to the size of a problem.

linear collection A collection in which each item has at most one predecessor and one successor.

linear search *See* **sequential search.**

linked list A list of data items in which each item is linked to the next one by means of a pointer.

list A linear collection that supports a wide range of operations, including insertions and removals at any position.

list iterator A special type of iterator used with lists that allows navigation to previous items.

load factor The number of items stored in the array divided by the array's capacity.

local host A server computer that runs clients to its servers.

local identifier A name whose value is visible only within a method or a nested block.

lock A mechanism whereby a thread obtains exclusive control of a data object. *See also* **monitor.**

logarithmic behavior An increase of work or memory in proportion to the number of times that the problem size can be divided by 2.

logical size The number of data items actually available in a data structure at a given time. *See also* **physical size.**

logical structure The organization of the components in a data structure independent of their organization in computer memory.

main (primary) memory Memory contained in the computer. *See also* **secondary memory.**

manifest interface The property of a method such that, when the method is called, the reader of the code can tell clearly what information is being transmitted to it and what information is being returned from it.

map A type of collection in which each item is associated with a unique key. *See also* **association list, dictionary, hash table,** and **keyed list.**

matrix A two-dimensional array that provides range checking and can be resized.

merge The process of combining lists. Typically refers to files or arrays.

mergesort A relatively fast sorting technique that subdivides a list and then merges the sublists into sorted order.

message A symbol used by a client to ask an object to perform a service. *See also* **method.**

metasymbols Symbols that a grammar uses to construct rules. Metasymbols express selection among optional items, iteration, and so forth.

method A chunk of code that can be treated as a unit and invoked by name. A method is called when a message is sent to an object. *See also* **class method** and **instance method.**

method heading The portion of a method implementation containing the function's name, parameter declarations, and return type.

model class A class that represents data or a real-world object. *See also* **model, view, controller pattern.**

model, view, controller pattern A design plan in which the roles and responsibilities of the system are cleanly divided among data management (model), user interface display (view), and user event handling (controller) tasks.

module An independent unit that is part of a larger development. Can be a method or a class (set of methods and related data).

module specifications In the case of a method, a description of data received, information returned, and task performed by a module. In the case of a class, a description of the attributes and behavior.

monitor An object used to control access to shared data among threads. *See also* **lock.**

mutator A method used to change the value of an attribute of an object.

neighbors Two vertices connected by an edge.

node A component of a linked structure, consisting of a data item and pointers to other nodes.

nonterminal symbols Symbols that a grammar uses to express phrases. *See also* **terminal symbols.**

null value A special value which indicates that no object can be accessed.

object A collection of data and operations in which the data can be accessed and modified only by means of the operations.

object heap An area of computer memory where storage for dynamic data is available. *See also* **free list.**

object-oriented programming The construction of software systems that use objects.

offset The quantity of cells added to a base address to obtain the address of an array cell. *See also* **base address.**

one-dimensional array An array in which each data item is accessed by specifying a single index.

one-way list A list that supports navigation in one direction only.

order of complexity A classification of the amount of work or memory consumed by an algorithm as a function of its problem size. *See also* **big-O notation.**

overloading The process of using the same operator symbol or identifier to refer to many different functions. *See also* **polymorphism.**

overriding The process of reimplementing a method already implemented in a superclass.

package A group of related classes in a named directory.

parallel arrays Arrays of the same length but with different component data types.

parameter *See* **argument.**

parameter list A list of parameters. An actual parameter list is contained in a method call. A formal parameter list is contained in a method heading.

parent The predecessor of a given node in a tree. *See also* **child** and **tree.**

parent class The immediate superclass of a class.

parse tree A data structure developed during parsing that represents the structure of a sentence or expression.

parsing The process of analyzing an expression for syntactic correctness.

path A sequence of edges that allows one vertex to be reached from another.

persistence The property of a data model that allows it to survive different runs of an application. *See also* **serialization.**

physical size The number of memory units available for storing data items in a data structure. *See also* **logical size.**

pivot A data item around which an array is subdivided during the quicksort.

pointer A reference to an object that allows one to access it.

polymorphism The property of one operator symbol or method identifier having many meanings. *See also* **overloading.**

port A channel through which several clients can exchange data with the same server or with different servers.

portable Able to be transferred to different applications or computers without changes.

postcondition A statement of what is true after a certain action is taken.

postfix A notation for writing expressions in which the operator follows the operands.

postorder traversal A tree traversal that visits the left child, visits the right child, and visits the item of each node.

precondition A statement of what is true before a certain action is taken.

prefix A notation for writing expressions in which the operator precedes the operands.

preorder traversal A tree traversal that visits the item, visits the left child, and visits the right child of each node.

primitive data type A data type such as `char`, `int`, `double`, or `boolean`, whose values are stored directly in variables of that type. Primitive data types are always passed by value when they are parameters in Java and copied during assignment statements.

priority queue A collection in which the items are ordered according to priority.

private method A method that is accessible only within the scope of a class definition.

private variable A variable that is accessible only within the scope of a class definition.

procedural programming A style of programming that decomposes a program into a set of methods or procedures.

program A set of instructions that tells the machine (the hardware) what to do.

program walk-through The process of carefully following, using pencil and paper, steps the computer uses to solve the problem given in a program. Also referred to as a *trace*.

programming language Formal language that computer scientists use to give instructions to the computer.

protected variable A variable accessible only within the scope of a class definition or within the class definition of a subclass.

pseudocode A stylized half-English, half-code language written in English but suggesting Java code.

public method A method accessible to any program component that uses the class.

public variable A variable accessible to any program component that uses the class.

quadratic behavior An increase of work or memory in proportion to the square of the size of the problem.

quadratic hashing A method of resolving collisions that involves repeatedly probing the position $k + r^2$. k is the original hash value that caused the collision, and r is incremented by 1 after each unsuccessful attempt.

queue A collection that allows the programmer to insert items only at one end and remove them from the other. Referred to as an FIFO (first-in, first-out) structure.

quicksort A relatively fast sorting technique that rearranges elements around a pivot element and recursively sorts these elements.

random access data structure A data structure in which the time to access a data item does not depend on its position in the structure.

range bound error The situation that occurs when an attempt is made to use an array index value that is less than 0 or greater than or equal to the size of the array.

ready queue A data structure used to schedule processes or threads for CPU access.

recursion The process of a subprogram calling itself. A clearly defined stopping state must exist. Any recursive subprogram can be rewritten using iteration.

recursive data structure A data structure that has either a simple form or a form that is composed of other instances of the same data structure. *See also* **linked list.**

recursive descent parsing A method of parsing in which each grammar rule translates to a method for processing a phrase.

recursive step A step in the recursive process that solves a similar problem of smaller size and eventually leads to a termination of the process.

recursive subprogram *See* **recursion.**

reference type A data type such as array, `String`, or any other Java class whose instances are not stored directly in variables of that type. References or pointers to these objects are stored instead. References to objects are passed when they are parameters in Java, and just the references, not the objects, are copied during assignment statements.

regression testing The process of rerunning a program on the test data to make sure that modifications have not unintentionally broken some feature that previously worked correctly.

rehashing A method of resolving collisions that uses several hash functions.

robust The state in which a program is protected against most possible crashes from bad data and unexpected values.

root The single node in a tree without a predecessor.

round-robin scheduling A method of scheduling that cycles processes in first-come, first-served order.

run-time stack An area of computer memory reserved for local variables and parameters of method calls.

scanning The process of picking words or tokens out of a stream of characters.

scope of identifier The largest block in which the identifier is available.

secondary memory An auxiliary device for memory, usually a disk or magnetic tape. *See also* **main memory.**

selection The process by which a method or a variable of an instance or a class is accessed.

selection sort A sorting algorithm that sorts the components of an array in either ascending or descending order. This process puts the smallest or largest element in the top position and repeats the process on the remaining array components.

semantics The rules for interpreting the meaning of a program in a language.

sentinel A data item that serves as a marker for locating a significant part of a data structure, such as the end of a string.

sequential access data structure A data structure in which the time to access a data item depends on its position in the structure.

sequential search The process of searching a list by examining the first component and then examining successive components in the order in which they occur. Also referred to as a *linear search*.

sequential traversal The process of visiting each data item in an array or a linked list from beginning to end.

serialization A mechanism that maintains the persistence of objects in a data model. *See also* **persistence.**

server A computational object that provides a service to another computational object. *See also* **client/server relationship.**

server daemon A thread that listens for requests from clients and dispatches these requests to client handlers. *See also* **client handler.**

set An unordered collection consisting of unique items. *See also* **unordered collection.**

shallow copy A method of copying an object wherein the copy shares references to the original object's data items. *See also* **cloning** and **deep copy.**

side effect A change in a variable that is the result of some action taken in a program, usually from within a method.

single-source shortest path problem A problem that asks for a solution that contains the shortest paths from a given vertex to all of the other vertices.

socket An object that serves as a communication link between a single server process and a single client process.

software engineering The process of developing and maintaining large software systems.

software life cycle The process of development, maintenance, and demise of a software system. Phases include analysis, design, coding, testing/verification, maintenance, and obsolescence.

software reuse The process of building and maintaining software systems out of existing software components.

sorted collection A linear collection whose items are arranged in sorted order.

sorted map A map that allows the client to access items in sorted order.

sorted set A set that allows the client to access items in sorted order.

spanning forest The spanning tree generated by traversing all the vertices of an undirected graph. *See also* **spanning tree.**

spanning tree A connected component of a graph that has the fewest number of edges possible.

sparse graph A graph that has relatively few edges and many vertices. *See also* **dense graph.**

stack A linear collection whose items can be accessed at only one end. Referred to as an LIFO (last-in, first-out) structure.

state The set of all the values of the variables of a program at any point during its execution.

static array An array whose memory is automatically allocated from the run-time stack. *See also* **dynamic array.**

stepwise refinement The process of repeatedly subdividing tasks into subtasks until each subtask is easily accomplished. *See also* **structured programming** and **top-down implementation.**

stopping state The well-defined termination of a recursive process.

string A linear collection of characters.

string buffer A Java class that allows the programmer to modify the contents of a string and efficiently increase its size.

string literal One or more characters, enclosed in double quotes, used as a constant in a program.

string tokenizer A Java class that allows the programmer to access text in a string one word at a time.

structure chart A graphical method of indicating the relationship between modules when designing the solution to a problem.

structured programming Programming that parallels a solution to a problem achieved by top-down implementation. *See also* **stepwise refinement** and **top-down implementation.**

stub programming The process of using incomplete functions to test data transmission among them.

subclass A class that inherits attributes and behavior from another class.

subgraph A subset of a graph's vertices and a subset of its edges.

subscript *See* **array index.**

substring A string that represents a segment of another string.

superclass The class from which a subclass class inherits attributes and behavior. *See also* and **inheritance** and **subclass.**

synchronization problem A type of problem arising from the execution of threads or processes that share memory.

syntax The rules for constructing well-formed programs in a language.

table *See* **association list, dictionary, hash table, keyed list,** and **map.**

tail-recursive The property that a recursive algorithm has of performing no work after each recursive step. *See also* **recursion.**

terminal symbols Symbols that appear in sentences in a language. *See also* **nonterminal symbols.**

thread A type of process that can run concurrently with other processes.

time slicing A means of scheduling threads or processes wherein each process receives a definite amount of CPU time before returning to the ready queue.

token An individual word or symbol.

top-down implementation A method for coding whereby you start with a top-level task and implement subtasks. Each subtask is then subdivided into smaller subtasks. This process is repeated until each remaining subtask is easily coded. *See also* **stepwise refinement** and **structured programming.**

topological order An ordering of vertices in a directed acyclic graph.

topological sort The process of generating a linear sequence of vertices that corresponds to a topological order.

trace *See* **program walk-through.**

tree A type of collection whose items have at most one predecessor.

tree iterator A special type of iterator that supports the traversal of a tree. *See also* **inorder traversal, level order traversal, postorder traversal,** and **preorder traversal.**

two-dimensional array An array in which each data item is accessed by specifying a pair of indexes.

2-3 tree A special type of search tree that supports $O(\log n)$ operations in the worst cases.

two-way list A list that supports navigation in both directions.

type *See* **data type.**

undirected graph A graph whose edges indicate no direction.

unit testing The testing of a component independently of other components in a software system. *See also* **integration testing.**

unordered collection A type of collection whose items are in no particular order.

user-defined class A new data type introduced and defined by the programmer.

user-defined method A new function introduced and defined by the programmer.

user-friendly A phrase that describes an interactive program with clear, easy-to-follow messages for the user.

user requirements The goals and needs of users of a software system, usually specified during the analysis phase of software development. *See also* **analysis.**

vector A one-dimensional array that supports resizing, insertions, and removals.

vertex A point or node in a graph.

view class A class involved in the display of information to a user. *See also* **model, view, controller pattern.**

virtual machine A software tool that behaves like a high-level computer.

visibility modifier A symbol (`public`, `protected`, or `private`) that specifies the kind of access that clients have to a server's data and methods.

void method A method that returns no value.

waterfall model A series of steps in which a software system trickles down from analysis to design to implementation. *See also* **software life cycle.**

weight An attribute, usually a number, that labels an edge in a graph and represents the cost of traversing that edge.

white box testing A type of testing that attempts to exercise all parts of a program. *See also* **black box testing.**

window object A computational object that displays an image, such as a button or a text field, in a window and supports interaction with the user.

wrapper class A class designed to contain a primitive data type so that the primitive type can behave like a reference type. *See also* **primitive data type** and **reference type.**

All items in bold face are computer font.